ONE HUNDRED
INDOOR GAMES
YOU CAN PLAY

EDITOR: PETER ARNOLD

CRESCENT BOOKS
NEW YORK

Dedicated to the memory of George Hervey

First published in Great Britain in 1981
under the title *The Complete Book of Indoor Games*
by The Hamlyn Publishing Group Limited

© The Hamlyn Publishing Group Limited, 1973, 1975, 1981

Sections of this book first appeared in *The Hamlyn
Illustrated Book of Card Games* and *The Illustrated
Book of Table Games*.

This 1988 edition published
by Crescent Books, distributed by
Crown Publishers, Inc.,
225 Park Avenue South,
New York, New York, 10003

By arrangement with Octopus Books Limited

Printed in Czechoslovakia

ISBN 0-517-65409-1

h g f e d c b a

Acknowledgment
The Publishers wish to acknowledge the kindness of
Waddingtons Playing Card Company Limited, who supplied
the cards for the card game illustrations.

Contents

Board and Tile Games

Dice Games

Roulette   308

Introduction

The first requirement of this introduction is to define the scope of this book in relation to its title. By 'indoor games' is meant those sedentary games which require no more physical energy than the laying of a card or the throwing of dice.

Bridge and poker players might claim that a long session requires stamina, but it does not need physical dexterity, athleticism or agility. Therefore such pursuits as table tennis, badminton and snooker, although played indoors, are not included. They are sometimes called indoor games, but might be more properly thought of as indoor sports.

Secondly the word 'complete' is not meant to imply that every game ever invented which uses cards, tiles, dice, counters and such like is included. No book has ever achieved such a feat, and none ever will. Nor would the reader wish to buy a book which used some of its space to describe how to toss a coin in a game of heads and tails, or how to play Noughts and Crosses or even Snakes and Ladders. Nor has it been thought feasible to include the proprietary games which proliferate annually, and many of which are in any case based on the old games.

The object has been to include those standard games which have stood the test of time and have so caught popular fancy as to have earned a right to be included, and those games which while they might not have become so widespread, yet have their followers and will repay those who make the effort to learn them. Anybody who masters all or most of the games in this book can claim with as much justification as the next man to be a complete games player.

The book has been based upon the great success of two earlier books, *The Hamlyn Illustrated Book of Card Games* and *The Illustrated Book of Table Games*. The best of each have been amalgamated, and some new games added. Thus there are a number of writers to be acknowledged. The late George F. Hervey wrote all the articles concerning card games. Paul Langfield wrote the articles on Chess and Checkers. Jeremy Flint wrote the article on Backgammon. Francis Roads wrote the article on Go. Rodney Headington wrote the article on Hex. David Pritchard wrote the articles on Reversi, Wari, Mah Jong and Dominoes. The present editor wrote the articles on Roulette and Dice games.

The largest part of the book concerns card games, and a description of the arrangement of them is best left to an extract from George Hervey's introduction to the book in which they originally appeared:

'Card games do not admit of a precise arrangement. In this book they have been arranged according to the number of players who may take part at one table; as, however, most card games can be played, in one form or another, by a varying number of players, it is more correct to say that the games have been arranged according to the number of players for which they are best suited; but party games and banking games are grouped separately, and among the party games some will be found suitable for members of the younger generation who may find that playing a game of cards is a less noisy pastime than playing an electric guitar. It is not an ideal arrangement, but it has the merit of convenience, and is less arbitrary than arranging the games in alphabetical order, and more practical than arranging them by their family resemblances. Most card games have a number of variations. Only the more popular ones have been given a place in this book, and, with some rare and inevitable exceptions, descriptions of them follow the description of the parent game.

The aim of the present writer is nothing higher than to explain how the various games are played; and when no authoritative organisation has laid down the scoring, rules of play and appropriate penalties for breaking them, the practice that he recommends is that of the majority of experienced players. If here and there he has broken form and given a few hints on skilful play, it is not to compete with the text books, but because without them the bare bones would be unreadable. When the play of a deal is summarized, the standard practice of underlining the card that wins the trick (the player leading to the next trick) is followed.'

George Hervey was one of the best of all writers on card games, and while he points out that his aim was 'nothing higher than to explain how the various games are played', his descriptions of sample games nevertheless convey the elements of good play.

This principle was also followed in the other parts of the book, and learners of new games will find that pointers on strategy will start them thinking along the right lines.

It is hoped that readers will find the articles on the games they already know entertaining and perhaps instructional, and that they will derive a lifetime's pleasure from learning some new games.

P.D.A.

Card Games

Bisley

SINGLE-PACK

Remove the four Aces from the pack and place them face upwards in a row on the table. Deal nine cards in a row to the right of them, and the rest of the pack in three rows of thirteen cards each, below them (see illustration). When the four Kings become available they are placed above their respective Aces.

The Aces are built on upwards and the Kings downwards in suit-sequences. It does not matter where the two sequences meet.

Only the bottom card of a column is available for play. It may be built either on its Ace- or King-foundation, packed on the bottom card of another column, or itself be packed on. Packing may be either upwards or downwards in suit-sequence, and the player may change this at his convenience. A space left vacant in the layout, by the removal of a card, is not filled.

In the layout below, the **K ♦** is played above the **A ♦**, the **2 ♠** is built on the **A ♠**, and the **2 ♥** on the **A ♥**. This exposes the **3 ♠** which is built on the **2 ♠**. The **Q ♦** is built on the **K ♦**. The **9 ♦** is packed on the **10 ♦**, and the **8 ♦** on the **9 ♦**. Now the **8 ♣** is packed on the **9 ♣**, exposing the **2 ♣** which is built on the **A ♣**. And so on.

Calculation

SINGLE-PACK

Calculation, or Broken Intervals, is a one-pack patience that is well-named, because it is necessary to calculate at the turn of every card, and it offers more scope for skilful play than any other patience.

Any **Ace**, any **2**, any **3** and any **4** are placed in a row on the table to form four foundations. The object of the game is to build, regardless of suits, the remaining forty-eight cards on them, as follows:

On the **Ace** in the order **Ace, 2, 3, 4, 5, 6, 7, 8, 9, 10, Jack, Queen, King**.

On the **2** in the order **2, 4, 6, 8, 10, Queen, Ace, 3, 5, 7, 9, Jack, King**.

On the **3** in the order **3, 6, 9, Queen, 2, 5, 8, Jack, Ace, 4, 7, 10, King**.

On the **4** in the order **4, 8, Queen, 3, 7, Jack, 2, 6, 10, Ace, 5, 9, King**.

The cards are dealt from the pack one at a time, and every card must either be built on a foundation or played to any one of a waste heap below each foundation. The pack is dealt only once, but play from a waste heap may continue after it has been exhausted. Only the top card of a waste heap may be played; it may be built on a foundation and may not be played to another waste heap.

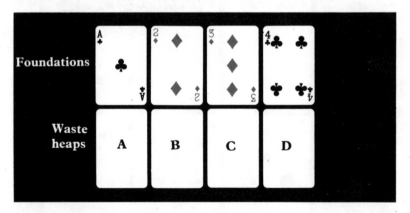

The cards in the pack are now dealt one at a time. Suppose a **10** is dealt, as it cannot be built on a foundation it is best played to waste heap **B**. Next a **6** is dealt; it is built on the 3-foundation. Next comes an **8**, and, of course, is built on the 4-foundation. The next card is a **King**. It must be played to a waste heap, but as a **King** is the last card to be built on a foundation it would be wrong to play it to waste heap **B** and so cover the **10.** It should be played to another waste heap, and many experienced players would now reserve this waste heap for Kings. Play continues in this way until all forty-eight cards have been dealt.

If the play is carefully thought out, by building on the waste heaps descending sequences of two to four or more cards, towards the end of a game excellent progress will be made.

Demon

SINGLE-PACK

Demon is probably the best known of all the many one-pack patiences. It is sometimes known as Fascination, sometimes as Thirteen, and, in America, as Canfield, because it was reputedly invented by Richard A. Canfield, a well-known gambler of the late 19th century, whose practice it was to sell the pack for $52.00 and pay $5.00 for every card in the foundation row when the game came to an end. It was not altogether as profitable as it may seem, because for every player he had to employ a croupier to keep an eye on him during the play.

Thirteen cards are dealt face downwards in a pile and the top card is faced. The pile is known as the heel, and four cards are dealt face upwards in a row to the right of it. The next card of the pack is dealt face upwards and placed above the first card of the row. It indicates the foundations.

The **10 ♦** is the first of the four foundations, and the **3 ♦** is the top card of the heel. As they become available, the other three 10s are played to the right of the **10 ♦**, and the object of the game is to build on them round-the-corner suit-sequences up to the 9s. The four cards to the right of the heel are packed in descending sequences of alternate colours. As a start, therefore, the **J ♦** is built on its foundation-card; the **4 ♣** is packed on the **5 ♥** and the **3 ♦** on the **4 ♣**. The card in the heel below the **3 ♦** is turned and, if it cannot be built on a foundation or packed on a card in the layout, is played to the space left vacant by the **J ♦**. The next card in the heel is then exposed.

The bottom card of the four columns may be built on a foundation, but a sequence may be moved from one column to another only as a whole, and then only if the sequence can be packed on the next higher card of a different colour.

The stock is dealt to a waste pile in batches of three cards at a time, but if there is less than three cards at the end of the stock they are dealt singly. The stock is dealt and redealt until the game is won, or lost because no further move can be made.

When all the cards in a column have been played, the space that is left must be filled at once with the top card of the heel and the next card of the heel exposed. A space must not be filled from the cards in hand, and when the heel is exhausted, spaces are filled from the waste heap, and the player need no longer fill a space at once, but leave it vacant until a suitable card is available.

Klondike

SINGLE-PACK

The demon (see page 13) and the Klondike are probably the two best-known and most popular of the one-pack patience games. In England the name of Canfield is sometimes attached to the Klondike. This name, however, is a misnomer, and to be corrected, because Canfield is the name that in America is given to the patience that we in England call the demon.

Twenty-eight cards are dealt face downwards in slightly overlapping rows of seven cards, six cards, five cards, four cards, three cards, two cards and one card. The bottom card of each row is turned face upwards (see below).

As they become available, Aces are played as foundations to a row above the layout; the object of the game is to build on the Aces ascending suit-sequences to the Kings.

An exposed card at the bottom of a column is available to be built on a foundation, or it may be packed in a descending sequence of alternate colour. A sequence may be moved from one column to another, but only as a whole and when the highest card of the sequence may be placed on the next higher card of another colour. When an exposed card is played, the face-downwards card immediately above it is turned face upwards; when a whole column is moved, the space must be filled by a King which may or may not have a sequence attached to it.

The stock is dealt one card at a time to a waste heap, of which the top card is available for building on a foundation or packing on a column in the layout. Only one deal is allowed.

An Ace must be played to the foundation row as soon as it becomes available, but all other cards may be left in position if the player prefers to wait on the prospect of finding a better move later in the game.

In the layout shown below the **5 ♦** is packed on the **6 ♣**, and the card under the **5 ♦** is turned face upwards. The **J ♣** is packed on the **Q ♥**, and the **K ♦** moved to fill the space vacated by the **J ♣**. The card under the **K ♦** is now turned face upwards. And so on.

Klondike has been the subject of several variations. One of the best is **JOKER KLONDIKE**. It is played in the same way as the parent game, but with the Joker added to the pack. Whenever the Joker becomes available for play it must be built on a foundation as the next card in sequence. Other cards, if in correct sequence, are built on it, but when the natural card that it replaces becomes available it is substituted for the Joker which is built on another foundation.

A player may choose on which foundation he will build the Joker. If it becomes available for play before a foundation has been started it must remain in its position until an Ace turns up and a foundation started.

La Belle Lucie

SINGLE-PACK

La Belle Lucie, or the Fan, is one of the classical one-pack patiences; it has a very pleasing layout. The entire pack is spread on the table in seventeen fans of three cards each and one of a single card, as illustrated.

As the Aces become available they are placed above the layout as foundations, to be built on in ascending suit-sequences to the Kings. Only the end card of each fan and the single card are available for play. They may be built on a foundation, packed on the end card of another fan in descending suit-sequence, or themselves be packed on in descending suit-sequences. A space made by playing off a complete fan is not filled.

When all possible moves have been made, all the cards except those played to the foundations, are picked up, shuffled, and redealt in fans of three. If one or two cards are left over they make separate fans. Two redeals are allowed.

In the layout illustrated the **A ♥** and **A ♣** are played to the foundation row. The **2 ♥** is built on the **A ♥**, and the **7 ♣** is packed on the **8 ♣**. This releases the **2 ♣** that is built on the **A ♣**. The **J ♦** is packed on the **Q ♦**, the **J ♥** on the **Q ♥**, and the **A ♠** followed by the **2 ♠** go to the foundation row. And so on.

Little Spider

SINGLE-PACK

The two red Aces and the two black Kings (or the two black Aces and the two red Kings) are placed in a row on the table to serve as foundations. The remaining forty-eight cards are dealt, face upwards, in two rows of four cards each, one above the foundation cards, the other below them.

The object of the game is to build ascending suit-sequences on the Aces to Kings, and descending suit-sequences on the Kings to Aces.

During the deal a card may be built from the upper row on any of the four foundation cards, but from the lower row only on the foundation card directly above it.

After every batch of eight cards has been dealt, the top cards of all eight piles are playable and may be built on any foundation cards or packed on any other pile in the layout. The piles are packed in ascending or descending, continuous sequences (an Ace ranks below a 2 and above a King) regardless of suit. A space made by removing an entire pile is not filled.

In the layout illustrated, the **Q ♣** may be built on the **K ♣** and the **2 ♥** on the **A ♥**. The **10 ♣** may be packed on the **J ♠**, and the **5 ♣** on the **6 ♠**. And so on.

Maze

SINGLE-PACK

Maze is an excellent patience because some skill is necessary if it is to be successful.

The fifty-two cards of the pack are dealt face upwards in two rows of eight cards each, and four of nine cards each. The four Kings are then discarded. This leaves four spaces, or six in all, because as well as the spaces left by the discard of the Kings, the spaces at the end of the first and second rows are taken into the layout for the play (see illustration).

The object of the game is to arrange the forty-eight cards in four ascending suit-sequences, from Aces to Queens, beginning with an Ace at the extreme left of the top row and ending with a Queen at the extreme right of the bottom row. The sequences follow on, from the end of one row to the beginning of the next, as in reading and writing. Only one card may be moved at a time.

The rules for moving a card into a space are:

1. The card must be in suit-sequence one higher than the card on the left of the space or one lower than the card on the right of the space, and it is to be assumed that not only are the rows continuous but that the bottom row is continuous with the top row.

2. When a space occurs on the right of a Queen it may be filled with any Ace, as an alternative to the card one lower in suit-sequence than the card on the right of the space.

Suppose the layout is as in the illustration. After the four Kings have been discarded, the space left vacant by the K♥ may be filled by any Ace, or with the 9♠ (by reason of the 10♠ on the right of the space) or the 8♠ (by reason of the 7♠ at the end of the bottom row). The space at the extreme right of the top row may be filled either with the 2♥ or 4♥, that at the extreme right of the second row either with the 10♥ or 10♠. The space left vacant by the K♦ may be filled either with the Q♣ or 5♠.

To begin the game. Play the A♠ to the top left corner of the layout, and the 10♥ to its vacant place. Play the 5♦ to the left of the 6♦ in the top row, and the J♦ to the left of the Q♦ in the bottom row. Play the 10♠ to the extreme right of the second row, and the 2♠ followed by the 3♠ to the right of the A♠ in the top row. Play the 5♠ to the left of the 6♠, the J♣ to the left of the Q♣ and the 4♠ to the left of the 5♠. The 5♥ is played to the left of the 6♥, the 9♥ to the left of the 10♥ and the 9♠ to the left of the 10♠. Now the 5♦ in the top row may be played to the right of the 4♦ and the 4♠ to the right of the 3♠ in the top row. With the A♠, 2♠, 3♠ and 4♠ in position, the game progresses well.

Paganini

DOUBLE-PACK

Paganini is a double-pack patience game, similar in principle to but more interesting than, the single-pack game known as spaces. It was composed by Mr Charles Jewell.

The entire pack is dealt face upwards on the table in eight rows of thirteen cards each, as shown in the accompanying illustration.

The object of the game is so to arrange the cards that each row consists of one suit beginning with an Ace (on the left) and ending with a King (on the right). No row is singled out for any particular suit; the player makes his own decision but, having made it, must not alter it.

Play begins by moving one of the Aces to the extreme left of a row. It will be appreciated, therefore, that as the game proceeds the whole of the layout is moved one space to the left so to speak. When a card is moved it leaves a space in the layout which is filled with the next higher card of the same suit as the card on the left of the space. Filling a space leaves another space in the layout. In turn this is filled in the same way, and so on, until a run is brought to an end by removing a card from the right-hand side of a King, because no card is available to be played to the space on the right of a King.

The game calls for a show of skill. To begin, a player has to decide which of the eight Aces he will move first and to the extreme left of which of the eight rows he will move it to. Then, whenever a card is moved in the layout, there is, at all events early in the play, a choice of two cards to fill the available space. It will be seen, therefore, that when all eight Aces have been moved to the extreme left of the layout, each move will offer the choice of filling one of eight spaces with either of two cards.

The layout in the illustration is not as difficult as it may appear. Indeed, with a little care the game should be won.

After a general survey of the possibilities in the game, the A ♥ in the bottom row should be moved to the extreme left of the row; the Q ♥ in the fifth row is moved to the space left vacant by the A ♥; and the 9 ♣ in the bottom row is moved into the space left vacant by the Q ♥. The space left vacant by the 9 ♣ may be filled either with the 2 ♥ in the second row or the one in the seventh row. Consideration shows that it should be filled with the one in the second row, because the 6 ♣ in the top row can be moved into the vacant space, the A ♣ in the fifth row can be moved to the extreme left of the top row, the 6 ♣ in the top row can be moved to the space in the second row left vacant by the 2 ♥, and either the 2 ♣ in the second row or that in the fourth row can be moved into the space (alongside the A ♣) left vacant by the 6 ♣. And so on.

Royal Parade

DOUBLE-PACK

Royal Parade is a popular two-pack patience with the alternative names of Financier, Hussars and Three Up.

Twenty-four cards are dealt in three rows of eight cards each (see illustration). Aces take no part in the game and are discarded. The cards in the layout must be arranged so that the top row consists of eight 2s, the middle row of eight 3s, and the bottom row of eight 4s, and these cards must be built on in suit-sequences at intervals of three cards, namely:

2	3	4
5	6	7
8	9	10
J	Q	K

In the layout illustrated the **A** ♦, in the top row, and the **A** ♣, in the bottom row, are discarded: the **4** ♠, in the middle row, is moved to the space in the bottom row left vacant by the discard of the **A** ♣, and the **7** ♠, in the top row, built on it. Either the **3** ♥ or **3** ♣, both in the top row, may be moved to fill the space in the middle row left vacant by the **4** ♠, and clearly the **3** ♥ should be chosen because the **6** ♥, in the bottom row may be built on it. And so on.

When all moves have been made, eight cards are dealt to waste heaps below the layout. Aces, as they are dealt, are discarded; other cards are used to build on the foundations or to fill spaces in the layout. Play continues in this way, making moves after each deal of eight cards to the waste-heaps, until the pack is exhausted. Only the top cards of the waste heaps may be moved to the layout.

Saint Helena

DOUBLE-PACK

Saint Helena, or Napoleon's Favourite, is a two-pack patience in which the packs are not shuffled together but used one after the other. Although the game gives a player some scope for ingenuity and the exercise of his memory, it is such a simple game that one rather doubts that it received its name because it was Napoleon's chief amusement during his last years.

An Ace and a King of each suit are arranged in two rows, the Kings above the Aces. Twelve cards are then dealt, clockwise, beginning above the left-hand King, as shown in the diagram:

The Kings are built on in descending suit-sequence to the Aces, and the Aces in ascending suit-sequences to the Kings; with the restriction that cards dealt to spaces 1, 2, 3, 4 may be built only on the Kings, cards dealt to spaces 7, 8, 9, 10 only to the Aces, and cards dealt to spaces 5, 6, 11, 12 to either.

When all moves have been made the spaces are filled from the pack, and when no further moves are to be made, another twelve cards are dealt to cover the cards in position.

When the pack has been exhausted, the restriction of play is lifted, and cards may be built on any foundation from any one of the twelve surrounding waste heaps. Also, the top card of each waste heap may now be packed on either in ascending or descending suit-sequence.

Three deals in all are allowed. The waste heaps are picked up in reverse order 12 . . . . 1, and turned face downwards, so that the bottom card of the twelfth waste heap becomes the top card of the re-made stock. No shuffling is allowed.

Spider

DOUBLE-PACK

There are several variations of Spider. The one described in this article is deservedly considered the best, and, indeed, among the best of all patiences, because it frequently calls for deep analysis. According to *Redbook Magazine* it was the favourite patience of the late President Franklin D. Roosevelt.

Forty cards are dealt to the table in four overlapping rows of ten cards each: the first, second and third rows face downwards, the fourth row face upwards, as in the illustration.

Foundation cards are not played to the centre. The game is to build within the layout, descending suit-sequences on the eight

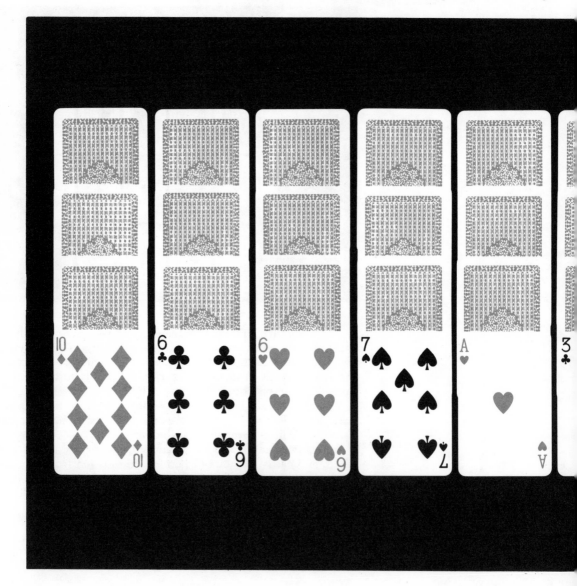

Kings to the Aces. A completed sequence is discarded, so that the game is won when the table is cleared of all cards.

The cards at the bottom of the columns may be packed in descending sequences irrespective of suit and colour, and when a card is moved from one column to another the face-downwards card immediately above it is turned face upwards and becomes available for play.

In the diagram any of the three sixes may be packed on the **7 ♠** and the **9 ♦** may be packed on either of the tens. Two cards will thus be exposed.

When all the cards have been moved from a column, the space may be filled by any exposed card or sequence of cards.

After all possible moves have been made, and spaces filled, ten cards are dealt from the stock, face upwards, one to the bottom of each column, overlapping the cards in position.

Play is continued in this way until the stock is exhausted. The last deal from the stock will, of course, be of only four cards.

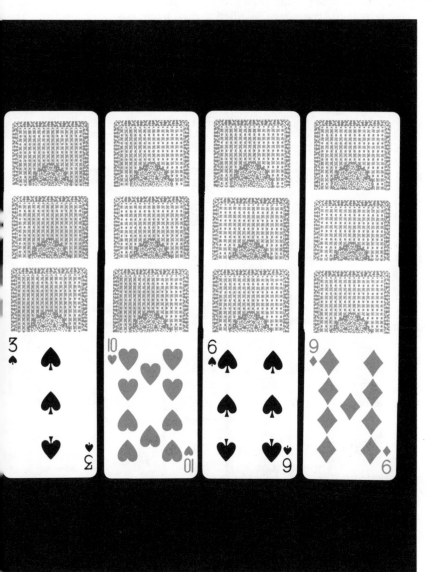

Sultan

DOUBLE-PACK

Sultan, sometimes, but rarely, known as Emperor of Germany, is a two-pack patience that calls for some skill if it is to be successful.

The eight Kings and one Ace of Hearts are removed from the pack and arranged on the table as shown in the illustration. With the exception of the central King of Hearts they serve as foundations to be built up in suit-sequences to the Queens, the Aces ranking between the Kings and the 2s.

On each side of the foundations, deal a column of four cards, as shown in the illustration. It is known as the divan, and the cards dealt to it are available to be built on the foundations. When one is played, the space is filled either from the stock or from the waste heap, but need not be filled immediately.

The pack is turned one card at a time to a waste heap, and may be dealt three times.

Management of the divan is of great importance. The general rule is not to fill a space with a card that is unlikely to be wanted during the immediate deal. If, for example, a foundation is built up to a 7, and both 8s are already buried, the 9s and higher cards should be played to the waste heap, because if used to fill a space in the divan they would be wasted.

Windmill

DOUBLE-PACK

The game known as Windmill or Propeller gets its name from the layout. Any King is placed face upwards on the table, and two cards are dealt above it, two below it, and two on each side of it, to form a cross (see illustration). The first four Aces that are dealt, whether to the layout or as the stock is turned, are played to the angles of the cross.

The object of the game is to build on the central King a descending, round-the-corner, sequence of fifty-two cards, regardless of suit and colour, and ascending suit-sequences, regardless of suit and colour, on the four Aces to the Kings.

In the layout shown, the A ♦ is played to an angle of the cross, the Q ♦ is built on the K ♠, and the J ♥ on the Q ♦. At any time a card may be taken from an Ace-foundation and played to the King-foundation, but only one card may be taken from each Ace-foundation during the building of any one sequence on the King-foundation.

The stock is turned to a waste heap, and a space in the layout must be filled from the waste heap, or from the stock if there is no waste heap.

There is no second deal, but when the stock is exhausted, the waste heap may be taken up and the first card dealt. If it can be played to a foundation, the next card is dealt, and so on. The game, however, comes to an end when a card can no longer be played to a foundation.

All Fours

All Fours is known in America as Old Sledge. It is a game for two players played with the full pack of fifty-two cards, which rank from Ace (high) to 2 (low). The game is won by he who first scores 7 points. The points are scored as follows:

High. The player who is dealt the highest trump in play scores 1 point.

Low. The player who is dealt the lowest trump in play scores 1 point.

Jack. The player who wins the Jack of trumps (if it is in play) scores 1 point.

Game. Each player counts the honours among the tricks he has won, and, counting the Ace as 4, the King as 3, the Queen as 2, the Jack as 1 and the Ten as 10, the player with the highest total scores 1 point. If there is equality the non-dealer scores the point.

The points are not counted until the end of the deal, but they should be understood from the start because they illustrate the object of the game.

Six cards are dealt in bundles of three to both players, and the thirteenth card is turned up to determine the trump suit.

The non-dealer now declares whether he will stand or beg. If he says 'I stand' he accepts the turned-up card as the trump suit and play begins. If he says 'I beg' he rejects the turned-up card as the trump suit, and the dealer must either accept or refuse the proposal to make another suit trumps. To refuse he says 'Take one'. The non-dealer then scores 1 point for gift and play begins. To accept he says 'I run the cards'. He deals three more cards to his opponent and three to himself, and turns up the next card to determine the trump suit. If this is the same suit as the original trump suit, he runs the cards again, and continues to run them until a different trump suit is turned up. In the rare, but not impossible, event of the pack being exhausted without a different trump suit being turned up, there is a redeal by the same player. If the turned-up card is a Jack, the dealer scores 1 point, and if when the cards are run, the turned-up card is again a Jack, the dealer again scores 1 point.

Play begins when the trump suit has been determined, and if the cards have been run, the players first discard from their hands enough cards to reduce the number held to six. The non-dealer leads to the first trick. His opponent must follow suit or trump. Unlike at most games, however, a player may trump even though he is able to follow suit, but he must not discard if he holds either a card of the suit led or a trump. If he does he has revoked and his opponent scores 1 point.

The winner of a trick leads to the next, and so on until all six tricks have been played. The players then turn up their tricks and score for High, Low, Jack and Game.

These four scoring features are fundamental to the game and are counted whenever it is possible to do so. If, for example, there is only one trump in play it counts 2 points, because it is both High and Low.

The deal passes in rotation.

ALL FOURS FOR FOUR PLAYERS is played with two players playing in partnership against the other two in partnership.

The method of play is the same as in the parent game, except that only the dealer and the opponent on his left (eldest hand) look at their cards to determine the trump suit. When they have done this, but not before, the other two players look at their cards and come into the game for play.

If a player exposes a card it is liable to be called by an opponent.

SEVEN UP is a variation of the parent game that receives its name from the method of scoring.

Both players (or both sides if four are playing) begin with seven counters each. Every time that a point is scored the player (or side) that wins it puts a counter aside, and the player (or side) who first gets rid of his counters wins the game. If both go out in the same deal, the winner is the one who first counts out when the points are scored for High, Low, Jack and Game.

ALL FIVES is a variation of the parent game that is played for 61 points up. For convenience the score is best kept on a cribbage board (see Plate 11).

The mechanics of the game are the same as those of the parent game, and points are pegged when the following trumps are won in a trick: Ace 4 points, King 3 points, Queen 2 points, Jack 1 point, Ten 10 points and Five 5 points. After the hand has been played, the honours are counted as in the parent game, to determine the point for Game, with the addition that the player who has won the 5 of trumps scores 5 points for it.

Bezique

The standard game of Bezique is played by two players, with two packs of cards from which the 6s, 5s, 4s, 3s and 2s have been removed. The cards rank in the order: **A 10 K Q J 9 8 7**.

Eight cards are dealt to each player in packets of three, two, three. The remaining forty-eight cards (the stock) are placed face downwards on the table, and the dealer exposes the top card to denote the trump suit. It is placed alongside the stock, and if it is a **7** he scores 10 points.

The non-dealer leads to the first trick. As at most games the winner of a trick leads to the next, but it is a feature of bezique that a player is under no obligation to follow suit to the card led. The object of the game is to score points for declaring certain cards and combinations of cards. The declarations, and the points that may be scored for them, are as follows:

Double Bezique = 500 points. Two **Q ♠** (or **Q ♣** if Spades or Diamonds are trumps) and two **J ♦** (or **J ♥** if Spades or Diamonds are trumps).

Sequence in Trumps = 250 points. **A 10 K Q J** of the trump suit.

Any Four Aces = 100 points.

Any Four Kings = 80 points.

Any Four Queens = 60 points.

Any Four Jacks = 40 points.

Bezique = 40 points. **Q ♠** (or **Q ♣** if Spades or Diamonds are trumps) and **J ♦** (or **J ♥** if Spades or Diamonds are trumps).

Royal Marriage = 40 points. **King** and **Queen** of the trump suit.

Common Marriage = 20 points. **King** and **Queen** of the same plain suit.

A player scores 10 points if he holds a **7** of the trump suit and exchanges it for the turn-up card; and 10 points are scored for playing a **7** of the trump suit.

When a player has won a trick he may declare by placing the appropriate cards face upwards on the table. He may make as many declarations as he chooses, always provided that the declarations do not involve the same cards. If the exposed cards show more than one declaration the player must announce which declaration he intends to score, and leave the other to be scored when he wins another trick. A card that has once scored cannot again be used to form part of a similar declaration. As an example, a player may expose **K ♠ Q ♠ J ♦** score 40 for bezique and announce 'Twenty to come' meaning that the next time he wins a trick he will score 20 points for the common marriage of the King and Queen of Spades. He may not expose a second Jack of Diamonds and score bezique with the Queen of Spades. The cards that have been declared, and so exposed on the table, remain a part of the player's hand and he may play them to later tricks.

Tricks should be gathered and kept by the player who wins them, because at the end of a deal a player scores 10 points for every Ace and every 10 that he has won. They are known as brisques.

When both players have played to a trick they replenish their hands from the stock: winner takes the top card, loser the next.

When the stock is exhausted the last eight tricks are played, and the game takes on a rather different character. Now, if a player has a card of the suit that has been led he must play it, and he must win a trick if he is able to. No further declarations may be made, and the aim of the player is to win brisques and the last trick for which 10 points are scored.

The deal passes to the other player, and so alternately, until one of them has reached an agreed number of points, usually 2,000.

The score cannot be kept satisfactorily with pencil on paper. It is best to use the special bezique markers that take the form of indicators marked as clocks on thin cardboard.

The following deal, played by two experienced players, illustrates many of the finer points of good play.

South dealt, and the hands were:

Clubs were trumps, the 10 of Clubs having been turned up.

The turn-up card is important because it is a sequence card, and a high one at that since it ranks immediately below the Ace.

The main features of North's hand are that he holds two sequence cards (the Queen and Jack of Clubs), a 7 of trumps to exchange for the valuable 10, and three Queens, which put him well on the way to a declaration of four Queens.

The main features of South's hand are a bezique Queen (the Queen of Spades) and three low trumps, including the 7; but, of course, as yet South does not know that North holds both the Queens of trumps, so that a sequence for him is impossible. It is South's lead, and it is necessary for him to win a trick to exchange the 7 of Clubs for the 10. An inexperienced player might be tempted to lead an indifferent card, such as the 7 of Hearts, hoping that North will have nothing to declare and will refuse to win the trick. This, however, is very artless play, and the better play is for South to lead his highest trump because it compels North to use a sequence card if he wants to take the trick and make a declaration. So . . .

Trick 1 South led the 9 of Clubs. North, who appreciated the importance of the turn-up card, won with the Queen of Clubs. This was North's best play, although it suffers from the defect that it reduces North's chance of declaring four Queens, and it informs South that virtually he has no hope of a sequence because North would hardly play a sequence card if he lacked a duplicate. North exchanged the 7 of Clubs for the turn-up card, and scored 10 points. He drew the King of Clubs (giving him no less than four of the five sequence cards), and South the 9 of Hearts.

Trick 2 North led the 9 of Diamonds, and South played the 7 of Hearts. North declared the royal marriage and scored 40 points, making his total 50 points. North drew the King of Hearts, and South the Ace of Hearts.

Trick 3 North led the 7 of Hearts, and South played the 9 of Diamonds. North declared the common marriage in Hearts and scored 20 points, making his total 70 points. North drew the Ace of Clubs, and South the Jack of Hearts.

Trick 4 North now held a sequence, but, in order to declare it, he had first to win a trick. A Heart must be led, and he chose the Queen. Undoubtedly it was the best lead. The Ace of Hearts is not a good lead, because, if trumped, it will cost North a brisque, and it is better for North to save for four Kings, instead of for four Queens, because not only does it gain 20 more points, but North had already played a Queen so the chance of drawing a Queen was slightly less than that of drawing a King. South played the 9 of Hearts. North declared his Ace, 10 and Jack of Clubs, and scored 250 points for the sequence, giving him a total of 320 points. South had not yet scored. North drew the 10 of Spades and South the Jack of Diamonds.

At this point the hands were:

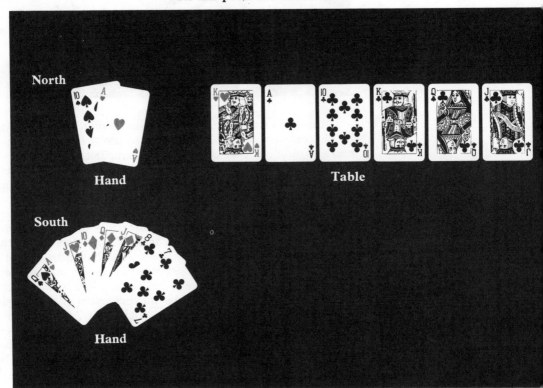

Trick 5 North's trumps were no longer of vital importance to him and could be played if desired. The two Kings were important, because North had made up his mind to save for Kings, and it is an error of tactics to change one's mind during the game. The Aces and 10s were important, because they furnish brisques. So North led the Jack of Clubs. South had a bezique in his hand, but unfortunately he could not win the trick and declare it. The best he could do was to play the Jack of Hearts. North drew the 8 of Diamonds, and South the Queen of Diamonds.

Trick 6 North led the 8 of Diamonds. South won with the 10 of Diamonds, putting away a brisque for himself, and declared bezique. South's 40 points for bezique was his first score, and he was a long way behind North's 320 points. South drew the 10 of Hearts, and North the Ace of Clubs.

Trick 7 South now had the lead. He chose the 7 of Clubs and scored 10 points, making his total 50. It was the best lead, because the lead of either Heart would probably be trumped and a brisque lost. He had to save for four Queens, and the Jack of Diamonds was out of the question since there was always the possibility of declaring double bezique. North was more or less compelled to win with the Queen of Clubs. North drew the 8 of Diamonds, and South the Queen of Spades.

Trick 8 North led the 8 of Diamonds, and South won with the 8 of Clubs and declared four Queens (60 points) giving him a total of 110. North, with a total of 320 points, was still well ahead, but he noted with some concern that South would be able to declare double bezique if he was lucky enough to draw the other Jack of Diamonds. South drew the 9 of Spades, and North the 8 of Spades.

Trick 9 South led the 9 of Spades, and North won with the 10 of Spades. North drew the Jack of Spades, and South the 8 of Spades.

Trick 10 North led the 8 of Spades, and South played the other 8 of Spades. North drew the 8 of Hearts, and South the Jack of Hearts.

Trick 11 North led the 8 of Hearts, and South won with the 10 of Hearts. South drew the King of Diamonds, and North the 8 of Hearts.

At this point the hands were:

The score was North 320 points, South 110 points.

Trick 12 South led the Jack of Hearts, and North played the 8. It would not have been good play for North to win with the Ace of Hearts because, though this would have given him a brisque, it is better for North to save for four Aces now that he held three. South laid down his King of Diamonds and scored a common marriage (20 points), giving him a total of 130 points. South drew the 7 of Spades, and North the Ace of Spades.

Trick 13 South led the 7 of Spades. North won with the Jack of Spades, and declared four Aces (100 points). This raised his total to 420, and he had a good lead on South, whose score was only 130 points. North drew the Jack of Clubs, and South the 9 of Spades.

The hands were now:

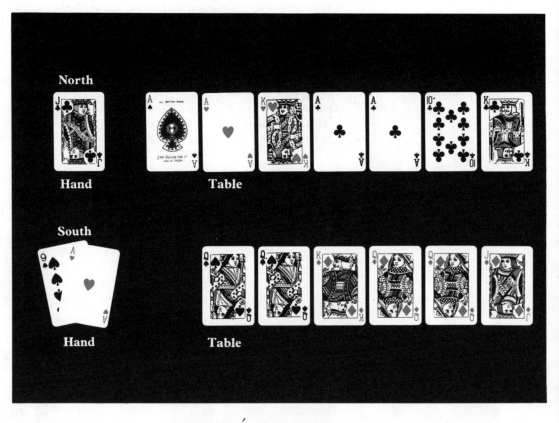

and South's hand with its three bezique cards was not without possibilities.

Trick 14 North led the Jack of Clubs, and South played the 9 of Spades. North drew the Jack of Spades, and South the 9 of Hearts.

Trick 15 North led the Jack of Spades, and South played the 9 of Hearts. North drew the King of Clubs, and South the Jack of Diamonds.

Trick 16 Now, of course, the whole game changed, because South held a double bezique, though he had to win a trick before he could declare it. If the stock is nearly exhausted it is proper for North to lead trumps in an attempt to prevent South from winning a trick. It was, however, too early in the game for these tactics, so North led the Ace of Spades, hoping that it would not be trumped, and South, who had no trump in his hand, discarded the married Queen of Diamonds. North drew the 10 of Diamonds, and South the 10 of Clubs, a vital card.

Trick 17 North, who by this time suspected that South held double bezique, led the Ace of Hearts, hoping that South would still not be able to trump. This time, however, he was doomed to disappointment, because, of course, South was able to win with the 10 of Clubs and declare double bezique. The score of 500 points for double bezique raised South's total to 630 and gave him a lead of 210 points because North's score was only 420 points. South drew the Ace of Spades, and North the King.

Trick 18 South, who had no further use for his bezique Jacks, led a Jack of Diamonds. North won with the 10 of Diamonds and declared four Kings (80 points), raising his score to 500 points. North drew the 9 of Clubs, and South the Ace of Diamonds.

Trick 19 North led the 9 of Clubs, and South played the Jack of Diamonds. North drew the 8 of Clubs, and South the Ace of Diamonds.

The hands were now:

Trick 20 North now suspected that South was on the point of declaring four Aces. His tactics, therefore, had to be aggressive, and, since the other 10 of Clubs had been played, his trumps were all winners, and he played them to prevent South from declaring. North led the Ace of Clubs, and South played the Queen of Spades. North drew one 7 of Diamonds and South the other.

Trick 21 North led the Ace of Clubs, and South played the 7 of Diamonds. North drew the Queen of Hearts, and South the 10 of Spades.

Trick 22 North led the 10 of Clubs, and South played the Queen of Spades. North declared the common marriage in Hearts (20 points) raising his total to 520 points. North drew the King of Spades, and South the 7.

Trick 23 North led the King of Clubs, and South played the 7 of Spades. North drew the King of Diamonds, and South the 10 of Hearts.

Trick 24 (last trick) North led the King of Clubs, and South played the Queen of Diamonds. North scored 10 points for the last trick bringing his total to 530 points. South's score was 630 points, and from the time that he declared double bezique North had little chance to overtake him. He did well, however, to prevent South from declaring four Aces and so adding another 100 points to his score. North drew the King of Hearts, and South picked up the 7 of Clubs exposed on the table.

After picking up their cards from the table, the hands of the two players were:

North   South

The play to the last eight tricks was:

North	South
K ♥	A ♥
7 ♦	A ♦
K ♦	A ♦
K ♠	A ♠
Q ♥	10 ♥
K ♠	10 ♠
8 ♣	K ♦
K ♥	7 ♣

South was lucky to win all his brisques, giving him a score of 100 points: North won six brisques for a total of 60 points. The final score, therefore, was: South 730 points; North 590 points.

Altogether a fine deal, and one worth studying, because it illustrates the importance of playing for double bezique. For the first half of the deal North was well ahead, but after South had won the highest prize that the game has to offer, it was practically impossible for North to win the deal, and all his efforts had to be directed towards preventing South from gaining an even bigger lead. North played well to reduce South's lead of 210 points (gained at the seventeenth trick) to 140.

RUBICON BEZIQUE has the advantage over the parent game that, as long ago as 1887, a committee of the Portland Club drew up a code of laws under which it should be played.

It is very similar to the parent game, and, like it, is a game for two players, but four packs of cards, not two, are used, and there are some differences in the preliminaries, the scoring and the routine of the game.

In the preliminaries, nine cards (not eight) are dealt to each player, either singly or in packets of three, and there is no turn up of the top card of the stock, so that the peculiar value of the 7 of trumps is lost.

The scoring is the same as in the parent game, with the following additions:

Carte Blanche = 50 points. If either player is dealt a hand without a court card he is entitled to score for carte blanche. Both players are entitled to score it. Before a player can score, however, he must show his hand to his opponent. Thereafter, each time that he draws a card from the stock he may show it to his opponent and score 50 points if it is not a court card.

Ordinary Sequence = 150 points. **A 10 K Q J** of any suit other than the trump suit.

Triple Bezique = 1,500 points. Three **Q ♠** and three **J ♦** (or **Q ♣** and **J ♥** if either Spades or Diamonds are trumps).

Quadruple Bezique = 4,500 points. Four **Q ♠** and four **J ♦** (or **Q ♣** and **J ♥** if either Spades or Diamonds are trumps).

Last Trick = 50 points.

The routine differs from that of the parent game in the following essentials:

1. A game is complete in one deal.
2. Trumps are determined by the first marriage or sequence declared by either player.
3. The tricks are left exposed on the table until such time as a brisque is played. After this the tricks are gathered and turned in the usual way.
4. If a card is played from a declared combination, subsequently the combination may be filled by adding an appropriate card and the declaration scored again.
5. If a player has declared two marriages in the same suit, he may rearrange the Kings and Queens on the table and declare two more marriages.
6. Brisques are disregarded for scoring except to break a tie or to save a player from being rubiconed.
7. If a player fails to score 1,000 points he is rubiconed. His score is added to (not subtracted from) that of his opponent, who adds a further 1,300 points (not 500) for the game. Further, if a player fails to score 100 points, the winner adds an extra 100 points to his score.

BEZIQUE FOR THREE PLAYERS is played with three packs of cards, and the players compete all against all. The play is the same as in the parent game with the addition of a score of 1,500 points for triple bezique.

BEZIQUE FOR FOUR PLAYERS is played with six packs of cards, or 192 cards in all. Two play in partnership against the other two.

The dealer places twenty-four cards face downwards in a pile on the table, and on this he places a marker so that the players will be warned when the stock is nearing exhaustion. He deals nine cards to each of the four players and places the remainder of the pack (132 cards in all) face downwards on top of the marker.

In general, the play follows that described under rubicon bezique (above) but there are some differences in the scoring and in declaring.

Carte Blanche = 100 points.

Double Carte Blanche = 500. Both partners being dealt hands without a court card.

Quintuple Bezique = 13,500 points. Five **Q♠** and **J♦** (or **Q♣** and **J♥** if either Spades or Diamonds are trumps).

Sextuple Bezique is so unlikely that no score has been alloted to it. Should it occur, the correct score is 40,500 points.

Any Four Aces = 1,000 points.

Any Four Tens = 900 points.

Any Four Kings = 800 points.

Any Four Queens = 600 points.

Any Four Jacks = 400 points.

The game bonus is 1,000 points, the rubicon 2,500 points and brisques are disregarded.

In all other essentials the scoring is the same as in rubicon bezique. The partnership principle, however, introduces two new features in the methods of declaring combinations. First, after winning a trick, a player may either declare or leave it to his partner to do so. Secondly, a player may declare a combination either with his own cards (including those on the table already declared by him) or with one or more of his own cards and one or more of his partner's declared cards. Indeed, since a player holds only nine cards, quintuple bezique (and sextuple bezique if it occurs) can only be declared with the help of partner.

The player on the left of the dealer leads to the first trick.

Beyond these additions, the play follows that of rubicon bezique.

SIX-PACK BEZIQUE, sometimes, but rarely, known as Chinese Bezique, is a game for two players, and generally considered the most popular variation of the family. Sir Winston Churchill was a keen player and an able exponent of the game.

Six packs are shuffled together and both players lift a part of the pack and show the bottom cards to determine choice of seat and deal. The one who shows the higher card has the choice, and would be advised to pass the deal to his opponent because there is a slight disadvantage in dealing. If equal cards are shown the players cut again.

The dealer takes a number of cards at random off the top of the pack, and the non-dealer estimates how many have been taken. If his estimate proves correct he scores 150 points. The dealer deals twelve cards, one by one, to his opponent and himself, and scores 250 points if he has taken exactly twenty-four cards from the top of the pack.

There is no turn-up to determine the trump suit. It is determined, as in rubicon bezique (above), by the first declared marriage or sequence by either player.

The declarations are scored for as follows:

Sequence in Trumps = 250 points.

Sequence in a Plain Suit = 150 points.

Royal Marriage = 40 points.

Common Marriage = 20 points.

Bezique = 40 points

Double Bezique = 500 points

Triple Bezique = 1,500 points

Quadruple Bezique = 4,500 points

If Spades are trumps bezique is **Q♠** and **J♦**; if Diamonds are trumps **Q♦** and **J♠**; if Hearts are trumps **Q♥** and **J♣**; and if Clubs are trumps **Q♣** and **J♥**.

Four Aces in Trumps = 1,000 points.
Four Tens in Trumps = 900 points.
Four Kings in Trumps = 800 points.
Four Queens in Trumps = 600 points.
Four Jacks in Trumps = 400 points.
Any Four Aces = 100 points.
Any Four Kings = 80 points.
Any Four Queens = 60 points.
Any Four Jacks = 40 points.
Carte Blanche = 250 points.

The non-dealer leads to the first trick. It is not compulsory to follow suit, and the card that is led holds the trick unless a higher card of the same suit is played or a trump is played to the lead of a plain suit. As points are not scored for brisques, nor for winning tricks, the tricks are not gathered and turned but left face upwards on the table in a pile. The winner of a trick may score for a declaration. He takes the top card of the stock (the loser takes the next card of the stock) and leads to the next trick.

A declaration is made by placing the appropriate cards face upwards on the table. They are left there and are available for play as though in the hand of the player. Declarations are scored when made, and the same card may be counted in a declaration more than once.

No declaration may be made after the last two cards of the stock have been drawn. The players then pick up any cards they have on the table and play off the last twelve tricks. As in the parent game, a player must now follow suit to the card led, and must win a trick if he is able to.

Every deal constitutes a game, and the player with the higher score wins. He adds 1,000 points to his score, and rubicons his opponent if he has failed to score 3,000 points.

EIGHT-PACK BEZIQUE is identical with six-pack bezique (above) except for the increased number of cards and the following differences in the routine and scoring:
1. Each player is dealt fifteen cards.
2. The scores for beziques are:
   Bezique = 50 points.
   Double Bezique = 500 points.
   Triple Bezique = 1,500 points.
   Quadruple Bezique = 4,500 points.
   Quintuple Bezique = = 9,000 points.
3. In the trump suit the scores are for:
   Five Aces = 2,000 points.
   Five Tens = 1,800 points.
   Five Kings = 1,600 points.
   Five Queens = 1,200 points.
   Five Jacks = 800 points.
4. A player who fails to score 5,000 points is rubiconed.

California Jack

California Jack is played with the full pack of fifty-two cards, the Ace ranking high the 2 low. It is a game for two players that derives from all fours (see page 28) but is generally considered an improvement on it.

The non-dealer cuts the pack and exposes the bottom card to decide the trump suit. The dealer deals six cards, one at a time, to each player, and places the remainder of the pack face upwards on the table, taking the precaution to square it up so that only the top card can be seen.

The non-dealer leads to the first trick. The winner of a trick takes the top card of the stock, the loser the next card. A player must follow suit if he can, and he loses 1 point if he revokes.

When the stock is exhausted and the last six cards have been played, the tricks won by each player are examined, and 1 point is scored for winning High (Ace of trumps), Low (2 of trumps), Jack (Jack of trumps) and Game (majority of points, counting each Ace won as 4 points, each King as 3 points, each Queen as 2 points, each Jack as 1 point, and each Ten as 10 points).

The game is won by the player who first scores 10 points.

The player should aim to keep both winning and losing cards in his hand because if the exposed card of the stock is valuable he will wish to win it, but if it is not, he will wish to lose the trick on the chance of the next card of the stock being a more valuable one. The Tens, of course, are the cards to go for.

A good California Jack hand. There are two good cards for trick-winning and three for losing

SHASTA SAM is a variation of the game in which the stock is placed face downwards on the table instead of face upwards. It is a less skilful game as, of course, the winner of a trick does not know what card he will draw.

Casino

Although Casino (sometimes erroneously spelt cassino) is essentially a game for two, played with the full pack of fifty-two cards, it may be played by three or four. The only difference is that if three players take part they play all against all, and if four take part two play in partnership against the other two.

The dealer deals two cards face downwards to his opponent, then two face upwards to the table, and then two face downwards to himself. This is repeated, so that both players end with four cards each, and there are four exposed cards (the layout) on the table. The remaining forty cards (the stock) are placed face downwards on the table.

The numeral cards count at their pip values. The Ace counts as 1, and the court cards are used only for pairing: they have no pip value.

The object of the game is to take in cards which score as follows:

The **10** ♦ (Great Casino) = 2 points.
The **2** ♠ (Little Casino) = 1 point.
The majority of cards (27 or more) = 3 points.
The majority of Spades (7 or more) = 1 point.
Each Ace = 1 point.
All cards in the layout (the Sweep) = 1 point.

Each player in turn, beginning with the non-dealer, plays a card until both players have exhausted their four cards. When this occurs, the same dealer deals four more cards to his opponent and four to himself, but none to the layout. Play continues in this way until the stock has been exhausted. In all, therefore, there are six deals to complete the game, and before making the final deal the dealer must announce it. If he does not, his opponent has a right to cancel the deal.

When a player plays a card from his hand he has the choice of several plays.

He may *Pair*. If, for example, there are one or more 5s in the layout, he may play a 5 from his hand and take it up as a trick with all the other 5s in the layout. A court card, however, may be paired with only one card of the same rank at a time.

He may *Combine*. It is an extension of pairing that allows a player to pick up cards from the layout of the total pip value of a card in his hand. Thus a player playing a 9 may take up a 7 and a 2, or a 6 and a 3 from the layout, or all four cards if they are in the layout.

He may *Build*. He may play a card to a card in the layout to make up a total that he is in a position to take with another card in his hand. If, for example, a player holds a 9 and a 2, and there is a 7 in the layout, he may build the 2 on the 7, so that the next time he plays (provided his opponent has not forestalled him) he may play the 9 and take all three cards as a trick. The build may be continued by either player up to a maximum of five cards, but a build can be taken only as a unit. The player who has built must take up the combination when next it is his turn to play, unless he prefers to win something else, or he decides to make another build.

He may *Call*. It is an extension of building that allows a player to earmark one or more combinations for subsequent capture. Suppose, for example, a player holds in his hand two 8s and that there is a 5 and a 3 in the layout (see illustration). He could, of

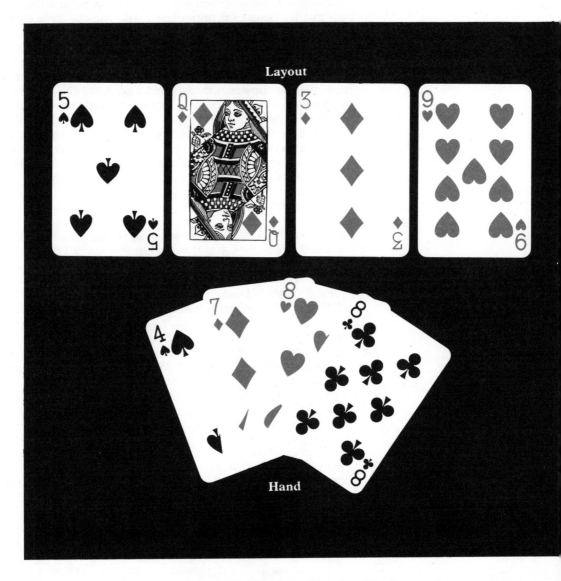

Layout

Hand

course, combine one of his 8s with the 5 and 3 in the layout, but this would only give him three cards in the trick. The better play, therefore, is for him to play one of his 8s to the layout and announce 'Eight'. Then, when next it is his turn to play, provided his opponent has not forestalled him, he may play his other 8 and pick up all four cards in the trick.

When a player cannot pair, combine, build or call, he must play one of his cards to the layout. It is known as trailing. It is advisable to play a low card, but not an Ace, little casino or a Spade.

When the last eight cards have been played any left in the layout are the property of the winner of the final trick, but it does not count as a sweep.

This ends the game, except for the formality of the players examining their tricks and counting their scores.

There is no penalty for making a build incorrectly, or for capturing cards to which a player is not entitled, because his opponent has the opportunity to see the error and demand that it is corrected. If, however, a player makes a build when he has no card in his hand to capture it or trails when he has a build in the layout, he automatically forfeits the game. If a card is faced in the pack, or if the dealer when dealing exposes a card, other than when dealing cards to the layout, the exposed card is played to the layout and the dealer plays the hand with fewer than four cards.

Casino is sometimes considered a game for children. It is, however, very far from being so. Among card players it is widely spoken of as one of the best of all two-handed games and it is often played for high stakes. To be successful a player needs an elephantine memory, and the capacity to deduce from the card played by an opponent what cards he is most likely to be holding in his hand.

ROYAL CASINO is an improvement on the parent game because the court cards play a more important part. The Aces count 1 or 14 (at the option of the player), the Kings 13, the Queens 12 and the Jacks 11, and they may be used for combining and building. Thus an 8 and a 4 may be taken with a Queen, a 6, a 4 and a 3 with a King, and so on.

Twenty-one points constitute the game.

In **DRAW CASINO**, after the first round of a deal, the forty undealt cards are placed face downwards on the table to form a stock. Then each player, after playing, draws a card from the stock to bring the number of cards in his hand up to four. When the stock is exhausted the hands are played out and the count made as in the parent game.

SPADE CASINO may be played either as royal casino (above) or as the parent game, with the addition that the Ace, Jack and 2 of Spades count 2 points each, and all the other Spades 1 point each.

Game is 61 points, and it is convenient and customary to keep the score on a cribbage board.

Comet

Two 52-card packs, with the same design on their backs, are used alternately. The packs must be prepared by rejecting all the Aces, putting all the red cards into one pack and all the black cards into another, and interchanging a red and a black 9.

Eighteen cards are dealt to each player, one at a time, and the remaining twelve cards are put aside; they play no part in the game. The non-dealer begins the game by playing one of his cards, face upwards, to the centre of the table. The players then, alternately, build up on it by rank only. Suits are disregarded. Any number of cards, provided they are of the proper rank, may be played in one turn. The four 8s, for example, may be built on a 7, the four Jacks on a 10, and so on. When a player is unable to build it is a stop, and his opponent begins a new sequence by playing any card he chooses. Obviously a King is always a stop.

The 9 of the opposite colour is called the comet. It may represent any card that the holder chooses, but may be played only in turn. It is a stop, and the player who plays it begins a new sequence.

The player who is first to get rid of all the cards in his hand is the winner. He scores the total of pips left in his opponent's hand, the court cards counting as 10 each. If both players are stopped and both are left with cards in their hands, both hands are counted. The lower hand wins and scores the value of his opponent's hand less the value of his own. If a player wins the hand while the comet is in the hand of his opponent he scores double. If a player wins by playing the comet, he doubles his score, and if he wins the hand by playing the comet as a 9 he quadruples his score.

COMMIT is a variation of the parent game that is suitable for more than two players. It is played with the standard pack of fifty-two cards from which the 8 of Diamonds has been removed, and as many other 8s and 7s as may be necessary for the players to be dealt an equal number of cards.

The players place an equal number of units into a pool.

The player on the left of the dealer begins by playing any card to the centre of the table. The others play cards on it as able, and not necessarily in rotation. The cards played must follow in sequence. Only the 6 of Spades may be played on the 5 of Spades, the 8 of Clubs on the 7 of Clubs, and so on.

The 9 of Diamonds is the comet and may be played either when all the players are stopped or when the holder of it has played regularly and is unable to continue the sequence. After it has been played, any player in rotation may either continue by playing the 10 of Diamonds on it, or the card next above that for which the comet has been substituted.

The player who plays the comet receives 2 units from each of the other players, and any player who plays a King receives 1 unit from each of the other players. The player who is first to get rid of his cards wins the pool, and receives 2 units from a player who has been left with the comet in his hand, and 1 unit for each King.

Cribbage

Cribbage is believed to have been developed out of the older card game of Noddy, by Sir John Suckling in the reign of Charles I. Originally it was a two-handed game, but variations for three and four players are now known.

The two-handed game is the most popular, and of it there are three variations: 5-card, 6-card and 7-card. Points won are marked with a peg on what is known as a noddy board. It is oblong in shape, has a double row of holes, thirty in each row, and is divided, for convenience in scoring, into groups of five holes. The board is placed between the two players; both start from the same end of the board and peg their scores first along the outer row of holes and then along the inner row—once round the board at the 5-card game, twice round at the 6-card game and three times round at the 7-card game. In each case the game ends when one player reaches the game hole from which he started. Thus, at 5-card cribbage the game is 61 holes, at 6-card 121 holes, and at 7-card 181 holes.

FIVE-CARD CRIBBAGE FOR TWO PLAYERS, which is the original game, is generally considered the most scientific of the variations. In the manner of scoring it is unique, and the play is different to that of most card games, because it calls for no effort of memory. Good judgement and concentration are the chief qualities that lead to success.

The full pack of fifty-two cards is used. The players cut for deal; the lower deals first. When cutting for deal, and for scoring sequences, the cards rank in order from Ace (low) to King (high), but, for counting, the King, Queen and Jack count 10 each and the other cards at their pip values. Five cards are dealt to each player, and the non-dealer pegs 3 holes (Three for Last) as compensation against the advantage of the first deal of a game.

The players look at their cards, and then place two of them face downwards on the right of the dealer. These four cards are known as the *Crib*. The non-dealer then cuts the pack, and the dealer turns up the top card of the cut and places it on top of the pack. The card is known as the *Start*, and if it is a Jack the dealer pegs 2 holes (Two for his Heels).

Scores are made partly in play and partly by the scoring values of the cards in hand. The latter, however, are not pegged until the play ends.

During the play of the hand, scores are made as follows:

If a player plays a card of the same rank as the previous one played, he pegs 2 for a *Pair*, but court cards pair only rank with rank—that is to say King with King, Queen with Queen and Jack with Jack.

If a player plays a third card of the same rank as a pair he pegs 6 for *Pair-Royal*.

If a player plays a fourth card of the same rank as a pair-royal he pegs 12 for a *Double Pair-Royal*.

A *Sequence* (or *Run*) is pegged at 1 for each card with a minimum of three cards and a maximum of seven. The cards need not be of the same suit, nor need they be played in sequential order, but, as the Ace is low, **A K Q** is not a sequence, and a sequence is destroyed by a pair or an intervening card. If the dealer plays a 7 and the non-dealer a 5, the dealer may now play a 6 and peg 3, and the non-dealer may continue either with a 4 or an 8 and peg 4.

If a player plays a card which, with those already played, adds up to *Fifteen* he pegs 2, and, again, if they total *Thirty-one* he pegs 2.

Out of this an important point arises. If, when the player whose turn it is to play cannot do so without exceeding thirty-one, he says 'Go'. His opponent then plays a card or cards up to the limit. If the cards that he plays bring the total up to exactly thirty-one he pegs 2; if not he pegs 1 (One for Last).

This ends the play, and the players, beginning with the non-dealer, count their scores by combining their own cards with the start. The dealer then exposes the crib (it is his exclusive property) and any values that he finds in it (making full use of the start) he pegs to his score. Should either player hold the Jack of the same suit as the start he pegs 1 (One for his Nob). If a player holds in his hand three cards all of the same suit he pegs 3 for a *Flush*, and 4 if the start is of the same suit. In the crib, however, nothing is scored for a flush unless, with the start, it is a flush of five; if it is the dealer pegs 5.

Two other features of the scoring call for special mention. First, a player must count his hand aloud, and if he overlooks any score, either in play or otherwise, his opponent may call 'Muggins', point out the omission, and peg the score for himself. Secondly, if a player reaches the game hole before his opponent has gone halfway round the board a *Lurch* is scored, that is to say the winner scores two games instead of only one.

Points are scored during the play by a player adding the value of the card played by the opponent to a card played from his own hand. Thus if a 10 or court card is led, and a player plays a 5, he scores fifteen and pegs 2 holes (Fifteen-Two as it is called for short). If a 6 is led, and he plays another 6, he scores for a pair and pegs 2. Again, a 4 is led, he plays a 6, and the opponent plays a 5: he pegs 3 for a sequence and 2 for fifteen. And so on.

The general principles of play may be illustrated in an elementary deal.

West   East

East is the dealer.

West holds a sequence of four. As a result the King of Clubs will go to the crib, and for his other card he must choose between the 6 of Clubs and the 9 of Hearts. There is not much in it, but as the 6 of Clubs is of the same suit as the King, there is a slight advantage in discarding the 9 of Hearts, because the 6 of Clubs (along with the King) might help to give East a flush in his crib.

East has an easy choice of discards. Indeed, it is obvious that he will discard the Ace of Clubs and 3 of Diamonds.

West cuts the cards, and East turns up the King of Spades.

The position is now:

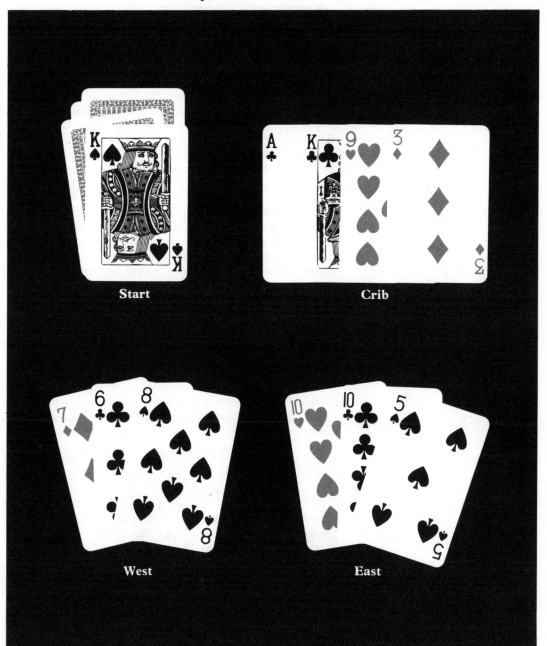

Start   **Crib**

West   **East**

West leads the **7** ♦ and says 'Seven'. It is his best lead because if East plays an 8 and pegs 2 for fifteen, West can play the **6** ♣ and peg 3 for sequence. He will not, of course, play the **8** ♠, because if East holds another 8 he will play it and not only peg for a pair-royal but for thirty-one as well.

In the event, East cannot play an 8 and score for fifteen. His best play, therefore, is the **10** ♣ announcing 'Seventeen'. This makes it impossible for a fifteen to be scored against him.

West has no better play than the **8** ♠ announcing 'Twenty-five', because the closer the total to 31 the better is the chance that East will be unable to play.

East plays the **5** ♠ announcing 'Thirty'.

West says 'Go' and as East has not got an Ace he pegs One for Last.

The hands are now counted.

West is not helped by the start. All he can score is 2 for fifteen and 3 for sequence. This with his Three for Last gives him a score of 8.

East pegs 6 for fifteen (two 10s and the **K** ♠ in the start, each combined with the **5** ♠) and 2 for the pair of 10s. In the crib he finds an Ace, a King a 9 and a 3. With the start this gives him 2 for the pair of Kings. He, therefore pegs 10 holes, making 11 in all as he has already pegged One for Last.

SIX-CARD and SEVEN-CARD CRIBBAGE FOR TWO PLAYERS. The 6-card and 7-card variations of cribbage differ very little from the 5-card game. There is, in fact, no difference in the play nor in the crib, and very little in the mechanics of the game. The only differences of importance, apart from the number of cards, are that the non-dealer does not receive Three for Last, that the cards are played out to the end (the player failing to score for go leading again, thus giving his opponent the chance of making a pair or fifteen) and that in the 6-card variation the play is twice round the board (121 holes) and in the 7-card three times round (181 holes).

The general principles explained for the parent game hold good at the 6-card variation. It is to be noted, however, that in the 6-card variation the number of cards in hand and in the crib are the same, from which it follows that it is not so important for the non-dealer to make an effort of trying to baulk the crib by his discard. The two objectives – preserving any values in hand and baulking opponent's crib – are in this case on the same level, and either objective may be preferred, as the nature of the hand dictates.

THREE-HANDED CRIBBAGE. Five cards are dealt to each player, and an extra one to the crib, to which each player contributes one card only. There is no Three for Last. The start is cut for in the usual way. The player on the left of the dealer plays first, and has first Show. He deals the succeeding hand. The score may be pegged on a triangular board open in the centre, or on the regular board furnished with a pivotted arm that permits a third player to peg. The game is once round the board.

FOUR-HANDED CRIBBAGE. Two play as partners against the other two, the partners sitting facing each other. Each player is dealt five cards and discards one to the crib, which is the property of the dealer. The player on the left of the dealer plays first. The others follow in clockwise rotation. Consultation between partners is not allowed, nor may they prompt each other, but a player may help his partner in the count of the hand or crib. The cards are played out to the end, as in the 6-card and 7-card variations. Game is usually twice round the board (121 holes).

Ecarté

Écarté is played with a 32-card pack; that is to say with a pack from which the 2s, 3s, 4s, 5s, and 6s have been removed. The cards rank in the order: King (high), Queen, Jack, Ace, 10, 9, 8, 7 (low).

The two players are deal five cards each, either in packets of three and two, or two and three, and the rest of the pack is placed face downwards on the table, between them. To determine the trump suit the top card of the pack is turned face upwards. After looking at his cards, the non-dealer either plays or proposes. If he proposes, the dealer has the choice of either accepting or playing, and if he accepts both players may exchange any or all of their cards for others from the pack. By agreement the exchange of cards may continue until the pack is exhausted.

The non-dealer has first lead. The object of the game is to win three tricks, called the Trick. The winner scores 1 point for this, and if he wins all five tricks (the Vole) he scores 2 points. The game is won by the player who first wins 5 points, and it is customary to count a treble if a player wins the game and his opponent has failed to score; a double if his opponent has scored only 1 or 2 points, and a single if his opponent has scored 3 or 4 points.

So far, then, *écarté* appears to be childishly simple. The game, however, lends itself to a number of refinements that raise it to the level of an adult game. If the non-dealer does not propose, but plays, and fails to make the Trick, the dealer scores 2 points instead of only 1. In the same way, if the dealer refuses a proposal, and plays, and fails to make the Trick, the non-dealer scores 2 points. The value of the Vole (2 points) is not affected by playing without proposing.

Another important feature of the game is that if the dealer turns up a King as trumps, or if a player is dealt the King of the trump suit, he scores 1 point. The point can be scored by the non-dealer only if he declares the King before he makes the opening lead, and by the dealer only if he declares it before he plays to the first trick. A player is under no compulsion to declare the King, and, indeed, sometimes it is better to sacrifice the point for declaring the King than to declare it and so disclose to the opponent that this important card is held against him.

With the score West 3 points, East 4 points, East deals and the 8 ♠ is turned up.

West   East

East decides to play and must win the game if he handles his cards correctly. In the event he loses the game by incautious play. He leads **K ♣** on which West plays **7 ♣**. West does not declare the **K ♠** because East has played without proposing and, therefore, will lose 2 points if he fails to win the Trick. On the other hand, if he wins the Trick, declaring the King will be of no help to West.

East is lulled into a false sense of security, and unaware that the **K ♠** is against him he assumes that it is safe to lead **Q ♠**. West wins with **K ♠**, leads **Q ♦** to force East to win with **J ♠**, and comes to the last two tricks, and with them wins the game, with **A ♠** and **A ♥**

There are a number of stock hands, holding which a player should play and not propose, and equally refuse the opponent's proposal. The more important of them are set out below. In all cases Spades are trumps:

1. Any three trumps supported by two inferior cards in outside suits— **♠ J 10 7 ♥ 8 ♦ 10**

2. Any two trumps supported by three cards in one outside suit— **♠ 10 8 ♥ J 8 7**

3. Any two trumps supported by the King and a low card in an outside suit, and one indifferent card in another suit— **♠ A 8 ♥ K 7 ♦ 9**

4. Any one trump supported by four cards headed by the King (or Queen) in an outside suit— **♠ J ♥ K 9 8 7** (or **Q J 8 7**)

5. Any one trump supported by three cards headed by a court card in an outside suit, and any high court card in another suit— **♠ 10 ♥ J 10 7 ♦ Q**

6. Any hand that contains three queens (or better) and even though it may lack a trump card— **♥ Q 7 ♦ Q 7 ♣ K**

7. Any hand that contains four high cards (King, Queen, Jack) and even though it may lack a trump card— **♥ K ♦ Q J ♣ Q 7**

These stock hands are based on the Law of Probability, supported by the experience of the best players, who set great store on them. So far as the dealer is concerned, they are the minimum types of hands for him to play on. In a number of cases he may do better if he follows his luck, or decides to play on what is called a hunch, but the non-dealer should never propose when holding a hand similar to one of the above types. The reason is that he has the opening lead, and, at écarté, the opening lead is of vital importance.

East deals and the **10 ♠** is turned up.

West   East

West plays and if he leads **Q** ♥ he wins the Trick no matter how East plays.

If, however, West had dealt, East would be on lead and if he led the **K** ♦ he would win the Trick no matter how West played. In fact, West would be hard put to save the Vole, and, indeed, would do so only if he retained the **J** ♣ and not the **Q** ♥. An experienced player would, of course, retain the **J** ♣ (although the **Q** ♥ is a higher card) because he holds three Hearts and only one Club, and since there are only eight cards in a suit it is about seven to five on that East's last card is a Club and not a Heart.

The deal is of some interest because it illustrates the danger of leading the Queen of trumps, unless the King has been turned up as trumps. It will be seen that if West decides to lead the **Q** ♠, East wins with the **K** ♠, runs his Diamonds (scoring the Trick) and West will save the Vole only if he retains the **J** ♣. On the other hand, it is to be noted that the lead of the singleton King of trumps is nearly always a good lead, and rarely damages the leader's hand.

As a general rule it is best for a player to play when he cannot see his way to discarding more than two cards; but if a player's hand guarantees him the Trick, or virtually so, he should propose or accept, because if the proposal is refused he is on easy street (since the Trick is more or less in his pocket) and if the proposal is accepted he has the opportunity to convert his hand into one on which he may win the Vole.

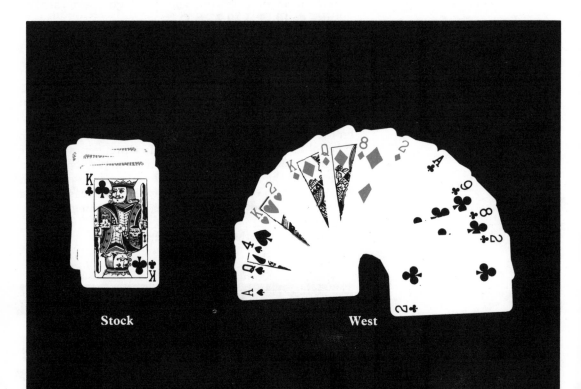

Stock   West

German Whist

German Whist is a very simple game. Each player is dealt thirteen cards. The remaining twenty-six cards are placed face downwards between the players and the top card is turned face upwards to denote the trump suit.

The non-dealer leads to the first trick. Thereafter the player who wins a trick leads to the next, and so on. A player must follow suit if he can. If he cannot he may either trump or discard. The winner of a trick takes into his hand the exposed card from the top of the stock: the loser takes the next card from the stock (he does not show it to his opponent) and turns up the next card of the stock.

When the stock is exhausted, the players play out the remaining thirteen cards, and at this stage of the game the player with a good memory will know exactly which cards his opponent holds.

The game is complete in one deal, and the player who wins the majority of tricks receives an agreed number of points per trick for all in excess of those won by his opponent. If both players win thirteen tricks, there is, of course, no score.

Although german whist is a simple game it offers good memory training for those who aspire to succeed at more advanced games, and, at the same time, gives exercise in the technique of card play.

If a player holds a strong trump suit he should lead his trumps early in the game so as to command the game in the later stages of the play, and if the exposed card is a trump it is always good play to make an effort to win it.

On the other hand, it is not always good play to win a trick. Much depends on the value of the exposed card. The 9♦ is exposed. West leads the **7♦** and East holds ♦ **Q63**. East should play **3♦**, and allow West to win the trick. It is not worth while wasting the **Q♦** which should be kept in hand for better things later in the game. By contrary, if the **J♦** is the exposed card, East should win the trick with the **Q♦**, because now he is exchanging the **Q♦** for an equivalent card and adding a trick to his total.

It is advisable to hold command of as many suits as possible, because it enables one to take a trick whenever the exposed card is worth winning, without losing control of the suit.

West holds the hand opposite.

Spades are trumps, and the exposed card is **K♣**.

The **K♣** is worth winning, but leading the **A♣** is not the best play. West will win the trick, but the value of his hand will remain unchanged. West should prefer to lead the **K♦**, because if it wins the trick his hand will be that much better, and if East is able to win the trick with the **A♦**, West's **Q♦** has been promoted to top Diamond.

Gin Rummy

Many variations of rummy (see page 139) are known, but for two players the one generally preferred is Gin Rummy with the Hollywood scoring, so called because during the war it was taken up with much publicity by the cinema stars.

The game is played with a full pack of fifty-two cards that rank from King (high) to Ace (low). The players cut to determine who deals first, but, thereafter, the player who wins a hand deals for the next one.

Ten cards are dealt to each player and the next card is turned face upwards and placed on the table between the players; it is known as the up-card. The rest of the pack is placed faced downwards alongside it.

The object of the game is to meld one's cards into sets of three or four of the same suit, and into sequences of three or more of the same suit. Sets and sequences must be independent of each other: a player is not allowed to meld the same card into a sequence and a set.

The non-dealer has first choice of taking the up-card into his hand. If he does not, he must offer it to the dealer. If either player takes the up-card, he discards a card from his hand face upwards on the table. If neither player takes the up-card, the non-dealer takes the top card of the stock and discards a card from his hand to cover the up-card. The dealer then has the option of taking into his hand either the card that the non-dealer has discarded or the top card of the stock. When he has taken one of them into his hand, he, too, discards a card from his hand. The discards are placed one on top of the other, so that only the card immediately discarded can be seen, and the discard pile must not be examined by the players while the deal is in play.

Play continues in this way—each player in turn either taking the top card of the discard pile or the top card of the stock—until one of them elects to go down (called knocking) or there are only two cards left in the stock. Neither may be drawn, and if the player who draws the fiftieth card discards without knocking, the deal is declared a draw; neither player scores and the same dealer deals again.

The player who knocks must do so after drawing a card and discarding, and his unmelded cards must not exceed a total of 10 points—court cards count 10 points each and the others their pip values.

Unless a player has declared gin (*i.e.* knocked with all his cards melded) his opponent can reduce his loss by adding cards from his hand to the melds exposed by his opponent.

North, who has not declared gin, knocks with the melds on the left.

South holds in his hand:

♠ **J 6 3 2**   ♥ **Q A**   ♦ **Q J**   ♣ **K 6**

and reduces his loss by adding the 6♠ and A♥ to North's sequences, and the K♣ to his set of Kings.

Play now ceases, and the score is made up as follows:

1. The unmelded cards of the players are totalled to determine their respective point-counts.
2. A player who has declared gin scores 25 points plus his opponent's point-count.
3. If gin has not been declared: if the knocker's point-count is less than that of his opponent's, the knocker wins the hand and scores the difference between the two point-counts; if the opponent's point-count is less than that of the knocker or if the two point-counts are equal, the opponent wins the deal and scores 20 points for undercutting plus the difference (if any) between the two point-counts.

The scores are recorded on a sheet of paper ruled as follows:

Every deal won and score entered is known as a box. The first time that a player scores he enters the points in the first column only. The second time that he scores he enters them in the second column and adds them to his score in the first column. The third time that he scores he enters them in the third column and adds them to the scores last entered in the first and second columns. Thereafter, every time that a player scores he adds his score to the scores last entered in all three columns.

When the score of a player in a column reaches a total of 100 points or more, the column is closed. The winner of a column scores 100 points for winning it, and a further 20 points for each box that he has won in excess of those won by his opponent. If, however, the opponent has won more boxes than the winner of the column, the opponent scores 20 points for each box that he has won in excess of those won by the winner of the column, and this score is deducted from that of the winner of the column.

If a player fails to score in any column he is blitzed, and the total score of the winner of the column is doubled. The player who has been blitzed in any column makes his first, or second, score in the next column which has not been won.

The game ends when all three columns have been won.

If a player wins all three columns, his final score is determined by adding together the total scores of all three columns. If a player wins two columns (his opponent one column) the final score is determined by adding together the total scores of the winner of the two columns, and subtracting the lower score from the higher.

Honeymoon Bridge

Thirteen cards are dealt to each player and the remaining twenty-six cards are placed face downwards between them.

The non-dealer leads to the first trick. Thereafter the player who wins a trick leads to the next. A player must follow suit if he can. The winner of a trick takes the top card of the stock, the loser takes the next card. The first thirteen tricks are played without a trump suit, and the tricks do not count in the final score.

When the stock is exhausted, the two players bid as in bridge (see page 83) the dealer first; bidding continues until one player passes a bid, double or redouble. The player who does not make the final bid leads to the first trick, and the play continues as in the regular game except that only two, instead of four, players are competing. The players score as in bridge.

If a player revokes during the play of the first thirteen tricks, or if he draws a card out of turn, or sees more than one card when drawing from the stock, his opponent, when it is his turn to draw from the stock, may look at the two top cards and take either. Other irregularities are governed by the laws of bridge.

In **HONEYMOON BRIDGE WITH A WIDOW** the players sit in adjacent seats and the cards are dealt into four hands (as in the regular game) of twelve cards each. The remaining four cards (the widow) are placed face downwards in the centre of the table.

The players bid as in the regular game (the dealer bids first) and when a bid has been passed, doubled or redoubled, the player who has won the declaration takes up the widow hand and, without showing it to his opponent, takes one card into his own hand, one into his dummy, and gives the other two cards to his opponent to take one into his hand and the other into his dummy.

The player who has won the declaration may demand the opening lead to be made either by his opponent or by his opponent's dummy.

Thereafter the play and scoring proceed as in the regular game.

In **SEMI-EXPOSED HONEYMOON BRIDGE** the players sit in adjacent seats and the cards are dealt as in the regular game, except that the first six cards to the dummies are dealt face downwards in a row, the remaining cards, six face upwards on top of them and one face upwards by itself.

The dealer bids first, and the bidding ends when a bid has been passed, doubled or redoubled. The hand on the left of the player who has won the declaration leads to the first trick. The play and scoring are as in the regular game, except that a player may play from his dummy only a face-upwards card. When a face-upwards card has been played, the card under it is turned face upwards, and becomes available for play.

Jo-jotte

Although Jo-jotte was invented by Ely Culbertson in 1937, it is not altogether a modern game, but a variation of the old French game of belotte in itself very similar to klaberjass (see page 61) and its several variations.

It is a game for two players, and played with the short pack, namely a pack from which all cards below the rank of 7 have been removed.

The rank of the cards varies. If there is a trump suit, the cards of the suit rank in the order: **J 9 A 10 K Q 8 7**. In plain suits, or if the hand is played in No-Trumps, the order is: **A 10 K Q J 9 8 7**.

Each player is dealt six cards (either singly, or in bundles of two or three) and the thirteenth card of the pack is placed face upwards on the table. It is known as the turned card.

There are two rounds of bidding. The non-dealer bids first. He may either accept the suit of the turned card as trumps, or pass. If he passes, the dealer has the same option. If both players pass, the non-dealer may name any suit, other than that of the turned card, as trumps, or he may declare No-Trumps or he may pass. If he passes for the second time, the dealer has the same option. If both players pass twice the hand is abandoned and the deal passes, but if either player names a suit as trumps, his opponent may overbid it by declaring No-Trumps, but not by naming another suit as trumps. Either player may double his opponent's declaration, and any double may be redoubled.

When the declaration has been determined (doubled, redoubled or passed) the dealer deals three more cards to his opponent and to himself, and he places the bottom card of the pack face upwards on top of the undealt cards of the pack. It has no significance in play but is solely informatory and, therefore, is known as the information card.

The player who has made the final declaration is known as the declarer: his opponent as the defender.

At this stage of the game the defender may announce that instead of defending against the declarer's contract he will himself become declarer at a Nullo contract; a contract, that is, to lose every trick. The declarer may now declare a Slam. It is a contract to win every trick either in the suit originally named by him (he cannot change the suit) or in No-Trumps.

The defender then announces his melds, if he holds any. A meld is four of a kind (except 9s, 8s and 7s at No-Trumps, and 8s and 7s in a suit declaration). A meld carries a score of 100 points and is scored (as at bridge (see page 126)) above the line. Only the player with the highest-ranking meld may score for it, and he may score for a second meld if he holds one.

Next, beginning with the defender, the players score for sequences, and for this purpose the cards take their normal rank of Ace (high), King, Queen, Jack, 10, 9, 8, 7. For a sequence of five cards the holder scores 50 points above the line, for a sequence of four 40 points, and for a sequence of three 20 points. If two sequences are of equal length, that headed by the highest card takes precedence. If both sequences are equal, a sequence in the trump suit wins over one in a plain suit; if both sequences are in plain suits neither is scored for. Only the player with the higher-ranking sequence may score for it, and he may score for any other sequences that he may hold.

Clubs are trumps. Defender scores 200 points above the line for his melds of 10s and Queens, and the declarer cannot score for his meld of Kings because in the trump suit the 10 is higher than the King.

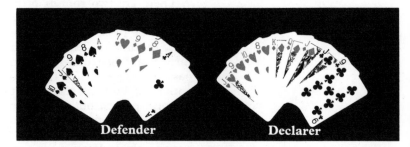

Hearts are trumps. Neither player has a meld. Defender declares his 4-card sequence in Spades but he cannot score for it because the declarer has an equal sequence in the trump suit (Hearts). The declarer, therefore, scores 40 points above the line for his 4-card sequence in Hearts and a further 20 points for his 3-card sequence in Diamonds.

Finally, it is to be noted that if the declarer elects to play the hand in the same suit as the turned card, either player if he holds the 7 of the suit may exchange it for the turned card.

The player who leads to a trick may lead any card that he chooses. The second player is limited in his play; for he must obey the three rules that follow:

1. He must follow suit if he can.
2. If a trump has been led he must not only follow suit if he can, but win the trick by playing a higher trump if he holds one.
3. If a plain suit has been led and he is unable to follow suit, he must win the trick by trumping if he can.

Second player may discard a worthless card only when he is unable to obey one or other of these three rules.

Winning a trick has no value in itself. What counts is winning tricks with certain cards in them: these are scored as follows:

For winning the Jack of trumps   20 points
For winning the 9 of trumps   15 points
For winning any Ace or 10   10 points
For winning any King or Queen   5 points
For winning the last trick (except at Nullo)   10 points

The example that follows is a simple one to illustrate the mechanics of the game.

Defender   Declarer

Hearts are trumps. The turned card is **K ♠**: the information card **Q ♦**.

Defender leads **A ♣**, and the play is:

Defender	Declarer
A ♣	**Q ♣**
10 ♣	**10 ♥**
8 ♦	**A ♦**
J ♦	**7 ♦**
8 ♣	**8 ♥**
9 ♥	**9 ♦**
10 ♠	**9 ♠**
Q ♠	**A ♥**
7 ♥	**J ♥**

Declarer scores for taking:

Jack of trumps (♥)	20 points
A ♥	10 points
A ♦	10 points
10 ♥	10 points
10 ♣	10 points
Q ♠	5 points
Last trick	10 points
	75 points

Defender scores for taking:

9 of trumps (♥)	15 points
A ♣	10 points
10 ♠	10 points
Q ♣	5 points
	40 points

In addition to the above, if a player holds the King and Queen of the trump suit (if there is one) he may score 20 points provided he announces 'Jo' when he plays the King and later 'Jotte' when he plays the Queen. He cannot score for the combination if he plays the Queen before the King.

Game is won by the player who first scores 80 points below the line, which may be made in one hand or in a series of part-scores, and the player who wins the rubber (best out of three games) scores a bonus of 300 points.

The declarer of a Nullo contract scores a bonus of 200 points if he loses every trick; if he takes a trick, however, his opponent scores 200 points for the first and 100 for every subsequent trick.

The declarer of a Slam scores a bonus of 500 points if he wins every trick; and if a player wins every trick but has not bid Slam he scores a bonus of 100 points.

Scoring below the line, towards game, is calculated as follows

1. If the declarer's total score, including melds, sequences, trick scores and bonuses (if any) is greater than the defender's total score, he scores his trick score below the line, and the defender scores his trick score above the line.

2. If the defender's total score is greater than the declarer's, the two trick scores are added together and scored by the defender below the line.

3. If the contract is doubled or redoubled, the player with the higher total scores both his and his opponent's trick score doubled or quadrupled, below the line.

4. If there is a tie in total points, the trick scores of both players are put in prison and awarded to the player who obtains the higher total in the following deal.

Klaberjass

Klaberjass is probably better known in America than in England, because under the names of Clabber, Clobber, Clubby, Klab and Klob, it occurs in Damon Runyon's amusing stories, and in 1937 a variation of the game, under the name of jo-jotte (see page 57) was publicized by Ely Culbertson. Despite the similarity of names it is not identical with the Hungarian game of kalabriás, which is a game for three or four players. There may have been a common ancestor, or possibly the game was taken to the New World by Central European immigrants and there adapted as a two-handed game with klaberjass as a bowdlerized version of kalabriás.

The game is played with a pack from which the 6s, 5s, 4s, 3s and 2s have been removed. In the trump suit the cards rank in the order **J 9 A 10 K Q 8 7**; and in the other three suits **A 10 K Q J 9 8 7**.

Six cards are dealt to both players, in two bundles of three cards each. The next card of the pack is turned face upwards on the table (it is known as the turn-up card) and the rest of the pack is placed face downwards so as partly to cover it.

The non-dealer bids first. He may *take-it* (*i.e.* accept the turn-up card as the trump suit); *pass* (*i.e.* refuse to accept the turn-up card as the trump suit); or *schmeiss* (*i.e.* offer to play with the turn-up card as the trump suit or throw in the hand, as his opponent prefers). If the opponent says 'Yes' to a schmeiss there is a fresh deal; if he says 'No' the hand is played with the turn-up card as the trump suit.

If the non-dealer has passed, the dealer may either take-it, pass or schmeiss.

If both players pass there is a second round of bidding. Now the non-dealer may name any one of the other three suits as trumps, or he may schmeiss (*i.e.* offer to name one of the other three suits as trumps or throw in the hand, as his opponent prefers), or he may pass. If he passes, the dealer may name one of the other three suits as trumps, or throw in the hand.

When a player accepts or names a trump suit, the bidding ends, and the player who has accepted or named a suit as trumps is called the maker.

There is never more than two rounds of bidding, and when the trump suit has been settled, the dealer deals three more cards, one at a time, to the two players. He then turns up the bottom card of the pack and places it on top of the pack. It takes no part in the play, and is put where it is only to be seen.

If either player has been dealt the 7 of the trump suit, he may exchange it for the turn-up card.

Only sequences are melded, and for melding the cards rank in the order from Ace (high) to 7 (low). A 3-card sequence counts 20 points, a 4-card or longer one 50 points.

The non-dealer begins by announcing the value of his best sequence. If his best sequence is of three cards he says 'Twenty'; if of four or more cards he says 'Fifty'. If dealer has a better sequence he says 'No good'; if he lacks a better sequence he says 'Good'; if he has an equal sequence he askes 'How high?'. The non-dealer then announces the top card of his sequence. The dealer then says whether it is good, no good, or if he has a sequence headed by an equal card. In this last event neither player scores unless one of the sequences is in the trump suit, which wins over a sequence in a plain suit.

The non-dealer leads to the first trick; thereafter the winner of a trick leads to the next. A player must follow suit if he can, and if he cannot he must play a trump if he holds one. If a trump is led, the second player must win the trick if he can.

After the first trick has been played, the player with the highest meld shows it and scores for all sequences in his hand. His opponent cannot score for any sequences that he may hold.

A player who holds the King and Queen of the trump suit may score 20 points so long as he announces 'Bella' immediately after he has played the second of them to a trick. If a player holds the Jack of the trump suit, as well as the King and Queen, he may score for the sequence as well as for bella.

When all the cards have been played, each player examines his tricks and scores points for winning in his tricks:

Jasz (the Jack of the trump suit)	20 points
Menel (the 9 of the trump suit)	14 points
Any Ace	11 points
Any 10	10 points
Any King	4 points
Any Queen	3 points
Any Jack (except Jasz)	2 points
Last Trick	10 points

If the maker's total, including melds and cards won, is higher than the opponent's, each scores all the points he has won. If the totals of the two players are equal, the opponent scores the points he has won, the maker nothing. If the opponent's total is higher than that of the maker's, the two totals are added together and the opponent scores them.

The player who first reaches 500 points wins the game.

KLABERJASS FOR FOUR PLAYERS is played in partnership, two playing against two. Eight cards are dealt to each player, and the dealer turns up his last card for trumps.

Each player in turn, beginning with the player on the left of the dealer, may either take-it or pass. There is no schmeiss. If all four players pass, there is a second round of bidding during which each player in turn has a right to name the trump suit. If all four players pass the second round of bidding there is a fresh deal.

The player who names the trump suit becomes the maker, and his side must score more than the opposing side.

The player on the left of the dealer leads to the first trick.

Pinocle*

Pinocle in its original form is a game for two players similar to bezique (see page 30). It is played with a pack of forty-eight cards, namely a pack that consists of **A 10 K Q J 9** (in this order) in each of the four suits, duplicated.

Twelve cards are dealt to both players, either three or four cards at a time, and the next card is turned face upwards to indicate the trump suit. The rest of the pack is placed face downwards on the table to half cover the exposed card.

The object of the game is to win tricks that include those cards which carry a scoring value when won in a trick, and to meld certain combinations of cards that carry a scoring value.

When taken in a trick each Ace scores 11 points, each 10 scores 10 points, each King 4 points, each Queen 3 points, and each Jack 2 points. The player who wins the last trick scores 10 points.

The values of the melds are:

Class A

A 10 K Q J of the trump suit	150 points
K Q of the trump suit (royal marriage)	40 points
K Q of a plain suit (common marriage)	20 points

Class B

Pinocle (**Q ♠** and **J ♦**)	40 points
Dis (**9** of the trump suit)	10 points

Class C

Four Aces – one of each suit	100 points
Four Kings – one of each suit	80 points
Four Queens – one of each suit	60 points
Four Jacks – one of each suit	40 points

The non-dealer leads to the first trick. Thereafter the winner of a trick leads to the next. It is not necessary for a player to follow suit to a led card. The winner of a trick replenishes his hand by taking the top card of the stock; the loser of the trick takes the next.

After a player has won a trick and before drawing from the stock, he may meld any of the above combinations. To meld he places the cards face upwards on the table in front of him, where they remain until he decides to play them to a trick, or until the stock is exhausted. Melding is subject to the three rules that follow:
1. Only one meld may be made at a turn.
2. For each meld, at least one card must be taken from the hand and placed on the table.
3. A card already melded may be melded again so long as it is in a different class, or in a higher-scoring meld of the same class.

---

*Pinocle is frequently spelt pinochle, but the Oxford Dictionary does not sanction the H.

That is to say, if Hearts are trumps a player may meld ♥ **K Q** and score for the royal marriage, and later he may add ♥ **A 10 J** and score for the sequence. He cannot first declare ♥ **A 10 K Q J** and score for sequence and later declare the royal marriage.

If the dealer turns up a dis as the trump card he scores 10 points. Thereafter a player holding a dis may count it merely by showing it when winning a trick. He may count the dis and make another meld at the same time. After winning a trick, the holder of a dis may exchange it for the trump card.

The player who wins the twelfth trick may meld if he is able to. He then draws the last face-downwards card of the stock and must show it to his opponent. The loser of the trick takes into his hand the card exposed on the table.

The last twelve tricks are now played off. During this period of play a player must follow suit if he can to the card led; if he cannot he must trump the trick if he holds a trump. If a trump is led the second player must win the trick if he can.

Melds are scored when they are declared. The score for cards won in tricks are added after the hand has been played out, a total of 7, 8, or 9 points is counted as 10.

Every deal may constitute a game, or the players may prefer that the winner will be he who first reaches an agreed figure.

At pinocle skill and experience count for much. An ability to remember which cards have been played contributes much towards success. When it comes to playing off the last twelve cards, the experienced player will never be in any doubt about which cards his opponent holds. Thus, when playing to the last trick before the stock is exhausted, a player should be able to weigh up the merits of winning the trick and melding, preventing his opponent from melding, or losing the trick and so obtaining the exposed trump card to add to his trump length in the final play off.

Piquet

Piquet is probably the best known of all card games for two players; there is no doubt that it is more skilful and interesting than any other. It is played with a 32-card pack, namely a pack from which the 6s, 5s, 4s, 3s and 2s have been removed, sometimes called the short or piquet pack. The cards rank from Ace (high) to 7 (low) and he who cuts the higher card has the right of first deal; he would be advised to take it because there is some advantage to be gained from it.

Twelve cards are dealt to both players in packets of either twos or threes, and the remaining eight cards (*talon*) are placed face downwards on the table between the players. The non-dealer may now exchange any five of his cards with the five top cards of the talon. He need not exchange as many as five cards, but he must exchange at least one, and, if he has not exchanged five cards, he may look at those that he was entitled to draw. The dealer may exchange cards up to the number that remain in the talon. He, too, must exchange at least one card. If he does not exchange all the cards, he may look at those that he was entitled to, but he must show them to his opponent if he does. The players place their discards face downwards on the table in front of them. The discards of the players should not be mixed together as, during the play of the hand, the players are entitled to look at their own discards.

The score is made up in three ways: the count of the hand; the count during the play of the cards; the extraordinary scores.

The hand is counted in the following way:

1. The *Point*, which is the number of cards held in the longest suit. The player who holds the longest suit wins the point, and scores 1 point for each card that he holds in it. If the number of cards in the suits held by the players is the same, the player with the highest count (Aces 11, Kings, Queens and Jacks 10 each, and other cards at their pip values) wins the point. If the count is equal neither player scores.
2. *Sequences*, which must not be of less than three cards of the same suit, are won by the player who holds the most cards in one sequence. As between sequences of equal length, the highest wins. For a sequence of three (tierce) 3 points are scored; for a sequence of four (quart) 4 points are scored. For a sequence of five (quint) 15 points are scored; for a sequence of six (sixième) 16 points; for a sequence of seven (septième) and for a sequence of eight (huitième) 18 points.
3. *Quatorzes* and *Trios* are any four or three cards of the same rank higher than the 9. The player who holds the superior quatorze or trio wins. Thus, a player who holds a trio of Aces will win even though his opponent may hold trios of Kings *and* Queens. In the same way, a player who holds trios of Aces, Kings, Queens and Jacks, will score nothing if his opponent holds a quatorze of 10s. Quatorzes are scored at 14 points each; trios at 3 points each.

The count of the hand must be declared in the order: point,

sequence, quatorze and trio, and, on demand, a player must show any combinations of cards for which he has scored. In practice, however, this is rarely necessary, because the opponent is usually able to infer from his own cards what cards are held against him by his opponent.

When counting the hand a player is not compelled to declare all that he holds. It is in order, and sometimes the very best play, to mislead one's opponent by declaring less than one holds in order to conceal one's strength. The practice is known as sinking. The player who holds a quatorze of Aces may declare only a trio. The opponent may inquire which Ace is not being reckoned, and the player may name any Ace he chooses, because the explicit reply: 'I do not count the Ace of Clubs' is not a guarantee that the player does not hold this card.

After the non-dealer has counted his hand he leads a card. The dealer then counts his hand and plays a card to the non-dealer's lead. Two cards constitute a trick, and it is compulsory for the second player to follow suit to the led card if he can do so. If not he may play any card he chooses, because there is no trump suit. The player who leads to a trick scores 1 point, and if his opponent wins it he scores one point for doing so (except in the case of the last trick, when he scores 2 points) and leads to the next trick, scoring 1 point for the lead. After all twelve tricks have been played, the player who has won most tricks scores 10 points for having done so (Ten for the Cards, as it is called). There is no score to either player if they win six tricks each.

There are four extraordinary scores:

1. *Carte Blanche*. If a player is dealt a hand that contains no court card he may claim carte blanche and score 10 points. It takes precedence over any other scoring combination, but the player must announce his carte blanche as soon as he picks up the cards dealt to him, and he must show his hand, though he need not do so until after his opponent has discarded.

2. *Pique*. If a player scores in hand and play 30 points, before his opponent scores anything, he wins a pique and scores 30 points for it. Only the non-dealer can win a pique, because he scores 1 point for the first lead before the dealer counts his hand; this, of course, automatically rules out the dealer from scoring for a pique.

3. *Repique*. If a player scores in hand alone a total of 30 points, before his opponent scores anything, he wins a repique and scores 60 points for it. Either player may score for a repique, because points in hand are counted in priority to those won in play.

4. *Capot*. If a player wins all twelve tricks he wins a capot and scores 40 points, not 10, for the cards. The capot, however, is not counted towards a pique because the points are not scored until the hand has been played.

The players deal alternately, and a *partie* (game) consists of six deals (three deals each). At the end of the *partie* the player with the higher score deducts from his score that of his opponent, and adds 100 points to the result. If, however, one player fails to score 100 points, he is rubiconed, and the player with the higher score adds the two scores together, and a further 100 points. If the score after six deals is equal, each player has one more deal, and if the score still remains equal the *partie* is a draw.

Most card games are played in silence. Piquet is a continuous dialogue. When a player counts his hand he declares his point, sequences, quartorzes and trios, and his opponent confirms whether they are 'Good', 'Not good' or 'Equal', and, if equal, the player announces the pip total which his opponent declares 'Good', 'Not good' or 'Equal'. Then, during the play of the hand, the two players announce their scores as each trick is played.

At piquet it is customary to call the non-dealer the elder (hand) and the dealer the younger (hand). The deal below (after both players have discarded) illustrates the method of scoring and is not to be accepted as an example of good play.

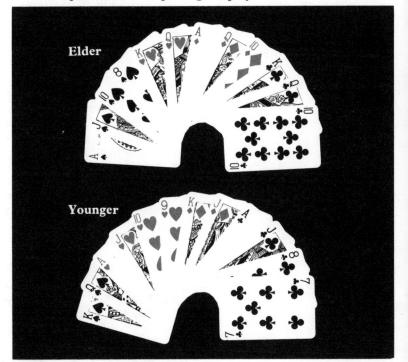

Elder : 'Point of four'.
Younger : 'Making?'
Elder : 'Thirty-nine.'
Younger : 'Not good.'
Elder : 'Queens and Tens—six'. (He counts his score for his trios without waiting for younger to confirm that the count is good. He knows that his trio of Queens is good because, from his own cards, he can see that younger cannot hold a quatorze or a better trio than one of Jacks. His announcement 'Queens and Tens' means that he holds three Queens and three 10s. If he held four Queens and three 10s he would announce 'Fourteen Queens and three Tens'.)

Elder, who has no more to count, leads the Ace of Spades—'Seven'.

Younger now counts his hand.

Younger : 'Point of four—forty,' (Elder has a right to ask in which suit the point is. In this case, however, he has no need because he knows from his own cards that it can only be in Hearts.) 'and tierce to the Jack—seven.' (Here, again, elder has no need to ask because, from his own cards, he knows that the tierce must be in Hearts.)

Younger plays the Queen of Spades on elder's Ace of Spades, and repeats his score—'Seven'.

The rest of the play is:

	Elder			Younger	
J	♠	'Eight'	K	♠	'Eight'
Q	♥	'Eight'	A	♥	'Nine'
K	♥	'Nine	J	♥	'Ten'
10	♠	'Ten'	7	♣	'Ten'
8	♠	'Eleven'	8	♣	'Ten'
K	♣	'Twelve'	A	♣	'Eleven'
10	♦	'Twelve'	10	♥	'Twelve'
Q	♦	'Twelve'	9	♥	'Thirteen'
Q	♣	'Thirteen'	J	♣	'Fourteen'
A	♦	'Fourteen'	J	♦	'Fourteen'
10	♣	'Fifteen'	K	♦	'Fourteen'

Elder, winning the trick–'Sixteen, and the cards twenty-six.' This ends the deal with the score at Elder 26, Younger 14.

A player's first consideration must be the point. The importance of scoring for the point cannot be over-estimated, because not only does it add to a player's score, but it protects him against a pique or repique, and, of course, scoring for point diminishes the opponent's score to the same extent. Normally, therefore, a player should retain his longest suit intact and discard from shorter suits. This, however, does not always hold good, particularly if the longest suit consists mainly of low cards, and the shorter suits of high ones. The inexperienced player who is dealt:

will be tempted to retain the Spades, and discard from the other suits, with a view to scoring for point and sequence. The experienced player will know that the better course is to discard all five Spades, because the Jack of Spades is the only card that will raise the suit from a quart to a sixième, and the odds are about three to one against drawing it. It is likely that retaining the Spades will win the point, but almost certainly it will result in the loss of the cards. This will make a big difference to the score, and always the cards must be considered together with the point. If the non-dealer holds a long suit headed by top cards, usually it guarantees the point and the cards. The suit, therefore, must be preserved at all costs, but this is of much less importance for the dealer because he may never obtain the lead.

A good general rule emerges. The discards of the non-dealer should be made towards obtaining an attacking hand; that of the dealer towards obtaining a defensive hand; that is to say a hand in which there is some strength in as many suits as possible.

Subject to these considerations, it is best to discard from as few suits as possible, and, once a player has made up his mind to discard from a suit, he should discard the whole of it, unless it is necessary to retain the suit guarded. Sequence cards should be retained in preference to non-sequence cards, and, of course, cards that help to make up trios and quatorzes should never be discarded if it is to be avoided.

Playing to the score is very important, particularly in the last deal of a *partie*. As an example: If a player is well ahead, and sees the opportunity to gain a rubicon, he should discard cautiously and play so as to prevent his opponent from saving the rubicon by scoring 100 points. By contrary, if a player is in danger of being rubiconed, he should be prepared to take some risks, since only a big score will save him. It must be remembered, however, that if a player is rubiconed his score is added to that of his opponent, so if there is no chance of saving the rubicon he should play to keep his score down. To this end he should declare only equities or those scores that will save pique and repique, and he should aim to divide the cards.

AUCTION PIQUET originated in Oxford, and was developed by some British prisoners of war during the war of 1914.

The bidding takes place before the discard. It is opened by the non-dealer. He may pass, and if he does and the dealer does also, there is a redeal by the same player. The lowest bid that may be made is one of Seven. It is an undertaking to win, or lose, seven of the twelve possible tricks. There is no penalty for a bid out of turn nor for an underbid, because these irregularities merely give information to the opponent.

The most interesting feature of the game is the minus bid. It is an undertaking to lose the stated number of tricks. It ranks neither above nor below a normal (plus) bid. In a minus deal the player scores everything good in his opponent's hand. A player may double a bid made by his opponent, and the player who has been doubled may redouble or shift to a higher bid.

After bidding, the players discard. The routine is the same as at the parent game except that there is no compulsion for the players to discard at least one card.

The declarations follow, and the players may declare the point, sequences, trios and quatorzes in any order they choose. Sinking is allowed in plus deals but not in minus ones.

The scoring is as follows:

The value of point, sequences, trios, quatorzes, cards and capot, are the same as in the parent game.

In plus deals pique (30 points) is obtained on the score of 29 and repique (60 points) on the score of 30. In minus deals both pique and repique are obtained on the score of 21.

The *partie* (six deals) is worth 150 points, and rubicon is under 150 points. In the event of a tie a seventh deal is played and the *partie* ends if it is tied.

A player scores 10 points for every trick won in a plus deal (or lost in a minus deal above (or below) the declared contract.

If a player fails to make his contract the opponent scores 10 points for every trick by which he is short.

Overtricks and undertricks are effected by doubling and redoubling, but scores in hand and play are not.

Although a player scores 1 point for winning a trick he does not score for leading a losing card, nor an additional 1 point for winning the last trick.

Tablanette

Tablanette is a game for two players that is easy to learn and worth learning because it is remarkably fascinating to play.

From a full pack of fifty-two cards, six cards are dealt face downwards to the two players, and four cards face upwards to the table between them. The rest of the pack is temporarily set aside. If any Jacks are dealt to the table they are removed, placed at the bottom of the pack, and the spaces filled with cards from the top of the pack.

The non-dealer plays first. If he plays a card of the same rank as any of the four cards on the table, he takes the card; or, if there are any two or three cards on the table whose values if added together equal that of the card played, he takes these cards. For this purpose a King counts 14, a Queen 13, and an Ace either 11 or 1. The Jack plays a special part in the game and its function will be explained later. The other cards count at their pip values.

If the cards on the table and the player's hand are:

he will play the **K ♥** and take the **K ♠** from the table. If he holds:

he will play the **A ♥** and take the **2 ♥** and **9 ♣** from the table, because together they total 11, a value of an Ace.

The card played and those taken from the table are kept in a pile, face downwards, on the table by the player who took them.

If at any time a player is able to take all the cards on the table (there may be only one, or there may be more than four) he announces 'Tablanette' and scores the total value of all the cards taken plus the value of the card he has played. If, for example, the cards on the table are:

and a player holds any of the other three Kings, he will be able to announce 'Tablanette', because his King will take the **K ♠** and the other three cards whose values total 14. The score for this will be 42 points (*i.e.* 14 × 3).

The special function of the Jack is that playing it allows the player to take all the cards on the table, but it does not allow him to score for a tablanette. Obviously, therefore, a Jack is an excellent card to hold, because playing it compels the opponent to play a lone card to the table and when there is only one card on the table the player whose turn it is to play is in a good position to score a tablanette.

The players play in rotation until they have exhausted their six cards. The dealer then deals another six cards to each, and so on until the pack is exhausted.

When the last batch of six cards has been played, any cards left on the table are taken by the player who last took a card from the table.

The players examine the cards they have taken, and score 1 point for the 2 ♣ and for every Ace, King, Queen, Jack and 10 (except the 10 ♦ which scores 2 points). Finally, if a player has taken 27 or more cards he scores 3 points.

The deal passes in rotation, and the game is won by the player who first scores a total of 251 points.

There is more skill in the game than may be apparent at first sight. If, for example, there is only an 8 on the table and the player holds:

his best play is the 4 ♥, because no one card has a value of 12 and the opponent, therefore, cannot score a tablanette.

As at all card games it is very important to keep in mind the cards that have been played. The opponent has scored a tablanette and the player holds:

He has to play a card to the table, and the natural tendency is to play the **3** ♥, because this will give the opponent a minimum score if he can again announce 'Tablanette'. But if no 3s have been played, but a 10 has, then it is better to play one of the 10s, because the chances are against the opponent holding the remaining 10, and there is a possibility that he holds one of the remaining three 3s.

TABLANETTE FOR THREE PLAYERS is played in the same way as the parent game, except that the players are dealt four cards (instead of six) at a time.

Black Maria

Black Maria, sometimes known as Black Lady and sometimes as Slippery Anne, is very similar to hearts and its several variations. (see page 111). It is considered best played as a game for three, but may be played by more.

The 2 of Clubs is removed from the pack, and seventeen cards are dealt to each player. The cards rank in the normal order from Ace (high) to 2 (low) and, after a player has looked at his cards, he passes three of them to his right-hand opponent and receives three from his left-hand opponent, which he must not look at until he has passed three on.

When the exchanges of cards have been made, the player on the left of the dealer leads to the first trick. Thereafter, the player who wins a trick leads to the next. A player must follow suit to the led card provided he can do so. Otherwise he may discard any card he chooses. There is no trump suit.

The object of the game is to avoid winning a trick which contains a penalty card. These cards, and the penalties that go with them, are:

Every card in the Heart suit—1 point each.

The Ace of Spades—7 points.

The King of Spades—10 points.

The Queen of Spades (Black Maria)—13 points.

The deal passes in rotation clockwise.

The game introduces two features: the discard and the play of the cards.

The inexperienced player, if he is dealt a high Spade, will assume that he cannot do better than pass it on to his right-hand opponent. It is, however, not always the best play. Provided a number of low Spades are held in support of the high ones, it is very often better to retain the high cards with a view to controlling the suit during the play of the hand. Indeed, a player who has been dealt any Spades or Hearts lower than the Queen would be well advised to keep them in order to protect himself against any top cards in the suits that may be passed on to him. The main principle of discarding should be to try and set up either a void suit—in order to get rid of penalty cards by discarding them during the play—or at obtaining long suits, provided low cards in them are held. A player who has been dealt:

cannot do better than pass on the three Diamonds. The Spades must be kept to protect against receiving a high card in the suit, the Hearts are adequately protected, and there is nothing to fear in Clubs.

An ability to count the cards is the first essential to success. Towards the end of a deal an experienced player will know pretty well which cards are still left to be played, and he will be able to make a shrewd guess who holds them. It is in the end-play, therefore, that opportunity comes for skilful play.

After fourteen tricks have been played the players should know who holds the remaining cards.

West is on lead and leads the **6 ♠**, North plays the **2 ♠** and East, perforce, wins with the **K ♠**. Now, if East returns the **5 ♦** West must win with the **7 ♦** and North saddles him with the **Q ♠** (Black Maria). If, however, East returns the **3 ♣**, North will have to win with the **6 ♣** on which West will have played the **A ♠**.

East's play will be directed by the score, and whether it is more advantageous to him to saddle West or North with all 20 points. The strategy is quite ethical so long as East puts his own interest first and is not moved by malice aforethought.

FOUR-HANDED BLACK MARIA is played in the same way as the parent game, except that no card is removed from the pack, and every player, therefore, receives thirteen cards. The players may play all against all, or two in partnership against the other two.

FIVE-HANDED BLACK MARIA is played in the same way as the parent game, but the 2 of Diamonds as well as the 2 of Clubs is removed from the pack. Each player, therefore, is dealt ten cards.

Cut-throat Bridge

Many suggestions have been made to make bridge (see page 83) suitable for three players. The most satisfactory is towie (see page 80) but what has become known as Cut-throat Bridge is the original and the simplest of the three-handed variations.

The players take seats at random and after drawing for deal, shuffling and cutting in the regular way, the dealer deals thirteen cards each to the three players and to a fourth hand that is temporarily set aside.

The auction, beginning with the dealer, is conducted as in the parent game, and when a player's bid, double or redouble has been passed by the other two players, the player on his left leads to the first trick. The player who has obtained the final contract then sorts the fourth hand, spreads it in front of him on the table, and plays it as his dummy, against the other two players in partnership with each other,

The play and scoring are the same as in the parent game, except that if a player loses his contract both his opponents score the penalty points. The winner of a rubber receives a bonus of 700 points if neither opponent has won a game, but 500 points if either has.

Very clearly the game is a gamble, because the players must bid in the hope of finding the cards they need in the dummy hand.

A variation designed to make the game less speculative is for every player to be dealt seventeen cards and the fifty-second card face downwards to the dummy. After looking at their cards, and before bidding them, every player contributes four of them, face downwards, to the dummy. This way, every player knows four out of the thirteen cards that he is bidding for.

In another variation, instead of bidding for the dummy, an agreed number of deals (that must be divisible by three) are played, and, in turn, every player plays the dummy against the other two playing in partnership.

In this variation rubbers are not played, but the player who bids and makes game scores a bonus of 300 points. There is no vulnerability.

Knaves

Knaves, a game for three players, is so called because the four Knaves are penalty cards and the object of the players is to avoid winning tricks that contain them.

Seventeen cards are dealt to each player and the last card is turned face upwards on the table to denote the trump suit. It takes no other part in the game.

The player on the left of the dealer leads to the first trick; thereafter the player who wins a trick leads to the next. A player must follow suit, if he can, to the card led. If he cannot he may either trump or discard a card of a plain suit.

The player who wins a trick scores 1 point for it, but 4 points are deducted from a player's score if he wins the Knave of Hearts, 3 points if he wins the Knave of Diamonds, 2 points if he wins the Knave of Clubs, and 1 point if he wins the Knave of Spades. The aggregate score for each deal, therefore, is 7 points (*i.e.* 17 points for tricks minus 10 points for Knaves) unless one of the Knaves is the card turned up to denote the trump suit. Game is won by the first player to score 20 points.

The players play all against all, but skilful play introduces temporary partnerships that add much to the interest of the game. If, for example, one player is in the lead and the other two are trailing behind, they will combine with the aim of preventing the leading player from winning still more, even if they cannot reduce his score by forcing him to win tricks that contain Knaves. In the same way, if two players have an advanced score, and the third is down the course, the two who are ahead will so play that such points as they cannot themselves win will go to the player with the low score rather than to the one with the high score.

The game, therefore, gives ample scope for clever play. Until the last Knave has been played, a player has to strike a balance between the incentive to take a trick, and so score a point, and the fear of being saddled with a Knave, resulting in a loss.

There is much more in the game than appears on the surface. Consider the hands on the left.

No score to anyone.

East deals and the **7 ♣** is turned up.

With his preponderance of trumps North appears to be in a position to score well. In reality his hand is far from being a good one, because, though the trumps give him the advantage of winning tricks, this advantage is more than offset by the fact that he is in the dangerous position of being forced to take Knaves. Indeed, North is very likely to come out with a poor score; against good play by West he will be hard put to avoid taking the Knaves of Hearts and Diamonds—for a loss of 7 points—and, in any case, he can hardly avoid taking one of them.

Ombre

Ombre is a Spanish game of considerable antiquity. It was introduced into England by Katherine of Braganza, who married Charles II in 1662, and it immediately became very popular. Nowadays it is rarely played in Great Britain, but it is popular in Denmark (which saw the publication of a book about it in 1965) and it is played in Spain under the name of trefillo and in Latin America as rocamber. It deserves to be more popular.

The game is played with a pack of forty cards *i.e.* the regular pack from which the 10s, 9s and 8s have been removed. It is not a difficult game to play, but it is first necessary to master the rather involved and unusual order of the cards.

In plain suits the cards in the *red* suits rank in the order: **K Q J A 2 3 4 5 6 7**; those in the *black* suits rank in the normal order: **A K Q J 7 6 5 4 3 2**.

In trump suits if a *red* suit is trumps the order of the cards is: **A ♠** (Spadille), **7** (Manille), **A ♣** (Basto), **A** (Punto), **K Q J 2 3 4 5 6**; if a *black* suit is trumps the order of the cards is: **A ♠** (Spadille), **2** (Manille), **A ♣** (Basto), **K Q J 7 6 5 4 3**.

The three top trumps, Spadille, Manille and Basto, are collectively known as Matadores. The holder of one need not follow suit with it to a trump lead, but he must play one if a higher matadore is led and his hand contains no other trump card.

To determine the dealer, a card is dealt face upwards to each player in turn, and he who is first to receive a black Ace is dealer. It is here to be noted that, as in all games of Spanish origin, in dealing and play the game progresses anti-clockwise.

Nine cards are dealt to each player in bundles of three. The remaining thirteen cards are placed face downwards in the centre of the table.

Each deal is complete in itself. One player (ombre) plays against the other two playing in partnership. The player on the right of the dealer has first option of being ombre. It carries two privileges: he names the trump suit, he may discard from his hand as many cards as he chooses and draw fresh cards from the stock. If the player on the right of the dealer wishes to become ombre he says 'I play'. His right-hand neighbour may then announce that he wishes to become ombre, and, by so doing, he tacitly agrees that he will play without exchanging any of his cards. The first player may then reconsider the position, and is entitled to remain ombre if he is willing to play without exchanging any of his cards. If the second player passes, the third player (the dealer) may announce that he wishes to play without discarding. Again, the first player has a right to reconsider and may remain ombre without discarding.

If all three players pass, that is to say, if none wishes to play ombre the deal is abandoned.

If the first player is allowed to play ombre unopposed, he discards as many cards as he chooses from his hand, and draws cards from the stock to replace them. The second player does the same, and then the dealer. If any cards are left in the stock after the three players have made their exchanges, the dealer is entitled to look at them. If he does he must show them to the other two players: if he does not, the other two may not.

Ombre now names the trump suit and leads a card. The game proceeds, anti-clockwise, every player following suit, if he can, to the led card, or trumping or discarding if he cannot. The winner of a trick leads to the next, until all nine tricks have been played.

At the beginning of a deal each player puts an agreed sum in a pool. Now . . .

Sacardo. If ombre wins more tricks than either of his opponents individually, he takes all that is in the pool.

Codille. If one of the opponents wins more tricks than ombre, ombre pays him a sum equal to the amount in the pool, and the amount in the pool is carried forward to the next deal.

Puesta. If ombre and one, or both, of his opponents win the same number of tricks, ombre doubles the amount in the pool and it is carried forward to the next deal.

The deal does not pass in rotation. After every deal the dealer for the next is determined by dealing the cards, face upwards, until one player receives a black Ace.

The deal that follows is a simple one to illustrate the mechanics of the game:

West	*North*	*East*
♥ K 7	♥ none	♥ 4 5 6
♦ 6	♦ 7	♦ 2 3 4 5
♠ 7 5	♠ J 6 4 3 2	♠ Q
♣ Ma Ba K 5	♣ Q J 6	♣ 7

North deals.

West says: 'I play'. East and North pass.

West discards 7 ♥ 6 ♦ 7 ♠ 5 ♠. He draws 3 ♥ Q ♦ A ♦ 4 ♣.

East discards 4 ♥ 5 ♥ 6 ♥. His hand is of no value and he hopes to end with a void suit. He draws Q ♥ A ♥ Spa.

North discards 7 ♦ J ♠ 6 ♠ 4 ♠ 3 ♠ 2 ♠. He draws J ♥ 2 ♥ K ♦ J ♦ K ♠ 3 ♣.

The hands are now:

West	*North*	*East*
♥ K 3	♥ J 2	♥ Q A
♦ Q A	♦ K J	♦ 2 3 4 5
♠ none	♠ K	♠ Q
♣ Ma Ba K 5 4	♣ Q J 6 3	♣ Spa 7

West names Clubs as the trump suit.

His hand is none too good, but the lead of a trump is called for. He, therefore, leads K ♣, and East wins with Spadille, because West would hardly have led the King of trumps if he did not hold Manille, and probably Basto as well. East has no better return than 7 ♣, on which North plays the **Jack**. West allows it to win, by playing 4 ♣, because he is aware that North holds the more dangerous hand, and that sooner or later a trick in trumps must be lost to him. North must keep his top Diamonds and K ♠, and he cannot safely lead a Heart. He, therefore, leads a Club. West wins with Basto, draws North's last trump with Manille, and continues with 5 ♣. It puts North on the spot. If he discards J ♦, West will lead the suit and later win K ♥ and a Diamond; if North discards 2 ♥ or K ♠, West will win K ♥, and continue with 3 ♥, so that he will either win Q ♦, or North and East will divide their tricks three-two. Either way it is sacardo, and West scoops the pool.

Towie

Towie was originated by J. Leonard Replogle as a variation of bridge (see page 83). It may be played by any number of players, but is most acceptable as a game for three because only three take an active part in each deal.

Four hands of thirteen cards each are dealt in the usual way; the one to the quarter opposite the dealer is the dummy hand to be bid for. After dealing, the dealer chooses (without looking at them) six cards from the dummy hand, and faces them.

The players, beginning with the dealer, bid as in the parent game, but part scores are not reckoned and if the bidding ends without a game or higher contract being reached, there is a goulash deal, with further goulashes if necessary.[*]

When the bidding ends the player on the left of the declarer makes the opening lead. The dummy hand becomes the property of the declarer who sorts it, exposes it on the table, and plays it against the other two players in partnership, as in the parent game.

The scoring is the same as in bridge with the following differences:

1. In No-Trump contracts the trick score is 35 points a trick.
2. For winning a first game the declarer scores a bonus of 500 points and becomes vulnerable. For winning a second game—and with it the rubber—a player scores 1,000 points.
3. The declarer who makes a doubled or redoubled contract scores a bonus of 50 points if not vulnerable, and 100 points if vulnerable.
4. For undoubled overtricks the declarer scores 50 points each. If doubled or redoubled he scores for them as in the parent game.
5. The penalties for undertricks are:

   Not Vulnerable
   Undoubled: 50 points per trick
   Doubled: 100 points for the first and second tricks
                200 points for the third and fourth tricks
                400 points for the fifth and subsequent tricks

   Vulnerable
   Undoubled: 100 points for the first trick
              200 points for the second and subsequent tricks
   Doubled: 200 points for the first trick
              400 points for the second and subsequent tricks

If the contract is redoubled the scores for doubled contracts are multiplied by two.

---

[*]For a goulash deal the players sort their cards into suits (the dealer sorts the dummy hand) and the hands are placed face downwards in a pile, one on top of the other, in front of the dealer. The cards are cut without being shuffled, and the same dealer deals the cards in bundles of five-five-three.

If there are more than three players participating in the game the inactive players are opponents of the declarer. They take no part in the bidding or play, but participate in the scoring, losing when the declarer makes his contract, and scoring the undertrick penalties when the declarer's contract is defeated.

At the end of a deal the declarer, whether he has won or lost his contract, retires from the table and his place is taken by one of the waiting players. The inactive players come into the game each in his turn, replacing the declarer of the previous deal. No vulnerable player, however, may re-enter the game if a non-vulnerable player is waiting to play.

The game ends when one player has won two deals.

Large penalties are not uncommon in towie because a player has no partner during the auction period and cannot do more than bid on the strength of his own hand, the six cards that he sees in dummy, and the seven cards that he expects to find there. Over-bidding is frequent, but risks must be taken, and the game is not for the chicken-hearted or cautious bidder. The play of the defence offers scope for skill, but, on the whole, the main object of a player must be to play the dummy, particularly when five are in the game.

The dummy hand after the face-down cards have been exposed

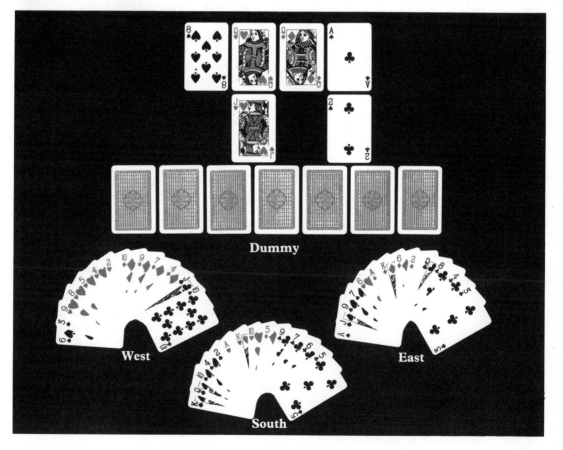

Dummy

West **East**

South

South and East were vulnerable, and South dealt. He bid a cautious One Spade, and, after a pass by West, East bid Three No-Trumps. South lacked the courage to bid Four Spades, and East, with dummy's cards opposite him, had an easy ride for his contract.

Auction Pitch

Auction Pitch, commonly known as Pitch and sometimes as Set Back, is a variation of all fours (see page 28). It is at its best and most popular when played by four players, each playing for himself.

As in the parent game, the cards rank in the usual order from Ace (high) to 2 (low), and six are dealt to the players in two bundles of three each. No card, however, is turned up to determine the trump suit.

The player on the left of the dealer bids first, and each player, in his turn, may either make a bid or pass. A bid must be for at least two points, and for more than the preceding bid, except for the dealer, who is entitled to buy the hand for the same number of points as the preceding bid. The maximum number of points in a deal is 4, and a player who expects to win them bids Smudge. The dealer cannot take the declaration from him.

The successful bidder is known as the maker, and he pitches (leads) to the first trick. The card that he leads determines the trump suit.

At each trick a player must follow suit to the card led, if he can, otherwise he may discard or trump. The winner of a trick leads to the next.

As in the parent game, points are scored as follows:

High. The player who holds the highest trump scores 1 point.

Low. The player who holds the lowest trump scores 1 point.

Jack. The player who wins the trick that contains the Jack of the trump suit (if it is in play) scores 1 point.

Game. Counting the Ace as 4, the King as 3, the Queen as 2, the Jack as 1 and the Ten as 10, the player with the highest total in the tricks he has won scores 1 point. If there is a tie no-one scores the point.

Every player records what he scores, and if the maker fails to reach his bid he is set back by the full amount of it. He records the score and if it reduces him to a minus score he encircles it. A player with a minus score is said to be in the hole.

The game is won by the player who first reaches 7 points, and if the maker and one or more of the other players reach 7 points in the same deal, the maker wins. As between the other three players, the points are counted in the order High, Low, Jack, Game.

A player who smudges and wins all four points automatically wins the game regardless of his score, unless he was in the hole when he smudged. In this event he scores only 4 points.

Bridge

Modern Bridge, more precisely Contract Bridge, but the 'Contract' has for long been dropped, was developed out of Auction Bridge and introduced to card players in the early 1920s. It took firm root quickly, and made rapid progress, to become the most popular game in the whole history of card-playing. To-day, half a century after its *début*, it is played by millions, rich and poor, from peers to peasants, and it has attracted to itself a vast literature in most European languages.

Bridge is played by four players, two playing in partnership against the other two, and with a standard pack of fifty-two cards. The cards rank in the order Ace (high) to 2 (low), and the Ace, King, Queen, Jack and Ten of a suit are known as the honour cards. The suits rank in the order Spades, Hearts, Diamonds, Clubs; the Spade and Heart suits are known as the major suits: the Diamond and Club suits as the minor suits. Although only one pack of cards is necessary, it is customary to use two, of different design or colour, and while one is being dealt the other is shuffled by the partner of the dealer, in readiness for the next dealer.

To determine partners, a pack is spread-eagled on the table. The four players draw cards from it, and the two who draw the two highest cards play in partnership against the other two. If two players draw cards of equal rank, precedence is determined by the rank of the suits. The player who draws the highest card has choice of seats and cards, and deals first. Thereafter the deal passes round the table clockwise. His partner sits opposite to him; the other two partners sit one on each side of him.

It is convenient to divide the game into two periods. The bidding, during which the two partnerships compete against each other to establish which suit shall be made trumps or whether the hand shall be played without a trump suit. The playing, during which the player who has won the contract strives to make it, playing his own hand and that of his partner exposed on the table, against the other partnership striving to prevent him.

The dealer bids first, and the bidding continues round the table clockwise. When a player bids he states the number of tricks in excess of six that he undertakes to win, and in the denomination that he undertakes to play. The lowest bid, therefore, is a bid of One (a contract to win seven tricks) and the highest is a bid of Seven (a contract to win all thirteen tricks). As No-Trumps takes precedence over the suits, and the suits rank in the descending order Spades, Hearts, Diamonds, Clubs, the lowest possible bid is One Club, and the ascending scale is: One Club, One Diamond, One Heart, One Spade, One No-Trump, Two Clubs, Two Diamonds . . . . Seven Hearts, Seven Spades, Seven No-Trumps. A contract of Six (to win twelve tricks) is called a small slam; a contract of Seven (to win all thirteen tricks) is called a grand slam.

In turn each bid must name either a greater number of tricks than the previous one, or an equal number of tricks in a higher denomination. If a player has no wish to contract to win tricks he says 'No Bid', and if all four players do so, the hand is thrown in and the deal passes.

In his turn any player may double a bid made by an opponent. The effect of a double is to increase the score whether the contract succeeds or fails: and the partnership whose contract has been doubled may redouble thereby increasing the score, win or lose, still further. Doubling and redoubling, however, do not increase the size of a contract: *e.g.* a bid of Four Clubs is inferior to a bid of Four Diamonds and remains inferior to it even though it may have been doubled and redoubled.

The bidding period continues until the last and highest bid has been followed by three passes. The player who first mentioned the denomination in the final contract then becomes the declarer.

It is usual to denote the four players by the cardinal points of the compass, and if we assume that South deals, a sequence of bidding to illustrate some of the points mentioned might be:

South	West	North	East
1 ♦	No bid	1 ♥	1 ♠
1 No-Trump	2 ♠	3 ♦	No bid
3 No-Trumps	Double	No bid	No bid
4 ♦	No Bid	5 ♦	Double
Redouble	No Bid	No Bid	No Bid

The final contract, therefore, is Five Diamonds, and the hand will be played by South, because he was the first on his side to mention Diamonds as the trump suit.

The playing period begins by the player on the left of the declarer leading to the first trick. As soon as he has done so, the partner of the declarer places his cards face upwards on the table as dummy. He takes no further part in the play except that he has a right to draw his partner's attention to certain irregularities, such as asking him if he has none of a suit when he fails to follow suit, and warning him against leading out of the wrong hand. The declarer plays the dummy hand as well as his own.

The play follows the normal routine of trick-taking games: if a player is able to do so he must follow suit to the card led; otherwise he may either discard or trump. The trick is won by the player who plays the highest card of the suit led, or the highest trump. The player who wins a trick leads to the next. Plate 13 shows the playing period of the game in progress.

When all thirteen tricks have been played, the players record their scores, and those of their opponents, on a marker, or sheet of paper, as shown in the accompanying diagram.

When a player makes his contract, the score for tricks won is entered below the horizontal line. All other scores are entered above this line.

A game is won when a partnership scores 100 points below the horizontal line, either in one or more deals. If a partnership scores less than game in one deal, it is said to have a part-score and if the opponents then score game the part-score cannot be carried forward towards the next game. When a partnership wins a game a line is drawn across the score sheet below it, and both partnerships begin the next game from a love score.

A partnership that wins a game becomes vulnerable and is subject to higher bonuses if it makes its contract, and increased penalties if it fails. Vulnerability, however, does not affect the points for winning the tricks contracted for.

The main object of the game is to win a rubber, which is the best out of three games.

If a partnership has bid and made its contract, it scores;

In No-Trumps: 40 points for the first trick and 30 points for each subsequent trick.

In Spades and Hearts: 30 points for each trick.

In Diamonds and Clubs: 20 points for each trick.

The scores for winning tricks are doubled if the contract has been doubled, and quadrupled if the contract has been redoubled.

If a partnership has made tricks in excess of its contract, it scores:

If undoubled:	trick value for each trick.
If doubled:	100 points for each trick if not vulnerable.
	200 points for each trick if vulnerable.
If redoubled:	200 points for each trick if not vulnerable.
	400 points for each trick if vulnerable.

If a partnership has failed to make its contract, it loses:

If undoubled:	50 points for each trick if not vulnerable.
	100 points for each trick if vulnerable.
If doubled:	100 points for the first trick; 200 points for each subsequent trick if not vulnerable.
	200 points for the first trick; 300 points for each subsequent trick if vulnerable.
If redoubled:	200 points for the first trick; 400 points for each subsequent trick if not vulnerable.
	400 points for the first trick; 600 points for each subsequent trick if vulnerable.

If a partnership wins a rubber, it scores:

In three games 500 points.

In two games 700 points.

A partnership scores bonuses of:

1,500 points, if vulnerable, for bidding and making a grand slam, 1,000 points if not vulnerable.

750 points, if vulnerable, for bidding and making a small slam, 500 points if not vulnerable.

150 points if either partner holds all four Aces in a No-Trump contract, or all five honours in a suit contract.

100 points if either partner holds any four honours in a suit contract.

50 points if a partnership makes a doubled or redoubled contract.

Bridge is not a difficult game unless a player makes it so by ill-advised bidding. Its most important feature is that a player scores below the line, towards game, only for the tricks that he has contracted to win, and, by a logical extension, he scores the big bonuses for slams only if the necessary number of tricks has been contracted for. It follows that it is of paramount importance for the partners to estimate the trick-taking power of their combined hands, and not only must a player estimate as accurately as possible the position of the adverse high cards and distribution (as revealed by the bids of the other players) but convey by his bidding as much information as possible to his partner. In short, bidding may be defined as a conversation between the partners, and both must speak the same language.

Most modern players value their hands by means of the well-known Milton Work count of 4 for an Ace, 3 for a King, 2 for a Queen, and 1 for a Jack.

The player who opens the bidding with a bid of One of a suit, promises to make a further bid if his partner responds with One in a higher-ranking suit, or Two in a lower-ranking suit. For this reason a player should not open unless he can see a sound rebid in his hand over partner's most likely response.

The strength to justify an opening bid varies, but in general it may be said that a hand totalling at least 13 points should be opened. It is clear, however, that the more points a player holds the less length does he need in the trump suit, and the fewer points in the hand the greater must be the length in the trump suit. With less than 13 points in the hand the practice is to open an 11- or 12-point hand with a reasonable 5-card suit, and with only 10 points in the hand, sometimes less, a player needs a reasonable 6-card suit, or two 5-card suits.

Open One Heart. The hand totals only 11 points, but the Heart suit is worth showing and if it is not shown at once it may be too late.

Open One Spade. The hand totals only 11 points, but is strong by reason of its distribution. With two suits of equal length it is proper to bid the higher-ranking before the lower-ranking one.

Open One Spade. The hand totals a mere 10 points, but the 6-card Spade suit is too good to be held back.

There are 40 points in the pack and experience has taught that if the combined hands have a total of 25 points game will be made, if 33 the small slam, and if 37 the grand slam. There are, of course, exceptions, but in the long run the rule is to be relied on.

A bid of One No-Trump is advised with a total of 16 to 18 points. The bid should never step outside the stipulated range, because partner needs to rely on it for his response. With 9 points he will jump to Three No-Trumps; with 7 or 8 he will bid Two No-Trumps and leave it to the opener to pass with a minimum, but bid Three with a maximum. A NoTrump range of 16 to 18 points is known as a strong No-Trump. Some experienced players favour, particularly when not vulnerable, a range of 12 to 14 points. It is known as a weak No-Trump. Whether a strong or a weak No-Trump is played is a matter of personal choice, but it must be agreed between the partners before play begins, because if a weak No-Trump is played partner must increase his responses by 4 points.

In the same way, an opening bid of Two No-Trumps is advised on 20 to 22 points, leaving it to partner to raise to Three if he holds 5 points, and to pass with less.

Opening bids of One No-Trump and Two No-Trumps postulate a balanced distribution of 4-3-3-3 or 4-4-3-2. A bid of Three No-Trumps is tactical. It shows a hand containing a solid minor suit, and altogether a hand that has a reasonable prospect of winning nine tricks if partner has one or two top cards in the right places.

The hand qualifies for an opening bid of Three No-Trumps. There is every prospect of making the contract; if not it will not cost a lot and there is the consolation that it has probably stopped the opponents from bidding a game that would have been a greater loss.

The partner of the player who opens the bidding with No-Trumps raises on a very precise number of points. The number of points, however, may be reduced slightly if the responder holds a 5-card suit. Over a bid of One No-Trump, partner holds:

The hand totals 8 points and 9 points are normally necessary to jump to Three No-Trumps. Here, however, the jump to Three No-Trumps is justified on the length of the Spade suit, and the good intermediate cards. It is unwise to bid Spades because if it is assumed that partner holds a balanced 16-point hand he is just as likely to win nine tricks in No-Trumps as the responder is to win ten in Spades. If Three No-Trumps cannot be made there is no reason to suppose that Four Spades can.

A jump take out into a suit is a game force. It does not, however, promise a very strong hand: rather it means that the responder, who knows the precise strength of his partner's bid, can foresee game for the partnership but cannot tell whether the combined hands will play better in No-Trumps or in a suit.

West	East
♠ Q J 4 3	♠ K 10 9 7 2
♥ A Q 2	♥ J 6 4
♦ K 9 3	♦ A J 8 2
♣ A 7 6	♣ 8

Bidding	Bidding
1 No-Trump	3 ♠
4 ♠	No Bid

Over West's opening bid of One No-Trump (16 to 18 points) East who has 9 points has enough to jump to Three No-Trumps. He prefers Three-Spades, however, which West raises to game, because game in Spades can hardly fail, but in No-Trumps will be defeated if a Club is led.

Another important feature of responding to a No-Trump bid is the Stayman convention. It is a bid of Two Clubs over partner's One No-Trump, or Three Clubs over his Two No-Trumps, made, irrespective of the holding in the suit, to ask partner to bid his better 4-card major suit, or, if he lacks one, to bid Diamonds.

West	East
♠ K Q 2	♠ A J 4 3
♥ A J 6 2	♥ K Q 8 4
♦ Q 6 4	♦ 3 2
♣ A Q 4	♣ J 8 5

Bidding	Bidding
1 No-Trump	2 ♣
2 ♥	4 ♥
No Bid.	

Without the convention East, with 11 points, would have no alternative except to jump his partner's opening bid of One No-Trump (16 to 18 points) to Three. The combined total of 29 points is more than adequate for the bid, but Three No-Trumps may be defeated if a Diamond is led and Four Hearts can hardly fail.

There is a large range of bids which show weakness and that may be recognized as such by the logic of the situation.

West	East
1 ♠	2 No-Trumps
3 ♠	?

East's bid of Two No-Trumps shows a count of from 11 to 13 points, and over it West cannot do more than repeat his suit. His hand, therefore, cannot be strong, and his bid of Three Spades no more than the cheapest way of keeping his promise to rebid, which he made when he opened with One Spade.

In the same way, if the bidding is:

West	East
1 No-Trump	2 ♠
?	

West should pass. East's bid must be showing a weak hand that he considers will play better in a suit than in No-Trumps, otherwise, over an opening bid of One No-Trump, it would be impossible for partner ever to play in Two of a suit.

Or we may consider the following sequences:

West	East	West	East	West	East
1 ♥	2 ♥	1 ♥	2 ♣	1 ♣	1 ♥
3 ♣	3 ♥	2 ♥	3 ♦	1 ♠	2 ♥
		3 ♥		2 ♠	3 ♥

In all these sequences the bid of Three Hearts shows weakness. A player cannot be holding much of a hand when he cannot do better than rebid his suit at the lowest level, and it is particularly pronounced when he rebids it twice.

An opening bid of Three of a suit is also a weakness bid. It is made with a hand that has little, if any, defensive strength, offers small chance of success of game, and with one long suit that, if trumps, is unlikely to be defeated by more than two tricks if vulnerable and three if not vulnerable.

This type of hand qualifies for an opening bid of Three Spades if only because, even if doubled and partner has no support, it cannot cost more than 500 points (two down). It is a reasonable loss if the opponents have a game in one of the other suits.

There is also a range of strong bids. The strongest of all is an opening bid of Two Clubs. It is strictly conventional and may be made even if the player is void in the suit. The bid guarantees either five or more high cards and distributional strength, or 23 or more points and a balanced distribution. With one exception the bid is forcing to game. Partner must respond no matter how weak his hand is, and with a weak hand he bids Two Diamonds. Any other response by him shows an Ace and a King or two King-Queen combinations or the equivalent in high cards. The exception to the bid not being forcing to game occurs when the opener has bid Two Clubs with a balanced hand and, after the negative response of Two Diamonds, has rebid Two No-Trumps.

West	East
♠ K J 3	♠ Q 6 2
♥ A Q 6	♥ 9 7 4
♦ A K 4	♦ 8 5 3 2
♣ A Q J 2	♣ 7 4 3

Bidding	Bidding
2 ♣	2 ♦
2 No-Trumps	No Bid

West, with 24 points, is too strong to open with any other bid than Two Clubs, and over East's negative response he cannot do better than rebid Two No-Trumps. East with only 2 points in his hand does well to pass, but another point in his hand would make a big difference and with 3 points or more he would bid Three No-Trumps.

The opening bid of Two in any other suit is forcing for one round, and shows a hand containing not fewer than eight playing tricks and at least one powerful suit.

This hand is best opened with Two Spades. If it is opened with One Spade there is no satisfactory way of coping with a response of Two Hearts.

A strong 2-suited hand also qualifies for an opening bid of Two. The higher-ranking suit is bid first.

A 1-suited hand may also be opened with a Two bid. This hand should be opened with a bid of Two Spades, and Three Spades should be bid over any response made by partner.

The responses to opening Two bids (of suits other than Clubs) are not so well-defined and clear-cut as the responses to an opening bid of Two Clubs. In general, if partner holds a biddable suit he should bid it at the lowest level. If he lacks a biddable suit, but has a total of from 10 to 12 points, he should bid Three No-Trumps. If he lacks a biddable suit and insufficient points to bid Three No-Trumps, but has adequate support (*i.e.* **x x x** or **Q x**) for partner's suit and a count of 5, he should give a simple raise in partner's suit. If he lacks a biddable suit, insufficient points for Three No-Trumps, and insufficient support for partner's suit, he should make the negative response of Two No-Trumps.

As well as an opening bid of Two Clubs there are several other bids that are forcing to game. The most frequent is a jump bid in a new suit.

West	*East*
♠ Q 8 4	♠ A K 6
♥ 9 2	♥ A Q J 10 6 4
♦ A J 3	♦ 8 2
♣ A K 9 3 2	♣ J 4
Bidding	Bidding
1 ♣	2 ♥

The situation is typical. East's bid of Two Hearts sets up a forcing situation. It is true that a bid of One Heart by East cannot be passed by West, but it is better for East to get the hand off his chest, and by bidding Two Hearts he makes certain that the bidding will not be dropped until a game level is reached.

It is much the same if the opener makes a jump in a new suit over his partner's response:

West	*East*
♠ K J 6	♠ A Q 9 2
♥ A K J 7 4	♥ 10 8 3
♦ 6	♦ K Q 9
♣ K Q J 7	♣ 10 6 3
Bidding	Bidding
1 ♥	1 ♠
3 ♣	

In this situation (or a similar one) West's bid of Three Clubs is a game force and East cannot pass it.

In many cases a forcing situation is set up by reason of the logic behind the bidding.

West	*East*
♠ A K 9 6 3	♠ Q 7 4 2
♥ K J 9 2	♥ Q 10 8 3
♦ A 8 4	♦ K 6 2
♣ 9	♣ 5 4
Bidding	Bidding
1 ♠	2 ♠
3 ♥	?

As West rebid at the level of Three, over East's weak response of Two Spades, and when there was no need for him to rebid, he must have a very strong hand, and East must make a further bid. He bids Four Hearts and West passes.

An inferential force is even more pronounced in a sequence such as:

West	East
1 ♥	1 ♠
2 No-Trumps	3 ♥
?	

West must not pass because East is very clearly inviting him to choose between playing the hand in Three No-Trumps or Four Hearts, whichever contract best suits him.

When the bidding of the partners shows that they hold between them the balance of strength, they should consider bidding a slam. As a guide it may be said that prospects of a slam are good when a player holds enough to make a positive response to a forcing bid; or when the point count of the combined hands totals at least 33; or when a player has enough for an opening bid opposite a partner who has opened with a bid of Two, or who has opened the bidding and made a jump rebid.

Before a slam can be bid with a measure of safety, it is essential for the partners to find out if they hold between them control of the vital suits. The Blackwood convention has been designed to enable the partners to learn how many Aces and Kings are held by the partnership.

When the trump suit has been agreed either directly by support or by implication, or if a forcing situation has been set up, a bid of Four No-Trumps by either partner asks the other to bid Five Clubs if he lacks an Ace or holds all four, Five Diamonds if he holds one Ace, Five Hearts if he holds two and Five Spades if he holds three. If the player who has bid Four No-Trumps, after his partner's response continues with a bid of Five No-Trumps, he is showing that he holds all four Aces and is asking his partner to bid Six Clubs if he lacks a King, Six Diamonds if he holds one King, Six Hearts if he holds two, Six Spades if he holds three and Six No-Trumps if he holds all four.

West | East

Bidding	Bidding
1 ♠	2 ♥
3 No-Trumps	4 ♠
4 No-Trumps	5 ♥
6 ♠	No Bid

Once East has shown that he has support for Spades, West, with support for Hearts, visualises a slam. His bid of Four No-Trumps asks East how many Aces he holds, and East's response of Five Hearts tells West that he holds two. It is important for West to bid the slam in Spades, because if East plays in Hearts and his two Aces are in Hearts and Clubs (as they are) the opening lead of a Diamond from South may break Six Hearts out of hand. When West plays in Six Spades, the King of Diamonds is protected against the opening lead and twelve tricks are assured.

As West knows that there is an Ace against the hand the grand slam is out of the question and West, therefore, has no need to bid Five No-Trumps to ask East how many Kings he holds.

The convention is a very useful one, but it must be used with discretion, because if partner lacks the necessary Aces the partnership may find itself carried out of its depth. As a rule, it may be said that if the final contract is to be in Clubs the bid of Four No-Trumps should not be made unless the bidder holds at least two Aces, and if the contract is to be in Diamonds he should hold at least one Ace.

A limit bid is a bid that informs partner of the precise strength of the hand, and so permits him to estimate the combined strength of the partnership, and drop the bidding if he can see no future for it.

No-Trump bids are limit bids because they are made on an agreed number of points in the hand. A single raise of partner's suit is a limit bid that shows moderate strength and support for the suit; a double raise of partner's suit shows that the hand is too good for a mere simple raise and invites him to bid game if his hand is above average; a triple raise is distributional, it promises good support for the suit and a few scattered points, but no more because with good support for the suit coupled with high-card strength it would be more in order to make a gradual advance to a possible slam.

When an opponent has bid a suit at the level of One, a player should enter the auction only if he can be reasonably sure that his bid, if passed out, will not be defeated by more than two tricks if vulnerable and three if not vulnerable. This general rule, however, must be accepted with some reservation. It would, for example, not be wrong for a player who holds

to bid One Heart over an opponent's One Diamond. The bid might prove costly, but not very often, and it is cowardly not to contest the part-score for fear of the worst happening. A player has a right to assume that even if his partner has a blank hand and only two or three low Hearts, the hand will win three tricks in Hearts and one in each of the black suits.

A jump overcall shows strength, and, though it is not forcing, partner is expected to take action if he holds the values that would justify a response to a bid of One.

An overcall should be based on a 5-card or longer suit, though it is reasonable to overcall with **A K Q x** or **K Q J x** at the level of One. It is nearly always very unwise to overcall with a broken suit.

In general, when an opponent has opened the bidding with a bid of One of a suit, it is better to counter it with a take-out double than with a weak overcall. A double in this situation shows weakness in the suit doubled and a total of about 13 or 14 points with a balanced hand and 11 or 12 with an unbalanced one. Postulating that the doubler's partner has not bid (if he has the double is for a penalty) the doubler invites partner to bid his best suit.

West	*East*
♠ K J 9 6 2	♠ 5 3
♥ K J 9 2	♥ A Q 8 3
♦ 6	♦ K 7 2
♣ A Q 7	♣ 10 8 6 2

If South has bid One Diamond, West should double. East bids Hearts and the good fit has been found. If West bids One Spade over South's One Diamond the Heart fit will never be found and a good result will be exchanged for a bad one.

If partner's best suit is the one that has been doubled, either he bids No-Trumps or passes for a penalty if he holds length in the suit.

A double of One No-Trump is made with a balanced hand and a count of about 2 points more than the No-Trump bidder's average. With a weak hand partner will take out into his best suit, but if the combined count totals 23 or more he will pass for a penalty.

A pre-emptive bid is defined as an opening bid at the level of Three or higher. It is a bid of great value because either it prevents the opponents from entering the auction or compels one of them to bid at a level that is dangerously high when he has no notion of what cards his partner may be holding. Postulating that the bid of Three is weak and that an opponent holds strength in the other three suits, the most practical way of countering the pre-empt is to bid Three Diamonds over Three Clubs and Three No-Trumps over Three Spades, Hearts or Diamonds. Either bid invites partner to bid his best suit.

When the bidding period ends, and the playing period begins, the player on the left of the declarer leads to the first trick. It is only after he has led that the partner of the declarer exposes his hand on the table as dummy. It follows, therefore, that the opening lead has to be made in the dark, since the player can see only his own hand and is left to judge the best lead from it, coupled with the information that he has obtained from the bidding. The opening lead must be chosen with care. It is of great importance, because quite often the choice of a good or bad lead will decide whether or not the declarer's contract will be made.

Against a No-Trump contract, if partner has bid a suit, leading it usually offers the best chance of defeating the contract, unless the player on lead holds only a singleton in the suit or he has a good suit of his own.

With two cards of partner's suit the higher should be led; with three cards the highest should be led, unless the suit is headed by the Ace, King, Queen or Jack, when the lowest should be preferred. With two honours in partner's suit the higher should be led; with a sequence (a combination of three or more cards of adjacent rank) the highest should be led. In all other cases the fourth highest should be led.

When a player leads his own suit, he should lead the fourth highest of his longest suit, unless he holds a sequence (when he should lead the highest), a long suit headed by the Ace and King and an entry in another suit (when he should lead the King), or an intermediate honour sequence *e.g.* **A Q J x** or **K J 10 x** (when the higher of the two touching honours should be led).

The reason for leading the fourth highest card of a suit is that if partner subtracts the number of the card from eleven, the remainder will be the number of higher cards held by the other three players. The Rule of Eleven.

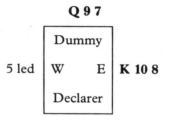

Q 9 7

	Dummy	
5 led	W E	**K 10 8**
	Declarer	

West leads the 5. As $11 - 5 = 6$, and East can see six cards higher than the 5 in dummy and in his own hand, he will know that the declarer cannot hold a card higher than the 4, so that whichever card is played from dummy he can win the trick by playing the card just higher.

Against a suit contract it is usually best to lead partner's suit, if he has bid one. If he has not, and the player on lead has to lead from his own suit, he should give preference to leading the top card of an honour sequence. He should avoid leading a card that may cost a trick *e.g.* leading the King from **K Q x**, or a card that may enable the declarer to win a trick with a card that might have been captured *e.g.* leading the Ace from **A Q x**. The lead of a trump is a good lead if the bidding has suggested that the dummy will be able to trump side suits.

After the opening lead has been made, and the dummy hand exposed, it is of first importance for the declarer, before he plays a card from dummy, to take stock of the position and decide upon the best way to play the cards.

West   East

Against West's contract of Three No-Trumps, North leads the Queen of Spades. At first sight it may seem immaterial whether West wins the trick with the Ace in dummy or with the King in his own hand. In the event, it matters a lot in which hand he wins the trick. If West gives consideration to the position he will appreciate that he must win the first trick with the King of

Spades in his hand, win the King, Queen and Jack of Clubs, reach dummy, by leading the 4 of Spades to the Ace, to win dummy's Ace and 7 of Clubs, and finally the two red Aces in his own hand. If West wins the first trick with dummy's Ace of Spades, he will lose the contract if the adverse Clubs fail to divide 3-2, because he has left himself with no side entry to the Clubs.

When the declarer is playing a No-Trump contract, usually his first aim should be to establish his longest suit. In many cases, however, it is better to develop a short and strong suit rather than a long and weak one.

North leads a Club against West's contract of Three No-Trumps. Consideration shows that West's best play is to win with the King of Clubs and play on Spades to knock out the Ace. This way, West makes sure of his contract with three tricks in Spades, three in Hearts, one in Diamonds and two in Clubs. The Diamond suit is longer than the Spade suit, but West cannot develop East's Diamonds without first losing the lead twice. By then the opponents will have set up the Clubs and broken the contract; in any case, only three tricks in Diamonds will be developed for eight in all, which is not enough.

In a suit contract, it is usually the right play for the declarer to draw the adverse trumps at the first opportunity. Trumps, however, should not be drawn if the declarer can find a better use for them.

West plays in Four Hearts, and North leads a Club. West wins the first trick with the Ace of Clubs, and if he draws the trumps at once his contract will depend on the finesse of the Queen of Spades being successful. It is no more than an even chance. The contract is a certainty if West, after winning the first trick with the Ace of Clubs, leads either the 7 or 3 of the suit. It does not matter whether North or South wins the trick, or what card is returned. Declarer wins the next trick and trumps a Club in dummy. Now the adverse trumps may be drawn, and West comes to ten tricks with one Spade, five Hearts, two Diamonds and one Club by straight leads, and the ruff of a Club on the table.

A valuable weapon in the armoury of the declarer is the ability to manage a suit to make the most tricks out of it.

West	*East*
A 9 3 2	K Q 10 5 4

In this position it is vital to play the King first. Then, if either North or South is void of the suit, there is a marked finessing position over the Jack, and five tricks in the suit will be made.

The unthinking player who first plays the Ace, on the assumption that it does not matter which high card he plays first because the outstanding cards will normally divide 3-1 or 2-2, will lose a trick in the suit whenever North is void and South holds **J 8 7 6**. It will occur about five times in every hundred.

West	*East*
A K 10 5 3	9 7 6

If West cannot afford to lose more than one trick in the suit, his play is to win either the Ace or King; if both opponents follow suit, he enters East's hand in a side suit, leads the 7 from the table and if South plays the 8, plays the 10 from his own hand. This protects him against losing two tricks in the suit if South started with **Q J 8 x**.

There is a percentage play or a safety play for almost every combination of a suit, and it may be found by analysing the division of the remaining cards in the suit.

West	*East*
♠ A K 4 2	♠ 5 3
♥ A 9 7	♥ 10 6 2
♦ A 9 4	♦ K 8 7
♣ K 7 6	♣ A 10 5 4 3

Against West's contract of Three No-Trumps, North leads a Spade. West can make his contract only if he wins four tricks in Clubs. After winning the first trick with the King of Spades, the right play is for West to win the King of Clubs. If North and South both follow suit, West continues with the 7 of Clubs and plays the 4 from dummy if North plays an honour, but the 10 if North plays a low card. If South follows suit, there is only one more outstanding Club and it will fall under East's Ace. If North shows out on the second round of Clubs, then South started with **Q J x x** of the suit and West cannot do anything about it. The directed play, however, guarantees that he will win four tricks in the suit if North originally held **Q J x x** of the suit.

Most important of all, however, is an ability to count the cards. It is not all that difficult, and, in the main, is largely a matter of drawing deductions from the bidding and previous play of the cards, coupled with training oneself to think along the right lines.

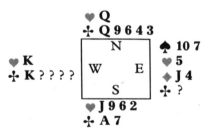

West deals at love all, and the auction is:

West	North	East	South
1 ♣	No Bid	1 ♦	1 ♥
2 ♦	2 ♥	2 ♠	4 ♥
No Bid	No Bid	No Bid	

West leads Diamonds and East wins the first two tricks with the Ace and King of the suit. A third round of Diamonds is ruffed by South with the 8 of Hearts.

As South has lost two tricks, it would seem that his contract is doomed, because West, by reason of his opening bid and lacking either the Ace or King of Diamonds, must surely be holding the Kings of Hearts and Clubs.

South, however, has a partial count of the hand that will enable him to make his contract if he knows how to take advantage of it. On the assumption that West almost certainly started with three Diamonds and probably five Clubs, he cannot have more than five cards in Spades and Hearts. South, therefore, wins the Ace of Hearts (in case the King is singleton) and when the King of Hearts does not come down, he leads a Spade to dummy's King, a Spade from dummy to the Ace in the closed hand, and then trumps his last Spade with dummy's 10 of Hearts. As West played the 7 of Hearts under South's Ace and followed to the three rounds of Spades, South may reconstruct the position as:

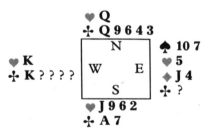

Now, by leading the Queen of Hearts from dummy, West is put on lead with the King, and as he must return a Club, South wins two tricks in the suit.

The play of the defenders is more difficult than that of the declarer, because a defender has to combine his hand with that of the unseen one held by his partner. They have the slight advantage of a partnership language that enables them to exchange information and advice, but, for the most part, success in defence comes mainly from drawing the right deductions from the bidding, and the cards that have been played to previous tricks.

To lead the highest card of a sequence, to win with the lowest, and to follow suit as the situation dictates, is a general rule that does not need to be enlarged on. Most of the general rules for defence play, however, have been handed down from the days when whist was the fashionable game. At bridge reservations have to be made, because the bidding and the exposed dummy hand allow for modifications of what were only broad generalities in the first place.

To return the suit that partner has led is not always the best play. Sometimes it is more important to take time by the forelock.

South deals and opens the auction with One No-Trump (12 to 14 points) and North jumps him to Three.

West leads the 3 of Hearts and East wins with the Ace. If East returns a Heart, South has no difficulty in making nine tricks, because dummy's 10 of Hearts protects the Jack in the closed hand and the defenders cannot win more than one trick in Spades and three in Hearts. With the 2 of Hearts on the table, East should appreciate that his partner cannot hold more than four Hearts and that they cannot be better than **K Q 9 3**, because if they were **K Q J 3** he would have led the King and not the 3. As once East gives up the lead he can never regain it, he must take advantage of the time factor, the tempo, and lead the Queen of Spades. The only chance of defeating the contract is to find West holding the Ace of Spades, and as South's bid of One No-Trump postulates a maximum of 14 points, East, who holds 7 points and can count 10 on the table, can count West with just enough room in his hand for the Ace of Spades as well as for the King and Queen of Hearts.

To cover an honour with an honour may be good play in many cases, but it is not when the honour has been led from a sequence.

The Queen is led from dummy. If East covers with the King, the declarer will win four tricks in the suit by winning with the Ace and returning the suit to finesse against West's 10. East, therefore, should not cover. The Queen will win, but now the defenders will always win a trick in the suit because if the declarer continues with dummy's Jack, the lead is no longer from a sequence and East covers it with the King. With **K x** only, East should cover the Queen, otherwise the declarer, after winning dummy's Queen may continue with a low Spade (not the Jack) from the table and East's King will be wasted.

Second hand plays low; third hand plays high, is another general rule that has been handed down from the past. It is, perhaps, a rule worth remembering, because exceptions when second hand should play high are few and far between, and when third hand sees only low cards on his right, there are virtually no exceptions to his playing high.

West leads the Jack. East should play the King like a man. He knows that the declarer holds the Queen (otherwise West would have led it in preference to the Jack) and if declarer holds the Ace as well the King is doomed. East, therefore, must play on the chance that West has led from **A J 10 x** and that declarer holds **Q x x**.

A very important weapon in the armoury of the defenders is the echo or peter, sometimes called the come-on or high-low signal. Reduced to its simplest terms, when a defender plays a higher card followed by a lower one of the same suit, it is a request to partner to play the suit. In many cases a defender can afford to play the suit only once. In such a case to play a 7 or a higher card is an encouragement to partner, and, by contrary, to play a lower card is a discouragement to him. Against a trump contract, the high-low play in a side suit shows that a doubleton is held and that the third round can be trumped. If the play is made in the trump suit itself, it shows that three trumps are held. Against a No-Trump contract, the echo shows length in the suit, usually four cards.

The defenders are frequently compelled to discard, and nearly always discarding presents them with a problem. The general rules to follow are not to retain the same suit as partner; not to discard from a suit in which you have the same length as dummy or suspect the declarer has in his hand; and never to discard so that the declarer is given information.

Counting the cards is, of course, as important to the defenders as it is to the declarer. In some ways, however, the defenders have it a bit easier. If the declarer is in a No-Trump contract he will have limited his hand to an agreed number of points. It follows, therefore, that if the declarer's limit is 16 to 18 points and he has shown up with 15 points, the defenders know that he has left in his hand no more than a King or its equivalent. In much the same way, in a suit contract the declarer and his dummy will rarely hold less than eight trump cards between them. It follows, therefore, that if a defender holds three trumps, he knows that his partner is probably holding not more than two.

In conclusion, it may be said that good defence consists in playing those cards that give as much information as possible to partner, and making things as easy as possible for him; by contrary, in playing those cards that give as little information as possible to the declarer and making things as difficult as possible for him. Whenever it is possible to do so, a defender should play the cards that the declarer knows are in his hand, and retain those of which he knows nothing. If all this comes as a counsel of perfection—the best bridge players are perfectionists.

Brint

Brint was originated by J. B. Chambers in 1929. It is a hybrid of bridge (see page 83) and vint, the national card game of Russia. It has been described as bridge with vint scoring, because the score that counts towards game, and recorded below the line, depends entirely upon the level to which the bidding has been carried. No-Trumps and the suits retain their rank, but each trick (over six) at the level of One is worth 10 points, at the level of Two 20 points, and so on up to Seven when each trick is worth 70 points.

The full scoring table is:

When the Contract is at the level of:	Each Odd-trick (whether Doubled or not) is worth:	When the Declarer is Not Vulnerable		
		Undoubled	Doubled	
		Penalty for each Undertrick	Bonus for Contract and each Overtrick	Penalty for each Undertrick
One	10	50	50	100
Two	20	50	50	100
Three	30	50	50	100
Four	40	100	100	200
Five	50	150	150	300
Six	60	200	200	400
Seven	70	250	250	500

The score for tricks made is unaffected by a double, but if a doubled contract is redoubled the trick score, as well as the bonus and penalty for a doubled contract, is doubled. The bonuses and penalties are increased by 100 points each if the player is vulnerable.

A game is won by the pair that first reaches a trick score of 160 points.

The bonuses for bidding and making slams and games, and for holding honours, recorded above the line as at bridge, are:

For a successful bid of Seven – 1000 points
For a successful bid of Six – 500 points
For a successful bid of Five – 250 points
For a successful bid of Four – 500 points if vulnerable
                                        250 points if not vulnerable
In a No-Trump contract for four Aces in one hand – 150 points
In a Suit contract for *five* honours in one hand – 200 points
In a Suit contract for *four* honours in one hand – 100 points
They are unaffected by vulnerability, doubling and redoubling.

Calypso

Calypso was invented by R. W. Willis of Trinidad: it dates from the mid-1950s, and though designed on entirely new lines, inevitably borrows some of the best features of bridge (see page 83) and canasta (see page 105).

The game is played with four packs of cards (with identical backs) shuffled together, but the cards are shuffled only at the start of a game, and a player holds only thirteen of them at a time.

Four players take part, and it is a novel feature of the game that each player has his own trump suit. Spades and Hearts play in partnership against Diamonds and Clubs. The players cut for seats and trump suits. The highest has choice of both, and his partner takes the corresponding suit and sits facing him. The choice of a trump suit conveys no advantage; it is purely a matter of personal preference.

Thirteen cards are dealt to each player, and the dealer places the rest of the pack to his left, ready for the next dealer after the hand has been played.

The player on the left of the dealer leads to the first trick. Thereafter the lead is made by the player who wins a trick. When playing to a trick a player must follow suit if he can; otherwise he may either discard or trump by playing a card of his own trump suit.

A trick is won by he who has played the highest card of the suit led, or by he who has trumped it, or over-trumped it by playing a higher trump of his own trump suit. If two or more players play identical cards, the first played takes priority for the purpose of winning tricks, and perhaps the most important feature of the game is that if a player leads a card of his own trump suit, he wins the trick automatically unless it is trumped by another player or over-trumped by still another player. To illustrate:

North ♣	*East* ♠	*South* ♦	*West* ♥
8 ♥	J ♥	10 ♥	3 ♥

North has led the 8 of Hearts, and East wins the trick because he has played the highest Heart.

4 ♦	6 ♠	7 ♦	3 ♦

North has led the 4 of Diamonds, and East wins the trick because he has trumped. South has merely followed suit to North's lead.

3 ♥	4 ♠	6 ♦	J ♥

North has led the 3 of Hearts, and South wins the trick, because although East has trumped, he has over-trumped. West has merely followed suit to North's lead.

9 ♣	J ♣	6 ♣	5 ♣

North has led the 9 of Clubs and wins the trick because Clubs is his own trump suit. That East has played a higher Club does not score.

North ♣	*East* ♠	*South* ♦	*West* ♥
6 ♣	7 ♠	9 ♦	5 ♣

North has led the 6 of Clubs, East has trumped, but South wins the trick because he has over-trumped.

6 ♥	Q ♥	Q ♥	10 ♥

North has led the 6 of Hearts, and the trick is won by East as his Queen of Hearts was played before South's.

The object of the game is to build calypsoes. A calypso is a complete suit (from Ace to 2) in a player's trump suit.

When a player wins a trick, he leaves exposed on the table, in front of him, any cards that will help him to build a calypso, passes to his partner any cards that will help him to build a calypso, and discards the others, face downwards, on his right.

North (whose trump suit is Clubs) leads the 4 of Clubs and wins the trick:

4 ♣	6 ♣	J ♣	6 ♣

North places the **4 ♣**, **6 ♣** and **J ♣** face upwards on the table in front of him, and discards the second **6 ♣**. He then leads the **8 ♣** and the trick is:

8 ♣	J ♣	7 ♣	8 ♦

Again North wins the trick. He keeps the **7 ♣** and **8 ♣** for his calypso, passes the 8 ♦ to his partner for his calypso, and discards the **J ♣** because he already has one.

The play continues until all thirteen tricks have been played; the next player then deals another hand of thirteen cards each.

A player may build only one calypso at a time, but once a calypso has been built the player may begin another. He may use any cards in the trick with which a calypso has been completed, but he cannot use any cards from his discard pile. These cards are dead.

The game ends when each player has dealt once. The score is then made up as follows:

For the first calypso—500 points.
For the second calypso—750 points ⎫ When obtained by
For any subsequent calypso—1,000 points ⎭ the individual players.
For each card in an incomplete calypso—20 points.
For each card in the discard pile—10 points.

The two partners add their totals together, and stakes are paid on the difference between the totals of the two sides.

A serious view is taken of revoking. A revoke does not become established until a player of the offending side has played to the next trick, and a revoke made in the twelfth never becomes established, but if established a revoke suffers a penalty of 260 points.

SOLO CALYPSO is played by four players but each plays for himself. The play is more or less identical with the parent game, the main difference between the two is that, in solo calypso, the players draw cards for choice of seats and trump suits; the highest has first choice, the lowest takes what is left.

CALYPSO FOR THREE PLAYERS is played with three packs of cards and one complete suit (it does not matter which) removed from all three packs. The game consists of three deals. Each player plays for himself.

Canasta

Canasta is a variation of rummy (see page 139) that was developed in South America as an independent game. It may be played by any number of players from two to six, but is at its most skilful when played by four. If two or three play each plays for himself; if four they play as two partners against the other two, the partners sitting facing each other; if five they play two against three, but of the three only two play at a time and rotate so that at each deal a different player sits out; if six play they play as three partners against the other three, the partners sitting alternately around the table.

The game is played with two 52-card packs and two Jokers to each pack. The four Jokers and the eight 2s are wild cards: they may be named as any other card.

The dealer deals eleven cards to each player * and the rest of the pack (the stock) is placed face downwards in the centre of the table. The top card is turned face upwards and placed alongside it. It is known as the up-card, and is the start of the discard pile. If it is a wild card or a red 3 it is covered with the next card of the stock, and if this also is a wild card or a red 3 it is covered with the next card of the stock, and so on.

The red 3s are bonus cards that count for or against the side to which they fall. They do not form part of a player's hand, and at his turn to play he who holds a red 3 must place it face upwards on the table in front of him and refill his hand by drawing the top card of the stock. If a red 3 is taken in the discard pile, it is similarly faced, but the player does not refill his hand from the stock.

The object of the game is to form melds of three or more cards of the same rank, with or without the help of wild cards. Sequences are not recognized as melds.

The player on the left of the dealer plays first. Thereafter play continues clockwise round the table. A play consists of a player drawing a card, melding (optional), discarding. A game in progress is shown in Plate 14.

The Draw The player takes either the top card of the stock or the up-card of the discard pile provided he can meld with it. In the latter case, however, he must take with it the whole of the discard pile subject to its not being frozen. At the beginning of the game the discard pile is frozen until a side has made its first meld; it is then unfrozen for that side only. Even for a side that has melded the discard pile is frozen at any time that a red 3 or a wild card is the up-card. It remains frozen until it is taken by a player, because the fresh discard pile is not frozen unless the player starts the fresh pile with a wild card. If a player plays a black 3 to the discard pile it is frozen for the next player only.

---

* If two play each is dealt fifteen cards; if three play each is dealt thirteen cards.

The Meld A meld is valid if it contains at least two 'natural' (*i.e.* not wild) cards of the same rank, and not more than three wild cards. Black 3s, however, may not be melded unless the player melds out in the same turn. Wild cards may not be melded separately from natural cards. A meld must be placed face upwards on the table, and the melds of the two partners are placed in front of only one of them. A player may add one or more cards of the same rank, or wild cards, to a meld previously faced by his side. A player may make as many melds as he chooses, including the addition of cards to melds made by his side; also he may not add cards to the melds of his opponents. Wild cards, once melded, cannot be replaced with natural cards.

A canasta is a meld of seven or more cards, and may be built up from an initial meld of three or more cards. If a canasta contains no wild cards it is a natural canasta; if it is formed with one, two or three wild cards it is a mixed canasta. Wild cards may be added in any number to a canasta, but other melds are limited to three (see illustration).

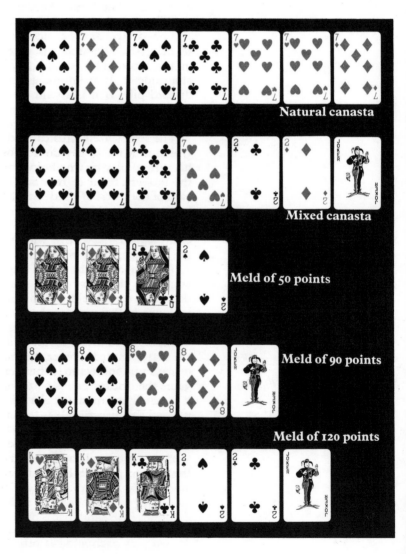

Natural canasta

Mixed canasta

Meld of 50 points

Meld of 90 points

Meld of 120 points

Every card melded has the following point value:
Jokers – 50 points each.
Aces and 2s – 20 points each.
Kings, Queens, Jacks, 10s, 9s and 8s – 10 points each.
7s, 6s, 5s, 4s, and black 3s – 5 points each.

These points count to the credit of a side if the cards are melded when a deal ends, and to its debit if they are not melded.

The red 3s have a value of 100 points each, unless a side holds all four of them, when each has a value of 200 points. At the end of the deal a side that has made any meld scores all its red 3s as a plus bonus: a side that has made no meld deducts the value of its red 3s from its score.

The first meld is governed by a strict rule. If the score of a side is under 1500 points the first meld must total at least 50 points; if the score is between 1500 and 2995 points it must total at least 90 points; and if the score is 3000 points or more it must total at least 120 points. There is no minimum total for a side that has a minus score.

The Discard. After a player has made a draw and melded if he has chosen to, he must play a card to the discard pile. The card must be played from hand and not from a meld on the table. The discard, however, is optional when the player melds every card in his hand (called melding out). It sometimes happens that a player is able to meld all his cards in one turn, he not having melded previously. It is known as melding out blind, and the bonus is doubled. Either way, however, a player must have, or be able to complete, a canasta, and as melding out may not suit partner he should first always ask him: 'May I go out?' Partner's reply to the question must be a simple 'Yes' or 'No', and, whichever it is, is binding on the partnership. Indeed, if the partner says 'Yes' and the player cannot, after all, meld out he suffers a penalty of 100 points.

The side that goes out totals the point values of the cards in its melds; adds a bonus of 100 points for melding out (200 points if it has melded out blind); 100 for each red 3 (800 points if the partnership holds all four red 3s); 500 points for each natural canasta and 300 points for each mixed canasta. From this is subtracted the total point value of the cards left in the hand of the partner.

The score of the side that did not meld out is determined in the same way, and it is deducted from that of the side that melded out. If it has not made a meld the value of its red 3s are deducted from, instead of added to, its total.

The game is won by the side that first reaches a total of 5,000 points, or the higher total if both sides pass 5,000 in the same deal.

The chief aim of a player must be to make canastas. If there is a choice, it is best to begin as many melds as possible, because each is a start towards a canasta. One should take advantage of the fact that, to fulfil the minimum count, a player may take two or more different melds at the same turn. At the same time, it is unwise to meld every meldable card as soon as you can. It depletes the hand and leaves you at the mercy of the opponents until you are able to go out. A good general rule is that it is unwise to make a first meld if it reduces the hand to less than six cards. A first meld should always be made if it can with the minimum number of cards.

A player should always try to retain at least one wild card in his hand, and, except to help complete a canasta, he should not add unnecessarily to a meld when there is the risk that the opponents will go out.

Nearly always it is unwise to discard Aces; they pull more weight when melded.

Since black 3s have no constructive value there is a tendency to discard them at the first opportunity. It is not bad play to do so, and it has the advantage of freezing the pack for one's left-hand opponent. In general, however, it is better to retain a black 3 until one is faced with the problem of finding a safe discard.

As the two partners hold between them only eleven cards, it stands out that at best they are unlikely to make more than one canasta out of them. There are, however, sixty-four cards that have not been dealt to the four players. Clearly, therefore, taking the pack must be to a player's advantage, because he can make so many more canastas out of it.

If your side wins the first pack, do not reduce your hand unnecessarily. Do not be frightened to discard from your longest holdings. By contrast, if your side loses the first pack your only defence is to play to go out. There is a very important difference between attacking and defending play.

When the pack is frozen, try to build up a hand in pairs. Pairs are very valuable, because every meld must contain at least two cards of the same suit—a pair that is.

THREE-PACK CANASTA, or Samba, may be played by any number of players from two to six, but is a satisfactory game only for six playing in three partnerships of two each. One player sits between two opponents, one of each of the other partnerships.

Three 52-card packs with two Jokers each are used. Thirteen cards are dealt to each player. Game is 10,000 points, and when a side reaches 7,000 its minimum count for its first meld is 150 points. Five red 3s have a value of 1,000 points; six 1,200 points. A side must have two canastas to meld out.

Euchre

Euchre, a game always more popular in the New World than in the Old, and made famous by Bret Harte's witty *Plain Language from Truthful James*, has several variations. The standard game is suitable for from two to six players, but is best for four, two playing in partnership against the other two.

The game is played with the 32-card or short pack, that is the regular pack from which the 6s and lower cards have been removed. The cards rank in the order from Ace (high) to 7 (low) with the exception that the Jack of the trump suit (Right Bower) takes precedence over all other trump cards, and the Jack of the suit of the same colour (Left Bower) ranks as the second highest trump.

There is some advantage in dealing. The players, therefore, must draw cards to decide who shall deal. The highest takes first deal, which, thereafter, passes round the table clockwise.

The dealer gives five cards to each player either in bundles of two then three, or three then two. It does not matter which, but he must be consistent throughout the game. The rest of the pack is placed face downwards in the centre of the table, and the top card is turned face upwards. It is the potential trump suit, and, beginning with the player on the left of the dealer, each player in turn has the option of either refusing or accepting it.

To accept it as the trump suit the opponents of the dealer say: 'I order it up'; the dealer's partner says: 'I assist'; and the dealer himself says nothing, but accepts by making his discard. To refuse the card as the trump suit, the opponents and partner of the dealer say: 'I pass'; the dealer signifies refusal by taking the card from the top of the pack and placing it, face upwards, partly underneath the pack.

If all four players pass on the first round, there is a second round. Beginning with the player on the left of the dealer, each player in turn may now either pass, or name any suit he likes (other than that of the turned up card) as trumps. If all four players pass on the second round, the hand is abandoned and the deal passes.

When the trump suit has been settled, the player who has named it (the maker) has the right to go it alone, but he must announce his intention to do so before a card has been led. His partner places his cards face downwards on the table, and takes no active part in the hand. The maker (he is the only one of the four who can go alone) plays his hand against the two opponents in partnership. If he wins the march (all five tricks) he scores 4 points; if he wins three or four tricks he scores 1 point; if he is euchred (*i.e.* fails to win at least three tricks) the opponents score 2 points each.

Euchre is a trick-taking game. The player on the left of the dealer (or the player on the left of the maker if he is going it alone) leads to the first trick. Thereafter the player who wins a trick leads to the next. A player must follow suit to the card led if he can, if not he may either discard or trump.

If the partnership that made the trump suit wins the march it scores 2 points; if it wins three or four tricks it scores 1 point; if it is euchred the opposing side scores 2 points. It is customary for each side to keep the score by using a 3 and a 4 (cards not needed in the game) as shown in the illustration. The side that is first to score five points wins.

TWO-HANDED EUCHRE is played in exactly the same way as the parent game except that the pack is reduced to twenty-four cards by removing the 8s and all lower cards, and, obviously, there is no declaration of going it alone.

THREE-HANDED EUCHRE is played in the same way as the parent game except that the maker of the trump suit plays against the other two in partnership. If the maker wins the march he scores 3 points; if he wins three or four tricks he scores 1 point; and if he is euchred each of his opponents scores 2 points.

CALL-ACE EUCHRE is a variation that may be played by four, five or six players, each playing for himself. It is played in the same way as the parent game with the exception that the maker has the option of either playing for himself or of calling for a partner by saying: 'I call on the Ace of . . .' and he names a suit. The player who holds the Ace of this suit then plays in partnership with the maker against the other players, but he does not reveal himself. It follows, therefore, that until the Ace is played, and it may not be in the deal, everyone except the holder of the Ace (if it is in play) is left to guess where his interest lies.

The scoring is rather different to that of the other variations as fundamentally the game is all against all. For winning the march a lone player scores 1 point for every player in the game; in a partnership hand the score is 2 points each if three or four players are in the game, and 3 points each if five or six players are in the game. For winning three or four tricks a lone player scores 1 point; in a partnership hand both players score 1 point. If a lone player or a partnership is euchred the other players score 2 points each.

Hearts

Hearts and its several variations is very similar in principle to black maria (see page 74) because the object of the game is to avoid taking tricks that contain certain specified cards. The play itself follows the general principles of trick-taking games: the player on the left of the dealer leads to the first trick, and thereafter the winner of a trick leads to the next; a player must follow suit to the card led if he can, and if he cannot he may discard any card that suits him.

The game may be played by any reasonable number of players, but it is at its most interesting and skilful as a game for four, each playing for himself. *

The Queen of Spades and all cards of the Heart suit are penalty cards. Every deal is a separate event, and the usual method of settling is to debit he who wins the Queen of Spades with 13 points, and those who win Hearts with 1 point for each card.

A revoke is heavily penalized. A player may correct a revoke if he does so before a card is led to the next trick; otherwise the revoke is established, the hand is abandoned, and the revoking player is debited with all 26 points.

The game is not a difficult one, but it calls for an ability to count the cards, read the distribution and visualize possibilities. It is instructive to consider the play in the deal below if West has to make the opening lead and assumes that the best lead is the 2 of Hearts because one of the other players will certainly have to win the trick.

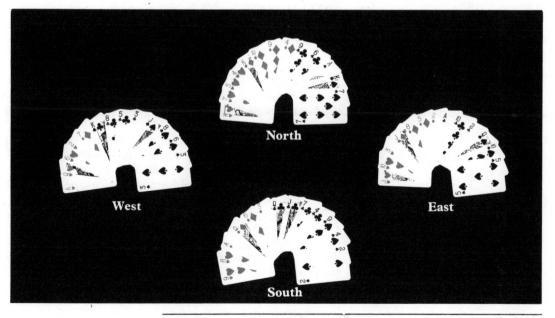

West

North

East

South

*When the game is played by three players or by more than four, low cards are removed from the pack to reduce it to a number that allows every player to be dealt the same number of cards.

Against West's opening lead of the 2 of Hearts the play will be short and sharp, and West will come off worst of all because good play by his opponents will saddle him with the Queen of Spades.

West	North	East	South
2♥	4♥	3♥	8♥
6♥	7♥	10♥	9♥
Q♥	K♥	J♥	A♦
A♥	5♥	Q♠	Q♦

A more experienced West would have kept off leading a Heart. It is probable that his best lead is the singleton Diamond, because he has nothing to fear in the Spade suit, and, once he has got rid of his Diamond, he gives himself the best chance to get rid of the dangerous Ace and Queen of Hearts.

In **DOMINO HEARTS** the players are dealt only six cards each, and the rest of the pack is placed face downwards in the centre of the table. The player on the left of the dealer leads to the first trick, and the game is played in the same way as the parent game except that if a player cannot follow suit to a card that has been led he must draw a card from the stock, and continue to do so until he draws a card of the suit led. Only after the stock has been exhausted may a player discard from his hand if he cannot follow suit to a lead.

Play continues until all the cards have been taken in tricks, each player dropping out as his hand is exhausted. If a player wins a trick with the last card in his hand, the next active player on his left leads to the next trick. The last player to be left in the game retains all the cards left in his hand, and takes into it any cards that may be left in the stock.

The Queen of Spades is not a penalty card; only cards of the Heart suit are, and 1 point is lost for each one taken in a trick or left in the hand of the surviving player.

In **GREEK HEARTS**, as in black maria (see page 104) each player, before the opening lead is made, passes three cards to his right-hand opponent and receives three from his left-hand opponent.

As in the parent game the penalty cards are the Queen of Spades and all cards of the Heart suit, and the penalties for winning them are the same; if, however, a player wins all the Hearts and the Queen of Spades, instead of losing 26 points, he receives 26 points from each of the other players.

The game calls for some considerable skill, because, before passing on his cards, a player has to decide whether he will take the easy road and play to avoid winning penalty cards, or try for the big prize by winning all. The decision is never an easy one, because by discarding a high Heart one may be helping an opponent to a better score, and oneself lose a good score if one receives the Queen of Spades and a couple of high Hearts from one's left-hand opponent.

HEARTSETTE is played in the same way as the parent game, but with a widow hand. If three or four take part in the game the 2 of Spades is removed from the pack, and if five or six take part the full pack is used.

When there are three players, each is dealt sixteen cards, when four, twelve cards, when five, ten cards and when six, eight cards. The remaining cards are placed face downwards in the centre of the table.

The player on the left of the dealer leads to the first trick and whoever wins it takes the widow and discards from his hand to reduce it to the proper number of cards. No-one else sees the widow nor the cards that have been discarded.

The play continues in the same way as in the parent game with the same penalty cards and penalties for winning them.

OMNIBUS HEARTS or Hit the Moon, combines most of the features that have been added to the parent game. Like it it is at its best when played by four, each playing for himself.

Thirteen cards are dealt to each player, and before the opening lead is made each player passes three cards to his right-hand opponent and receives three from his left-hand opponent.

The play is the same as in the parent game. All the Hearts and the Queen of Spades are penalty cards, but a novel feature is that the 10 of Diamonds is a bonus card. A player loses 1 point for every Heart that he wins and 13 points if he wins the Queen of Spades. By contrary, he wins 10 points if he takes the 10 of Diamonds, and if he wins all the Hearts, the Queen of Spades and the 10 of Diamonds (known as hitting the moon—no longer such a feat as it once was) he wins 26 points instead of losing 16.

The game is won by the player who has the highest plus score, or lowest minus score, when one player reaches a score of −100.

The game calls for skill both in discarding to the right-hand opponent and in the play. Good discarding is dictated by the fact that only the Club suit is neutral and harmless. Every Heart is a liability and top Spades are dangerous (unless adequately supported by low cards) though top Diamonds are advantageous the low ones may be liabilities.

In play it is necessary to aim at forcing the lead into the hand of the least dangerous opponent. All the time temporary partnerships must be formed. If the score stands at: North −83, East −41, South +32, West +47, it is obvious that West will be doing his best to win the game by driving North to −100 as quickly as possible. A skilful South, therefore, will enter into a tacit partnership with North to try and save him by prolonging the game and so give himself more time to pull ahead of West. The strategy is perfectly proper because both players are acting in their own interests.

PIP HEARTS is played in the same way as the parent game, but the Queen of Spades is not a penalty card and the penalty for winning a Heart is increased to the pip value of the card, the court cards counting Jack 11, Queen 12, King 13 and Ace 14.

Pinocle

(see footnote page 63)

Pinocle has much in common with bezique (see page 30) and originated in Europe. It has, however, long since crossed the Atlantic, and, if we exclude the ubiquitous bridge (see page 83) it shares with poker (see page 133) the honour of being the national card game of the U.S.A.

In its original form, pinocle is a game for two players and is described on page 63. American card-players, however, have developed a number of variations suitable for more than two. The most popular is Auction Pinocle, a rather remarkable game because though fundamentally a game for three it makes a better game when played by four.

In every deal only three players take an active part. If four play the dealer deals no cards to himself; and if five wish to take part the dealer deals no cards to the second player on his left as well as none to himself. The inactive players, as they are called, take no part in the bidding and play, but participate in the settlement.

The pinocle pack consists of forty-eight cards, namely the **A 10 K Q J 9** (in that order) of each suit, duplicated. The dealer deals fifteen cards face downwards to the active players, either in five bundles of three each, or in three bundles of four each and one of three, and after the first round, three cards face downwards to the table as a widow-hand.

A bid is a contract to score either by melds, by cards won in tricks, or by both, the number of points named, and the player on the left of the dealer makes the first bid which must be at least 300. After this, each player in turn may either pass or make a higher bid. Bids must be in multiples of ten, and once a player has passed he cannot re-enter the auction. When two players pass a bid the player who made it becomes the bidder, his bid the contract, and the other two players his opponents.

If the opening bid of 300 is passed by the other two players the bidder may concede defeat by throwing in his cards without looking at the widow. He pays 3 units to the kitty (but nothing to his opponents) and the deal passes to the next player.

If the bid is for more than 300, or if the bidder does not wish to concede defeat, he shows the widow to his opponents and takes the cards into his hand. He then names the trump suit, and places on the table in front of him his melds. They are scored for as follows:

Class A
A 10 K Q J of the trump suit = 150 points
K Q of the trump suit (royal marriage) = 40 points
K Q of a plain suit (common marriage) = 20 points

Class B
Pinocle (**Q ♠** and **J ♦**) = 40 points
Dis (**9** of the trump suit) = 10 points

Class C
Four Aces – one of each suit = 100 points
Four Kings – one of each suit = 80 points
Four Queens – one of each suit = 60 points
Four Jacks – one of each suit = 40 points

No card may be used twice in melds of the same class, but the same card may be used in two or more melds of different classes. Only the bidder melds. He then discards face downwards (buries) three cards from his hand in order to reduce it to fifteen cards: later the cards that he discards will be counted for him as won in a trick. The discards must be made from the cards in his hand, not from those in his melds, but before he leads to the first trick he may change the cards that he has discarded, change the melds and the trump suit.

When the bidder and his opponents have agreed on the value of the melds and how many more points (if any) he needs to fulfil his contract, the bidder leads to the first trick. If, however, he thinks he will not be able to make his contract he may concede defeat (called *single bête*) and pay to the players, active and inactive, the value of his bid.

When playing to a trick a player must follow suit if he can, and if he cannot he must play to win the trick by trumping or over-trumping it. Only if he has no card of the suit led and no trump card may he discard. If a trump is led, the subsequent players must try to win it. A trick is won by the highest card of the suit led or the highest trump if the led card has been trumped. If two identical cards are played the one first to be played wins the trick, if the trick is to be won by the card.

When all the tricks have been played, the players score for each Ace 11 points, each Ten 10 points, each King 4 points, each Queen 3 points, each Jack 2 points, and for winning the last trick 10 points. It gives a total of 250 points to be won in tricks.

Every deal is a separate event and settlement is made before the next deal begins. It is usual to reduce the contract to units on which payment is made.

Contract	*Unit Value*	
300–340	3	
350–390	5	If Spades
400–440	10	are trumps
450–490	15	the unit
500–540	20	values are
550–590	25	doubled.
600 and more	30	

The bidder pays double (called *double bête*) if his score for melds and cards taken in tricks fails to equal his contract; he receives if his score equals or exceeds his contract, but he does not receive more than the unit value of his contract.

Payment is made to and from all players, active and inactive, and to and from a kitty if the contract is for 350 or more.

The kitty is a separate account and is the common property of the players. They make good any deficiency if it owes, and divide any surplus when the game breaks up.

As the name implies **PARTNERSHIP PINOCLE** is played by four players two playing in partnership against the other two. The partners face each other.

The 48-card pinocle pack is used. The dealer gives each player twelve cards in bundles of three each, and turns up the last card dealt to himself to determine the trump suit. In turn, beginning with the player on the left of the dealer, any player who holds the dis (9 of the trump suit) may exchange it for the turned-up card, and if the dealer turns up the dis as the trump card he scores 10 points. Each original holder of a dis, whether or not he exchanges it with the turned-up card, scores 10 points for it.

The players expose their melds on the table in front of them, and in addition to the melds for auction pinocle (page 160) melds and the scores for them are as follows:

Double Trump Sequence **A 10 K Q J**	1,500 points
Double Pinocle	300 points
All Eight Aces	1,000 points
All Eight Kings	800 points
All Eight Queens	600 points
All Eight Jacks	400 points

When the players have shown their melds and scored for them, they return them to their hands. No meld, however, finally counts unless the partnership wins a trick, and when a trick is won both partners score for their melds.

The player on the left of the dealer leads to the first trick, and the play continues as in auction pinocle.

When all twelve tricks have been played, the players count 10 points for every Ace and 10 won, 5 points for every King and Queen, and 10 points for winning the last trick. As in auction pinocle the total is 250 points.

The game is won by the partnership that first wins 1,000 points in melds and cards won in tricks, but if both partnerships reach 1,000 or more points in the same deal the game continues to 1,250 points, and, if it happens again, to 1,500 points, and so on.

At any time during the game a player may claim that he has scored 1,000 points or more and won the game. Play is brought to an end and the claim is verified. If the claim is found to be correct his partnership wins the game; if the claim is found to be wrong his partnership loses the game. In either case, what the opposing side has scored makes no difference to the result.

PARTNERSHIP PINOCLE FOR MORE THAN FOUR PLAYERS is played with two 48-card pinocle packs shuffled together. Six players form two partnerships of three players each sitting alternately at the table: eight players form two partnerships of four players each sitting alternately.

The dealer gives 16 cards to each player in bundles of four each and turns up the last card dealt to himself to denote the trump suit.

The game is played in the same way as partnership pinocle, but in addition to the melds opposite, melds and the scores for them are as follows:

Triple Trump Sequence **A 10 K Q J**	3,000 points
Double Trump Sequence **A 10 K Q J**	1,500 points
Four Kings and Four Queens of the same suit	1,200 points
Three Kings and Three Queens of the same suit	600 points
Two Kings and Two Queens of the same suit	300 points
Quadruple Pinocle	1,200 points
Triple Pinocle	600 points
Double Pinocle	300 points
Fifteen Aces, Kings, Queens and Jacks	3,000 points
Twelve Aces	2,000 points
Twelve Kings	1,600 points
Twelve Queens	1,200 points
Twelve Jacks	800 points
Eight Aces	1,000 points
Eight Kings	800 points
Eight Queens	600 points
Eight Jacks	400 points

FIREHOUSE PINOCLE is played as a partnership game for four, two playing in partnership against the other two. Twelve cards are dealt to each player. As in auction pinocle the trump suit is bid for; the player on the left of the dealer bids first; each player has only one bid or pass, and the minimum bid is 200. The bidder makes the trump suit and leads to the first trick. Game is won by the partnership that first reaches 1,000 points. The score of the bidder's side is counted first, and the game is played to the end. A partnership cannot concede defeat.

CHECK PINOCLE was developed some say in Texas, out of firehouse pinocle, and is considered one of the best and most skilful of all partnership games, not excluding bridge.

The game is played by four players, two playing in partnership against the other two, with the regular 48-card pinocle pack.

Twelve cards are dealt to each player in bundles of three at a time, and each player in turn, beginning with the player on the left of the dealer, must either bid or pass. The lowest bid is 200, subsequent bids must be made in multiples of ten, and once a player has passed he may not re-enter the bidding. None of the first three players may make a bid unless he holds a marriage (King and Queen of one suit) but if all three pass the dealer must bid at least 200 and he does not need a marriage to do so; if, however, he wishes to make a higher bid than 200 he must hold one. The bidding ends when a bid has been passed by the three other players, and the bidder then names the trump suit.

The players then expose their melds on the table. The melds and the scores for them are the same as in auction pinocle (page 114) and the partners add the values of their melds together and record the total as a single score.

Some melds have what is known as a check (chip) value; a Trump Sequence (**A 10 K Q J**) and Four Aces each of a different suit are each worth 2 checks, Four Kings, Four Queens, Four Jacks each of a different suit, and Double Pinocle are all worth 1 check. Check values are paid across the table as the game procedes.

The players return the melds to their hands, and the play is the same as in partnership pinocle. When all twelve tricks have been played a partnership scores 10 points for every Ace and 10 that it has won, 5 points for every King and Queen, and 10 points if it has won the last trick.

The bidding side adds these points to those that it has already scored for its melds, and if the total is at least equal to the bid the contract has been made and the partnership scores for everything that it makes; if its total is less than its bid the amount of its bid is deducted from its score. In all cases the opposing side scores for everything that it makes.

The game is won by the partnership that first scores 1,000 points. The score of the bidding partnership is counted first, and as the game is over when it reaches 1,000 points, the opposing partnership scores nothing in the final deal.

At the end of each deal a partnership is entitled to checks on the following scale:

Contract	If Made	
200–240	2 checks	If the contract is
250–290	4 checks	defeated the
300–340	7 checks	bidding partnership
350–390	10 checks	pays double checks
400–440	13 checks	to the opposing
and 3 added checks for		partnership.
each series of 50 points.		

A partnership that wins all twelve tricks in a deal receives 4 checks; for winning the game it receives 7 checks and 1 check for each 100 points (or part thereof) by which the score of the winning partnership exceeds that of the losing partnership; and if the losing partnership has a net minus score, the winning partnership receives an additional 4 checks.

Polignac

Polignac is sometimes played as a party game with the 52-card pack. It is, however, better as a serious game for four, playing all against all, with the 32-card pack – the 6s and lower cards removed.

Eight cards are dealt face downwards to each player. The player on the left of the dealer leads to the first trick. Thereafter the player who wins a trick leads to the next. A player must follow suit to the card led, if he can, otherwise he may discard.

The object of the game is to avoid taking tricks that contain a Jack, and 1 point is lost for every Jack taken, with the exception of the Jack of Spades (Polignac) which costs the winner 2 points.

The usual method of scoring is to play a pre-arranged number of deals (that should be a multiple of four) and he who loses the least number of points is the winner.

It is a very simple game, but some skill is called for particularly in choosing the best card to lead after a trick has been won, correct discarding when unable to follow suit, and deciding whether or not to win a trick when the choice is available.

Slobberhannes

If we may judge by its name, Slobberhannes is either of Dutch or German origin. It is a very simple game that is played in exactly the same way as polignac (see above). The only difference is that a player loses 1 point if he wins the first trick, 1 point if he wins the last, 1 point if he wins the trick containing the Queen of Clubs, and a further 1 point (making 4 points in all) if he wins all three tricks.

Solo Whist

Solo Whist, more commonly called Solo, is one of the classical games for four players. It is played with the full pack of fifty-two cards. Thirteen cards are dealt to each player in three bundles of three cards each, and the last four cards singly. The dealer turns up the last card to indicate the trump suit.

Each player in turn, beginning with the player on the left of the dealer, must either pass or make a bid. The bids (declarations) are:

Proposal. The player who makes a Proposal asks for a partner with the object of making eight tricks in partnership with him against the other two players. In turn, any other player may Accept, and the two play as partners from the seats in which they are sitting. The declaration of Proposal and Acceptance is usually called Prop and Cop.

Solo is a declaration to win five tricks against the other three players.

Misère is a declaration to lose all thirteen tricks. The hand is played without a trump suit.

Abundance is a declaration to win nine tricks against the other three players; the declarer chooses his own trump suit. A player who wishes to play abundance with the turned-up suit as trumps may overcall with Royal Abundance, but the stake value of the bid remains unchanged.

Open Misère is a declaration to lose every trick, and after the first trick has been played with his cards exposed on the table in front of him. There is no trump suit.

Declared Abundance is a declaration to win all thirteen tricks with a trump suit of his own choice.

Every bid must be higher than the previous one, and with the exception of the player on the left of the dealer, who may accept a proposal after passing, no player may re-enter the bidding once he has passed. The bidding ends when a bid has been passed by the other three players.

If the final bid is Declared Abundance, the declarer leads to the first trick. Against any other declaration the opening lead is made by the player on the left of the dealer. The play follows the general principles of trick-taking games: a player must follow suit if he is able to, otherwise he may either discard or trump, and the winner of a trick leads to the next.

Stakes are scaled to the value of the bids:

Proposal and Acceptance = 2 units * Abundance = 4 units
Solo = 2 units   Open Misère = 6 units
Misère = 3 units   Declared Abundance =
                                                    8 units

---

*Proposal and Acceptance does not carry equivalent stakes to Solo because they are paid by and received from two players, whereas in Solo (and higher declarations) they are paid to and received from three players.

Solo is a combination of whist and nap(oleon). It is a fairly simple game, and by far the simplest of the declarations is Proposal and Acceptance. As no player will propose without some strength in trumps, the partnership hardly ever fails to make eight tricks. It is a notoriously dull contract, therefore, and most modern players reject it.

The declaration of Solo is another that is-fairly easy to win, though it must never be forgotten that the player has to compete against three. It is unwise to bid Solo without a good trump suit, and the dealer is in the ideal position to bid it with success because he plays last to the first trick: it gives him the best chance to win it and make an immediate attack on the trump suit.

Misère is not such an easy declaration as it may seem. A 5-card suit, unless it contains the 2, is likely to spell defeat. If a player holds **7 6 5 4 3** of a suit he will usually be defeated if another holds four of the suit including the 2.

Abundance should not be attempted without a very good trump suit, and Declared Abundance is best avoided by any except an experienced player.

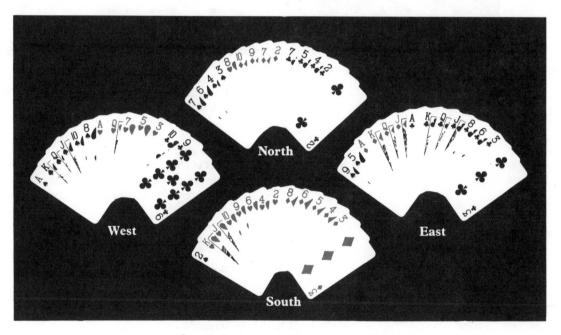

South deals and turns up the 2 of Spades.

West	North	East	South
Solo	Misère	Abundance	Open Misère
Pass	Pass	Pass	

West's Solo is the obviously correct bid. He cannot fail to win less than five tricks and it is too much to expect the Hearts to develop three tricks to make Abundance a good call.

North's Misère is optimistic. Had he been left to play it, the opening lead of a Heart would have broken him out of hand.

East's Abundance is a certainty with eleven tricks (and him needing only nine) for the taking of them.

South's Open Misère is not to be advised. As already pointed out a 5-card suit missing the 2 is a danger spot. As it happens it is the Heart suit that proves his downfall.

West leads the 10 of Clubs, and the play is:

West	North	East	South
10 ♣	7 ♣	J ♣	K ♥
9 ♣	5 ♣	A ♣	J ♥
A ♠	4 ♣	3 ♣	10 ♥
A ♥	8 ♥	A ♦	6 ♥

The position is down to:

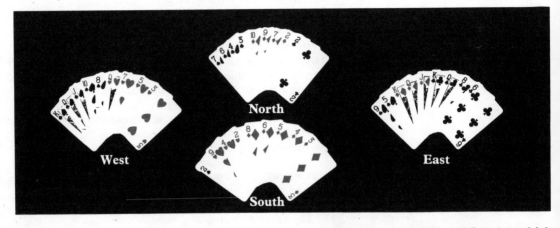

South is doomed because West wins the **7 ♥** and **5 ♥** (on which South plays the **4 ♥** and **2 ♥**) and continues with the **3 ♥** which South must win with the **9 ♥**.

As solo is limited to a mere handful of declarations, the variation known as **AUCTION SOLO** is much to be preferred, because it permits of a larger number of declarations and, therefore, makes a more interesting and skilful game. In ascending order the declarations are:

Proposal and Acceptance.
Solo of Five in own suit.
Solo of Five in trump suit.
Solo of Six in own suit.
Solo of Six in trump suit.
Solo of Seven in own suit.
Solo of Seven in trump suit.
Solo of Eight in own suit.
Solo of Eight in trump suit.
Misère.
Abundance of Nine in own suit.
Abundance of Nine in trump suit.
Abundance of Ten in own suit.
Abundance of Ten in trump suit.
Abundance of Eleven in own suit.
Abundance of Eleven in trump suit.
Abundance of Twelve in own suit.
Abundance of Twelve in trump suit.
Open Misère.
Declared Abundance with no trump suit (bidder has the lead).
Declared Abundance in the original trump suit (bidder does not have the lead).

Such, at least, are the declarations in the original version of the game, but modern players do not recognize all of them. Proposal and Acceptance are nearly always omitted, so also are Solo of Five in own suit, and Declared Abundance in the original trump suit.

Once the players have agreed on which declarations are admissible and which not, the game is played in the same way as the parent game.

Settlement is made in the following way:

Proposal and Acceptance
> For success: receive 6 units each plus 1 unit for each overtrick.
> For failure: pay 6 units each plus 1 unit for each undertrick.

Solo
> For success: receive 6 units from each player plus 3 units for each overtrick.
> For failure: pay 6 units to each player plus 3 units for each undertrick.

Misère
> For success: receive 12 units from each player.
> For failure: pay 12 units to each player.

Abundance
> For success: receive 18 units from each player plus 3 units for each overtrick.
> For failure: pay 18 units to each player plus 3 units for each undertrick.

Open Misère
> For success: receive 24 units from each player.
> For failure: pay 24 units to each player.

Declared Abundance
> For success: receive 36 units from each player.
> For failure: pay 36 units to each player.

The stake-values of Solo and Abundance are unchanged whether the contract is for five, six, seven or eight, or nine, ten, eleven or twelve tricks, overtricks and undertricks count from the number of tricks that are contracted for.

The method of scoring appears to encourage underbidding. In practice, however, it is not so and as first bidder a player would be well advised to declare his full strength at once, especially if his hand is worth no more than six tricks. With six tricks in a plain suit a player should bid it at once, no matter what his position at the table, but if the tricks are in the original trump suit it is reasonable to bid only a Solo of Five: he may get away with it, and, if not, a Solo of Six in the trump suit will overcall an opponent's Six in a plain suit. The penultimate player should make it a rule always to bid his hand to the limit; if he does not the last player will and then there may be no second chance.

Whist

Whist developed out of the sixteenth-century game of triumph. At first its practice was confined to the lower classes, but in 1718 it was taken up by a party of gentlemen, Lord Folkestone among them, who met at the famous Crown Coffee House, and they, with the help of Edmond Hoyle, introduced the game to fashionable society. At this time the game was known as whisk: soon after it was changed to whist in order to underline the silence in which it was proper to play the game.

During the eighteenth and nineteenth centuries it was by far the most popular card game of the English-speaking nations, but at the close of the nineteenth-century it lost much of its popularity due to the introduction of bridge (see page 83). It is, however, still extensively played.

In principle whist is a very simple game, played by four players, two playing in partnership against the other two. The partners sit facing each other. Thirteen cards are dealt singly to each person, and the dealer exposes the last card to denote the trump suit. He takes it into his hand after he has played to the first trick.

The player on the left of the dealer leads to the first trick. Thereafter the player who wins a trick leads to the next. A player must follow suit to the card led if he can, if not he may either discard or trump.

The object of the game is to win a rubber (best out of three games), and a game is won when one side has won 5 points. The first six tricks (the book) do not count for scoring: a side scores 1 point for each trick that it wins over six. The Ace, King, Queen and Jack of the trump suit are known as honours, and any side that is dealt all four of them scores 4 points, and any three 2 points. If, however, at the beginning of a deal a side has a score of 4 points it cannot score for honours.

The deal passes in a clockwise rotation.

Skill at whist is largely a matter of playing in close collaboration with one's partner, and estimating from the cards held and those that have been played, the most likely position of those that remain to be played.

To this end, there are a number of recognized plays which should be departed from only under special circumstances, to be learnt by experience. It is, for example, good tactics for second player to play low and third high; a player should not finesse against his partner; and if an opponent plays an honour it is usually profitable to play a higher honour on it.

A player who holds five or more trumps in his hand should make it a rule to lead one; and if a player fails to lead a trump and wishes his partner to do so, he calls for the lead of one by first playing an unnecessarily high card in a suit and following it with a low card in the same suit.

The lead is a good opportunity for a player to give his partner information about his hand, and the leads listed in the table opposite are standard practice and should be known to all players.

In plain suits:

Holding	1st Lead	2nd Lead
A K Q J	**K**	**J**
A K Q	**K**	**Q**
A K x and more	**K**	**A**
A K	**A**	**K**
K Q J x	**K**	**J**
K Q J x x	**J**	**K**
K Q J x x x and more	**J**	**Q**
A x x x and more	**A**	4th best of remainder
K Q x and more	**K**	4th best of remainder
A Q J	**A**	**Q**
A Q J x	**A**	**Q**
A Q J x x and more	**A**	**J**
K J 10 9	**9**	**K** (if **A** or **Q** falls)
Q J x	**Q**	
Q J x x and more	4th best	

In the trump suit:

Holding	1st Lead	2nd Lead
A K Q J	**J**	**Q**
A K Q	**Q**	**K**
A K x x x x x and more	**K**	**A**
A K x x x x	4th best	

Lacking any of these combinations the fourth highest of the longest suit should be led.

In the deal below the mechanics of the game are illustrated.

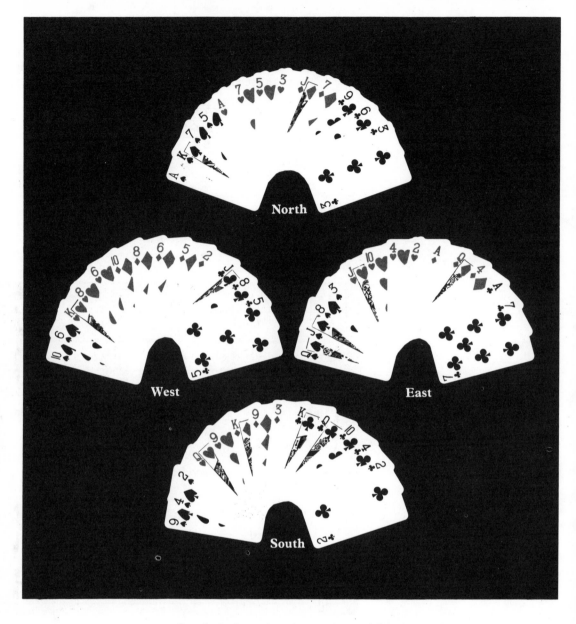

South deals and turns up the 4 of Spades to denote trumps. West leads the 5 of Diamonds, and the play is:

West	North	East	South
5 ♦	J ♦	A ♦	3 ♦

West leads the fourth highest of his longest suit, commonly called fourth-best. East wins with the **A ♦**. It would be finessing against his partner if he played the **Q ♦**. In the event it makes no difference, because East has no better play than to return his partner's suit, and it is proper to lead the highest from an original holding of three.

2 ♦	7 ♦	Q ♦	K ♦

South, therefore, wins the second trick, instead of the first, with the **K ♦**

West	North	East	South
5 ♣	3 ♣	A ♣	K ♣
8 ♣	6 ♣	7 ♣	Q ♣

East has no better lead than the **7 ♣**. He knows that South holds the **Q ♣**, because without it South would not have led the **K ♣** at the previous trick, but it offers a chance of trumping if West can take the lead early in the play.

West	North	East	South
10 ♦	5 ♠	4 ♦	9 ♦
6 ♠	A̲ ♠	3 ♠	2 ♠
10 ♠	K̲ ♠	8 ♠	4 ♠
J ♣	9̲ ♣	2 ♥	2 ♣

North has no better lead than the **9 ♣**.

West	North	East	South
8 ♦	3 ♥	J̲ ♠	4 ♣
6 ♦	7 ♠	Q̲ ♠	9 ♠

East pulls the remaining trumps.

West	North	East	South
K ♥	A̲ ♥	J ♥	Q ♥

The end position has come down to:

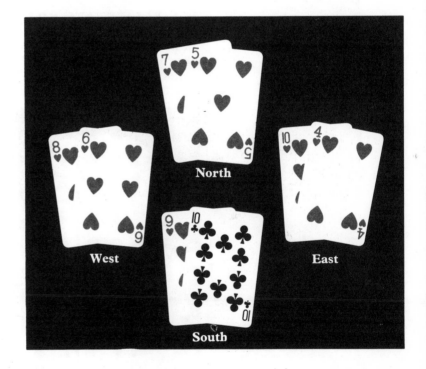

It is North's lead. North and South have won six tricks, East and West five tricks. North, therefore, leads the **5 ♥**. If East wins with the **10 ♥** his side will win the odd trick as West will win the last trick with the **8 ♥**. North's only hope is that East will make the mistake of playing the **4 ♥**, because then South will win with the **9 ♥** and the last trick with the **10 ♣**.

West	North	East	South
6 ♥	5 ♥	10̲ ♥	9 ♥

East makes no mistake.

West	North	East	South
8̲ ♥	7 ♥	4 ♥	10 ♣

East and West, therefore, have won the odd trick and score 1 point. There is no score for honours as both sides held two.

Brag

Brag is almost certainly the ancestor of poker (see page 133) and itself probably derived from the Spanish game of primero, the popular card game of Tudor England and, so far as we can trace, the first card game to be played scientifically in this country.

The game is played with the full 52-card pack, and by any number of players from five to eight. The general principle of the game is quite simple. The players stake on the respective merits of their cards, and the best hand is determined by certain arbitrary rules. Bluffing is an important feature of the game. The Ace of Diamonds, Jack of Clubs and 9 of Diamonds are known as braggers, and rank as Jokers or wild cards.

In **SINGLE-STAKE BRAG** the dealer puts up a stake to the agreed limit, and deals three cards face downwards to each player. In turn, beginning with the player on the left of the dealer, each player must either drop out of the game for the round in progress, or put up a stake at least equal to that of the dealer's. If he chooses he may raise the stake, in which event, any player coming into the

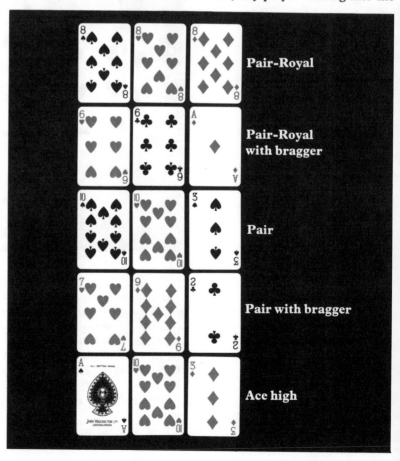

Pair-Royal

Pair-Royal with bragger

Pair

Pair with bragger

Ace high

The classes of brag hands, the highest at the top

game, or already in the game, must raise his bet to as much as the highest individual stake, or drop out of the game and lose what he has already staked. If no-one meets the dealer's stake he withdraws it, and receives an agreed amount from the other players. The deal then passes to the next player.

Unlike at poker, there is no discarding and drawing more cards. When all those who wish to play have raised their bets to an equal amount, the cards are shown and the player with the best hand collects all the stakes.

Flushes and sequences are of no value. The best hand is a Pair-Royal; it consists of three cards of equal rank (the Aces high the 2s low) and a hand of three natural cards takes precedence over one with braggers. The next best hand is a Pair, with a preference for a natural pair over one with a bragger, and if two players have equal pairs the one with the higher third card wins. If no player holds either a Pair-Royal or a Pair, the player with the highest single card wins and if two players hold exactly equal hands the winner is he who was first to stake.

In **THREE-STAKE BRAG** the game begins by each player putting up three separate stakes; the dealer then deals two cards face downwards and one card face upwards to each player.

The first stake is won by the player who is dealt the highest face-upwards card. For this round of the game the braggers take their normal position in the pack, and if two or more players are dealt cards of equal rank, precedence is determined as in the single-stake game.

The hand is next played as in single-stake, and the winner takes the second stake. If no-one bets, the hands are exposed and the highest hand wins.

Finally, the players expose their cards and the third stake is won by the player whose cards most nearly total 31 (over or under) the Aces counting 11, the court cards 10 each and the other cards at their pip values. A player whose hand totals less than 31 may draw a card from the remainder of the pack, but if his total then exceeds 31 he automatically loses the game.

Coon Can

In the U.S.A. Coon Can is known as Double Rum. It is no bad name for it because it is a variation of rummy (see page 139) played with two packs of cards shuffled together with two Jokers.

The game may be played by any number of players up to eight; each plays for himself.

Ten cards are dealt face downwards to each player. The rest of the pack (the stock) is placed face downwards in the centre of the table, and the top card of it is turned face upwards and placed alongside it to start the discard pile.

The object of the game is to get rid of all the cards held, by melding them face upwards on the table, either in sets of three or more of the same rank, or in sequences of three or more of the same suit, the Ace either high or low but not round-the-corner. A Joker may be used to represent any card that the holder chooses.

Each player, beginning with the one on the left of the dealer, plays in turn. He is under no obligation to meld, but he must take into his hand either the top card of the stock or the top card of the discard pile, and discard a card to reduce his hand to ten cards. If he chooses to meld he must do so between drawing a card and discarding one, and as well as melding, at the same time, he may add cards to melds that he has already made, and to those of his opponents.

A Joker may be moved from one end of a meld to the other, provided the player has the natural card to replace it. If, for example, a sequence is: **6 ♠ 7 ♠ 8 ♠ Joker**, a player who holds a **9 ♠** may play it in room of the Joker and transfer the Joker to represent the **5 ♠**. Once moved, however, a Joker cannot be moved a second time and a player who holds a **5 ♠** cannot play it in room of the Joker and place the Joker elsewhere. Nor can a Joker be moved if it is in the interior of a sequence, as in **4 ♠ 5 ♠ 6 ♠ Joker 8 ♠**. The Joker cannot be replaced by a **7 ♠**. When a Joker cannot be moved it is customary to place it cross-wise, as a reminder to the other players.

The game is won by the player who is first to meld all his cards. The remaining players pay him the same number of units as the pip value of the unmelded cards left in their hands—a Joker counting 15, an Ace 11, the court cards 10 each, and all other cards their pip values.

Rarely it happens that the stock will be exhausted before the game has been won. In this event the game continues and the players draw cards from the discard pile, discarding a different card to that drawn. If this proves insufficient to finish the game, the pip values of the hands are counted and placed into a pool to be scored by the winner of the next hand.

Napoleon

Napoleon, usually called Nap, is one of the simplest of all card games. It is played with the full pack of fifty-two cards, by any number of players up to six, each playing for himself.

Each player is dealt five cards, and, beginning with the player on the left of the dealer, every player in turn must either pass or declare to win a specified number of tricks in the ascending order: Two, Three, Four and Nap (a declaration to win all five tricks).

The player who has contracted to win most tricks leads to the first trick and the card that he leads determines the trump suit. Play follows the usual routine of trick-taking games: a player must follow suit if he can, otherwise he may discard or trump, and the player who wins a trick leads to the next.

Stakes are paid only on the number of tricks contracted for. Those won above, or lost below, the number contracted for are ignored. The usual method of settlement is by means of a level-money transaction:

Declaration	Declarer wins	Declarer loses
Two	2 units	2 units
Three	3 units	3 units
Four	4 units	4 units
Nap	10 units	5 units

Payment is made to, and received from, all players at the table.

Nap(oleon) is such an elementary game that in some circles interest is added to it by introducing a number of extraordinary declarations:

Misery is a declaration to lose every trick. It ranks between the declaration of Three and Four, and though normally it is played without a trump suit, some play it with a trump suit, determined as in the parent game by the opening lead. It pays and wins 3 units.

Wellington is a declaration to win all five tricks at double stakes. It cannot be declared, however, except over a declaration of Nap.

Blücher is a declaration to win all five tricks at triple stakes. It cannot be declared, however, except over a declaration of Wellington.

Peep Nap sanctions the player who has declared Nap (or Wellington or Blücher if these declarations are permitted) to exchange the top card of the pack for a card in his own hand.

Purchase Nap sanctions each player before declaring to exchange any number of cards in his hand for fresh cards, by paying into a pool 1 unit for every card exchanged. The pool is carried forward from deal to deal and taken by the first player to win Nap (or Wellington or Blücher if these declarations are permitted).

SEVEN-CARD NAPOLEON is a variation of the parent game in which seven cards are dealt to each player, and a player cannot contract to win less than three tricks. There is no Wellington and no Blücher. Misery is optional and, if permitted, ranks between Nap and Six.

Apart from these amendments, the game is played in the same way as the parent game.

Settlement is made as follows:

Declaration	Declarer wins	Declarer loses
Three	3 units	3 units
Four	4 units	4 units
Nap (five tricks)	10 units	5 units
Misery (if played)	10 units	5 units
Six	18 units	9 units
Seven	28 units	14 units

Payment is made to, and received from, all players at the table

Poker

Poker is not a difficult game to learn, but by no means an easy one to play well because skill at the game is born only of experience coupled with some knowledge of arithmetic. Fundamentally, poker is a game of calculating chances.

The parent game, commonly called straight poker, but more correctly straight draw poker, is played with the 52-card pack by any reasonable number of players: five, six or seven is considered the ideal number.

Each player is dealt five cards face downwards, and the object of the game is to make the best hand by an exchange of cards, and then bet on it against the other players.

The cards rank in the order from Ace high to 2 low, suits are equal and in ascending order the nine classes of poker hands, together with the approximate odds against their being dealt to a player, are:

Highest Card : any five odd cards. Evens.
One Pair : two cards of the same rank and three odd cards. 15 to 11.
Two pairs : two cards of the same rank, two other cards of the same rank and an odd card. 20 to 1.
Threes : three cards of the same rank and two odd cards. 46 to 1.
Straight : any five cards in sequence, not of the same suit; An Ace may be either high or low. 254 to 1.
Flush : any five cards of the same suit. 508 to 1.
Full House : three cards of the same rank and two other cards of the same rank. 693 to 1.
Fours : four cards of the same rank and an odd card. 4,164 to 1.
Straight Flush : a sequence of five cards all of the same suit: an Ace may be either high or low. 64,973 to 1.

Examples of each hand are illustrated. They are valued on the highest combination, and if the combination of two or more players is equal, by the highest odd card. In the event of two or more players holding exactly equal hands the stakes are divided.

The player on the left of the dealer begins the game by putting up an agreed amount, known as the ante. For convenience we will assume that it is 1 chip. The player on his left then puts up a straddle of 2 chips.*

The dealer now deals, face downwards, to each player five cards. After looking at his cards, the player on the left of the straddle has the option of playing or not. If he decides not to play he throws his cards face downwards towards the centre of the table, and takes no further interest in the deal in progress. If he decides to play he puts up 4 chips. The player on his left now has the choice of

---

* Throughout the game every player puts his chips on the table in front of him.

The classes of poker hand, the highest at the bottom. The numbers of possible ways in which each hand can be made up are as follows:

highest card:	1,302,540
one pair:	1,098,240
two pairs:	123,552
threes:	54,912
straight:	10,200
flush:	5,108
full house:	3,744
fours:	624
straight flush:	40

throwing in his hand, coming into the game for 4 chips, or doubling (*i.e.* coming into the game for 8 chips). In the same way, in turn, every player has the choice of throwing in his hand, coming into the game, for the same stake as the previous player, or raising the stakes until the agreed maximum is reached.

When staking reaches the ante and straddle, they can either throw in their hands and sacrifice what they have already put up, or come into the game by raising their stakes to the appropriate amount.

If no player comes into the game, the straddle recovers his 2 chips and takes the 1 chip put up by the ante.

Staking continues for some little time, because if a player has come into the game and a subsequent player has doubled, it is open to those who have already staked to increase their stakes, and this progressive staking continues until no-one increases the stakes or the agreed limit is reached.

When all have staked, those left in the game have the chance to improve their hands by exchanging cards. The dealer ignores those who have already thrown in their hands, but gives all the other players in turn as many cards as they wish after they have discarded those cards that they do not wish to retain. A player may discard any number of his cards, but no experienced player would remain in the game to exchange four cards, and only one who has taken leave of his senses will do so to exchange all five cards. Most players will exchange one, two, or three cards.

When cards have been exchanged, the player who was first to come in begins the betting. Either he throws in his hand (sacrificing the stake he has already made to come in) checks (signifies his intention to remain in the game without increasing his stake) or raises (increases his stake to any amount up to the agreed limit).

If he checks, all the players who follow him have, in their turn, the same choice. If no-one raises those left in the game show their cards and the player with the best hand takes all that has been staked. If a player raises, the subsequent players, in turn, have the option of throwing in their hands, putting up sufficient chips to meet the raise, or raise still further.

In this way the betting continues until the final bet is either called or not. If the final bet is called, the players left in the game show their cards and the player with the best hand wins all that has been staked: if the final bet is not called, the player whose bet has not been called wins all that has been staked with no need to show his hand.

Poker falls naturally into two parts: the staking and the betting. The staking is the easier part of the game because it is open to a precise arithmetical analysis. We may suppose that a player is dealt:

$$10 \spadesuit \quad 6 \spadesuit \quad 5 \spadesuit \quad 2 \spadesuit \quad 9 \heartsuit$$

Since a pair of 10s is of small value, the player's aim must be to discard the 9 of Hearts hoping to draw a Spade to fill the flush.

There are 47 cards from which to draw, and of them only 9 are Spades, the other 38 are non-Spades. It follows, therefore, that the odds against drawing a Spade are 38 to 9, or approximately $4\frac{1}{4}$ to 1. If three players have come into the game with 4 chips each, making 15 chips on the table with the ante and straddle, it is not worth while playing because it costs 4 chips to come in so that the table is offering odds of 15 to 4 ($3\frac{3}{4}$ to 1) and the chance of improving is $4\frac{1}{4}$ to 1. If, however, four players have come in it will be just worth while coming into the game, because now there will be 19 chips on the table so that the table is offering odds of $4\frac{3}{4}$ to 1, which is better than the odds against improving.

Poker players should study very carefully the mathematical chances, because the whole theory of staking may be summed up by asking oneself two questions: What are the chances of improving my hand? What odds are the table laying me? Then, if the answer to the first question is greater than to the second the player should come in, if it is not he should throw in his hand.

The betting is the more difficult part of the game because it is largely psychology. At the same time, a player has to be gifted with the quality that we call judgement because his betting must be dictated by the manner in which the other players are betting, and how they, on their part, will interpret his betting. Particular note should be taken of the number of cards drawn by each of the other players and deductions drawn from the information gained. The subsequent betting should go a long way towards confirming whether the deductions are correct or not, and whether the player has improved on the draw.

A good poker player is inscrutable and unpredictable, because he varies his game to make the most with his good hands and lose the least with his bad ones. He profits by the advice of Saint Matthew—'let not thy left hand know what thy right hand doeth'—and he is always imperturbable, because there is no future in gloating over a win and wailing over a loss. If he thinks that he holds the best hand he bets on it boldly: if he thinks that he is beaten he throws in his cards and cuts his losses.

Pot-Deals, commonly called Pots, are widely played, and are an important feature of all variations of the game. When a pot is played there is no ante and no straddle; instead every player contributes an agreed amount to a pot, or pool, that is independent of the staking and betting. The player on the immediate left of the dealer has first decision whether to open the game by staking or not. If he does not open, the option passes to the player on his left, and so on.

The essence of a pot is that a player is debarred from opening the game, by putting up a stake, unless his hand qualifies him to do so by a pre-arranged standard. If no player opens, the deal passes, and the players sweeten the pot, by adding to it, for the next deal. If the pot is opened, other players may come in even if their hands are below standard, and he who wins the deal also wins the amount in the pot as well as all the stakes put up by the other players. The player who opened the game must show that his hand qualified for opening.

In a *Jackpot* a player must have a pair of Jacks, or better, to qualify for opening.

In a *Progressive Jackpot*, if no-one opens the first deal, the second deal is a Queenpot, and if no-one opens it the next is a King-pot, and so on. Some stop at Acepots, others continue to two pairs before beginning again at a Jackpot if no-one has opened the game.

In a *Freak Pot*, sometimes called Deuces Wild, all the 2s are wild cards and may be used to represent any cards that the holder chooses. Fives (five cards of the same rank) is now a possible hand, and it is classed above a straight flush, but is beaten if the straight flush is headed by an Ace.

In a *Double Pot*, or Legs, any type of pot is chosen, but a player must win it twice before he may take his winnings.

WILD WIDOW is a variation of the parent game, but, after four cards have been dealt to each player, a card is turned face upwards in the centre of the table and is left there for the duration of the deal. The dealer then gives each player one more card, and the game is played with the three other cards of the same rank as the exposed card wild.

In **SPIT IN THE OCEAN** only four cards are dealt to each player. A card is then dealt face upwards in the centre of the table. Each player considers this card as the fifth card of his hand. It is a wild card, as also are the other three cards of the same rank.

STUD POKER is a variation of the parent game the main feature of which is that some of the cards are dealt face upwards and some face downwards. There are several ways of playing the game.

In *Five-card Stud* there is no ante unless agreed on. The dealer gives each player a card face downwards (it is known as the hole card) and then a card face upwards. The deal is then interrupted for a betting interval. After the betting interval the dealer gives each active player another three cards face upwards, and after each there is a betting interval. If two or more players remain in the game after the last betting interval, they turn up their hole cards and the player with the best hand wins.

Each betting interval begins with the player who holds the best combination of cards exposed, and if two or more players have equal combination the one nearest to the dealer's left bets first. At the first betting interval the player who opens must make a bet; at subsequent intervals he may check. Any player who drops out of the game must turn his exposed cards face downwards.

Seven-card Stud, sometimes called Down the River, or Peek Poker, is played in the same way as five-card stud, except that the dealer first deals to each player two cards face downwards and one card face upwards. There is a betting interval, and, after this, the active players are dealt three cards face upwards and one face downwards, with the deal interrupted for a betting interval after each round of dealing. At the showdown, a player exposes his hole cards and selects five of his seven cards to form his hand.

WHISKY POKER is so called because it was originally played in the American lumber camps to decide who should pay for the drinks.

Every player contributes an agreed amount to a pool. The dealer deals an extra hand (widow) to the centre of the table, immediately before dealing cards to himself. The player on the left of the dealer, after looking at his cards, may either exchange his hand for the widow, pass (in which case the option of taking the widow passes to his left-hand neighbour) or indicates, by knocking the table, that he will play with the cards dealt to him.

If the player on the left of the dealer (or any subsequent player) takes the widow, he puts his own cards face upwards on the table as a new widow. The player on his left may now either take the whole of the exposed widow in exchange for his own hand, take one or more cards from it in exchange for cards in his hand, or knock. A player, however, cannot draw cards from the widow and knock at the same turn, and the option to exchange the widow or cards with it, continues until a player knocks. As soon as a player does so, the remaining players have one turn each to exchange their hands or cards for it. After the player on the right of the knocker has had his turn, the players expose their cards and the best hand wins the pot.

If no-one takes the widow before it is the turn of the dealer, he must either take the widow or turn it face upwards on the table. Even if he decides to knock, without making an exchange, he must still turn up the widow.

In **KNOCK POKER** every player puts up an ante. The dealer gives every player five cards, as in the parent game, and the rest of the pack (the stock) is placed face downwards in the centre of the table. The player on the left of the dealer draws the top card of the stock and discards a card from his hand. Thereafter each player in turn draws either the top card of the stock or the top card of the discard pile, and discards a card from his hand.

At any time after drawing a card and before discarding one, a player may knock the table. He then discards a card from his hand. The other players have one more turn each to draw and discard a card, or drop out of the game by paying the knocker the amount of the ante. After the player on the right of the knocker has drawn and discarded, or dropped out of the game, all players remaining in the game show their cards and settlement is made as follows:

1. If the knocker has the best hand, all who are in the game pay him twice the ante.
2. If the knocker and one or more other players have equal hands they divide the winnings except for the amount paid to the knocker by those who dropped out of the game.
3. If the knocker does not have the best hand he pays twice the ante to every player remaining in the game, and the player with the best hand wins the antes.

HIGH-LOW POKER. Any variation of poker may be played high-low. As a rule the hand is played as a pot. The player plays his hand for either high or low, but does not have to announce which until the last card is dealt. The highest and the lowest hands divide the pot between them. An Ace is always high and cannot be counted as a low card except as part of a sequence in the high hand.

In **STRIP POKER** the dealer deals five cards, face downwards, to each player. There is no ante and no straddle. After an exchange of cards (as in the parent game) the players expose their cards and the one with the worst poker hand pays the table by removing an article of clothing.

The game, with all its voluptuous prospects, is said to be at its best in mixed company during a heat wave!

Rummy

Rummy, the name is frequently truncated to Rum, is one of the most popular of all card games. It is played with the full 52-card pack, and is suitable for any number of players up to five or six, each playing for himself. More than six players should prefer coon can (see page 130) or the variation known as continental rummy.

Ten cards are dealt to each player if only two play; seven cards if three or four play; and six cards if five or six play. The rest of the pack (the stock) is placed face downwards in the centre of the table, and the top card of it is turned face upwards and laid alongside it to start the discard pile.

Each player in turn, beginning with the one on the left of the dealer, must take into his hand either the top card of the stock or the top card of the discard pile, and discard a card from his hand, but if he has drawn the top card of the discard pile he must not discard it in the same turn.

The object of the game is to make sets of three or more cards of the same rank, or sequences of three or more cards of the same suit (the Ace being low) and declare them by exposing them on the table, after drawing a card from the stock or discard pile and before discarding a card from the hand. At the same time a player may add one or more proper cards to sequences and sets already declared either by himself or the other players.

If the stock is exhausted before any player declares all his hand, the discard pile is turned face downwards and becomes the stock.

The player who is first to declare all his cards wins the hand, and the other players pay him for every court card left in their hands 10 points each, for every Ace 1 point, and for every other card its pip value. If a player declares all his cards in one turn he scores rummy and is paid double.

Rummy is a very simple game that has lent itself to a number of improvements.

In **BOATHOUSE RUMMY** a player may draw the top card of the stock; or he may draw the top card of the discard pile and then either the top card of the stock or the next card of the discard pile. He may, however, discard only one card from his hand.

In a sequence the Ace may be either high, low, or round the corner.

The play does not come to an end until a player can declare his entire hand in one turn.

A losing player pays only for the unmatched cards in his hand, but Aces are paid for at 11 points each.

CONTINENTAL RUMMY is a variation of the parent game that is suitable for any number of players up to twelve. If two to five play two packs with two Jokers are used; if six to eight play three packs with three Jokers are used; and if nine to twelve play four packs with four Jokers are used.

Each player receives fifteen cards. A player may not declare until all fifteen of his cards are melded either in five 3-card sequences, or in three 4-card sequences and one 3-card sequence, or in one 5-card, one 4-card and two 3-card sequences. Sets of three or more cards of the same rank are of no value. A Joker may be used to represent any card. The Ace may be high or low, but not round the corner.

There are many ways of scoring, but generally the winner collects from all the other players 1 unit from each for winning, and 2 units from each for every Joker in his hand.

GAMBLER'S RUMMY is so called because it is the variation of the parent game that is most frequently played for high stakes.

Only four players take part and each is dealt seven cards. The Ace is low and, as in the parent game, counts only 1 point in the settlement. A player is not allowed to declare all his hand in one turn. He must declare it in at least two turns, but he is not debarred from going out second turn even if on his previous turn he played off only one card on another player's declaration.

The stock is gone through only once. When it is exhausted the players must draw the top card of the discard pile, and the game ends when a player refuses it.

KNOCK RUMMY, or Poker Rum, is played in the same way as the parent game, but a player does not declare his sequences and sets by exposing them on the table. Instead, after drawing a card, he knocks on the table, and then discards. Play comes to an end. The players separate their matched cards from their un-matched ones, and each announces the count of his unmatched cards, as reckoned in the parent game. The player with the lowest count wins the difference in counts from all the other players. If a player ties with the knocker for the lowest count he wins over the knocker. If the knocker does not have the lowest count he pays a penalty of an extra 10 points to the player with the lowest count. If the knocker goes rummy (has all his cards matched when he knocks) and wins, he receives an extra 25 points from all the other players.

Stock   Discard pile

The player should take the 5 ♠ and discard 9 ♣, as 5 ♠ offers alternative chances of melding: either with 5 ♥ or 6 ♠

Scotch Whist

Scotch Whist, sometimes called Catch the Ten because one of the objects of the game is to win the trick that contains the 10 of the trump suit, is played with a pack of thirty-six cards. The 2s, 3s, 4s, and 5s are removed from the standard pack. The cards rank from Ace (high) to 6 (low) with the exception that the Jack of the trump suit is promoted above the Ace.

The game is suitable for any number of players from two to eight, but, as every player must begin with the same number of cards, if five or seven players take part the 6 of Spades is removed from the pack, and if eight take part all four 6s are. If two, three, five or seven play, each plays for himself. If four, six or eight play they may either play each for himself, or form into partnerships.

Dealing varies with the number of players taking part in the game. If two play each receives eighteen cards that are dealt in three separate hands of six cards each, to be played independently; if three play each receives twelve cards that are dealt in two separate hands of six cards each, to be played independently; if four or more play the cards are dealt in the normal clockwise rotation. In every case the dealer turns up the last card to indicate the trump suit.

The player on the left of the dealer leads to the first trick. Thereafter the player who wins a trick leads to the next. Play follows the usual routine of trick-taking games: a player must follow suit, if he can, to the suit led, if he cannot he may either trump the trick or discard on it.

The object of the game is to win tricks containing the five top trump cards, and the player, or partnership, that does scores 11 points for the Jack, 4 points for the Ace, 3 points for the King, 2 points for the Queen, and 10 points for the Ten. Over and above this, each player, or partnership, counts the number of cards taken in tricks, and scores 1 point for every card more than the number originally dealt to him, or it.

The game ends when a player, or partnership, has reached an agreed total, usually 41 points.

It stands out that a player must direct his play towards winning tricks that contain the top cards of the trump suit, particularly that which contains the 10, since the Jack can only go to the player to whom it has been dealt, and usually the luck of the deal determines who will win the tricks that contain the Ace, King and Queen.

In a partnership game the player who has been dealt the 10, either singleton or doubleton, would be well advised to lead it. It gives a good score if his partner is able to win with the Jack; if an opponent wins the trick the partnership must hope to recover by aiming to win as many tricks as possible. If the game is being played all against all, the player who has been dealt the 10 should try and get rid of all the cards in his shortest suit, so that he can win the 10 by trumping with it.

Spoil Five

Spoil Five, sometimes called Forty-five, is an excellent game for any reasonable number of players, but is best for five or six, as it calls for some show of skill.

It is played with the full pack of fifty-two cards, but that it is rarely, if ever, played outside its native Ireland may be ascribed to the eccentric order of the cards. The 5 of the trump suit is always the highest trump, the Jack of the trump suit is the second highest, and the Ace of Hearts the third highest. Thereafter, if a black suit is trumps the cards rank in the order **A K Q 2 3 4 6 7 8 9 10** and if a red suit is trumps in the order **A** (if Diamonds are trumps) **K Q 10 9 8 7 6 4 3 2**. In plain suits, the black suits rank in the order **K Q J A 2 3 4 5 6 7 8 9 10**; the red suits in the order **K Q J 10 9 8 7 6 5 4 3 2 A** (except in Hearts). It is concisely expressed as 'highest in red; lowest in black', but even with this help it is all rather involved.

Five cards are dealt to each player either in bundles of two then three, or three then two. The next card is exposed to determine the trump suit. A pool is formed to which every player contributes an agreed amount, and it is usual to fix a maximum and, after the first deal, only the player whose turn it is to deal contributes to the pool.

The object of the game is to win three tricks, and, at the same time, prevent another player from winning them.

The player who wins three tricks takes the pool; and if no-one wins three tricks (a spoil) the deal passes to the next player. When a player has won three tricks the hand ends and the deal passes, unless the player who has won them declares 'Jinx'. It is an undertaking to win the remaining two tricks. Play then continues and if he fails to win the two tricks he loses the pool; on the other hand, if he wins the two tricks not only does he take the pool but the other players each pay him the amount that they originally contributed to the pool.

The player on the left of the dealer leads to the first trick. Thereafter the winner of a trick leads to the next. The rules of play are precise and peculiar to the game:

1. If the card turned up to denote the trump suit is an Ace, the dealer may rob. He may, that is, exchange the Ace for a card in his hand, but he must do so before the player on his left leads to the first trick.
2. Any player who has been dealt the Ace of the trump suit may exchange any card in his hand for the turn-up card, but he need not do so until it is his turn to play.
3. If a trump is led a player must follow suit if he can, but the 5 and Jack of the trump suit and the Ace of Hearts are exempt from following suit to the lead of a lower trump. It is called reneging. It means that the 5 of the trump suit need not be played if the Jack of the trump suit is led, and the Jack of the trump suit need not be played if the Ace of Hearts is led; if, however, the 5 of the trump suit is led no trump can renege.
4. If a plain suit is led a player may follow suit or trump as he

chooses, but he must not discard from another plain suit if he is able to follow suit or trump.

5. If a player misdeals the deal passes to the next player.

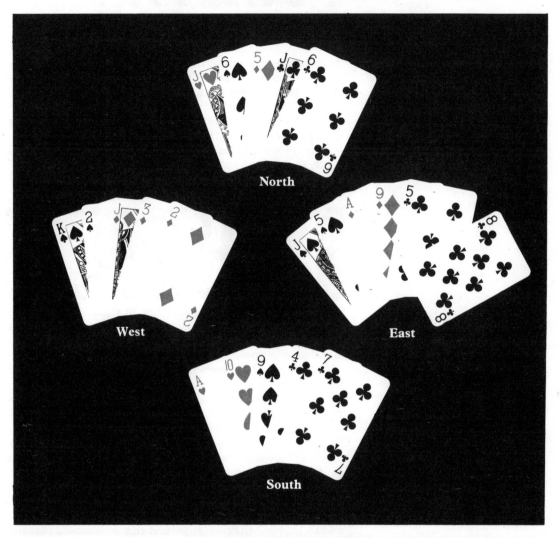

North

West

East

South

East is dealt the 8 ♣, but exchanges it for the 9 ♦

In a 4-handed game, South deals and turns up the **9 ♦**.

West leads the **J ♦**. North may renege the **5 ♦**, but it would hardly be good play not to use it to win the second highest trump, so he plays it. East, who holds the **A ♦**, robs by exchanging the **8 ♣** for the **9 ♦** and, of course, plays it. West who started with the hope of a jinx is now not so sure that he will win even three tricks. His prospects, however, improve when South, perforce, plays the **A ♥**. At least South cannot hold another trump.

North leads the **J ♣**, East plays the **5 ♣**, South the **7 ♣**, and West wins with the **2 ♦**.

West leads the **K ♠**, North plays the **6 ♠**, and East sees the possibility of himself winning three tricks. He trumps with the **A ♦**, and South plays the **9 ♠**. With any luck East should be able to win the last two tricks with the **J ♠** and **5 ♠**.

As it happens, however, East's play has enabled West to win three tricks, because when East leads the **J ♠**, West wins with the **3 ♦** and the last trick with the **2 ♠**.

Newmarket

Newmarket is a modern variation of the old game of pope joan (opposite) and is known by a number of other names – Boodle and Stops in England; Chicago, Michigan and Saratoga in America.

It is an excellent game for from three to eight players that is easy to learn and contains an element of skill that guarantees the better player winning in the long run.

The game is played with a full pack of fifty-two cards, and an Ace, King, Queen and Jack (each of a different suit) from another pack. These four extra cards are known as the boodle cards, and are placed, face upwards, in a row in the centre of the table.

Before the deal each player has to stake an agreed number of chips (usually, but not necessarily, 10) on the boodle cards. He may stake his chips as he pleases, but he must not stake more nor less than the agreed number.

The dealer then deals the cards one at a time to each player in rotation, and to an extra hand or dummy. As the players must each receive the same number of cards, any over-cards are dealt to the dummy hand which remains face downwards on the table throughout the deal.

The cards rank in the order from Ace (high) to 2 (low) and the player on the left of the dealer makes the first lead. He may lead a card from any suit, but it must be the lowest card that he holds in the suit. The players do not play in rotation round the table. The next play is made by the player who holds next higher cards in the suit, then the next higher card is played by the player who holds it, and so on, until the run is stopped either because a player plays the Ace of the suit, or the next higher card is in the dummy hand. Either way, the player who played the last card leads the lowest card of another suit, and if he has no other suit the lead passes to the player on his left.

When a player plays a card that is identical with one of the boodle cards he collects all the chips that have been staked on it.

The object of the game, however, is not only to win the chips that have been staked on the boodle cards, but to get rid of all one's cards, because the player who is first to do so receives one chip from each of the other players. If no player gets rid of all his cards, the one who holds the fewest number of cards wins the hand, and if two players are left with an equal number of fewest cards they divide the winnings.

If when a deal comes to an end the chips on one or more of the boodle cards have not been claimed, because the corresponding cards to the boodle cards are in the dummy hand, they are carried forward to the next deal.

Pope Joan

Pope Joan is a very old card game that at one time was exceptionally popular in Scotland. The 9 of Diamonds is given the name of Pope, and as the Pope was the Antichrist of Scottish reformers, there is reason to think that it was for this reason that the nickname of Curse of Scotland became attached to the card.

The game is played with a standard pack of fifty-two cards from which the 8 of Diamonds is removed. Originally a special board, consisting of a circular tray divided into eight compartments, and revolving about a central pillar, was used with counters. To-day these boards are museum pieces, and modern players must make do with eight saucers labelled: *Pope* (**9** ♦), *Ace, King, Queen, Jack, Matrimony, Intrigue, Game,* placed in the centre of the table.

Each player begins with the same number of counters of an agreed value, and the dealer places six in the saucer labelled Pope (**9** ♦), two each in Matrimony and Intrigue, and one each in Ace, King, Queen, Jack and Game. It is called dressing the board.

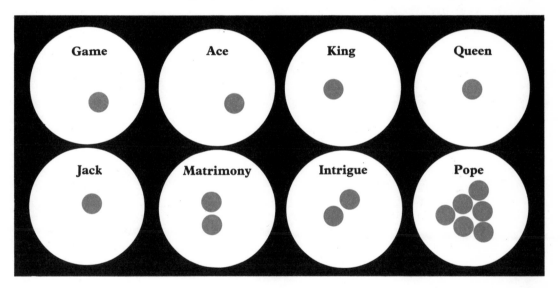

Cards are then dealt to the players and to an extra hand (widow) in the centre of the table. The number of cards dealt to each player and the widow depends on the number of players in the game. The players must each hold the same number of cards, so any over-cards go to the widow. The last card is turned face upwards to denote the trump suit, and if it is either the Pope (**9** ♦) or an Ace, King, Queen or Jack, the dealer wins the counters in the corresponding saucer.

The player on the left of the dealer leads to the first trick. He may lead any card he chooses, and at the same time he announces it. Suppose it is the 6 of Clubs. Then the player who holds the 7 of Clubs plays it and announces it, the player who holds the 8 of Clubs plays it and announces it, and so on, until the run comes to an end.

The four Kings are stop cards, and in the Diamond suit the 7 is as well, because the 8 has been removed from the pack. In practice, of course, any card may be a stop card on account of the cards in the widow hand, and because the next higher card may already have been played.

When a run comes to an end, the player of the stop card starts a fresh run by leading any card he likes. In this way the game continues until one of the players has played all his cards. He is then entitled to the counters in the Game saucer, and, in addition, he receives from each player 1 counter for every card left in his hand. The player who is left with the Pope (9 ♦), however, is exempt from paying the winner so long as he holds the card in his hand. If he has played it in the course of the game he loses this advantage.

During the course of the game, any player who plays the Ace, King, Queen or Jack of the trump suit, or the Pope (9 ♦), wins the counters in the corresponding saucers; if the same player plays the King and Queen of the trump suit he wins the counters in matrimony, and if the same player plays the Queen and Jack of the trump suit he wins those in Intrigue.

The deal passes round the table clockwise, and any counters that have not been won in a deal are carried forward to the next.

Ranter Go Round

Ranter Go Round is an old Cornish game with the rather more appropriate alternative name of Cuckoo.

It may be played by any reasonable number, with a standard pack of fifty-two cards. The cards rank in order from King (high) to Ace (low); the suits have no rank. Each player begins with an agreed number of units, usually three. The dealer deals one card face downwards to each player. The object of the game is to avoid being left with the lowest card.

The player on the left of the dealer begins the game. He may either retain his card or offer it to his left-hand neighbour with the command 'Change'. There is no choice about it. The player so commanded must exchange cards with his right-hand neighbour unless he holds a King, when he says 'King', and the game is continued by the player on his left.

When an exchange has been made, the player who has been compelled to do so may pass on the card he has received in the same way, and so on, clockwise round the table, until the card is brought to a halt either by a King or by a player receiving a high card in exchange, so that he has nothing to gain by passing it on.

Any player giving an Ace, 2 or 3, in obedience to the command 'Change', must announce the rank of the card.

The dealer is last to play, and if he wishes to exchange his card, he does so by cutting the remainder of the pack and taking the top card of the cut.

If in doing this he draws a King he loses the hand and contributes one unit to the pool. If he does not draw a King, all the players expose their cards and the one with the lowest contributes one unit to the pool. If two or more tie for lowest card, all contribute to the pool.

When a player has contributed all his units to the pool, he retires from the game. The others continue, and the game is won by he who is left with at least one unit in hand.

Red Dog

Although in Red Dog, or High-card Pool, players stake on their cards, it is usually accepted as a party game, rather than a banking game, because the players stake against a pool and not against a banker.

The game may be played by any number up to ten, with the standard pack of fifty-two cards, ranking from Ace (high) to 2 (low). The suits have no rank.

The players contribute to the pool an agreed number of units and each player is dealt five cards (only four cards if nine or ten players are in the game). Beginning with the player on the left of the dealer, each in turn stakes a minimum of one unit and a maximum that must not exceed the number of units in the pool, that he holds a card that is higher than, and in the same suit as the top card of the stock when it is his turn to play.

The dealer faces the top card of the stock. If the player can beat it, he shows his card and is paid out of the pool. His remaining cards are not seen. If he cannot beat it, his stake is added to the pool and his cards are shown to the other players.

If at any time a player's winning bet takes all in the pool, a new pool is started as at the beginning of a game.

Widow   A   B

Rockaway

Rockaway or Go Boom is a game that may be played by any reasonable number of players.

Two packs of cards are shuffled together, and the dealer deals seven cards, face downwards, to each player. The next card (the widow) is placed face upwards in the centre of the table, and the rest of the pack (the stock) is placed face downwards on the table.

In turn, and beginning with the player on the left of the dealer, each player covers the widow either with a card of the same rank, of the same suit, or with an Ace, drawn from his hand. If he has no card in his hand to comply with the rule he draws a card from the stock and continues to draw one until he draws a card that permits him to cover the widow.

The card that covers the widow then becomes the widow for the next player, and so on, round the table in a clockwise direction.

When the stock is exhausted, the players play out the cards in their hands, and a player who cannot cover the widow misses his turn.

The hand comes to an end when a player has exhausted the cards in his hand. The remaining players expose their cards, which are scored against them: an Ace counting 15 points, a court card 10 points, and all other cards their pip value.

The deal passes round the table in a clockwise direction, and the game comes to an end when every player has dealt an equal number of times, by arrangement before the game begins.

E dealt. A, therefore, leads first, and the play is:

A	B	C	D	E
6 ♣	2 ♣	2 ♦	K ♦	A ♠

As an Ace counts 15 points against a player who is left with it, E plays A ♠ rather than one of his Diamonds.

| 10 ♠ | 9 ♠ | J ♠ | 8 ♠ | ? |

As E has no Spade, no 8 and no Ace in his hand, he must draw from the stock, and continue to do so until he draws a playable card.

It can be seen that E was foolish to play his Ace first round. As no opponent can go out in less than seven rounds, E would have been wise to keep his Ace for six rounds at least. He would not then have found himself in such a bad position on the second round. Usually, an Ace should not be played if another choice is available.

Spinado

Top: **matrimony**
Centre: **intrigue**
Bottom: **spinado**

Spinado is a less complicated version of pope joan (see page 145). No board is necessary (if you could find one) and there are only three pools: Matrimony, Intrigue and Game.

Before dealing, the dealer contributes 12 counters to the Matrimony pool, and 6 each to the Intrigue and Game pools. The other players contribute three counters each to the Game pool.

Matrimony is the King and Queen of Diamonds: Intrigue is the Queen and Jack of Diamonds.

The four 2s and the 8 of Diamonds are removed from a standard 52-card pack, and the dealer deals the cards to the players and to an extra hand (widow). As the players must each hold the same number of cards, over-cards go to the widow hand.

The player on the left of the dealer starts the game by playing any card that he chooses, and the other players continue by playing the next higher cards in succession until a stop is reached. The player who plays the stop card then starts a new run by playing any card that he chooses.

The Ace of Diamonds is known as Spinado, more usually truncated to Spin, and whoever holds it may play it at any time that he chooses provided that he accompanies it with the proper card, and announces that he is playing Spinado. It constitutes a stop, and he receives 3 counters from each of the other players.

During the game, the player who plays the King of Diamonds receives 2 counters from each of the other players, and if he plays the Queen of Diamonds as well he wins the Matrimony pool. The player who plays the Queen of Diamonds and the Jack of Diamonds wins the Intrigue pool, and those who play the Kings of Spades, Hearts and Clubs receive 1 counter from each of the other players.

The game is won by the player who is the first to play all his cards. He takes the counters in the Game pool and is exempt from contributing to the pools in the next deal, unless it is his turn to deal.

A player who is left with Spinado in his hand pays the winner of the game double for each card he is left with.

Spinado, therefore, should not be kept back too long. On the other hand, it is not always advisable to play it with one's first card. If, for example, a 10 is led, and the player who holds Spinado also holds the King and Jack, it is an error of judgement to play Spinado with the Jack, because if the Jack proves to be a stop there was no need for the play of Spinado, and the King is the natural stop if another player follows with the Queen.

It is better to hold up Spinado to be played with some card that is not known to be a stop.

Thirty-One

Thirty-one may be played by any number of players up to fifteen. It is played with the full pack of fifty-two cards, the Aces ranking high the 2s low.

Before each deal the players contribute an agreed amount to a pool.

Three cards are dealt face downwards to each player, and three cards are placed face upwards in the centre of the table. It is known as the widow hand.

In turn each player, beginning with the one on the left of the dealer, must exchange one of his cards with a card from the widow. He cannot pass, nor can he exchange more than one card. Counting the Ace as 11, the court cards as 10 each and all the other cards at their pip values, the object of the game is to hold three cards of the same suit which will add up to 31. Next in value is a hand that contains three cards of the same rank. Failing either, the pool is won by the player who holds the highest total in any one suit.

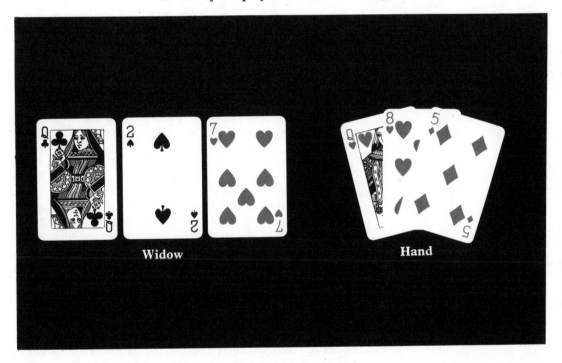

Widow   Hand

The player might be advised to exchange his 5 ♦ with the 7 ♥ and rap, since 25 is not a bad score

The exchange of cards with the widow-hand continues until a player has obtained a 31-hand. When a player holds such a hand he exposes it on the table, claims the pool, and the deal passes. At any stage of the game, however, a player who thinks he has a hand good enough to win, may rap the table. The other players now have the right, in turn, either to stand pat with the cards that they hold, or exchange one more card with the widow. The players then expose their cards and the one who holds the best hand wins the pool.

Baccarat

Baccarat, more correctly Baccarat Banque, is a game of chance that is played in casinos everywhere.

The game may be played by any number up to thirty or more. The banker sits midway down one of the sides of a long, oval table (opposite), and the players sit in equal numbers on both sides of him. Those for whom there is no room to sit, stand behind them.

Six packs of cards are shuffled together, in Las Vegas eight packs are used, cut and placed in an open-ended box known as a shoe, designed to release only one card at a time. The court cards rank in value at 10 points each; all other cards at their pip values.

The banker, who is also the dealer, puts his stake on the table in front of him, and any player who wishes to bet against the whole of it, calls 'Banco'. If two or more call, the one nearest to the banker's left makes the bet. If no-one calls, the players combine their bets to equal the stake put up by the banker.

The banker then gives a card face downwards to the player on his right, a card to the player on his left and a card to himself. He repeats the operation so that the three of them have two cards each.

The object of the game is to form in two or three cards a combination counting as nearly as possible to 9. In counting the total, ten is disregarded; if, for example, a player's two cards total 15 it counts as a point of 5.

The banker looks at his two cards and if he has a point of 8 or 9 he shows his cards and wins the hand. If he has not got a point of 8 or 9, he announces that he will give and the player on his right looks at his cards. If he has a point of 8 or 9 he shows his cards and announces his natural. If he has not got a point of 8 or 9 he may ask for one more card which the banker gives to him face upwards. The player on the left of the banker goes through the same performance, and then the banker may, if he chooses, take one more card. Finally, the banker wins or loses to each player according to whose point is nearer to 9; equality neither wins nor loses.

To illustrate. The banker holds 10 ♠ and A ♥, making a point of 1, and he, therefore, must give. The right-hand player holds 5 ♣ and 3 ♣. He faces his cards, announces his natural point of 8, and must win. The left-hand player holds 9 ♠ and 4 ♣, making a point of 3. He must draw and the banker gives him 8 ♦, reducing his point to 1. For the moment, however, the left-handed player does not announce his point. The banker faces his cards, and, as he holds no more than a point of 1, he draws a card. It is the 8 ♣, which raises his point to 9.

The banker, therefore, wins from the left-hand player, but loses to the right-hand player because though the banker has a point of 9, against the point of 8 held by the right-hand player, a natural beats any point made by the addition of a drawn card.

The rules of play are strict. They should never be deviated from because the player who is holding the cards is playing for all on his side of the table. If he deviates from the rules, and thereby loses the hand, he is liable to make good all losses incurred through his error. A player must not look at his cards until the banker has either announced that he holds a natural or that he will give cards. When a player looks at his cards, if he holds a natural he must expose his cards and declare his natural at once. If a player does not hold a natural, he must draw a card if he holds a point of 4 or less, stand if he holds a point of 6 or 7, and use his discretion to draw or stand only if he holds a point of 5.

The layout of the staking table used in baccarat and *chemin de fer*

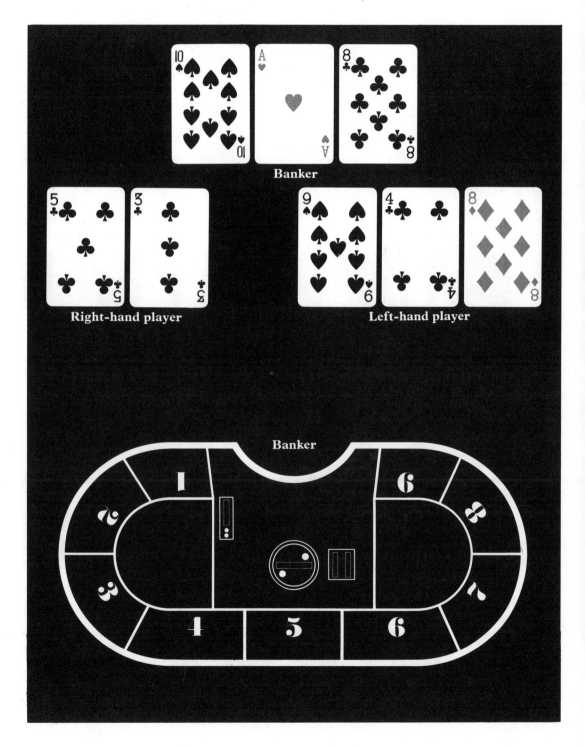

Banker

Right-hand player

Left-hand player

Banker

Blind Hookey

Blind Hookey may be played by any number of players with a single pack of fifty-two cards.

After the pack has been shuffled by one player and cut by another to the banker, it is passed to the player on the left of the banker, who removes a few cards (not less than four) from the top of the pack, and places them in a pile face downwards on the table in front of him. He then passes the pack to his left-hand neighbour who does the same thing, and so on until all the players (the banker last) have placed a small pile of cards in front of them.

Without looking at the cards, all the players (except the banker) stake to an agreed limit and turn their piles face upwards to expose the bottom card. The banker wins from all whose exposed card is lower than or equal with his and loses to all whose card is higher. By agreement, the Ace may be high or low.

Play continues with the same banker if he wins more than he loses, but passes to the next player if the banker loses more than he wins.

Banker

The banker wins from A, B, C and F and loses to D, E and G. Overall he loses 3 units and, therefore, the bank passes to the next player

Another way of playing the game is for the banker to cut the pack into three piles. The players place their stakes on either of two piles, and the third pile is taken by the banker. The three piles are turned face upwards and the players receive from the banker or lose to him according to whether the bottom cards of their piles are higher or lower than the bottom card of his pile.

Chemin de Fer

Chemin de Fer, nearly always called Chemmy, is the same game as baccarat (see page 152) modified for social play, because in all games of chance the banker has an advantage to a greater or lesser degree, and his advantage at *chemin de fer* is nothing like what it is at baccarat because he plays against one hand instead of against two.

For all practical purposes the difference between baccarat and *chemin de fer* is that at the latter game the bank passes in rotation round the table, the banker holding the bank until he loses a coup when it is passed to the player on his left; and the banker deals only one hand, not two, to the players, the hand being held by the one who has made the largest bet.

As the banker plays against only one hand, he may not use his judgement whether to draw or stand. The rules for play are precise and strict:

1. If his point is 8 or 9 he declares a natural.
2. If his point is 7 he stands whether the player draws any card or stands.
3. If his point is 6 he draws if the player draws a 6 or a 5, but stands if the player draws any other card or stands.
4. If he holds a point of 5 he draws if the player draws a 7, 6, 5, 4, 3, or stands, but stands if he draws any other card.
5. If he holds a point of 3 or 4 he draws if the player draws a 7, 6, 5, 4, 3, 2, or Ace or if he stands, but stands if he draws any other card.
6. If he holds a point of 0, 1 or 2 he draws whether the player draws any card or stands.

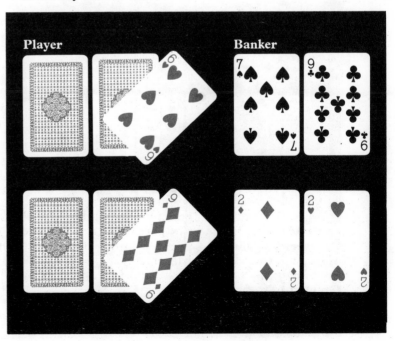

Banker's point is 6. Player has drawn a 6, so banker must draw

Banker's point is only 4, but as player has drawn a 9 he must stand

Easy Go

Easy Go is a very simple game of chance played by any number up to nine with a single pack of fifty-two cards.

The banker deals five cards face upwards to every player, except himself. He now faces a card and any player who holds a card of the same rank pays into a pool 2 units if it is the same colour and 1 unit if it is different. In all the banker faces five cards in turn, and for the second card the players pay into the pool 3 units if the cards are of the same colour and 2 if they are different; for the third card they contribute 5 units if the cards are of the same colour and 4 if they are different; for the fourth card they contribute 9 units if the cards are of the same colour and 8 if they are different; for the fifth card they contribute 17 units if the cards are of the same colour and 16 if they are different.

There is now a second show of five cards by the banker, but this time the players take out of the pool at the same rate as they paid into it.

After this, anything left in the pool is taken by the banker, but if there is not enough in the pool to meet the requirements of the players he must make it good.

The bank passes clockwise round the table.

Overall result of this game of easy go:
A wins 1 unit;
B wins 5 units;
C wins 3 units;
D wins 2 units;
E loses 3 units;
banker loses 8 units

First five cards faced by banker

A pays   0 units to the pool
B pays   1 unit to the pool
C pays 13 units to the pool
D pays   7 units to the pool
E pays   5 units to the pool

Second five cards faced by banker

A receives 1 unit from the pool
B receives 6 units from the pool
C receives 16 units from the pool
D receives 9 units from the pool
E receives 2 units from the pool

Hoggenheimer

Hoggenheimer, or English Roulette, is played with a pack of cards from which the 2s, 3s, 4s, 5s and 6s have been removed, and the Joker (or one of the rejected cards) added.

After the pack has been shuffled and cut, the banker deals the cards, face downwards, in four rows of eight cards each, and places aside, also face downwards, the thirty-third card. Great care must be taken when dealing that no-one sees the face of any of the cards.

The top row is for Spades, from Ace to 7; the second row for Hearts, from Ace to 7; the third row for Diamonds, from Ace to 7; the bottom row for Clubs, from Ace to 7.

The players now stake their money. They may stake on a single card being turned up (even chance), or two touching cards being turned up (2 to 1 chance), or all four cards in a column or any group of four touching cards being turned up (4 to 1 chance), or all eight cards in a row being turned up (8 to 1 chance).

When the players have placed their bets, the banker picks up the thirty-third card and shows it. If it is the Joker he wins all the money on the table and there is a redeal. If, as is more likely, it is another card, he places it in its appropriate place in the layout, exposes the card that it replaces and transfers this card to its appropriate place in the layout; and so on until the game is brought to an end when the banker exposes the Joker.

The banker then collects the money on those chances that have not materialised in full, and pays out on those chances that have.

Hoggenheimer in progress. Stake 1 is on 10 ♠ being turned up; Stake 2 on 9 ♠, 8 ♠; Stake 3 on all four Queens; Stake 4 on 10 ♦, 9 ♦, 10 ♣, 9 ♣; Stake 5 on all Clubs; Stake 6 on 7 ♥ and 7 ♦

Lansquenet

Lansquenet, of German origin, is a game of pure chance that derives its name from the seventeenth-century German mercenary (*landsknecht*) with whom the game is said to have been popular.

Any number may play. The banker places the two top cards of the pack (hand cards) face upwards on the table. He then deals a card face upwards to himself, and one face upwards to the players. If either card is of the same rank as one of the hand cards it is put with them and another card dealt in its place.

The players place their bets, and the banker covers them. He then draws cards from the pack, face upwards, one at a time. If he draws a card of the same rank as the players' card he wins the bets on it; if he draws a card of the same rank as his own card he loses all the bets on the other card; and if he draws a card that matches neither card nor the two hand cards it is placed on the table and the players may bet on it.

When the players' card is matched the banker withdraws both cards and deals another card to the players. Cards that match the hand cards are placed with them. The game ends when the pack is exhausted unless the banker matches his own card first.

First card drawn from pack: Q ♠. The card is placed on the table and players may bet on it. Second card drawn: 8 ♦. The card is added to the hand card pile. Third card drawn: K ♥. The banker wins the two units staked on K ♦

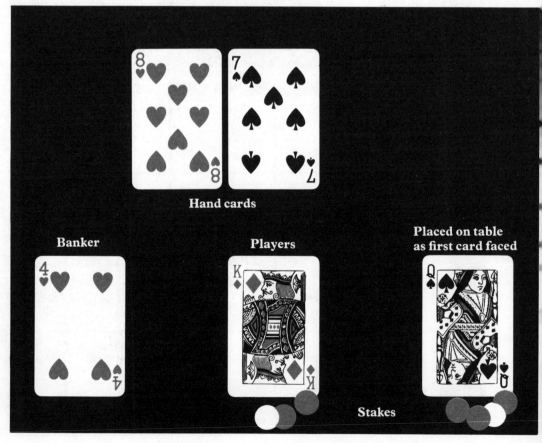

Hand cards

Banker

Players

Placed on table as first card faced

Stakes

Monte Bank

In principle Monte Bank is a game of chance that is very similar to lansquenet (opposite).

It is played by any number of persons, with a pack of cards from which the 8s 9s and 10s have been removed.

After the cards have been shuffled and the pack cut by one of the players, the banker draws the two cards from the bottom of the pack and places them face upwards on the table (the bottom layout), and then the two cards from the top of the pack and places them face upwards on the table (the top layout).

The players place their bets up to an agreed maximum on whichever layout they choose. The banker then turns the pack face upwards and if the exposed bottom card (known as the gate) is of the same suit as any of the four cards in the layouts, he pays all bets on that layout, and collects all bets on a layout that shows no card of the same suit as the gate.

The layouts and gate are then discarded, and the game is continued with new layouts and gate. The bank passes after five coups.

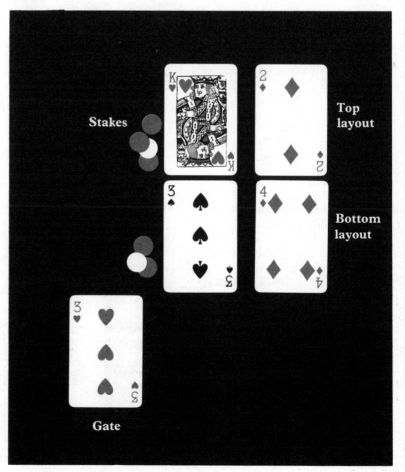

Stakes

Top layout

Bottom layout

Gate

Banker pays four units to players who stake on the top layout and collects the three units on the bottom layout. If the gate had been a Diamond, all players would have won; if a club all would have lost

Racing

Racing is played with the standard pack of fifty-two cards. The four Aces are placed in a row on the table. The remainder of the pack is shuffled and cut, and the banker draws the top seven cards from the pack and lays them in a vertical column immediately below the Aces, so that the lay out takes the form of a T (see illustration).

The banker deals the remaining cards one at a time, and each time that the card of a suit is dealt the Ace of the same suit is moved one card forward, the winner being the Ace that is first to pass the seventh card.

Players place their stakes on whichever Ace they choose. The race ends when the first Ace passes the seventh card.

Racing layout. The banker might offer evens on a suit if there are no cards in the layout, 2-1 if there is one card (as with Clubs and Hearts here), 3-1 if there are two cards (Diamonds here), 5-1 if there are three cards (Spades here) and 10-1 if there are four cards. If there are five or more cards of a suit in the layout, it is impossible for that suit to win, and there must be a redeal

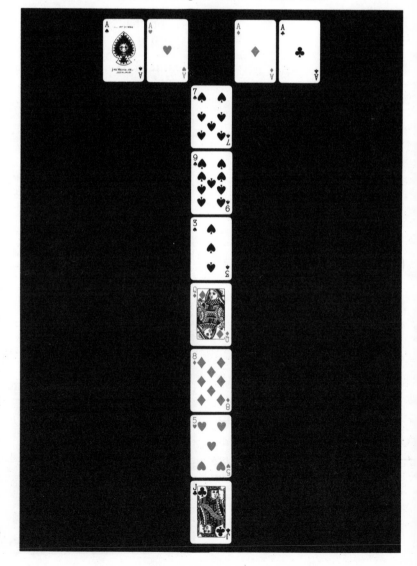

Slippery Sam

Slippery Sam or Shoot, as it is sometimes called, may be played by any number from two upwards, but the game is best for from six to eight players. It is probably the only banking game which favours the player rather than the banker, because the player has the advantage of seeing his cards before he bets and, therefore, can calculate whether the odds are in his favour or against him. Provided he bets with intelligence he should come out a winner.

The game is played with the standard 52-card pack, the cards ranking from Ace (high) to 2 (low).

The banker places an agreed sum in a pool and then deals three cards, one at a time, face downwards, to each player. The remainder of the pack (the stock) he places face downwards on the table in front of him and topples it over to make it easier to slide off the top card.

The player on the left of the dealer, after looking at his cards, bets that at least one of them will be in the same suit as, and higher than, the top card of the stock. He may bet all that is in the pool or any part of it, but he may not bet less than an agreed minimum. When he has made his bet, the banker slides the top card off the stock and exposes it. If the player has won his bet he exposes his card and takes his winnings out of the pool. If he has lost his bet he pays the amount that he betted into the pool and does not expose his card. The four cards are then thrown into a discard pile, and the opportunity to bet passes to the next player.

Meanwhile: a player must not look at his cards until it is his turn to bet; if the pool is exhausted the bank immediately passes to the next player, otherwise the banker holds the bank for three full deals round the table, and then he may either pass the bank to the player on his left or hold the bank for one more, but only one more, deal round the table.

Since the player wins if a red card or a Club lower than the 10 is exposed, and loses only if a Spade or the Ace, King, Queen or Jack of Clubs is exposed, he has 32 chances of winning and 17 of losing: he should stake heavily

Trente et Quarante

Trente et Quarante, or *Rouge et Noir*, is a game of pure chance and, like baccarat (see page 152) is essentially a casino game. It is played on a long table, each end marked as in the accompanying diagram. The banker sits midway down one of the sides, the players sit, and some stand behind them, at each end.

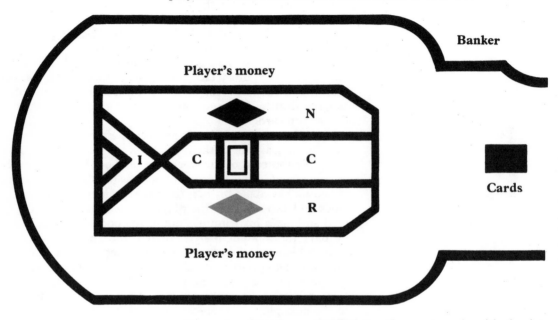

Six packs of cards are shuffled together, cut, and–with the Ace counting as 1, the court cards 10 each, and other cards their pip values–the banker deals a row of cards until the total exceeds 30. He then deals a second row immediately below it in a similar manner. The top row is *noir* (black) the lower *rouge* (red) and whichever row adds up to the lesser total wins. Apart from these two chances the players can bet on whether the first card dealt will be the same colour as the winning row (*couleur*) or the opposite colour (*inverse*). All four are even chances, but if both rows add up to 31 it is a *refait* (drawn game) and the player may either halve his stake with the bank, or allow the whole of it to be put in prison. He has the right to choose between the red and black prisons, and if his stake wins on the next deal he withdraws it.

All other identical totals end in the deal being declared void, and leave the player at liberty to withdraw his stake or leave it on the table to win or lose the next deal.

Vingt-et-Un

Vingt-et-Un, or Twenty-one, is a leading game in the casinos of America where it is known as Black Jack. Although it is a game of chance, in which the odds on winning are heavily in favour of the banker, in Great Britain it is far more of a social pastime and, under the name of Pontoon (almost certainly an easy corruption of punting) it was exceptionally popular in the trenches during the war of 1914–1918.

The game is played with a standard 52-card pack, by any number of players up to ten: if more than ten take part two packs of cards shuffled together should be used.

The banker deals one card face downwards to each player and to himself, and the players, after looking at their cards, stake any amount up to the agreed maximum.

The object of the game is to obtain a total of 21, or as near to it as possible, but without exceeding it. For this purpose an Ace counts 11 or 1 (at the option of the holder) a court card 10, and any other card its pip value.

When the players have made their bets, the banker looks at his card, and has the right to double. In this event the players must double their bets.

The banker then deals another card, face downwards, to all the players and to himself. If a player holds a pair he may announce his intention to split. He stakes the same amount as his original bet on both cards, and the banker deals a second card to each. The player plays both hands separately. The banker may not split pairs.

If the banker holds a natural (an Ace and a court card or a 10) he turns the two cards face upwards and receives from the players double what they have staked, except that if a player also holds a natural he loses only his original stake. The hands are thrown in, and the banker deals another hand.

If the banker does not hold a natural, but a player does, the banker pays him double his stake, and, after the deal has been completed, the bank passes to him. The bank, however, does not pass on a split natural. If two or more players hold naturals, the one nearest to the banker's left takes the bank.

When all naturals (if any) have been declared and settled, the banker asks each player in turn (beginning with the one on his left) whether he wants more cards or not. The player has three options. He may *Stand*; that is he elects to take no more cards. He may *Buy*; that is he increases his stake for the advantage of receiving a card face downwards. He may *Twist*; that is he does not increase his stake and receives a card face upwards. The rules to be observed are:

1. A player may not stand if he holds a count of 15 or less.
2. A player may not buy for more than his original stake.
3. If a player has twisted a third card he may not buy a fourth or fifth, though a player who has bought a third card may twist subsequent cards.
4. A player may not increase, though he may decrease, the amount

for which he bought a previous card.

5. If a player has received four cards he may not buy a fifth if the total of his four cards is 11 or less.

Five cards is the most that a player may hold, and if they total 21 or less the banker pays him double, unless the banker also holds five cards that total 21 or less when the banker wins.

The player who makes a total of 21 with three 7s, receives from the banker triple his stake. The banker does not have this privilege.

When the total of a player's cards exceeds 21 he turns his cards face upwards and the banker wins all that he has staked.

When all the players have received cards, the banker turns his two cards face upwards and deals himself as few or as many cards as he chooses. If when doing so he exceeds a total of 21 he pays the players their stakes. At any time, however, he may elect to stand and agree to pay those players who have a higher total and receive from those who have a lower or equal total.

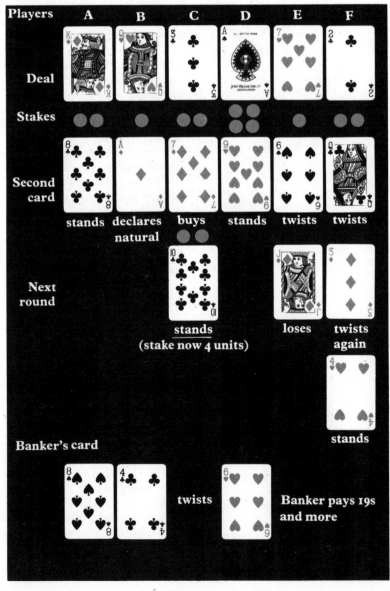

Banker pays B
(double), C, D and F
Banker wins from
A and E
Banker loses 9 units
on deal

Board
and Tile Games

Chess

The game of chess as played today has an interesting if somewhat obsure history. Originally evolved as a game for four players, various changes have taken place over a period of many centuries and it is generally agreed by modern players that the game as played today can hardly be improved upon.

Most authorities attribute invention of the game to the Hindus but no precise date can be given. It was probably devised during the fifth century A.D. and during the next hundred years spread from India to Persia. In the course of time it reached North Africa, Italy, Spain and by the tenth century most of Europe. England has the Norman Conquest to thank for the introduction of the game and the earliest chess book to be published here was Caxton's *The Game and Playe of the Chesse* which is dated 1474.

Originally called *Chaturanga* the pieces used represented the four divisions of an Indian army – elephants, mounted horsemen, horse-drawn chariots and footsoldiers. Originally the game was played with a dice which decided the piece a player should move. In course of time this was dropped and it was generally agreed that the player must decide which piece had best be moved to effect a Checkmate.

A number of changes have taken place during the centuries that the game has been played. The Queen was once a male figure in the shape of some sort of minister or adviser to the King. When chess reached the European Continent this piece became a Queen and much greater powers were conferred upon her. Whereas the male adviser to the King was limited to one square at a move the newly crowned Queen was granted the sweeping powers of both Bishop and Rook. This piece could now move across the board as far as the player wished using ranks, files or diagonals.

The rook has had many different shapes and forms in the past. Sometimes a chariot, sometimes an elephant, it is today represented as a castle turret. Bishops too have had changes of form and power. Once an elephant, the piece became a Bishop when chess reached England. In France however the change was to that of a court jester and the piece became 'le fou'.

Knights seem always to have been associated with cavalry and today the piece is represented by a horse's head. When Nathaniel Cook designed the pieces most of us play with today he persuaded his friend the eminent chess player Howard Staunton to allow the set to be named after him. The Knight in the Staunton set is a horse's head said to have been based on the famous Elgin marbles.

Pawns were foot soldiers in the original game and they appear as such in many chess sets today. The Staunton pieces represent the Pawn as a small ball on a bell-shaped base.

When learning to play chess it is best to use Staunton pieces because these are now used in chess clubs and at all chess tournaments throughout the world.

The Board and the Pieces

Chess is played on a board of 64 squares of which 32 are White and 32 are Black. It is very important that players ensure that the board is the right way round before they set up the pieces. Each player should have a White square at his right hand corner.

The squares are coloured light and dark—usually White and Black but sometimes Cream and Brown or even White and Green. They are not identified by letters or numbers except in theory. To be able to record games both letters and numbers have been given to the squares and the item on notation explains the two main systems. It is possible to play the game without knowing either of them but a player wishing to improve his play would do well to master both because not all books use the same system.

Object of the Game

The object of the game is for a player to defeat his opponent by capturing his King. In fact the King is not removed from the board, but as soon as he is manoeuvred into a position from which he cannot escape, the game is over and the player who has made the capture has won.

Players move alternately and, except when making a special move called 'castling' which will be explained later, only one piece is moved at a time. A piece can be moved to a vacant square or to one occupied by a hostile piece which is then removed from the board in this same move.

The player who has the White pieces has a slight advantage and decision as to who plays White is decided by lottery. It is usual for one of the players to hold a Pawn of each colour in his closed hands and for his opponent to point to or touch one of the hands. Whichever colour he has selected he plays in the first game and thereafter the players alternate.

Value of the Pieces

The rules of chess decree that not all pieces move in the same way and therefore some pieces are stronger than others. A player should know the value of the pieces he is using or he will very soon find that, even if he knows the moves and can play a game, he will have difficulty in winning.

You need not remember the following points which experts have agreed should be awarded to the pieces, but you should be able to list the pieces in your mind in descending order of value. Here are the values:

Queen 9 points
Rook 5 points
Bishop 3 points
Knight 3 points
Pawn 1 point
King ?

Clearly the Queen is your strongest piece and then come your Rooks. If your opponent has a Queen and King left on the board at the end of the game, and you have two Rooks and a King, then theoretically you have the edge on him – by one point.

Bishops and Knights come next and are equal in value in the early part of the game but the position of pieces in the end game may give the advantage to one or the other of these pieces.

Pawns have the least value but players should not underestimate them. After all each one qualifies for exchange to a Queen if they can reach the opponent's back row! Furthermore a well positioned Pawn in the end game may tip the scales to victory for a player.

It is not really possible to give a reliable point value to a King. He is not a powerful piece but he is valuable. If you lose your Queen you can still play on. Lose your King and you lose the game!

Check and Checkmate
Your opponent's King is said to be in Check if, having made a move you find you are able to capture the King in your next move. It is required that the player say 'Check' so that his opponent is aware that some action must be taken to save the threatened King. If a player finds that his King is in Check and that there is no way of saving the King then that is Checkmate and the game is over.

The Figures
The figures in this article have been designed to show the movements of the various pieces and, for simplicity, only those pieces involved in the move with the hostile King are shown. In a game of chess there would probably be many more pieces on the board but

it was thought that these, if shown, would only confuse or distract the reader.

Notation

There are two different ways of recording chess games and it will repay the reader to master both. Neither is difficult to learn and once the shorthand is understood a player can record his own games and, just as important, play out on his own board the games played and recorded by the experts.

The system in common use in the English speaking countries is known as Descriptive Notation (or English Notation) but most other countries use what is called Algebraic Notation.

Descriptive Notation

A very simple code is used to designate the pieces. Each is referred to by its initials as follows:

King – K
Queen – Q
King's Bishop – KB
Queen's Bishop – QB
King's Knight – KKt or KN
Queen's Knight – QKt or QN
King's Rook – KR
Queen's Rook – QR

The Pawns are named after the piece they stand before, thus:

King Pawn – KP
Queen Pawn – QP
King's Bishop Pawn – KBP
Queen's Bishop Pawn – QBP
King's Knight Pawn – KKtP or KNP
Queen's Knight Pawn – QKtP or QNP
King's Rook Pawn – KRP
Queen's Rook Pawn – QRP

Now for the board. Each square has a number for White and a number for Black. White's squares are numbered from the bottom of the board on all illustration figures and Black's from the top. The numbers run from 1 to 8 in each file and the files are identified by the names of the pieces which occupy them at the start of a game. Hence you get K1 and Q1 in the centre of the back rank and K1 goes to K8 up the board for White. K1 for Black runs down the board to K8. The same applies to all the other files.

BLACK

QR1 / QR8	QKt1 / QKt8	QB1 / QB8	Q1 / Q8	K1 / K8	KB1 / KB8	KKt1 / KKt8	KR1 / KR8
QR2 / QR7	QKt2 / QKt7	QB2 / QB7	Q2 / Q7	K2 / K7	KB2 / KB7	KKt2 / KKt7	KR2 / KR7
QR3 / QR6	QKt3 / QKt6	QB3 / QB6	Q3 / Q6	K3 / K6	KB3 / KB6	KKt3 / KKt6	KR3 / KR6
QR4 / QR5	QKt4 / QKt5	QB4 / QB5	Q4 / Q5	K4 / K5	KB4 / KB5	KKt4 / KKt5	KR4 / KR5
QR5 / QR4	QKt5 / QKt4	QB5 / QB4	Q5 / Q4	K5 / K4	KB5 / KB4	KKt5 / KKt4	KR5 / KR4
QR6 / QR3	QKt6 / QKt3	QB6 / QB3	Q6 / Q3	K6 / K3	KB6 / KB3	KKt6 / KKt3	KR6 / KR3
QR7 / QR2	QKt7 / QKt2	QB7 / QB2	Q7 / Q2	K7 / K2	KB7 / KB2	KKt7 / KKt2	KR7 / KR2
QR8 / QR1	QKt8 / QKt1	QB8 / QB1	Q8 / Q1	K8 / K1	KB8 / KB1	KKt8 / KKt1	KR8 / KR1

Fig. 1   **WHITE**

Figure 1 shows the numbering for both White and Black. When recording movements always use the minimum shorthand. For example, if White's King Pawn opens the game by moving two squares forward this is written as P–K4. There is no point in identifying the Pawn as KP because it is the only one that can move to this square at this stage of the game. The dash (–) indicates 'moves to'. Other shorthand you should know is equally simple. The letter x = captures.

Therefore P x P simply means Pawn takes Pawn and this would apply if there is only one Pawn that can take another. If two Pawns have the option of capturing a hostile Pawn the one making the move should be identified such as BP x P (Bishop Pawn captures Pawn) or QP x P (Queen Pawn captures Pawn).

There are a few other simple symbols you should know about. Any move by any piece which puts the hostile King in jeopardy – that is to say a move which means that the King could be captured in the next move – is one that puts the King in Check. The player who has made this move must announce this by saying Check. It is recorded as simply ch after the move (example Q–R8 ch. The Queen has been placed in the eighth rank and in her next move could capture the King).

The move known as castling which will be fully explained later is recorded as O.O if made on the King's side of the board and O.O.O if on the Queen's side. The only other shorthand you need to know is the ! normally put after a good move by an analyst (example

Fig. 2

QxR ch ! which simply means Queen captures Rook and puts the King in Check, a good move) and ? which implies a move of doubtful worth, or a bad one. Sometimes one gets a combination of these last two such as R x B !? which means Rook captures Bishop—a daring move of doubtful wisdom depending on further moves by both players.

Algebraic Notation

Many players and especially chess writers prefer this system which is popular on the Continent. There is much to be said in its favour but, until it is more widely used in the English speaking countries, the reader would do well to master Descriptive Notation.

Algebraic Notation is easy to follow. The board is (in theory but not in practice) numbered from 1 to 8 up the files and from a to h across the ranks as shown in Figure 2. The history of this system goes back to Medieval times and was reintroduced about the middle of the 18th century.

The pieces with the exception of the Pawns are represented by their initials as in Descriptive Notation. The eight files have the letters a to h. The eight ranks have the numbers 1 to 8 starting from White's first rank. Black's first rank therefore is No. 8. The squares are therefore identified by a combination of letter and number.

A move is written as the initial of the piece plus the identification of the square it leaves and the square to which it moves. As in Descriptive Notation the act of moving a piece is shown as a hyphen or dash. To capture is shown as x.

Descriptive Notation gives the Ruy Lopez opening as follows:

White	Black
1) P–K4	P–K4
2) Kt–KB3	Kt–QB3
3) B–Kt5	and so on

Algebraic Notation of these moves is as follows:

1) e2–e4	e7–e5
2) Kt–g3	Kt–c6
3) B–b5	and so on.

Very few chess books in the English language use Algebraic Notation so the reader may think it best to concentrate on Descriptive Notation first.

Kings

Each player has a King. He is not the most powerful piece on the

PAWNS   QUEEN KING   PAWNS
   BISHOP   BISHOP
 KNIGHT   KNIGHT
 ROOK   ROOK

QUEEN'S   KING'S
SIDE   SIDE

 ROOK   ROOK
  KNIGHT   KNIGHT
   BISHOP   BISHOP
PAWNS   QUEEN KING   PAWNS

Fig. 3

board but he is certainly the most valuable. This is explained by fact that you may lose any other piece or pieces and carry on playi but, if your King is captured, you lose the game.

Movement of the King is restricted to one square at a time exc when making a special move known as castling which will be plained later. For the present, regard your King as valuable, s moving and vulnerable. Take heart from the fact that this also app. to your opponent's King.

A King can use ranks, files or diagonals provided that he mo no further than one square in a move. Why should a player wish move his King? The answer is that if a King is under attack a *can be taken* in the next move then the player under pressure m do one of four things. He must:

1) Move his King to a square which is not under attack—wh explains why you might want to move him, or

2) the player must capture his opponent's attacking piece with King. This he may not be able to do because the attacking pi may not be on a square adjacent to that of the King so he migh

3) move another piece to place it between the attacking piece a the beseiged King. Alternatively the player whose King is attack may be able to

4) remove the attacking piece with one of his other pieces.

If any of these moves can be made the game goes on. If not King is Checkmated and the game is over.

Pawns

Each player has eight Pawns and these are placed directly in fr of the other pieces as shown in Figure 3. For recording the mo ments of a game Pawns take the name of the piece they stand front of and reading from left to right they are as follows: Quee Rook Pawn (QRP), Queen's Knight Pawn (QKtP), Queen's Bish Pawn (QBP), Queen's Pawn (QP), King's Pawn (KP), Kin Bishop Pawn (KBP), King's Knight Pawn (KKtP) and King's Rc Pawn (KRP).

The rules governing Pawn movements are quite simple and ap| to all Pawns. They always move forward and, except when maki a capture, they always keep to the file in which they are placed the beginning of the game. A Pawn is always moved one square a time except in its first move when the player has the option moving it two squares.

Pawns capture diagonally and this they can only do if there i

Fig. 4

Fig. 5   Fig. 6

hostile piece on the square ahead of them in the left or right adjacent file. Look at Figure 4. White has moved his Queen Pawn two squares forward as his first move and Black has replied with the same move P–Q4. The result is that both Pawns are blocked and can make no further move until one is captured and removed or makes a capture. Suppose that White now decides to move his King Pawn and to take advantage of the rule allowing a Pawn being moved for the first time to go forward two squares. Figure 5 shows his move P–K4. It is Black's move and because Pawns capture diagonally he takes White's Pawn as shown in Figure 6. If White had moved his King Pawn only one square it would not have been taken. Furthermore it would have been one square diagonally behind his Queen Pawn guarding it. In other words the King Pawn could capture any piece which took the Queen Pawn.

Pawns can capture any hostile piece in this way except the King but they can threaten the King. A Pawn can put a King in Check.

Promoting Pawns

There is one other very important thing you must know about Pawns. Although they are the least powerful pieces on the board, every one of them is a potential Queen. To achieve this promotion it is necessary for a player to get a Pawn to his opponent's back rank. This is never easy because there are so many hostile pieces waiting to attack any advancing Pawn. It is worth trying to achieve a second Queen because, as we shall shortly see, a Queen is more powerful than any of the other pieces and to have two on the board means almost certain victory. A strong player may well achieve this if playing against a beginner but good players of equal strength usually ensure that advancing Pawns are dealt with before they become eligible for promotion.

It should be mentioned that a Pawn reaching the eighth rank does not automatically become a Queen. The player can elect to exchange it for any other piece he cares to choose except, of course, a King.

Most sets of chessmen do not contain more than one Queen for each player so that if a Pawn is exchanged for a second Queen the player must improvise. If there is a Rook off the board at the time it is usual to use this with a Pawn balanced on top of it. More often than not a Pawn becomes a Queen late in the game when the player's Queen has been captured and is already off the board. She can now be taken back into service and is placed on the square which the successful Pawn reached.

Fig. 7

Fig. 8

Fig. 9

Rooks

The movements which a Rook may make are very easy to learn. In a way it is the most straightforward piece on the board. A Rook can travel as far across the board as the player wishes provided that it is kept to a rank or a file. In other words the Rook can be moved forwards or backwards in a file or to the left or right in a rank. A Rook can put the hostile King in Check from the other side of the board. Look at Figure 7. The Black King is not in Check from the Rook because he cannot be captured in White's next move. Suppose White moves his Rook to the square shown in Figure 8 (R–K1). Now the Black King *is* in check and Black's next move must be to rescue his King. The arrow shows the path White Rook would take to capture the King.

Rooks can capture any hostile piece on the board by moving along the ranks or files and removing the piece from the square they travel to. Look at Figure 9. Black Rook can travel across the rank and capture White Bishop as shown by the arrow. If Black makes this move then White Pawn can capture Black Rook! This was a bad manoeuvre for Black because Rooks are more valuable than Bishops. This is where tactics come into chess. Only make a capture if it is really to your advantage to do so. Be sure you understand the relative values of the pieces and do not sacrifice a strong piece for the capture of a piece relatively weaker! If the protecting Pawn had not been in the position shown and the Bishop had been isolated, then the Rook capture would have been worthwhile.

Bishops

The movements which a Bishop is allowed to make are as simple as those of the Rook. The difference is simply that Bishops are confined entirely to the diagonals on the board. They move across the corners but never across ranks or up and down files. Like the Rook a Bishop can be moved as far as the player wishes provided that his path is unobstructed. Bishops capture by occupying the square of a hostile piece which is removed from the board.

One of your Bishops starts, and remains throughout the game, on a White square and the other on a Black square. This, of course, also applies to your opponent's Bishops.

As long as he is kept to diagonals a Bishop can advance or retreat provided the way is clear. When he takes a piece he occupies the square on which he made the capture and he remains on that square until moved again–or until he is captured.

Fig. 10   Fig. 11

In Figure 10 the White Bishop is in a position to capture either the Black Knight or the Black Pawn. The Black Knight is protected by another Black Pawn so that if the Bishop does take the Knight he will be captured by Black Pawn. On the other hand if the player elects to capture the lone Black Pawn the Bishop is still safe. This would normally be the better move. It is a capture rather than an exchange.

In some circumstances an exchange would be the better move. In Figure 11 the White Bishop has the same choice of victims and elects to capture the Knight. If Black Pawn captures the Bishop the pathway is clear for White Rook to capture Black Queen and call Check. In fact, it is Checkmate because the Black King cannot escape from the back row. He is hemmed in by his own Pawns. White has made the sacrifice of a Bishop to win the game.

Knights

The movements of the pieces so far described have been simple to describe and should be easy to learn. The movement of a Knight does call for a little concentration because it is not quite so straight-forward in its mode of progress across the board. A Knight moves two squares forward and one to the side every time it moves. It cannot elect to go one or two squares and then stop. It must make this L-shaped move or not move at all. Knights can advance or retreat and the movement across the squares can be two across a rank and one up a file or two up a file and one across a rank. Figure 12 shows a Knight moving out from its starting position and the arrow shows the square to which the player has elected to move it. Note

Fig. 12   Fig. 13

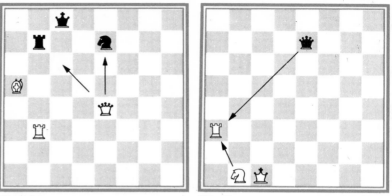

Fig. 14   Fig. 15

that from this starting position there is one other square available to it and this is marked with a cross. Figure 13 shows a Black Knight in one of the centre squares. From this position the Knight can move to capture any one of the White Pawns round him. It should be remembered that Knights are the only pieces on the board which are allowed to hop over other pieces – and this applies to your own or those of your opponent.

Queens

Each player starts the game with a Queen. She is the most powerful piece on the board and the good player will ensure that, whatever move he makes throughout the game, his Queen is safe from capture. There are positions in which it may pay the player to sacrifice his Queen in order to ensure a Checkmate, but we will deal with this later.

Now for the movements a Queen is allowed to make. She combines the movements of both Rook and Bishop. That is to say a Queen may use ranks or files like a Rook or, if the player wishes she may use diagonals like a Bishop. She may be moved backwards or forwards across the board. Queens capture pieces in the same way as Bishops, Rooks or Knights. They occupy the square of the hostile piece and the latter is removed from the board. It should be mentioned that the Queen cannot make the Knight move. She is confined to ranks, files or diagonals.

In Figure 14 the White Queen is in a position to capture Black Rook or Black Knight as the arrows show. If the player elects to capture the Knight the game could go on with Black moving to get out of his difficulties. On the other hand if White Queen captures the Black Rook it is Checkmate. The Black Knight is not in a position to capture the White Queen and Black King cannot take her because if he did he would be moving into Check from the White Rook. The only escape square which might have been available to him is covered by the White Bishop.

If a Queen is in a position to make a capture always watch closely to ensure she does not put herself in jeopardy. In Figure 15 the Black Queen can capture White Rook and in the same move put White King in Check. Not a good move this because White Knight would then very promptly capture Black Queen! It is usually considered bad play to bring a Queen out into the open early in the game. She is powerful but like any other piece the Queen is vulnerable too.

Fig. 16   Fig. 17

Special Moves

There are two special moves a player should know about before he starts to play a game. The first of these is the En Passant move which is seldom made but nevertheless it should be understood perchance the player has the opportunity of making it.

En Passant

Stated briefly it is simply this. Any Pawn on the board when making its first move can go two squares forward but it cannot escape capture if it moves alongside a hostile Pawn. In Figure 16 White Pawn is about to be moved for the first time and there is a Black Pawn which in this position cannot capture White. If White takes advantage of the rule which allows him to go forward two squares then Black can capture White as if White had moved only one square. Figure 17 shows the move White Pawn has made and an arrow shows the square to which Black Pawn can now go and at the same time White Pawn is removed from the board. The result is a Pawn capture for Black as if White Pawn had moved forward only one square. The En Passant move does not crop up very often but the other special move does and the player should master it before starting to play. This is known as castling and it is usual for both players to make this move early in the game.

Castling

Each player is allowed to castle once during a game and experienced players usually aim to do it by about the tenth move – or soon after. In the one move the King is placed at the side of the back rank and a Rook is brought towards the centre of this rank. The object is to get the King to a place of greater safety and, at the same time, bring a powerful piece into active play towards the centre of the board. A player may castle on either side of the board depending on whether or not the way is clear for him to do so.

On the King's side the Bishop and the Knight must have vacated their squares before the player can castle. On the Queen's side the Queen herself must also have left her starting square. Figure 18 shows White ready to castle on the King's side and the arrows indicate the move about to be made. Note that after the move there is one White square at the corner. When castling is completed on the Queen's side there is both a White and Black square in the back rank corner. Figure 19 shows White ready to castle on the Queen's side (the arrows show the move). Figure 20 shows the move completed.

Fig. 18

Fig. 19

Fig. 20

A player cannot castle if his King is in Check, nor can he do so if either the King or the Rook have already made a move in the game. He cannot castle if the square he is to occupy or the one he crosses is under attack from a hostile piece. In other words he cannot move into or across 'Check'. The illustrations show the moves for the White pieces and exactly the same applies to the Black pieces.

Openings

There are many different ways of opening a game and a beginner would do well to study some of the well-known and well-tried variations. Games are named after the manner in which players use their pieces in the first few moves and have sometimes acquired the names from players who have introduced the opening or who were well-known for their use of it. Sometimes the place of origin gives its name to an opening and in some cases the name indicates the type of play expected. The Ruy Lopez opening is named after a sixteenth century Spanish priest who published an early textbook on the game and who was patronised by Philip II. The Spanish King invited Lopez to his court for games of chess. The Vienna Opening dates back to the Vienna Chess Congress of 1873 when it was used in tournament play and thereafter became popular with chess masters from Vienna. Examples of openings which anticipate the likely course of the game are Queen's Gambit Accepted and Queen's Gambit Declined. There are many variations on these openings and the beginner cannot be expected to master more than one or two openings to start with.

It is however worth studying the first few moves of some of the standard openings and some of these are given here.

Ruy Lopez

This is probably the most widely used opening of all. The moves start as follows:

White	Black
1) P–K4	P–K4
2) Kt–KB3	Kt–QB3
3) B–Kt5	

and depending on Black's third move the variations have additional titles such as Bird's Defence, Classical Defence and so on.

Examine carefully the first two moves for each player. White opens with a centre Pawn and Black replies with this same move P–K4 to stop the advance of White and give himself equality in the centre squares. White's second move Kt–KB3 is a threat to Black's Pawn and whereas Black could make a similar threat by copying White's move he in fact brings out his Queen's Knight. This is a defending move which shows White that Black will capture White's Knight if White dares to take the Pawn. Exchanging a Knight for a Pawn is a very poor move for White so he now goes B–Kt5. This is a threat to Black's Knight though the Knight is protected by two Pawns. If White Bishop captures Black Knight then Black Pawn takes White Bishop. Black's third move could be P–R3 (Morphy's Defence) which would drive the Bishop away or Kt–Q5 (Bird's Defence) which is an escape for the Knight and gives him a centre square.

For readers who would like to pursue further the Ruy Lopez opening here are some variations to try out.

Ruy Lopez   Classical Defence

	White	Black
1)	P–K4	P–K4
2)	Kt–KB3	Kt–QB3
3)	B–Kt5	B–B4
4)	P–B3	KKt–K2
5)	P–Q4	P x P
6)	P x P	B–Kt5 ch
7)	B–Q2	B x B ch
8)	Q x B	P–Q4
9)	P x P	Kt x P
10)	B x Kt ch	P x B

The eleventh move could be for both players to castle. In terms of material captured, the players are equal. They both have more or less equal domination of the centre of the board. There is still room for development for both.

Ruy Lopez   Morphy Defence

	White	Black
1)	P–K4	P–K4
2)	Kt–KB3	Kt–QB3
3)	B–Kt5	P–QR3
4)	B–R4	Kt–B3
5)	O–O	Kt x P
6)	P–Q4	P–QKt4
7)	B–Kt3	P–Q4

8) P x P   B – K3
9) Q – K2   Kt – B4
10) R – Q1   P – Kt5

This would follow on with (11) White B – K3, Black Kt x B and (12) RP x Kt for White. Here again the material captured gives equality to both players and domination of the centre squares is about equal. White has the advantage of having castled but the disadvantage of doubled Pawns in his Queen Knight file.

English Opening

This opening acquired its name because it was used on various occasions by the famous British nineteenth century player Howard Staunton. Its usual feature is that White opens with a Bishop Pawn leaving Black the opportunity to play for centre domination in the early moves. In theory White can counter this and by opening with a Bishop Pawn he is able to strengthen his position by quick development of his pieces. Here is one of the English openings:

English Opening   Four Knights' Variation

White	Black
1) P – QB4	P – K4
2) Kt – QB3	Kt – KB3
3) Kt – B3	Kt – B3
4) P – Q4	P – K5
5) Kt – Q2	Kt x P
6) KKt x P	Kt x Kt
7) Kt x Kt	B – Kt5 ch
8) B – Q2	B x B ch
9) Q x B	Kt – K3

In the first nine moves each player has captured a Knight, a Bishop and a Pawn. Black has put White in Check twice and is already in a position to castle. Note that in the fourth move White offered a Pawn which Black refused and Black pressed on to threaten White's Knight. Having driven Black's Knight back, White must now continue development of his other pieces. It is anybody's game.

There are many other openings to study and readers who intend to take the game seriously should obtain a copy of one of the many books on chess openings.

Middle Game

This is the most difficult area to cover as far as instruction and

Fig. 21   Fig. 22

advice are concerned. There are so many different positions in which pieces may be placed on the board that it is only possible to give general guidance relating to a few common dangers to avoid. The beginner must always watch his Queen. Whatever move is contemplated he should look at it in the light of how does it leave his Queen when the move is made. He should also anticipate the next move of his opponent and make sure that, if it is an attack on the Queen, she can be saved before it is too late. This, of course, is in addition to safeguarding his King!

Pins

A piece which cannot or should not be moved is said to be pinned. Figure 21 shows a White Rook which is pinned by a Black Bishop. If White moved his Rook he would put his own King in Check which the rules do not allow. Figure 22 shows a White Knight pinned by a Black Bishop. If White moves his Knight, which he is allowed to do, he would lose his Queen to the Bishop.

A player who has a piece pinned should consider the following possible action:

1) capture the piece which is causing the pin.
2) move the piece which is being guarded to free the pinned piece.

Forks

If a piece is in a position from which it can capture either one of two pieces it is said to have them in a fork. Figure 23 shows a White Queen which in one move has put the Black King in Check and has forked Black Knight and Rook. When Black moves his King out of

Fig. 23

Fig. 24

Fig. 25

Fig. 26

Fig. 27

Check White Queen can capture either the Knight or the Rook.

A particularly deadly fork is a Knight attack on King and Queen as shown in Figure 24. Black must move his King and then White captures Black's Queen.

Skewers

A skewer is an attack on one piece which, when moved to avoid capture leaves the attacker in a position to take another piece. In Figure 25 White Bishop has put Black King in Check. The King must move and then Bishop captures Black Queen. From this example it is clearly dangerous play to position your King in front of your Queen. Sometimes it is possible to force a King into this position. Figure 26 shows a Black Rook about to force the White King to move from the Rook file. Figure 27 shows that Black's second Rook can now Check Black King forcing it to move again so that Black Rook can capture White Queen. A skewer can take place on a diagonal, a rank or a file.

End Game

The final stages of a game offer opportunities to the beginner for worthwhile study. It is disappointing to capture material, avoid pins forks and skewers but fail to effect a Checkmate. Study the simple mates to start with. If a Queen can safely occupy a square adjacent to that of the hostile King when he is at the edge of the board then that is a certain mate. Figure 28 shows that White King is not in Check but it is Black's move. Figure 29 shows the winning move. White King cannot capture Black Queen because he would

Fig. 28

Fig. 29

Fig. 30

Fig. 31

Fig. 32

move into Check from the Bishop. There is no escape square to which he can now move.

A simple mate is often effected with two Rooks. The hostile King must be driven to the edge of the board. Figure 30 shows Black King in Check from one White Rook and he must move. The only rank available to him is the back rank because the second White Rook stops him coming forward. Figure 31 shows that he has retreated and now White moves his second Rook to the back rank and this is mate. Figure 32 shows the move.

It has been stressed that players should always keep a wary eye on their Queens to ensure that these are not captured. In the part dealing with Queen movements it was stated that in some positions a player may decide to sacrifice his Queen to ensure a Checkmate. Here is an example which is worth playing out on your board. The game has reached the 17th move (Figure 33). White goes P–QKt4 and Black brings a Bishop to call Check B–B7 ch. White must move his King. He cannot capture the Bishop with his King because this would put his King in Check from Black's Knight. White's move is K–QR1. Now comes Black's surprise move. He feels that his position is strong enough to risk his Queen and he goes Q–K8! (Figure 34).

Note that White could capture Black Queen now but his position is so desperate that he feels it is more important to get his King out of the blocked position it is in. He must make an escape route and to do so he moves P–R3. Black's next move is another surprise. It is Kt x B! (Figure 35). There is nothing to stop White Rook capturing Black Queen now. This, of course, is what he does. Move

Fig. 33

Fig. 34

Fig. 35

Fig. 36

Fig. 37

Fig. 38

Fig. 39

Fig. 40

Fig. 41

Fig. 42

Fig. 43   Fig. 44

20 is R x Q for White. Black's reply is R x R ch! (Figure 36). White King is still on the run. He cannot capture the Rook so he must move. His foresight in moving out the Rook Pawn enables him to move K – R2. Black continues to press his relentless attack with B – KKt8 ch! (Figure 37). White King forlornly goes to KKt3 but Black hounds him with his Rook. The move for Black is R – K6 ch! (Figure 38). Once more the weary White King moves, this time to KKt4. This time Black does not put White King in Check but he rescues his Knight and brings it into the attack. His move is Kt – K7 (Figure 39).

White should really be concerned to rescue his King but he seems to hope for a distraction by threatening Black's Rook. He moves Kt – KB1. Black ignores this and continues to build up his attack on the King. This time he moves a Knight Pawn and threatens White's Queen, P–KKt3! (Figure 40). White saves his Queen by Q – Q5 and Black calls Check again with P – KR4! (Figure 41). White King goes to KKt5 and Black brings his own King into the fray. White's move is K – KKt5 and Black's K – KKt2 (Figure 42).

Because he is not actually in Check and because he aimed to do it a long time ago, White now captures Black's Rook. Black calls Check again by P–KB3 ch (Figure 43). If you put yourself in the position of the player with the White pieces you will see that White's next move is the only one open to him. He has to move his King and there is only one square available. There are five vacant squares of which four are under fire from Black pieces. So White moves K – KR4 and Black moves up his Bishop, B–KB7 ch! (Figure 44). Now comes White's last despairing move. It is P–KKt3 (Figure

Fig. 45

Fig. 46

45). He is out of Check for only a matter of seconds. Black now captures this Pawn and calls Checkmate (Figure 46).

Study the position carefully. Black Bishop is Checking White King and it cannot be taken by any White piece. The King cannot capture it without moving into Check from Black Knight. The White Queen is on a wrong diagonal. White King cannot move to the only adjacent vacant square because this would be a move into Check from a Black Pawn!

For ten moves Black has managed without his Queen and in half of those moves he has been able to call Check.

In giving the value of pieces earlier in this article it was mentioned that although a Queen is the strongest piece on the board, a well positioned Pawn can tip the scales at the end of a game. This, indeed was just such a game!

And now to resignations, draws and stalemates. If either player is fairly sure that his opponent will soon effect a Checkmate and if he himself cannot possibly win he may well think it pointless to continue the game. He is therefore well-advised to resign and, of course, this means his opponent has won. On the other hand both players may find themselves without sufficient strength in pieces to effect a mate and it is usual for them to agree a draw.

On the other hand there is one form of draw which players with mating material on the board should strenuously avoid. This is stalemate. If it is your turn to move and the only moves open to you would mean exposing your King to Check when he is not already in Check, then that is a stalemate. You cannot move so you cannot win or lose. The result is therefore a draw. In Figure 47 the player with the White pieces cannot possibly win because he is reduced to a lone King. Black on the other hand has his Queen, a Rook, a Knight, a Bishop and a Pawn on an open file that might have become another Queen. But the result is a stalemate because it is White's move and he cannot move his King without moving into Check. Note that White is not in Check *before* his move. White therefore claims a draw.

Clearly this is a rather exaggerated position and Black has played very badly to allow this position to come about. To avoid a stalemate you must be sure that your opponent *can* move a piece without having to move his King into Check. You may hope for a stalemate if you are losing and your opponent is strong but it can only be a hope. There is no way of forcing your opponent to make the supreme blunder.

A Complete Game Analyzed

Here is a complete game with comments on the moves of both players. If you play this out on your own board you will find it easier to see whether or not you would have made the same moves.

Irregular Defence

    White   Black

1) P–K4   P–K4

White makes a standard opening move with a Pawn placed in the centre of the board. Black's reply follows the convention of stopping the opening Pawn from going any further. Black also achieves equality in the game by occupying a centre square.

2) Kt–KB3   Kt–QB3

White brings out his King Knight. The position it now occupies is a threat to Black's King Pawn. Black's reply is bring out his Queen Knight to protect his Pawn. If White captures Black Pawn, Black would capture White Knight! Both players now have opening Pawns in the centre and each has a Knight ready for attack or defence.

3) B–B4   P–Q3

White advances his Bishop to a square from which it could take a Black Pawn (B x BP ch) and put the Black King in Check. This would be throwing the Bishop away if White makes it his next move because Black would reply with K x B. Losing a Bishop to take a Pawn is a poor exchange! On the other hand if White could in move 4 advance his King Knight to Kt5 he could *then* make the Bishop move with safety because the King would be unable to capture except by moving into Check which the rules do not allow. Black's reply is P–Q3. This move serves two purposes. Firstly it frees Black's Knight from its protective role guarding the King Pawn. Black's Queen Pawn now does this. Secondly it opens the diagonal for Black to bring out his Queen Bishop.

4) P–B3   B–Kt5

White's Pawn move is aimed at discouraging Black's Knight from advancing either to the centre (Kt–Q5) or to the Queen's side (Kt–Kt5). White's Pawn is ready to capture Black Knight if he jumps to either of these positions. White has also opened up another diagonal for his Queen.

    Black's Bishop has now come out as we anticipated that it might. Black Bishop threatens White Knight but not very seriously because if B x Kt then P x B. But Black has pinned White Knight unless White is prepared to sacrifice his Queen. If White moves his King Knight then Black Bishop captures White Queen!

5) Q–Kt3   Q–Q2

White now takes advantage of the new diagonal for his Queen and goes to Kt3 on the same diagonal as his Bishop. Now if in his next move White Bishop captures Pawn it would be Check and Black King could not capture the Bishop because he would be moving into Check from White Queen.

Black can see this danger and moves his Queen one square so that, if necessary, she can capture Black Bishop if the Pawn is taken.

6) Kt–Kt5   Kt–R3

White is free to move the Knight that was pinned and he brings this up to support the attack he has mounted with his Queen and Bishop. The square under fire is KB7 for White or KB2 for Black. White now has two pieces either of which can capture the Black Pawn on this square. The White Bishop supports the Knight and White Queen supports the Bishop.

Black's reply to White's attack is to bring out his King Knight to a square from which it can capture any piece which dares to take the Pawn which is under threat.

7) BxP ch   KtxB

Now comes White's attack. By taking the Black Bishop Pawn with his Bishop he puts the King in Check. As expected Black captures White Bishop with his Knight. White continues to press the attack.

8) KtxKt   QxKt

In capturing Black's Knight with his own, White knows that Black King cannot be used against him because the King must not move into Check. If Black Queen takes White Knight there could then be an exchange of Queens. This is a risk Black is prepared to take and, though his King is not in Check he decides to capture White Knight with his Queen.

9) QxP   K–Q2

White now switches his attack to the Queen's side of the board. Having failed in his attack on the Black King he elects to gain advantage in material by first of all snatching a Pawn. Black brings his King forward to Q2 to avoid Check if White now captures Black's Queen Rook.

10) QxR   Q–QB5

Throughout the game so far White has done the attacking and Black has defended. In this tenth move the pattern starts to change. As expected White's new attack is aimed at gains in material and

Fig. 48

capturing Black's Rook without loss appears good until you study Black's reply. The move to QB5 is the beginning of Black's winning attack. Study the position carefully. He already has a Bishop covering his K7 square and White has no escape paths open to him. He must start a brisk defence now or lose the game.

11) P–B3   BxP

White's Pawn move is a threat to Black's Bishop and halts the immediate attack but Black keeps the pressure on by capturing the Pawn even though he knows he must surely lose his Bishop. White must capture Black Bishop if he is to stay in the game.

12) PxB   Kt–Q5

White Pawn captures Black Bishop. In terms of material captured White is ahead but the pressure is on and Black's move Kt–Q5 is a further threat and at the same time a possible sacrifice. White should take the Knight with his Bishop Pawn.

13) P–Q3   QxQP

This is White's fatal mistake. By threatening Black's Queen with his Queen Pawn he had hoped to capture Black's Knight without loss. Black simply captures the threatening Pawn and waits for the kill. It is not far away.

14) PxKt   B–K2

So White now captures Black Knight. He is still gaining material but to little effect. Black's reply only tempts him to further indiscretion. By moving his Bishop from the back rank Black has exposed his Rook to danger from White's Queen. In fact this does not matter as the next move by both players clearly shows.

15) QxR   B–R5 mate!

White has fallen for the bait while Black has manoeuvred his Bishop into a winning position. White Queen captures Black Rook but Black Bishop moves to R5 and calls Check–in fact it is Checkmate (Figure 48). White has no piece to effectively intervene. White King is in Check and there is no escape square for him.

A short game this in which there are a number of noticeable features. Neither White nor Black castled in this game which is unusual for players of this stature. White did all the attacking in the earlier part of the game but Black's defence was always adequate. White gained more material but allowed himself to fall into fatal traps. Good aggressive play by White and brilliant cleverly calculated play by unruffled Black. The players were White Rodzynski and Black one of the really great chess players of all time, the legendary A. Alekhine.

Summary

Chess is not a game which is difficult to play nor is it really a difficult game to learn. There are, however, many rules to remember and a beginner should find the following At-a-glance A–Z useful when playing with an opponent who is also a beginner. A glance at the appropriate heading should lead to a quick answer to queries which may crop up in a game. There is also general chess information here.

At a Glance A–Z of Chess

Algebraic notation. This is a system of recording the moves in a game widely used on the continent but not much favoured in English-speaking countries.

The eight files are given the letters a to h from left to right for White and the ranks are numbered 1 to 8. The numbering starts from White's back rank. A move is recorded as the piece (not Pawns) identified by its initial and the combined letter-number of the square of departure and the square of arrival.

Back row. The back row is White's first rank and Black's first rank – that is the first line of squares running from left to right across the board and nearest to each player.

Bishops. Each player has two Bishops one of which is confined to White squares and the other to Black squares. All Bishops are confined to diagonals when they move but, provided the squares are unoccupied, they can move as many squares as they like in one direction. They can, of course change direction in the next move. Bishops capture by occupying the square of a hostile piece. They can put a King in Check if the diagonal from Bishop to King is unoccupied by White or Black pieces. One Bishop starts at the side of the King and the other at the side of the Queen. They are identified respectively as King's Bishop and Queen's Bishop.

Board. There are 64 squares on the board – 32 White (or light coloured) and 32 Black (or dark coloured). When the pieces are set up for a game each player must have a White corner on the right of his back rank.

Capture. When any piece makes a capture it occupies the square of the hostile piece which is, in the same move, taken off the board.

This applies to all pieces from Pawns to Kings. A capture is indicated by a cross (x).

Castling. This special move is open to each player once in any game. The conditions governing the move are: The King must not have made a move before castling. The Rook must not have made a move before castling. The squares between King and Rook must be vacant. The King must not pass across a square under attack from a hostile piece. The King must not move into Check. The King must not be in Check. On the King's side the King moves two squares towards the corner of the board and the Rook two squares towards the centre and ends up therefore on the King's other side. To castle on the Queen's side of the board the King moves two squares towards the corner and the Rook three squares towards the centre of the board ending up on the King's other side.

Check. If a hostile King can be captured by a player in his next move then the King is in Check and it is customary for the player to say 'Check'. His opponent is obliged to get the King out of Check by moving the King to a safe square or capturing the attacking piece *or* placing a piece between the attacking piece and the King. The game can then proceed.

Check, discovered. If a player moves a piece which leaves the hostile King in Check from another piece then this is known as a Discovered Check.

Check, double. It is possible for a player to double Check the hostile King. An example is when a Bishop starts in front of a Rook which is in the file occupied by the King. The latter is not in Check but when the Bishop moves to a square of which the diagonal is in direct line to the King then there is a double Check – one from the Rook and the other from the Bishop. The King must escape from both.

Checkmate. If a King is put in Check and cannot escape from the Check, then that is Checkmate and the end of the game.

Chess clock. In tournament chess it is customary to decide before play begins how many moves a player must make within a given time. Special clocks are available with two faces and White's clock is started as soon as play commences. When he has made his move White presses a button to start Black's clock having stopped his own. Players keep a record of their moves and can see from their clocks how well they are keeping within the time limit for the game.

Descriptive notation. Sometimes called the English Notation because it is largely used in the English speaking countries, this is the method of recording games most likely to be of use to the reader. The files are identified by the initials of the pieces which occupy them at the beginning of the game. The ranks are numbered from 1 to 8 for both White and Black starting from the back rank of each. White's King square is K1 and this square, if Black reaches it is K8. In chess literature, White always plays from the bottom of the diagram. The pieces are identified by their initials and Pawns by P unless it is necessary to distinguish between two in which case they are further identified with the initials of the piece they stand in front of at the beginning of the game. A dash means 'moves to', and x means captures. Check is abbreviated to ch. (!) means a good move, (?) a bad move.

Diagonals. Moving across the diagonals of a board simply means moving across the corners. Bishops are confined to diagonals throughout the game. Queens have the option of using the diagonals as do the Kings though the latter, except when castling, are confined to moving only one square at a move.

Development. From the first move in the game each player endeavours to bring out his pieces to positions of advantage on the board. This is known as development. It can be impeded if a player's opponent gains an early advantage and plays an aggressive game. This inevitably means that defence and consolidation are called for and the player may be delayed in developing his pieces satisfactorily.

Draws. If neither player has sufficient strength to Checkmate it is customary for them to agree a draw. A draw can be requested by a player if the same position appears three times as a result of the same move being made by that player.

A draw can be claimed by either player if fifty moves have been made and no piece has been captured and no Pawn has been moved – an unlikely eventuality!

En passant rule. If a Pawn when making its first move advances two squares and avoids capture by drawing alongside a hostile Pawn then it can be captured as if it had moved only one square. The capturing move must be made immediately after the Pawn's two square advance and cannot be postponed until later in the game.

Forced move. This refers to the position a player finds himself in when the move he makes is the only possible move.

Exchange. When a player captures a hostile piece and then loses his own piece it is said to be an exchange. An exchange in which equivalent pieces are lost and won is an even exchange. An exchange in which a Knight or Bishop is captured for the loss of a Pawn is said to have been won—if the Pawn was captured in exchange for the Knight or Bishop the exchange is said to be lost.

Files. The rows of squares which run in line from your back row to your opponent's back row. In chess charts the files are the lines of vertical squares.

Files, open. An open file is one which is unoccupied by Pawns of either colour. Rooks do well in these.

En prise. A piece under attack and which is undefended is said to be *en prise*.

Fork. A fork is a double attack when a piece can, in its next move capture either one of two hostile pieces. To counteract a fork the player should consider a counter attack such as putting the hostile King in Check or capturing the piece responsible for the fork.

Gambit. A gambit usually means to offer a piece for possible positional advantage, and to enable the player making the offer to get early advantageous development. Some named chess openings have the word gambit in them such as Queen's Gambit Accepted or Queen's Gambit Declined.

Interpose. To interpose a piece is to place it between an attacking piece and the King to get the King out of Check. It also applies to relieving other pieces from attack such as placing a Pawn on a diagonal between an attacking Bishop and a Queen. The Bishop would then have to take the Pawn first and, if that square is safe, the Queen might then take the Bishop.

J'adoube. When a player has occasion to touch a piece in order to place it properly on its square and not to move it he should correctly say '*J'adoube*' or, more informally 'I adjust'.

Knights. These are the only pieces in chess which have the power to jump over other pieces (of either colour). The Knight's move is two squares in one direction and then one square in a different direction. He thus makes an L shaped move. The Knight can go two squares up a file and then one across a rank or two across the rank and one into the file. Knights can move forwards or backwards.

Kings. Kings are limited in their moves to one square in any one move except when castling takes place. The two Kings in a game must never be placed on adjacent squares. There must always be one square between them though this need not be vacant. King's can advance or retreat.

King's side. All squares on the right hand side of the board for White and left hand side for Black are referred to as the King's side.

Mate (see Checkmate).

Middle game. After the known moves of an opening and the final moves of the end game comes the major battle which is loosely referred to as the middle game. No precise number of moves constitutes either opening, middle game or end game.

Notation. The two most widely used systems of recording Chess games are Descriptive Notation (also known as English Notation) and Algebraic Notation. Both are described in this book.

Openings. The number of ways of playing the first ten moves of a game are some astronomical figure and the beginner cannot be expected to remember many of them, but he will remember a few as he becomes familiar with them.

Openings have been named after Master players with whom they have become associated, places or tournaments, or in some cases they have been named to indicate the likely course of play.

Pawns. The least powerful of the chess pieces, Pawns do have the chance of promotion if they can be safely taken to the opponent's back rank. The movement of the Pawn is one square forward in its own file except when it is moved for the first time when the player may, if he wishes, advance the Pawn two squares. Pawns capture diagonally and remain in the file on which the capture was made. Pawns never retreat and never hop over other pieces. Pawns can give check to a hostile King.

Pawn, blocked. A Pawn is said to be blocked if it can make no further progress forward because a hostile piece occupies the square immediately in front of it.

Pawns, doubled. When two Pawns of the same colour occupy the same file, as a result of a capture, the player finds he has Doubled Pawns. This impedes satisfactory play and development and should be avoided if possible. Doubled Pawns are weak Pawns.

Pawn, passed. A Pawn which has a clear run in its own file and no hostile Pawns on its adjacent files is known as a Passed Pawn.

Pieces. In this book, and many others, the term pieces refers to any of the chessmen including Pawns. Purists, however, limit the term to Queens, Rooks, Bishops and Knights. The Queens and Rooks are classified as major pieces and the Bishops and Knights as minor pieces.

Pin. A piece is said to be pinned if it cannot or should not move. A Bishop which stands in front of a King to stop a Check from a hostile Rook cannot be moved and is forcibly pinned. A Knight standing in front of a Queen is pinned if he prevents the Queen being captured. The player may have the right to move the Knight but would be well advised not to.

Promotion. When a Pawn reaches the end of its file (the 8th rank) it can be changed to any other stronger piece the player decides on. It is usual to choose a Queen. This is promotion.

Queens. Queens are the most powerful pieces on the board. This is because they can do more than other pieces. They can use ranks, files or diagonals and can move as many squares as the player chooses provided the way is clear, of course. They combine the powers of Rooks and Bishops. They are, like all other pieces, vulnerable and loss of a Queen is more often than not, loss of the game.

Queen's side. All squares on the left hand side of the board for White and right hand side for Black are referred to as the Queen's side.

Ranks. The lines of squares which run from left to right across the board are the ranks. In chess charts the ranks are the lines of horizontal squares.

Rooks. Second only to the Queen in power the Rooks are confined to ranks and files. They never move diagonally nor do they hop over other pieces. Rooks can travel as far as the player decides provided the squares are free and they capture by occupying the square of a hostile piece which is, in the same move, taken off the board.

Sacrifice. A player who allows a piece to be captured is said to make a sacrifice. This is done in the hope of obtaining an advantageous position which is not always obvious to the opponent.

Skewer. A skewer is an apparent attack on one piece whereas it is in fact an attempt by the player to capture a more valuable piece which is in the same line of squares but lying behind the piece attacked.

Stalemate. When a player can move no piece on the board except his King and if the King is not in Check but would move into Check if moved at all, then that is stalemate and the game is declared a draw.

Threat. If a piece can capture a hostile piece that is a threat.

Touched piece. If a player touches a piece the laws of chess decree that he must move it. An exception is when he is adjusting it on its square and this he must announce to his opponent (see *J'adoube*).

White, who plays? The decision as to which player has the White pieces is decided by lottery. It is usual for one or other of the players to conceal in each hand a Pawn of the two colours. His opponent then points to or touches one of the closed fists and plays whichever colour is revealed when the hand is opened.

Checkers

In Great Britain the game is called draughts and is played with Black and White pieces on a Black and White board. In the United States it is called checkers and the pieces are usually red and white and the board dark green and buff. The method of play is the same on both sides of the Atlantic though there are other variations such as Spanish draughts, German draughts, Russian draughts and Polish draughts. Other alternatives to the normal game are losing draughts and diagonal draughts.

The game is played on a board of 64 squares of which 32 are White (or light coloured) and 32 are Black (or dark coloured). Each of the two players has 12 pieces or men and these are round wooden or plastic discs coloured White (or light coloured) and Black (or dark coloured).

The discs are placed on the three rows of Black squares nearest to each player. Before setting out the pieces always ensure that the board is the correct way round by looking to make sure you have a White square in the right hand corner nearest to you (Figure 1). This is exactly the same as for Chess.

All play takes place on the Black squares and movement of the pieces is confined to moving forward on diagonals (across the corners of the squares). The pieces all have the same value and are all confined to the same type of move until they are advanced to the opponent's back row when they are crowned kings. This is done by placing a second disc on top of the successful one so that it is distinguished from the ordinary men. Kings can move in any direction on the diagonals and can retreat as well as advance.

Capturing is achieved by hopping over an opponents piece or pieces and in order to do this the piece to be captured must have a vacant square beyond it (Figure 2). The piece hopped over or captured is taken off the board in the same move. A piece making captures may continue to move for as long as there are hostile pieces to hop over and, in doing so, the piece may change direction (Figure 3). The arrows indicate the move Black makes to capture two White men in one move.

The object of the game is to defeat your opponent by removing from the board as many of his men as possible and to immobolize any pieces he is left with. Each player moves alternately and Black always starts a game. To decide who plays Black in the first game one of the players takes a piece of each colour and conceals these in his clenched fists. He then offers his closed hands to his opponent who chooses (by pointing at or touching) one or the other. Which-

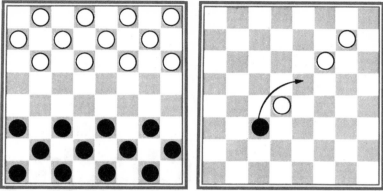

Fig. 1   **Fig. 2**

ever colour is revealed to the player making the choice is the colour he must play. Thereafter players alternate colours in subsequent games played at the same session. Players make their moves alternately and the rules say that if a piece is touched it must be moved. Once a player removes his hand from a piece that has been moved he cannot move it again until his opponent has made his move. In other words you must make sure that you capture all the pieces you can in one move before taking your hand off a piece.

A player who fails to take a piece that could have been taken may be 'huffed' by his opponent. This must be done by the opponent immediately and he can insist that the piece which should have made the capture is removed from the board. A 'huff' is not a move and the player who has claimed the huff then makes his own move. If you have failed to take a piece which could be taken your opponent does have an alternative to 'huffing' you. He can, if he chooses, insist that you take back the move you have just made and he can make you take the piece you have overlooked.

You may find that you have two pieces on the board which can each make a different capture. In this case the choice is yours and if you take a hostile piece you cannot be 'huffed' provided that the piece you moved made all the captures available to it.

Good general advice is that when a game is under way it is usually better to move towards the centre of the board. From here your pieces can attack in two directions instead of being limited to one direction from the side of the board. Always study the position of the pieces very carefully before making a move and do not give your opponent the chance to 'huff' you. Try to follow up the move of a piece with other pieces to stop your opponent capturing lone men. In other words keep your pieces up together especially towards the end of a game. If you are ahead in captures you should go in for equal exchanges, that is be prepared to lose a man to capture one of his.

In competition draughts you should move within five minutes if it is your turn otherwise your opponent may call 'Time' and then you have only one minute to move or lose the game.

The system of recording games is quite simple and the serious draughts player would do well to master it. Figure 4 shows the numbering of the board. The Black squares which are the only ones used for play are numbered from 1 to 32 starting from Black's back row and the sequence in each row is from right to left. The Black pieces are placed on squares 1 to 12 and White on 21 to 32. Figure 1

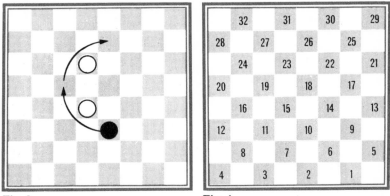

Fig. 3   **Fig. 4**

shows the pieces set up ready for a game. In Draughts diagrams Black is always shown at the bottom.

The movement of each piece is simply given as the number of the square a piece moves from followed by a dash and then the number of the square the piece finally settles on. Figure 2 shows a Black piece moving to capture a White piece. This is written as 11–18. Captures are not mentioned in the notation. As in chess, opening moves in draughts have acquired names such as the Bristol which is 11–16 or the Edinburgh 9–13. Black, who starts the play has seven moves to choose from. Thereafter his play will depend on White's moves.

Here is a game between players of equal strength which, as you might expect, ends in a draw. If you play this out on your own board you will readily see how good draughts players think ahead. Black opens with 11–15 and White replies with 23–19. Neither player can capture yet. Black's second move is 8–11 to back up the first man moved. White goes 22–17 bringing a second front row piece into play and moving to the side of the board. Black now goes 4–8 continuing to back up his front men. White continues to the side of the board with 17–13. He cannot be 'taken' here. Black ventures into enemy territory with his next move which is 15–18 and White goes 24–20.

The game proceeds as follows: 11–15, 28–24. 8–11, 26–23. 9–14, 31–26. 6–9, 13–6 (first capture). 2–9, 26–22. 1–6, 22–17. 18–22, 25–18. 15–22, 23–18. 14–23, 27–18. 9–13, 17–14. 10–17, 21–14. 6–10, 30–25. 10–17, 25–21. 22–26, 21–14. 26–30 (1st King) 19–15. 30–26, 15–8. 26–22, 32–28. 22–15, 24–19. 15–24, 28–19. 13–17, 8–4. 17–22, 4–8. 22–26, 19–15. 26–30 Drawn.

Players who tire of conventional draughts may care to try some of the variations on the game.

Losing Checkers

This game follows closely the rules and regulations of ordinary draughts except that each player aims to lose his own pieces instead of trying to capture those of his opponent. To 'huff' becomes a little different and even more important in this game and a player who fails to take a piece is made to take back his move and capture the piece or pieces he did not take. In the early moves it is safe enough to go in for equal exchanges allowing your opponent to take one of your men for each of his that you capture. Thereafter try to move

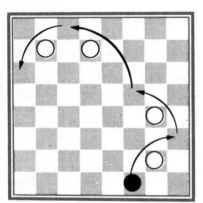

Fig. 5

your men out from your back row and leave spaces between them and the pieces in front of them. The player who first loses his pieces or cannot move those remaining on the board is the winner.

Spanish Checkers

It is usual to turn the board for this game so that each player has a Black square in the right hand corner of his back row. The pieces are set out on the Black squares as for ordinary Draughts and they move in the same way – diagonally forward. Kings, however have greater power in this game. Readers who play chess will be familiar with the Bishops' move, which is through as many squares as the player chooses provided the diagonal is clear. In Spanish draughts a King also has this 'long move' but there must be a vacant square beyond the piece the King wishes to capture so that he can hop over the piece to take it. Kings making the long move need not stay on the vacant square immediately behind the piece taken but may move on along the diagonal to any other vacant square. It is, of course, compulsory to take any pieces available in any one move. Having hopped over all pieces that are available in the one move these are then removed from the board. Once a piece reaches the opponent's back row it is crowned and remains on that square until it is the player's turn to move again. Figure 5 shows the move of a Black King to capture four White pieces in the one move. Other than this the rules for ordinary draughts apply.

German Checkers

In this game the rules of draughts apply and Kings have the same power as they have in Spanish draughts. Kings can move along a diagonal as far as the player likes provided the squares are clear and provided there is a vacant square beyond the piece the King hops over and takes. Movements of the ordinary pieces are, however a little different. They move forward on diagonals but if capturing pieces they can move backwards as well. A piece reaching the opponents back row is crowned in the ordinary way *unless* it can take more men by coming back across the board. In this case the piece continues its move and is not crowned. If there is a choice in the pieces which you can move and which will make captures, you must move the piece which can take the most hostile men in the one move.

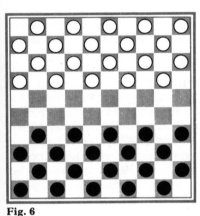

Fig. 6

Russian Checkers

This is similar to German draughts and the same rules apply except the one about pieces becoming Kings. In this game any piece reaching the opponents back row is crowned and then proceeds to complete its move by capturing any other men available to it. The players do not have to make the largest number of captures possible but are free to choose whichever piece they care to move.

Polish Checkers

This differs from the previous games described in that a board with a hundred squares is used (50 White and 50 Black). These are sometimes available in compendiums of games but the reader may find it necessary to make one. Each player has twenty pieces and the decision as to who plays Black is decided as for conventional draughts. The board is placed between the players so that each has a white square in the right hand corner nearest him. The pieces are set up as shown in Figure 6. Black has the first move.

All play is confined to the Black squares and the pieces move diagonally forward. Any piece can capture either forward or backward provided there is a vacant square beyond the piece being taken. A piece is crowned when it reaches the opponents back rank and it then becomes a Queen. As in conventional Draughts crowning is a matter of placing another piece on top of the man who then remains on the square until moved again. If a piece reaches the back rank but can still capture, it must do so and is not crowned. It is compulsory to capture the maximum pieces available. A Queen in Polish Draughts has the same powers as a King in Spanish Draughts. She is entitled to the long move, and can advance or retreat along a diagonal of squares provided they are unoccupied. She captures by hopping over an enemy piece and can either remain on the vacant square immediately beyond that piece or she can continue along other vacant squares.

Maximum capture being compulsory you would have to take an enemy Queen rather than a piece if both were available. When a Queen captures a number of pieces in one move these are left on the board until the move is completed. In this sort of move you cannot hop over the same piece twice. You may, however jump empty squares more than once in the same move. This is a refreshingly different game and one that is well worth trying.

Backgammon

Backgammon is a game in which men are moved round a board according to the throw of dice. Games with this principle have been known for at least 5,000 years, the earliest recorded example being discovered in a royal cemetery of the Sumerian civilisation in Mesopotamia.

Backgammon in most of its modern features has been played at least since the fifteenth century, and there are several backgammon boards in existence that date back to the sixteenth century. The name 'backgammon' itself dates back to 1645, though the games of 'tric-trac' (still the name used in France) and 'tables' were essentially what we know as backgammon.

However there is one very important feature of modern backgammon that was invented as recently as the 1920s, and that is the idea of *doubling*. This is a method by which the stakes can be raised during the course of the game, and it is the biggest single factor in making backgammon the action-packed game it is.

The Rules

Backgammon is a board game played between two players. Figure 1 shows the board set up in the starting position. Each player has fifteen men (variously referred to as pieces, chequers, stones) and the object of the game is to move the pieces round the board and then off the board. The player who first achieves this object is the winner.

Each player has two dice, and he makes his moves according to his dice throws.

The Board

The twenty-four elongated triangles shown in Figure 1 are referred to as 'points'. They correspond to the squares in other board games like chess or snakes and ladders. They are normally painted alternate colours to make it easier to count out the moves. There is no other significance in the different colours.

The board is divided into two halves by a central partition referred to as the 'bar'. In the configuration shown in Figure 1 the points on the right hand side of the bar make up the 'home board' and those on the left of the bar are the 'outer board'. White's home and outer boards are at the bottom of the diagram, while Black's are at the top.

The points have been numbered 1 to 12 starting from the right hand end of the board. This is to facilitate the description of the

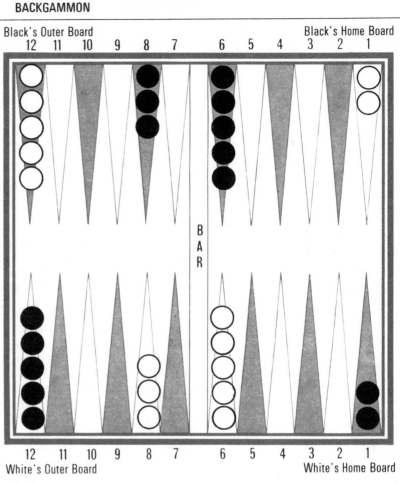

Black's Outer Board   Black's Home Board

12 11 10 9 8 7 6 5 4 3 2 1

B
A
R

12 11 10 9 8 7 6 5 4 3 2 1

White's Outer Board   White's Home Board

Fig. 1

moves; actual backgammon boards are not numbered. Points 1 to 6 are the 'home board' points, and 7 to 12 the 'outer board' points.

The Starting Position

At the beginning of a game each player sets up his men as shown in Figure 1. Notice that each player starts with five men inside his home board, on his 'six point' – i.e. on the sixth point counting from the right hand end. Each player has three men in his own outer board, on the eight point; and five men in his opponent's outer board, on the opponent's twelve point. Finally each player starts with two men in his opponent's home board, on his opponent's one point.

The player playing White sits at the bottom of the board, and Black at the top. Notice that White's home board is on his right, while Black's is on his left. The board can be set up in the mirror image position, such that White's home board is on his left. It makes no difference to the play; throughout this article we will use the set-up of Figure 1. Numbers thrown by the dice are printed in red.

The Play

Each player moves his men round the board towards his home

board. White moves anti-clockwise and Black clockwise. Thus the two sides are moving in opposite directions past each other. When a player has brought all his men into his home board (i.e. all his men are distributed somewhere on the points 1 to 6) he can then start to remove them from the board. The first player to remove all his men is the winner.

The players move alternately, and their moves are controlled by dice. Each player has two dice, and preferably a cup for shaking them, and when it is his turn to play he rolls the dice into the half-board on his right. Thus White rolls on the home board side of the bar, and Black on the outer board side. For a throw to be legal dice must come to rest flat on the surface of the board on the side on which they were thrown. If a die finally comes to rest on top of a man, or tilted against the side of the board, it is said to be 'cocked', and *both* dice must be thrown again.

For the first roll of the game, and the first roll only, each player throws one die. The player who rolls the higher number makes the first move, and takes as his roll the numbers shown on the two dice.

Moving the Pieces

When a player has thrown his dice, he must move his men according to the numbers showing on the dice. He considers each number separately: for example, if he rolls a 3−2 he must make a move of 3 and a move of 2, not a move of 5. If a player throws a double (i.e. 1−1, 2−2, 6−6 etc.) he must move the number four times.

There are three types of move: moving round the board, re-entering from the bar, and removing the men at the end of the game.

Moving round the board. Let us assume that the game is about to start. White throws a 5 and Black a 2, so as White has thrown the higher die he has the first move, and takes as his opening roll a 5−2. He must move one of his men five spaces, and one two spaces. He is allowed to move the same man, or he can move two different men. For example, two possible moves that White could play for his five would be to move from Black twelve point five spaces to his own eight point; or he could play a man from White eight to White three. (In future we will refer to Black's twelve point as 'B12' and so on.) For the two White could move any of his men. Figure 2 indicates the possible plays.

There are two restrictions on the movement of men round the board. The first is they cannot be moved past the one point – it is as

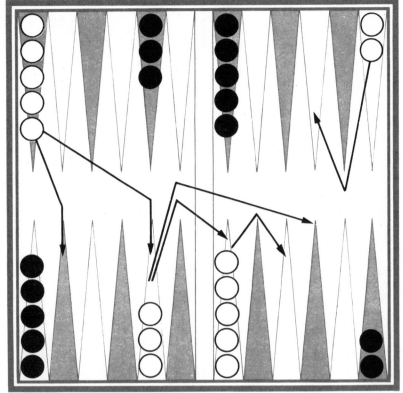

Fig. 2

if the pieces moved on a track which starts at the opponent's one point and ends at the player's own one point. For example, the men on W6 cannot be moved six spaces, as that would entail moving past W1.

The second restriction is that a man cannot be moved to a point occupied by two or more of the opponent's men. So for our example opening roll of 5−2 White could not move from B1 to B6 for the five, as B6 is already held by Black. Similarly if White played from B1 to B3 for the two, he could not then move on from B3 to B8, as B8 is also held by Black in the starting position. So in the starting position White can move from B1 with any number except a five; from B12 with any number except a one (ones being blocked by Black's men on W12); from W8 with any number; and from W6 with any number except a five or a six (fives are blocked by Black's men on W1, and a six would take the man past W1).

Re-entering moves. To introduce the second type of move, let us assume that White played his opening 5−2 by moving one man from B12 to W8, and one from B12 to W11. This leaves the situation shown in Figure 3. The isolated man at W11 is referred as a *blot*.

It is now Black's turn, and we will assume that he rolls a 6−4. One of the ways he can play the roll is to move from W1 to W5, and then onwards to W11. Remember if W11 had been occupied by two or more White men, Black would not have been able to move to that point. However, in this instance there is only one White man at W11, and in this case Black *is* allowed to move there. Furthermore, when the Black man lands on top of him the White blot is said

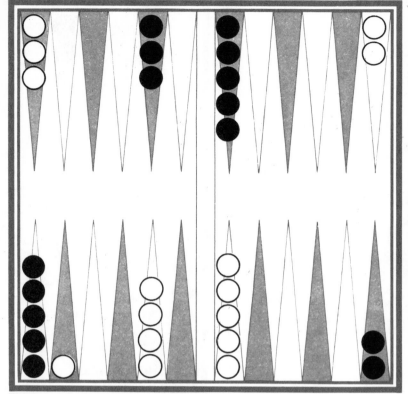

Fig. 3

to be hit. The White man is removed from the board, and has to be brought back into play at White's next turn. While the White man is in this limbo condition he is put on the bar.

When a player has a man on the bar he must bring it back into play at the first available opportunity. Until he does so he is not allowed to make any other moves. The man must be re-entered on one of the six points in the opponent's home board, as always according to the numbers shown on the dice. For example, if White has a man on the bar and he rolls a 6−2 he must re-enter the man either on B6 or on B2. As for the first type of move, he is not allowed to re-enter the man on a point held by his opponent. So if it happened that Black held B6 (as he does in the starting position) White would be forced to re-enter his man on B2. And if Black held both B6 and B2, White would not be able to re-enter at all with his 6−2, and he would lose his turn.

You will see that the more points a player manages to make in his home board the more difficult it will be for a man on the bar to re-enter. For this reason good players try to make as many home board points as possible (see below).

Bearing off. When a player has brought his men round the board and into his home, such that all fifteen of them are distributed somewhere on his own one to six point, he can start to remove them from the board. This process is called *bearing off*. As with the other types of move it is controlled by the dice, and in some respects it is the reverse process to re-entering. For example, if during the bearing off a player rolls 3−1 he is allowed to remove a man from his three point and a man from his one point, provided he has men on those points. Instead of removing a man from a given point he would also be allowed to move a man from a higher-numbered point.

An additional rule is required to cover the situation in which a player rolls a number corresponding to a vacant point. For example, a player may roll a three when he has no man on his three-point. Then if he has men on higher points he must move one of those; but if he has no men on higher numbered points he must bear off a man from the lower occupied point. This process is described more fully in the example game.

The Doubling Cube

The single feature that makes backgammon such an exciting game is the way in which the stakes can be periodically doubled during the game. The normal and most convenient way of recording the stake is with a *doubling cube*. This cube is usually rather larger than the dice, and on its six faces it has inscribed the numbers 2, 4, 8, 16, 32 and 64. At the beginning of the game the stake is one unit; as there is no 1 on the doubling cube this is signified by placing the cube half-way between the players with the 64 face uppermost.

As the game goes on, the player whose turn it is to roll may offer his opponent a 'double'. This means that the player who is doubled has the option of continuing the game at double the current stake, or of stopping the game and paying out his opponent at the current stake. If the player who is doubled accepts, the cube is turned to show twice the previous stake (e.g. to 2 for the first double of the game) and is placed on the doubled player's side of the table. The next double can only come from the player who accepted the last double.

As an example, after three rolls of a game White may decide to double. If Black accepts, the cube is turned to 2 and placed on his side of the table. The next double can only come from Black. Then if Black redoubles later in the game and White accepts, the cube is turned to 4 and placed on White's side of the table. The double to 8 can only come from White.

Scoring

In a normal game the player who first bears off all his men wins the number of points shown on the doubling cube. So if the stake was £1 a point and the cube was at 8, the winner would get £8.

A second type of win is a *gammon*. If one player removes all his men before his opponent removes any, the winning player is said to have gammoned his opponent, and he collects twice the number of points shown on the doubling cube.

A third degree of win is the *backgammon*. White would win a backgammon if Black had not removed any men and in addition still had Black men in White's home board when the last White man had been removed. In such a case Black would have to pay three times the number of points shown on the cube. In the U.K. it is quite common not to play backgammons—a player can never lose more than twice the doubling cube. Whether backgammons are played is a matter of agreement between the players.

In a normal three or four hour session between good players the margin at the end would be unlikely to be more than thirty points; between bad players it could be higher, as there tends to be more doubling cube activity in a weaker game.

An Example Game

For the opening roll, White throws a 6 and Black a 5, so as his first roll White gets a 6–5. He uses it to move a back man via Black's seven point to Black's twelve point. This will be written in shorthand:

1W. 6–5. B1–B7–B12.

It is now Black's turn, and he rolls a 3–1. He uses it to make his five point by moving a man from Black eight and one from Black six:

1B. 3–1. B8–B5, B6–B5.

The five point is the most important point to make in the early game.

2W. 6–3. B1–B7–B10.

White runs out with his other back man.

2B. 4–3. W12–B9, W12–B10 (hit).

Black hits the White blot at B9, and brings down another man into his outer board. This leaves the position shown in Figure 4.

White now has a man on the bar, and his first duty is to bring it back into play.

3W. 5–2. Bar–B2, B12–W8.

White has to re-enter on B2, and moves down from B12 with the five. Notice that if White had rolled 6–6, 6–5 or 5–5 he would not have been able to re-enter. He would then have lost his whole turn.

3B. 6–2. B10–B4, B6–B4.

Black makes another point in his home board.

4W. 5–5. B2–B7–B12, 2(W8–W3)

White is lucky in that he is able to escape with his back man to B12,

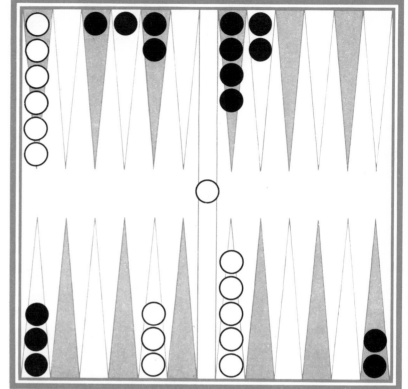

Fig. 4

and to make a point in his own home board. Remember that if you roll a double you move the number *four* times.

4B. 6–6. 2(W1–W7), W12–B7, B9–B3.

Black also gets a double, and uses it to bring his back men out to White's seven point (or *bar point*) and to move two other men towards home.

5W. 5–1. B12–W8, W6–W5.

White brings one man down and starts his five point. Now that both sides have rescued their back men they will try to avoid leaving blots where their opponent could hit them. Since the blot on W5 is behind Black's rear-most men it is safe.

5B. 4–4. 2(W7–W11–B10)

Black manages to escape from White's bar point.

6W. 6–5. B12–W7, B12–W8.

6B. 5–4. W12–B8, W12–B9.

7W. 3–3. 2(W8–W5), 2(B12–W10).

This leaves the position shown in Figure 5. In the last three moves both players are simply moving round the board and getting their men in as fast as possible. To accelerate this rather boring phase of the game we will give both sides double sixes:

7B. 6–6. 2(B10–B4), B9–B3, B8–B2.

8W. 6–6. 2(W10–W4), B12–W7, W8–W2.

8B. 5–5. 2(B8–B3), B7–B2, B5–off.

Black brings his last three men into his home board. Having done that, he still has one five to play, and he bears off a man from his five point.

9W. 6–2. W7–W1, W8–W6.

Fig. 5

Fig. 6

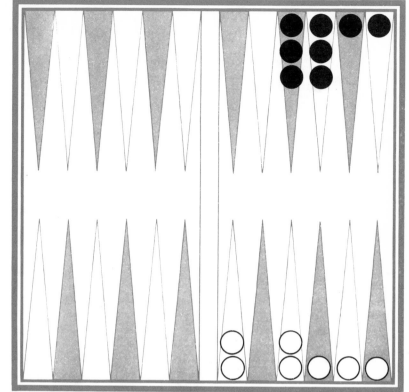

Fig. 7

This leaves the position shown in Figure 6.

Up to this stage neither side has had much of an advantage. But Black's 5-5 makes him a distinct favourite; it is now his turn to roll, but before he does so he *doubles*. White has the option of either conceding one point and getting on with the next game, or of playing on with the stake now at two points. White choses to accept, whereupon he takes the doubling cube over to his side of the table and turns it to 2.

9B. 5-1. B5-off, B6-B5.

Black takes a man off from the five point; since he has no man on the one point he must move a man from a higher point for the one. He chooses to move from the six point.

10W. 2-1. W7-W5, W1-off.

A miserable roll for White. He brings in his remaining man to his five point and takes a man off the one point.

10B. 5-3. B5-off, B3-off.

11W 6-3. W6-off, W3-off.

11B. 5-2. B6-B1, B2-off.

Black has no man on the five, so as he has a man on a higher point (i.e. the six point) he must move from there.

12W. 6-5. W6-off, W5-off.

12B. 6-4. B6-off, B4-off.

13W. 5-5. 3(W5-off), W6-W1.

White takes off his three men on the five point, and then has to move from the six point with the five. This leaves the position shown in Figure 7.

13B. 5-4. 2(B4-off).

Now a new rule comes into operation. Black has no man on his five point, but since he also has no man on a higher point he must bear off a man from the next lower occupied point – in this position, his four point.

14W. 5–5. 2(W6–W1), 2(W4–off).

For his first pair of 5 s White has to move to his one point; but for the second pair, as he now has no more men on his six point he is allowed to take two men off his four point.

14B. 5–4. B4–off, B3–off.

15W. 6–2. W3–off, W2–off.

15B. 2–1. B2–off, B1–off.

This leaves the following position: White, three men on W1. Black, two men on B3. It is White's turn to roll, but as he is now favourite, before he rolls he doubles. Black accepts, so the doubling cube goes back to Black's side of the table at 4.

16W. 2–1. 2(W1–off).

White would have won the game outright if he had rolled a double at throw 16. He is still slightly favoured, as Black will not get off if he rolls a one or a two (apart from double 2).

16B. 6–1. B3–off, B3–B2.

Black fails to get both men off. Since White is bound to get his man off now, White wins and receives four points (the number showing on the doubling cube).

This was rather a tedious game as there was only one hit in the whole game (Black's move 2), and both sides managed to get their back men out easily.

More exciting games occur when there is more blot hitting and when one side or the other manages to block in their opponent's back men.

The Elements of Good Play

The object of the game is for a player to remove all his pieces before his opponent. There are two broad ways in which the player can approach this objective: he can do so directly, by simply running his men round the board at every opportunity while taking little notice of what his opponent is doing; or he can take a more indirect line, and play to slow down his opponent by forming barriers and hitting blots wherever possible. If a player follows either of these techniques exclusively, he will probably lose. In most games a good player will use a combination of these tactics, adapting his game to suit the situation.

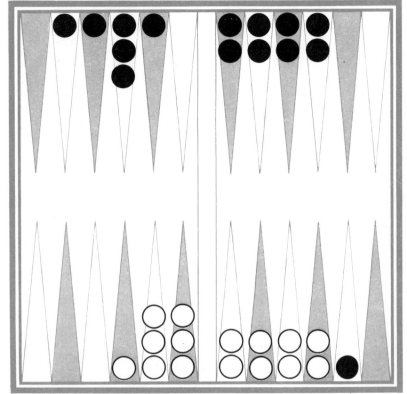

Fig. 8

Blocks and primes. The most powerful blockade against an opponent is six points in a row. Look at Figure 8. The Black man on W2 cannot move as all the points between one and six spaces away from him are held by White. (Remember, if Black throws say a 6 – 4, he cannot play a ten but must move a separate six and four.) White's succession of points running from W8 down to W3 is called a *prime*.

The lesson to be learnt from this is that it is a good thing to build up groups of consecutive points. In the starting position each player already holds two good points for blocking (his eight and six points), and much early play revolves round building up a block starting with this framework.

Home board points. Look at Figure 9. It is Black's turn and he has a man on the bar. He needs to get specifically a 1 to re-enter his man, odds of about five to two against. But change the position by moving the two men on W2 back to W7 and those on W3 to W8, and now Black only needs a 1, 2 or 3 to re-enter, odds of three to one on. The message here is that the more home board points a player has, the more serious it is for his opponent to be hit. So good players build up their home board whenever they can.

Blots. Clearly when the opponent has a strong home board a player will try to avoid leaving blots where they can be hit. But it is a mistake to play too cautiously, particularly in the early part of the game, and it is often good play in the first few moves to leave blots in order to gain greater flexibility. In a high quality game most of the risks are taken early on.

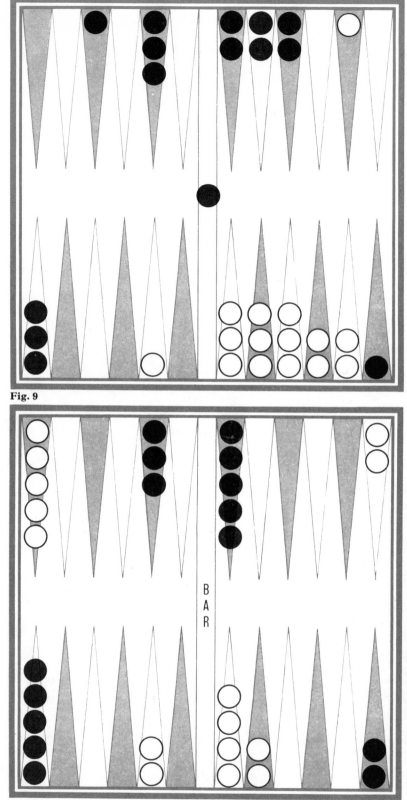

Fig. 9

Fig. 10

The Opening Moves

This general preamble brings us on to the best way of playing the early rolls. This is quite an instructive topic, as many of the ideas are useful for the later parts of the game.

The opening rolls fall into three principal categories: (i) point-making rolls, which are ones that enable the player to make a useful point immediately; (ii) extrication rolls, which are used to start the back men on the road to freedom; (iii) building rolls, which are used to set up the men to make a useful point at the player's second turn. We will consider them all from White's point of view.

Point-making rolls. 3–1, 6–1, 4–2, 5–3.

With all these rolls it is best to make a point down in the vital area of the board between W8 and W3.

3–1. W8–W5, W6–W5. Figure 10 shows the play of this most desirable opening roll. The five point is the most important point, as it adds to the block already started by W8 and W6, and on top of this is a home board point.

6–1. B12–W7, W8–W7. This roll enables White to make his seven point, or *bar point*. The bar point is the best purely blocking point, as it fills in the gap between the points already held; and as it is six spaces away from Black's back men it blocks 6–6 and 6–5, the best escaping rolls.

4–2. W8–W4, W6–W4. Like the five-point, the four point pulls weight in two ways, as a blocker and as a homeboard point.

5–3. W8–W3, W6–W3. Not such a good point, as it is too far forward to have much blocking effect. However it improves in strength if White subsequently makes his five or four point.

Running rolls. 6–5, 6–4, 6–3.

All are played by running out a back man from B1. With a 6–5 the man gets to safety at B12, with the other two White has to leave a blot either at B11 or B10.

Building rolls. 6–2, 5–1, 4–1, 2–1; 5–4, 5–2, 4–3, 3–2.

None of these rolls does anything appetising immediately; they are used to prepare the ground for making a point at the next turn.

6–2, 5–1, 4–1, 2–1. All these rolls are used to put a blot onto the five point, the idea being that if it is not hit by Black at his first turn White may be able to cover it at his second turn.

6–2: B12–W11–W5.

5–1 : B12–W8, W6–W5.
4–1 : B12–W9, W6–W5.
2–1 : B12–W11, W6–W5.
5–4, 5–2, 4–3, 3–2. All these rolls are played by moving two men from B12 down into White's outer board. The idea is that if the blot or blots so exposed survive, White will be well placed to make a good point at his next turn.

The play of doubles. The rules do not allow the first player to get doubles. If the second player gets a double as his first roll, the best way to play them is as follows (again from White's point of view).
6–6. 2(B1–B7), 2(B12–W7). White makes both bar points. A good roll.
5–5. 2(B12–W8–W3). White makes his three point from White's twelve point. But if Black had split his back men at his first turn, then it is usually better to play 2(W8–W3), 2(W6–W1) if by so doing White can put a Black man onto the bar.
4–4. 2(B1–B5), 2(B12–W9). White makes Black's five point, a powerful point for defensive operations; and brings down two men into his own blockade.
3–3. 2(W8–W5), 2(W6–W3). White makes two good home board points.
2–2. 2(B12–W11), 2(W6–W4). White brings down two builders, makes a home board point.
1–1. 2(W8–W7), 2(W6–W5). An extremely fine roll, as it enables White to make his bar and five points immediately.

Another consideration in the first few rolls is that it may be possible to hit an opponent's blot. It is usually correct to do so anywhere outside the player's own home board.

Otherwise the players concentrate on the twin themes of extricating their own back men while attempting to trap the opponent's back men.

Other Forms of the Game

Chouette. Though normally backgammon is played between two people, it is possible for more people to play in one game. In such a case one player (the 'man in the box') plays by himself against the others. One of the other players is called the 'captain'. If the captain's side wins a game, the captain becomes the man in the box, the next person in the queue becomes the captain, and the previous man in the box goes to the bottom of the queue. If the man in the box wins, he stays in the box and the captaincy is taken over by the next in line. The players can debate amongst themselves the best way to play a particular roll, or whether or not to double, but the captain has the deciding vote. While the players cannot double the box individually, they may accept or refuse the box's doubles individually.

Tournaments. Backgammon tournaments are becoming increasingly popular. The usual form is to play a knock-out. The winner of each match in the various rounds of the knock-out is the first player to reach a given number of points. The winners of each match are paired against each other in the successive rounds, until finally there is only one unbeaten player.

Go

Most Go players believe that theirs is the most interesting and profound of all board games. Go has been played for thousands of years in the Far East, but it is only in the last decade or two that it has achieved international status, with national Go organisations in most Western countries. The basic rules are simple and elegant, yet the number of possible developments is so astronomically large that the game can never become stereotyped or predictable.

The Equipment
A standard size Go board is ruled with 19×19 horizontal and vertical lines (Figure 1). Play takes place on the 361 points of intersection of these lines, and not on the squares. A theoretically limitless supply of black and white men known as 'stones' are used for

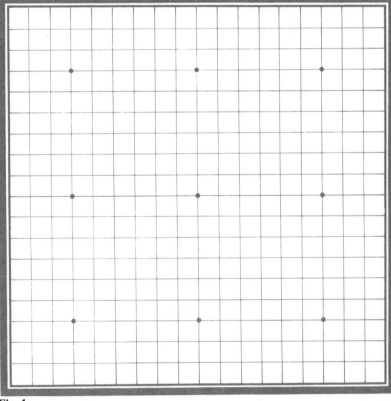

Fig. 1

play. Traditional Japanese stones are bi-convex in shape, and beautifully made from slate and shell. A full set comprises 181 black and 180 white stones. Western players are usually less particular about their equipment, and often improvise sets from counters, buttons, drawing pins, etc., and boards made of hardboard or card.

The Moves

Play starts with the board empty. Players move alternately, Black playing first. A move consists of placing a stone on any unoccupied intersection of the board, subject to two restrictions described below. Once played stones are not moved unless they are captured by the opponent's in which case they are removed from the board. Thus the board gradually fills up with stones during a game.

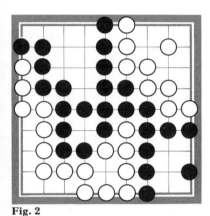

Fig. 2

The Object

The primary object of the game is to surround vacant space on the board, with a secondary object of capturing the opponent's stones. When the end of the game is reached each player scores one point for each unoccupied intersection on the board that he surrounds with his stones (usually referred to as his 'territory') plus one point for each enemy stone captured. The player with the higher total score wins. The margin of points is not regarded as important—a win by a single point carries the same credit as a win by 100.

Figure 2 shows the end of a game played on a 9×9 board. (Smaller boards such as this are often used by beginners or those who want just a quick game.) Black has surrounded nine vacant points near the upper edge, five near the lower right corner, and an odd one in the middle making 15 in all. White has eight in the upper right corner, six in the lower left corner, and one near the lower edge, also totalling 15. However, the game was not tied as Black captured one white stone during the game while White made no capture, so Black won by 16 points to 15.

It is important to note that it is the *vacant* points which count as territory, not the ones actually occupied by the stones, and that points along the edge and in the corner all count as territory.

Captures

Captures are made by closely surrounding enemy stones. A single stone in the middle of the board is said to have four 'liberties', i.e. the four horizontally and vertically adjacent points marked with crosses in Figure 3*a*. If at any time the opponent can occupy all four of these points with his stones the original stone is captured. Figure 3*b* shows the black stone with only one liberty left, and 3*c* shows the position after White occupies the last liberty and removes the stone. Stones removed like this are retained as 'prisoners' by the player who makes the capture, to add to his score at the end of the game.

Figure 4*a* shows how a stone on the edge of the board has only three liberties, and one in the corner has only two. Figure 4*b* shows the positions after White has occupied the liberties of these stones and captured them.

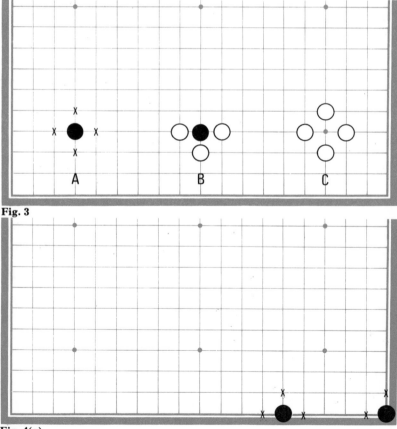

Fig. 3

Fig. 4(a)

Armies

If a player plays a stone on a liberty of one of his own stones already on the board, the two form a connected unit called an army (see Figure 5a). Armies can be extended in size without limit by connection via liberties. Further examples of armies are given in Figures 5b, c and d. It is important to realise that diagonally adjacent stones are not connected. The two white armies in Figure 6 would require another stone at 'x' or 'y' to connect them into a single unit.

Fig. 4(b)

Fig. 5

The Capture of Armies

Armies have more liberties than single stones, but the principle involved in capturing them is similar. When the last remaining liberty is occupied by an enemy stone the whole army is removed at once – it cannot be captured piecemeal. Figure 7 shows the armies in Figure 5 with all their liberties bar one (marked with 'x') occupied by enemy stones, i.e. subject to capture on the next move. (Go players often use the Japanese term 'atari' to describe this situation – chess players will recognise the analogy with 'en prise'.) If the opponent is able to occupy this last liberty each army is captured and immediately removed from the board, leading to the positions shown in Figure 8. Note that armies such as 5*d* with an internal space have to be surrounded internally as well as externally before they are captured.

It is worth mentioning one of the basic tactical principles of Go at this stage. Clearly the more liberties an army has the harder it is to capture. It is therefore usually good play to separate your opponent's stones into small units as much as possible, while keeping your own in positions where they may be easily linked together if necessary.

The Suicide Rule

As mentioned above, there are two prohibitive rules in Go. The first of these, the 'Suicide Rule', forbids a player to play so as to leave any of his own stones or armies with no liberty, i.e. in the sort of position where they would be captured if the opponent had brought it about. To put it another way, he must not capture his own stones.

Points 'a', 'b', and 'c' in Figure 9 are all examples of illegal moves for White. A play at 'a' would leave that stone with no liberty; a play at 'b' would leave a three-stone army with no liberty; and a play at 'c' would unite the white stones into a five-stone army with no liberty. However, point 'd' represents a different case, as by

Fig. 6

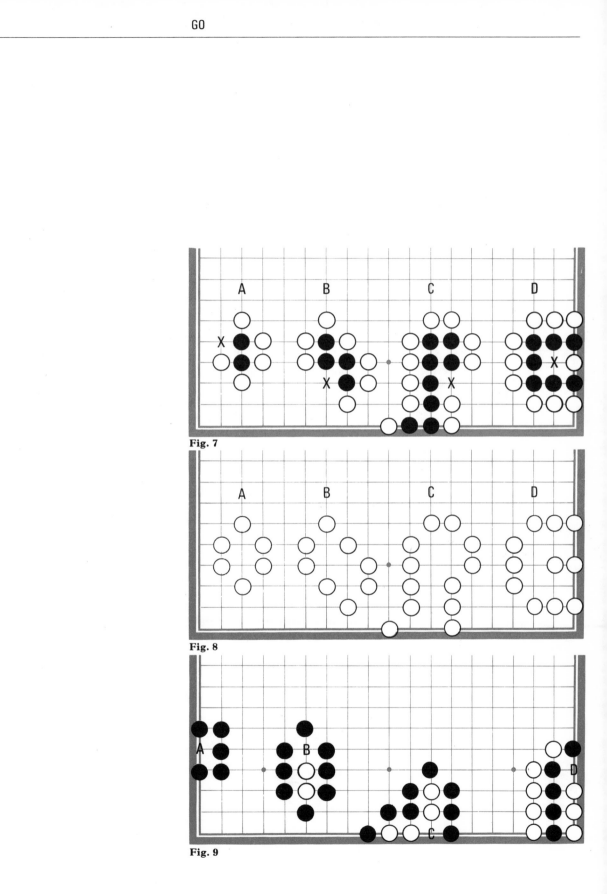

Fig. 7

Fig. 8

Fig. 9

Fig. 10

playing there White captures some black stones and creates some new liberties for his army. In cases like this the move is permitted. Figure 10 shows the position resulting from this move and the capture of four black stones.

The Ko Rule

The second prohibitive rule is designed to prevent repetition of the same position. Its name derives from the Japanese word 'Ko', which signifies 'eternity'. Figure 11a shows when it applies. White may capture at 'x' if he wishes, leading to the position in Figure 11b. The move is not suicide, as he has created a new liberty for his stone at 'y'. If Black were now to recapture at 'y', this move would lead straight back to the position in Figure 11a. However, the Ko rule forbids him to make this recapture immediately; he must make at least one move elsewhere on the board first. This will give White the chance to end the Ko situation if he wishes by playing at 'y' himself on his next move, leading to Figure 11c. If White chooses to play elsewhere on the board, Black will be at liberty to recapture at 'y' whenever he wishes. Locally this will repeat the position, but over the board as a whole the position will have been altered by the addition of at least one stone of each colour.

Fig. 11

Fig. 12

Figures 12*a* and *b* show how Ko positions can occur on the edge of the board or in the corner.

The rule states further that if, despite the prohibition, the same position should occur twice in a game, the game is drawn. This can only occur in certain specialised positions which will occur very rarely.

The End of the Game

The theoretical formula for ending the game is that either player may at any time pass his turn to play, and when both players pass in succession the game ends. If one player wishes to continue making moves while the other passes, the passing player should surrender one stone from his supply to his opponent as a prisoner for each move passed.

In practice, however, experienced players nearly always end their games by mutual agreement, when both can see that further moves cannot benefit either of them. This point is reached when all the available territory has been securely surrounded either by black or by white stones, and when there is no doubt in either player's mind whether or not a particular stone or army can be captured.

If one player does pass, while his opponent continues to move, one of the players is making a mistake. If the player who is still making moves is not increasing his score thereby he is wasting his time; if he *is* increasing his score then his opponent should not be passing but making suitable counter-moves.

End-of-game Customs

There are certain customs associated with the end of the game which, while not embodied in the rules, are usually observed by Go players.

When the game is nearing its end there are usually a number of 'neutral points'—a sort of no man's land between opposing armies which cannot be surrounded by either player and where it is of no significance who plays. When there are no better moves available than these neutral points they are usually filled in very rapidly by the players without taking strict turns. Figure 13 shows the game in Figure 2 at the stage just before the filling in of neutral points— the points marked 'x' were filled in in the manner described.

After filling in neutral points it is customary for each player to allow his opponent to remove from the board as captives any stones which, although still on the board, he acknowledges to be in a hopeless position where they could not escape ultimate capture if the game were to continue further. These now count as prisoners along with other stones captured during play. Such stones are often referred to as 'virtually dead' while they remain on the board.

Territories are then rearranged into convenient rectangles for ease of counting. Prisoners are usually used to fill up the opponent's territory, as the margin of points will be the same whether they are added to their captor's territory or subtracted from the opponent's. Figure 14 shows the game in Figure 2 rearranged in this way, with the white captive used to fill up a point of White's territory.

An Actual Game

The game shown in Figure 15 was played by two players of intermediate strength. It has been chosen because the strategy is very simple and it is free from any gross blunders, although the moves chosen were not always the best. To understand it is best to play the moves through in order on a board.

Moves 1–5. These moves take advantage of the fact that territory is easiest to acquire in the corners and along the edge.

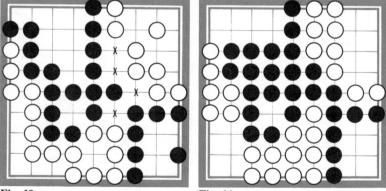

Fig. 13   Fig. 14

White 6. This tries to reduce the size of Black's potential territory sketched out with 1, 3, and 5.

7 and 8. Black counterattacks and White strengthens his own framework along the lower edge.

9–15. Now Black makes a series of threats to enter the potential white territory. White consolidates, but after his 15 White 6 is cut off from the main group. Both players know that this stone cannot now avoid ultimate capture, so both leave it alone. White does not wish to waste more stones in a hopeless rescue attempt, and there is no hurry for Black to effect the capture.

16 and 17. White 6 still has an effect on the game. White 16 threatened a further play at the point Black occupied with his move 17, which would have left the black stones 9, 11, 13, and 15 with no means of escaping capture, so Black had to protect himself.

18–21. White expands his territory and reduces Black's, while Black prevents any further incursion and prepares a counter-offensive.

22–24. White carries out a similar operation on the other side of the board.

25. A good move – the intention behind his 21. White would like to cut this stone off from Black 21 by playing at the point occupied by 27, but Figure 16 shows the disaster that would ensue for White. So he has to play defensively at 26 and 28, after which Black will be immediately captured if he plays at 'x'.

Figure 16: this Black 27 cuts off five white stones and places them in 'atari'. They are then virtually dead – even if the sequence continues up to Black 31 White cannot escape as Black has the altern-

Fig. 15   Fig. 16

Fig. 17

atives of capturing at '25' or at 'x' if White connects at '25' himself.

Moves 29–30 (Figure 15). These moves fill the last remaining gaps in the defensive chains around the players' territories. There were no neutral points in this game. White now allowed Black to remove the virtually dead stone White 6 as a captive. The territories were rearranged as in Figure 17, the white captive being used to occupy a point of white territory. Black won by five points.

Many games of Go are more complex than this one, with the territories more fragmented, and perhaps more stones being captured, but one does sometimes find this simple style of play in master games.

Secure Territory

Beginners often find it hard to know when a certain area can be regarded as secure territory, or whether additional stones are needed to secure it. A useful definition of secure territory is as follows: a player can regard any area as securely surrounded if he is sure of being able to capture any enemy stone that should be played within it. Figure 18a shows a secure Black area of six points—no further black stones are needed here. If White tries to invade as in Figure 18b, Black can capture White's stones. After Black 4 White cannot play at either 'x' or 'y' because of the suicide rule, and as Black could take off the white stones at any time with a play at 'x' they are virtually dead.

Figure 19a shows territory that is not yet quite secure—Black can press back White's frontiers somewhat as shown in Figure 19b,

Fig. 18

reducing the territory by a couple of points. (I leave the reader to examine why White 6 is needed.)

Figure 20*a* shows a worse form of insecurity. At first sight there appear to be no gaps in White's border, but when Black plays at 1 in Figure 20*b* three white stones are in 'atari' and have no means to avoid capture. (If White plays on the point occupied by Black 5 he loses four stones instead of three.) So the best White can do now is to let these stones go, and save what territory he can with his 2 and 4. Black 5 captures the three stones. Of course White needed a play at 'x' in Figure 20*a* to secure all the territory.

Secure territory is an area where neither player should play stones.

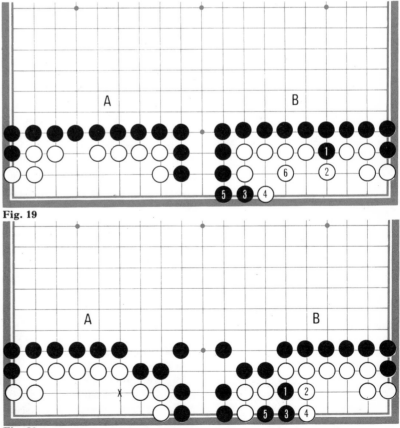

Fig. 19

Fig. 20

If a player puts stones within his own secure territory, he reduces his score by one point for each stone he plays there (remember, it is only the *vacant* points that count). If he puts them within his opponent's secure territory, then by the above definition they become virtually dead as soon as played. Even if he forces the opponent to make defensive moves within his territory, thereby filling in his own points, he is still supplying him with an extra prisoner for each defensive move he forces him to make, leaving the final score unchanged. (See Figure 18 for an example of this process.)

A Common Misconception

Beginners sometimes imagine that by refusing to surrender virtually dead stones at the end of the game, and insisting on the opponent's occupying all their liberties before removing them, he can be forced to fill in extra points within his own territory. All the opponent would need to do in such a case would be to wait until the neutral points were all filled and then proceed with filling in the liberties of the virtually dead stones. What is the first player to do meanwhile? If he passes, he will have to surrender a prisoner to his opponent each move: if he plays, he must either play within his own territory or his opponent's, in each case losing one point each play. The result must always be to leave the final score unchanged.

If you examine the final positions shown in Figures 2 and 15 you can confirm that neither player can play again anywhere without incurring a loss of one point. This stage is always the end of the game.

Basic Capturing Techniques

Certain methods of capturing stones are so common that every Go player needs to be aware of them.

When a single stone is in 'atari' in the middle of the board (see Figure 21a), it can at least temporarily avoid capture by a play on its own last liberty (i.e. at 'x'). But when this situation occurs on the second line, facing the edge (Figure 21b), adding further stones does no good at all, as the sequence in Figure 21c shows. The stone was virtually dead to start with, and White has only increased his loss in trying to save it.

Figure 22a shows another common position. After Black plays at 'x' there is no way to save the white stone, as Figure 22b illustrates.

Figure 23a shows an interesting capture called the 'ladder attack'. If Black is foolish enough to try to save his single stone with a play

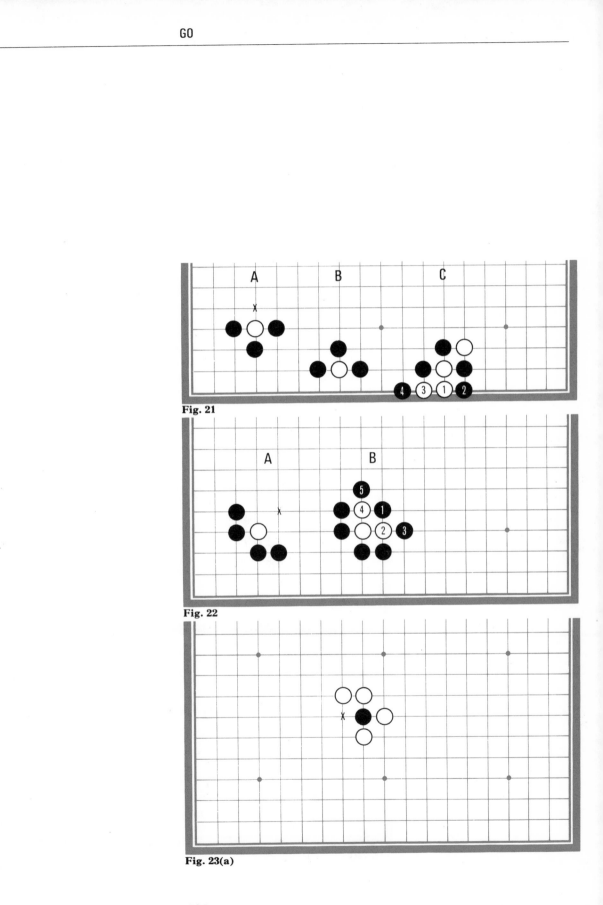

Fig. 21

Fig. 22

Fig. 23(a)

at 'x', and then persists in this policy, Figure 23*b* shows how with each move White can keep the growing black army in 'atari', until the sequence reaches the board's edge. White 24 then captures the 13-stone army, and such a loss in an actual game would usually call for Black's immediate resignation.

In Figure 23*c* there is a black stone 'x' in the path of the ladder attack. In this case Black can rescue his attacked stone, and it is White that would be wrong to persist with the attack – Figure 23*d* shows what will happen. After Black 15 he can no longer place Black in 'atari', and his own stones are now very vulnerable to capture with moves such as 'y' and 'z' which place two stones in 'atari' at once.

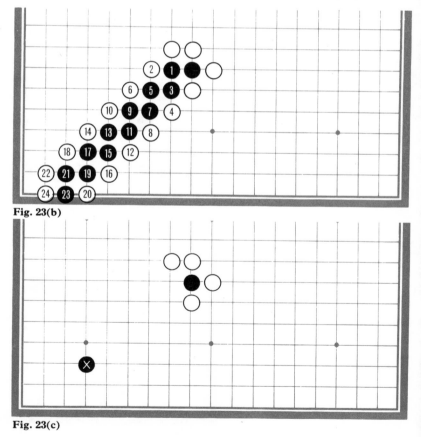

Fig. 23(b)

Fig. 23(c)

A white stone in the path of the ladder can cause it to end before the edge of the board (see Figure 23e). As misjudged ladder attacks cause such immense losses, understanding them is an important part of a Go player's tactical skill.

Invulnerable Armies

Figure 18b shows a particular case of a general rule about armies that are permanently safe from capture. We have seen from Figure 5d that an army with an internal space has to be surrounded internally as well as externally to be captured. Because of the suicide rule, the play which actually captures the army must be on one of the internal liberties. If White had tried to occupy all the internal

Fig. 23(d)

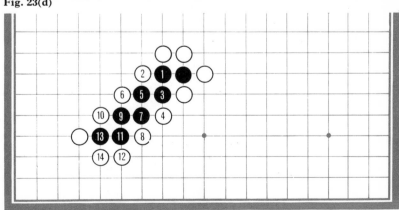

Fig. 23(e)

liberties first, as shown in Figure 24, he would have contravened the suicide rule with White 2. Such moves are only permitted when they have the effect of capturing the army, i.e. when all the external liberties are already filled.

If this army had a second, separate internal space, as shown in Figure 25a, then White has no way to effect the capture. He can fill up all the external liberties and all except one liberty within each space as shown in Figure 25b, but either of the moves 'x' and 'y' would now be suicide and illegal. He cannot play 'x' until he has played 'y' and he cannot play 'y' until he has played 'x'! Any army that has two *separate* spaces like this is permanently safe from capture. This tactical principle is of fundamental importance.

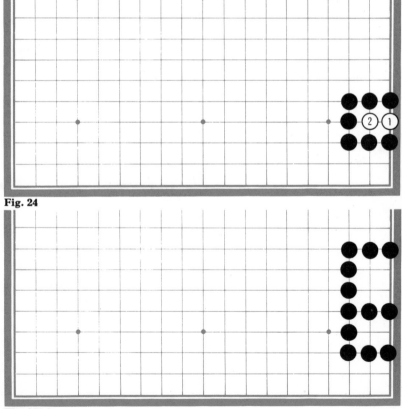

Fig. 24

Fig. 25(a)

Figure 26 shows further examples of invulnerable black armies. The two separate spaces are often referred to as the army's 'eyes'. Eyes can be of any size, and they may or may not contain some virtually dead enemy stones.

False Eyes

Figure 27*a* shows two examples of white armies with so-called 'false eyes'. At first they appear to be invulnerable, but some of the stones are not properly connected (remember that there are no connections along diagonals), and part of each group can be captured separately. Plays at 'x' and 'y' lead to the positions in Figure 27*b* where each army has clearly only one eye.

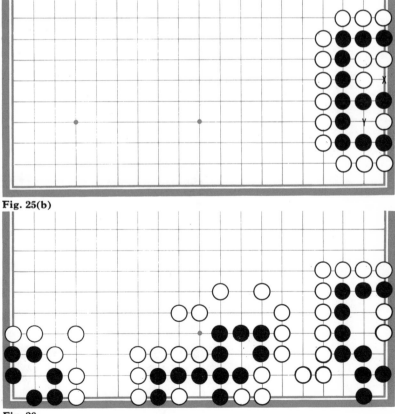

Fig. 25(b)

Fig. 26

When to Make Eyes

Any army with a large internal space can be fairly certain of being able to divide it in two in the event of an attack, and it is bad play to waste stones making two eyes before it becomes really necessary. All the armies in Figures 2 and 15 are invulnerable—indeed, it is one of the features of the end of the game that every army on the board must be invulnerable or virtually dead.

However, when the internal space is a small one, the ability to make two eyes becomes critical. Figure 28a shows an army with only three internal points, and Black must at once play 'x' to save his army. If he fails to do so White will play there himself as in

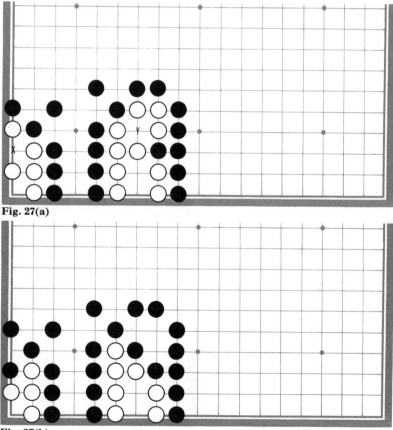

Fig. 27(a)

Fig. 27(b)

Figure 28*b*. Black may capture this one stone as in Figure 28*c*, but now White could play back at 'x' and capture the whole army. If the army had some external liberties White could not capture it at once, but it would still be virtually dead. Figure 29*a* shows another example. If Black plays at 'x' he has two eyes; if White plays there as in Figure 29*b* Black's attempt to divide his territory in two is doomed to failure.

Figure 30 shows a black army that does not require another stone for safety. It has only one eye at present, but if White plays at 'x' to try to prevent the formation of two eyes Black just plays at 'y', or vice versa.

Fig. 28

Fig. 29(a)

Fig. 29(b)

Fig. 30

Over-large Territories

Sometimes a territory is so large, or has so many weaknesses in its boundary, that there is room for the opponent to play inside it and make an invulnerable army. Figure 31a shows how White could invade a rather improbable Black territory. The sequence up to 5 is a standard corner opening, and the white stones will have no trouble in making two eyes in the corner should Black continue his attack. However, White can easily capture any black stones played in his territory in Figure 31b – there is not enough space for Black to make two eyes if White makes appropriate counter-moves.

Life and Death Struggles

Sometimes two armies are in such a position that neither can make two eyes without capturing the other. Such a position is described

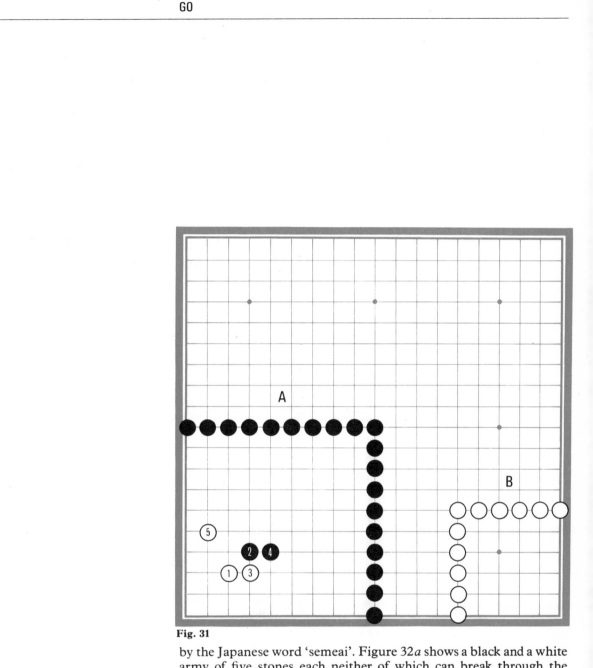

Fig. 31

by the Japanese word 'semeai'. Figure 32*a* shows a black and a white army of five stones each neither of which can break through the encircling enemy stones and neither of which can make even one eye without capturing the enemy army. In cases like this it is generally the army with the more liberties that wins the struggle. Here Black has four liberties and White only three, so even if White plays first Black wins the fight. With Black 6 in Figure 32*b* he captures the five white stones, thereby making his own safe.

In an actual game the players would not play out these moves as both would know that this fight must inevitably be won by Black, and therefore the white stones are already virtually dead.

When the fighting armies have some common liberties, there can be a rather surprising result. Figure 33*a* shows a position similar to

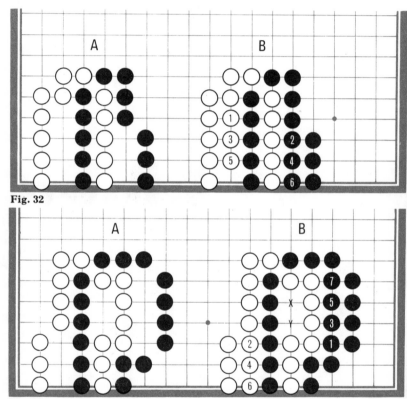

Fig. 32

Fig. 33

Figure 32*a*, and as White's stones have six liberties to the black stones' five, you might expect White to win the fight even when Black moves first. However, after Black 7 in Figure 33*b* White dare not play on one of the common liberties 'x' and 'y' as he would be immediately captured by his opponent's play on the other. When it is Black's turn, he dare not play on either of these points for the same reason. The position has reached a local stalemate (often known by the Japanese term 'seki') and the players will leave the stones as they are until the end of the game. The points 'x' and 'y' will be filled in then as neutral points, but neither army is regarded as captured.

In a case like this the moves might well be played out in an actual game. If Black fails to play 1, White will still play at 2 and then he will be one liberty ahead, and in time to capture the black army.

There are other types of seki, and I leave the reader to investigate for himself the relative numbers of external and common liberties required to produce a seki. It is also interesting to examine the effect on life-and-death struggles if one or both armies has a single eye.

One rule about the seki needs to be mentioned. If a seki is left on the board at the end of a game (as it usually would be) territory surrounded by the two armies is not counted towards the scores.

Ko-fights

In the Ko position already shown in Figures 11 and 12, usually only one stone is at stake. As it takes two plays to capture and keep one stone in such a position, it is not very profitable as a manoeuvre, and is usually left right until the end of the game.

However, sometimes more is at stake than one stone. Figure 34a shows a position where the fate of a whole army depends on the outcome of a Ko position. White would like to play at 'x', making one of the black army's eyes into a false one, so that the army would be virtually dead.

It is Black to play, however, and he will of course capture at 'x' leading to Figure 34b. If he could play at 'y' on his next move his army would have two good eyes and be invulnerable. White can only prevent this by recapturing at 'y', but the Ko rule prevents his doing this at once. What is White to do?

White must make some threat, elsewhere on the board, that is so compelling that Black must answer it at once, in preference to

Fig. 34(a)

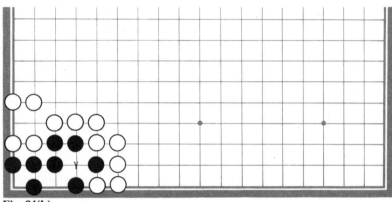

Fig. 34(b)

playing at 'y'. After Black has answered it, White will be allowed to recapture at 'y', leading back to Figure 34a. If Black does not want to give up the struggle, it will then be his turn to seek a 'Ko-threat'.

Let us see how this works in an actual game. Figure 35a shows a game nearing its end, but with the Ko position of Figure 34a still unresolved in the lower left corner. If Black can make two eyes for his army there he will have at least ten points (two in that corner, seven in the lower right area plus one prisoner), while White has only nine (four in the top left corner, four in the middle left area plus one prisoner already taken), and Black will win.

Black 1 captures at 'x' (see Figure 35b) and White plays at 2 as a Ko-threat. This move threatens to cut off and capture nine black

Fig. 35(a)   **Fig. 35(b)**

stones, giving White an easy victory. Therefore Black must answer at 3 in preference to playing 'y'. White 4 recaptured Black 1 in the Ko at 'y', and now Black needed a strong threat himself to stop White killing his army on the next move. Black 5 sufficed, as it threatened to capture two white stones, thereby making the necessary second eye and taking some white territory away. So White had to answer at 6, and with his 7 Black could now capture at '1' once again. White's next Ko threat 8 threatened thirteen black stones, so Black 9 was essential, and White could recapture at 'y' once again with his 10. Black 11 threatened to stop White from making two eyes for his corner army (cf. Figure 30) so White played 12 to make them. Black 13 recaptured at '1' in the Ko yet again, but then White had no further Ko-threat available. All he could do was to fill in a neutral point such as 14. So Black filled in the Ko at 'y' with his 15, made his second eye, and won the game by one point. If White had had one more threat available, he would have won the Ko-fight and the game, as Black had no more threats himself.

Ko-fights can be very complex if they occur in the middle game, when many threats are available. Plays such as Black 5 and 11 are quite pointless as ordinary moves as they gain nothing, but as stalling moves to enable the player to recapture in the Ko without infringing the Ko rule they are very valuable.

Efficiency
Since both players play the same number of stones, but one ends with more territory than the other, he must have used his stones more efficiently than his opponent, i.e. he has a better ratio of stones

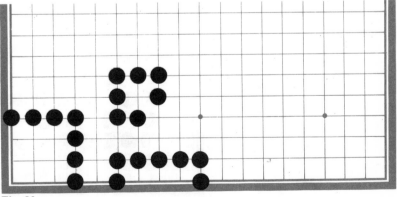

Fig. 36

played to points surrounded. This concept is of importance throughout the game, but never more so than in the opening.

If we take a seven stone army as an example, Figure 36 shows how in the centre such an army can surround only one point, on the edge three, and in the corner as many as nine points. This gives an idea why the opening struggle in Go is for control of the corners, and then the sides, the centre being the least important part of the board.

A Full-board Opening
The full-board opening shown in Figure 37 was played by two of the strongest European players, Z. Mutabzija (Jugoslavia) and H. de Vries (Holland) at the European Go Congress in Bristol in 1971. Mutabzija played Black.

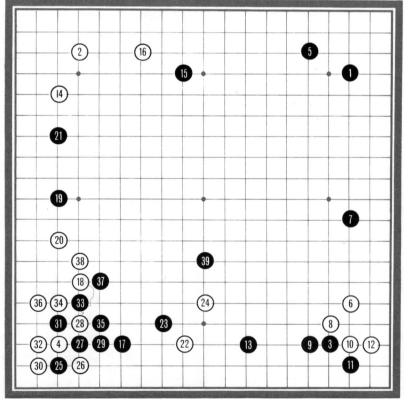

Fig. 37

Black 1 and 5, and White 2 and 14 make standard corner enclosures. Black was able to build up a wide but loose framework with his 7 and 15, the one White made with his 16 being smaller but tighter.

The sequence from 6–13 is a standard corner opening or 'joseki'. Many thousands of these have been worked out, and this one is typical, the corner being more or less evenly divided.

19 and 21 are a standard side formation. It encloses little territory, but can be fairly sure of making two eyes if required.

White 22 attacks 17 by severing it from the strong stones in the lower right corner. 23 is a strong counter attack, and 24 is defensive.

The sequence 25–38 is not standard, and in fact includes one or two doubtful moves. 25 becomes virtually dead–this stone and White 28 are deliberate sacrifices. The result is that White makes secure territory in the corner and along one side, but Black's group on the outside is very strong. Black now uses this strength together with his lower right group to mount an attack on White 22 and 24, with his 39. Now the middle game is under way.

Note how Black 39 is the first stone to pay any attention to the middle of the board–most of the opening plays are on the 3rd and 4th lines from the edge. Note also how territory is thinly sketched out at first, stones only being played next to each other when a tactical encounter develops.

Standard Corner Openings (Joseki)
The standard Japanese reference work on joseki lists some 21,000 variations. No amateur player ever comes close to knowing them all–what is more important is to understand the principles that underlie them. A few examples are given here to illustrate some of the tactical principles that apply not only in the opening but throughout the game.

The most frequently played opening move in a corner is on the '3–4' point (see Figure 38). The player's intention is to add another stone at 'a', 'b', 'c', or occasionally 'd' to make one of the standard two-stone fortifications of the corner or 'shimari'. (See the top left and top right corners of Figure 37 for examples). The best way for the opponent to challenge his hold on the corner is to attack by occupying one of these points himself.

Figure 39 shows a joseki where Black at once counter-attacks White 2 with Black 3. A move like this is called a 'squeeze' or 'pincers' attack for obvious reasons, and the idea is to stop White

Fig. 38

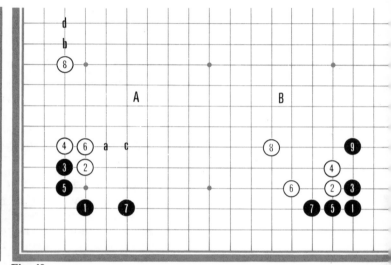

Fig. 39

Fig. 40

from stabilizing his stone with an extension such as that betwe
moves 19 and 21 in Figure 37. Points 'a', 'b', 'c', 'd', and 'e' are
alternative squeeze plays against White 2.

White then uses moves 4 and 6 to stabilize his stones, wh
Black sketches out territory with 5 and 7. Later White hopes
counter-attack Black 3 from somewhere in the region of 'f', a
'g' is also a good point for either player.

Figure 40a shows one of the joseki that results from White
attack at 'a' in Figure 38. Black takes territory in the corner, a
White builds a strong side position.

White 8 is the optimum extension from the two stones 4 and
Had there been another white stone at or about 'a', the corre
extension would be to 'b', and with stones at or around 'a' and
the correct extension is to 'd'. In theory the opponent has no mea
of disconnecting such extensions. Note that they are made alo
the third line from the edge—extensions made in the middle of t
board usually need to be somewhat closer.

Figure 40b shows a typical joseki resulting from an initial pl
on the '3–3' point. Black has taken all the corner territory, b
White's stones are said to have an 'influence' towards the cent
and lower edge of the board, which will be useful to him in t
middle-game. White has also won the initiative from Black—nc
he can play first at some other important point (see also Figure 3

246

g. 41

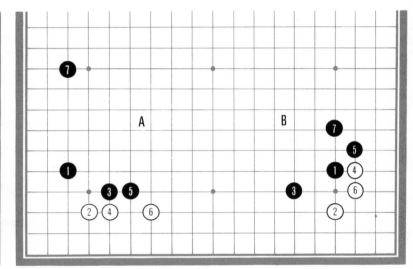

Fig. 42

for another popular '3–3' point joseki).

The other most commonly chosen opening points in the corner are the '4–4', '3–5', and '4–5' points. Figures 41, 42*a* and 42*b* respectively show a typical joseki from each opening.

Summary of Principles of Sound Play

Always consider efficiency. In the opening, sketch out territory thinly at first on the third and fourth lines from the edge, controlling first corners, then sides, lastly centre.

A move which serves several functions is always better than one with only one purpose. Never use two stones where one will do, and never play a move that gains a few points when another move elsewhere would gain more.

Always consider for each manoeuvre whether it retains or loses the initiative. Losing the initiative is not bad in itself, but only give it up for a worthwhile advantage.

Stones which could easily be linked together are hard to attack, while disconnected ones are usually an easy prey. Remember that by the end of the game all your stones are going to need to have been connected into armies that could make two eyes if needed (except in the case of the 'seki'). Don't play good stones after bad in trying to rescue stones that are virtually dead – you will only increase your loss.

Keep your options open as long as possible, e.g. which areas of territory you intend to defend, which endangered stones you are prepared to rescue, etc. Likewise, limit your opponent's options as much as possible.

Remember a one point advantage is enough to win. If you are winning, don't take chances – if losing, complicate the position.

If you are stuck for a move, imagine where your opponent would play if it were his turn. Very often your best play is at or near that point.

The Handicapping System
One of the great advantages of Go, at least from the weaker player's

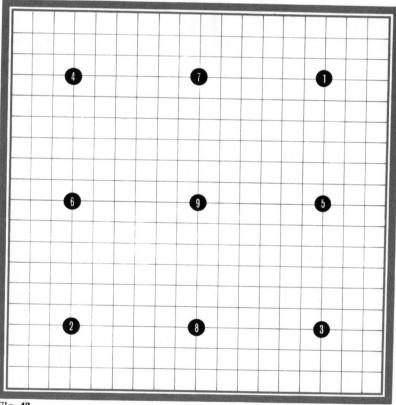

Fig. 43

point of view, is that it has a built in handicapping system, which enables two players of widely differring playing strengths to enjoy a game in which each has an equal chance of winning.

In Figure 1 you can see the nine 'handicap points', the ones marked with small dots. In a handicap game, the weaker player plays, as his first move, from two to nine stones on certain of these points to give himself just sufficient advantage to compensate for the difference in playing strengths. The handicap points are points of great strategic value and give a very considerable advantage to the Black player. The maximum normal handicap is nine stones (see Figure 43), The order of placing them shown is the traditional Japanese one.

If a player receiving a nine-stone advantage were to defeat his opponent (say) three times in succession, his opening advantage would be reduced to eight stones – the one he would lose would be the centre one (No. 9). For a seven-stone advantage stones 7 and 8 are omitted; for six stones, omit stones 7, 8, and 9; for a five-stone advantage, omit 5, 6, 7, and 8. A four stone advantage uses only stones 1, 2, 3, and 4; a three stone advantage 1, 2, and 3; two stones, 1 and 2. A 'one-stone advantage' consists of giving Black the advantage of moving first: however, this move does not have to be on a handicap point.

When players of equal strength play, it is usual to add $5\frac{1}{2}$ points to White's score at the end of the game. This compensates him for Black's advantage in moving first, and prevents a tied score.

The Grading System

All serious Go players have a grade which is somewhere on the scale shown in Figure 44. Note that the 'Kyu' (intermediate) grades are better the lower the number, whereas in the 'Dan' (master) grades the reverse applies. Handicaps are worked out according to grade, e.g. if a 2-dan player plays a 5-kyu player, the difference in grade is six (not seven, as the scale has no zero), and the 5-kyu player would play six stones on the appropriate handicap points as his first move. If a 1-dan player played a 1-kyu, the weaker player would simply have the advantage of moving first. In either case, if the players are correctly graded, each should have a 50 per cent chance of winning.

Professional players have a quite separate grading system going up to 9-dan. A professional 1-dan is about the same strength as an amateur 5-dan!

DAN GRADES (Master)	5	GO - DAN
	4	YON-DAN
	3	SAN-DAN
	2	NI-DAN
	1	SHO-DAN
KYU GRADES (Beginner and Intermediate)	1	
	2	
	3	
	4	
	5	
	6	
	7	
	8	
	9	
	10	
	11	

Fig. 44

How To Learn Go

There has only been space here for the rules and the most elementary tactics and strategy of Go. One of the great joys of the game is that while it can be played and enjoyed after ten minutes' study of the rules, if you want to take it seriously, it can occupy a lifetime of study. Professional Go players in Japan and Korea (there are about 500 of them) are apprenticed to a master player in their early teens and thereafter spend most of their waking hours playing and studying Go.

There are plenty of books in English nowadays for both the beginner and intermediate player. Advanced players have to turn to Japanese literature to some extent, but this is easier than you might think as much of the information can be gained from the diagrams, with little or no knowledge of the Japanese language.

As well as studying the literature it is necessary to play against strong players to really improve. Beginners whose only opponents are other beginners, though they may thoroughly enjoy their Go, tend to remain at a rather low playing strength. There are however plenty of opportunities to meet strong players at local Go clubs and in tournaments. In Britain it has become the tradition for even the strongest players to welcome beginners at all Go functions.

Beginners are strongly advised to start playing on the 9×9 board, then to progress to the intermediate 13×13 board, and to delay tackling the 19×19 board until they have really understood the basic tactics of Go. One really does learn more soundly this way.

Go is rooted in the culture of China, Korea and Japan and followed with a fervour accorded to no comparable Western game. (There are eight million players in Japan alone.) Two World Chess Champions, Bobby Fischer and Emmanuel Lasker, have been Go players, and the latter's namesake Dr. Edward Lasker (the author of a book on Go), predicted that Go would eventually replace chess as the leading intellectual game of the West, and that Western Go players would eventually rival the top Oriental players. Only time will prove him right or wrong, but Go is certainly here to stay!

Hex

Hex is a board game of pure skill for two players. Its rules are very simple, but it is a game of considerable interest, and deserving of more attention than it has yet received.

Hex is played on a diamond shaped board ruled into equilateral triangles, the standard size board having ten triangles along each edge (see Figure 1). Play takes place on the points of intersection of the lines as in Go, and not within the triangles.

Algebraic notation is used to define points, and for this purpose vertical lines are ignored. Thus the central point is referred to as F6, and not F11 or L6.

Moves are also made as in Go–starting with the board empty players alternately place men on any vacant point, Black moving first. Once played men are not moved, and there is no capturing.

Each player's object is to build a continuous chain of adjacent men linking any point on one of the sides marked with his colour

Fig. 1

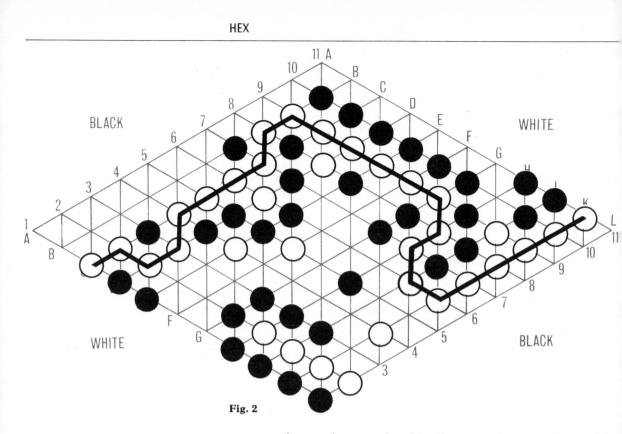

Fig. 2

to any point on the opposite side. Corner points may be used by either player to reach his side.

Figure 2 shows the end of a game of hex which White has won. The heavy black line picks out the continuous chain of men with which he has linked his two sides. Note that a winning chain can turn and double back as much as it likes as long as it has no gaps. Notice also that a game of hex cannot be drawn. There is no way Black could now connect his two sides without the chain crossing the white one somewhere.

We will now examine the game which ended as in Figure 2. You are advised to play the moves through on a board.

Moves 1–20 (see Figure 3)

Black 1: The strongest opening move is on the centre point—however, as this gives Black a considerable advantage it is customary to bar opening there, or sometimes on the entire short diagonal. The latter rule was in force in this game.

White 2: A typical reply.

Black 3: This makes a 'double connection'—the two black men cannot be disconnected because as soon as White plays F7 or F8 Black plays the other.

White 4: Tries to block Black 3 from the lower right side.

Black 5–White 9: More double connections by Black, and more blocks by White. Black has a rather inflexible position, but White has a weak point at K5.

Black 9–Black 15: Black cuts White off from the lower left side, and the following plays look rather submissive on Black's part. However, he is being chased in the direction he wants to go (towards A1), so

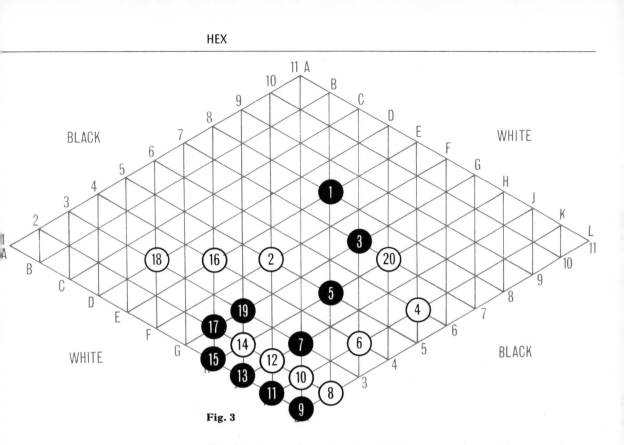

Fig. 3

Black is happy knowing that White cannot keep this up too long.

White 16: This man threatens to connect both to the lower left side and to White 14.

Black 17: Threatens to break both these connections, so;

White 18: Preserves the possibility of connecting to the lower left side, and hints at a possible winning chain via the C9 area.

Black 19: Carrying out the threat to disconnect 14 from 16.

White 20: A subtle move, threatening to link the white men (and therefore disconnect the black ones) with a play at H4. Without White 20 Black could parry this threat by disconnecting White at his weak point of K5 e.g. White H4, Black K5, White H6, Black G6, White J5, Black H7, White J6, Black J8, etc. However, White 20 protects this weakness at K5.

Moves 21–40 (see Figure 4)

Black 21: A very solid reply.

White 22: He has to play somewhere in this area as Black 1 is now potentially connected, via double connections and directly, to L1 on the lower right side, and he must therefore disconnect it from the upper left side.

Black 23: Trying to block White 22 from the upper right side, but;

White 24–White 34: In a forced sequence White connects his 22 to the upper right side using his 20 and 4 on the way. Of course the chain still has some gaps, but these are all of the 'double connection' variety, so Black has no way to break through.

Black 35–White 36: Black's only hope is to push through between White 2 and 22, and White's defensive block at a distance is usually the right way to handle such a frontal assault.

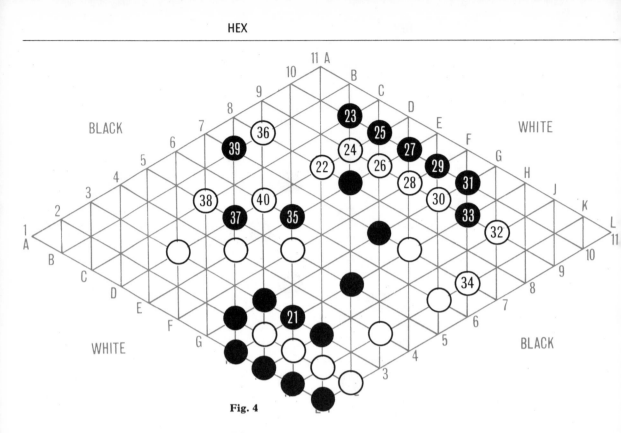

Fig. 4

Black 37–White 38: White is prepared to abandon his 2 and 16.
He doesn't mind which way his winning chain runs!
Black 39: An attempt to confuse the situation.
White 40: Probably best, but . . .

Moves 41–68 (see Figure 5)

Black missed a chance to win with 41 D4. After missing this chance,
the game goes downhill for him—he plays his remaining moves only
in the hope of a mistake by White.

After White 44 he threatens a double connection with the upper
right side with B10 or A11. Black 45 prevents this, but White just
plays 46 and uses the connection he established with moves 24–34.
White 50 and 52 are standard replies to an attempt to break a double
connection to a side point. The remaining moves are trivial as they
consist of threats to break double connections and their replies.

As in most games of strategy, it pays in hex to keep your options
open as long as possible. Black lost this game because of a too solid
style of play, especially in over-reliance on the double connection in
the opening stages.

Hex was invented in Denmark in the 1940s and enjoyed a brief
vogue there and subsequent pockets of interest in the U.S.A.
However, there is almost no literature on the game, and at the time
of writing the game is not manufactured. It is however quite easy
to make a board and to use Go stones or counters for the men, or
you can play with a pencil on isometric drawing paper.

Some players prefer a board drawn as a tesselation of hexagons,
playing inside the hexagons instead of on the intersections as in
the version shown here. The game comes to the same thing, but

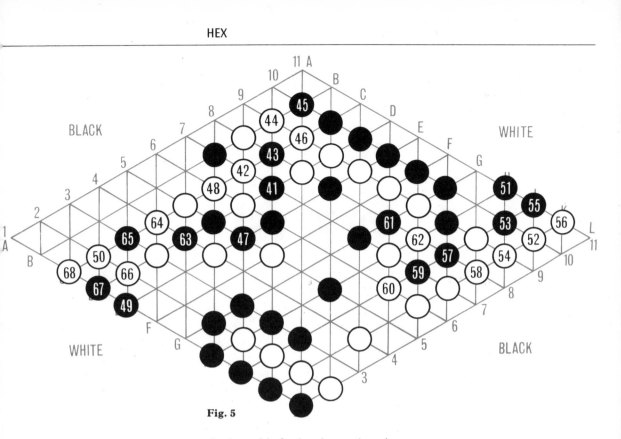

Fig. 5

the board is far harder to draw!

Other size boards than the one shown may be used. I think that as the game comes to be studied more larger boards may well be used.

The lack of hex literature is an advantage for the player who likes a game that depends mainly on over-the-board ability rather than prior book study. It is of course an irony of this and all such games that as general interest in it grows, so also will the amount of book work required to become a stronger player.

Reversi

Reversi is a board game for two using an ordinary draughtsboard (chequerboard) and 64 identical men similar to draughtsmen with the two sides of each man in contrasting colours usually, as here, black and red.

The game was invented in England in the late nineteenth century when it became briefly popular. It continues to enjoy a modest following but should be better known as it is skilful and fast-moving with dramatic changes of fortune and is also a good family game.

Many variations of Reversi have been tried (for example, on different size boards) but the version given here is the standard one. Cheap sets are readily obtainable but the men may easily be improvised.

81	82	83	84	85	86	87	88
71	72	73	74	75	76	77	78
61	62	63	64	65	66	67	68
51	52	53	54	55	56	57	58
41	42	43	44	45	46	47	48
31	32	33	34	35	36	37	38
21	22	23	24	25	26	27	28
11	12	13	14	15	16	17	18

Fig. 1

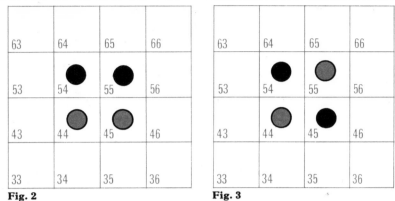

Fig. 2   **Fig. 3**

Preparation for Play

Players toss for colour then each takes 32 men and arranges them in front of him, own colour uppermost.

The board is placed between the players without regard to orientation as the colours of the squares have no significance in the game.

Before we go further it is necessary to annotate the board for reference. An adequate notation is shown in Figure 1 with the colours of the squares omitted for clarity. It will be seen that each row (rank) is numbered progressively up the board in tens, and each column (file) progressively from left to right in units.

The board is now dressed by the players alternately placing two men, one at a time, on the four central squares. Clearly only two arrangements are possible, with like men either side-by-side (Figure 2, preferred by experts) or diagonally opposite (Figure 3).

Play

Red plays first and places a man on any vacant square orthogonally or diagonally adjacent to a square already occupied by a black man such that the black man is flanked by two red men. It can be readily seen that Red has four, and only four legal plays in either of the two initial arrangements. When a man has been trapped in this manner it is reversed to show the colour of its captor. For example, if the board were dressed diagonally (black men on 45 and 54), and Red played first on 35, the black man on 45 would be turned over, when there would be four red men on the board and only one black man (on 54).

Now it is Black to play and he can occupy 34, 36 or 56, reversing one red man in each case.

Object of the Game

The object of the game is to have a majority of your colour on the board at the end. Play ceases when all the squares have been filled or when neither player has a legal move (i.e., cannot make a capture). If at any time one player is unable to move, he misses his turn.

Strategy

As the board fills up from the centre, opportunities will occur to capture several men in a single play. Men captured are determined solely by the last piece played, when every enemy man in an unbroken line between it and the next friendly man *in any and every*

Fig. 4

direction are captured and reversed. Theoretically, as many as 19 men can change sides in one play though about half this number is the usual maximum.

Figure 4 shows a game in progress with Red to move. In this position, Red has five plays:

25 – reversing the two men on 35 and 45
33 – reversing the two men on 34 and 35 and the man on 44
42 – reversing the three men on 43, 44 and 45
53 – reversing the man on 54
64 – reversing the men on 34, 44 and 54

Remember that the man played alone dictates the men captured. Thus if Red here plays 33, then after reversal of 34, 35 and 44 the black man on 45, although surrounded, is not reversed.

All captured men must be reversed at once but there is no requirement to make the numerically largest capture.

Notice that if there is a gap anywhere in a line of men flanked by two men of the opposite colour, either between the men in the line or between one of the end men and a flanking man, then none of the men is reversed. Similarly, a line of men cannot be trapped if one of them is on the board edge as then it is impossible to satisfy the conditions of capture. However, if the line runs along the board edge, then the men can be captured unless a corner square is occupied by one of the group when capture again becomes impossible.

It will be seen from this that certain squares can be more valuable than others. Figure 5 identifies best squares to occupy (white) and worse (red) with shading showing relative values of the others.

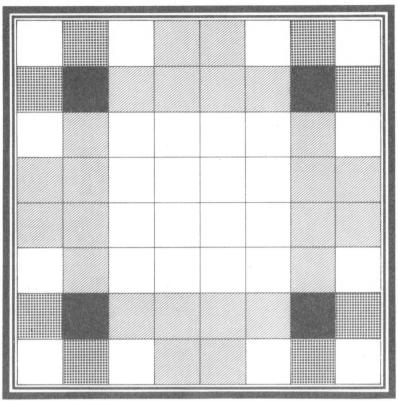

Fig. 5

It will be seen that the four squares diagonally in from the corners are especially to be avoided because their occupancy is likely to allow the opponent into the strong corners securing all adjacent men in three directions.

This is only a relative guide however, useful as all such guides are useful, but not to be followed slavishly as positions can often arise where square values may vary from those shown.

The concept of key squares nevertheless remains at the root of Reversi strategy and it is usually better to forgo the capture of, say, five men, if an important square can be gained for, say, the capture of only two or three men.

Generally speaking, one should aim at filling in the centre before expanding outwards to the sides (notice in Figure 5 that the 12 squares that surround the four dressed squares in the centre are all classed as valuable).

It is not easy to see ahead accurately more than a move or two in Reversi except in the closing stages of a game, but with practice one can develop a feel for good and bad formations—and unlike so many games, Reversi, because of its fluctuating fortunes, can never be dull.

Wari

There is a whole family of games, commonly referred to generically as Mancala, whose common features are that they are games of skill, usually for two players, in which a number of stones or beans, initially distributed among two, three or four rows of cups, are redistributed or 'sown' according to certain rules; contents of cups are captured from time to time by one or other of the players, the winner being the player who acquires more than half of the available stones.

Mancala has been described as the national game of Africa and has a good claim to being the oldest board game extant as it is believed to have been popular during the Empire Age of Ancient Egypt well over 3,000 years ago. There are at least two hundred recorded regional variants of Mancala, each with its own local name. One of the most widely played is Wari, originating in West Africa where the 'boards' are often simply holes scooped out of the ground (though boards are also carved from wood, often elaborately) with the 'stones' usually beans, pebbles or shells.

A Wari board consists of 12 cups arranged in two parallel rows of six with a large cup at each end, one for each player, to keep prisoners (Figure 1).

Fig. 1

Play

The two players face each other across the board which is placed lengthways between them, each player assuming control of the row of six cups nearest to him.

The board is dressed by placing four stones in each of the 12 cups, there being no differentiation between the stones of the two sides.

The players decide who shall start, and the first player lifts *all*

Fig. 2

the stones from any cup of his choice *on his side of the board* and sows the stones one at a time into successive cups in an anti-clockwise direction starting with the cup immediately to the right of the emptied cup and continuing round his opponents cups if necessary. The second player then takes all the stones from one of the cups on *his* side of the board (4 or 5 as the case may be) and sows them similarly, still in an anti-clockwise direction.

Play continues in this way until one player puts the *last* stone from one of his cups *into* an opponent's cup that contains *one* or *two* stones (i.e., two or three stones after distribution has been completed). The player is entitled to all the stones in this cup as prisoners. He scoops them out and puts them in his large hole at the end of the rows. If there are also precisely two or three stones in the *preceding* cup, and this cup is also on the opponent's side, then these stones too are taken prisoner. Similarly with the next cup. If any cup has less than two or more than three stones in it, however, then these stones are immune from capture as are the stones of any cups which preceded it in the distribution, regardless of their contents. Some simple examples will serve to explain these points.

Let us call the players White and Black, and annotate the cups on White's side A–F and those on Black's side a–f, from left to right looked at from White's side in each case. The starting position is then as shown in Figure 2. The arrows indicate direction of play.

Supposing White starts and elects to pick up the stones in cup E. He must pick up *all* the stones. He then sows them anti-clockwise, dropping the first stone in F, the second in f, the third in e and the fourth in d. As d does not now contain either two or three stones, no captures are made and the turn ends. We can record this simply as E(4), the letter indicating the cup emptied and the number of stones in it. There is no need to indicate the player, as each can only empty a cup on his own side of the board and can only capture stones on his opponent's side. Let us continue a move or two: f(5); B(4); a(5)

The position is now as shown in Figure 3. Black's last play was into cup E which now has two stones in it. Accordingly, these stones are removed and are now Black's prisoners. If D had had 2 or 3 stones in it, Black would have captured these as well. If each of the cups A–E had had either 2 or 3 stones in them after the distribution from a, then Black would have taken the contents of all these cups.

There are only a few other rules. If a cup contains more than 11 stones and hence at least one circuit of the board is completed, the

Fig. 3

cup from which the stones were lifted must remain empty. Thus if 12 stones were distributed, the last stone would be dropped into the cup immediately beyond the starting cup.

A player may not empty or leave empty *all* the cups on his opponent's side. He must play so as to leave at least one stone for his opponent to sow (it is hard to find a parallel of this compassionate rule in European games). If he is unable to do so, he (the player) takes all the stones remaining (which must perforce be on his side of the board) and adds them to his prisoners and the game is over.

Sometimes in the late stages of a game a position arises where no further meaningful plays are possible (for example, if White has only one stone left at C and Black only one stone left at c, these two stones will simply follow each other round). In this case, the players take up the stones on their respective sides of the board and the game is over.

Hints on Play

There is no chance in Wari, so theoretically a 'best play' can be calculated in any position. In practice, of course, the possibilities to be considered are astronomical except in the late stages of a game so precise computation is out of the question.

Simple tactics become evident after a game or two. For example, a cup containing two stones is obviously vulnerable to an enemy cup that contains the correct number of stones to reach it. The weakness can be defended by (a) emptying a cup that will allow a stone to be added to the two thus making that cup impregnable; or (b) playing so as to add a stone to the enemy cup so that it will overshoot its target; or (c) emptying the cup and distributing the two stones. This last is not usually satisfactory as the second player has only to feed one stone into the empty cup to make it vulnerable again.

An aggressive game calls for a build-up in your right-hand cups. If the number of stones in any cup is such that the last stone in that cup will be sown in home territory, then clearly that cup is inoffensive and the stones in it poorly deployed. Aim to get several of the opponent's cups simultaneously under attack.

Mah Jong

Mah Jong is a game for four players (two- and three-player versions exist but are unsatisfactory). Mah Jong has affinities to the card game, Rummy, and like that game, the element of luck is considerable while still leaving scope for skilful play.

Mah Jong in its present form is probably about a hundred years old, a development of early Chinese card and domino games, themselves derived from ancient Chinese paper money. Mah Jong cards (narrow strips of pasteboard) are still used, but the game is commonly played with tiles, once made of ivory or bone and often backed with wood, particularly bamboo, but now almost invariably manufactured of plastic.

The game is widely played today throughout the Far East and among Chinese communities everywhere. One of the distinctive sounds in the back streets of Singapore and Hong Kong is the audible shuffling of the tiles–'the twittering of the sparrows'.

Mah Jong was first introduced to the West as a card game before the turn of the century but it was not until after the First World War, when it reappeared in its present form, that it acquired any popularity. The Mah Jong craze of the 1920s, particularly evident in America, soon passed, a victim of proliferating rules and the rising appeal of Contract Bridge.

Rules

There are two basic games; the uncomplicated Mah Jong of the East, essentially a gambling game, and the Western version which has many 'special hands', more elaborate scoring and sometimes extra tiles. Although a number of attempts have been made to codify Mah Jong, there are no universally acknowledged rules, certainly for the Western game, though the version offered here, a compromise between the two extremes, has achieved wide acceptance. Nevertheless, rules should always be agreed before play to avoid misunderstandings.

Equipment

Tiles. A modern set comprises 136 tiles of which 108 are 'suit' tiles and 28 are 'honour' tiles.

There are three suits in Mah Jong; Bamboos (commonly called 'sticks'), Characters (sometimes called 'numbers') and Circles ('dots'). There are 36 tiles in each suit, four of each number from one to nine.

The honour tiles consist of four each of Winds (East, South,

Fig. 1

West and North) and Dragons (Red, Green and White). The reverse side of all tiles is uniform, invariably plain. The 34 different values are shown in Figure 1. Notice that the ones and nines of each suit are known as terminals.

A few sets also have decorative tiles known as Flowers and Seasons, each tile different and numbered. These earn bonus points but otherwise have no part in the play and these days they are little used.

Bones. These are really counters or chips, but are long and thin with the value of each stamped on it. Common denominations are 10, 100 and 500.

Dice. Two conventional dice are used in the preliminaries.

Wind Disc. This is simply a marker to show 'prevailing wind' (i.e., the dealer).

Racks. Sets often include racks to hold the hands of each player. Tiles can also be stood on end, blank side facing the other players, or held in the palm of the hand.

Fig. 2

Preliminaries

Few games can have such elaborate preliminaries as Mah Jong.
Some enthusiasts consider these add flavour to the game.

1) One player takes one each of the wind tiles and shuffles them face
down. Each player then picks up a tile, the shuffler taking the last
one. East is first dealer, who chooses his seat. South sits on his
right, North on his left and West opposite him. Note that this does
not correspond to our arrangement of the compass points.

2) The 136 tiles are now mixed face down with all players taking
part in the shuffling. Each player then builds a wall 17 tiles long and
2 high, all tiles face down. When the walls are complete they are
moved together to form a hollow square. This is the Great Wall of
China, secured against demons (Figure 2).

3) The dealer (East Wind) now throws the dice, adds the two
numbers together and counts round the walls *anti-clockwise*,
beginning with his own. Thus if East threw a 2 and a 5, totalling
seven, he would count 'East 1, South 2, West 3, North 4, East 5,
South 6, West 7'. To determine the point at which the wall will be
broken, West (or whichever player at whom the count ended) then
throws the dice and adds the total to that of East's throw. If West
threw two 3's, for example, making 13 in all, West would then start
counting along the tiles of his wall *from right to left*, breaking the
wall between the 13th and 14th tiles. (If West had thrown a double
6, making a total of 19, he would have continued counting round
the corner onto South's side.)

4) The players now draw their hands from the wall in the following
manner. East, as dealer, first takes the four tiles (two stacks of two)

immediately beyond the break. Each of the other players do likewise in turn (South, West, North), the wall thus being dismantled clockwise. This procedure is repeated three times when each player has twelve tiles. East then takes the next two tiles and the other players in turn take one more each from the wall, always the tile nearest the break and top before bottom. The hands, which are concealed from the other players, are now complete and play can start.

Object of the Game

The aim of each player is to make the highest score which is usually synonomous with being the first to go Mah Jong (go out), similar to Rummy. A player may go out when he has arranged his hand into four sets and a pair, or completes a special hand (see below).

There are three kinds of sets:
1) A sequence (CHOW); any three consecutive tiles of the same suit
2) A triplet (PUNG); any three identical suit or honour tiles
3) A four (KONG); any four identical suit or honour tiles.

A pair is any two identical tiles.

In the hand shown in Figure 3, the player is waiting for a North Wind or an 8 of Characters to go out.

Play

1) Dealer starts by discarding a tile of his choice face up inside the wall. All players now hold 13 tiles. Dealer's subsequent discards are laid face up in a continuous row so that the other players can see what he has discarded and in what order. The other players follow the same procedure. An alternative system is for discards to be placed face up at random within the wall.

2) After the dealer has discarded, and assuming no other player wants his discard (see below), play will continue anti-clockwise. South will take the next tile from the wall (at the point where North removed the last tile for his hand), discarding at will, and so on until a player goes Mah Jong, or Wu as it is sometimes called.

3) A set can be made in two ways:
a) It can be picked up in the initial hand, or drawn from the wall, or a combination of these. This is known as a *concealed* Chow, Pung or Kong.
b) It can be completed by picking up the third tile (or fourth in the case of a Kong) discarded by another player. This is known as an

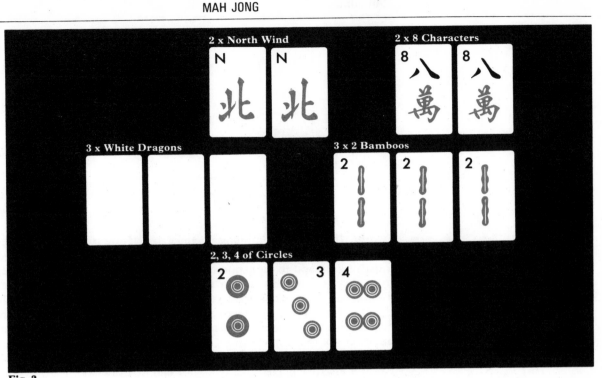

Fig. 3

exposed or open Chow, Pung or Kong. (An exposed Kong can also be obtained by adding a tile drawn from the wall to an exposed Pung but not by claiming a discard to add to an exposed Pung.)

4) Concealed sets (except Kongs, see below) are not disclosed until the end of play. They are worth double exposed sets (except Chows). Exposed sets are placed face up in front of the owner, between the rack and the wall.

5) Only the discard of the last player can be claimed, and that before the next player has picked up a tile. Only the next player in sequence can claim a discard to complete a Chow, but any player can claim a discard to complete a Pung or a Kong or to go Mah Jong (completing a set *or* the necessary pair to go out). The player or players requiring the discard shout 'Chow', 'Pung', 'Kong' or 'Wu', as appropriate. Precedence is in ascending order of value, with a player claiming a Chow having lowest priority and a player calling Wu, highest. Where more than one player is claiming Wu, the player first in rotation of play has prior right.

6) A player who wins a discard takes the tile into his hand and *at once* completes a set, which is then exposed, or goes out. If he does not go out, he must himself discard before completing his turn. A discard may not be claimed to keep in hand nor to add to an exposed Pung. The turn of play then passes to the player immediately to the right of the player claiming the discard. Thus if East throws away and North legally claims the discard, then play will again pass to East; South and West having effectively lost their turns.

7) A special procedure occurs when a player completes a Kong. If this is picked up in the initial hand, then the player must wait until his turn when he declares it, placing it on the table, the two central tiles face up and the outside tiles face down to show that it is a concealed set. He then draws a tile from the wall *but does not*

discard. If a player completes a concealed Kong during play and claims it, or claims a discard to make an exposed Kong, or draws the fourth tile to add to an exposed Pung, he must draw a further tile from the wall and discard in the usual way when his turn ends. This procedure is designed to ensure that the right number of tiles are always in hand to go Mah Jong (four sets and a pair). A player with an exposed Pung may hold the fourth tile in his hand but elect not to complete the Kong (because, for instance, he wants the fourth tile for a Chow). In this case he cannot claim points for a Kong if another player goes Wu, nor can he draw another tile. He may subsequently, however, decide to convert his Pung into a Kong when he follows the procedure set out above.

8) If nobody has gone Mah Jong when the wall has been reduced to 14 tiles (the 'dead wall', often separated slightly from the main wall at start of play), the game is abandoned without scoring.

Scoring

Scoring, like the preliminaries, can be complicated. First, the winner (the player to go out) adds up his points as below.

Scoring Table

Points awarded for	Amount scored
−going Mah Jong	20
−going Mah Jong and drawing last tile from wall (i.e., not a discard)	2
−going Mah Jong with the last tile from the wall (excluding the 14 dead tiles)	2
−an exposed Pung of	
simple tiles (2−8)	2
terminal tiles (1, 9)	4
honour tiles	4
−an exposed Kong of	
simple tiles	8
terminal tiles	16
honour tiles	16

Concealed Pungs and Kongs count DOUBLE.
Chows score NOTHING, whether concealed or exposed.
Pairs score as follows:

Dragons	2
Dealer's (prevailing) wind	2
One's own wind	2

Notice in particular that Chows earn nothing while Pungs and Kongs of terminals earn the same as honour tiles, and concealed sets are worth double exposed sets. Certain pairs can also earn points, as shown. They score the same whether the pair was concealed or completed from a discard to go out. Some schools allow a number of additional bonuses but these are omitted in this description for simplicity.

When the points are added, they are *doubled* for *every time* that the following conditions can be satisfied:
1) Holding a Pung or Kong of:
a) Dragons
b) Dealer's (prevailing) Wind
c) Own Wind
2) The tile to go out is drawn from the wall
3) The tile to go out is the last tile of the wall (excluding the 14 dead tiles)
4) The hand is all of one suit with Winds or Dragons
5) The hand is all Pungs

They are *doubled twice* whenever the hand contains a triplet or four of the player's wind *when he is dealer* and *doubled four times* when the player's hand is all of the same suit or all terminals or all honours tiles.

Payment
Only the player who goes Mah Jong scores his hand. The other players each pay him the total score, rounded up to the nearest ten. The dealer (prevailing wind) pays *double*, but if he is the player who goes Mah Jong all the other players pay him double.

Some players score every hand, each player settling the difference between his score and those of the other players, but this is very confusing and is not recommended.

It is usual to agree a limit score for a hand. This is usually 500.

Example of Scoring
East is dealer and goes Mah Jong, drawing his last tile from the wall, with the following hand:
　　Concealed Kong of East Wind
　　Exposed Pung of Red Dragons
　　Concealed Pung of 1 Circles
　　Concealed Chow (3, 4, 5 of Bamboos)
　　Pair of Green Dragons

He scores:

Going Mah Jong	20
Drawing last tile from wall	2
Concealed Kong of East Wind	32
Exposed Pung of Red Dragons	4
Concealed Pung of 1 Circles	8
Concealed Chow	0
Pair of Green Dragons	2
	68

He doubles his hand once for:

Pung of Dragons

Going out with tile from the wall

He doubles his hand *twice* for:

Kong of dealer's wind when dealer

The hand thus earns four doubles, making a total well in excess of the limit hand, hence the total score for payment is 500. But East is dealer, so each of the other players must pay him 1,000 points. There are no other payments.

Special Hands

Many consider that Mah Jong was suffocated by the proliferation of 'special hands' introduced from time to time 'to make the game more interesting'. However, certain of these hands, including one or two admitted in the Chinese game, have achieved general acceptance and are given below. They are all 'limit' hands.

1) *Concealed Triplets* Four Pungs and a pair, ALL tiles drawn from the wall. Sometimes Kongs, if concealed, are also allowed in this hand.

2) *Four Big Winds* Four sets of Winds plus a pair.

3) *The Snake* 1–9 of a suit plus one of each of the Winds with any tile paired. All tiles except the last must be drawn from the wall.

4) *Heavenly Hand* (Dealer only) Go Mah Jong with the 14 tiles dealt; i.e., without any play taking place.

5) *The Gates of Heaven* A Pung of 1's, a Pung of 9's, and one each of the tiles 2–8, one of them doubled and all tiles of the same suit.

6) *All Pair Honour Hand* 7 pairs of honour and/or terminal tiles.

Hints on Play

It is necessary to strike a balance between building a high-score hand and going Mah Jong as soon as possible. The dealer (whose awards and penalties are doubled) should always strive to go out.

As with Rummy, discards can be important indicators of opponents' hands—watch them.

It is always advisable to monitor the pool of dead tiles—it is not much use waiting for a second Green Dragon to complete your pair if three have been discarded!

An open-ended consecutive suit pair—say, 4 and 5 of Circles—obviously offers better chances of a Chow than a pair with only one end open (say, 1 and 2) or a split pair (6 and 8).

Defer the discard of a tile you think may be wanted—particularly the dealer's wind.

Be alert for the tiles you want—a good player plays quickly to prevent the other players claiming discards.

If a game has been going on for some time, strive to go out rather than trying to improve your hand—other players are likely to be near Mah Jong. Most winning hands, unlike the example given above, are low-scoring.

Dominoes

Dominoes, like playing cards, are not a game but a whole family of games of varying complexity and suitable for almost any number of players.

The history of dominoes is obscure but they likely came from China where they have been in use for many hundreds of years. It is interesting that Chinese dominoes and playing cards are virtually indistinguishable. The origin of the name is also clouded and there are several theories, but none of them is particularly convincing.

Domino games are generally simpler than other games in this book because their scope is more limited but it is nevertheless possible to develop considerable skill in play.

Most games of dominoes are played with a double-six pack which consists of 28 tiles (see Figure 1). The tiles themselves are black or white with the spots—known as 'pips'—in a contrasting colour, usually white or black respectively. Each tile is divided into two, each half representing a number between 0 (blank) and 6. Notice that if the blanks are excluded the other tiles correspond to every possible combination of the throws of two dice. One can consider the single blank tiles as the throws of a single die with the double-blank to complete the set. (There are no blanks in the Chinese pack.)

Double-nine and double-twelve packs are used in some multi-player games but are not discussed here as these packs are not seen very often.

Certain procedures are common to all or most domino games:

1) The pack is first shuffled face down, all the players taking part.

2) Players each draw a domino from the pack to determine first lead. Highest double takes precedence, or if there are no doubles, highest domino (total pips). Tiles are again shuffled before play, which is clockwise.

3) A number of dominoes are now drawn by each player, the manner of dealing and the numbers taken depending on the game. Tiles in hand are concealed from the other players.

4) In almost all games, players take it in turns to put a domino face up on the table; second and subsequent dominoes are joined to form one continuous chain or 'leg' with pips matching on adjacent dominoes and with doubles placed at right angles to the leg. Thus there are two open ends to a domino chain which can be conveniently made to turn corners to keep the playing area manageable.

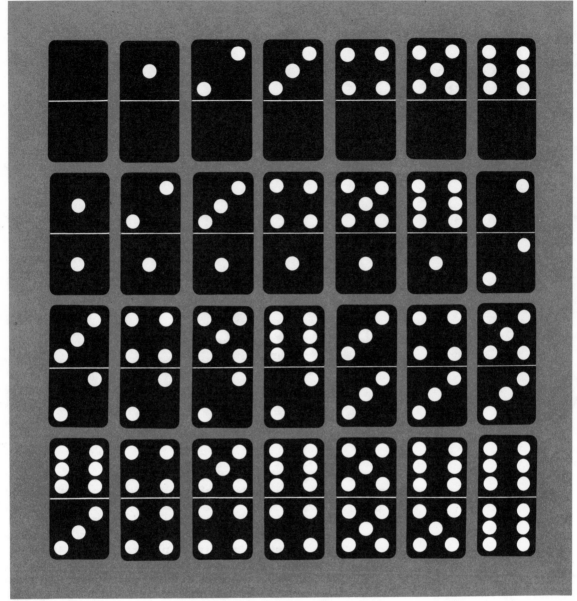

Fig. 1

5) When a player cannot match from hand either of the dominoes at the ends of the chain, he is blocked and signifies this by knocking on the table. In some games he may draw a tile from the stock, or 'boneyard' as it is usually called, or receive one from another player, but otherwise misses his turn.

6) The object of most games is to be the first to go out – i.e., get rid of all one's tiles – but in some games this is secondary to making scoring plays.

7) Partnerships are usual in four-player games. Partners sit opposite each other as in Bridge.

8) The score may be kept on paper but a cribbage board is often used for this purpose, particularly in pub games and it has the advantage of allowing all players to see easily the state of the score.

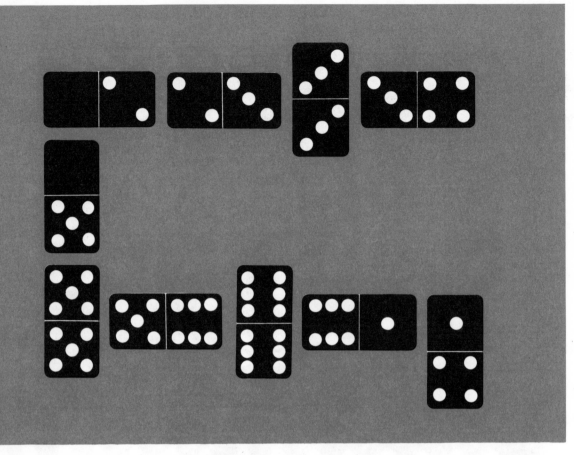

Fig. 2

The Block Game

The Block Game can be played by two, three or four players (in partnership), and is probably the most widely played of all domino games.

Preparation for the two-player variant is as above. Each player takes seven dominoes from the boneyard into hand. The holder of the highest double plays first by placing it in the centre of the table. If neither player holds a double the tiles are reshuffled.

The second player places a domino, one end of which must match the 'starter', with this end against the double but at right angles to it. The first player on his second turn has a choice between placing a matching domino against the starter or against the end of the second player's domino. Play continues in this fashion, doubles always being placed at right angles to the leg. A player who is unable to play must pass his turn. If both players are unable to add to the leg, the hand ends; the player with the smaller total number of pips on the tiles remaining in his hand is the winner and he scores the difference between this total and the total of his opponent's pips. If one player goes out (or 'domino') he scores the total of his opponent's remaining tiles. Thus if A goes out and B has the 6−3 and 4−1 left, A scores 14. A game is played to an agreed total−50 or 100 is common.

Each player also draws seven tiles in the three- and four-player variants. In the latter, all the dominoes are in play so the hand must be started with a double 6. The hand ends when *one* player goes out; the partnership scoring the total pips of the opponents' dominoes *less* the pips of the remaining partner.

Figure 2 shows a two-handed Block game in progress. Play was started with a double-6. Both ends of the leg are 4-spots so only a domino with a 4-spot can be played. Half the dominoes are, of course, out of play in the boneyard.

The Draw Game

This is very similar to the Block Game except that the starter may be any domino and a player may, on his turn, *whether he can add to the leg or not* draw one or more dominoes from the boneyard *except that the last two may not be touched*. Thus if player A in a two-player Draw Game puts down the 5–4, B may elect to draw a tile from the boneyard. He can then put down a domino or draw another tile from the boneyard, and so on. Only when a player has drawn *all* the remaining tiles in the boneyard (except the last two) can he pass. Thus if B cannot play to the leg and there are three tiles in the boneyard he must draw one tile and must play this tile if he can do so, otherwise he may pass. In the four-player version, players draw only six dominoes each at the start, leaving four in the boneyard. Scoring is the same as for the Block Game.

Fives-and-Threes

This game is also for two, three or four players (in partnership). Each player draws seven tiles, as for the Block Game. Lowest double takes first drop (starts). Every time the combined total of both ends of the leg is a multiple of three or five, the player completing the total, scores according to the following table:

Total at *both* ends	Score
3	1
5	1
6	2
9	3
10	2
12	4
15	8
18	6
20	4

Each 3 or 5 in the total scores one point; hence 15 is the top-scoring total (five 3's plus three 5's). When a player is blocked he

Fig. 3

must pass. The player (or partnership) who goes out scores an additional point.

Figure 3 shows a two-player game of Fives-and-Threes in progress. The plays, with points scored, were as follows:

Player A – double 1 (no score)
   B – 1–6 (no score)
   A – 1–3 (3 points)
   B – 6–2 (1 point)
   A – 2–blank (1 point)
   B – double 3 (2 points)
   A – 3–5 (1 point)
   B – 5–6 (2 points)
   A – blank–3 (3 points)
   B – double 6 (8 points)

Thus with ten tiles down, B leads by 13 points to 8.

The Star

The Star, or Cross, also known under several other names, is best as a four-player, non-partnership game.

Each player draws seven tiles and whoever holds the double-6 places it in the centre of the table. The next player must play a 6-spot but may place it *either* at right-angles to the starter *or* in line with it. The next three plays must add 6-spots to the starter so that a cross is formed. Once the cross has been formed players continue and score as in the Block Game. Any player holding the two remaining 6-spots has an advantage as he can secure one arm of the cross for at least one round.

Bergen

A good game for two, three or four players. In the two- and three-player versions, each draws six dominoes; four players draw five.

Lowest double is played and holder scores 2 points. If all doubles are in the boneyard, lowest tile is played but the owner does not score for it. Play rotates as usual except that if a player cannot match, he draws one tile which he must play if he is able. If he still cannot play, he passes.

The object of the game is to match both ends of the leg. When this is done, the player scores two points for a 'double-header'. If the domino at one end is a double, then the player matching it, or playing the double, gets 3 points for a 'triple-header'. (Hence the 2-point score for the double starter.)

The first player to get rid of all his tiles scores an additional point.

It pays to hold back doubles in this game in order to cap a double-header with a triple-header. As in most domino games, one cannot opt to pass.

There are a whole fund of other domino games, many drawn from oral tradition and with regional differences that are a social study in themselves. There are a few solitaire games. A very simple one calls for the player to draw five tiles from the pack. Starting with any domino, he plays from his hand as long as he can. When he is blocked, he again makes his hand up to five by drawing from the boneyard. He wins if he succeeds in playing out the whole pack.

Hints on Play

1) In most games it pays to go out first, so this is a primary aim.

2) With choice of plays, select from the longest suit. This enhances the chance of being able to add to the leg in the next round, particularly in a two-player game. As an extreme case, if every 5-spot were held, three tiles could be put down in succession without interference (a 5-spot at the end of the leg followed by the double-5 and another 5-spot). Naturally, if both legs can be controlled in this way there is considerable advantage.

3) Always conceal whether a play is made from choice or necessity.

4) With a little practice it is often possible to form some idea of opponents' hands. In a two-player game, if one player passes the second player may be able to identify certain tiles in the boneyard.

5) Mental arithmetic and a quick sight of exposed tiles are particularly useful in the harder games (e.g., Fives-and-Threes).

Halma

Halma was invented as a proprietary game in the late 19th century, and was very popular. It is still played, even though the patent has long since lapsed. It has not received such detailed analysis as games like Chess and Go, but is a game with considerable scope for skill. Since the 1930s a game based on Halma, Chinese Checkers, has taken some of its popularity. Chinese Checkers is usually played on a board in the shape of a six-pointed star, and is suitable for from three to six players.

The Board and Pieces
The board is a square of 256 small squares. At each corner heavy lines mark off enclosures, called camps, as shown in Figure 1. The camps mark off 13 squares, but in two diagonally opposite corners the camps are enlarged to mark off an additional six squares. The pieces are counters of a different colour for each player.

The Players
The game is for two or four players. With two players, each has 19 pieces, which are set up in the larger camps as shown in Figure 2. With four players, each has 13 pieces set up in the smaller camps as shown in Figure 3. With four players, each may play for himself, or they may play in pairs, partners sitting diagonally opposite each other, and assisting each other in the manner described later.

The Object of the Game
The object of the game is to move all of one's pieces from their starting camp to that diagonally opposite. The first player to do so wins. In partnership play, the first pair to transfer all their pieces wins.

The Play
Players move one piece at a time, in turn clockwise. There are two ways to move. The *step* is a move to an adjacent square in any direction, along a file or column, or diagonally. The *hop* is like a taking move in draughts, whereby a piece may hop or jump over an adjacent piece, again in any direction, to a vacant square beyond. A hopping move may continue, and a piece may hop over as many other pieces as possible. The pieces hopped over may be one's own, or one's partner's or opponent's. There is no taking, and pieces hopped over remain where they are on the board. No move may combine a step and a hop. Hopping is not compulsory. Stepping and hopping moves are shown in Figure 4, A showing how a piece may step in any

one of eight directions, and B showing a piece in a continuous hop over friendly and opposing pieces.

Strategy

Halma is a race game, so strategy must consist in devising ways of moving pieces across the board as quickly as possible. Clearly hopping is the quicker way, and as Figure 4 indicates, the formation of 'ladders' suitable for hopping will enable pieces to advance several squares at a turn. Of course ladders can equally be used by opponents moving in the opposite direction. Players should attempt to form ladders more suitable for themselves than opponents, and to block opponent's ladders. A new dimension is added to partnership play in that partners can form ladders of use to each other.

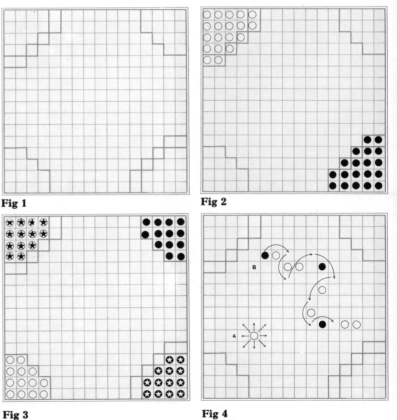

Fig 1

Fig 2

Fig 3

Fig 4

Nine Men's Morris

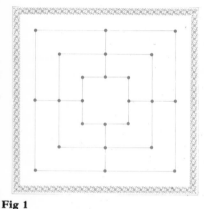

Fig 1

Nine Men's Morris is a game with its origins in ancient history. Layouts have been found on articles, in manuscripts and in tombs dating from various times, including one cut into roofing slabs at Kurna dating from around 1400 BC. It is called the Mill in the United States and Germany (*Muhle*) and is also known as *Morelles* or *Merels*. It has similarities to the children's game Noughts and Crosses, or Tit Tat Toe. It was at its most popular in the 14th century and acquired the name Morris in England possibly due to the board resembling the patterns made by Morris dancers. Three Men's Morris and Six Men's Morris are also played. Each game is for two players.

The Board and Pieces

The layout of the board is shown in Figure 1. It will be seen that there are three concentric squares, with four joining lines, which make 24 intersecting points arranged in 16 lines of three points each. Each player has nine counters, with contrasting colours for each player. No counters are on the board at the start of the game.

The Object of the Game

Play takes place on the 24 intersecting points on the board. Each player attempts to arrange three of his pieces in a line on the board. Such a line is known as a *mill*. This entitles him to remove any one of his opponent's pieces from the board, except any that are themselves forming a mill. A player who can reduce his opponent to two pieces only or blocks him from making a legitimate move wins the game.

The Play

The play is in two distinct phases. In the first phase, players alternately lay each piece onto one of the 24 points. A player making a mill is entitled to capture any enemy piece, which becomes dead. A possible end to the first phase, with all pieces in position and none so far captured, is shown in Figure 2. In the second phase players alternately move one piece along a line to an adjoining vacant point, still attempting to make a mill. A mill can be made any number of times by moving one of the pieces on one turn (called opening the mill) and moving it back on the following turn, thus closing the mill again and removing another opposing piece. A player with only three pieces left, forming a mill, must open the mill on his turn, even if it means losing a piece and thus the game.

Fig 2

Fig 3

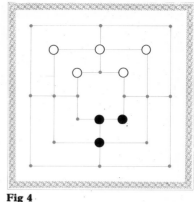

Fig 4

Strategy

To discuss strategy, it is necessary to number the points on the board, and this is done in Figure 3. As an example of the way the game progresses, consider the position in Figure 2, with all pieces played. Black can form a mill in three moves, by moving 12-7, 11-12 and 17-16. White cannot prevent this mill, if Black moves first. On the other hand, White can form a mill in two moves, by moving 5-8 and 6-5. However, Black can prevent this mill by moving 4-5 as soon as point 5 becomes vacant. So if both players attempt these mills, the game might proceed: B 12-7, W 5-8, B 4-5 (to prevent the mill), W 15-3, B 11-12, W 10-11, B 17-16 (forming a mill). Black then removes W 11. White must now attempt to block 11 and 17 to prevent Black opening and closing this mill, so W 20-17, B 12-11, W 22-10, B 11-12 (forming a mill). Black removes W 8, again has two points (11 and 8) on which to open and close the mill, and is on the way to victory.

Let us imagine what might happen should it be White's turn to move first from Figure 2. Suppose White attempts to complete a mill on 2,5,8 with the piece on 18. The game proceeds W 18-13, B 12-7, W 13-9, B 7-8. Black must form a mill first, as White still cannot prevent the mill on 16,12,7. Therefore White's best procedure is W 5-8, B 4-5, W 8-7. White has prevented the threatened mill, and the game should develop into a long battle.

It is believed that, like Noughts and Crosses, with correct play by each player Nine Men's Morris will be a draw. Probably the best points to occupy in the first phase of the game are 5,11,14,20. From each of these a piece may move in four directions. The eight points allowing three moves are probably more valuable than the 12 allowing only two.

If the first player begins on one of the four favoured points (say 5) and the second player fails to respond with a piece on an adjacent point (in this case 2,4,6 or 8), then the first player can force a mill. This, too, has similarities to Noughts and Crosses. However, in this case, the first mill does not guarantee a win. Play out the following: W 5, B 11, W 8, B 2, W 9, B 7, W 13, B 18, W 14, B 15, W 6, B 4, W 21. White now has a mill on 6,14,21. Whatever piece he removes, Black replaces. Let us say White removes B 11. The game proceeds B 11, W 19, B 20. White now has one piece left. He cannot place it on 12 or 17, or Black will play B 16 and he will be unable to move next turn, and so lose the game. If he places it on 16, Black will put his last piece on 12 or 17, and White has only one more move. If White places his

Fig 5

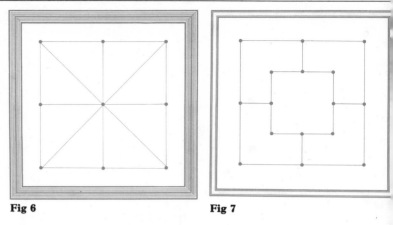

Fig 6   **Fig 7**

last piece on any vacant point on the outside square, Black will plac
his last piece on an adjacent square, and follow White's piece roun
the board until White can move no further. So Black wins withou
having made a mill. It must not be assumed, however, that a mil
made in the first phase of the game will lead to defeat.

A player who forms two mills will almost certainly win, and
double mill is particularly deadly. Positions to try to achieve ar
shown in Figure 4. Black's triangle of pieces allows two opportunitie
for mills to be made on 16 and 23, a valuable position in the firs
phase. White's position allows mills to be made on every turn in th
second phase, by moving the piece on 5 to 8 and back.

Variation
It is sometimes allowed that a player reduced to only three pieces ma
on his turn move any piece to any vacant point, not being restricted t
a point adjacent to the piece to be moved. Since this convention onl
enables a well-beaten player occasionally to win, it is not recom
mended.

Three Men's Morris
Three Men's Morris is played on a smaller board, as shown i
Figure 5. Each player has four pieces, which are alternately placed o
the intersections, each player trying to form a mill, which wins th
game. Once the pieces are played, they are not moved, and lik
Noughts and Crosses, correct play by both sides means every game i
drawn.

A refined version uses the board shown in Figure 6. Each playe
has three pieces, and once they are played to the board, pieces ar
moved along the lines to adjoining points, in an effort to form a mil
A player forming a mill wins. Correct play ensures a win for th
player going first.

Six Men's Morris
Six Men's Morris is played on the board shown in Figure 7. Eac
player has six pieces, and the game proceeds in two phases, as fo
Nine Men's Morris. The lines connecting the two squares are for th
purposes of moving pieces, and a piece at each end of any of thes
lines is not a mill, which has to be of three pieces in a line.

Dice Games

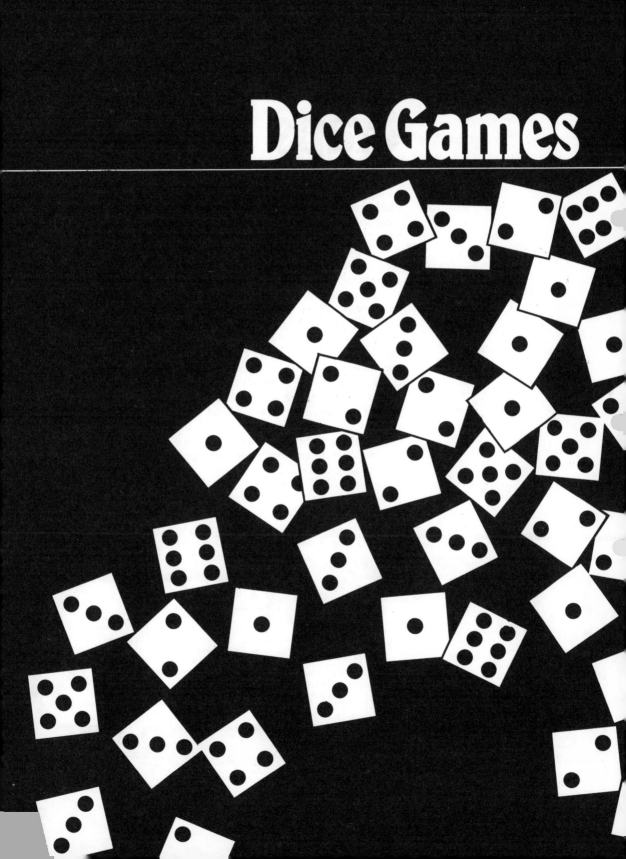

Craps

Craps is a gambling game played with two dice, perhaps the oldest of all gambling implements. Early dice players used astragals, the ankle bones of cloven-footed animals (usually sheep), which have distinct faces. The modern game of craps developed during the twentieth century from an old English game called Hazard, which was popular all over Europe (but was not the game Chuck-a-Luck, which is sometimes called Hazard). Craps is now the most popular dice game, and in Las Vegas, the gambling capital of the world, the craps tables usually are the busiest. It is also the gambling game with the fastest 'action'.

Craps can be played either in casinos or privately. In casinos there will be a staking table (of about 10 feet by five feet) and the game will be operated by employees. All bets will be made against the bank. In private games, the only equipment necessary is the dice, and bets will be made amongst the players. In private games, therefore, the range of bets allowed will normally be smaller than that in casinos, and the odds paid for each bet will also differ, since there is no need to build in a percentage profit for the casino. The casino game will be described first, as it is the more complicated. In this article all numbers which represent a total thrown by the dice are printed in red.

Casino Craps

Craps in a casino will be played on a table like that in Figure 1. There are many different styles of layout, but that in the illustration is typical, and will serve to describe the bets. Seated at the centre

Fig. 1

TOTAL	POSSIBLE COMBINATIONS	NUMBER OF WAYS	ODDS AGAINST
2		1	35—1
3		2	17—1
4		3	11—1
5		4	8—1
6		5	31—5
7		6	5—1
8		5	31—5
9		4	8—1
10		3	11—1
11		2	17—1
12		1	35—1

Fig. 2

of the table (at the top in the diagram) will be the boxman, who controls the game and keeps watch on all transactions. Opposite him will be the stickman who handles the dice and looks after the betting on the centre section of the table. On each side of the boxman will be a dealer, who looks after all bets at his end of the table. The gamblers stand round the table to left and right of the stickman, and use the casino's chips, which will usually vary in colour with the denomination.

The player who throws the dice is the shooter. He rolls the dice across the table so that they hit a backboard (which surrounds the table) before coming to rest. The first roll is known as his 'come-out' roll. The totals 7 and 11 are 'naturals', and should either be thrown the shooter wins immediately. The totals 2, 3 and 12 are 'craps', and mean the shooter loses. Should any other total appear it becomes the shooter's 'point', and the dealers at each end of the table place a marker in the box containing that number. The shooter then continues to roll the dice in an attempt to throw his point before he throws a 7. If he throws his point, he wins; if he throws a 7 he loses. Other totals do not count. A 7 therefore is a natural and a winner on the come-out roll, but a loser thereafter. Should the shooter win, the dice are said to 'pass' and a bet on this is called a 'right' bet. It is possible to bet that the dice 'don't pass' or 'miss-out', and this is a 'wrong' bet.

On this simple base is built a complex betting structure. However, the game remains one of chance only, and its main attraction to games players lies in examining the probabilities concerning the outcome of throwing two dice and comparing them with the various odds offered against the bets allowed. Figure 2 shows the 36 ways a pair of dice may fall, and lists the true odds against any total appearing. There are eight ways in which a shooter may come out with a natural 7 or 11, so that in the long run twice in every nine rolls the shooter will win immediately. There are a total of four ways in which the come-out roll may be a crap 2, 3 or 12, a loser for the shooter on one roll in nine. On the remaining six rolls in every nine, the shooter will make a point, and his chance of winning will vary with his point. To discover the shooter's overall chance of winning, a total of 1980 rolls must be considered to avoid fractions. Table 1 summarizes these rolls.

Table I: Shooter's Probability of Passing

Come-out roll	Number of times thrown	Number of winning coups	Number of losing coups
2 crap	55	—	55
3 crap	110	—	110
4 point	165	55	110
5 point	220	88	132
6 point	275	125	150
7 natural	330	330	—
8 point	275	125	150
9 point	220	88	132
10 point	165	55	110
11 natural	110	110	—
12 crap	55	—	55
Totals	1980	976	1004

Thus, in the long run, of every 1980 come out rolls, the shooter will win 976 and lose 1004, and since the bank offers even money for a pass bet, it will enjoy an advantage over the shooter of 1·414 per cent.

Using the table above, it is possible to calculate the bank's percentage advantage in all the craps bets it will allow.

The bets and advantages are as follows:

Win, Do, Pass or Front Line. This is a bet that the shooter will pass, and the stake is placed on the space marked 'line' on the table. This line might on other tables be marked 'pass line' or 'win'. The odds offered are even money. As calculated above, the bank's advantage is 1·414 per cent.

Lose, Don't, Don't Pass or Back Line. This is a bet that the shooter will lose, and the stakes are placed on the 'Don't Pass' space. The odds are again even money. As there are more ways in which the shooter can lose than win, the bank must adjust the bet to retain its advantage. The 'Don't Pass' line in Figure 1 states the adjustment: 'Bar 6, 6'. This means that if the shooter comes out with a double-6, don't pass bets are void, and await a further throw. A double-6 will occur 55 times in the total of 1980 rolls listed in Table 1, and if these are barred, the shooter can lose only 949 times, while still winning 976 times, so the don't pass bettor finds that the casino keeps its advantage, although it is slightly less, 1·403 per cent. Some casinos bar double-1 rather than double-6, and their advantage remains the same. Others bar 1, 2, which occurs twice as often as double-1 or double-6, and their advantage rises to 4·385 per cent.

Come. This is a bet made when the shooter has already established his point. It is the same as a pass bet, except that the shooter's next roll will be considered as his come-out roll. The stake is placed in the box marked 'come'. If the shooter's next roll is a natural, the come bettor wins immediately. Similarly he loses if the next roll is a crap. Alternatively, the next roll might establish a point for the come bettor, in which case the dealer will move the stake to the appropriate point box. The bet is then the same as a pass bet, except that the shooter and the come bettor will have different points and will win or lose at different times in the sequence of rolls. The odds offered are even money. The bank's advantage is, as for pass bets, 1·414 per cent.

Don't Come. This bet is the opposite of a come bet, made when the shooter has established his point. As with a don't pass bet, the double-6 is barred (or the double-1 or 1, 2 as explained earlier). The don't come stake is placed in the box marked 'don't come', and moved by the dealer to the blank square below the appropriate point square when the shooter has made a new point for the don't come bettor. The odds offered are evens. The casino's advantage is 1·403 per cent (or 4·385 per cent if the 1, 2 is barred).

Big Six and Big Eight. These are bets that a 6 or an 8 will appear before a 7, and the stakes are placed in the appropriate box. Reference to Figure 2 shows that a 7 will be thrown six times to every five for a 6 or an 8. The odds offered are even money, so the bank enjoys an advantage of 9.091 per cent.

Field. This is a bet that any of a group of numbers will appear on the next roll. The stake is placed on the space marked 'Field' on the table. The group of numbers on the table in Figure 1 is 2, 3, 4, 9, 10, 11, 12. Figure 2 shows that one of this group will appear 16 times in 36. The odds offered are even money, but to give the bettor a fairer bet, the double-6 and double-1 are paid double, i.e. at odds of 2−1. This means that the bettor on the field can expect a return of 34 chips for every 36 staked, an advantage to the bank of 5·556 per cent. The field varies, and some casinos will offer the 5 instead of the 4 in the field, but will not pay double on the double-1 and double-6 The bank's advantage remains the same.

Hardway. This is a bet that 4, 6, 8 or 10 will be made the hard way, i.e. by means of a double, before it is made any other way or before a 7 is thrown. The bets are placed in the appropriate place in the centre of the table, where it will be seen that the bank offers 8 *for* 1 (7 *to* 1) on hardway 4s and 10s, and 10 *for* 1 on hardway 6s and 8s. Since there are eleven ways in which a 6 or 7 can be thrown, and only one is a double-3, the correct odds for a hardway 6 are 10−1. In offering 10 *for* 1, the bank thereby takes an advantage of 9·091 per cent, and takes the same for hardway 8s. The bank's percentage on hardway 4s and 10s is 11·111 per cent.

Place or Box Numbers. These are bets that a chosen number will be thrown before a 7. Stakes are placed on the line above or below the respective point number. On 4 and 10 the bank pays odds of 9−5. Reference to Figure 2 shows the correct odds to be 2−1, so the bank's advantage is 6·667 per cent. On 5 and 9 the bank pays 7−5, its advantage being 4·000 per cent. On 6 and 8 the bank pays either 7−6, in which case its advantage is 1·515 per cent, or even money in which case its advantage is 9·091 per cent. Note that if the casino offers odds of 7−6 on place 6 and 8 bets, it is pointless backing Big Six and Big Eight at even money, where the bank enjoys nearly six times the advantage.

Buy or Lay Bets. A buy bet is similar to a place bet in that the player bets that a point number will appear before 7. The difference is that on the buy bet the casino will pay winners at the correct odds: for points 4 and 10 at 2−1, for 5 and 9 at 3−2, and for 6 and 8 at 6−5. However, it will exact a commission of 5 per cent of the stake. Since the minimum commission will be the minimum stake, the gambler must stake 20 times the minimum or pay a higher percentage commission. The casino's advantage on these bets is 4·762 per cent. Reference to the percentages for place bets shows that the player does better to buy bets on 4 and 10 and to place them on 5, 6, 8 and 9. Lay bets are the opposite of buy bets, i.e. the player bets that 7 appears before the point. The true odds are paid: for points 4 and 10 at 1−2, for 5 and 9 at 2−3, and for 6 and 8 at 5−6. The 5 per cent commission is this time exacted on the winnings rather than the stake, i.e. 1 chip commission will be levied on a stake of 40 on points 4 and 10, 30 on points 5 and 9, and 24 on points 6 and 8, since each of the bets will win 20 chips. The casino's advantage is respectively 2·439 per cent, 3·226 per cent and 4·000 per cent. The bets are made by the player placing his stake on the table and calling the point he wants. The dealer removes the house commission (called 'vigorish') from the stake and places the stake in the correct box.

Other Bets. There are various other bets or combinations of bets possible at craps. A few are shown on the table in Figure 1. Most are 'one-roll action' bets, and are settled on the result of one roll. For instance, a gambler can back 7 to appear on the next throw. The odds are 5 *for* 1, and the bank's advantage 16·667 per cent. Odds of 30 *for* 1 are offered for double-1 and double-6, with the same advantage to the bank. Odds of 15 *for* 1 are offered for 3 and 11, the advantage still being 16·667 per cent. All craps are offered at 8 *for* 1, an advantage to the bank of 11·111 per cent.

Free or Odds Bets. When the shooter has a point, casinos allow players who have bet on pass, don't pass, come or don't come to double their bets, and the second half of the bet is paid at the correct odds. Thus pass or come bettors will get 2−1 on points 4 and 10, don't pass or don't come bettors will get 1−2. The odds offered on 5 and 9 will be 3−2 and 2−3 respectively, and on 6 and 8, 6−5 and 5−6. For example, a come bettor with a point of 6 and a stake of five chips will be allowed a free or odds bet of five chips on 6, to be paid at odds of 6−5. As the casino will not deal in fractions of a chip, the stake on this particular free bet must always be in multiples of five, and the player will be allowed to round up or down his stake to the nearest multiple of five. If his stake is only one or two chips he will not be allowed a free bet at all. The casino allows the free bet to speed up the action, and takes no commission on it. Thus the player should always accept it for the maximum stake allowed, and correspondingly reduce the bank's advantage on the total bet. Free bet stakes are not placed flat on the table, but overlap the edge of the original stake.

The bank's overall advantage on the bet can be calculated by reference to Table 1. Of the 1980 rolls summarized, the bank returns to the pass line bettor 976 × 2 chips (assuming one chip per bet), or 1952 chips. The table shows that 1320 of the 1980 rolls will result in a point and if the pass bettor takes the free bet each time he will stake a further 1320 chips, and, since the bets are paid at the correct odds, can expect 1320 chips back in return. Thus, if he always accepts the free bets, his total stakes on the 1980 rolls will be 1980 + 1320, or 3300 chips, from which in the long run he will expect 1952 + 1320 back, or 3272. So he will expect to lose only 28 chips in 3300, a casino advantage of only 0·848 per cent. Don't pass bettors will do even better, with an advantage to the bank of only 0·832 per cent. This is the lowest advantage the casino takes in crap games, except for some casinos in Reno, where free bets are allowed of double the original stake. A player making full use of these bets will reduce the casino's advantage to 0·606 per cent on pass or come bets and 0·595 per cent on don't pass or don't come bets.

Private Craps

Craps played privately is a much simpler game than casino craps. The only essential equipment is a pair of dice, although a blanket or carpet might be used to roll them on, and a backboard for the dice to rebound from is advisable. Because of the lack of a staking table, the bets are fewer and simpler.

The first shooter places a sum of money before him as his 'centre' bet, and the other players are invited to 'fade' it. The shooter is betting he will win; the other players put up an amount equal to his stake to bet he will lose. It is an even money bet. As in the casino game, the shooter wins if he throws a natural 7 or 11, loses if he throws a crap 2, 3 or 12, and continues to roll if he establishes a point.

Meanwhile, the other players bet among themselves on whether the shooter passes or not. Come and don't come bets are also made. Once a shooter has thrown his point, he and other players may bet that he will or will not make it. The correct odds are paid, i.e. 6–5 that he will make 6 or 8, 3–2 that he will make 5 or 9, and 2–1 that he will make 4 or 10. Sometimes even money is bet on the shooter making a point of 6 or 8, but this is incorrect, and gives the wrong bettor a tremendous advantage. Hardway bets are common. If the shooter's point is 4 or 10, 8–1 are the odds against making it the hard way. It is 10–1 against making a hardway 6 or 8. The players may make other bets among themselves, but those already mentioned are the commonest.

The shooter keeps the dice while winning; as soon as he misses out he passes the dice to the next player in rotation.

Strategy
Craps is a game of chance, and skilful play consists only of knowing the proper odds and probabilities for each bet, and making bets which are arithmetically sound. In private crap games the wrong bettor generally has an advantage of 1·414 per cent, a significant advantage over a long period. In casino games, a sound bet is merely one with a small advantage to the casino. The player will therefore avoid, for example, Big Six, Big Eight and hardway bets. Wrong bettors face a slightly smaller disadvantage than right bettors. If the free or odds bets are made whenever possible, the casino's advantage can be kept below 1 per cent.

Dice Games

In this section are described a selection of games which require only dice and sometimes a sheet of paper on which to keep a score. Most dice games are very simple, many are games of chance only, and even those games which allow skill to be exercised depend considerably more on chance. This leads to many of them needing a gambling element for their attraction, and some are indeed pure gambling games. Nevertheless the simplicity of dice games can be an asset when an awkward number of players of varying standards require games needing only intermittent concentration.

The games are arranged in order according to the number of dice required, beginning with two games requiring only one die.

It is advisable to play all dice games with a dice cup, which should be shaken before the dice are thrown. When players throw from their hands, sooner or later one player will develop secret or outspoken suspicions about another player's lucky throw.

Twenty-one

Any number may play, and only one die is required. It is not necessary to keep a score sheet. Players each roll a die to determine who takes first throw, lowest first. Play then proceeds clockwise.

Each player on his turn throws the die as often as he wishes, adding his scores together, in an attempt to score 21, or as near to 21 as possible, without exceeding it. A player may stop when he likes, when the turn passes to the next player clockwise. A player who exceeds 21 is out of the game. The player nearest to 21 at the end of the round wins. Should two or more players be equal, they play off a deciding game between them.

Strategy A player with a score of 18 has an even chance of improving his score by taking another throw. It would therefore be unwise for an early player to stop with a score lower than 18. Once a target has been set, later players will continue to throw until they have at least equalled or bettered it. The later his turn in the round, the better a player's chance of winning.

Variation To speed the game up, two dice might be used until a player reaches a score of 14, when he discards one and continues his turn with one die. Of course, he might exceed 21 before changing to one die.

Gambling When played as a gambling game, all players begin by contributing one chip to a pool. Additionally, each player who exceeds 21 must add another chip to the pool. This alters the strategy only a little, as a player playing last and facing a total of 21 would be advised to risk an extra chip attempting to improve even from a score of 20, provided there were ten or more chips in the pool. The extra chip has the effect of reducing the early player's disadvantage, as a good score could force the later players to exceed 21. It might be decided that in the gambling game players who tie should share the pool rather than play off. After the first round, the first player should be the player to the left of the first player in the previous round, and play should continue until all players have played first an equal number of times.

Pig

Any number may play Pig and one die is used. Players throw for turn, the lowest throwing first, and the turn passing clockwise. A player may throw the die as often as he wishes, adding together his scores. When he decides to stop, his score is entered against his name on a score sheet. However should he throw a 1, his turn ends and he scores nothing for the turn. The first player to reach 100 wins.

Variation The game can be played with two dice. A player throwing a 1 with either die loses his score for the turn. A throw of a double carries a bonus. A throw of double 1 scores 25 for the turn, irrespective of how many had already been accumulated by previous throws on that turn, and the dice pass to the next player. However, any other double thrown doubles the score shown for the throw (i.e. double-4 counts 16), and the player may continue throwing if he so desires.

Strategy A player must decide when to be satisfied with his score. The state of the game will influence the decision. A player well behind will find it necessary to take a risk in attempting a big score. Generally, anything above 15 is a reasonable score, but runs of 50 or so are not rare. It would be a brave player who continued beyond 50.

Gambling Pig is not usually played as a gambling game, but if desired players can either contribute to a pool, to be taken by the winner, or losers can pay off the winner at an agreed amount per ten points.

Barbudi

Sometimes known as Barbooth, Barbudi is a gambling game played in Mexico and Eastern Europe, which requires two dice. Any number may play and bet, but only two players at a time are involved in the action. Traditionally, miniature dice are used, but any dice are suitable.

The players throw a die, and the highest thrower becomes the *shooter*. The player to his right becomes the *fader*. (In Barbudi, the 'action' passes anti-clockwise). The fader puts up a stake of whatever amount he wishes (unless maximum and minimum amounts are agreed beforehand) and places it in the centre of the table. The shooter covers as much of the stake as he wants. If all is not covered, the player to the fader's right has the option of covering all or some of the remainder, and so on round the table until the stake is covered. If any remains uncovered, the fader withdraws it. The shooter may give up his opportunity to be shooter and pass the dice to the player on his right, who becomes shooter. Similarly, the fader may decline to put up a bet, in which case the player on his right becomes fader. In placing his bet, the fader stipulates a one-shot or two-shot decision, the meaning of which will become clear later.

When the fader's bet has been covered, the shooter and the fader throw alternately, shooter first, to decide the fate of the bets.

In a one-shot decision game, either player wins if he throws double-6, double-5, double-3 or 6-5 (see Figure 1). Either player loses if he throws double-1, double-2, double-4 or 1-2 (see Figure 2). Bets are immediately settled. If the shooter wins, he remains shooter for the next round, and the fader remains fader. If the fader wins, he becomes shooter for the next round, and the player on his right is the new fader.

In a two-shot decision game, a throw of 6-5 wins only half the bet, and a throw of 1-2 loses only half. Either player can then decide to end the round there, with winners taking only half the opposing stake as winnings, and losers retaining the other half. If the shooter won, he remains shooter, otherwise the fader becomes shooter for the new round.

On the other hand, both players can agree to continue to shoot for the second half of the stake. In this case all stakes are left on the table. If the shooter won the first half, he remains shooter for the second half. If the fader won the first half, the players reverse roles for the second half of the bet, and the old fader has the privilege of shooting first as the new shooter. When the decisive throw is cast, if the same

Fig 1

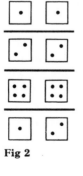

Fig 2

side won both halves of the bet they collect their winnings. If each side won one half of the bet, then each bettor withdraws his own stake. When the second half of a two-decision game is contested, both the shooter and the fader lose their roles, whoever wins, and the shooter for the next round is the player to the original fader's right.

Variation Some players find the one-shot or two-shot decision needlessly complicates the game, and ignore it, treating all games as one-shot games, where all bets are immediately settled on a winning or losing throw. However, the 6-5 and 2-1 throws retain some significance, as a shooter who loses by throwing 2-1 or by the fader throwing 6-5 can retain his position as shooter for the next round.

Gambling The game can only operate as a gambling game. Played privately, it is an even game, with no advantage to either shooter or fader. However, it is a popular game in clubs and casinos in some parts of the world, and in these games the gambling house usually takes 5 per cent of the losing bets before paying out the winnings, in effect taking $2\frac{1}{2}$ per cent commission on all money staked. This is a heavy commission to attempt to overcome over a long period.

Four-Five-Six

Four-Five-Six is cometimes called See-Low, and is derived from a Chinese game called Strung Flowers, which is described as a variation later. It is a banking game suitable for any number of players and requires three dice. All players throw the three dice, the highest thrower becoming first banker.

The banker puts up a stake, or bank, and players in turn to his left may cover all or part of it, until it is all covered, or until no more players want to bet. If any part remains uncovered, the banker withdraws it. The banker then throws the dice, and continues to throw until he achieves one of the following significant throws:

1.   A throw which wins all bets immediately. These are (a) any triplet; (b) 4-5-6; (c) any pair with a 6.

2.   A throw which loses all bets immediately. These are (a) 1-2-3; (b) any pair with a 1.

3.   A throw which establishes a point for the banker. These are any pair with 2, 3, 4 or 5.

In the last case, the odd die represents the banker's point, and the play on the round continues.

The first bettor to the banker's left throws the dice, and continues to throw until he throws a significant throw. If he throws a combination listed in (1) above, he wins. If he throws a combination listed in (2) above, he loses. If he throws a point for himself, as listed in (3) above, he wins if his point is higher than the banker's, loses if it is lower, and ties, and recovers his stake, if his point is the same. The next bettor to his left then settles his bet in the same way, and so on until all bets are settled.

The banker retains his bank for the next round, unless (a) he loses the whole bank in the course of the play, in which case the bank passes to the player on his left or (b) a player throwing against the banker's point throws a triplet or a 4-5-6 combination, in which case the bank passes to him on the next round, the banker withdrawing any of the bank which is remaining after the round has been completed.

Strategy Four-Five-Six is a game of chance, and no strategy applies but it should be recognised that the banker holds an advantage of about 2.47 per cent, due to the fact that in his initial roll there are 27 outright winning throws against 21 outright losing throws, and of 60 point-making throws he will win 25, lose 28.33 and tie 6.67. Half of all possible throws of three dice produce a significant throw.

Variation The Chinese game Strung Flowers has the following variations:

1. All players throw the dice for choice of first banker, and the player who throws most 4s becomes banker. Players who tie throw again until a decision is reached.

2. Players place their stakes in front of them, and the banker covers each in turn. This assures that all players who wish to do so can play on each round. It is advisable to agree on a maximum stake beforehand.

3. All stakes are made in multiples of three, for reasons which will become clear immediately.

4. When both the banker and player throw a point, the bet is settled according to the difference in the two points. Thus if the difference is one point, only one third of the stake is won and lost; if two points, two thirds; if three points, all the stake. This has the effect of very slightly increasing the banker's advantage.

5. The banker loses his bank only when he makes a point which is beaten by a player's point. The bank then passes to the banker's left at the end of the round.

This last variation ensures that by agreement a game can continue until all the players have enjoyed the bank an equal number of times.

In the Chinese version, a throw of 4-5-6 is known as *Strung Flowers*, 1,2,3 as the *Dancing Dragon*, and a pair with an ace as *Ace Negative*. Many will think it a more pleasing version of the game than Four-Five-Six.

Buck Dice

Buck Dice is a game which finds a loser rather than a winner. Any number can play, and three dice are used. Players throw the dice to decide (a) who takes first throw and (b) who establishes a *point number*. The lowest player throws one die, and whichever number he throws becomes the point number for the game. The highest player then takes the first throw. Play proceeds clockwise.

The first player throws all three dice, and scores one point for each point number that he throws. He continues to throw the three dice, keeping count of his points, until he fails to score on any throw, when his score for the turn is entered on a score sheet and the dice pass to the player on his left. A player who throws a triplet, other than the point number, scores a *Little Buck*, which is worth five points. A triplet of the point number is *Big Buck*, and all the thrower's previous scores are wiped out and he is given a total of 15.

As players reach 15 points, they retire from the game, so Big Buck earns immediate retirement. The last player left is the loser. Each player must end exactly on 15, and if during a turn a player scores points which take him beyond 15 (for example by throwing two points or Little Buck when his score is already 14) he loses his score for that round and passes the dice to the next player.

Variation This variation is played as a gambling game. All players contribute one unit to a pool, and the game produces a winner, who takes the pool, rather than a loser, as above.

The first thrower also establishes the point. He throws a single die, and a throw of 4, 5 or 6 establishes the point number. Should he throw 1, 2 or 3 (on this throw called a *Mulligan*), he must throw again, and must continue to throw until he establishes a point of 4, 5 or 6. However, after the Mulligan, which is 'free', each time he fails to establish a point he must add another unit to the pool. This counters the big advantage a player has in going first.

Once the point is established, the first player throws the three dice and rethrows them each time he scores, until a throw fails to produce a score, when his score for the turn is entered on the score sheet and the dice pass to the next player, clockwise. Scoring is more varied than in the parent game. Each point number scores one, but a player who scores two point numbers in one throw is credited with Little Buck, worth five points. Any triplet other than the point number is also Little Buck, and scores five points. A triplet of the point number is Big Buck, and wins the game immediately irrespective of the current score.

Also any combination of smaller numbers thrown which add up to the point number score a point. Thus if the point number is 6, a throw of 1,2,3 earns a point; 2,4,6 earns two points; 3,3,1 earns a point.

A player must score 15 exactly to win (but need not complete his turn once a throw has taken his score to 15). Should a throw take his total past 15, he loses the score for that throw only, and his turn ends.

Unless the game is won with Big Buck, a player failing to score at the end of the game must add one unit to the pool. Some will think it a weakness of the game that occasionally a player will win on his first turn, leaving other players to contribute an extra unit to the pool without having had a turn – but at least before the first player is decided, all players have an equal chance.

Chuck-a-Luck

Chuck-a-luck is a banking game, using three dice. It is basically the same game as Crown and Anchor, once popular with the Royal Navy, and now occasionally to be found operated illegally on street corners and racetracks.

The game cannot be played without gambling, and a layout should be made on which stakes can be placed. This is shown in Figure 3. Players place their bets on whichever number they fancy will appear at least once in a throw of the dice.

The banker then throws three dice, and pays out as follows: on all single numbers thrown, he pays out bettors at even money; on all pairs, he pays out bettors at 2-1; on a triple he pays bettors at 3-1. He collects losing bets, and another round begins.

Fig 3

Fig 4

This game is popular in casinos, where instead of throwing the dice the banker may tumble a birdcage (see Figure 4). An advantage is held by the casino (or the banker in a private game) arising from the fact that doubles should be paid at 14-1 and triples at 215-1. This amounts to an advantage to the banker of 7.87 per cent. It is advisable therefore in private games for the bank to circulate.

Sometimes casinos and carnivals, particularly in America, will operate a wheel called a Chuck-a-Luck wheel or Big Six Wheel, in which combinations of three dice are shown on a giant upright wheel, which is spun to decide the winning combination. These wheels do not show all 216 possible results of a throw of three dice. They might show, for instance, just the 56 different combinations (ignoring the fact that with three dice, 4,3,2, for instance, can be thrown six ways), in which case the operators enjoy an advantage of 12.50 per cent. Other wheels have a casino advantage of 22.22 per cent. All these wheels are to be avoided.

Yacht

Yacht is one of the most interesting dice games, calling for judgment. It is one of many 'category' games, some others of which are described later. Any number may play. Five dice are required. A special score sheet must be ruled up (Figure 5) showing the players and the various categories in which they may score.

Players throw to determine who goes first – lowest starts. Each player has up to three throws at each turn. After the first throw of the dice, he may set aside any that he wishes to keep, and rethrow the remainder. He may do the same after the second throw, but after the third throw the five dice represent his score. He may, if he wishes, stop after the first or second throw. He must then decide into which category on the score sheet to enter his score. The categories and scores are:

Yacht (five of a kind): scores 50.

Big Straight (2,3,4,5,6): scores 30.

Little Straight (1,2,3,4,5): scores 30.

Four of a Kind   scores the total
Full House (three of one kind, two   number of pips
   of another   showing on the
Choice (any five dice)   five dice.

Sixes: scores six points for every 6 thrown. Similarly *Fives* scores
   five points for every 5, and so on.

The play ends after 12 rounds with each player having entered a

	CHRIS	MARY	KAREL	JOHN	
YACHT					
BIG STRAIGHT					
LITTLE STRAIGHT					
FOUR OF A KIND					
FULL HOUSE					
CHOICE					
SIXES					
FIVES					
FOURS					
THREES					
TWOS					
ACES					
TOTAL					

Fig 5

score in each category. A player must select a category, even if he scores nothing for it, and once a category is filled, the score for that category cannot be superseded by a later, higher score. For instance, if a player throws 5,5,5,5,3 and already has his categories for *Four of a Kind* and *Fives* filled, he must decide whether to score 23 for *Choice*, three for *Threes*, or zero in any other category. Players often dispense with awkward throws by entering zero in the *Aces* category, as maximum score for this category is only five.

After 12 rounds, the scores are added for each player, the highest being the winner.

Strategy Players should attempt to score the big scores at the top of the list of categories. A player with 2,3,4,5 has two chances of completing a straight with one throw to come, the odds against achieving either *Big* or *Little Straight* being 2-1. However an 'open' straight (e.g. 2,3,5,6) presents only a 5-1 chance of completion. Players with a triplet on the first or second throw will probably throw the other two dice, attempting *Yacht*, *Four of a Kind* or *Full House*. A player ending with, say, 4,4,4,4,2, will usually do better to score it in *Four of a Kind* rather than *Fours*, since a later throw of 4,4,4,6,3 could then score 12 in *Fours* where it would be useless elsewhere, unless *Choice* were still open, in which case 21 would be scored. As mentioned above, players often dump a poor throw in *Aces* or *Twos*, since these categories cannot score highly. Occasionally, near the end of a game, a player might register a poor throw as zero for *Yacht*, since most players in a game will not score for *Yacht*. Naturally, a

	LEIGH	SUE	GLYN	IAN	
SMALL GENERAL	60				
FOUR OF A KIND		40			
FULL HOUSE		30		30	
STRAIGHT	20		20		
SIXES		18	18	24	
FIVES	15		15		
FOURS	12				
THREES					
TWOS					
ACES		0	0	3	
TOTAL					

Fig 6

player will bear in mind which categories are still open to him when re-throwing his dice. For instance, if the only two categories left are *Fives* and *Big Straight*, it would be pointless retaining a pair of 6s.

Gambling If gambling is required, players usually pay the winner according to the points difference, at an agreed sum per 10 points.

General

This is another 'category' game, played on the same lines as *Yacht* but with different categories and a different scoring system. The system of play is the same.

The categories are shown in the score sheet (Figure 6). Some scores have been entered as if a game were in progress. The scoring for the first four categories varies according to the throw on which the score was made.

Big General is five of a kind made on the first throw of any turn. It is not entered on the score sheet, as a throw of Big General wins the game immediately.

Small General is five of a kind made on the second or third throw, and scores 60.

Four of a Kind scores 45 on the first throw, 40 on the second or third.

Full House scores 35 on the first throw, 30 on the second or third.

Straight (either 1,2,3,4,5 or 2,3,4,5,6) scores 25 on the first throw, 20 on the second or third.

Sixes, Fives, Fours, Threes, Twos and *Aces* are scored as in Yacht.

An ace in one category only is 'half-wild'. In *Straight*, an Ace may be counted as a 2 or 6, but not 3,4, or 5. Thus 1,3,4,5,6 or 1,1,3,4,5 can both count as a *Straight*.

General is an extremely popular game among Puerto Ricans. The strategy is similar to that of Yacht.

	PETER	CAMILLA	KIM	IAN
CRAG				
THIRTEEN				
HIGH STRAIGHT				
LOW STRAIGHT				
EVEN STRAIGHT				
ODD STRAIGHT				
THREE OF A KIND				
SIXES				
FIVES				
FOURS				
THREES				
TWOS				
ACES				
TOTAL				

Fig 7

Crag

Crag is a 'category' game included here because the principles are similar to Yacht and General, but it is interesting because it is played with only three dice and is a quicker game than the others. Any number may play.

In Crag, a player may make only two throws per turn. The categories are shown in the score sheet (Figure 7).

Crag is any pair plus a third die in which the three dice total 13, e.g. 4,4,5 or 6,6,1, and scores 50.

Thirteen is any three dice totalling 13, and scores 26.

If a *Crag* is thrown, and the *Crag* category is already filled, the throw may score as *Thirteen*.

High Straight (4,5,6), *Low Straight* (1,2,3), *Even Straight* (2,4,6) and *Odd Straight* (1,3,5) all score 20.

Three of a Kind scores 25.

Sixes, Fives, Fours, Threes, Twos and *Aces* score as in Yacht.

Drop Dead

Drop Dead is a fast, simple game using five dice, especially suitable for games involving children. Players throw a single die to decide the order of play, lowest going first. Ties are rethrown.

The first player throws the five dice, and if no 5s or 2s appear, he scores the total of the numbers thrown, and rethrows the five dice. However if any dice show a 5 or 2, he scores nothing for that throw,

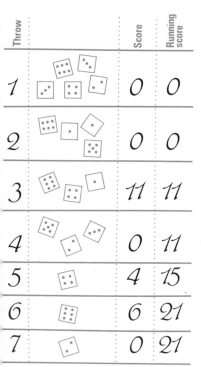

Throw		Score	Running score
1		0	0
2		0	0
3		11	11
4		0	11
5		4	15
6		6	21
7		0	21

Fig 8

puts aside the dice showing 5 or 2 and rethrows the remainder. Each throw he makes without a 5 or 2 scores the total showing, and he continues to throw until all dice are eliminated. His score is then noted on the score sheet and the dice pass to the left for the next player to throw. A specimen turn is shown in Figure 8. When all players have thrown, the player with the highest score is the winner.

The game provides lower scores than might be imagined, and anything over 20 is a good score. It is interesting to note that the odds against scoring with five dice are 211-32 (about 13-2), against scoring with four dice are 65-16 (about 4-1), against scoring with three dice are 19-8 (nearly 5-2) and against scoring with two dice 5-4. With one die remaining, there is a 2-1 on chance of scoring. Therefore players tend to discard dice quickly, but occasionally run up a score with only one die remaining. A player who scores with five dice is in a strong position.

Variation For a longer game play might continue until each player has had five turns.

Qualify
Qualify is a banking game, using five dice. When played socially each player should hold the bank in turn. First banker is decided by each player rolling one die, highest becoming banker.

Each player puts up a stake, which is covered by the banker. It is advisable to agree a maximum stake. The banker takes no part in the play. Each bet is settled in turn, beginning with the player to the banker's left.

The object of the game is to score 25 points or more.

The first player throws the five dice, and sets aside the highest die as a contribution to his score. He then rethrows the four remaining dice, again setting aside the highest, and so on until he throws the last die singly, and totals his score.

If his score is 25 or more, he wins his bet; 24 or lower and the banker collects his stake.

Although 25 seems a high number for five dice, the thrower should be in with a chance on his last die (i.e. have a score of 19 or more) in about three-quarters of his turns, and should have an even or better chance (21 or more) in about half his turns. No less an authority than Ely Culbertson thought the banker had no advantage, but experience suggests that it might approach as much as 20 per cent.

Number of times point number appears	Odds paid
26	4–1
27	5–1
28	6–1
29	8–1
30 or more	10–1
13	5–1
10 or fewer	10–1

Fig 9

Twenty-six

Twenty-six is a game for any number, which uses ten dice. It is a banking game. Players throw a single die to decide first banker: highest wins.

The player on the left of the banker puts up a stake (it is advisable to agree on a maximum beforehand) and chooses a point number, from 1 to 6, which he announces. He then throws all ten dice from a cup 13 times, keeping a running count of how many times the point number appears. It is best if the banker writes down the running total after each throw, so that no argument arises as to how many throws have been taken. Should the thrower score 26 or more, he wins; less than 26 he loses his stake to the banker, unless he scores 13 or fewer than 11, in which case he wins. The banker pays winners according to the table in Figure 9.

The odds quoted are thought to be fairest. Wherever Twenty-six is played, the odds vary from game to game, and a game operated by a gambling house will offer considerably shorter odds.

In effect, the number of times a point would be 'expected' to be thrown is 21.67, so a score of 26 or more is difficult to achieve, and the bank should show a profit in the long run. At the end of each round the bank passes to the next player clockwise.

Variation Fourteens is a similar game to Twenty-Six, also using ten dice. However, in Fourteens, a player nominates his point number *after* his first throw. Should his first throw produce a triplet or better, the number of the triplet or better becomes his point number, and he is credited with the number of times it appears. Should his first throw not produce a triplet or better, then he can choose and announce any point number, and is credited with a score of three for his first throw.

He has four further throws, totalling the number of times he throws his point number, and wins if he scores 14 or more, when he is paid at odds of 8-1. If his last four throws fail to produce a point number, he also wins and is paid at 8-1. Again, the bank should show a profit.

Poker Dice

Poker Dice is played with a special set of five dice, whose six faces are shown in Figure 10. It can be played with standard dice. The first player is chosen by lot, and thereafter for each round, the player on his left throws first. Later players have an advantage over earlier players. Players contribute to a pool, to be taken by the winner.

Fig 10

On his turn, a player throws the five dice, and can set aside any he wishes to keep, and throw the remainder a second time. The object is to get the highest ranking poker hand. The rank of the hands are shown in Figure 11. Hands without a pair are of no value.

The first player's throw is noted, and subsequent players must attempt to beat it. When the throw is beaten, the new highest hand is noted. The player to have the highest hand at the end of the round wins.

With all hands except the two straights it is necessary to note the value of the hand within the rank to distinguish between hands of equal rank. For example, Four Queens will beat Four Jacks. With a Full House, the value of the triplet decides the winner, and the value of the pair decides only if another throw produces the same triplet. For example, Three Tens and Two Queens beats Three Nines and Two Aces, but loses to Three Tens and Two Kings. Similarly if two hands produce Two Pairs, the value of the higher pair has first importance. With Four of a Kind, Three of a Kind, Two Pairs and One Pair, the value of the odd dice are not significant. It should be decided beforehand whether, in the event of a tie, the winners play off or divide the pool.

Liar Dice

Liar Dice is a game for two players, using two sets of Poker Dice whose faces are illustrated in Figure 10. It is an awkward game to play, because each player throws separately, and neither player must see his opponent's hand until the showdown, so a screen must be erected between the two players. It is also a game of bluffing, and of all dice games most resembles the card game Poker. Standard sets of dice may be used. Each player throws a single die, higher becoming first *caller*.

Each player then throws his five dice, so that his opponent cannot see them. The caller then announces whether or not he is satisfied with his hand. If he is, play continues. If he announces he is dissatisfied, his opponent has the right to decide to play or not. The caller may announce 'either way' leaving the option to his opponent.

	Rank of hands in Poker Dice
1	Five of a kind
2	Four of a kind
3	Full house
	(three of a kind plus a pair)
4	High straight
	(A,K,Q,J,10)
5	Low straight
	(K,Q,J,10,9)
6	Three of a kind
7	Two pairs
8	One pair

Fig 11

If play is to continue, the caller announces his hand. Here the element of bluff enters, because the caller (and either player on subsequent announcements) may announce any hand he pleases, higher or lower than the actual hand held. Announcements must be in full, and specify each die, for example 'Three Kings, Ace, Jack' or 'Two Tens, Two Nines, Queen'.

If his opponent thinks the caller is bluffing, he may remove the screen immediately, and wins if the caller's hand is lower than announced. If the caller's hand is as announced or better, the caller wins. However if the caller's announcement is accepted, then the opponent must announce a higher hand. Now the caller has the choice of accepting or removing the screen. Removing the screen clearly is tantamount to calling one's opponent a liar, hence the name of the game.

Should the caller now accept his opponent's call, he may set aside any of his dice he wishes to keep, and rethrow the remainder. He must then announce a higher hand than his opponent, whose options are once again as on the first round. Play continues thus until each player has had two re-throws (i.e. three throws including the initial throw). After his opponent's third throw, the caller must remove the screen.

The game is usually played best of three or best of five hands, the loser paying the winner an agreed stake.

Strategy The object of announcing a lower hand than that held is to keep a little in hand as the hands improve through the play. The object of announcing a higher hand than held is to hope that the opponent accepts it and fails to beat it in his turn. A bluff should not be so high as to invite the opponent to remove the screen, as he wins if he does. The most difficult choice arises when either player announces three of a kind on his first roll, as this is a better hand than can be expected, but not high enough to be a fairly sure bluff. Always announce a Straight correctly, and remove the screen on your first option, as this hand is extremely difficult to improve with a re-throw. It is usually best to announce high hands, such as Full House or better, correctly and remove the screen on your turn. If the caller has a good hand on his first throw, an announcement of 'either way' risks his opponent not playing, but if the call is accepted, the caller knows he has a better hand than his opponent expects.

Roulette

Roulette

Roulette is a gambling game of chance, in which the winning and losing is decided by a ball falling into a numbered pocket on a wheel which spins in one direction while the ball rolls in the other. Although no skill is required to play it, it has a fascination for games players with a liking for arithmetic because of the ingenuity of the systems which gamblers have invented for years in an effort to make their fortunes. The search for an infallible system continues despite periodic and mistaken claims that it has been found. Roulette is primarily a casino game, but home sets are marketed widely, and it is possible to hire full-size wheels and tables.

The use of a pocketed wheel and a ball for gaming dates back to about the year 1700 when a game called hoca became popular in casinos on the continent of Europe. In England a game called E.O. was played in which, instead of numbered compartments, all the pockets were lettered E or O (for even or odd). A game more similar to modern roulette was developed in Europe in the eighteenth century. Called boule, and still played today, it consists of a stationary wheel set in a bowl around which a ball is rolled. There are eighteen pockets numbered 1 to 9, two pockets for each number. Gamblers can back any number to win (and be paid 7 to 1 if successful), or back various groups of four numbers at even money. The number 5 is always a loser on these even-money bets. The bank thus can expect to retain over 11 per cent of all money staked, a much worse proposition for the gambler than playing roulette.

Roulette itself has also been played since the eighteenth century, and became very fashionable towards the end of the nineteenth, when the casino at Monte Carlo began to flourish and receive patronage from the royal families of Europe.

The Equipment

The basic equipment for roulette consists of the wheel and ball, and the table on which the bets are made. The wheel used in the Monte Carlo casino (Figure 1) has 37 pockets, numbered 1–36 and 0 (zero). The pockets are alternately red and black, except the zero pocket which is green. The numbers are arranged so that the high and low numbers, and the odd and even numbers also alternate as far as possible. In American casinos, the wheel is different (Figure 2). It has an additional zero pocket, numbered 00. As will be seen later, the effect of this extra pocket is to make betting on roulette much less attractive in American casinos than elsewhere, where a single zero is used. The arrangement of the numbers is

Fig. 1

Fig. 2

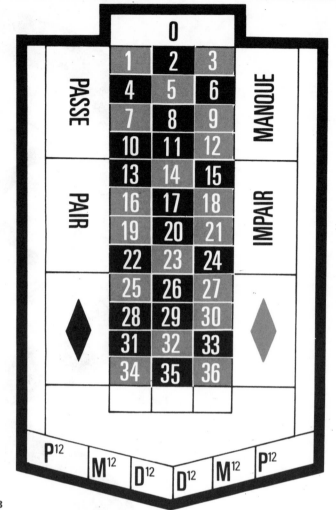

Fig. 3

different on the American wheel, although the eighteen red numbers on the Monte Carlo wheel are also red on the American wheel.

The table is of green baize cloth, marked in red, black and gold, although again the conventional layout differs in Monte Carlo and America. The layout of the table has no effect on the game, and indeed in Britain, where the Monte Carlo wheel is used, the table found in many casinos will be of the American pattern (but without the 00 space). The Monte Carlo table is illustrated in Figure 3 and the American table in Figure 4. The table in casinos might be double-ended, i.e. there will be a staking layout each side of the wheel, the zero being closest to the wheel at each end. The double-ended table allows more players to make bets in comfort.

The Casino Game

In a casino, roulette will be operated by croupiers, who will spin the wheel, rake in losing bets and pay out the winners. Bets will be made with the casino chips, which will usually be of a different colour for each player. When a game is in full swing, the wheel will be spun approximately every two minutes. Soon after setting the

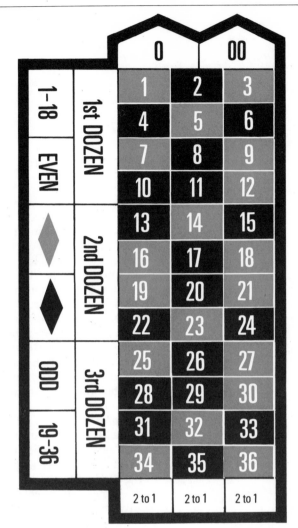

Fig. 4

wheel and ball in motion the croupier will call '*Rien ne va plus*' and no more bets may be made on that spin. The French language is traditionally used in describing roulette, although in English-speaking countries and particularly America this custom might not be observed, and '*Rien ne va plus*' becomes 'No more bets'.

The bets allowed fall into two categories, the even-money bets and those offering other odds.

The even-money bets are as follows:
Rouge, which is a bet that a red number will win
Noir, which is a bet that a black number will win
Pair, which is a bet that an even number will win
Impair, which is a bet that an odd number will win
Manque, which is a bet that a low number, 1–18, will win
Passe, which is a bet that a high number, 19–36 will win.

The stake is placed on the appropriate place on the table layout.

A player making a successful bet on one of these combinations will win an amount equal to his stake. An important difference between European and American casinos arises regarding these bets. In most European casinos, should zero turn up, the stake is not automatically lost. It is put 'in prison' and remains on the table for another spin. Should the bet win on the second spin, the player is allowed to retain his stake, but does not collect any winnings. This is equivalent to the player losing half his stake should zero turn up, and in some casinos he may be allowed to withdraw half his stake and forfeit half. In American casinos, the bet will automatically be lost should zero or double-zero win. This convention puts the American gambler at a considerable disadvantage compared to the European gambler.

The other bets are as follows:

En plein (straight). This is a bet on a single number, and the stake is placed on the number on the table. It is allowable to bet on zero, and, on the American wheel, the double-zero. The odds paid are 35−1. The American gambler is still at a disadvantage since whereas the true odds are 36−1 on the European wheel, they are 37−1 on the American wheel, there being an extra pocket. The same disadvantage applies to the remaining bets.

A cheval (split). This is a bet on two adjacent numbers on the table layout (not adjacent numbers on the wheel), and the stake is placed on the line between the two numbers. Zero or double-zero can be combined with a number adjacent to it. The odds paid are 17−1.

Transversale pleine (street). This is a bet on any three numbers in a horizontal line on the table, such as 22, 23, 24. The stake is placed on the outer line of the row. Zero or double-zero may be combined with any two adjacent numbers by placing the stake on the corner common to the three numbers. The odds paid are 11−1.

En carré (square). This is a bet on a block of four numbers forming a square on the table, such as 13, 14, 16, 17. The stake is placed on the corner common to all four numbers. Zero in Europe can be backed in conjunction with 1, 2, 3 by placing the stake on the outside corner common to the zero and the row 1, 2, 3. The odds paid are 8−1.

Transfersale simple or *sixaine* (line). This is a bet on six numbers comprising two horizontal rows, such as 31, 32, 33, 34, 35, 36.

The stake is placed on the outer corner common to the two rows. It is impossible to include the zero or double-zero in a *transversale simple*. The odds paid are 5−1.

Colonne (column). This is a bet on one of the three vertical columns of twelve numbers on the table. The stake is placed in the blank box at the foot of the column on the Monte Carlo table. On the American table (Figure 4) the three columns are marked '2−1', and these are the odds paid.

Colonne à cheval (split column). This is a bet on two adjacent columns, the stake being placed on the line between the two boxes at the foot of each. The odds paid are 2−1 on, or 1−2.

Douzaine (dozen). This is also a bet on twelve numbers. The alternatives are the low numbers, 1−12, the middle numbers, 13−24 or the high numbers, 25−36. The stake is placed on the Monte Carlo table on P (première) for 1−12, on M (moyenne) for 13−24, or D (dérnière) for 25−36. On the American table, the stake is placed on 1st Dozen, 2nd Dozen or 3rd Dozen respectively. The odds paid are 2−1.

Douzaine à cheval (split dozen). This is a bet on any two adjacent dozens, the stake being placed on the line between the appropriate two boxes on the table. The odds paid are 2−1 on, or 1−2.

In the casino game, the odds offered for each bet ensure an advantage to the casino. Where a wheel with one zero is used, and bets on even-money chances are placed in prison when zero wins, as in Europe, the casino will expect, in the long run, to win 1·35 per cent of all money staked on even money bets, and 2·7 per cent on all other bets. In American casinos, with a wheel with two zeros, and no in prison rule, the casino will expect to win 5·26 per cent of all stakes. The casino will impose a minimum and maximum stake for all bets.

The Private Game

When roulette is played privately, the bets and odds are exactly the same as in the casino game. This means that in most cases, the bank will show a profit at the end of the session. It may be that the host, or the supplier of the equipment, will take on the role of the bank, in which case he will expect to win. However, it is possible for all players to share the bank, thus giving each an equal chance of winning or losing.

The way to do this is for each player to contribute an equal amount before play begins to the bank. The total sum contributed forms the bank's capital. At the end of the game the money remaining in the bank is divided equally among the players. Since the bank expects to win, this will usually be more than the amount contributed.

It may be, of course, that not every player will wish to share in the bank. In this case, players may have unequal shares in the bank. For ease of calculation let us say there are ten players. Fix the bank's capital as 1,000 units (which might be £10 or £100, or $1,000), and offer each player 100 units. Say only six players wish to have a share in the bank, and all take 100 shares. This leaves 400 shares over. If all six players would like further shares in the bank, then lots may be drawn to decide which four may purchase a second hundred shares. The total of 1,000 shares, and the lots of 100 per player, are suggested so that the ultimate sharing-out of the bank's capital becomes easier. For example, if the capital in the bank at the end of the game is 4,200 units, each holder of 100 shares receives 420 units in the share-out. Another system is to allow each player to buy as many shares as he likes, up to a maximum. The only disadvantage is that if the total shares taken are, say, 730, the final sharing-out will involve awkward fractions.

If during the course of the game the bank runs out of capital, then the players holding shares must replenish it by the same amount as their original shares.

As in the casino game, minimum and maximum stakes should be set. The following table suggests minimums and maximums in units.

	Minimum	Maximum	Odds
En plein (single number)	1	2	35–1
A cheval (two numbers)	1	4	17–1
Transversale plein (three numbers)	1	6	11–1
En carré (four numbers)	1	8	8–1
Transversale simple (six numbers)	1	12	5–1
Colonne and Douzaine (twelve numbers)	2	25	2–1
Even-money and other bets	4	100	

The game would operate more conveniently if counters were

Roll	Winning Number	Colour	Odd or Even	High or Low	Column	Dozen
1	3	R	O	L	3	1
2	17	B	O	L	2	2
3	8	B	E	L	2	1
4	14	R	E	L	2	2
5	36	R	E	H	3	3
6	0	-	-	-	-	-
7	9	R	O	L	3	1
8	17	B	O	L	2	2

Fig. 5

used as stakes rather than currency. Four colours might be used, to represent one, two, five and ten units. There should be a good supply of counters, so that players running out during the game may purchase more. All money collected for counters, including those forming the bank should be kept to one side. At the end of the game, when the counters in the bank have been distributed among the shareholders, all players cash in their counters.

It is an advantage if one member of the party, instead of playing, acts as banker and croupier. If the party plays regularly, the banker might be decided by rotation. Should nobody be willing to perform this task, then one of the players may look after the bank, but he must be careful to keep his own capital and the bank's separate. If the banker plays, the game will be slowed down.

A fixed period of play should be agreed beforehand. This prevents embarrassment should some players wish to stop when others wish to continue. If about four hours is agreed for the session, then it might be divided into two halves of 50 spins each, with an interval for refreshment. The host should prepare a ruled sheet of paper with 100 lines numbered 1–50 and 51–100, with three columns for each line. After each spin he should enter in the columns the winning number, the colour, and whether it is odd or even. This will ensure that the agreed number of spins are made, and it will enable system players to check the sequences. If the players wish it, three additional columns might be added to indicate whether the winning number is high or low or in which column or dozen it is contained. Figure 5 shows the beginning of such a full chart. It is because the croupier has to spin the wheel, settle the bets, keep the chart and generally see that the game proceeds properly, that it is advised that he should not play himself.

Systems

For games players who prefer their fortunes to depend on skill, or skill allied to chance, rather than on chance alone, the pleasure of roulette comes from an appreciation of staking systems, and the invention or choice of a plan and putting it into operation.

It is impossible, of course, to devise a system which will guarantee to win. On every bet made at roulette, the bank enjoys an advantage of at least 1·35 per cent, and no clever manipulation of numbers is going to alter that.

The best known and simplest of all staking systems is the martingale, or 'doubling-up' system. It is used on the even-money

315

bets, as listed above. The player stakes one chip on, say, red. If it loses he doubles his stake and his next bet is two chips. Another loss and he stakes four chips. Eventually, he will win, and when he does his win will equal all his previous losses plus one chip. Since ultimately a win is a certainty, the system cannot lose. However, the 1, 2, 4, 8, 16 progression very rapidly reaches large numbers. After ten successive losses, the player has already lost 1023 chips and must stake 1024 on the next spin. Red once came up 28 times running at Monte Carlo, so even a Rockefeller, had he been backing black, would have needed to send for more funds. In practice, of course, a run of losers soon necessitates a stake above the maximum allowed, so the martingale is unworkable.

The system is more fun played in reverse. Instead of doubling losing stakes, winnings can be left on the table to double, and will mount as quickly as the stake does in the martingale system. If it is decided to collect the winnings only after eight successive wins, the number of chips taken will be 256. And as the stake is never more than one chip, it will take a long time to pay back 256 chips.

Another popular system is to increase the stake by a chip after a loss, and to decrease it by one after a win. The idea, as with the martingale, is to have the larger stakes on the winners, and if winners and losers alternate there will be one chip more on each winner than each loser. Unfortunately sequences are never as neat as that, but the system has the merit of keeping stakes within reasonable limits.

There are fewer systems for backing single numbers, and they usually rely on the fallacious 'law of averages'. The most popular is backing 'sleepers', which are numbers which have not won for some time and are consequently considered 'due'. A number can be expected to win, on a 37 number wheel, once in 37 spins on average. The *systémier* waits until a number has not appeared for 111 spins (3 × 37) and then backs it 37 times with a single stake, then increases the stake to two chips, and after a further 37 spins to three chips. The theory is that numbers rarely sleep for as many as 222 spins, but it will be noticed that the system does not necessarily show a profit when the expected win comes. In any case, the system is based on the premise that past results will affect future ones, which on a fair wheel is clearly erroneous.

A more valid system, perhaps the most interesting of all, is another based on the even chances, the 'cancelling-out' system. The player begins by writing down a short series of numbers, say

1, 2, 3, 4 or 2, 2, 2 or 1, 1, 2, 2. He backs one of the even money chances, and his first stake is the sum of the two outside numbers of his series. Were the series 1, 1, 2, 2, his first stake would be $1+2 = 3$. Should he win, he cancels the two outside numbers, leaving his series as 1, 2. His stake is therefore again 3, and should he win again his whole series is cancelled, and he is six units to the good. Should his second bet lose, he adds the losing stake, 3, to his series, which becomes 1, 2, 3 and his next stake is again the sum of the outside terms, in this case $1+3 = 4$. The beauty of the system is that every time the player wins, he cancels two numbers in his series, and every time he loses he adds only one, so that his series will always ultimately be cancelled out. And every time it is, he will win the sum of the numbers in his series–in the example followed, six units. The system's only drawback is that when a long adverse sequence occurs the stake can mount quickly.

The variety of roulette bets allows the player to invent systems as simple or complicated as he pleases. It will be noticed, for instance, that the third column on the roulette table contains eight red numbers and only four black. Suppose the player backs this column at odds of 2–1. He can expect to lose roughly twice for every win, but he can hedge his bet by also backing black. If his column bet wins, he must win at least one chip overall, perhaps three. When his column bet loses, his bet on black stands a better than even chance of saving his total stake, because there are 14 possible black winners in the first two columns to only ten reds. The backer has 26 of the 37 numbers on his side. It sounds an attractive plan, but it is a snare. The column bet will lose one chip in 37 to the bank, the bet on black one chip in 74, and there is no way of adding the two losses together to make a win.

Although the advantage in roulette must always be with the bank, the game is an enjoyable way to lose money, and serious students get their pleasure from the never-ending search for a plan which offers the promise of a good win with minimal losses.

Index

cluding one applicant with extremely agile fingering. William decided on a stratagem. English organs did not yet have pedals for bass notes, as continental organs did. So, unseen, William placed lead weights on the organ keyboard, thus achieving a fullness of sound that impressed and mystified the judges.[2] William won the position, but he stayed in Halifax only three months. Late in 1766 he was appointed organist and choir director for the Octagon Chapel in the resort city of Bath. Music students flocked to him because of his skill and amiability, and he found himself giving as many as 46 lessons a week. With two full-time jobs, he was now earning a good living.

In 1767 William's father died, and his musically talented younger sister Caroline found herself trapped as cook, seamstress, and cleaning woman for her family. William tried to extricate her. In 1772 he finally persuaded his mother to allow his sister to return with him to England by providing enough money so that his mother could hire a servant to replace Caroline. Caroline was forever grateful.

She went from managing one household to managing another that was even more demanding. But now she was happy. She was studying music. Then, in 1773, William plunged into the hobby of astronomy. It began as an effort to improve his musicianship. To help himself understand harmonics, he studied mathematics. After spending 14 to 16 hours a day with music, he would relax at night by solving calculus problems. Math got him interested in optics. Optics got him interested in astronomy. He bought some lenses and assembled a telescope to view the heavens but was very disappointed. He wanted to see more and realized that a larger instrument would be required. But in his day, refracting telescopes were small because the lenses caused colored haloes to appear around every star.[3] The bigger and thicker the objective lens, the worse the problem was. The less the lens curvature, the less the problem of chromatic aberration but the longer the telescope became. Herschel fashioned one 30 feet in length and abandoned it as unwieldy.

So he turned to reflecting telescopes. The large light-gathering lens for a refracting telescope has to be ground on both sides and needs a perfect interior as well, whereas the mirror for a reflecting telescope requires the polishing of only one surface. In fact, the mirror for a reflecting telescope need not be made of glass. Perhaps, thought Herschel, he himself could fashion a decent-size mirror with acceptable reflective qualities in order to collect more light. He experimented with metal alloys until he found one good enough to serve as the mirror of a reflector. His younger brother Alexander, a cellist, had joined him at Bath in 1766, and brother Jacob had returned for a visit to enjoy the musical opportunities that William could arrange. Alexander assisted with the new project, contributing his valuable engineering skills. Caroline also joined in faithfully, partaking in every aspect of the work, despite the shambles it made of their house. During the day, Herschel's home was a school of music. Suddenly, it was a telescope factory as well. During the night, it was an observatory.

THE HERSCHEL SCHOOL OF MUSIC AND TELESCOPE FACTORY

To make a telescope satisfactory to him, Herschel needed to craft a better instrument than had yet been made. He wanted to make a large telescope, so he rejected the Galilean type of refractor, which used a lens to gather light, because he judged that a large lens could not in his day be ground well enough. To gather more light, he turned to reflecting telescopes of the kind that Newton had pioneered a century earlier. He experimented with different metal alloys in an attempt to find one of high reflectivity, fair resistance to tarnishing, and reasonable ability to hold its shape through daily temperature changes.

He turned his entire house into a telescope laboratory, much to the dismay of his sister Caroline: ". . . it was to my sorrow that I saw almost every room turned into a workshop." Telescope tubes and stands were fabricated in the drawing room. An optical lathe for grinding eyepieces took over a bedroom. The kitchen became the smelter.

On one occasion, in August 1781, a hot mirror mold (made of horse dung) broke, spilling molten metal that cracked the flagstone floor and sent pieces flying like shrapnel in every direction. The Herschels and their workmen fled for their lives. Herschel fell exhausted on a heap of bricks. Miraculously, everyone escaped injury.

In spite of occasional mishaps, Herschel found an acceptable speculum metal from which to make his mirrors—71 percent copper and 29 percent tin. In 1778 he completed an excellent 6.2-inch telescope with a focal length of 7 feet (frequently referred to as the 7-foot telescope) and used it to make his second and third complete surveys of the heavens.

In 1782, a year after Herschel found Uranus with

Herschel's house at 19 New King Street, Bath. It was here on March 13, 1781, that Herschel discovered Uranus.
William Herschel Society, Bath, England

this telescope, it was taken to Greenwich for comparison with the telescopes at the Royal Observatory. Nevil Maskelyne announced that Herschel's telescope was clearly superior.

Astronomy became William's passion. He cut back on his music teaching. English weather being what it is, every clear night had to be used to its fullest. No time was to be lost. William would not pause from telescope making or observing for meals. So, while he worked, Caroline placed morsels of food in her brother's mouth. William also didn't seem to need much rest. Caroline wrote: "If it had not been sometimes for the intervention of a cloudy or moon-light night, I know not when my Brother (or I either) should have got any sleep . . ."[4]

One evening in December 1779, Herschel was in front of his house observing the Moon with his 6.2-inch (7-foot focal-length) reflector when a man came up and asked if he might have a look. Herschel as always was very accommodating. The man later introduced himself as Dr. William Watson. He and his father, physician to the king, were both members of the Royal Society. A deep lifelong friendship began.

Perhaps a Comet

By March 13, 1781, William Herschel, with help from the Watsons, was beginning to become known in English scientific circles. He had completed a survey of the skies with a 4.5-inch reflector in which he cataloged every star of 4th magnitude or brighter. (All these stars were visible to the naked eye, but they were up to 100 times fainter than Sirius, the brightest nighttime star.) That "review," as Herschel called it—the first of four he was to complete in his lifetime—and reports about the size and quality of his telescope had generated much interest. If anyone was most likely to be the first person since the beginning of recorded history to discover a planet, it was William Herschel.

And he did. It happened during his second great all-sky survey. He was using the 6.2-inch reflector he had built after his initial test search. "In the quartile near Zeta Tauri," he wrote in his observing journal, "the lowest of two is a curious either nebulous star or perhaps a comet. A small star follows the comet at ⅔ of the field's distance."[5] For more than a month Herschel continued to think the object he found was a comet. Previous comet orbits as computed by Newton, Halley, and others were long ellipses resembling parabolas. But a parabola failed to correctly predict where Herschel's newly found object would be located a few days or weeks later. Its orbit was not cometlike.

Nevil Maskelyne, the English astronomer royal, was the first person on record to suspect that the object was a planet. He received news of the discovery from Dr. William Watson, Herschel's friend in Bath. After observing for three nights, he wrote to Watson on April 4, 1781: "[The object's motion] convinces me it is a comet or a new planet, but very different from any comet I ever read any description of or saw."

On April 23, he wrote to Herschel:

Nevil Maskelyne, astronomer royal and friend of William and Caroline Herschel
Royal Greenwich Observatory

I am to acknowledge my obligation to you for the communication of your discovery of the present Comet, or planet, I don't know which to call it. It is as likely to be a regular planet moving in an orbit nearly circular round the sun as a Comet moving in a very eccentric ellipsis. I have not yet seen any coma or tail to it.[6]

The mathematical proof came independently that summer from Anders Johan Lexell, a Swedish astronomer working at Saint Petersburg in Russia, and from Jean Baptiste Gaspard Bochart de Saron and Pierre Simon de Laplace in France. When they fitted the observations to a circular, more planetlike orbit, the object moved more nearly as predicted. Laplace and Pierre François André Méchain calculated the first elliptical orbit for Uranus in 1783.

SONG OF THE HEAVENS: CAROLINE HERSCHEL (1750–1848)

"I never forgot," wrote Caroline Herschel, "the caution my dear Father gave me against all thought of marrying, saying as I was neither handsome nor rich, it was not likely that anyone would make me an offer, till perhaps, when advanced in life, some old man might take me for my good qualities."[1]

So Caroline dreamed of a career to keep her from being dependent on family members. She had a good singing voice. She came from a musical family. But her mother disapproved of careers for women. Anna even frowned on the liberal education that Isaac, the father, gave their sons. It would inflate their expectations. She did her best to limit her two daughters to the purely practical matters of cooking, sewing, and household management. Isaac quietly slipped in a few language and music lessons for the girls whenever he could.

But when Isaac died in 1767, Anna Herschel relegated her younger daughter Caroline, age 17, to the position of household drudge. Five years passed slowly and unhappily. Finally, her brother came to rescue her and brought her to England to live. He bought her freedom by providing money

Caroline Herschel at the age of 79 (1829)
National Maritime Museum Greenwich

for their mother to have a paid servant. Wilhelm— he called himself William now—had managed to establish himself in the resort city of Bath as a church organist, music teacher, and concert performer. Caroline was forever grateful to her brother and plunged into intensive training under his direction.

Caroline's day began with breakfast at 7 A.M. or earlier, much too early to suit her. On the breakfast

[1]This and a second quotation from Caroline are from Constance A. Lubbock, ed., *The Herschel Chronicle* (Cambridge: Cambridge University Press, 1933), pp. 45, 137. The spelling and punctuation of this quotation have been modernized. Caroline had mild scarring from smallpox.

Half a year after he found it, Herschel's comet was acknowledged by most astronomers to be a large new planet. Its calculated orbit placed it more than twice as far from the Sun as Saturn. Herschel had doubled the size of the solar system.[7] The disk of the new planet, as measured by Herschel, was a little over 34,000 miles (54,700 kilometers) across, more than four times the diameter of the Earth. Herschel's estimate was not too far from the modern measure of 31,800 miles (51,200 kilometers).

English astronomy, which had generally led the way since Newton a century earlier, now had a brilliant new discovery in its crown and an amateur scientist who was becoming the greatest astronomer of his age.

The Royal Society, England's venerable scientific organization, gave Herschel its coveted Copley Medal in 1781 and made him a member.

---

table, from her brother, were "Little Lessons for Lina"—mathematics problems for her to solve and discuss with William over breakfast. Following breakfast, Caroline took cooking lessons from the housekeeper, whose job she would soon have. Then followed a lesson in English and then another in math, emphasizing bookkeeping. Next she practiced music, playing the harpsichord while singing with a gag in her mouth to improve her projection and enunciation. This was the first of two or three music lessons each day. Finally, she was allowed some relaxation, by which William meant the study of astronomy. That was Caroline's daily schedule up till noon.

Within five years, Caroline became a noted soloist. But her career didn't last long. William was seized by a dangerous and demanding hobby—astronomy. He started building telescopes. Larger and larger telescopes. And observing with them. One night he fell off the scaffolding and narrowly escaped grave injury. Thenceforth Caroline stayed up nights with him, at first taking down observing notes, then making her own observations. During the day, after a full night of observing, she ran the household while her brother taught music students and performed. She also entertained guests, helped her brother prepare astronomy papers for publication, and polished telescope mirrors. Her singing career was over.

While helping William to prepare a telescope for

observations after a snowfall on New Year's Eve 1783, she slipped on the ice and fell against a large metal hook used for lifting the telescope. The hook pierced her right leg six inches above the knee. Her brother and a workman extricated her, but "not without leaving near 2 oz. of my flesh behind." The doctor told her that her injury would have kept a soldier in the hospital six weeks, but she was back in action within days, rejoicing that her incapacity had not cost her brother any good observing weather.

But the turning point had already come. In 1781 her brother had discovered the planet Uranus. William Herschel became world-famous. The next year, at age 44, he abandoned the profession of music and turned all his energies to astronomy.

Caroline Herschel followed her older brother into a new career. The king allotted her a subsidy of 50 pounds a year, making her the first woman to be a professional astronomer. She never married, but the distinguished French astronomer Joseph Lalande made two visits to see Herschel's giant telescope at Slough, "possibly as much because of Caroline as the 40-foot."[2] In eleven years, she discovered eight comets and what we now know is a satellite galaxy of the Great Spiral in Andromeda.

---

[2]Colin Ronan, *Astronomers Royal* (Garden City, New York: Doubleday, 1969), p. 90.

Royal Observatory
Greenwich about 1781,
when Herschel
discovered Uranus and
his telescope was
brought to the
astronomer royal for
inspection
*National Maritime Museum
Greenwich*

On its own initiative, the society waived his annual dues so that he would have extra money to continue his research.

Herschel's achievement in discovering Uranus by recognizing its tiny disk as different from the stars stunned the astronomical community. Admirers urged King George III to give Herschel an annual subsidy so that he could devote all his time to science. But others could not believe the claims Herschel made for his instruments. They urged that the 6.2-inch telescope Herschel had made for his second sky survey—the telescope he was using when he found Uranus—be inspected to see if he could possibly be telling the truth about its performance and the discoveries he was reporting, which they could not verify with their own instruments.

In late May 1782, Herschel visited the king and showed him the heavens through his telescope. By mutual agreement, Herschel then stopped by the Royal Observatory at Greenwich so that the astronomer royal and other astronomers could have a look. The word was quick in coming. Maskelyne and other English astronomers pronounced the telescope far superior to those owned by the Royal Observatory or any others they had tested.

Herschel immediately wrote home to his sister to share the news:

> These two last nights I have been star-gazing at Greenwich with Dr.
> Maskelyne and Mr. Aubert [Alexander Aubert, a prominent amateur]. We

have compared our telescopes together, and mine was found very superior to any of the Royal Observatory. Double stars which they could not see with their instruments I had the pleasure to show them very plainly, and my mechanism is so much approved of that Dr. Maskelyne has already ordered a model to be taken from mine and a stand to be made by it to his reflector. He is, however, now so much out of love with his instrument that he begins to doubt whether it *deserves* a new stand.[8]

A little later Herschel visited Aubert's observatory for a similar side-by-side comparison. It was no contest. "I can now say," he wrote to his brother Alexander, "that I absolutely have the best telescopes that were ever made."[9] Self-taught astronomer and optician William Herschel was not only making the best telescopes in the world, he was also using them in a rigorous observing program like none ever attempted.

Herschel pretty much ignored the fame that followed his discovery, but he was bothered by the impression that the finding was an accident. Because his second all-sky survey, begun in August 1779, had been both comprehensive and precise, Herschel felt any object he found was not due to luck. He was recording the position and brightness of every star down to magnitude 8, about 40 times fainter than the dimmest star in his first all-sky survey. The faintest of these stars was five times too dim for the best human eye to see and ten times fainter than Uranus. As he later explained:

> It has generally been supposed that it was a lucky accident that brought this new star to my view; this is an evident mistake. In the regular manner I examined every star of the heavens, not only of that magnitude but many far inferior, it was that night *its turn* to be discovered. I had gradually perused the great Volume of the Author of Nature and was now come to the page which contained the seventh Planet. Had business prevented me that evening, I must have found it the next, and the goodness of my telescope was such that I perceived its visible planetary disc as soon as I looked at it . . .[10]

The Need for a Name

By the fall of 1781, six months after the discovery, most astronomers had convinced themselves that Herschel's object was a planet, and the need for a name seemed urgent. How should a new planet be named? There was no precedent. No planet had ever been discovered in the course of recorded history.

Sir Joseph Banks, president of the Royal Society, urged Herschel to make a suggestion, lest the French, who had helped to prove that the new object moved like a planet rather than a typical comet, seize the glory:

> Some of our astronomers here incline to the opinion that it is a planet and not a comet; if you are of that opinion it should forthwith be provided with a name [or] our nimble neighbours, the French, will certainly save us the trouble of Baptizing it.[11]

Herschel ignored the request. Meanwhile, the French were indeed engaged in bestowing a name. Joseph Jérôme Le Français de Lalande, one of the orbit calculators, generously and unpolitically suggested that the new planet be named Herschel.

Another proposal came from Johann Elert Bode, editor of the *Berliner Astronomisches Jahrbuch* (Astronomical Yearbook of Berlin). He suggested the name Uranus, because Uranus was the father of Saturn, just as Saturn was the father of Jupiter and Jupiter the father of Mars, Venus, Mercury, and Apollo (the Sun). Uranus was also god of the sky and husband of Earth. The name Uranus would thus keep all the planets part. of one mythological family.

These two proposals and many others—including Neptune, Cybele (wife of Saturn), Astraea, and Minerva—were published and debated, with still no response from Herschel. The Royal Society, whose name told of its patronage, saw a good public relations opportunity slipping away. Intent on securing royal assistance for Herschel's research in any case, the society may have encouraged King George III to believe that Herschel wanted to name the new planet after him, while telling Herschel that the king wanted to give him an annual subsidy and that it would therefore be appropriate for him to name the planet after George.

These machinations were delayed somewhat by the insistence of some skeptical society members that Herschel's telescope first be tested. Once the verdict was in, Herschel wrote the king to ask if he might honor him in the planet's name. The royal pension for Herschel came through in the summer of 1782. His subsidy of 200 pounds a year was two-thirds the salary of the astronomer royal, and Herschel had only one official duty: to live close enough to Windsor Castle so that he could show the king and his family the heavens from time to time.[12] This stipend was livable but not comfortable. Herschel was not overwhelmed by the king's munificence. He was earning about twice that amount in Bath by teaching music and making telescopes. Nevertheless, he accepted the appointment because he welcomed the opportunity to devote all his energies to astronomy and because he could continue to supplement his income through the sale of telescopes. The king, in fact, immediately ordered five 10-foot focal-length telescopes to dispense as gifts.

Herschel soon wrote an effusive letter of praise to King George, proposing that the new planet be called Georgium Sidus (George's Star) because of the king's generosity to him and to science and because the name would remind people that the planet was found in England during the reign of George III.

The name was instantly unpopular wherever George III did not reign. Astronomers resented the name's political symbolism and cumbersome length, and they pointed out that George's Star was not a star. Each coun-

William Herschel holds a diagram of the Georgian Planet (Uranus), orbited by the two moons (Oberon and Titania) that he also found.
Courtesy of Special Collections, San Diego State University Library

try went its own way. The new planet was Uranus in Germany; it was called Herschel (and then gradually Uranus) in France; and for the next 60 years in Britain it was known as the Georgian Planet. Bode's recommendation finally prevailed, but the new planet remained officially "The Georgian" in Britain until after the discovery of Neptune and through the 1847 publication of the *Nautical Almanac* for 1851.

How serious was Herschel about the planet name he had suggested? His gracious letter to the king sounds sincere. Yet when Bode wrote in 1783 to congratulate him and to argue that Uranus was a better name, Herschel responded: "When I named it Geo[rgium] Sidus I hardly expected that this name would become generally accepted, because we already know by experience that the first names of the satellites of Jupiter and Saturn were soon changed."[13] Was Herschel just being diplomatic and standing aloof from partisan disputes, or was he acknowledging that his proposed name was a gesture to his benefactor and of little interest to him?[14] There is no way to tell. Whatever Herschel's intentions, he left no evidence that he wanted the planet named after himself.

In accordance with the terms of his royal pension, Herschel immediately moved close to Windsor. In 1786 he settled in Slough, within sight of the castle, where he spent the rest of his life. He gave up music and devoted his remaining 36 years to astronomy.

The Amateur Turns Professional

Even in his occasional duty as astronomy tutor to the royal family, Herschel demonstrated his characteristic creativity and resourcefulness. For example, if the court was anxious to observe but the weather was uncooperative, Herschel would rig up a model Saturn at a distance and illuminate it by a lantern so that the expectant royalty could look through the telescope anyway and enjoy at least a simulated view.[15]

Herschel was 42 years old when he found Uranus, an age when most scientists' major discoveries are behind them. But, for Herschel, 40 years of sustained scientific productivity lay ahead. From 1781 until 1821, when his health finally failed, he led the way in virtually every branch of astronomy.

In 1788, at age 49, Herschel married a 37-year-old widow named Mary Pitt, and in 1792 their only child, John, was born. Even as a boy, John began helping his father and Aunt Caroline, and he grew up to be one of the most renowned astronomers of his age. In the meantime Mary saw to it that William now took time for meals and vacations. For a time, Mary's place in William's affections strained her relations with Caroline, who had so selflessly devoted her life to her brother. But eventually both women, to their credit, came to like each other.

A serious illness in 1808 caused Herschel, at age 70, to cut back his observing schedule somewhat, but he remained active until 13 years later, when his health began to decline steeply. In June 1821, Caroline served as his observing assistant for the last time. Herschel died on August 25, 1822, just short of 84 years old. His life was almost exactly the length of one revolution of the planet he had discovered. Uranus had nearly returned to the place in the skies where it had stood at his birth.

Throughout most of the eighteenth century, research in astronomy meant the confirmation and application of Newton's work. Professional astronomers often became bureaucrats, endlessly logging the precise time that the Sun, Moon, stars, and planets crossed the north-south line in their transit telescopes so that they could improve the measurement of time, determine geographical longitude, and refine the orbits of the planets.

It was amateur astronomer William Herschel and three generations of others like him who changed the course of astronomy and revitalized

HERSCHEL'S TELESCOPES

The discovery of Uranus brought Herschel a flood of inquiries about his instruments and techniques. Only then did it begin to dawn on him that he, William Herschel, an amateur isolated in Bath, England, was the best-equipped astronomer in the world. Despite Herschel's sale of telescopes, the world did not catch up with him in his lifetime. Because other astronomers did not check his observations on stars and faint nebulae, they could not appreciate his work on the structure of the heavens.

After he came under patronage from the king, Herschel began work on the largest telescope the world had ever known—a 40-foot-long instrument with a 48-inch mirror. This endeavor was subsidized by an initial grant of 2,000 pounds from King George III. A second 2,000 pounds followed to complete the job, and 200 pounds a year was allocated to maintain the instrument. Herschel supervised every detail of the work, which sometimes required 40 workers. It took 12 men working together to handle the grinding and polishing tool. Herschel had three mirrors cast, each weighing almost a ton, before he was reasonably satisfied. The telescope was three and a half years in the making.

The 50-foot-high scaffolding for the huge tele-

Herschel's 40-foot (48-inch) reflecting telescope
Royal Greenwich Observatory

scope attracted many visitors, and Herschel lost much time showing distinguished guests, including the king, his work. People especially liked to walk through the 40-foot-long tube as it lay on the ground. One day the king brought the archbishop of Canterbury to see the project and led him it. For 60 years after Herschel discovered Uranus in 1781, progress in astronomy came almost entirely through the efforts of amateurs.

Herschel was acclaimed around the world and is still recognized as the father of stellar astronomy. He made four highly successful complete surveys of all the stars visible through his ever-improving telescopes. He discovered the existence of binary star systems—stars revolving around one another. He realized that stars were much farther away than previously thought. He pioneered the study of the shape and extent of the stellar universe, thus founding the field of observational cosmology. He proved that the Sun was moving in space, toward a point in the constellation Hercules. He discovered infrared light. All these breakthroughs came after he found the planet Uranus. "The history of astronomy," wrote historian Michael Hoskin, "knows great telescope builders, great observers, and great theorists; but only William Herschel falls indisputably into all three categories."[16]

---

through the tube, saying, "Come, my Lord Bishop, I will show you the way to Heaven."[1]

Completed in 1789, the 48-inch reflector remained the largest telescope in the world for more than half a century until William Parsons, the lord of Rosse, made a 72-inch reflector in 1845. Herschel's 48-inch telescope was larger than any optical telescope in operation in Britain today.[2]

On his second night of viewing through his 48-inch telescope, Herschel discovered a sixth moon of Saturn (Enceladus). Three weeks later he discovered a seventh (Mimas). Yet Herschel was disappointed with this instrument. It was clumsy to operate, the English weather was seldom good enough to allow the large mirror to perform well, the mirror distorted under its own weight when tilted, and it tarnished rapidly. With only a hundred hours a year of truly excellent seeing conditions,[3] Herschel had at last exceeded the limits of contemporary technology and the weather of his adopted country. He returned to his 20-foot focal-length

(18.8-inch) reflector (the "large 20-foot," completed in 1783), one of the finest telescopes ever made. He used it constantly for 20 years.[4] The 40-foot monster was left mostly for visitors to gawk at.

Another of Herschel's finest telescopes was the 25-foot-long, 24-inch-diameter reflector ordered by the king of Spain for the Madrid Observatory. Herschel was paid 3,150 pounds. Unfortunately, most of the people who bought a Herschel telescope did so for prestige and as a work of art. Little astronomical use was ever made of this exquisite instrument, and it was destroyed in the Napoleonic wars.

The giant 40-foot telescope stood erect until 1839, when the rotting timbers of the scaffolding compelled John Herschel to have the instrument taken down. The tube, mirror in place, was laid on the grass, and the family gathered inside the tube for a requiem, using music composed by John. The tube was then sealed against the elements. A tree felled by a storm in the 1860s crushed most of the tube, but the mirror and a fragment of the tube are still displayed at Herschel's home in Slough today.

---

[1]Mary Cornwallis Herschel, *Memoir and Correspondence of Caroline Herschel* (New York: D. Appleton, 1876), p. 309.

[2]Pointed out by Michael Hoskin, *William Herschel and the Construction of the Heavens* (New York: W. W. Norton, 1963), p. 26.

[3]According to Herschel, cited by Henry C. King, *The History of the Telescope* (Cambridge, Massachusetts: Sky Publishing, 1955), p. 133.

[4]His son John Herschel refurbished this telescope under his aged father's supervision, resurveyed his father's nebulae and star clusters with it, and then took this instrument to the Cape of Good Hope to survey the southern skies, his most famous contribution to astronomy.

CHAPTER 2

The Fervor for New Planets

"Can one believe that the Founder of the Universe left this space empty? Certainly not."
Johann Elert Bode
(1772)

Before the discovery of Uranus, no one thought that there were any planets beyond Saturn. Almost no one thought that there were unknown planets closer to the Sun than Saturn. But with the discovery of Uranus in 1781, horizons suddenly broadened. Maybe there were other planetary bodies in the solar system yet to be found. Attention focused on something called Bode's Law.

Popularized by the same man who provided Uranus with its name, Bode's Law began as a curiosity—the relative distances of the planets from the Sun expressed as an arithmetic progression. Two-thirds of a century later, it was once again just a curiosity. But during the intervening 65 years, Bode's Law was a major driving force in solar system research. The distance of newly discovered Uranus was in good agreement with the law's numerical sequence, and this gave the progression credibility.

Titius' Approximation

Bode's Law, however, is neither Bode's nor a law. More properly, it should be (but seldom is) known as the Titius-Bode Rule. In 1766, Johann Daniel Titius, a mathematics professor at Wittenberg, translated from French to German a work by Swiss naturalist Charles Bonnet entitled *Reflections on Nature.*[1] Bonnet was trying to show the handiwork of God in the order of nature, and he began with the example of the solar system.

14

The example was too diffuse, however, and Titius decided to help Bonnet by quietly interposing a paragraph that offered an intriguing progression in the distances of the planets from the Sun.[2] His finding can be stated like this:

- Start with the series 0, 3, 6, 12, 24, 48, 96, . . . in which, beginning with 3, each succeeding number is twice the one before it.
- Add 4 to each number.
- Divide each number by 10.[3]

The result is a good approximation of the distances of the then-known planets from the Sun in astronomical units (an astronomical unit is the mean distance of the Earth from the Sun—now set at 92.96 million miles, or 149.6 million kilometers).

Johann Daniel Titius
Archive of the Archenhold Observatory

DISTANCE FROM THE SUN
(in astronomical units)

	Titius-Bode Law		*Actual as of 1790*
Mercury	$\frac{0 + 4}{10}$ =	0.4	0.39
Venus	$\frac{3 + 4}{10}$ =	0.7	0.72
Earth	$\frac{6 + 4}{10}$ =	1.0	1.00
Mars	$\frac{12 + 4}{10}$ =	1.6	1.52
———	$\frac{24 + 4}{10}$ =	2.8	(nothing known)
Jupiter	$\frac{48 + 4}{10}$ =	5.2	5.20
Saturn	$\frac{96 + 4}{10}$ =	10.0	9.54

Titius noted that his numbers worked well except for a gap between Mars and Jupiter where there was no known planet. "But did the Lord Architect leave that space empty?" he asked. "Not at all," he answered.[4] This space must be occupied by undetected satellites of Mars and perhaps of Jupiter.

This exercise by Titius, buried in another author's book, would probably have attracted no attention had not Johann Elert Bode happened across it. Bode was a young, energetic, self-taught astronomer who, at the age of 21, had published a very popular introduction to the heavens.[5] In 1772 he had just been hired by the Berlin Academy of

Johann Elert Bode
Archive of the Archenhold Observatory

Sciences to work on its annual astronomical almanac. The academy relied on this publication for revenue, but it was selling poorly. Bode quickly transformed it from a money loser to a high-profit item by correcting the publication's inaccuracies and by supplementing the usual numbers, dates, and times of an astronomical almanac with astronomy and general science news from around the world. He thereby made the *Berliner Astronomisches Jahrbuch* (Astronomical Yearbook of Berlin) into a major reference work. He continued as editor from 1774 (age 27) until his death in 1826.

Bode came across the planetary distance relationship in the first German edition of Bonnet, translated by Titius in 1766. Titius inserted it into the text of the book without a note, so that it appeared to be by Bonnet.[6] Bode reprinted the relationship with only a few very minor changes in phrasing and without credit to Bonnet or Titius in the second edition (1772) of his introductory astronomy book. "Can one believe," said Bode, "that the Founder of the Universe left this space empty? Certainly not."[7] Instead of satellites of Mars or Jupiter in the gap, however, Bode proposed that a major planet lay undiscovered there and enthusiastically promoted this planet spacing relationship every chance he got.

Bode continued to fail to credit Titius in the next two editions of his popular astronomy book and in his 1778 technical survey of astronomy as well. He finally acknowledged Titius as the source for Bode's Law in 1784, three years after Uranus was discovered, when he wrote a monograph on the new planet. Bode pointed out that if his rule about planet distances had been carried one step further, it would have predicted a planet at 19.6 astronomical units and that Uranus was actually found at 19.2. Suddenly, this curious rule acquired the aura of credibility. And this formulation of planet spacings became tightly coupled to Bode's name.

Celestial Police

Based on the apparent validation of Bode's Law by Uranus, Bode began plans to search for the planet that the law predicted should lie between Mars and Jupiter. The object had to be faint, or as close as it was, it would be plainly visible to the unaided eye.

Bode's confidence that a planet existed in the Mars-Jupiter gap was matched by that of the Hungarian astronomer Franz Xaver von Zach. On September 21, 1800, Zach convened a meeting of astronomer friends in Lilienthal, Germany, at the home of the town's chief magistrate, Johann Hieronymus Schröter.[8] The village of Lilienthal was about 12 miles (20 kilometers) from Herschel's birthplace in Hanover. Schröter was an amateur astronomer who made outstanding telescopes himself and who had purchased a superb reflector with a 27-foot focal length. This gave him the largest telescope on the European continent. Schröter was one of the few people to use a Herschel telescope for research rather than display.

King George III, ruler of Hanover as well as Great Britain, subsidized both Herschel and Schröter. The king encouraged Schröter's research by buying all of Schröter's instruments and leaving them in his hands until his death. He also provided money for Schröter to hire an assistant, just as Herschel received a stipend for Caroline. Schröter is regarded as the father of selenography for his long-term work on the features of the Moon.

The six astronomers[9] who met at Lilienthal adopted a plan previously proposed by Lalande to find the missing planet. Since all the known planets lay near the ecliptic, within the zodiacal band, they reasoned that the undiscovered planet might also be found there. So they divided the sky into 24 sections along the zodiac and assigned the search of each 15-degree section to an astronomer they felt would want to participate in this project. Zach dubbed the group the Lilienthal Detectives. Letters went out to astronomers all over Europe notifying them of their assignments.

It was too late. Before the letter to Giuseppe Piazzi arrived at the observatory he directed in Palermo, Sicily, he had made and reported a puzzling discovery.

Piazzi was a priest and mathematician by training. When he was appointed a professor at Palermo in 1780, he was encouraged to establish an observatory. In the late 1780s he went to England so that he could buy the best instruments available. He spent time with the astronomer royal and then went on to visit William Herschel. While observing with Herschel, he fell off the scaffold and broke his arm. Astronomy can be a dangerous profession.

Back in Sicily with his new equipment, he launched a lengthy, painstaking, but valuable project to determine the exact astronomical coordinates of several thousand stars. He was 11 years into this project when, on the night of January 1, 1801, the first day of the nineteenth century, he noticed a very faint, starlike object in Taurus that wasn't in the catalog he was checking.

He observed it again the next night and the night after that. The object was moving slowly against the background stars. A few more days of observations assured him that the object was indeed a member of the solar system—but what was it? He began to notify colleagues. To Lalande and Bode he described his discovery as a comet. But in his letter of January 24, 1801, to his close friend Barnaba Oriani, director of the Brera Observatory in Milan, Piazzi confided:

Franz Xaver von Zach
Archive of the Archenhold Observatory

Johann Hieronymus Schröter
Archive of the Archenhold Observatory

Giuseppe Piazzi
Courtesy of Special Collections, San Diego State University Library

I have announced this star as a comet, but since it is not accompanied by any nebulosity and, further, since its movement is so slow and rather uniform, it has occurred to me several times that it might be something better than a comet. But I have been careful not to advance this supposition to the public. I will try to calculate its elements when I have made more observations.[10]

On February 11, Piazzi fell seriously ill, and before he had recovered, the object had moved too close to the Sun's position to be observed. Mail delivery could be absurdly slow in those days, and it was two or three months before Oriani, Bode, and Lalande received their letters. Bode immediately suspected that Piazzi's discovery was the planet the Detectives had hoped to find, and he spread the news. Zach was delighted.

For philosopher Georg Wilhelm Friedrich Hegel, however, the news was embarrassing. Early in 1801, before word of the discovery was received, he had published his *Dissertatio Pholosophica de Orbitis Planetarum* (Philosophical Dissertation on Planetary Orbits), in which he proved by logic that only the seven known planets could exist and that Bode's Law was absurd.

But now there was a serious problem with the object that Piazzi had found. By the time Bode, Lalande, and Oriani received notification and Piazzi was well enough to resume work, the object was lost. Piazzi had observed it over a period of 41 days, which covered 3 degrees of its orbit. Such a small percentage of an orbit made the calculation of the object's position after it emerged from the brightness of the Sun extremely uncertain. True, it was less uncertain than the position of Uranus after half a year of observation (by which time it had shown itself to be a planet), but Piazzi's object was much harder to find because it was of 8th magnitude, about ten times fainter than Uranus. It was on the fringe of visibility with most of the telescopes available, and it exhibited no telltale planetary disk. Searches were in progress everywhere, but the new object eluded detection, even by Herschel. Astronomers began to despair.

But then a brilliant 23-year-old German mathematician stepped in: Carl Friedrich Gauss. The problem of recovering Piazzi's object fascinated him. In the fall of 1801 he developed a new method of calculating orbits from a minimum of observations. Late that year he delivered his orbit calculation and position prediction to Zach. On December 31, 1801, the last night of the year of its discovery, Zach found the object only half a degree from where Gauss had calculated it would be.[11]

Gauss's calculation also confirmed what had been suspected: The object had the nearly circular orbit of a planet, not the elongated orbit of a comet. And Gauss confirmed that the object's distance from the Sun was 2.77 astronomical units—almost exactly the 2.8 figure that Bode's Law promised.

Carl Friedrich Gauss, later in life, on the terrace of the Göttingen Observatory
Courtesy of Special Collections, San Diego State University Library

Piazzi proposed to name the object Ceres Ferdinandea—Ceres of Ferdinand. Ceres was the Greco-Roman goddess of agriculture and patron goddess of Sicily. Ferdinand was the ruler of Sicily. But the length of the name and its political connotations quickly resulted in the use of Ceres only.

But soon new trouble arose. Ceres was relatively close, showed no appreciable disk, and was extremely faint. It had to be small. Was it too small to be the expected planet?

Then, on March 28, 1802, Wilhelm Olbers found a new object with very similar behavior. Olbers, a physician and skillful amateur astronomer, was also one of the Lilienthal Detectives. He had been searching to recover Ceres and thus had made himself very familiar with the part of the sky (Virgo) where Ceres might be expected to reappear. In fact, Olbers had independently recovered Ceres on January 1, 1802, the night after Zach's success.

Olbers was looking for comets when he saw what he named Pallas (another name for Athena, sometimes regarded as goddess of medicine). His familiarity with that part of the sky allowed him to recognize this faint interloper from among hundreds of stars in his field of view.

The discovery of Pallas complicated matters. Bode's Law predicted one planet at 2.8 astronomical units. Now there were two. And neither was of normal planetary dimensions. Herschel estimated the diameter of Ceres

Too Small to Be a Planet

Wilhelm Olbers
Archive of the Archenhold Observatory

at 162 miles and Pallas at 110. Modern measurements are kinder: 617 and 335 miles (993 and 540 kilometers), but these two bodies are still much smaller than the smallest planet, Pluto, which is about 1,457 miles (2,345 kilometers) in diameter.

Herschel wrote to Piazzi and Olbers to suggest that it was possible to save Bode's Law only by reckoning that Ceres and Pallas were a new class of solar system members, too small to be designated planets. He proposed to call them *asteroids* because of their starlike appearance, which did not readily reveal a planetary disk. The name stuck, even though asteroids have nothing to do with stars. Planetary scientists now prefer to call them *minor planets* or even *planetoids*, the name proposed by Piazzi in 1802 to avoid the "starlike" connotation of *asteroid*.

Olbers accepted Herschel's diminutive measurements for the two new objects and adopted the term *asteroid* in his reply to Herschel in June

AN EARLY APPLICATION OF AUTOMATION TO ASTRONOMY
by Ruth S. Freitag, Library of Congress

After Piazzi came across the first (and largest) asteroid in 1801, three more were found by Olbers and Harding in the ensuing six years; then nearly four decades elapsed without any further discoveries. However, once the search was resumed by a new cast of characters armed with better star maps, the numbers began to accumulate, beginning in 1845. From 1847 on, not a year passed without the identification of yet another asteroid or two, or six, or eleven. By mid-1873, more than 130 were known. After considering carefully the hardships that dedicated asteroid seekers had to endure, the Bavarian satirical weekly, *Fleigende Blätter*, announced in its issue of September 19, 1873, the development of an indispensable new accessory:

An Automatic Asteroid Finder

We have succeeded in building an instrument that discovers asteroids, comets, and other unknown celestial bodies by purely mechanical means. The arrangement is as follows: An instrument resembling a telescope, the lens combination of which is designed like that of the camera obscura, is set up facing the sky. This instrument projects all the heavenly bodies within its field of view onto a long strip of paper, which stretches between two rollers and is carried along past the focal point of the instrument, by means of a clock drive, at the same speed as that of the stars in the field. All the known fixed stars, planets, and asteroids are shown as dark spots on this paper strip, exactly like a celestial map. The rest of the paper is chemically treated in such a way that the least amount of light falling upon a spot that is not blackened will set the paper on fire. If this rolling chart of the heavens is correctly oriented, the light from a star will fall upon the corresponding black spot on the map; but if there is a star (asteroid or comet) anywhere in the sky that is not yet shown on the map, i.e., not yet discovered, a point of light will fall on the chemically prepared part of the paper; the paper will catch fire, sparks will fall on a fuse treated with powder that connects with the touch hole of a small cannon, and a shot will go off. By means of the shot the astronomer quietly sleeping in an adjoining room will awaken, jump up, rush to the instrument, and, in the field of view of a telescope set up parallel with the camera-telescope, he will see the newly discovered star. Klinkerfues, Luther, and all the other famous asteroid discoverers need no longer expose

1802. But Olbers, a clever mathematician, offered an intriguing idea in his letter: that Ceres and Pallas might be fragments of a large planet that had been destroyed by internal explosion or by collision with a comet. He proposed that astronomers search the two regions in the sky where the orbits of Ceres and Pallas came closest to intersecting in the hope of finding other fragments, since an explosion might throw debris in all directions, but the orbits of the fragments would bring them back to the site of the explosion at each revolution. The intersections were in Cetus and Virgo.

On September 2, 1804, Carl Ludwig Harding, an assistant at Schröter's observatory and himself one of the Lilienthal Detectives, discovered Juno in Pisces, very close to Cetus, and on March 29, 1807, Olbers, taking his own advice, found Vesta in Virgo.

It was an embarrassment of riches. All four asteroids were small. Even

Automatic Asteroid Finder

themselves to the night air during frosty winter evenings with their comet-seekers and catch colds and chills from their tiresome work. Unfortunately it has not yet been possible to bring this epoch-making instrument to the international exhibition. It can be expected, in view of the large number of small planets that are to be found between Mars and Jupiter, that every quarter of an hour a shot will sound, announcing to the earth's entire population the discovery of yet another new asteroid.

(Translation by Ruth S. Freitag)

Fliegende Blätter, founded in November 1844, poked fun at German social, cultural, and political life with great success during the nineteenth century. Some of its contributing artists, such as Wilhelm Busch and Carl Spitzweg, achieved independent fame. As the years passed, the journal was overtaken by rapidly changing times to which it could not adapt; it expired, finally, in 1944—the only German periodical of its kind to last for a century.

if they were fragments of a larger planet, all of them put together and all the other pieces that could reasonably be imagined to exist were not enough to form one decent-sized primary planet. Today, the total mass of the asteroid belt (3,700 known asteroids and all those remaining to be identified, plus debris and dust) is estimated to amount to less than 5 percent of the mass of the Moon. It would take almost 2,000 such asteroid belts to equal the mass of the Earth. The zone of minor planets continues to fragment and reduce itself to dust through collisions, but it seems never to have contained a planet of major size.

Nevertheless, most astronomers in the early nineteenth century felt that Bode's Law was extremely powerful. Why it worked remained a mystery, but Uranus was found at the distance the law predicted, and a search of the gap given by the sequence produced the discovery of the asteroids. Some astronomers even used Bode's Law to suggest that a planet lay beyond Uranus.[12]

Confidence in Bode's Law was great enough so that when John Couch Adams and Urbain Jean Joseph Le Verrier attempted to calculate the existence and position of a planet beyond Uranus, both adopted the rule's prediction that a trans-Uranian planet would lie at a distance of 39 astronomical units.

Neptune was found where Adams and Le Verrier, using Bode's Law to postulate its distance, had predicted it would be in the sky, but Neptune proved to be closer than expected—30.06 astronomical units—an error in the law of 23 percent. And Pluto, whose mean distance from the Sun is close to where Neptune should have been, is only half the distance that the Law would predict for a ninth planet.

Ironically, the very success of Bode's Law in helping with the discovery of Neptune led directly to its discrediting. Undermined at the peak of its popularity, Bode's Law returned to the status of a curiosity.[13]

CHAPTER 3

Trouble with Uranus

"Who can say but your new star (Uranus), which exceeds Saturn in its distance from the sun, may exceed him as much in magnificence of attendance? Who knows what new rings, new satellites, or what other nameless and numberless phenomena remain behind, waiting to reward future industry . . . ?"
Sir Joseph Banks, president, Royal Society, on awarding Herschel the Copley Medal (November 1781)

Uranus required a major conceptual leap for the public and the scientific world. A new planet. A solar system twice the size previously thought. The law of gravity extending deeper into the universe.[1]

Then, to further complicate matters, Uranus would not cooperate. It seemed to be violating the law of gravity. In 1781, soon after Uranus was discovered, Lexell, Bochart de Saron, and Pierre Simon de Laplace had calculated circular orbit approximations for Uranus which demonstrated that the object, unlike any known comet, was in a planetary orbit. Laplace and Pierre François André Méchain calculated the first elliptical orbit for Uranus in 1783. That orbit allowed astronomers to predict more accurately where Uranus would be. But still there was considerable error.

New calculations were made, some improvement resulted; and most astronomers presumed that more observations would lead to better ephemerides.[2]

They didn't. In fact, Uranus seemed to be increasingly wayward.

When it is closest to Earth, Uranus has a visual magnitude of about 5.5, barely visible to excellent human eyesight under perfect observing conditions without optical aid.[3] With even a modest amateur telescope, however, Uranus is relatively bright, one of the 2,000 brightest objects among the million or so stars visible with a small instrument. Late in 1781, soon after Herschel's newly discovered object was generally acknowledged to be a planet, Bode raised the question of whether Uranus had been seen previously but mistaken for a star. Such prediscovery observations could be very useful for the refinement of orbital calculations. The position of Uranus had been recorded since its discovery for only a little over six months—too small a span of the 84-year orbit to be confident of its size and period. Additional sightings from earlier years could be helpful in reducing the orbital uncertainties.

Those Who Missed

Bode began a search through historical records and found two occasions when astronomers had recorded a star of the proper brightness that was no longer at its marked position. The motion of Uranus, calculated backward along its orbit, seemed to place the planet near enough to those positions to indicate that earlier astronomers had—not surprisingly—mistaken Uranus for a star. Telescopes prior to Herschel's could not have shown astronomers a planetary disk, which would distinguish it from the stars. Even in Herschel's day, famed observers such as Charles Messier identified Uranus only with great difficulty by noting on consecutive nights which starlike object in the proper field of view had moved against the starry background. Unless they had an instrument like Herschel's, an exacting eye like Herschel's, and an observing program like Herschel's where every single object in the sky, even objects ten times fainter than Uranus, would be recorded—unless they had provided themselves with all these advantages—their chances of discovering Uranus were minimal at best.

Herschel had not been looking for a planet at all. He was conducting his all-sky "review" in search of double stars that might be useful for parallax measurements to determine the distances to stars. He was not specifically looking for motion within the star field from one night to the next, which would indicate a nearby object such as a planet or a comet. He did not recognize Uranus because of its motion but because, to his trained eye and with his matchless instrument, Uranus showed a very small disk and therefore did not quite look like a star.

Bode announced that Tobias Mayer had unknowingly seen Uranus in 1756. So had John Flamsteed, the first astronomer royal, as far back as 1690.[4] With observations now spanning almost a century—more than one orbit of Uranus—several astronomers attempted to calculate an orbit that would allow the accurate prediction of future positions. The calculations worked marginally for a few weeks and then steadily faded into uselessness. Other astronomers joined in the hunt through historical archives for earlier sightings. Pierre Charles Le Monnier examined his own records and found that he had seen Uranus nine times before its discovery without recognizing that it was not a star. He was so embarrassed that he published only four.[5]

New orbital calculations were made that tediously incorporated the gravitational perturbations on Uranus by Jupiter and Saturn. The result still wasn't quite right, but it was an improvement, and astronomers turned their attention to other matters, such as how to avoid the guillotine following the French Revolution. Jean Baptiste Gaspard Bochart de Saron, who had computed one of the first orbits for Uranus, was beheaded. He spent his last night in prison calculating a refined orbit for Halley's Comet.

Troublemaker

Later, 22 years after Le Monnier's death, French astronomer Alexis Bouvard reexamined earlier observational records in an attempt to compute a better orbit for Uranus. He published a list of 17 prediscovery sightings[6] of Uranus and 40 years of postdiscovery observations. These tables (1821) provided position markings along the orbit of Uranus that stretched for 130 years, from 1690 to 1820—more than one and a half revolutions for the planet. With so much coverage, it should have been possible at last to calculate an orbit that truly matched the planet's motion.

But using all the data, Bouvard could find no decent fit. It was frustrating. If all the positions were included, the old observations would correspond, but the new ones wouldn't. If the modern observations alone were used in the calculations, then the old observations wouldn't fit. Bouvard saw no alternative but to exclude the prediscovery sightings from his orbital calculation on the grounds that the observations of Flamsteed, Mayer, James Bradley, and Le Monnier could not be as accurate as modern ones.

Bouvard pointed out that 12 of the 17 prediscovery sightings belonged to Le Monnier, including 4 on consecutive nights in January 1769. Bouvard attributed Le Monnier's misfortune less to lack of luck than to his sloppiness and his failure to compare his notes on star positions from one night to the next. A story circulating at the time said that Le Monnier scribbled one of his unrecognized observations of Uranus not in an observing journal but on a paper bag that had contained hair powder.

The story was not true, but Le Monnier was an easy butt of ridicule. He had an irascible personality and fought frequently with colleagues. Besides, it was in Bouvard's interest to cast aspersions on the non-discoverers of Uranus because he needed to discredit their observations in order to calculate an orbit that seemed to fit the planet's motion.

Le Monnier did not recognize Uranus, but the positions he recorded for this starlike object had an average error in longitude of only 6 arc seconds—ten times smaller than the errors that Bouvard wished to attribute to him.

On the surface, it looked like Le Monnier had indeed been inexcusably inattentive and sloppy. In less than a month, between December 27, 1768, and January 23, 1769, he had seen but not recognized Uranus eight times. Yet during this period of time Uranus was just coming out of retrograde motion and was at a stationary point. Le Monnier did not notice the motion of Uranus through the star field because, at that time, Uranus was virtually not moving.[7]

By excluding prediscovery sightings from his orbital calculations, Bouvard was dismissing the work of some of the guiding lights of positional astronomy. The typical observational uncertainties by all four "ancient" astronomers who had seen Uranus prior to its recognition as a planet were seven to ten times too small to warrant such drastic action. As Le Verrier proved later, the "ancient" data were good. Bouvard wrote unhappily:

> . . . I leave to the future the task of discovering whether the difficulty of reconciling the two systems results from the inaccuracy of the ancient observations, or whether it depends on some extraneous and unknown influence which may have acted on the planet.[8]

Having explained his exclusion of older data, Bouvard then used the 40 years of "modern," more reliable data to establish a new, improved orbit for Uranus. There remained discordances of a fraction of a minute of arc, but additional observations, he felt, could be expected to solve the problem. It seemed promising at first.

But additional observations only exacerbated matters. By 1824, the failure of Uranus to operate on schedule was so aggravating that the distinguished German mathematician Friedrich Wilhelm Bessel expressed his opinion that the "mystery of Uranus" would be solved by the discovery of an outlying planet. He began advocating a search for it.

Throughout this period, Uranus was running fast. It was consistently and increasingly ahead of its predicted position. Then, just as the positional errors seemed intolerably large, the problem began to vanish. Uranus was running less and less ahead of schedule. For about two years, 1829 and 1830, Uranus was almost exactly where calculations forecast. Temporarily, astronomers forgot about the planet's many years of unruly and unexplained behavior.

Then, just as complacence was setting in, Uranus fell off schedule again—but this time it was running slow. Slow, and getting steadily worse.

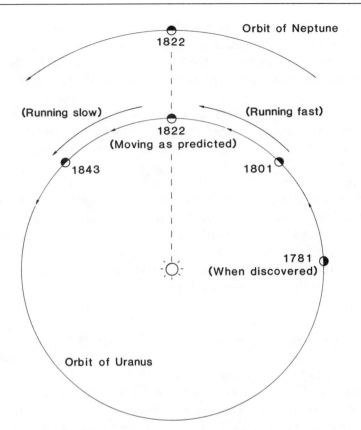

1822
Orbit of Neptune

(Running slow)   (Running fast)

1822
(Moving as predicted)

1843   1801

1781
(When discovered)

Orbit of Uranus

From the time of its discovery until about 1821, Uranus moved *faster* along its orbit than provided by calculations using the gravitational attractions of the known planets. Around 1822, Uranus moved as expected. Thereafter, it moved too *slowly.* The reason was an unknown planet beyond Uranus— Neptune.

The effort to explain the problem shifted from observational accuracy to some force acting on Uranus. Several forces were proposed and swatted down. One idea, revived from Descartes, was that a cosmic fluid with vortices filled the space between heavenly bodies. It was discarded, as before, because there was no evidence for such a fluid and no way that it could bring about the perturbations observed.

The second idea proposed that Uranus was being disturbed by a large satellite. This theory was abandoned because, to produce the observed disturbance, the moon would be too big to be undiscovered, and because any moon's period of revolution would be too short to cause such long-period perturbations.

A third proposal was that a comet struck Uranus about the time of its discovery, changing its orbit, so that old and new observations could not be reconciled because the planet now moved in a slightly different path. But this impact theory failed because Uranus was now significantly off schedule according to calculations based solely on modern positional measurements.

The fourth proposal was more tenacious: that the motion of Uranus couldn't be handled adequately by the law of universal gravitation because gravity was not universal. Instead, said some scientists, gravity operated as described by Newton on Earth and from the Sun out to Saturn, but at greater distances the law needed modification. The intractability of Uranus was an example of the breakdown of Newtonian physics. This idea, dating from Newton's time, was proffered whenever a stubborn scientist encountered a phenomenon or developed a theory that didn't immediately seem to reconcile with gravity. Yet in every case over a century and a half, Newton and gravity had prevailed.

Among those who doubted the universal validity of gravity was George Biddell Airy, appointed astronomer royal of England in 1835. For the most part he kept his suspicions quiet, but this bias and his efforts to be the man who fixed Newton's work were to have profound consequences for the lives of several astronomers and the history of astronomy. Yet nearly all of the most productive scientists saw ample evidence that gravity operated in the same way everywhere.

Toward an Explanation

As the 1830s passed, only one proposal to explain the peculiar motion of Uranus remained attractive to those gripped by the problem: that Uranus was being disturbed by a more distant planet.

The idea of unknown planets had surfaced without generating much attention even before Uranus was discovered. In 1758, when Alexis Claude Clairaut, Lalande, and Nicole Reine Étable de Labrière Lepaute had calculated the date when Halley's Comet would pass closest to the Sun on its first predicted return, Clairaut had noted "that a body which travels into regions so remote, and is invisible for such long periods, might be subject to totally unknown forces, such as the action of other comets, or even of some planet too far distant from the Sun ever to be perceived."[9]

Of course, Bouvard had timidly raised the possibility of "some extraneous and unknown influence" on Uranus that was causing his tables for the planet to fail. By 1836 he had embraced this concept rather than blaming discrepancies in the orbit of Uranus on observational errors by earlier astronomers.

Apparently Bouvard had been speculating privately by 1834 about the possibility that the course of Uranus was being disturbed by an undiscovered planet. Thomas John Hussey, an English clergyman and amateur astronomer, raised this possibility with Bouvard on a visit to France. When he returned to England, Hussey wrote to George Airy, soon to be astronomer royal, that he and Bouvard independently agreed that there must be an outlying planet. Hussey sought advice about how to find it. Airy discouraged such thoughts, informing Hussey that mathematics was unequal to the task of calculating the position of such a planet.

> It is a puzzling subject, but I give it as my opinion, without hesitation, that it is not yet in such a state as to give the smallest hope of making out the nature of any external action on the planet. . . . But if it were certain that there were any extraneous action, I doubt much the possibility of determining the place of a planet which produced it. I am sure it could not be done till the nature of the irregularity was well determined from several successive revolutions.[10]

In other words, since the revolution of Uranus required 84 years, Airy was telling Hussey to wait several centuries.

In 1835, Halley's Comet arrived at perihelion a day later than predicted. Trying to account for this discrepancy, Benjamin Valz wrote: "I would prefer to have recourse to an invisible planet, located beyond Uranus; its orbit, according to the [Bode's Law] progression of planetary distances . . ." The planet's perturbations on the comet over four or five revolutions might then reveal its location. "Would it not," sighed Valz, "be admirable thus to ascertain the existence of a body which we cannot even observe?"[11]

Friedrich Bernhard Gottfried Nicolai responded to the same stimulus with almost the same reaction. He observed that the delay of the comet in reaching perihelion had been noted previously. "One immediately suspects," wrote Nicolai, "that a trans-Uranian planet (at a radial distance of 38 astronomical units, according to the well-known rule) might be responsible for this phenomenon."[12]

In 1837, Bouvard set his nephew Eugène to work on collecting new position measurements for Uranus to attempt a fresh orbit calculation. Eugène wrote to Airy at the Royal Observatory at Greenwich, explaining that his uncle thought the unruly perturbations were the result of an undiscovered planet. Airy replied that he was confident that the problem could be traced to the adopted distance from Uranus to the Sun. It was too small, he was sure. He urged the young astronomer to concentrate on that possibility instead. Eugène did, and he showed that even with a larger orbit for Uranus, there was still no reconciliation between observation and theory. Nevertheless, Airy continued to hold that the problem lay in the distance from the Sun attributed to Uranus. Thus Airy, who had done much to publicize the discrepancies between the predicted and actual positions of Uranus, was increasingly isolated in his opinion about the cause. By 1838 the existence of a trans-Uranian planet was a major topic in astronomy.

Two astronomers, Niccolò Cacciatore, director of the Palermo Observatory, and Louis François Wartmann, owner of a private observatory in Geneva, thought that independently they might have caught sight of a planet beyond Uranus.[13]

By the end of the 1830s, most astronomers were convinced that an unseen and troublesome planet lurked beyond Uranus. Astronomers such as Johann Heinrich von Mädler expressed "the hope that analysis will at some future time realize in this her highest triumph, a discovery made with the mind's eye, in regions where sight itself was unable to penetrate."[14]

Friedrich Bessel, who for almost 20 years had blamed the trouble with Uranus on an unseen planet, told John Herschel in 1842 that he and his student Friedrich Wilhelm Flemming were preparing to attack the problem, beginning with a new analysis of positional observations of Uranus. But Flemming died suddenly, and soon thereafter Bessel's health failed.

In 1841 a young mathematics student at Cambridge University was browsing in a bookstore and came across Airy's 1832 presentation of the predicament. A week later he wrote himself a note in which he resolved to take on the problem as soon as he finished his degree. This young man was destined to solve the problem and suffer one of the most excruciating frustrations in the history of astronomy. His name was John Couch Adams.

CHAPTER 4

Neptune:

The Planet Found on a Sheet of Paper

"(The Uranus problem is) not yet in such a state as to give the smallest hope of making out the nature of any external action . . ."
George Airy discouraging T. J. Hussey in his hope that Neptune could be found by calculation (1834)

"That star is not on the chart."
Heinrich d'Arrest's response as Johann Galle called off stars in the search for Neptune (1846)

John Couch Adams was lucky to have survived his early education. His parents, Thomas and Tabitha, meant well. They were devoted to one another and their seven children. John was born June 5, 1819, on a farm near Laneast in Cornwall, England, where his father was a tenant farmer. The family was "respectable"—not poor, but with very limited means.

John's first school was in a farmhouse in Laneast, but at age eight he was placed under the tutelage of R. C. Sleep, newly arrived in southwestern England, who was known to advertise himself as

> Professor of Caligraphy, Stenography, Mathematics, French, Hebrew, etc. . . .
> Mr. Sleep Challenges any man in England for Caligraphy, Stenography or the Mathematics.[1]

Little did Mr. Sleep reckon on finding a youngster like John Adams in the provinces. When the boy was ten, student and "professor" sat down for the first time to study from Mr. Sleep's one and only mathematics book, an old algebra text. John was almost immediately far ahead of his teacher.

In 1830, at the age of 11, John accompanied his father on a visit to a relative in Devon. The relative noted John's precocity in comparison to his own bright son and arranged a competition between John and the town's schoolmaster, who had a local reputation as a mathematician. It was a humbling experience for the older man.

The next year, the Adamses removed their son from Mr. Sleep's tutelage and sent him off to a school in Devonport headed by Tabitha's cousin. The school was strong in the classics but weak in mathematics. John, age 12, took the matter into his own hands. He spent every possible moment in the nearby town hall, which housed the library of the Devonport Mechanics Institute. There he devoured books and encyclopedia articles on astronomy and, by himself, worked his way through differential calculus.

He was thrilled by the sight of Halley's Comet in 1835 and wrote his first scientific publication for a local newspaper on a lunar eclipse in 1837. Several London papers reprinted the article, much to the delight of the author and the local editor. By now John was reading mathematics texts and devising new solutions to the problems presented. He was seriously preparing himself for college, not only in his studies but also by tutoring the sons of local wealthy families to supplement what little tuition money his family could provide. A local minister who had a Cambridge University education and some competence in math helped him along in his scholastic preparation. In October 1839, John, age 20, left for Cambridge to take the examinations for a sizarship, a scholarship offering financial assistance in exchange for work at St. John's College.

John Couch Adams at about the time that Neptune was discovered (1846)
National Maritime Museum Greenwich

Adams at College

Unlike the stereotypical gifted student, John was modest and gracious. He made friends easily despite the class-conscious and competitive environment at Cambridge. Archibald Samuel Campbell was also there to take the exams and was one of Adams' first acquaintances:

> He and I were the last two at a viva-voce [oral] examination; he broke the ice by asking me to come to his rooms to tea. I went and we naturally had a long talk on mathematics, of which I knew enough to appreciate the great talent of my new friend. I was in despair, for I had gone up to Cambridge with high hopes and now the first man I meet is something infinitely beyond me and whom it was hopeless to think of my beating. If there were many like him, my hopes of success were gone. A few days experiences soon relieved me and I knew what a wonderful man I had met. If I could keep *near* him in the examinations I should do very well.[2]

St. John's College, Cambridge University, as it was when John Couch Adams attended. The first doorway to the right of the tower led to Adams' rooms.
The Master & Fellows of St. John's College, Cambridge

Adams won every scholastic honor available in math as well as first prize in Greek Testament every year he was at Cambridge. During the summers he tutored other students to ease the financial burden on his parents. But he firmly set aside one month each summer to be with his family.

In his student diaries, John sometimes rebukes himself for allowing his interest in astronomy to distract him from other work. In 1840 he and two friends walked from Cambridge to London in 30 hours, in part to visit the Royal Observatory at Greenwich. In the spring of 1841 he at last permitted himself to tour the Cambridge Observatory, with its 11.75-inch (30-centimeter) Northumberland equatorially mounted refracting telescope. He and his friend Campbell soon returned to examine it more closely. A few months later John Adams assigned himself an extraordinary project that set the course of his life and gave that telescope a crucial role in his future.

On June 26, 1841, Adams was browsing in a Cambridge bookshop when he chanced upon an 1832 report by George Airy that mentioned the increasing frustration of astronomers with the errant behavior of Uranus. A week later Adams wrote a note to himself on a slip of paper:

> 1841. July 3. Formed a design, in the beginning of this week, of investigating, as soon as possible after taking my degree, the irregularities in the motion of Uranus, wh[ich] are yet unaccounted for; in order to find whether they may be attributed to the action of an undiscovered planet beyond it; and if possible thence to determine the elements of its orbit, &c approximately, wh[ich] w[oul]d probably lead to its discovery.[3]

John Couch Adams' memorandum to himself on July 3, 1841, in which he resolved to locate, using mathematics, an undiscovered planet that he thought was causing irregularities in the motion of Uranus
The Master & Fellows of St. John's College, Cambridge

Adams drove straight for his objective. He completed his undergraduate degree in 1843 by taking first place in the Mathematical Tripos, a fearsome ordeal of 12 tests, each three hours long, strewn with original problems of extraordinary complexity. Only the top-ranking students, candidates for mathematical honors, were admitted to this examination, which determined postgraduate fellowships and often scientific careers, and occasionally caused nervous breakdowns in excellent students.

Adams emerged as senior wrangler, the foremost student in mathematical science, with a total of 4,000 points. Francis Bashforth, who went on to assume an endowed professorial chair in mathematics, finished second with fewer than 2,000. There was a greater gap in points between Adams and Bashforth than between Bashforth and the worst of the candidates who took the exam. Campbell, by now Adams' close friend, placed fourth. Adams followed this honor by winning the First Smith's Prize, the university's top award in mathematics. He was then elected a fellow of St. John's College.

It was now the spring of 1843, and Adams was anxious to begin work on the Uranus problem. But he felt obligated to his parents because of their sacrifices for his education, so he spent as much time as he could tutoring students and sending the money home to repay his family and to help with the education of his two younger brothers. Only his vacation time was allocated to Uranus. Nevertheless, in the spring of 1843 he outlined his project to James Challis, director of the Cambridge Observatory, and received encouragement.

The problem that John Adams was attacking was so difficult that most mathematicians had written it off as insoluble or, at least, too much of a gamble with their time and careers. Adams didn't know it, but George Airy, the astronomer royal, was already firmly on record that the mathematics could not be done. When noted amateur astronomer Thomas J. Hussey had enthusiastically written to him in 1834 that the perturbations of Uranus pointed to the existence of an outlying planet whose position might be calculated, Airy strongly discouraged the idea, insisting that the motion of Uranus was still much too poorly known to point toward a planet. Even if an outlying planet was disturbing Uranus, he doubted that mathematics could calculate the planet's position. Airy counseled waiting a few centuries until the planet completed several revolutions. And, with characteristic obstinancy, Airy kept his mind closed.

Yet Airy had been senior wrangler and First Smith's prizeman at Cambridge in his college days, then professor of astronomy and director of the observatory there before his appointment as astronomer royal in 1835.

James Challis, who succeeded Airy as Plumian Professor of Astronomy and director of the Cambridge Observatory, had also been senior wrangler and First Smith's prizeman in his time (1825). Yet Challis privately saw no hope in finding a planet based on the motion of Uranus. As he explained later, it was "so novel a thing to undertake observations in reliance on merely theoretical deductions . . ."[4]

Throughout this period, France and Germany produced a succession of noted mathematicians, but no one, until 1845, saw any promise in attacking the problem.

In the standard gravitational problem, it was possible, knowing the existence of Uranus, to calculate the gravitational disturbance it would cause in the motion of Saturn. The relative distances of Saturn and Uranus from the Sun were known. The relative mass of Uranus was known from the revolution of the first of its moons to be discovered. The positions of Uranus and Saturn in their orbits were known from observations and hence the distance and direction from which the gravitational force of Uranus would be exerted. Using these factors to calculate the perturba-

Adams' First Assault

James Challis, director of the Cambridge Observatory
Royal Greenwich Observatory

tion in Saturn's motion caused by Uranus was tedious and required care, but it was straightforward, thanks to Newton.

What Adams had to do was to solve the problem in reverse: Here were irregularities in the motion of Uranus. Subtract the perturbations caused by its moons and by Jupiter and Saturn. Now use the remaining irregularities to deduce exactly where the disturbing force is coming from, how fast and along what path that body is moving, how far away it is, and how massive it is. It was an intimidating project. If the disturbance was coming from a more distant planet, that planet would also be in motion around the Sun and therefore its distance and position with respect to Uranus would be constantly changing. Thus the direction and magnitude of its gravitational force would always be changing too. Nevertheless, calculate the position, orbit, and mass of the disturbing planet, making sure that the unseen object moves along its path so that it causes precisely the perturbations recorded in the motion of Uranus at every point throughout its observed history.

Of course, the farther away the disturbing body is, the more massive it must be to cause those perturbations. But there is no way of knowing the distance or mass of the disturber at the beginning. So start by assuming a distance. Adams did the obvious and picked 38.4 astronomical units, twice the distance of Uranus and in good agreement with the prediction of that mysterious but thus far effective Bode's Law.[5] Next, consider that the undiscovered body does not travel in a perfectly circular orbit, so refine the calculation to take into account the unseen planet's elliptical path. Finally, use the calculated orbit for the new planet to predict where it can be found in the sky for confirmation by telescope.

To handle all the simultaneous variables, the problem required the invention of a new form of mathematical analysis. There weren't many people capable or willing to face that challenge.

By October 1843, at the age of 24, Adams had produced a preliminary solution of the problem that confirmed the existence of a planet beyond Uranus. He shared the results with Challis and asked his help in obtaining the best and latest positional observations of Uranus from the Greenwich Observatory so that by mathematics he could pinpoint where the unseen planet could be found. Challis wrote to Airy, the astronomer royal, on February 3, 1844, to say that Adams was working on the Uranus problem and to request the data Adams needed. Airy responded to Challis with a wealth of information and an invitation for Adams to write him directly.

Adams continued his efforts diligently as time permitted, but he was slowed by his tutorial workload. The Göttingen Academy of Sciences was offering a prize for the best mathematical paper on Uranus and Professor

William Hallowes Miller urged him to enter, but Adams didn't have the time to write up his work in progress.

By the summer of 1844, Adams was working fitfully on his second analysis, which attempted to merge the best current Greenwich observations of Uranus with the old prediscovery plottings and to determine an elliptical rather than a circular orbit for the disturbing planet.

By mid-September 1845 he had completed his new solution to the Uranus problem. He could not know it, of course, but the position he predicted for the unknown planet was accurate to within 2 degrees.

Again he gave his results to Challis, including the predicted position—and from that moment and for the next two years everything that could go wrong with Adams' professional career did.

Response from Above

Challis, who possessed excellent mathematical credentials himself, knew of Adams' reputation for brilliance. Here, confronted with emphatic evidence of Adams' skill, Challis might have immediately undertaken a telescopic search or at least advised the young man to publish his results. He did neither. Instead he suggested that Adams send his results to Airy. Since Adams was about to leave on his monthlong visit home to see his family, Challis provided a letter of introduction so that Adams could deliver his findings to Airy personally.

Adams arrived at the Greenwich Observatory at the end of September and found that Airy had gone to Paris for a meeting of the French In-

Royal Observatory Greenwich about the time that John Adams tried to deliver his calculations for a trans-Uranian planet to George Airy
Royal Greenwich Observatory

stitute on a harbor-improvement project for the port of Cherbourg. So Adams left his letter of introduction and went on to Cornwall. Upon his return from France, Airy wrote Challis that he was sorry to have missed Adams, that he was very much interested in the subject, and that he would welcome correspondence.

Adams returned to Greenwich on October 21, 1845, on his way back to Cambridge. It was early afternoon, and Airy was in London at a meeting on the standardization of railway track gauges for Britain. But he was expected back soon. Adams left his card and a short statement of his results, saying that he would return later. The card was probably delivered to Mrs. Airy, who may have forgotten to pass the message to her husband. Richarda Airy could have had a lot on her mind. A week later, she gave birth to their son Osmund.[6]

Airy returned soon after Adams left, and at precisely 3:30 in the afternoon he and his wife sat down to dinner. It was Airy's unique and unpublicized custom to have dinner in the middle of the afternoon because his doctor had prescribed this ritual for his supposedly frail patient (who lived to age 90).

Adams returned an hour later, as promised, with the hope of meeting the astronomer royal at last and discussing what he had accomplished. He was met at the door by the butler. Dr. Airy was at dinner and could not be disturbed. No, the astronomer royal had left no message for the young man. What could Adams think? Airy knew his name from correspondence with Challis. Airy had his letter of introduction from Challis. Airy had the summary of his research. The visitor had timed his return to be far from the traditional dinnertime or even teatime. Adams left deeply disappointed.[7]

The astronomer royal may have been unaware of Adams' treatment in his three thwarted visits, but he was in possession of Adams' results. The astronomer royal was unimpressed. His attitude toward Adams was probably compounded of two factors: his dislike of the theoretical approach to scientific research and his snobbishness.

Despite his considerable mathematical abilities, Airy thought that astronomy and all science should proceed by collecting observations and then using mathematics as the language to express the findings. The procedure should not be reversed; mathematics should not be used to point toward observational breakthroughs. Such a theoretical approach was just playing with numbers. A mental game with no basis in reality. A waste of time. He distrusted and even intensely resented such efforts.

Airy's unresponsiveness to Adams was also a product of the snobbishness he had cultivated from his youth. In his view there were two kinds of people in the world: those who had succeeded and those who had not. Successful people were potentially of use and therefore worth cultivating. Those who had not succeeded or had not yet succeeded (such as younger people) were of little use and therefore not worthy of consideration.[8]

Nevertheless, one week later, Airy showed Adams' note summarizing his results to William Rutter Dawes, a clergyman, physician, and extremely skillful amateur observer. Dawes was impressed, but perhaps because he was erecting and furnishing his new observatory, he did not undertake a search himself. He did, however, pass the information and the planet's predicted position along to William Lassell, a successful brewer in Liverpool and the builder of a 24-inch reflector—the largest operational telescope at that time in England. Dawes recommended that Lassell take on the project. Lassell would have liked the challenge, but he was confined to bed with a severely sprained ankle. Before he could return to observing, the letter had disappeared and Lassell lost the opportunity.[9]

Dawes' very positive reaction to Adams' work impressed Airy not at all. The astronomer royal, compulsively orderly and prompt, who always answered his mail immediately, remained so negative to Adams' work that he delayed his response to Adams' paper. On November 5, 1845, more than two weeks after Adams had been turned away from his door, Airy finally replied to the young man with a rejection in the form of a question. Referring to Adams' calculations as assumptions, Airy asked whether Adams' work could explain why Uranus was slightly farther from the Sun than previously calculated. From Adams' point of view, the question was trivial and besides the point. Adams' research could specify the location of the planet disturbing the motion of Uranus. Recent observational data had shown that Uranus was moving more slowly than expected. According to Kepler's third law, the slower a known planet moves, the farther it must be from the Sun. But the problem at hand was the *location* of the *planet disturbing Uranus.* The observed motion of Uranus, whether slow or fast, formed the data from which the location of the disturbing planet was calculated—and this was what Adams had accomplished. Airy's question was essentially irrelevant.

What was apparent was that Airy had completely and inexplicably misunderstood the essence of Adams' work. Adams had *calculated* the planet's existence from royal observatory data that Airy had furnished. He had not *assumed* that the planet existed and guessed at a possible orbit. Airy knew this from the letter of introduction that Challis wrote for Adams, which emphasized that the young man had calculated a planet beyond Uranus using observational data that Airy himself had furnished. The letter also acknowledged Adams as a very competent mathematician. Airy must have read Adams' summary in a most cursory manner.

As he looked at Airy's reply, Adams saw no flicker of recognition or interest in his project, which the astronomer royal had known about for a year and a half. There was no offer to undertake a search. There was no suggestion that his work was worth publishing. With no interest in a search expressed by Challis or Airy, Adams was uncertain how to proceed. He didn't respond immediately to Airy's inane question.[10] Instead, he resolved to rework his calculations to get a prediction so impressive that it could not be ignored.

Adams' failure to reply immediately gave Airy just the excuse he sought to drop the matter: "Adams' silence . . . was so far unfortunate that it interposed an effectual barrier to all further communication. It was clearly impossible for me to write to him again."[11]

On the Continent	The erratic motion of Uranus bothered French, German, and other European astronomers no less than the English. The dean of French astronomers was Jean Dominique François Arago. He was popular with

GEORGE BIDDELL AIRY: ASTRONOMER ROYAL

Young George was not popular with his classmates at school because, he said, he had very little "animal vitality." He was also snobbish and conceited. But his classmates endured him when he created useful gadgets for mischief such as peashooters.

At the age of 12, George, already concerned for his own advancement, conspired with his mother's brother, a wealthy and well-educated farmer, to adopt and hide him from his family without informing them so that he would have better social contacts. His father, depressed over the loss of his job with the tax office, declined to block the arrangement.

At the age of 18, Airy was off to Cambridge University with a scholarship and a very high opinion of himself. He made no friends, and professors judged his abilities to be limited, but Airy worked doggedly and carried off the two big science and mathematics prizes as senior wrangler and First Smith's prizeman in 1823. He thought well enough of himself by this time to write his first autobiography.

Just as meticulously as he recorded his younger days, so he carefully plotted his future life. He kept a complete daily record of his activities and thoughts. His financial accounts were personally kept by double entry throughout his life, and he regarded their keeping as one of his greatest joys.[1] He never destroyed a document and preserved all his old checkbook stubs, bills, and receipts from merchants in chronological order. A colleague at Cambridge quipped, "if Airy wiped his pen on a piece of blotting-paper, he would duly endorse the blotting-paper with the date and particulars of its use, and file it away amongst his papers."[2]

As a fellow of Trinity College in 1824, he set his sights on the position of astronomer royal and refused to accept an assistantship at the Royal Observatory because assistants had not previously been promoted to the post. Instead he fought his way upward through professorships at Cambridge, campaigning successfully for higher pay. In 1835

[1]George Biddell Airy, *Autobiography*, edited by Wilfrid Airy (Cambridge: At the University Press, 1896), p. 2.

[2]This story, told by Augustus De Morgan, appears in E. Walter Maunder, *The Royal Observatory Greenwich* (London: Religious Tract Society, 1900), pp. 116–117.

the public because of his clear, enthusiastic, and engaging way of explaining science. He was popular with astronomers because he liked to identify interesting scientific problems and pass them along to young astronomers for solution. He would then encourage and assist them with his insight and his encyclopedic knowledge of the scientific literature. He also helped to find them jobs.

In the summer of 1845, Arago urged Urbain Jean Joseph Le Verrier to take on the problem of the motion of Uranus. Arago was a shrewd judge of talent who could pair the scientific difficulty of a problem with the intellectual capability of a scientist.

Le Verrier, like Adams, had come from a family of modest means in the provinces. He was born in Saint-Lô in Normandy on March 11, 1811. His father, an estate manager, did all he could to foster his son's intellectual pursuits, and Urbain responded by reaching the top of his class at high school in Caen. He then took the highly competitive exam for the École Polytechnique in Paris, but there were gaps in his provincial education

Urbain Jean Joseph Le Verrier
Royal Greenwich Observatory

George Biddell Airy, astronomer royal
National Maritime Museum Greenwich

he received the call he expected as the seventh astronomer royal. He immediately set to work restructuring the Royal Observatory in his mold. Airy was an organizer rather than a scientist.[3]

Under his direction the Royal Observatory was a superb servant of the Navy, providing tables for celestial navigation of improved precision. Greenwich expanded into meteorological and magnetic record keeping. But among staff members, Airy tolerated no independent thought or research. Observers were often required to work 21 hours straight. Young boys hired to do arithmetic calculations were kept at their desks for 12-hour shifts with no breaks except for one hour at midday. Morale was poor. But Airy's efficiency and discipline at the Royal Observatory were admired in England and copied by many other countries, which led years later, particularly in England, to a conspicuous lack of creativity in observational astronomy.

Airy declined knighthood three times, complaining about the initiation fees and the cost of maintaining the expected life-style, but finally accepted the honor in 1872. He retired as astronomer royal in 1881 at the age of 80 and spent his remaining ten years filing (but not organizing the contents of) his papers.

[3]Olin J. Eggen, "George Biddell Airy," *Dictionary of Scientific Biography* (New York: Charles Scribner's Sons, 1974).

and he was not admitted. Urbain's father thereupon sold the family house for cash to enroll his son in the Collège de Saint Louis in Paris for additional preparation in 1830. Urbain rewarded his father's sacrifices by winning the annual mathematics prize sponsored by the École Polytechnique in 1831 and gaining admission to the school. He was never again below the first rank of scientists. He graduated with highest honors, a wide range of scientific interests, and a reputation for tenacity.

His first job was with the Ministry of Tobacco. He had decided on a career in chemistry, and his objective was to work with renowned chemist Joseph Louis Gay-Lussac. Le Verrier fell so in love with Paris and his future wife that he left government service two years later rather than accept the usual tour of duty in the provinces. He spent a year teaching and then rejoined Gay-Lussac when his mentor was appointed to the École Polytechnique faculty and created an assistant's position for him.

Le Verrier's first published papers were in chemistry. Gay-Lussac saw talent there, but even greater skills in mathematics. When a professorship in astronomy opened at the École Polytechnique in 1837, he arranged for Le Verrier to be appointed and encouraged his colleague, now 26 years old, to switch fields. Le Verrier did, studying astronomy with his characteristic ferocity and applying his mathematical incisiveness to it. He worked extremely hard so that his initial publications in astronomy would be worthy of his distinguished predecessor Félix Savary, of his mentor Gay-Lussac, and of his own high standards. Le Verrier's first two papers showed extraordinary analytical powers, and he was befriended (as most promising young scientists were) by Arago in 1840.

Arago gave him the problem of the motion of the planet Mercury, which was always ahead of where its calculated orbit predicted it would be. Le Verrier worked on the problem for three years and explained most of the variance as perturbations caused by other planets. But he was left with a small discrepancy that he could not explain.

With the Mercury problem initially intractable, Le Verrier turned his attention to cometary orbits with great success. In June 1845, Arago approached him again—this time with the most difficult and intriguing puzzle facing contemporary astronomers: the motion of Uranus. Le Verrier was now 34, eight years older than Adams. He was already internationally known for his mathematical analysis of astronomical problems.

Le Verrier began with an exhaustive analysis of the motion of Uranus as presented in Bouvard's *Tables*. On November 10, 1845, Le Verrier presented to the Paris Academy of Sciences the first of three papers on Uranus. It dealt exclusively with old and modern observations and demonstrated that they were irreconcilable—there really was a problem with the planet's motion, not with the quality of the observations. He

François Arago, director of the Paris Observatory
Royal Greenwich Observatory

would, he announced, analyze those outside causes in a second paper soon. He also pointed out that Bouvard was wrong in ignoring the positions of Uranus observed prior to its recognition as a planet.

On November 10, 1845, while Le Verrier was giving his preliminary report on the project that Arago had encouraged him to undertake, Adams was receiving his astronomer royal's most discouraging response to his calculation of where a new planet could be found.

The insult, intentional or careless, was compounded a few weeks later when Airy visited Challis at Cambridge University. Neither Challis nor Airy invited Adams to meet Airy at last and discuss his work with him.

Meanwhile, in France, Le Verrier was hard at work preparing his second paper on Uranus. He presented it to the Paris Academy of Sciences on June 1, 1846. This paper demonstrated that the irregularities in the motion of Uranus could be induced only by an unknown planet farther from the Sun. What had been suspected now had a solid mathematical basis that had been announced to a wide scientific community.

Le Verrier then went on to calculate the planet's position, ending with the hope that "we will succeed in sighting the planet whose position I have just given."[12] The academy praised this new analysis, but to Le Verrier's amazement, no one offered or even suggested that a search should be undertaken.

Airy received a copy of Le Verrier's second paper on June 23 or 24, 1846. He immediately noticed that Le Verrier's prediction agreed to within one degree of Adams'. "To this time," wrote Airy, "I had considered that there was still room for doubt of the accuracy of Mr. Adams's investigations . . . But now I felt no doubt of the accuracy of both calculations . . ."[13]

Airy responded immediately with a letter to Le Verrier expressing enthusiasm and delight. Le Verrier was eight years older than Adams and an established scientist. He was worthy of notice. Airy's response was also in character, wrongheaded and neglectful. Had Le Verrier considered the possible need to modify the length of the Uranus radius vector (the Sun-to-Uranus distance)? It was the same inane question he had asked Adams. But Airy didn't bother to mention that Le Verrier's fine work had been matched eight months earlier by a young mathematician at Cambridge. And, of course, Airy did not bother to share his "delight and satisfaction" with Adams.

Airy Begins to Move

Airy must have been even more impressed than his reply to Le Verrier indicated, because three days later, when the Board of Visitors (the commission that conducted periodic inspections) of the Royal Observatory convened at Greenwich on June 29, Airy proclaimed "the extreme probability of now discovering a new planet in a very short time . . ." He was confident because Adams' and Le Verrier's calculations of the position of the planet disturbing Uranus coincided so closely. Still Airy made no effort to notify Adams, nor did he bother to authorize a search. Serving on this board, hearing these words, were James Challis and John Herschel.[14]

Upon hearing this news, Challis behaved inexplicably. Instead of finally recognizing the opportunity that had been staring him in the face for a year, instead of starting a search on his own, Challis now lost whatever little interest he had in the matter and what little confidence he had in Adams' predictions. Perhaps he thought that Airy had preempted the project.

Le Verrier received Airy's reply on June 28. Since he had dealt with Airy only a few times previously, he was impatient rather than discouraged. He immediately informed Airy in firm icy tones that the astronomer royal's question was irrelevant because his calculations dealt with perturbations on Uranus and where they were coming from, hence the exact distance of Uranus from the Sun was corrected for "automatically." Having dismissed the astronomer royal's objection, Le Verrier went on to offer to send specially calculated position predictions to simplify the quest for the new planet if Airy had "enough confidence in my work to search for the planet in the sky . . ." Airy received the offer on July 1 and again responded immediately. He declined Le Verrier's offer because, he said, he was about to leave for business on the continent. His trip was actually scheduled for August 10, five and a half weeks away.

The next day Airy again visited Cambridge University. He was in the company of visiting astronomer Peter Andreas Hansen, director of the Seeberg Observatory near Gotha, Germany (which Zach had helped to build and had directed). Despite Le Verrier's recent letter and despite his own statement to his observatory's Board of Visitors that the irregular motion of Uranus would soon lead to the discovery of a new planet, the astronomer royal made no effort to contact or meet with Adams. It happened anyway, but accidentally. That evening Airy and Hansen encountered Adams on St. John's Bridge. Airy introduced Adams to Hansen but was very cool and made no mention of Adams' calculations for a new planet. He cut off the conversation after about two minutes and moved on.

A few days later, on July 6, Airy spent some time at Ely with George Peacock, his old professor at Cambridge, and the subject of Uranus was broached. Airy told his mentor about his correspondence. Peacock was dumbfounded by his former student's negligence and urged him to act.

Airy finally got the message, and three days later, on July 9, he wrote James Challis to request an urgent search. Presuming Challis' answer would be negative, because such a project would likely be time-consuming and tedious, Airy offered an assistant from the Royal Observatory to help. The situation, said Airy, was "almost desperate," neglecting to acknowledge that he had delayed a search for nine months.

Four days later, without waiting for Challis to reply, Airy wrote again, this time sending him a complete set of instructions for the search. Nothing except emergency unpostponable observations should be allowed to intervene, said Airy, because "the importance of this inquiry exceeds that of any current work . . ."

Challis was away from Cambridge when the letters arrived. When he returned, he was of course offended by Airy's imperious and condescending manner. In his reply of July 18, Challis told Airy that he had already decided to look for the planet himself and therefore declined an assistant.

It made sense for the Cambridge Observatory, rather than the Greenwich Observatory, to conduct the search. Greenwich primarily had transit telescopes, which could pivot up and down but not side to side. They were locked into position along the meridian so that they could observe exactly when a star, planet, the Moon, or the Sun crossed the north-south line for purposes of calculating time, longitude, and orbits. The Cambridge Observatory had the 11.75-inch (30-centimeter) Northumberland Telescope, equatorially mounted so that it could be aimed at any point in the sky and with more than enough light-gathering power for this kind of search.

Challis Begins to Act

But for the next week and a half Challis did nothing. Then, late in July, Challis told Adams of the projected search. Adams provided updated position predictions for the planet and gave Challis very encouraging news: The planet should be large enough to show a disk. Thus a careful observer would be able to recognize the new planet as other than a star without having to wait a day or so to see if the suspected object moved among the background stars.

On July 29, 1846, Challis began his search, resigned to the prospect of a long, tedious, and fruitless task because mathematics was no way to find a planet. Placing no confidence in the quality of Adams' or Le Verrier's calculations and ignoring Adams' advice that the planet should show a disk, Challis agreed with Airy that it was useless to concentrate on the positions that Adams and Le Verrier had predicted. Instead he prepared to search a swath of sky 30 degrees long and 10 degrees wide— 15 degrees to the east and west and 5 degrees to the north and south

of the predictions. Challis' plan was to sweep this region steadily, recording all but the dimmest stars, and then to return to that region a few days
later to reexamine each star to see if one had moved. Such a search would
require mapping at least 3,000 stars and would consume at least 300 hours
of telescope time—approximately eight straight weeks of good observing weather. This was the only way, unless he was to value the work
of Adams and Le Verrier and concentrate his search on the region of the
sky where they predicted the planet would be. If he had, his efforts would
have succeeded within a few nights.

On August 12, 1846, two weeks into his search, but on only his fourth
night of acceptable observing conditions, Challis and his assistants recorded in his notebook the new planet almost exactly where it was
predicted. But Challis failed to recognize his target.

Le Verrier's second paper, identifying an outlying planet as the source
of Uranus' peculiar motion and predicting its position, circulated widely. Sears Cook Walker, a young astronomer at the United States Naval
Observatory in Washington, D.C., read of Le Verrier's work and proposed
to search. But Matthew Fontaine Maury, superintendent of the observatory, rejected the proposal because of his facility's heavy schedule.

Final Predictions

Le Verrier kept pushing forward. On August 31, 1846, he presented his
third and final paper on Uranus to the Paris Academy of Sciences, this
time laying out the orbital elements, the mass, and the position of the
planet that was disturbing Uranus. His refined positional calculation dif-
fered only slightly from his previous prediction. The planet, he said, was
about 5 degrees east of Delta Capricorni. To encourage a search, Le Verrier stressed that the planet was just past opposition—closest to Earth
and visible almost all night long. The planet was big enough to show a
disk, so that a long, tedious mapping of stars would not be necessary.
He received polite applause from his scientific audience and, once again,
not a single offer to search for the planet from any astronomer, not even
his champion Arago.

Adams did not know of Le Verrier's third paper when, on September
2, he sent Airy his sixth solution to the problem, refining a little bit further his prediction of where the disturbing planet would be found. This
calculation explicitly included a correction for the distance of Uranus
from the Sun, the matter about which Airy had previously expressed concern. Airy was now actually away on his trip to the continent, and Adams
received a mindless reply from Robert Main, Airy's chief assistant, offering more observational data on Uranus.

Adams now at last resolved to lay his work before the scientific community. He decided to present his findings at a meeting of the British Association for the Advancement of Science in Southampton in mid September. But when he arrived on September 15, he found that there had been a confusion in the conference announcement. The astronomy session had already concluded, and there was no other appropriate forum for him. The irony was overwhelming when Adams heard that John Herschel had opened the conference with his valedictory address as president of the association by heralding the prospect of a new planet: "Its movements have been felt . . . with a certainty hardly inferior to that of ocular demonstration."[15]

Johann Galle

In France, Le Verrier was also frustrated. His countrymen praised his mathematical virtuosity, but no one was willing to invest time in a search for the planet. Airy in England had declined to search, as far as he knew. Then Le Verrier remembered a doctoral dissertation he had received from Johann Gottfried Galle, an assistant at the Berlin Observatory. Almost a year had passed and Le Verrier had failed to acknowledge the gift. On September 18, 1846, Le Verrier picked up his pen, praised the young astronomer, and enclosed his position predictions for the new planet with the request that Galle attempt a search.

The letter reached Galle on September 23, 1846. He rushed into the office of Johann Franz Encke, the director of the Berlin Observatory, to request permission to use the institution's fine 9-inch (23-centimeter) refracting telescope for the project. It took considerable pleading before Encke gave way. It was Encke's birthday and he intended to celebrate at home with his family, so he had no personal plans for the telescope that night.[16] Heinrich d'Arrest, a young graduate student at the observatory, overheard the discussion in progress, boldly joined in, and begged to be allowed to help. "Let us oblige the gentlemen in Paris," said Encke finally, and departed.[17]

Berlin

Johann Encke, director of the Berlin Observatory

Galle and d'Arrest could scarcely wait for nightfall. They opened up the observatory dome and started looking for the new planet. As d'Arrest stood by, Galle searched the region around the position specified by Le Verrier—right ascension 21 hours 46 minutes, declination −13 degrees 24 minutes—in hopes of identifying the planet by its disk. But the planet was not immediately evident in the field of view and in surrounding fields.

Then d'Arrest suggested that they use a star map and compare stars in the sky with those on the chart to find one that wasn't plotted. Galle was reluctant. The star maps he had been using (such as those by Carl Ludwig Harding) were not very reliable. Nevertheless, there seemed to be no other choice.

The Berlin Observatory
as it was about the
time that Neptune was
discovered

Galle and d'Arrest hunted through the map files. There, to their delight, they found an excellent new chart of the region in Aquarius that they needed. They had not known that this particular map existed. Prepared by Carl Bremiker, their own observatory's staff mathematician and map-maker, this chart was a product of the Berlin Observatory's involvement with other German observatories in a full-sky mapping project inaugurated in 1830 at the urging of Friedrich Wilhelm Bessel to help with the search for more asteroids. (No new minor planets had been discovered since 1807.) Bremiker's chart of Hora XXI (right ascension hour 21 and one hour to either side) had been printed earlier that year but had not yet been released for distribution, possibly so that the Berlin Observatory could enjoy a temporary advantage.[18]

The two astronomers went back to work: Galle with his eye to the telescope, calling out each star in his field of view; d'Arrest off in a corner with a dim lamp shielded from Galle's eyes, matching each star as it was announced with one of the right position and brightness on the map.

"On the chart," he would respond. Galle would call another.

Star map by Carl Bremiker that Johann Galle and Heinrich d'Arrest used to find Neptune. The position circled is marked *Neptun beobachtet* ("Neptune observed"). The position with a square around it is labeled *Neptun berechnet* ("Neptune calculated").
Archive of the Archenhold Observatory

"On the chart," d'Arrest would say again.

Galle moved the telescope slightly to widen the search by one degree and resumed calling.

"On the chart," came the answer.

"Right ascension 21 hours 53 minutes 25.84 seconds; magnitude 8," said Galle.

"That star is not on the chart," said d'Arrest.

They had examined only a few stars. It was under an hour since they started observing. The object was less than one degree from where Le Verrier had predicted.[19]

They ran to find Encke, breaking up the birthday party. The three of them observed until the early morning hours when the object set, but they could not yet be sure that it was moving against the background stars, nor could they be sure that it showed a disk.

Encke joined Galle and d'Arrest for the commencement of observing the next night, September 24, 1846. The observing conditions were even better than the night before. The first look told the story. The object had moved. Moveover, it displayed a tiny disk, just as Le Verrier had predicted.

Galle sent notification to Le Verrier the next morning, September 25, beginning exuberantly, "The planet whose position you have pointed out *actually exists.*"[20] Concluding his praise for Le Verrier, Galle suggested that the new planet be named Janus.

Meanwhile, Encke began notifying the German astronomical community, with credit for finding the planet to Galle and himself, while omitting acknowledgment for the graduate student d'Arrest.

The Berlin Observatory's 9-inch refracting telescope with which Johann Galle and Heinrich d'Arrest found Neptune, based on the calculated position furnished by Le Verrier. The telescope is now on display at the Deutsches Museum in Munich.

Meanwhile . . .

News of the planet's discovery reached Airy while he was still on the continent, returning the visit of Peter Andreas Hansen at the Seeberg Observatory he directed near Gotha. It was September 29, two days before the news reached England. Airy's reaction was not recorded.

Meanwhile, in England, James Challis was plodding along with the search assigned to him. On September 29, 1846, he finally received a copy of Le Verrier's third paper on Uranus, giving the position of the unknown planet and the prediction that it would exhibit a disk. Challis had ignored that suggestion when it came from Adams but now he began looking for the disk. That very night, he found an object with a disk and noted its position, but didn't bother to follow up—to examine the object at higher magnification to be sure. Perhaps the next evening.

At dinner on September 30,[21] Challis mentioned the search and the disk he thought he saw to the Reverend William Towler Kingsley of Sidney Sussex College. Kingsley surprised Challis with his great excitement and asked to see it for himself at a higher power. Challis proposed a look after dinner. They reached the observatory building, which also served as the Challis home, under clear skies. When they arrived, Mrs. Challis insisted on serving them tea. By the time they finished their refreshment, the sky had clouded over. The days that followed, Challis felt, would find the Moon interfering with observations in that part of the sky, so no observations were attempted.

On October 1, 1846, the *Times* of London announced the discovery of the new planet, confirmed by John Russell Hind, an observer in London, who found it easily with a 7-inch (18-centimeter) telescope despite the moonlight and hazy skies.

Challis reexamined his records and found that he had seen the new planet twice in his first four days of searching but had not recognized it. In a letter to Airy, he confessed: "after four days of observing, the planet was in my grasp, if only I had examined or mapped the observations."[22] He had seen it again as a disk on September 29.

France

In Paris, Le Verrier was soaking up the adulation and pondering a name for the planet. On October 1 he wrote to Galle: "I thank you cordially for the alacrity with which you applied my instructions to your observations of September 23rd and 24th. We are thereby, thanks to you, definitely in possession of a new world."[23]

But Le Verrier was annoyed by Galle's suggestion of the name Janus. That was trespassing on the discoverer's right to name the planet. So he appended a postscript to the letter stating that the French Bureau of

Longitudes had named the planet Neptune. It was not true. The idea was Le Verrier's. He may have mentioned it to friends of his at the bureau who unofficially thought the name a good one, but the bureau had no official role in assigning astronomical names. Le Verrier was content that he had headed off Galle's proposal with one that seemed to carry the weight of authority.

But during the next few days Le Verrier had a change of heart. He decided that the planet should be named after himself. Yet he had already sent out notifications of his previous choice of the name Neptune to a number of astronomers. How could he undo this damage?

He went to see François Arago, the dean of French science, his friend, and the man who had sent him on the quest for this suspected planet. Arago was reluctant at first. He thought Neptune was a sensible name. But he was so impressed with Le Verrier's work that he agreed, on one condition: He would propose and urge the adoption of Le Verrier as the planet's name if the name of Uranus could be changed to Herschel (the name the French had originally proposed when Uranus was discovered).

It was a shrewd political approach. It was also very awkward and unseemly. Le Verrier's collected papers on Uranus, nearing publication, received a new title: *Recherches sur le mouvement de la planète Herschel (dite Uranus)* (Research on the Motion of the Planet Herschel [called Uranus]), but the text of the article was too far along for alteration and used the name Uranus exclusively. Le Verrier appended a note: "In my future researches, I shall consider it my strict duty to eliminate the name Uranus completely, and to call the planet only by the name *Herschel*."

On October 5, Arago announced to the Paris Academy of Sciences that Le Verrier had invited him to name the new planet and that he had chosen the name Le Verrier. He made the best possible case for this choice in an emotional speech. Comets were named after their discoverers. Why not planets, which are much greater discoveries and particularly this planet, found by such "an admirable and unprecedented method."[24] So the planet Uranus ought to be called Herschel, and the asteroid Juno ought to be Olbers (to satisfy English and German pride). Such names, he argued, represented legitimate patriotism.

The idea was harshly rejected by the international astronomical community, which had already informally adopted Le Verrier's original suggestion of Neptune. For the moment, the most serious problem had become the name for the planet.

Le Verrier and his admirers strutted their victory for the glory of France. Letters poured in. H. C. Schumacher's comment on Le Verrier's work was typical: "It is the most noble triumph of theory which I know of."[25]

The English Claim

John Herschel
Courtesy of Special Collections, San Diego State University Library

Little did the French expect that the English were about to rain on their parade. John Herschel wrote to set the record straight and give Adams appropriate credit. Airy and Challis wrote to exonerate themselves and to stake out their places in history.

On October 3 an article by John Herschel appeared in the London weekly magazine *Athenaeum*. After congratulating Le Verrier, Herschel quoted his speech three weeks earlier at the meeting of the British Association for the Advancement of Science in which he forecast that the predicted planet would soon be found. Just one such calculation would not have given him the confidence to make that prediction, he explained. He had heard from Airy that Adams had made a similar calculation earlier:

> But it was known to me, at that time, (I will take the liberty to cite the Astronomer-Royal as my authority) that a similar investigation had been independently entered into, and a conclusion as to the situation of a new planet very nearly coincident with M. Le Verrier's arrived at (in entire ignorance of his conclusions), by a young Cambridge mathematician, Mr. Adams—who will, I hope, pardon this mention of his name (the matter being one of great historical moment)—and who will, doubtless, in his own good time and manner, place his calculations before the public.

On October 5, Challis wrote to Arago to say that he had been searching for the new planet since July 29 and that, upon receiving Le Verrier's third paper on September 29, he searched for and found that night a star with a disk—prior to his hearing about the Berlin Observatory discovery six days earlier. Challis was trying to grab a bit of the fame for himself.

What Challis omitted from his letter says much about his character. He did not mention that the search that he began on July 29 was based on Adams' computations. In fact, Challis made no mention of Adams and his work at all. Challis also neglected to admit that he had seen the planet twice previous to its identification at the Berlin Observatory but had not bothered to check his work and therefore failed to recognize the planet. He also failed to mention that he had not bothered to positively identify the new planet when he saw it on September 29.

While the astronomers involved were congratulating or positioning themselves, other observers were examining the new object. William Lassell, the brewer and amateur astronomer who might have discovered Neptune a year earlier if he had not been incapacitated by an ankle injury and if his copy of Adams' position predictions had not been lost, went to work examining Neptune with his 24-inch (61-centimeter) reflector. On October 10, 1846, two and a half weeks after Neptune was found, Lassell discovered that Neptune had a moon. But before this moon could be positively confirmed (there weren't many other telescopes capable of seeing so faint an object), the Sun intruded too close to the planet's position in the sky for favorable observation. The moon of Neptune, now called Triton, was not confirmed until July 1847.

Airy Maneuvers

On October 14, 1846, it was Airy's turn to stake out his position. He realized he was trapped and was trying to shape the circumstances to his best advantage. He began his letter to Le Verrier with effusive congratulations. Then came the bombshell:

> I do not know whether you are aware that collateral researches had been going on in England and that they led to precisely the same results as yours.

Of course, Le Verrier didn't know of Adams' work. During his correspondence with Le Verrier on Uranus and its unseen disturber, Airy had deliberately withheld mention of Adams. Then Airy tried to have his cake and eat it too, and in so doing, he committed another inexcusable denigration of Adams' work.

> I think it probable that I shall be called on to give an account of these. If in this I shall give praise to others, I beg you will not consider it as at all interfering with my acknowledgements of your claims. You are to be recognized beyond doubt as the real predictor of the planet's place. I may add that the English investigations, as I believe, were not quite so extensive as yours. They were known to me earlier than yours..[26]

Even so, Airy, in his letter, still could not bring himself to mention Adams by name.

Finished with that, Airy continued his maneuvers. He answered a letter from Challis in which the Cambridge professor reported on his failed search and then suggested the name Oceanus for the new planet. Airy pretended to be unconcerned about the failure—"these misses are sometimes nearly unavoidable"—and then went on to recommend that Challis present the name Oceanus to Le Verrier, even though Airy had privately and in correspondence lent the weight of his opinion to the name Neptune and even though he knew that Le Verrier already had his own name in mind for the planet. It was a rather shabby diversionary tactic. Airy could see the scientific and political storm gathering. Having lulled Challis into a sense that no harm was done, Airy asked Challis for permission to publish his report on the planet search. Airy then wrote to Adams to make the same request so that England and "individuals" would receive "justice." Airy proposed to prepare this report himself for the Royal Astronomical Society "because I know nearly all the history and yet have taken no part in the theory or the observations."[27] Airy, who knew "nearly all the history," sent this request to the "Rev. W. J. Adams." Adams' initials, of course, were J. C., and he was not ordained.

Airy's letter reached Le Verrier on October 16. About the same time he learned of Herschel's article in the *Athenaeum*. Le Verrier was furious. If this Adams had done the work, why had neither Airy nor Challis ever mentioned him? Who was this Adams? He was professionally unknown. If he had done the work, why had it not been published? And why had nothing been heard from Adams himself? Le Verrier wrote to Airy to pose these embarrassing questions and to ask the astronomer royal to defend his claims.

The next day, on October 17, Challis published an account of his investigation in the *Athenaeum*, mentioning Adams' first solution of the Uranus problem in 1843. He also proposed the name Oceanus for the new planet.

Resentments

That did it. On October 19, 1846, the Paris Academy of Sciences met and fumed like a hall of politicians over what seemed like a British effort to usurp their nation's honor. Arago used his gift of rhetoric to discredit the English claims and to inflame the academy members. Arago was surprised by Herschel's remarks, "in complete contrast with the usual courtesy and reserve of Mr. Herschel."[28] But he reserved his venom for Airy and Challis. The astronomer royal was an authority on celestial mechanics. It was impossible to believe, if Airy had really seen Adams' work, that he could have doubted the existence of a trans-Uranian planet.

As for Challis, he was doomed by the inconsistencies in the reports he had filed. In his October 5 letter to Arago, Challis had mentioned only Le Verrier as a spur for his search. But in the October 17 *Athenaeum* article, Challis claimed to have been guided by Adams' work. This discrepancy made Challis appear either dishonest or deranged.

Since Adams had not published, said Arago, he had no claim. Concerning Oceanus as a name for the planet, which Arago thought had come from Adams, it was the height of arrogance for someone who had contributed nothing to try to horn in on the glory. "Mr. Adams has no right to figure in the history of the discovery of the planet Le Verrier, neither by a detailed citation, nor by the slightest allusion." This discovery, concluded Arago, "one of the most magnificent triumphs of astronomical theory," was a contribution to posterity from France.[29]

The French press picked up the issue and the tone and began a series of vicious attacks on Adams, Airy, Challis, Herschel, and England generally. It got so ugly that Arago and Le Verrier soon disavowed their sympathy with the papers.

While the dispute was raging, the influential scientists on the continent quietly, through correspondence, settled on the name Neptune for the planet and repudiated the use of Le Verrier's name.

The Investigation

On November 13, 1846, the Royal Astronomical Society held an inquiry into what now appeared as the Neptune scandal. How had the English scientific establishment let this prize slip through their fingers? Airy presented his "Account of Some Circumstances Historically Connected with the Discovery of the Planet Exterior to Uranus." Challis followed with his "Account of Observations at the Cambridge Observatory for Detecting the Planet Exterior to Uranus." Then Adams offered "An Explanation of the Observed Irregularities in the Motion of *Uranus* . . . ," complete with the position, mass, and orbit of Neptune—presenting an abstract of the work that he had tried in vain for more than a year to bring to the attention of the scientific establishment.[30] Adams had also computed the first orbit for Neptune, using the three unrecognized sightings by Challis, and had sent it to Airy on October 15.

Adams expressed no disappointment or bitterness, only praise for Le Verrier:

> I mention these dates merely to shew that my results were arrived at independently and previously to the publication of M. Le Verrier, and not with the intention of interfering with his just claims to the honors of the discovery, for there is no doubt that his researches were first published to the world, and led to the actual discovery of the planet by Dr. Galle, so that the facts stated above cannot detract, in the slightest degree, from the credit due to M. Le Verrier.[31]

At last Adams received some measure of acclaim. Challis and Airy were sharply criticized. Why hadn't Challis begun a search in September 1845 when Adams first gave him the planet's position? Challis' answer was lame—he lacked confidence in theoretical calculations. Why hadn't Challis reviewed his search data? "[P]artly," he said, "because I thought the probability of discovery was small till a much larger portion of the heavens was scrutinised, but chiefly because I was making a grand effort to reduce the vast number of comet observations which I have accumulated; and this occupied the whole of my time when I was not engaged in observing." No one doubted that Challis had told the truth, but the truth cost him his credibility as a scientist.

Airy stood convicted even in the minds of his friends of "unreasonable incredulity and apathy toward Adams," as his colleague Adam Sedgwick, a geologist, informed him:

> Had the results communicated to you and Challis been sent to Berlin, I am told, they came *so near the mark* that to a certainty the new planet would have been made out in a very few weeks, perhaps a very few days, and the whole business settled in 1845—Adams the sole, unadvised, unassisted discoverer. . . . To say the very least of it, a grand occasion has been thrown away.[32]

And that was from a friend writing to him. Others were far less restrained and less private in their judgment of Airy.

But Airy's high opinion of himself sustained him through the crisis. As always, he felt he had done his job with distinction.

Recognition

It was now annual awards time, and the Royal Society gave its Copley Medal for 1846 to Urbain Jean Joseph Le Verrier for the discovery of Neptune. It had made joint awards before but now declined to honor Adams because it considered his claims too uncertain for notice. The Royal Astronomical Society, having just completed its extraordinary investigation, decided in exhaustion not to award its Gold Medal to anyone in 1846.

Gradually, through the early months of 1847, more of the facts emerged. The hurt feelings and wounded national pride slowly healed. Newspapers called off their vendettas. The accomplishments of Adams and his gentlemanly behavior through the entire proceeding began to be appreciated.

In June 1847, at a meeting of the British Association for the Advancement of Science, Adams and Le Verrier met one another for the first time at a party given by John Herschel. Some guests held their breath. Within minutes, Adams and Le Verrier were off by themselves talking animatedly and laughing. They formed a lifelong friendship.

In 1848, trying to make up for its injustice two years earlier, the Royal Society gave Adams its Copley Medal. The Royal Astronomical Society, too, was ready for a reassessment, but its response was peculiar. For 1848, it gave no Gold Medal but instead awarded "testimonials" to 12 scientists, including Adams, Le Verrier, and Airy, while omitting Galle, d'Arrest, and Challis.

History has been generally kind to Adams. Textbooks and reference works today usually credit Adams and Le Verrier or Adams, Le Verrier, and Galle with the discovery of Neptune, although d'Arrest is still almost always overlooked.

The discovery of Neptune by mathematical calculation—the planet found on a sheet of paper—was the greatest triumph for gravitational theory since 1758, when the comet of 1682 returned just as Edmond Halley had predicted in 1705 using Newton's laws. Ever since, that object has been known as Halley's Comet. Other historians of science argue that the discovery of Neptune was the greatest triumph for Newton's gravitational theory since its publication in 1687.

The discovery of Neptune in 1846 was a turning point in the history of astronomy, as mathematics and theory now took the lead in the way astronomical research was pursued. The greatest epoch, begun with William Herschel's discovery of Uranus in 1781, of discoveries and progress in astronomy led by amateur astronomers was ending. Amateurs would still make contributions, but astronomy was more and more a highly specialized mathematical and physical discipline.

And what did life bring for the major participants in one of the most dramatic and scientifically significant events in the history of astronomy?

Thereafter

Johann Gottfried Galle continued in the position of special assistant that Encke had created for him at the Berlin Observatory in 1835. In 1851 he accepted appointment as professor of astronomy and director of the observatory at the University of Breslau. It was wrenching to leave Encke and the well-equipped Berlin Observatory for a modestly equipped observatory in a provincial town. But there Galle remained for the rest of his life, contributing significantly to binary star, comet, and meteor studies, and when the city lights and obsolete equipment rendered his observatory useless, he shifted with effectiveness into the study of meteorology. When he died in 1910 at the age of 98, he was still sharp of mind and active in astronomy, revered by three generations of Breslau students, and had the unique distincition of having observed Halley's Comet as a professional astronomer at two different apparitions—in 1835 and 1910.

Johann Galle in old age
Archive of the Archenhold Observatory

Heinrich d'Arrest was not mentioned in Encke's report on the discovery of Neptune at the Berlin Observatory in 1846. Following his internship at the Berlin Observatory, d'Arrest moved on to the Leipzig Observatory in 1848, where he continued his fine work on comets and asteroids. In 1858 he was named professor of astronomy and director of the new observatory at the University of Copenhagen. There he expanded his scientific reputation with his studies of nebulae and his exploration of the new field of spectroscopy until his untimely death at the age of 52. It was not until 1877, two years after his death, that Galle finally clarified the important role that d'Arrest had played in the detection of Neptune.

George Biddell Airy, astronomer royal, stubbornly rode out the criticism of his role in the Neptune scandal. There is no indication that he ever felt ashamed or regretful or even uncertain of his treatment of Adams or his handling of the quest for Neptune. Airy was impervious because he never doubted himself. Under his direction the Royal Observatory continued to be a model of efficiency as a source of accurate astronomical

George Airy in 1852, six years after Neptune was discovered
National Maritime Museum Greenwich

tables for British navigators. He remained unpopular with his assistants because he treated them as drudges and tolerated no independent thought. He trained no young astronomers. He was an organizer and a bureaucrat rather than a scientist. In 1881, at the age of 80, he retired from duties as astronomer royal and died, still organizing his papers, in 1892 at the age of 90.

It had been a swift and promising ascent for James Challis from senior wrangler and First Smith's prizeman as an undergraduate at Cambridge to Plumian Professor of Astronomy and director of the Cambridge Observatory in 1836 at the age of 32. Yet no notable science appeared. The Neptune incident focused the attention of the faculty at Cambridge and astronomers in England and abroad to the fact that Challis was something of a kook. His ideas and scientific claims became ever more overblown, perhaps in an effort to extricate himself from the Neptune failure. He claimed that he had generalized Newton's law of universal gravitation to include all physical forces and was about to publish. He never did. Only his friendliness and Cambridge tradition dissuaded critics from stripping him of his distinguished position as Plumian Professor of Astronomy. He did surrender his directorship of the Cambridge Observatory to Adams in 1861. As one historian observed: "Challis was a spectacular failure as a scientist, and ironically, this failure has immortalized him."[33] He died in 1882, just before his seventy-ninth birthday.

Honors continued to pour in for Le Verrier. Professorial chairs in celestial mechanics and astronomy were created for him at the Sorbonne. He continued his study of planetary perturbations for the remaining 31 years of his life, refining the orbits and masses of the planets. He completed this vast project of more than 4,000 pages one month before his death. Le Verrier hoped that other planets would be found the way he and Adams found Neptune.

With typical tenacity, Le Verrier also returned to the problem of Mercury's motion that had stymied him in 1843. Mercury's perihelion was advancing along its orbit as a rate of about 9 minutes 26 seconds a *century*—less than one-third the apparent diameter of the Moon as seen from Earth. In 1843, Le Verrier had been able to explain about 90 percent of this motion by the gravitational perturbations on Mercury of the other planets in the solar system. But 38 (now known to be 43) seconds of arc per century defied his efforts at a complete solution based on the gravity of known objects.

In 1859, 19 years after Arago had handed him the problem, Le Verrier offered an answer. The codiscoverer of the outermost known planet proposed that inside the orbit of Mercury lay an undiscovered innermost planet—or a group of asteroids.

Soon after he published his results, Le Verrier received a letter from

Urbain Jean Joseph Le Verrier
Courtesy of Special Collections, San Diego State University Library

a French country doctor and amateur astronomer named Edmond Modeste Lescarbault who claimed to have seen this planet passing across the face of the Sun. Le Verrier rushed to meet Lescarbault and was convinced that an intra-Mercurian planet had been found, duplicating his planet-predicting triumph with Neptune. A name appropriate for a planet so close to the Sun was already waiting—Vulcan, the Roman god of fire.

Once again, it seemed, Le Verrier had saved the integrity of Newton's law of universal gravitation. But the sighting was not confirmed by other observers at the time or duplicated by later observers. Through the years, various amateur and professional astronomers claimed to have seen Vulcan transiting the Sun or near the Sun during a total eclipse, but these reports conflicted with Lescarbault's sighting and with one another, or they were better explained as misidentified stars.

Ironically, in the carefully observed and analyzed motion of Mercury, astronomers this time had uncovered a real defect in Newton's law of gravity. The problem of Mercury's orbit was not solved until Einstein published his General Theory of Relativity in 1916. The excessive precession of Mercury's perihelion was the most detectable difference in solar system motion between the predictions of Newton and Einstein. And the anomaly that Le Verrier had pointed out provided one of the crucial proofs that Einstein was correct.[34]

Following the death of Arago, Le Verrier became director of the Paris Observatory in 1854. Not only did he continue to lead astronomy from that position, but he was one of the founders of modern meteorology. He set up an international network to warn sailors of approaching storms.

Le Verrier was admired for his absolute integrity in scientific matters, but people close to him found him edgy and authoritarian. His tenure at the Paris Observatory was stormy. He was dismissed in 1870 for repressing staff creativity and devoting too little of observatory funds to astronomy. He was reinstated in 1873 when his successor and enemy Charles Eugène Delaunay died. Thereafter Le Verrier devoted full attention to celestial mechanics. He died of a progressive liver ailment in 1877 at the age of 66.

Appropriate recognition for Adams was slower in coming. His fellowship at St. John's College, Cambridge, expired in 1852 because he had not joined the clergy. He became a fellow at Pembroke College, Cambridge, in 1853. He applied for the position of superintendent of the *Nautical Almanac* in 1853 but was not chosen.[35] Finally, in 1858, he was appointed professor of mathematics at the University of St. Andrews. Upon that appointment, Cambridge University repented its snub and, in that same year, brought Adams back as Lowndean Professor of Astronomy and Geometry. In 1861, Challis was eased out as director of the Cambridge Observatory and Adams was appointed in his place.

John Couch Adams in middle age
The Master & Fellows of St. John's College, Cambridge

In 1863, at the age of 44, Adams married Eliza Bruce from Dublin. They had no children. He was the first president of the Association for Promoting the Higher Education of Women in Cambridge and helped in the establishment of Newnham College in 1880, the first residence for women at Cambridge. He was one of the first professors to open his lectures to women.

Following his codiscovery of Neptune, Adams continued to do distinguished work in astronomical mathematics, bringing him additional renown—and controversy. He carefully studied the gradual acceleration and deceleration in the Moon's motion evident in historical records of eclipses and caused by the changing ellipticity of the Earth's orbit. He found that the analysis of Laplace, the great French celestial mechanician, had been faulty. This caused very hard feelings among French astronomers until, by 1861, independent investigations showed that Adams was right.

He was offered knighthood in 1847 and the position of astronomer royal when Airy retired in 1881 but declined both. The modesty that had cost him fame early in his career endeared him to friends and colleagues throughout his life. John Couch Adams died in 1892 at the age of 72.

CHAPTER 5

Percival Lowell and Planet X

(On possible names for Neptune): "The name 'Janus'
would imply that this planet is the last one in the solar
system, and there is no reason to believe that this is so."
U. J. J. Le Verrier
(September 1846)

"(A)fter thirty or forty years of observing the new planet
(Neptune), we will be able to use it in turn for the
discovery of the one that follows it in order of distance
from the Sun."
U. J. J. Le Verrier
(c. 1846)

(On the clustering of certain comet orbits): "This can
hardly be an accident; . . . it means a planet out there as
yet unseen by man, but certain sometime to be detected
and added to the others."
Percival Lowell
(1903)

The discovery of Uranus and Neptune tantalized astronomers with the
prospect that still more distant planets lay undetected. Le Verrier believed
that analysis of the motion of Neptune would reveal the existence of
another planet, but not in his lifetime. Neptune crept along its orbit so
slowly that even at the beginning of the twentieth century its path was
not known with sufficient precision to reveal the perturbations of an outlying planet.

The discovery of Neptune solved the mystery of the anomalous motion of Uranus—almost. When the actual motion of Uranus was compared to predictions that took account of all known gravitational disturbances, tiny discrepancies remained—only a few percent the size of the errors that enabled Adams and Le Verrier to calculate the existence and position of Neptune. Were these "residuals" meaningful? Did they reveal the existence of yet another planet, or were they just minute errors in measuring the exact location of Uranus, resulting perhaps from inaccurate positional data for the background stars? The obstacles to calculating and searching for trans-Neptunian planets were so formidable that few astronomers tried. Many doubted that a planet lurked beyond Neptune. Still, an occasional astronomer attempted some crude calculations that suggested the unexplained inconsistencies in the motion of Uranus (the residuals) pointed to a more remote planet.[1]

The Patrician Amateur

Percival Lowell
Lowell Observatory photograph

On March 13, 1855, Percival Lowell was born into a wealthy Boston family, the oldest of five children. His brother Abbott Lawrence Lowell became president of Harvard University. His youngest sister Amy became a famous poet. Percival graduated with honors in mathematics from Harvard and amassed his own fortune during six years of business work for his grandfather's wide-ranging enterprises, which included cotton mills, financial institutions, and utility companies. Then, in 1883, he began a ten-year series of extended visits to the Far East as a travel writer. He served as foreign secretary and general counselor for the first diplomatic mission from Korea to the United States.

During a trip to Japan in 1893, Lowell learned that Giovanni Schiaparelli, the noted Italian astronomer, was going blind and had been forced to terminate his observations of Mars. It was Schiaparelli who in 1877 had first described thin, straight, crisscrossing features on the surface of the red planet. He named them *canali,* meaning "channels." Channels could be natural or artificial features. The English-language press, however, translated *canali* as "canals," implying that they were built by intelligent beings.

The controversy over artificial features on Mars had long fascinated Lowell. He returned to Boston and began to use his wealth to establish an observatory whose major effort would be the investigation of the Martian "canals."

Lowell chose as his site a pine-forested mesa one mile west of Flagstaff in remote Arizona Territory at an elevation of 7,250 feet (2,210 meters), where his observatory could "see rather than be seen."[2] His was the first permanent observatory in the world to be purposely situated away from city lights and in a climate tested for good seeing conditions.[3]

The Lowell Observatory opened on June 1, 1894. Lowell, an excellent public speaker and writer, was soon lecturing about life forms on Mars whose canals gave proof of their intelligence and global unity but also demonstrated that this peaceful civilization was doomed by drought. Most astronomers were skeptical of Lowell's interpretations of the Martian features; some were harshly critical. Lowell hired a small cadre of talented scientists to operate his observatory and gave them sufficient time for their own research. They left the flamboyance, controversy, and public relations to Lowell and concentrated on meticulous work that brought its own recognition to the Lowell Observatory. In 1905, the permanent scientific staff consisted of Vesto M. Slipher and Carl O. Lampland. Slipher's younger brother Earl C. Slipher soon joined the full-time staff.

A Trans-Neptunian Planet

But Lowell's attention was not exclusively focused on Mars. All the planets intrigued him. His interest in the possibility of a planet beyond Neptune stemmed from his college training by Benjamin Peirce, who created a long-standing controversy by claiming that the discovery of Neptune was an accident because although the position predictions of Adams and Le Verrier were correct, all their other predictions about the planet's distance, orbit, brightness, and mass were in error. Peirce was wrong. Adams and Le Verrier had correctly used perturbations in the motion of Uranus to pinpoint Neptune.

Now, with the means to conduct a telescopic search, an enduring interest in mathematics, and knowledge of previous efforts to hypothesize a ninth planet, Lowell was ready to attack this high-profile problem. Lampland felt that Lowell sought the "prestige of mathematically predicting a new planet . . . in order to gain more respectability for his theories about Mars" and to enhance the prestige of his observatory, which, because of Lowell's claims for canals on Mars, had become "virtually an outcast in professional astronomical circles."[4]

From 1902 on, Lowell's lectures and writings give evidence of his belief that a trans-Neptunian planet would eventually be detected.

His first search for a ninth planet began in early 1905 and proceeded sporadically as his time permitted for four years. The quest began as a photographic survey along the mean plane of the solar system; later a dimension of theory and calculation was added in an attempt to narrow the search. But the observational and theoretical components of the search were seldom integrated. Each time Lowell made a new computation, he altered the hypothetical planet's predicted location and would send his colleagues in Flagstaff a new position to be searched. The photography, completed in September 1907, was performed by a succession of three

University of Indiana astronomy students. Lowell examined the resulting 440 plates but found nothing. Lowell was worried that his project would be stolen by others, so, unlike his other well-publicized ventures, he kept his search for a trans-Neptunian planet as quiet and secretive as he could, referring to it in correspondence with his staff as the "invariable plane" work because the search was conducted along the mean plane of the solar system, thought to be the most likely orbital path for the suspected planet. Eventually, when he found that the complexities of the search were so great that no one could jump in opportunistically, he dropped his secrecy. By late 1908 he was referring to his trans-Neptunian quarry as Planet X.

Competition

In mid November 1908, Lowell received some startling and troubling news. He attended a lecture by William H. Pickering of Harvard, who for a few months had helped him initiate the Mars observation project when the Lowell Observatory opened in 1894 and who was now a critic of his Mars theories. Pickering had used a graphical plot of the residuals of Uranus to predict the existence and position of a trans-Neptunian "Planet O." This graphic approach had first been used and its value demonstrated by John Herschel to refine the orbit of Neptune and to show how its existence and location had been deduced from the residuals of Uranus. His method first appeared in his popular textbook *Outlines of Astronomy* in 1849.

Pickering's 1908 prediction for Planet O gave it a distance of 51.9 astronomical units, a period of 373.5 years, and a mass twice that of Earth. Its disk was estimated to be about 0.8 arc second in diameter and its magnitude either 11.5 (if reflective like Neptune) or 13 (if less reflective like Mars). Two brief telescopic searches had failed to find the planet.

Pickering sought Lowell's help with the search, but Lowell declined, neglecting to mention that he had been calculating and searching for a ninth planet for more than three years himself. Lowell realized that he had serious competition in his quest—and from a scientific adversary whose calculations seemed to be ahead of his own. The shock of discovering Pickering's interest in a trans-Neptunian planet caused Lowell to plunge ahead with all the energy and resources he could spare from his Mars work.

In March 1905, Lowell had hired a moonlighting U.S. Naval Observatory mathematician named William T. Carrigan to assist him with the extraction and analysis of the residuals of Uranus and Neptune. Lowell initially urged Carrigan on, but in May 1909 dismissed him, saying that he had reached his own theoretical solution to the orbit and location of a ninth planet without using any of Carrigan's four years of calculations. Lowell complained that Carrigan was overly meticulous. The planet, Lowell wrote to Carrigan, lay 47.5 astronomical units from the Sun, had an orbital period of 327 years, a magnitude of 13 or fainter, and a mass two-fifths of Neptune's.

Lowell never published this prediction, nor did he use it to search for a planet. His anxiety about Pickering's lead subsided when he read Pickering's published work and found his approach superficial. In annotating his copy of Pickering's paper, Lowell derided his former colleague's efforts, concluding: "This ninth planet is very properly designated O [and] is nothing at all."[5]

Assessment

A year was to pass before Lowell returned to the problem of Planet X. He began by assessing the shortcomings of his first search. First, there was a problem of instrumentation. The observatory's 5-inch (13-centimeter) telescopic camera, the latest and most promising of four telescopes employed in the search, was inadequate to the task. It recorded a sharply defined field only about 5 degrees across. What Lowell could not know was that the undetected planet was then too far south of the ecliptic to be within the search zone and had a brightness of only 16th magnitude (10,000 times too faint for the unaided human eye to see), at the recording limit of his photographic plates.[6]

A second problem with the initial search for Planet X was technique. Lowell's method of examining the plates was unlikely to yield results. The search produced plates of the same region of the sky taken a few days apart so that a planet would reveal itself by its change of position. Lowell would take these glass plates, superimpose them, offset them slightly, and then examine each pair of images with a magnifying glass in search of motion. It was cumbersome, unsystematic, and imprecise.

About a year into the first search, Lampland had suggested that Lowell buy a new invention called a blink microscope for the inspection of the plates. With a blink microscope (also called a blink comparator), two plates could be placed side by side and viewed through an eyepiece that optically superimposed the two plates and magnified them. A shutter inside the system then alternated views so rapidly that the shift from one plate to the other was almost undetectable to the eye. If the plates to be compared were identical in images and exposures and if the plates were aligned so as to superimpose accurately, the blink microscope would show what appeared to be just one plate with nothing moving, jumping, or pulsating. But if an object had moved or changed in brightness from one plate to the next, the object that changed would appear to jump

Percival Lowell observing Venus in the daytime with the 24-inch Clark refractor at the Lowell Observatory
Lowell Observatory photograph

back and forth or pulsate as the shutter inside the blink microscope alternated views, while the rest of the images remained unchanged. Lowell decided against an investment in a blink microscope.

Instead Lowell decided that if he were to have any hope of succeeding, the quest would require the most thoroughgoing mathematical analysis possible. A graphical plot of the residuals of Uranus would not do. He would have to repeat and even amplify the rigor that Adams and Le Verrier had applied in their pursuit of Neptune. He faced, he felt, a problem even greater than Adams and Le Verrier had confronted because for them Neptune was the solution, while for him it was part of the problem.

Lowell was ignoring the fact that Adams and Le Verrier had to invent their own mathematical analysis, whereas he could study their methods and employ one of their already proven systems. Nevertheless, he faced some very real problems in his search for Planet X. He ticked off the difficulties:

(1) The residual errors in the predicted versus actual positions of Uranus were now, with Neptune's influence accounted for, very small.

(2) Neptune had not been observed long enough along its huge orbit for perturbations of its motion by an outlying planet to be evident. Therefore he would have to rely on the presumably smaller perturbations exhibited by Uranus.

(3) A ninth planet might have a highly eccentric orbit, and that orbit might be sharply inclined to the ecliptic. (Here Lowell was using the analogy of Jupiter, Saturn, and their satellites as miniature solar systems. The outer moons of Jupiter and Saturn have markedly elliptical orbits that are notably inclined to the equators of their planets.)

(4) The orbit of Uranus (and any planet) cannot be known with absolute precision because of the constantly changing perturbations on it and the difficulty of astronomical measurements. The resulting inaccuracies are incorporated into any calculation using that planet's position.[7]

Lowell reviewed the differences in the methods by which Adams and Le Verrier had attacked the Neptune problem and then chose Le Verrier's. Adams' approach was "direct and masterful," he thought, but Le Verrier's was "simpler and more complete."[8]

A New Attack

The second search began in July 1910 with a mathematical assault by Lowell, assisted by Elizabeth Langdon Williams, who had been editing publications in his Boston office for at least five years previously. Lowell assumed that Planet X traveled around the Sun in the same plane as Uranus and was 47.5 astronomical units from the Sun, the same distance he had used for his initial search.[9] Using the residuals of Uranus, he sought to calculate the orbital eccentricity, the longitude of perihelion, and the mass of Planet X.

On March 13, 1911, Lowell celebrated his fifty-sixth birthday (and the one hundred thirtieth anniversary of the discovery of Uranus) by sending a telegram to Lampland, his assistant director at the Lowell Observatory, requesting him to begin a new photographic survey along the ecliptic for Planet X. Lowell promised that his computations to focus the search would soon follow. Lampland proposed again that the analysis of the photographs would greatly increase in efficiency and precision if the Lowell Observatory had an instrument like a blink comparator. This time, Lowell bought one immediately and it was shipped back and forth between Boston and Flagstaff as needed.[10]

Lowell's first new computations for the position of the ninth planet were not ready until late April. The photographic search proceeded sporadically because Mars was nearing opposition (the point at which the Earth and Mars are closest that occurs every two years) and Lowell and his colleagues were making their usual plans for detailed studies of the red planet.

In 1911, Pickering published his prediction of the existence of three more trans-Neptunian planets beyond his Planet O, designating them P,

WILLIAM H. PICKERING AND PLANETS O, P, Q, R, S, T, AND U

William H. Pickering (1858–1938) made and published more predictions for the existence of trans-Neptunian planets than any other astronomer.

Like Percival Lowell, Pickering was born in Boston, came from a family of social and intellectual distinction, was well educated (M.I.T.), and had travel and adventure in his blood (Pickering especially liked primitive areas and mountain climbing). Like Lowell, Pickering was a bundle of energy. Besides leading four solar eclipse expeditions as a staff member of the Harvard College Observatory, he set up stations of the observatory in Arequipa, Peru (1891), and Mandeville, Jamaica (1900), and helped in 1894 to build the observatory in Flagstaff for Percival Lowell.

He had more than average scientific accomplishments. He was a pioneer in new celestial photography technology. In 1899 he discovered Phoebe, the ninth moon of Saturn and the first satellite to be found photographically. He also produced the first complete photographic atlas of the Moon (1903).

Unlike his older brother Edward Charles Pickering, director of the Harvard College Observatory, William was less rigorous in his work and prone to sudden enthusiasms. This caused considerable friction between the brothers, and William was never promoted beyond assistant professor.

Approaching age 50, Pickering became more and more consumed with predicting the existence and location of trans-Neptunian planets. Although his 1919 prediction of the position for Planet O was as close to where Pluto was found as was Lowell's prediction for Planet X, Pickering's credibility was not high, because of the number of new planets he

William H. Pickering
Harvard University Archives

predicted, the less-than-rigorous method he had for predicting them, and the speed with which he abandoned or substantially modified his predictions.

In 1924 he retired from the Harvard College Observatory, and the observatory he had established for Harvard in Mandeville, Jamaica, became his private observatory.[1]

---

[1]See especially William Graves Hoyt, "W. H. Pickering's Planetary Predictions and the Discovery of Pluto," *Isis* 67 (1976): 551–654.

Q, and R. Planet Q had a mass 20,000 times greater than Earth, which would have made it 63 times more massive than Jupiter and about one-sixteenth (6 percent) the mass of the Sun—close to a star of minimal mass rather than a high-mass planet. Q , said Pickering, had a highly elliptical polar orbit.

Now, as in 1908, competition with Pickering altered none of Lowell's opinions but caused him to intensify his project. He gave orders to accelerate the photographic search and hired four more mathematical assistants to help him and his chief computer, Miss Williams, in Boston. (In those days, computers were human.) All five assistants were at work in November 1912, but Lowell wasn't. He had been pressing so hard on the problem that late in October he collapsed from nervous exhaustion."[11] It was two exasperating months for Lowell before he could return to work for even short periods.

Waiting for a Telegram

In Flagstaff the photographic search proceeded by examining the areas specified by the continually modified calculations. From 1911 to 1914, Lowell conducted the hunt on his observatory's largest instrument, a 40-inch (102-centimeter) reflector, installed in 1909, but its field of view—only one square degree—was too small for an efficient search. In April 1914, Lowell and his colleagues turned to a 9-inch (23-centimeter) Brashear photographic refractor that they borrowed from Swarthmore College's Sproul Observatory near Philadelphia without initially revealing to Swarthmore the exact nature of the project.

The project's intensive computational phase ended in April 1914. Approximately the same orbits and positions for Planet X were recurring in repeated calculations. Lowell sent two of his mathematical assistants to Flagstaff to step up the photographic search, discharged the others, and retained Miss Williams for whatever calculations might yet be needed. Lowell was optimistic when he and his wife set sail in May for their usual spring vacation in Europe. He telegraphed his observatory a new most probable location to search for Planet X, requesting, "Don't hesitate to startle me with a telegram—FOUND!"[12]

But no such telegram arrived. Many years of calculations and searching had not produced the expected planet. Lowell began to get discouraged. He wrote an account of his theoretical and observational efforts for presentation in 1915 to a meeting of the American Academy of Arts and Sciences. Two weeks before the speech, he notified his staff of a newly revised position for Planet X, adding: "I am going to give my work before the Academy on January 13. It would be thoughtful of you to announce the actual discovery at the same time."

Publication and Response

Percival Lowell at his observatory in Flagstaff
Lowell Observatory photograph

Lowell's paper—logical, mathematical, and conservatively phrased—gathered little attention from the press, the general public, or other astronomers. The academy even declined to publish it, and Lowell was irked at having to issue it as a Lowell Observatory publication at his own expense. With the failure of his search and the lack of interest exhibited in his research on a trans-Neptunian planet, Lowell showed his discouragement in his typical way: He turned to other matters and seldom mentioned or took an active part in the project again. "No news from X?" he inquired in July. An entry in the observation log for October 8, 1915, mentions that "Dr. Lowell paid a visit to the 9-inch." But after Lowell published his efforts to find a trans-Neptunian planet in September 1915, Planet X disappeared from his writings and his interviews with the press.

On July 2, 1916, the entry in the observation log read "Lunch." Sky conditions prevented any further work that night. And that was the end of the second photographic search for Lowell's trans-Neptunian planet. The 9-inch telescope was needed back at Swarthmore.

On the nearly 1,000 plates exposed in this second search were 515 asteroids, 700 variable stars—and 2 images of the ninth planet. On March 19 and April 7, 1915, Thomas B. Gill, one of Lowell's former mathematical assistants in Boston, now an assistant observer at Flagstaff, had recorded the sought-after trans-Neptunian planet as part of the ongoing photographic search, but the object went unrecognized. Lowell had predicted that Planet X would be about magnitude 13; these images were between 15th and 16th magnitude—about five times fainter. They were just barely visible on the plates. Lowell probably never examined these plates himself. At this stage in his career, he left such tedious work to his assistants.

Lowell concluded from this second search that the object he was seeking was fainter than 13th magnitude and that therefore the 9-inch telescope used for the search was probably too small. He also concluded that the distance of the trans-Neptunian planet was less than the 47.5 astronomical units he had previously clung to.[13]

He would never know how close he came to Planet X.

On November 12, 1916, Percival Lowell, 61 years old, died of a massive stroke at the Lowell Observatory.

CHAPTER 6

The Discovery of Pluto

"Lunch."
Final entry in the observation log for the 1905–1916 Lowell Observatory telescopic search for a ninth planet

"We think he is going to develop into a useful man. He has several good qualities that are going to make up for his meager training."
Vesto M. Slipher on newly hired Clyde Tombaugh
(1929)

"Young man, I am afraid you are wasting your time. If there were any more planets to be found, they would have been found long before this."
Visiting astronomer to Clyde Tombaugh
(June 1929)

In his will Lowell provided quite handsomely for his wife, appointed Vesto M. Slipher as observatory director, and left an endowment of more than a million dollars for the support of his observatory. His staff, despite their less flamboyant scientific styles, respected Lowell and wanted to proceed with his projects, including the search for Planet X. But work was slowed not only by World War I but by the lengthy court battle that ensued when Lowell's widow bitterly contested the will. By the time the litigation ended, legal fees had swallowed a substantial fraction of the estate.

If a new search for Planet X were to be mounted, a larger telescope specifically designed for sky survey work would be needed. As soon as the estate was settled in 1927, the Lowell Observatory arranged for the fabrication of a 13-inch (33-centimeter) photographic refractor, made possible by a gift of $10,000 from Abbott Lawrence Lowell, president of Harvard and Percival's brother. The new telescope was assembled and tested at Flagstaff in 1929 and found to be an exceptionally fine instrument, with its wide field providing extremely clear images across a 12-by 14-degree region.

A Kansas Farm Boy

But there was no one to conduct the search. The Lowell Observatory core scientific staff of Vesto M. Slipher, Carl O. Lampland, and Earl C. Slipher professed confidence in Lowell's computations for a ninth planet, but none had room among his existing projects for the time and tedium entailed in a comprehensive photographic search for Planet X.

Vesto Slipher wanted to hire a new assistant observer who was not a research astronomer, lest the observer's own interests distract him from the trans-Neptunian planet search. In 1928, Slipher had received a letter from a young high school graduate in Kansas named Clyde W. Tombaugh. His summers were taken up by farming with his family, but his winters and all clear evenings were devoted to his hobby of astronomy. He had built three reflecting telescopes with mirrors ranging from 7 to 9 inches (18 to 23 centimeters) in diameter, the last two of excellent quality. His drawings and notes about his observations indicated commitment and precision. Despite Tombaugh's lack of formal astronomical training, Slipher decided to give him a chance and invited him to join the staff as an assistant observer on a trial basis.

Clyde Tombaugh, age 22, arrived in Flagstaff on January 15, 1929, without knowledge of the project he would be assigned. He quickly impressed the staff astronomers by his enthusiasm, his willingness to learn, and his painstaking work. The third search for Planet X began with Clyde Tombaugh at the 13-inch refractor on April 6, 1929.

Tombaugh quickly found that the staff astronomers were so busy that he could not rely on them for improvements to the prescribed search procedure. So, after a few weeks, he took the project ever more in hand and made the needed modifications himself.

Planet X was expected to be magnitude 12 to 13 or, as Lowell suspected at the conclusion of his second search, perhaps somewhat fainter. The 13-inch telescope could reach stars of 17th magnitude with a one-hour exposure. But, Tombaugh realized, if seeing conditions were poor, the exposure time would require another 15 to 20 minutes. In order to use the blink microscope to compare star fields in search of an object that shifted position from one picture to the next, it was crucial that the plates be made within about a week of one another and that the exposures be made and developed under as nearly similar conditions as possible. This

Clyde Tombaugh with the 13-inch telescope that he used to discover Pluto. (He is looking through the eyepiece for the guide scope.) This photograph was made in 1931, the year after the discovery.
Lowell Observatory photograph

The Lowell Observatory administration building as it was when Clyde Tombaugh arrived in 1929
Lowell Observatory photograph

Dome for the 13-inch telescope with which Clyde Tombaugh discovered Pluto
Lowell Observatory photograph

The 13-inch photographic survey telescope that Clyde Tombaugh used to discover Pluto. This astrograph, made possible by a gift from A. Lawrence Lowell, Percival's brother, was being installed at the Lowell Observatory in 1929 as Tombaugh arrived to take up observing duties on a trial basis.
Clyde W. Tombaugh

procedure would assure that the background stars on each plate would be as close to identical as possible during blinking so that a real planet (or asteroid or variable star) would stand out. Tombaugh chose a relatively bright star near the center of each star field to serve as a guide star so that the telescope would remain correctly targeted while it turned to track the westward-wheeling stars as the Earth rotated. His plan was

CLYDE TOMBAUGH GOES TO FLAGSTAFF

Clyde Tombaugh, the eldest of six children, was born on a farm near Streator, Illinois, on February 4, 1906. He enjoyed exploring the heavens with his Uncle Lee and his 3-inch telescope. Clyde virtually memorized the popular astronomy book his uncle loaned him. In 1920 his father and Uncle Lee bought a new 2.25-inch scope from the Sears-Roebuck catalog for them to share.

When Clyde was 16, his family moved to a rented farm near Burdett, Kansas, and his uncle insisted that he take the new telescope with him. So much work needed to be done on the farm that Clyde dropped out of school for a year to help. In 1925 he graduated from Burdett High with a longing to be a college professor. But even a college education seemed out of reach. He was needed for farmwork.

Yet the lure of astronomy was strong. In 1926, Clyde fashioned an 8-inch reflecting telescope. He made the mirror out of ship porthole glass, the tube out of pine boards, and the mount out of discarded farm machinery. But the curvature of the mirror was not very good, and he was disappointed with his view of the features on Mars.

With his father's help, Clyde built a storage and storm cellar that could also provide the stable air needed for telescope-mirror testing. He then made a fine 7-inch reflector and sent it to his Uncle Lee. His uncle paid him, and Clyde plunged the money into a 9-inch mirror of his own. His days belonged to farmwork, but his nights were devoted to observing the skies and carefully sketching the planets. He completed his excellent new telescope in time to enjoy the 1928 close passage of the Earth by Mars.

The growing season of 1928 was developing in-

to one of the best the family had ever known when a sudden hailstorm ruined the crop just before harvest. Clyde decided against a career in farming. He was 22 years old. He needed to get a job to earn some money to help his family through the crisis. He weighed joining the railroad as an apprentice fireman or trying to start a telescope-making business. He sent a few of his meticulous sketches of Jupiter, Saturn, and Mars off to the Lowell Observatory for appraisal. "It was the only planetary observatory I knew of," he confessed years later.[1]

His letter arrived at an opportune time. Vesto Slipher, the observatory director, was looking for a committed young observer to resume the photographic search for a trans-Neptunian planet suspected by observatory founder Percival Lowell and upon which he had invested so much effort. Slipher, his brother Earl, and Carl Lampland, the three professional astronomers on the Lowell Observatory staff, had all grown up doing farmwork. Slipher invited Tombaugh out to Arizona on a three-month trial basis. Clyde's family drove him 30 miles to the nearest railroad station. His father advised him, "Clyde, make yourself useful, and beware of easy women." The Kansas he left had for its state motto *Ad astra per aspera*—"To the stars through difficulties."

Tombaugh arrived in Flagstaff on January 15, 1929, after a train ride of 28 hours. He didn't have enough money to sleep in a Pullman berth. He didn't have enough money for a train ride home.

---

[1]This and the following quotation are from Clyde W. Tombaugh and Patrick Moore, *Out of the Darkness: The Planet Pluto* (Harrisburg, Pennsylvania: Stackpole Books, 1980), p. 25.

to photograph each region three times. The two most nearly identical plates would be blinked against one another. The third plate and pictures taken by a 5-inch (13-centimeter) telescopic camera mounted piggyback on the telescope tube would be kept for comparison and—hopefully—verification.

Tombaugh started in Cancer, to the east of Lowell's predicted location

Clyde Tombaugh with his homemade 9-inch telescope on his family's farm in Kansas. The year is 1928, and Tombaugh is 22 years old.
Clyde W. Tombaugh

Slipher met him at the station, and Tombaugh moved into a bedroom at the observatory.

The lens for the 13-inch telescope to be used for the search had not yet arrived, so Clyde was pressed into service showing tour groups around the observatory, stoking the furnace in the administration building (as all the staff did), carefully pushing snow off the canvas dome for the 42-inch telescope, and painting the 13-inch telescope tube red.

The lens arrived in February. Slipher coached him through the photographic process, and quickly Tombaugh was on his own. He faced a series of problems that threatened the very precise work necessary. When the clock drive of the telescope (to keep it pointed at the proper star field as the Earth rotates) turned through a particular position, one of the telescope axes slipped slightly, creating double images of each star. Such a photograph was useless for blinking. A second problem was that the glass photographic plates he was using shattered in the numbing cold—and with a crack so loud Tombaugh feared that the expensive telescope lens had broken. It was up to him to find the cause and invent a fix for each problem. He did. For the axis slippage problem, he ran the telescope ahead and then backed it up through the problem point so that there would be no slippage when it ran forward. For the problem of the photographic plates that cracked, he found a new way to fasten them onto the telescope so that the corners could expand or contract before being tightened down.

Slipher was pleased with Tombaugh's progress. "We think he is going to develop into a useful man. He has several good qualities that are going to make up for his meager training. . . . He has a good attitude: careful with apparatus, willing to do anything to make himself useful and is enthusiastic about learning and wants to do observing."[2]

---

[2] Letter of February 7, 1929, to Roger Lowell Putnam, Percival's nephew and sole trustee of the observatory. Quoted by William Graves Hoyt, *Planets X and Pluto* (Tucson, University of Arizona Press, 1980), p. 181.

for Planet X. Each exposure captured 50,000 stars. Then Tombaugh pushed on into Gemini, closer to the Milky Way. Now each plate provided 400,000 stars to be inspected.

Five days into his search, on April 11, 1929, Tombaugh exposed plate number 10 and captured the object he was seeking. He captured it again on April 30, its companion plate for comparison. But the ninth planet went unnoticed by the Lowell Observatory astronomers who were responsible for the blink comparator examination. Plate 10 had cracked in the brutal cold of winter at high altitude. It was still blinkable, but the plates were not sufficiently well matched in background star brightness for successful comparison. Gemini was also too close to the horizon, so that light from that broad region passed through significantly varying amounts of the Earth's atmosphere, dimming the stars closer to the horizon more. Further, Planet X was expected to be significantly brighter than it was. There was little point in spending much time with such unpromising plates.

Blinking

Originally, Tombaugh was supposed to do only the photography. The blink microscope work would be left to the more experienced staff. But by the beginning of summer, 1929, almost no plates had been blinked. The experienced staff had been too busy with other duties. The summer rains set in, reducing Tombaugh's observing time, so Slipher asked him to take over responsibility for plate comparisons on the blink microscope as well. "I was overwhelmed," Tombaugh recalled. "It had become evident to me that the one doing the blinking carried the heavy responsibility of finding, or not finding, the planet."[1]

Clyde Tombaugh using the blink comparator with which he discovered Pluto. This photograph was taken in 1938, as Tombaugh continued his full-sky survey.
Lowell Observatory photograph

Tombaugh spent half of each month at the telescope and the other half, when the presence of even the crescent Moon above the horizon made the sky too bright for such sensitive telescopic photography, at the blink microscope. His sessions at the blink microscope would last three to six hours; beyond that the numbing routine was so exhausting that he could not stay alert. The average star count per photograph was 160,000.[2] Areas of the sky toward the center of the Milky Way yielded plates filled with a million stars. "I came to dread the Milky Way regions," said Tombaugh.

He divided the plates so that he could blink a few hundred stars at a time, examining each one for a telltale change in position. Tiny irregularities in the concentration of silver grains in the photographic emulsions gave rise to dozens of false planet suspects on every plate. There were numerous variable stars that were visible at maximum brightness but invisible at minimum. They too could look like stars that had moved.

But "even more appalling" were the problems caused by asteroids.[3] These minor planets in orbit around the Sun had a motion similar to but generally faster than the planet he was seeking. Yet when the Earth caught up with and passed each minor planet, it would appear to stop, go backward (retrograde motion), and then move forward again. When traveling slowly near a transition point to and from retrograde motion, the asteroids closely mimicked the movement of a trans-Neptunian planet. Often in the course of examining each star on every plate, Tombaugh saw a starlike object that changed position, but each time it proved to be an asteroid.

After much thought, Tombaugh solved the problem by photographing the sky 180 degrees from the Sun's position (part way up the southern sky at midnight). Here the retrograde motion of a distant planet and an

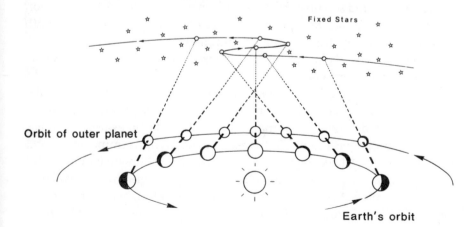

As the Earth catches up with and passes a slower-moving outer planet, that planet appears to stop and back up (move westward) in the sky. As the Earth moves ahead of the other planet, it appears to stop its retrograde motion and resume its direct motion eastward among the stars.

asteroid would be most noticeable In fact, at opposition all the asteroids moved enough during the one-hour exposures to create a trail on the photographic plates, thus allowing him to discriminate them from the planet he sought.

Each photographic plate required a one-hour exposure. Each pair of plates required three days to a week or more of blinking. It was maddening work.

But potentially the worst discouragement of all that Tombaugh faced was the skepticism about a trans-Neptunian planet that he heard from visiting astronomers. Most of Lowell's ideas were branded as fanciful, and Pickering's planet predictions were thought to be wild speculations. Tombaugh remembered poignantly when a visiting astronomer privately confided to him, "Young man, I am afraid you are wasting your time. If there were any more planets to be found, they would have been found long before this."

Expanding the Search

By early September, Tombaugh decided to search not just the area where Lowell had predicted the planet would be but the entire zodiac. He had little confidence in Lowell's predictions because they were based in part on the idea that the location of a ninth planet could be at least roughly established by the trans-Neptunian aphelia (far points in their orbits) of a family of comets. He resolved to make his search so thorough that "if nothing was found, I would be able to state such a planet does not exist."

Late in January 1930, Tombaugh was photographing the western portion of the constellation Gemini. His search of the zodiac had now come full circle. He had returned to the region that he began with.

On January 21, he exposed Negative 161, centered on the star Delta Geminorum. The sky transparency was good but heavy atmospheric turbulence provided seeing conditions of 0 on a scale of 0 to 10—very poor.

He returned to the Delta Geminorum region again on January 23, with Negative 165. This time seeing conditions were very good.

He made his third plate of the area, Negative 171, on January 29. Again, the seeing was very good.

The January 23 and January 29 plates were taken under the most similar conditions, so he planned to blink them against one another as soon as time permitted. There were many other plates to be examined first.

Tombaugh began the blink analysis of the Delta Geminorum plates on February 15. Three days later, late in the afternoon, he had made his way through one-quarter of the stars on these photographic plates. Then, at 4:00 P.M. on February 18, 1930, two weeks after his twenty-fourth birthday, Clyde Tombaugh saw a star shifting back and forth as the blink microscope cut the view from one optically superimposed plate to the

The discovery of Pluto. Here are small sections of the plates on which Clyde Tombaugh discovered Pluto on February 18, 1930. The photographs were taken on January 23, 1930 (left), and January 29, 1930 (right). Pluto, marked by an arrow, revealed itself by its motion.
Lowell Observatory photograph

other. It was 15th magnitude—fainter than the object expected. "That's it," Tombaugh said to himself.

> A terrific thrill came over me. I switched the shutter back and forth, studying the images. Oh! I had better look at my watch and note the time. This would be a historic discovery. . . .
>
> For the next forty-five minutes or so, I was in the most excited state of mind in my life. I had to check further to be absolutely sure.

They were no defects on the photographic plates. The two dots didn't look like two different variable stars. The change in position between January 23 and January 29 was right for a trans-Neptunian planet in retrograde motion. He checked for the object on the January 21 plate and on the simultaneous photographs made by the 5-inch telescopic camera mounted piggyback on the 13-inch. The object was real.

For 45 minutes he had been the only person on Earth to know of the existence of a ninth planet. At 4:45 P.M. Tombaugh called across the hall to Lampland that he had found a trans-Neptunian planet. Yes, said Lampland, "I heard the clicking of the comparator suddenly stopped, then a long silence." Lampland immediately began studying the images. "Then," said Tombaugh,

> I walked down the hall to V. M. Slipher's office. Trying to control myself, I stepped into his office as nonchalantly as possible. He looked up from his desk work. "Dr. Slipher, I have found your Planet X." I had never come to report a mistaken planet suspect. He rose right up from his chair with an expression on his face of both elation and reservation. I said, "I'll show you the evidence."
>
> He immediately hurried down the hall to the comparator room. I had to step lively to keep up with him.

"[T]he air was tense with excitement," Tombaugh recalled.[4] Vesto Slipher insisted that there should be no announcement until the obser-

Plate 1. With its giant dark spots, bright white clouds, and banding in its atmosphere, Neptune showed *Voyager 2* more visible features than Saturn or Uranus. Neptune rotates eastward (toward the right) on its axis once every 16 hours 7 minutes, but the spots move at different speeds within the atmosphere.
NASA/Jet Propulsion Laboratory

Plate 2. Voyager 2 at Neptune and Triton (Artwork by Don Davis)
NASA/Jet Propulsion Laboratory

Plate 3. Voyager 2 launch, August 20, 1977
NASA/Jet Propulsion Laboratory

Plate 4. Voyager 2 images of Uranus. On the left is Uranus in real color. No atmospheric details are visible. On the right is a computer-enhanced image of Uranus, with false color added to bring out detail. Now the atmosphere shows bands that run parallel to the equator. The south polar atmosphere of Uranus (pointed toward and a little to the left of us) is slightly darker in color.
NASA/Jet Propulsion Laboratory

Plate 5. A *Voyager 2* image of Uranus, with computer enhancement and false color added, shows a very large cloud (more than 5,000 miles [8,000 kilometers] long) in the planet's atmosphere in the one o'clock position. The south pole of Uranus is pointed almost directly at us, so this cloud lies near the equator. (The doughnut-shaped rings in the picture are caused by dust in the camera.)
NASA/Jet Propulsion Laboratory

Plate 6. Uranus and its ring system seen from Miranda. Separate *Voyager 2* images have been used to simulate what a spacecraft near Miranda would see of Uranus.
NASA/Jet Propulsion Laboratory

Plate 7. From above the north pole of Uranus, artist Ron Miller visualizes the narrow Uranian rings which circle the planet's equator.
© *Ron Miller*

Plate 8. Voyager 2 found fault valleys up to 12 miles (20 kilometers) deep on the Uranian moon Miranda. Artist MariLynn Flynn imagines astronauts at the bottom of this canyon with a crescent Uranus in the sky.
© *1987 MariLynn Flynn*

PLATE 1

PLATE 2

PLATE 3

PLATE 4

PLATE 5

PLATE 6

PLATE 7

PLATE 8

PLATE 9

PLATE 10

PLATE 11

PLATE 12

PLATE 13

PLATE 15

PLATE 14

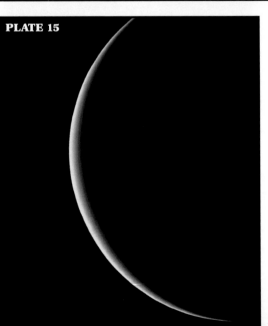

Plate 9. CRAF (Comet Rendezvous Asteroid Flyby) mission near a comet as surface ices vaporize. Astronomer and artist William K. Hartmann imagines that the comet's high carbon content gives it a reddish color.
© *Painting by William K. Hartmann*

Plate 10. The formation of the solar system: Planetesimals accrete to form planets.
© *Painting by William K. Hartmann*

Plates 11 and 12. Charon casts a shadow on Pluto. Here, artist Joe Shabram views the eclipse from two angles: from Charon and at a distance from both. Pluto, with polar ice caps, reflects more light than Charon. Nighttime on Charon is not completely dark because of sunlight reflected from Pluto. That sunlight, in turn, is reflected from Charon back to Pluto and keeps the shadow cast by Charon from being completely black. Note the size of Charon (and its shadow of equal diameter) compared to Pluto.
© *1988 Joe Shabram*

Plate 13. Astronomer and artist William K. Hartmann depicts Chiron, the outermost known asteroid, passing over the pole of Saturn. Chiron roams from just inside the orbit of Saturn to almost the orbit of Uranus.
© *Painting by William K. Hartmann*

Plate 14. The nucleus of a comet was seen for the first time when the European Space Agency's *Giotto* spacecraft used its Halley Multicolor Camera to photograph Halley's Comet during its flyby on March 13, 1986. Comet Halley's nucleus is jet black in color and irregular in shape—about 10 miles (15 kilometers) wide. Gases from vaporizing surface ices carry dust grains outward in jets. Comets may be planetesimals left over from the formation of the outer planets and their moons.
© *1986 Max-Planck-Institut fur Aeronomie, Federal Republic of Germany; courtesy of H. U. Keller*

Plate 15. Looking back at Uranus, *Voyager 2* took this farewell picture as it began its 3.5-year journey to Neptune. Uranus is never visible as a crescent from Earth.
NASA/Jet Propulsion Laboratory

vation could be thoroughly confirmed. "Don't tell anyone until we follow it for a few weeks," said Slipher. "This could be very hot news."

Tombaugh didn't even tell his parents. They found out about their son's discovery after the formal announcement almost a month later, when the editor of their county newspaper called.

Confirmation

Carl O. Lampland, assistant director of Lowell Observatory
Lowell Observatory photograph

To confirm the existence of the new planet, the Lowell astronomers decided to rephotograph the region where the suspect had been found. But that night, February 18, was overcast. Tombaugh, trying to fill the time, went off to Flagstaff to see Gary Cooper in *The Virginian.* "There would never be another day like that one," Tombaugh reckoned late in life.

The weather cooperated at least to some degree on the next four nights. Tombaugh captured the object with the 13-inch telescope on February 19, 21, and 22. On February 20, Slipher, Lampland, and Tombaugh examined Pluto visually with the 24-inch (61-centimeter) refractor. The next night, Lampland photographed the suspect with the 42-inch (107-centimeter) reflector[5] under seeing conditions listed as poor. The object had no discernible disk, the tip-off of a planet. Yet it lacked the tail, fuzzy coma, and other features of a comet. Sadly, there was no satellite visible, which would have quickly confirmed it as a planet and would have offered a means to measure its mass.

Although everyone on the Lowell Observatory staff was confident about the discovery, Slipher delayed the announcement so that further confirmatory observations could be made. He also wanted to get a head start on the computation of the planet's orbit so that the Lowell Observatory could be the first to publish it. He wanted as well to gather as much information on the new planet as possible before the observatories with larger telescopes overpowered their work. Slipher invited John A. Miller to come to Flagstaff to compute the planet's orbit. Miller, director of the Sproul Observatory at Swarthmore College, was a specialist in celestial mechanics and had taught the Sliphers and Lampland at Indiana University.

On March 12, 1930, at 10:00 P.M. Arizona time—midnight in Boston—Slipher sent a telegram to the Harvard College Observatory, clearinghouse for the announcement of astronomical discoveries. The discovery of a trans-Neptunian planet was announced the next day—March 13, 1930. It was the seventy-fifth anniversary of the birth of Percival Lowell and the one hundred forty-ninth anniversary of William Herschel's discovery of Uranus. The ninth planet had been found within 6 degrees of the spot predicted by Percival Lowell in 1915.

The story was front-page news around the world, and the scale of public interest amazed the Lowell staff. Harlow Shapley, director of the Harvard College Observatory, was scheduled to deliver a talk on astronomy to a small audience in Philadelphia on the evening of March 14. He decided to include mention of the new planet. The lecture had to be moved to a ballroom so that a thousand extra people could be accommodated. When he showed a slide of Percival Lowell, the audience gave a thunderous ovation—greater, Shapley felt, than any Lowell had received in his lifetime.[6]

But Shapley and others were annoyed at and soon critical of the Lowell Observatory for withholding all but one position for the new planet. Slipher had released enough information for other observatories to confirm the planet's existence but not enough so that other astronomers could compute the orbit of Pluto without accumulating their own positional observations over a period of a month or so. By hoarding their January-through-March observations, the Lowell Observatory astronomers had, they hoped, given themselves enough data so that their orbital computation could be better than others.

Even so, two orbital computations appeared before that of the Lowell Observatory. The first (released April 7) was from Armin Otto Leuschner, Ernest C. Bower, and Fred L. Whipple at the University of California, Berkeley, which gave a cometlike parabolic orbital approximation for the new planet. Its distance from Earth, they computed, was 41 astronomical units and the inclination of its orbit was 17 degrees. On April 8 a cir-

Vesto M. Slipher, director of the Lowell Observatory after Lowell's death
Lowell Observatory photograph

LOWELL'S CALCULATIONS AND MY SEARCH
by Professor Clyde W. Tombaugh

It has been stated by some writers of the Pluto story that Percival Lowell's calculations greatly aided my finding Pluto. Quite to the contrary, when I found out in the latter part of 1929 how Lowell had drastically changed his predicted position of Planet X from Libra to Gemini, this indicated to me that considerable uncertainty was involved, and I could not take the prediction seriously.

At the start of my trans-Neptunian planet survey at the Lowell Observatory in the spring of 1929, I photographed the region where Lowell had predicted Planet X to be and the two Sliphers blinked the three pairs of plates I had taken, spanning Gemini. As it turned out, the Pluto images were on the Delta Geminorum pair, but the Sliphers missed them. Since the Sliphers failed to detect the Pluto

images on these plates, I wrote Gemini off and concluded that Planet X might be anywhere in the zodiac belt, if indeed Planet X existed at all. I intended to thoroughly search the entire zodiac. After I became experienced in blinking in the fall of 1929, I realized that the Sliphers had scanned the plates too hastily and that I should rephotograph the Gemini regions again, this time under the proper observational strategy, and then thoroughly blink the new plates.

I rephotographed Gemini when it returned to opposition in January 1930. I was blinking one of the pairs of plates when I found Pluto two-thirds of a degree east of the star Delta Geminorum on February 18, 1930.

cular orbital approximation from the Cracow Observatory in Poland was published in the United States.

On April 12, 1930, Slipher was ready and the Lowell Observatory released its provisional orbit along with a number of planet positions. This work, led by Miller, calculated that the ninth planet had an extremely elliptical orbit (eccentricity of 0.909) and a period of 3,000 years. These initial calculations cast some doubt on whether the object was a planet or not. The problem was that a decent orbit was hard to calculate when the object had moved such a tiny amount along its path. On May 9, British astronomer Andrew C. D. Crommelin reported that the new planet was part of a field photographed at the Royal Observatory of Belgium at Uccle on January 27, 1927, thereby extending the recorded arc of the planet's motion by more than three years. The new calculation showed a much less elliptical orbit (eccentricity 0.287) and a period of 265.3 years. The trans-Neptunian object now had a clearly established planetary nature, and this status was never again seriously challenged. These figures, now close to the actual values for the ellipticity and period of Pluto's orbit, were also close to Lowell's prediction for Planet X.

Naming the Planet

Venetia Burney, age 11, from Oxford, England, was studying mythology in school when she heard about the discovery of the ninth planet and proposed the name Pluto.
Mrs. E. Maxwell Phair

Meanwhile, suggestions for names flooded the observatory. Mrs. Lowell first proposed Zeus, then decided that the old gods were worn out and that the planet should be named Percival. Then she changed her mind again and proposed her own first name—Constance. In a final effort, she urged the name Planet X. Again, Slipher refused to be pressured into a quick announcement. He personally favored the name Minerva, goddess of wisdom, but decided that that name was too firmly attached to an asteroid. Acceptable alternatives, he felt, were Cronus and Pluto. But Cronus was suggested by "a certain detested egocentric astronomer," so this name was discarded.[7] (The rejected name had come from Thomas Jefferson Jackson See, an early and abrasive Lowell Observatory staff member.) The name Cronus (or Kronos) was also considered less than optimal because Cronus is the Greek equivalent of Saturn, who was already well represented in the sky.

The name Pluto was officially proposed by Slipher on May 1, 1930. Pluto had actually been one of the first name suggestions received at the Lowell Observatory. It had come from Venetia Burney, an 11-year-old schoolgirl in Oxford, England, who was learning about Greek and Roman mythology in school and thought that such a dim and gloomy planet should be named for the god of the underworld.[8] As a symbol for Pluto, Slipher proposed PL, formed from the letters P and L, the first two letters in the word Pluto. They were also the initials of Percival Lowell.

William H. Pickering, author of many outer-planet predictions, was

initially unhappy with the choice of Pluto as a name. From his retirement home and private observatory on the island of Jamaica, he complained that he had intended to use the name Pluto when his Planet P
was found (although he had never published his intention). Eventually
he reconciled himself to the name Pluto and its PL symbol, comment-
ing to a visiting astronomer, "That's a good name—Pickering-Lowell!"[9]

Whom to Credit

Once Pluto was shown to have a planetary orbit, the question arose as
to whether Lowell or Pickering had been more accurate in his predictions. Granted, it was solely Lowell's calculations that had spurred the
search that led to the discovery of Pluto at his observatory, but Pickering's fairly similar predictions had lent some credibility to the search.

Lowell's predicted orbital elements for Pluto were reasonably close
and, in fact, except for the critical element of location, better overall than
Adams' and Le Verrier's predictions for the orbit of Neptune. Pluto was
found within 6 degrees of the locations specified by both Lowell and
Pickering (in his 1919 prediction of Planet O). Pickering was actually 0.1
degree closer.

A diagram of the actual
orbit of Pluto compared
with the orbits
predicted by Lowell in
1914 and Pickering in
1928. The orbits are
approximated by circles
with the positions of
their centers noted.
Dennis Rawlins

Lowell's prediction was more nearly correct than Pickering's in the planet's distance from the Sun, orbital eccentricity, longitude of perihelion, perihelion date, and period. Pickering's 1919 prediction was closer to the mark in orbital inclination, longitude of ascending node, mass, and magnitude.

Pickering had revised his Planet O prediction in 1928 so markedly that the anticipated object was very different from his 1919 planet. The 1928 prediction foresaw an object with a mass of only 0.75 (still closer to the truth) and with a most unusual orbit that crossed inside of Neptune's. All other aspects of Pickering's 1928 Planet O prediction were conspicuously wrong.

At first it looked as if the roles of Adams and Le Verrier had been replayed: Two dedicated researchers had independently solved a problem that the scientific community had doubted could be solved, and their insight had been vindicated by a striking discovery.

But as more data flowed in, the question became whether Pluto, found where Lowell calculated it would be, was actually the Planet X he had had predicted. The overwhelming problem, right from the beginning, was one of mass. Pluto showed no disk to observers, even with the largest telescope at that time—the 100-inch (2.5-meter) one on Mount Wilson. Thus Pluto had to be small, far smaller than the 6.6 Earth masses that

LOWELL'S AND PICKERING'S PREDICTIONS FOR PLUTO[1]

Orbital Elements	Lowell's Planet X 1914	Pickering's Planet O 1919	Pluto 1930
Mean distance (astronomical units)	43.0	55.1	39.5
Eccentricity	0.202	0.31	0.248
Inclination	about 10°	about 15°	17.1°
Longitude of node	(not predicted)	about 100°	109.4°
Longitude of perihelion	204.9°	280.1°	223.4°
Period (years)	282	409.1	248
Perihelion date	February 1991	January 2129	September 1989
Longitude (1930.0)	102.7°	102.6°	108.5°
Mean annual motion	1.2411°	0.880°	1.451°
Mass (Earth=1)	6.6	2.0	less than 0.7
Magnitude	12–13	15	15

[1]Based on William Graves Hoyt, *Planets X and Pluto* (Tucson: University of Arizona Press, 1980), p. 221.

Lowell had predicted; even smaller than the 2.0 Earth masses that Pickering (1919) had predicted. The mass could certainly be no greater than that of our planet. Then how was it possible that distant Pluto could have noticeably disturbed the motion of Uranus, a billion miles (1.6 billion kilometers) away at its closest—as far as the Earth is from Saturn?

Yet, could it be that two independent researchers would so nearly coincide in their predictions and that their predictions would so nearly coincide with reality unless their work was valid?

The controversy continued for many years.[10] Throughout those years new telescopes and techniques kept whittling away at the size of Pluto. Measurements by University of Hawaii astronomers in 1976 found spectroscopic evidence of methane frost on its surface. Such an icy covering could give Pluto a high albedo (reflectivity). But a high reflectivity meant that the planet was still smaller than previously expected—smaller than our Moon. Under those circumstances, Pluto's mass could be only a few thousandths that of Earth.

CLYDE TOMBAUGH AFTER PLUTO

Clyde Tombaugh took leave from the Lowell Observatory each school year beginning in the fall of 1932 to formally study astronomy at the University of Kansas on a scholarship. He entered as a 26-year-old freshman and tried to enroll in the freshman astronomy class. But the head of the department was adamant: "For a planet discoverer to enroll in a course of introductory astronomy is unthinkable."[1]

At the end of spring semester 1934, he married Patricia Irene Edson from Kansas City, and they spent their honeymoon in Flagstaff. They had two children. In 1939, Tombaugh received a master's degree in astronomy.

As his planet search through the entire sky from Flagstaff neared completion, Tombaugh was drafted, in July 1943, the middle of World War II, to teach navigation for the Navy at Arizona State College at Flagstaff.

Following the war he was visiting professor of astronomy at UCLA for a year and then, in 1946, went to the White Sands Missile Range in New Mexico as the supervisor of the Optical Tracking Section. There he developed a tracking telescope that could see the tail fins on V2 rockets at an altitude of 100 miles (160 kilometers). Tombaugh's work led to the tracking cameras that follow manned and unmanned rockets from launch to orbit today and that, aboard spacecraft, look down on Earth to provide pictures with incredible detail.

In 1955 he was appointed associate professor at New Mexico State University, where he helped to found the Department of Astronomy. He became a full professor in 1956. He has been professor emeritus since 1973 and continues to inspire students with his lectures on astronomy.

In honor of his service and achievements, New Mexico State University is establishing a Clyde Tombaugh Scholars Endowment to assist postdoctoral astronomy students and an endowed professorship, the Clyde Tombaugh Chair in Astronomy.

[1]Dinsmore Alter, quoted in Clyde W. Tombaugh and Patrick Moore, *Out of the Darkness: The Planet Pluto* (Harrisburg, Pennsylvania: Stackpole Books, 1980), p. 160.

A Bulge

The matter was settled in June 1978 when U.S. Naval Observatory astronomer James W. Christy was examining pictures of Pluto taken on April 13 and 20 and May 12, 1978. These photographic plates had been exposed at the Naval Observatory's station in Flagstaff, Arizona, only four miles from the Lowell Observatory, where Pluto was discovered. Christy found a bulge in the image of Pluto—a bulge that had shifted position on the second plate. Christy immediately interpreted this bulge as a satellite in revolution around Pluto, and examination of earlier survey photographs verified it.

As a name for Pluto's moon, Christy chose Charon, the boatman in Greek mythology who ferries the souls of the dead across the rivers of woe and lamentation to Pluto's underworld. Beyond its mythological appropriateness, Christy was especially fond of the name because his wife's name is Charlene—nickname: Char.

The presence of a moon in orbit about Pluto allowed for the calculation of the mass of the combined Pluto/satellite system. This calculation, by Christy's Naval Observatory colleague Robert S. Harrington, showed a mass of about two-tenths of one percent (0.002) of the Earth. Pluto was only about 20 percent the mass of our Moon.

The mass of the Pluto-Charon system was hopelessly inadequate to produce measurable gravitational perturbations on Uranus or Neptune. Pluto could not be Percival Lowell's Planet X. The planet found was not the planet sought. What had seemed to be another triumph of celestial mechanics turned out to be an accident.

Or, rather, Pluto had been found not by theory but by the intelligence and thoroughness of Clyde Tombaugh's search.

CHAPTER 7

Toward Uranus

"Fate often smiles kindly upon great endeavors."
Charles Kohlhase, *Voyager* Mission Design Manager

A flashlight provides more light in one second than Uranus has provided to Earth in the 200 years since it was discovered by Herschel in 1781.[1] No wonder that two centuries passed before Uranus was revealed in detail.

A Long Wait

Watching Uranus as scarcely more than a dot in the skies had told astronomers about its orbit. Watching its moons in orbit had told astronomers the mass of Uranus and that the planet was lying on its side as it revolved about the Sun. Nearly every time a large new telescope went into operation, it was trained on Uranus (and Neptune) to try to see details, to measure a rotation period, and to discover new satellites. Uranus was uncooperative.

Astronomers settled into a routine. The size of Uranus was refined. The orbits and periods of the Uranian satellites were refined. The mass of Uranus, calculated from its satellites' periods, was refined.

Claims to have seen surface markings on Uranus were made and not confirmed and made again later by others. But ever-improving telescopes still could not confirm details on the face of Uranus.

Uranus as seen from Earth is the size of a golf ball seen at a distance of 1.5 miles (2.5 kilometers). With no distinct atmospheric clouds, bands, or storms to provide contrast, the period of rotation for Uranus—the length of its day—was difficult to measure. Even spectroscopy—breaking down

An excellent view of Uranus from Earth, showing the five moons known before the visit of *Voyager 2* in 1986. The satellites are the bright, starlike objects closest to Uranus. Titania is at the one o'clock position; Miranda is at four o'clock, almost lost in the glare of Uranus; Umbriel is at seven; and Oberon and Ariel are at eleven, with Oberon the more distant. The south pole of Uranus is pointed almost directly at us, so these moons revolve like a spot on the hand of a clock. This picture was taken by W. Liller on June 12, 1977, with the 158-inch (4-meter) telescope at the Cerro Tololo Inter-American Observatory in Chile. *National Optical Astronomy Observatories*

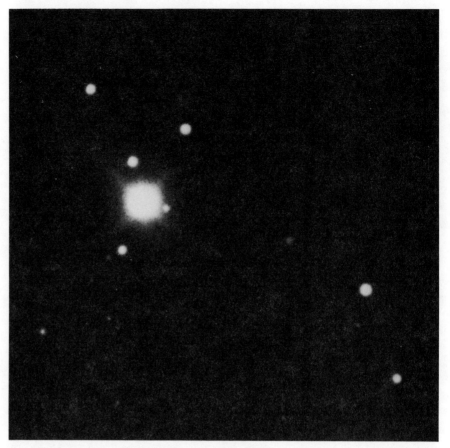

light into its component wavelengths to study subtleties such as composition, temperature, and atmospheric flow—was very difficult and prone to error for such a small, faint object at a distance of almost 2 billion miles (3 billion kilometers).

As the bicentennial of the discovery of Uranus neared, the number of moons known for Uranus had risen to five. The atmosphere, as expected from the example of Jupiter and Saturn, was known to be predominantly hydrogen. The pale bluish-green color of the planet could be assigned to a very small percentage of methane in the atmosphere that absorbed red light. Spectroscopy indicated a rotation period for Uranus of about 10 hours 50 minutes.[2]

And that was pretty much all that was known. But the distance and faintness of Uranus did not stop Earth-bound astronomers from using every technique at their disposal to wring more secrets from the tilted world. A big surprise came unexpectedly from a flying telescope.

On March 10, 1977, several independent teams of astronomers were in the Southern Hemisphere to watch as Uranus passed in front of a star. Since the position and speed of Uranus in orbit were well known, a timing of the occultation could provide improved information about the size of the planet. Observation of the way the star's light faded as Uranus eclipsed it could reveal the nature of the planet's atmosphere.

An American team of astronomers, led by James Elliot, was aboard NASA's Kuiper Airborne Observatory, a converted military C-141 Starlifter cargo jet carrying a 36-inch (0.9-meter) telescope and photometry equipment. They were flying over the southern Indian Ocean at 41,000 feet (12,500 meters) to surmount as much as possible of the Earth's turbulent atmosphere and especially its water vapor, which absorbs the infrared light that could provide information not obtainable from the surface of Earth. Because the position of the star to be occulted was not known with the greatest exactitude, the sensing equipment was turned on 47 minutes early to avoid missing the event.

The action began immediately. The light from the star dimmed, brightened, then dimmed again, flickering at least five times. Yet the edge of Uranus had not yet encroached upon the star. And no flaw in the instruments could be found. What was going on? Had a series of undetected Uranian satellites caused the flickers?

As Uranus moved on in its orbit and the star emerged from behind its disk, the flickers repeated themselves in reverse order. Such symmetry could not be the result of moons. The Kuiper Airborne Observatory team

Dimmings

NASA's Kuiper Airborne Observatory. The rings of Uranus were discovered in 1977 using the 36-inch (91.5-centimeter) telescope aboard this converted C-141 jet transport. By flying high above the clouds, astronomers can study infrared radiation from celestial objects. These wavelengths are absorbed by water in the air before they reach the ground.
NASA

joked about the possibility of a ring system immediately but dismissed the idea because narrow rings were unknown and thought to be implausible. Elliot hit upon the correct interpretation four days later, soon after he returned to the United States. No other conclusion was possible: Uranus had a ring system.[3] Saturn was not unique.

Careful analysis of the flickers showed nine rather than five rings for Uranus—all very thin and dark compared with the rings of Saturn observed from Earth. It was the first ring system to be discovered for a planet in more than 350 years.

But how could such narrow rings be preserved? Collisions between particles in the rings should spread them out into a broad, flat band of debris like the rings of Saturn. So, typical for science, a major new discovery raised challenging new questions. How and when had such a strange ring system developed around Uranus? And how could it persist?

To Uranus and Neptune, Maybe

By the time that the rings of Uranus were discovered, two *Voyager* spacecraft were already at the Kennedy Space Center being prepared for launch. The prime objectives of the *Voyagers* were Jupiter and Saturn. Each probe would fly past both planets. *Voyager 2* could then be sent on to Uranus and Neptune, but only if *Voyager 1* succeeded at Saturn. If *Voyager 1* failed, *Voyager 2* would be retargeted for a look at Saturn's moon Titan, a satellite with an atmosphere. Even if *Voyager 1* succeeded and *Voyager 2* could travel on to Uranus and Neptune, there was no assurance that the spacecraft could continue operating long enough.

Yet if *Voyager 2* could survive, it could collect in six hours close to Uranus far more information about the planet than had been possible to gather in the 200 years since it was discovered. The spacecraft could:

- Measure more exactly the size and mass of Uranus.
- Analyze the atmosphere of Uranus.
- Detect a magnetic field of Uranus.
- Examine the known moons and rings of Uranus and look for undiscovered ones.
- Search for clues to explain the axial tilt of Uranus, the origin of its rings, and the evolution of the Uranian system.

A Grand Tour

On August 20, 1977, America's *Voyager 2* space probe rode a Titan-Centaur rocket away from Earth on a trajectory that could carry it by Jupiter in such a way that the largest planet's gravity would sling the craft on to Saturn. With care, it would have the right path so that the gravity of Saturn could, in turn, hurl the vehicle on toward Uranus. Again, with just the right position and time of encounter, *Voyager* could use the gravity of Uranus to venture on to Neptune. It was a Grand Tour of the four largest planets in the solar system.

Only once every 175 years do the outer planets align themselves so that a spacecraft can, with minimal fuel, use the gravity of one to change its course to another and repeat that process twice more so that four successively more distant planets can be reached. Through most of two centuries, a rocket leaving Earth can visit only one or occasionally two outer planets. But for a very brief period once in every 175 years, space engineers and scientists can squeeze four planetary visits out of one space probe—if that craft can last more than 12 years and still function in an environment where diminishing sunlight plunges the temperature toward 400° below zero Fahrenheit (−240° Celsius).

The *Voyager 2* Grand Tour mission to four planets almost didn't happen—three times.

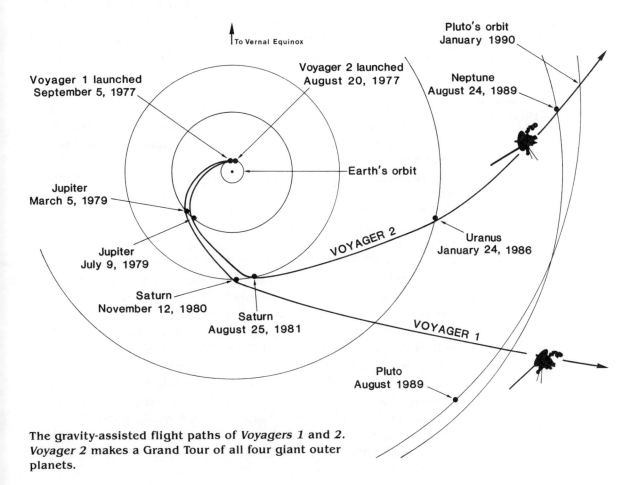

The gravity-assisted flight paths of *Voyagers 1* and *2*. *Voyager 2* makes a Grand Tour of all four giant outer planets.

The opportunity began to take shape in 1965 with discoveries by Gary Flandro and Michael Minovich that the gravity of the giant planets could be used to change the speed and course of a spacecraft so that it could fly on to a new destination. Specifically, Flandro determined, a spacecraft could use the gravity of Jupiter to accelerate on to an outer world with little or no further expenditure of fuel and with a great savings in time.

Most fascinating of all, Flandro found that the outer planets would be positioned in 1977 for a four-planet trip. A standard rocket journey direct from Earth to Neptune without gravitational assist would have required 40 years.[4] The Grand Tour, as Flandro named it, would allow a spacecraft to visit the four giant planets in 12 years.[5]

But there was a severe constraint. The last time the four giant planets had been favorably positioned for a Grand Tour was during the presidency of Thomas Jefferson. The next opportunity centered on 1977.[6] Could a spacecraft be built in time to take advantage of this rare planetary lineup? The challenges were formidable. In 1965, man had not yet walked on the Moon. Only one spacecraft, NASA's *Mariner 4*, had reached as far as Mars. To fly a 12-year mission so far from the Sun would not just stretch capabilities, it would require the development of new technologies.

Obstacles

With substantial power needs and yet sparse sunlight in the outer solar system, it would not be possible to use solar panels to provide electricity for the spacecraft. Instead the project would require miniature nuclear generators.

At such great distances from Earth, the spacecraft's onboard computer would have to be able to recognize and handle emergencies, since radio communication with the Earth would require hours.

Finally, the spacecraft systems and scientific instruments would have to last at least 12 years—a duration of time in 1965 that was longer than the space age was old.

As daunting as the challenge of the Grand Tour was, the problem of congressional approval was greater. The mission was canceled in December 1971. Most of the technical problems of a Grand Tour had been solved—Pluto had even been added to the itinerary—but Congress balked at a price tag of nearly $1 billion. The United States had reached the Moon but had no long-range plan for space exploration.[7]

In the summer of 1972, Congress voted $360 million for a less ambitious project: a flight to Jupiter and Saturn by two probes patterned after the Mariner probes that had successfully flown past Mars and Venus. The Jet Propulsion Laboratory in Pasadena, California, operated for NASA by the California Institute of Technology, would be the lead center for the project.

The shorter two-planet flight required spacecraft designed for only a 4-year mission—not 12. The *Mariner Jupiter-Saturn* project would use a gravitational assist at Jupiter to reach Saturn, but the Grand Tour mission to encompass four planets was dead.

DISCOVERY OF THE GRAND TOUR *VOYAGER* MISSION PROFILE
by Dr. Gary A. Flandro

PART 1

The work that led directly to the Grand Tour began at the Jet Propulsion Laboratory in 1965 when I was given a summer position to supplement my Ph.D. stipend as a graduate student in aeronautics at the California Institute of Technology. I had worked at JPL several times previously doing engineering work on missile trajectories, aerodynamics, and guidance systems. I learned as much from working there as from any of my formal graduate studies. The outstanding engineers at JPL had been a major inspiration for me to pursue graduate studies in space science.

My supervisor was Elliot "Joe" Cutting, with whom I had worked earlier on some trajectory problems. Joe assigned me the task of identifying possible unmanned missions to the outer planets. That was quite a leap at a time when America's longest spaceflight had been *Mariner 4* to Mars. The mere thought of missions to Saturn and beyond caused spacecraft engineers to tremble. The great distances to those bodies required long flight times. In 1965 the problem of building reliable mechanical and electronic devices with lifetimes long enough for trips to Mars (about 9 months) had not been truly solved. Missions that required vehicles to perform flawlessly for 9 years or longer were thought to be beyond our technical capability. Flights to Jupiter would take about 2 years, possibly just within our grasp, but missions to Neptune or Pluto would require approximately 40 years with the minimum energy transfer trajectories used in most space exploration. Another very worrisome problem was the difficulty of communicating over such vast distances. In light of these and other practical considerations, NASA and JPL management

Gary A. Flandro
Courtesy of Gary A. Flandro

had little interest in outer-planet exploration in 1965.

It was a great challenge to try to make exploration of the outer planets practical. I examined the conventional spaceflight trajectories to reach an outer planet with the least energy expended, in which a spacecraft is treated as a miniature planet in an elliptical orbit around the Sun. The vehicle's perihelion is the Earth's orbit, its aphelion is the target planet's orbit, and the flight is timed so that the spacecraft will arrive at the target planet's orbit just as the planet itself reaches that position. For trips beyond Jupiter, the flights took too long. We needed more speed, but we could accelerate the payload in a major way only during the rocket burn following launch. After that, a spacecraft bound for the outer planets constantly loses speed because of the Sun's gravity. To get more launch energy required either larger and more expensive rockets or much smaller and lighter space vehicles. Practical limits in both those directions had apparently already been reached. Was there some other energy source that could be tapped en route to increase the speed of the spacecraft? That was the key realization.

Astronomers had known since the late 1600s that when a comet passes close to a massive planet like Jupiter, its kinetic energy is changed tremendously and its orbit is greatly perturbed. Spaceflight pioneers understood this but did not realize its potential. The earliest study of "indirect" trajectories that used intermediate planets to mold the flight path in a desirable way was by Walter Hohmann in his book *Die Erreichbarkeit der Himmelskorper* (The Accessibility of the Celestial Bodies), published in 1925. He called these multiplanet trajectories the "Hohmann route" and designed the first Earth-Mars-Venus-Mercury flight paths.

In this work also, he first described the Hohmann minimum energy transfer orbit—the cost-effective trajectory utilized by a majority of planetary space missions.

Much later, indirect trajectories were proposed by Gaetano Arturo Crocco, the Italian scientist and aviation pioneer. He discovered that flight paths between the Earth, Mars, and Venus could be designed to utilize energy losses and gains in repeated close flybys to keep a space vehicle continuously in what he called the Grand Tour of the inner solar system. Crocco described his discovery in 1956 to the Seventh International Astronautical Congress in Rome.

The space age began the next year, but scant attention was paid at first to such trajectories in the technical literature on spaceflight. An exception was Krafft Ehricke, one of the original Peenemunde scientists. In *Space Flight* (1962), his voluminous work on applied celestial mechanics, he described the physical situation most clearly: "One rule, however, remains generally valid: *If at all possible, maneuvers for changing the heliocentric orbital elements should be carried out during the hyperbolic encounter with a planet, rather than in heliocentric space*. The greater the planet's mass, the greater the energy saving." But attention in the early 1960s was focused on the completion of simple one-target missions, so multiplanet flight paths did not attract much attention.

By 1965, however, JPL investigators were examining gravity-assist flight paths. Joe Cutting and Francis Sturms had devised a trajectory to the innermost planet Mercury that used a flyby at Venus to drop the spacecraft in toward the Sun. This concept became *Mariner 10*, the first successful multiplanet mission, and returned fantastic pictures of Mercury's surface.

Also working on gravity-assist possibilities that summer at JPL was Michael Minovich, a UCLA graduate student in astronomy, but our paths seldom crossed because he preferred to work at night. He was studying trajectories that used close flybys of Jupiter for the purpose of either escaping the solar system or making close approaches to the Sun. If a spacecraft caught up with a planet from behind, it gained energy and was flung outward at an increased speed instead of returning to the inner solar system on its original elliptical trajectory. If a spacecraft crossed in front of a planet, it lost energy and fell in closer to the Sun. Joe Cutting suggested that I examine gravity assist as a means for reaching the outer planets.

Strange as it now seems, many JPL engineers had misconceptions about gravity assist in 1965. They knew that because of gravity a spacecraft would gain speed as it approached a planet and lose speed as it coasted away, but they thought that there would be no net change in the spacecraft's energy relative to the Sun. They failed to consider that the planet was in motion around the Sun and could itself lose energy as it accelerated the spacecraft.

Another misconception was that multiplanet trajectories took a spacecraft out of the most direct orbital course to its final target and that therefore a gravity assist would *increase* rather than *decrease* flight time. This was a natural conclusion reached from examination of Hohmann's calculations and early multiplanet concepts such as those used in

Mariner 10. For *Mariner 10* to travel from the Earth inward toward the Sun required that kinetic energy be *reduced.* The net result was that flight time to Mercury via Venus was longer than a direct elliptical transfer would require.

The work of Minovich on solar system escape trajectories demonstrated that these were truly misconceptions. It became clear to me that the key to the outer solar system was to utilize the gravity-assist method. It was also obvious that Jupiter, with its enormous mass to bend spacecraft trajectories, was the best energy supply station, since its distance was reasonable, requiring typically a two-year flight time.

With these considerations in mind, I began detailed studies of Earth-Jupiter-Saturn trajectories. Previous work of this sort had been elementary, aimed just at establishing the feasibility of such orbits. My task was to calculate realistic mission profiles so that estimates of actual flight times, payloads, and planetary approach distances and speeds could be made. Of greatest importance was to identify "launch windows," periods during which such missions could be initiated.

In July 1965, I found that the best launch dates for a Jupiter-Saturn trajectory occurred in the late 1970s, perfect timing for the developing space-exploration program. I located the optimum launch dates by drawing graphs of the planetary longitudes for all of the outer planets.

It was at this time that I discovered something that had apparently not been noticed earlier: In the early 1980s, all of the outer planets would be on the same side of the Sun and in amazingly close proximity. This conjunction of the outer planets provided the inspiration for the Grand Tour mission concept. I could see immediately that a single spacecraft could explore all four giant outer planets by using each planet in succession to modify the spacecraft's trajectory as necessary to rendezvous with the next planet in the series.

PART 2

This was a rare moment of great exhilaration. Instantly it was mixed with a considerable amount of skepticism; I found myself doubting that anything practical could be done with the Grand Tour in view of our nation's slow progress in attaining spaceflight capability. However, ten years were available to overcome the engineering difficulties, and on second thought, motivation supplied by a goal like this one could have a real impact on progress.

I immediately began work to determine if practical multi-outer planet trajectories could be located. The trajectory computer programs available were not truly adequate for the job. I evolved a hand method using tabulations and graphs for "matching" the trajectories across each planetary encounter. Later, conic trajectory programs were developed that automated this tedious process. I set up a sequence of about ten trajectory runs each night and submitted these to the programmer (it was a job-shop computer operation in those days) and picked up the results the next morning. I would then examine these results to determine the next set of runs.

It took about a thousand trajectories to map out the original mission profiles and launch dates for the Grand Tour. These were plotted on graphs showing launch dates versus arrival dates, with spacecraft launch energy as the variable. This made it easy to visualize when and how the best mission possibilities would occur. The best launch window was in September 1978, with acceptable windows in 1977 and 1979. The actual launch dates used in the *Voyager* missions were virtually the same as those worked out by primitive methods in 1965.

Convincing others that the Grand Tour constituted a real mission opportunity was the most difficult part of the job. Cutting saw the possibilities immediately, but there were many naysayers in the ranks at JPL. They scoffed at designing a space vehicle that could survive many years and a close passage at Jupiter.

Eventually I was asked to present the Grand Tour concept to Homer Joe Stewart, one of my professors at Caltech, who also worked at JPL as director of the advanced concepts group. He saw the potential instantly.

The very next day, JPL issued a press release

describing the Grand Tour to the outer planets. Serious consideration of a multi–outer planet mission at JPL had begun. It eventually culminated in the successful *Pioneer 11* and *Voyager 1* and *2* missions.

Public opposition to the Grand Tour appeared at once. A hippie group, upon reading in the press release that the energy for flinging the spacecraft outward came at the expense of Jupiter's orbital energy, decided to organize the Pasadena Society for the Preservation of Jupiter's Orbit. They paraded in downtown Pasadena carrying signs, one of them wearing a flowing black cape and top hat, and held meetings for a short time in a good-natured way. But the real problems for the mission came later.

PART 3

The summer was over. My direct involvement with Grand Tour planning was finished, although for several years I continued to aid in the marketing of the mission concept by presenting technical papers and answering questions from the press. There was widespread acceptance of the idea with such notables as Wernher von Braun and President Nixon indicating support. In 1972, I received the annual Golovine Award of the British Interplanetary Society in recognition of my work in celestial mechanics. I had been nominated for this award by William H. Pickering, the JPL director.[1]

---

[1] William Hayward Pickering (b. 1910) is no relation to William Henry Pickering (1858–1938), predictor of trans-Neptunian planets.

In the meantime, things had not gone well for the Grand Tour mission. The original very ambitious JPL plan involved a spacecraft that would have ejected atmospheric probes and orbiters at each intermediate planet. That mission was canceled in 1971 because of NASA budget restraints, but then a less ambitious *Mariner*-class spacecraft design was substituted. This "plain vanilla" plan was still based on the original Earth-Jupiter-Saturn gravity-assist flight path.

When it became apparent that the outer-planet Grand Tour mission would indeed fly, several individuals came forth claiming to be the originators of the idea. Truly, the multi–outer planet mission concept is the outcome of the work of many people. Walter Hohmann, originator of the multiplanet trajectory, and G. A. Crocco deserve as much credit as anyone for suggesting the use of gravity assist in planetary mission design and for the name Grand Tour. The solar system escape and close solar probe study by Mike Minovich demonstrated the benefit of the Jupiter gravity-assist maneuver.

The two *Voyager* spacecraft proved so reliable in the first legs of their flights that the *Voyager 2* flight plan was extended to perform the full four-planet Grand Tour mission, which culminated when *Voyager 2* made its final encounter, at Neptune, in August 1989, 24 years after my memorable summer at JPL.

Resurrection

Almost, but not quite. NASA began plans for a third *Mariner* probe to be launched on a Jupiter-Uranus mission in 1979. In 1975, the Jupiter-Uranus project and the third spacecraft were canceled for lack of funds.

In 1977, the *Mariner Jupiter-Saturn* project was given a more manageable name—*Voyager*. And the *Voyager* management team took a final fond look at the Grand Tour plan. The highest priority objectives at Jupiter and Saturn included not just data from the planets but also close-up pictures and measurements of Jupiter's innermost large moon, Io, and Saturn's largest moon, Titan.

It was still possible, with a 1977 launch, to fly the Grand Tour but only by sacrificing optimum views of Io and Titan. If *Voyager 1* flew suitably
close to Io, it would acquire so much velocity from Jupiter that it would
arrive at Saturn too soon to be diverted on to Uranus. If *Voyager 1* flew
suitably close to Titan, it would leave Saturn headed in the wrong direction to reach Uranus.

But if *Voyager 1* gave up its option for a Grand Tour, it could examine
both Io and Titan close up as the central mission objectives required.
That would leave *Voyager 2* in a backup position—ready to undergo midcourse correction to fill in for *Voyager 1* if it failed at Saturn. But if *Voyager
1* succeeded at Saturn and Titan, *Voyager 2* could follow up and broaden
the coverage at Saturn as it would at Jupiter while maintaining course
for a Grand Tour mission on to Uranus and Neptune.

The flight to Uranus and Neptune, already twice canceled, was on
again. It required no extra money, at least not immediately. It was only
a contingency plan. A hope. A dream.

Voyager 2 was launched first, on August 24, 1977. *Voyager 1* lifted off
on September 5, 1977, on a slightly more direct and hence faster route
so that it would reach Jupiter and Saturn ahead of its sister ship. But project managers still considered a successful Grand Tour a long shot.

Voyager 1 succeeded brilliantly at Jupiter. It documented in detail the
turbulent flow of the Jovian atmosphere, especially near the Great Red
Spot, a centuries-old storm that is at least twice the size of Earth. *Voyager
1* found that Jupiter has a faint dusty ring.

**Winds flow turbulently
around the Great Red
Spot on Jupiter, as
seen by the *Voyager*
spacecraft**
*NASA/Jet Propulsion
Laboratory*

Exploring Jupiter's moons, *Voyager 1* discovered active volcanoes on Io, the surface of Europa covered by cracked ice, parallel ridges and grooves on Ganymede, and a surface on Callisto so heavily cratered that new impacts erase as many craters as are formed.

A Grand Tour for *Voyager 2* was still a possibility.

Voyager 1 again performed splendidly at Saturn. It learned that the fabled ring system was composed not of a few but of thousands of rings. Winds in Saturn's atmosphere reached speeds of 1,000 miles per hour (1,600 kilometers per hour).

Voyager 1 discovered that Jupiter has a faint, dusty ring. The tiny particles showed up best as *Voyager* looked back through the ring toward the Sun to see sunlight scattered by the dust.
NASA/Jet Propulsion Laboratory

Voyager 1 discovered that Io, Jupiter's innermost large moon, has more active volcanoes than any other body in the solar system. A volcano on the horizon hurls ejecta more than a hundred miles above Io's surface.
NASA/Jet Propulsion Laboratory

Jupiter's moon Europa has the smoothest surface of any body in the solar system. The cracks in its water ice crust do not jut upward to appreciable height. *NASA/Jet Propulsion Laboratory*

Jupiter's Ganymede, the largest moon in the solar system, has a highly wrinkled surface that suggests extensive movement of crustal plates. *NASA/Jet Propulsion Laboratory*

This high-resolution mosaic of Callisto, Jupiter's outermost large moon, shows that it is saturated with craters. Except for impact cratering, little has happened to Callisto since it formed. *NASA/Jet Propulsion Laboratory*

The *Voyagers* found that Saturn's ring system was composed of thousands of rings.
NASA/Jet Propulsion Laboratory

Computer-enhanced image of Saturn's atmosphere as seen by the *Voyagers*. The spots are smaller versions of Jupiter's Great Red Spot, but on Saturn the jet-stream winds flow three times as fast.
NASA/Jet Propulsion Laboratory

The *Voyagers* revealed for the first time surface details on the moons of Saturn. This is Dione.
NASA/Jet Propulsion Laboratory

Among Saturn's moons, Titan was known to have an atmosphere. *Voyager 1* found that this atmosphere was denser than Earth's and that its principal constituent was nitrogen. It revealed for the first time details on the other moons of Saturn, a wild variety of terrains with abundant evidence that, despite their modest size, these worlds had experienced internal evolution long after formation. *Voyager 1* discovered two new rings at Saturn and confirmed the theory that a narrow ring could be stabilized by small shepherd moons.

The Grand Tour for *Voyager 2* now loomed large.

On August 25, 1981, *Voyager 2* successfully cleared Saturn on course. The Grand Tour was on.

On—but again threatened, this time by problems with the spacecraft.

CHAPTER 8

The Grand Tour of *Voyager 2*

"The space program has done more to stimulate the growth of human knowledge than any other aspect of life on Earth."
Ellis D. Miner, Assistant Project Scientist for *Voyager*

Voyager 2 is legally deaf, chronically arthritic, and just a touch senile.[1]

A few months after *Voyager 2* set out for Jupiter, one of its radio receivers, vital for the spacecraft to receive instructions from Earth, failed outright and the backup receiver lost its tuning ability.

Voyager spacecraft
NASA/Jet Propulsion Laboratory

High-Gain
Directional
Antenna

Cosmic Ray
Analyzer

Plasma Analyzer

Magnetometer (1 of 4)

Extendable
Boom

Wide-Angle TV

Narrow-Angle TV

TV Electronics

Ultraviolet
Spectrometer

Infrared
Interferometer
Spectrometer
and Radiometer

Photopolarimeter

Planetary Radio
Astronomy and
Plasma Wave Antenna

Low-Energy
Charged Particles Detector

Thrusters (16)

Electronic
Compartments

Science Instrument
Calibration Panel
and Shunt Radiator

Propulsion
Fuel Tank

Radioisotope
Thermoelectric
Generators (3)

Planetary Radio
Astronomy and
Plasma Wave Antenna

Voyager spacecraft instruments and equipment
NASA/Jet Propulsion Laboratory

As it flew by Saturn, the *Voyager 2* scan platform, which turns the cameras and some of the other scientific instruments toward their targets, seized up.

Throughout most of the mission outward, a small portion of the spacecraft's computer memory has been inoperable.

Yet by the time it reached Uranus on January 24, 1986, after a flight of eight and a half years, *Voyager 2* was a better spacecraft than when it left home. The Jet Propulsion Laboratory scientific and engineering team had redesigned the spacecraft in flight.

Seven and a half months after launch, en route to Jupiter, a power surge on *Voyager 2* permanently destroyed the primary radio receiver and damaged the backup so badly that it could not tune to receive different frequencies from Earth. Before the failure the receiver had been able

Almost Showstoppers

to scan across a 100,000-hertz range and lock onto the signal. This capability was necessary to compensate for the varying wavelengths caused by the Doppler Effect as the spacecraft moves away from Earth at varying speeds. Because of gravity, the spacecraft's speed gradually increases as it approaches a planet or moon and gradually slows down after passing it. The receiver's scan/lock-on feature was also necessary to compensate for variation in receiver temperature, which alters what wavelengths the radio can receive.

After the power surge aboard *Voyager 2*, the tiny remaining range of frequencies that the receiver could accept was only ±96 hertz. The bandwidth for reception had been cut a thousandfold. A change of 0.5°F (0.25°C) was enough to render the spacecraft deaf. This problem was severe and scary. Without the ability to update the spacecraft's instructions, the mission was lost. The flight team solved the problem by carefully adjusting the transmitted wavelengths to compensate for the Doppler Effect and expected temperature so that *Voyager 2* could receive all its messages within a single small bandwidth, the only frequency it could hear. The flight team would transmit to *Voyager 2* only when the craft was in normal cruising mode. After spacecraft maneuvers that generate heat within the probe, the flight team would wait 48 hours before sending messages to *Voyager 2*.

This radio reception problem meant that *Voyager 2* would be deaf to Earth commands during the close phases of the Uranus and Neptune encounters. No matter. A message from Earth to *Voyager* at Uranus and a confirming message from *Voyager* to Earth required five and a half hours—almost the entire length of the *Voyager 2* close encounter with Uranus. The spacecraft would have to be very carefully preprogrammed with instructions for the entire close-in data-gathering and picture-taking sequence at Uranus and Neptune in order to enjoy a successful flyby. By the time some instructional error was revealed during the encounter, there would be no time to correct it. And there would be no second chance.

And just in case this final frequency fails, the flight team always keeps *Voyager 2* loaded with the latest instructions to carry out the Neptune flyby without further update from Earth.

The technical challenge of getting good information from Uranus was intimidating. Uranus lies at twice the distance of Saturn, so there is only one-fourth as much sunlight at Uranus to provide illumination for pictures. Thus long exposures are necessary. But long exposures of moving objects lead to smeared images unless the camera is moved to track the target.

Unfortunately, the scan platform on which *Voyager 2*'s cameras were mounted had jammed as it pivoted rapidly to follow targets one and a half hours after its closest approach to Saturn on August 25, 1981.[2] A number of pictures and measurements scheduled to be made were lost because the spacecraft could not point its instruments in the right direction. Lubrication gradually seeped back into the gears and the system seemed to be working again at slow and moderate speeds, but the mission team wanted to take no chances. The Uranus encounter would be so brief that even one picture was too precious to be lost. So whenever fast or even moderately fast slews were required of the scan platform to track the targets, the entire spacecraft was rolled to follow the action.[3] Rolling the entire craft provided smoother motion besides. But it was tricky. *Voyager 2* would rush by the moon Miranda at 20 times the speed of a rifle bullet while the whole spacecraft rolled to pan its cameras to an accuracy of better than one-tenth of a degree.

The enhancement of *Voyager* to meet the challenge of Uranus and Neptune did not stop with an understanding of and a compensation for the scan-platform problem. In the weak sunlight at Uranus and with *Voyager* moving as fast as 56,000 miles per hour (25 kilometers per second), additional care had to be taken to make the craft as steady as possible during picture taking. Even the starting and stopping of *Voyager's* tape recorder was a problem. Every time the recorder turned on, the start-up of the spinning reels created equal and opposite momentum in the spacecraft. The spin induced in *Voyager* was very tiny because of its much greater mass, but the spin was nevertheless very real and could blur pictures and foul up other directional measurements. When the tape recorder stopped, the spacecraft picked up that momentum and began to spin slowly in the direction that the reels had been turning. For every action, there is an equal and opposite reaction. It was a textbook demonstration of Newton's third law of motion. It was also a troublesome obstacle to quality pictures and other measurements expected from *Voyager 2*. The mission team solved the problem by programming *Voyager 2* to fire tiny bursts of gas from its thrusters to counteract the torque created by the starting and stopping of the onboard tape recorder.

Voyager 2 also ran afoul of a computer memory problem when a computer chip failed in one of the two scientific computers. The damage was irreparable and cost that computer 3 percent of its memory capacity. For this problem, there was no "fix" except to moderate demands on the computer.[4]

Thus, on its way to Uranus, *Voyager 2* developed three potentially showstopping technical problems—with radio reception, with its scan platform, and with its computer memory. From Earth, millions of miles away, these problems had been detected, diagnosed, and worked around so that *Voyager 2* lost very little of the capabilities built into it and did not have to forgo any of the experiments planned for it to execute.

But the ground team went much further than restoring the spacecraft to its initial proficiency. They actually made it better.

Enhancements

As *Voyager 2* sped farther from Earth, its radio signal became weaker. At Jupiter, the signal was weak but adequate. At Saturn, almost twice as far away, the signal was four times weaker. At Uranus, more than twice the distance of Saturn, the signal upon which all the data would be received on Earth was four times weaker than from Saturn and sixteen times weaker than from Jupiter. The result was that in order to avoid a jumbled message, *Voyager 2* could not pack its data so tightly for transmission, just as a speaker talks more slowly to make certain he is understood.

Especially critical were the images to be transmitted, which required vast amounts of transmission time. All *Voyager* pictures are black-and-white, but taking multiple pictures through different filters allows scientists back on Earth to combine filtered pictures to make color images. Even so, transmitting black-and-white pictures requires enormous quantities of bits. Each *Voyager* image is a television picture formed from an array of 800 pixels (picture elements, dots) across and 800 pixels down—a total of 640,000 pixels. And the darkness or lightness of each of these pixels is described by 8 binary bits to provide a gray scale of 256 shades. Thus each picture to be transmitted required $640,000 \times 8 = 5,120,000$ bits of information—over 5 million bits.

At Jupiter, *Voyager*'s X-band transmitter could start and finish broadcasting a picture to Earth within 48 seconds.[5] At Saturn, where distance forced *Voyager 2* to use a lower data transmission rate, the time between the start and finish of a single picture broadcast was about two and a half minutes. At Uranus, the transmission time for a single image would rise to ten minutes—unacceptably long. When *Voyager* rolled so that its cameras could track a target, its antenna would be turned away from Earth and its tape recorder would store the images until they could be transmitted. With transmission times so long, there was danger that the recorder would be quickly overwhelmed and precious pictures and other data would be lost.

The computer scientists at the Jet Propulsion Laboratory came up with a solution—a computer innovation called data compression. Instead of describing the exact shade of gray of each pixel in an image, only the first pixel in each line would be precisely described. Each pixel that followed in that row would then be described only in terms of how much lighter or darker it was than the one preceding it. This data compression carried risks. An error (due to electronic noise) at the beginning of a row would create errors in all the other pixels in that row. And an error in any pixel in the row would make the values of all following pixels in that row wrong. The image as a whole, however, ought to reveal such defects by contrast.

There was another risk. Data compression would have to be performed by the computers aboard *Voyager 2*, and the computer program to compress the data was so extensive that it would require one of *Voyager's* two scientific computers to be completely dedicated to this function alone.

Yet it was worth the risk. The data-compression system reduced the number of bits required to send an image by 60 percent. Instead of 12 minutes to broadcast one picture from Uranus, it would now take only 5.

But data compression was not the only improvement to *Voyager 2* made en route to Uranus. *Voyager* engineers also worked out a new system for shorter bursts on the thrusters to stabilize the craft, making it smoother in its maneuvers. *Voyager 2* became able to take steadier pictures while becoming more conservative of fuel.

So as *Voyager 2* got older, it actually did get better, thanks to the ingenuity of a lot of scientists and engineers on Earth.

And facilities on Earth improved as well. They had to if they were going to hear the puny radio signal of *Voyager* all the way from Uranus. "Clearchannel" radio stations in the United States broadcast on 50,000 watts of power. *Voyager 2* transmits its data to Earth on 22 watts. But that signal spreads out during its journey from Uranus so that by the time it has traveled 1.75 billion miles (2.8 million kilometers), a 210-foot (64-meter) dish receiver on Earth captures only one-billionth of one-millionth of a watt.

To receive *Voyager 2's* information from Jupiter and Saturn and to transmit instructions to the spacecraft, NASA had used its Deep Space Network—three tracking stations scattered a third of the way around the world from one another. One is at Goldstone, California, 100 miles (160 kilometers) northeast of Los Angeles. The second is near Madrid, Spain. The third is near Canberra, Australia. Each Deep Space Network site was equipped with a steerable parabolic dish antenna 210 feet (64 meters) in diameter.

For the Uranus encounter those dishes weren't enough. NASA augmented their receiving capability by linking the giant dishes to smaller 112-foot (34-meter) dishes at each station. It worked like an old-fashioned ear horn for a partially deaf person: the more receiving area, the more signal captured. At Madrid, a single 112-foot antenna was arrayed with a 210-foot dish, boosting reception by about 28 percent.

Bigger Ears

NASA's large Deep Space Network radio receiving dish at Goldstone, California
NASA/Jet Propulsion Laboratory

The timing of the encounter placed the greatest burden on the Canberra and Goldstone sites. There, two 112-foot antennae were arrayed with the 210-foot dish, and receptivity was increased by about 56 percent. At Canberra, the receiving site for *Voyager*'s data from Uranus at closest encounter, a further enhancement was made. The Australian government linked its 210-foot (64-meter) Parkes radio telescope with the three-dish array of NASA's Deep Space Network at Canberra to form a combined antenna with the reception power of a 400-foot (100-meter) dish.

Bull's-eye

In addition to the chronic ailments of its remaining radio receiver, its scan platform, and its computer memory, and in addition to the greater distance that affected the strength of the radio signal from *Voyager 2* and the time for instructions to reach the spacecraft, *Voyager 2* faced a special challenge at Uranus because of the planet's orientation.

The two *Voyager* probes had previously encountered Jupiter and Saturn, planets that, like Earth, travel around the Sun with their rotational axes nearly perpendicular to their orbital planes. Because they travel around the Sun "standing up," their equators lie nearly in their orbital planes. All the rings and a great majority of the moons in the solar system revolve around their planets' equators. So the rings and most of the moons of Jupiter and Saturn lie nearly in the plane of revolution for that planet, which is extremely close to the orbital plane of the Earth and hence essentially the plane formed by flight of *Voyager 2*. Thus as *Voyager 1* and *2* approached Jupiter and Saturn, it was a little like approaching a city on a flat map. *Voyager* first found itself in the suburbs, able to shoot a snapshot of one moon and then prepare for the next. In sequence, the spacecraft passed one moon after another, then closest to the planet, and then outward past additional moons one at a time. The Jupiter and Saturn close encounters were each spread out over several days.

Uranus was not so accommodating. *Voyager 2*'s closest encounters with Uranus, its rings, and all of its moons were crammed into a period of less than six hours.

The rings and moons of Uranus revolve almost precisely around its equator, just as most of the moons and all of the rings of the other planets do. The problem is that Uranus lies on its side as it revolves around the Sun. So the orbits of its moons and rings are tilted, like the planet, almost perpendicularly to the orbital plane of Uranus. Even so, if the equator of Uranus had been more or less edge on to *Voyager* as it approached (which is approximately the case for about half of the 84-year period of Uranus), *Voyager* could have passed across that orbital plane and the moons could have been studied sequentially on approach and departure.

But the planetary alignment that allowed *Voyager 2* to bounce from

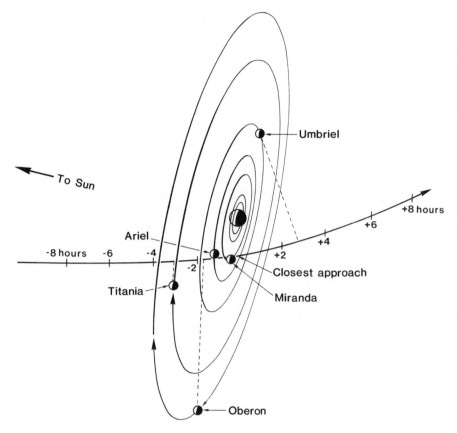

To Sun

-8 hours -6   -4   -2 +2 +4 +6 +8 hours

Umbriel

Ariel

Titania

Closest approach

Miranda

Oberon

Voyager 2's flight past Uranus. *Voyager 2* passed nearly perpendicularly through the Uranian system because Uranus lies on its side as it orbits the Sun and its moons orbit above its equator. At the time of *Voyager 2*'s arrival, Uranus had its south pole pointed toward the spacecraft and the Sun and thus presented a bull's-eye target to its visitor. Because of this geometry, *Voyager 2*'s closest approaches to Uranus, its rings, and each of its moons (its opportunities for best pictures and measurements) were squeezed into a period of less than six hours.

Jupiter to Saturn to Uranus to Neptune just happened to catch Uranus with its south pole pointed toward the Sun, the Earth, and the approaching robot ambassador from Earth. *Voyager 2* saw Uranus, its rings, and its moons laid out before it like a target with a bull's-eye and concentric rings. The spacecraft plunged perpendicularly through the Uranian system like a dart thrown at a paper target. The time when *Voyager 2* was closest to Uranus was also very nearly the time when *Voyager 2* had its closest view of each moon. The picture taking and scientific measurements that could be spread over several days at Jupiter and Saturn were compressed into a little over five hours at Uranus. While each image was made, another important target was near its best viewing.

It had taken four and a half years for *Voyager 2* to fly from Saturn to Uranus. Working against formidable obstacles of distance, darkness, and planetary orientation at Uranus; working against a crippled radio receiver, a sticky scan platform, and a degraded computer onboard the spacecraft,

Solo

scientists meticulously planned every aspect of the Uranus encounter so that *Voyager 2* could take full advantage of the first practical opportunity since the dawn of the space age to examine in detail the realm of Uranus.

At Jupiter and Saturn, *Voyager 2* had been the backup craft, following up on *Voyager 1*'s discoveries and duplicating measurements from a different angle. Now, at Uranus, *Voyager 2* was the only spacecraft, traveling where no spacecraft had ever gone before. With each passing moment, *Voyager 2* was expanding the absolute frontier of planetary journeys.

On January 24, 1986, eight and a half years outbound from Earth, NASA's *Voyager 2* spacecraft passed 50,700 miles (81,600 kilometers) above the cloud tops of Uranus. Uranus was 1.75 billion miles (2.8 billion kilometers) from Earth, and the data radioed from *Voyager* took two and three-quarters hours to reach home traveling at the speed of light.

Astronomy had come a long way in the 205 years since Herschel had caught sight of a tiny disk in his homemade telescope.

CHAPTER 9

Triumph at Uranus

"What do we learn about the Earth by studying the planets? Humility!"
Planetary scientist Andrew P. Ingersoll
(1986)

The blue-green planet that *Voyager 2* approached in January 1986 had clouds, but not in brilliant earth-tone colors like those of Jupiter. It had rings, but not in bright, broad belts made of thousands of ringlets like those of Saturn. It had moons, but none as large as Jupiter's Big Four or Saturn's Titan. Uranus was more subtle, yet every bit as puzzling. Its atmosphere seemed bland, its rings were narrow and dark, its largest moons were quite modest in size. It would take a connoisseur to appreciate this planet—and a great many imaginative and clear-thinking scientists to understand it.

The atmospheres of Jupiter, Saturn, Uranus, and Neptune are basically the same. It is their temperatures that make them look so very different. Their atmospheres are composed overwhelmingly of hydrogen and helium, with only traces of other chemicals. All have clouds made of some of those trace elements. All have an obscuring haze layer formed as sunlight breaks up methane molecules (CH_4), allowing the carbon to recombine into more complicated and less transparent hydrogen-carbon compounds, such as acetylene (C_2H_2) and ethane (C_2H_6).

Each of these gas giant planets has a well-mixed atmosphere rich in chemicals. On Earth, most of those chemicals are dissolved in the oceans

Atmospherics

or have been compounded to form rocks and hence have been extracted from the air. But on Jupiter, Saturn, Uranus, and Neptune, all those chemicals are gases in the atmosphere and will condense to form clouds if the temperature is right. On Earth, only water condenses and forms white clouds. On Jupiter, temperatures at various levels are cold enough to form ice clouds of water (white); ammonia (white); and compounds of ammonia (white), phosphorus (reddish brown), sulfur (red, orange, yellow, blue, and black), and various more complex organic compounds (usually reddish). At Jupiter, heat from the Sun and from deep within the planet creates updrafts in the atmosphere. These rising gases expand, cool, and then sink back to lower, warmer levels. As each gas in the atmosphere reaches its special temperature of condensation, it freezes out of the air to form clouds of ice particles—different colors for different chemicals.

Each of the gas giant planets produces clouds according to the heat it receives from the Sun and its own internal sources of heat. The colder a planet is, the less vertical atmospheric motion it has and the fewer cloud patterns and features.

But another factor is at work on the gas giants that determines what cloud features are visible when the planet is viewed from a distance. That factor is the hydrocarbon smog. This obscuring haze is present on all four gas giants at a level where the atmospheric pressure is about one-hundredth to one-tenth the pressure at sea level on Earth. In the comparative warmth on Jupiter, the clouds billow up above the smog to create a planet that looks like an abstract painting in riotous colors. At Saturn, there are still patterns, storms, and eddies to be seen but less distinctly

Using false color, clouds were detected in the Uranian atmosphere; one is visible here near the one o'clock position close to the planet's edge (near Uranus' equator). The small doughnut-shaped features are not real; they were caused by dust in *Voyager 2*'s camera.
NASA/Jet Propulsion Laboratory

and less colorfully. Saturn's lower temperature creates less cloud activity, and much of it is buried out of sight beneath the smog.[1]

Over the decades that preceded the visit of *Voyager 2* to Uranus, several Earth-based astronomers had claimed to see clouds in its atmosphere, but their contemporaries had been unable to confirm these findings. *Voyager 2* did indeed find clouds drifting in the Uranian atmosphere, but these clouds were visible only through special filters and with contrast enhanced by computers. They are invisible at ordinary optical wavelengths because, with so little solar or internal heat at Uranus, the clouds lie deep in the atmosphere below the thin high haze of hydrocarbon smog that veils the planet. Below the haze is a cloud deck two to three miles thick of tiny methane ice crystals floating in the planet's predominantly hydrogen atmosphere.

The Weather on Uranus

Uranus lies on its side as it revolves around the Sun. How would this orientation affect the weather *Voyager 2* would find on the planet?

The tilt of Uranus means that during the course of a year on the planet—equal to 84 Earth years—the Sun stands directly or almost directly above every point on Uranus.[2] Thus, for several years out of each 84-year orbital cycle, the north and south poles on Uranus are treated to sunlight beaming down from near the top of the sky—a circumstance unique to Uranus and Pluto among planets in the solar system.

The orbit of Uranus causes the position of the Sun to appear to slowly swing from pole to pole during the course of a Uranian year. As the Sun

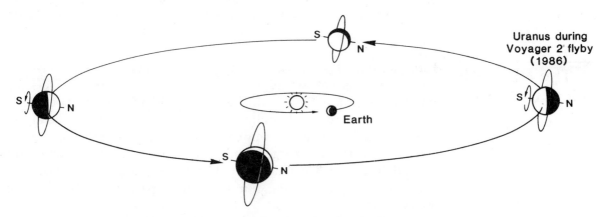

The seasons of Uranus. Uranus lies on its side as it orbits the Sun. This axial tilt means that the Sun can stand almost directly above the planet's north and south poles. For 42 years, the south pole receives continuous sunlight. Then, for the next 42 years at the south pole, the Sun is never visible.

is hovering nearly over each pole, the seasonal cycle of the Sun's north/south apparent motion in the sky is in the process of slowing, stopping, and reversing itself. At midcycle, when the Sun is over the equator, the seasons are changing fastest. Therefore, the polar regions of Uranus actually receive slightly more solar warmth than the equator. Not much, because the Sun provides precious little heat at Uranus, but scientists expected that the sunlit pole would be a few degrees warmer than the equator.

It wasn't. *Voyager 2* found that the temperatures around the planet, poles and equator, day and night, were within 3° Fahrenheit of being identical—about 366° below zero Fahrenheit (−221°C; 52°K). The sunlight is so weak that what little heat is received is quickly spread rather evenly around the planet by its winds.

But how would winds, if any, flow on a planet where the region around the south pole is currently receiving the most direct sunlight? On Earth, the Sun's radiation falls most vertically and hence most intensely, near the equator, where it heats the surface air and causes it to rise. Cooler air farther from the equator flows in to form the principal wind circulation. The west-to-east rotation of the Earth then causes those air currents to curve so that the prevailing winds blow west to east.

But with maximum heating on Uranus at the south pole, would the prevailing winds on that planet be north to south? No, *Voyager* found, the winds blow east to west because of the rapid east-to-west rotation of Uranus.[3]

Meterologists were startled. The angle of sunlight is less important than planetary rotation in generating the motion of weather systems. The jet-stream winds in the upper atmosphere of Uranus flow at 200 miles per hour (300 kilometers per hour), about twice the speed of those on Earth.

The Magnetic Field of Uranus

Perhaps the greatest surprise afforded by the planet itself was its magnetic field. A magnetic field was expected because Uranus is very massive—14.5 times more massive than Earth. The mass of Uranus is great enough that its gravity can create a hot interior. This heat makes atoms shed electrons so that they are electrically charged. The rotation of the planet then spins this electrically charged fluid interior to generate a magnetic field around the planet. The magnetic field changes the courses of incoming charged particles from the Sun and ionized particles in the planet's atmosphere.

But from Earth it had not been possible to detect a magnetic field for Uranus. *Voyager 2* did the honors—and raised some eyebrows. The magnetic field of Uranus was greater than the Earth's. It was also absurdly tilted. The magnetic poles of Earth correspond roughly with the poles of rotation. They are offset from one another by only about 11.7 degrees. The same is true for Jupiter and Saturn. But not for Uranus. The magnetic axis of Uranus is tipped 60 degrees to the poles of rotation, meaning that the north and south magnetic poles lie closer to the equator than to the geographic poles.

But that wasn't all that was strange. The magnetic axis of the Earth passes very nearly through the exact center of our planet. (It misses by less than 300 miles [500 kilometers]). So it is at Jupiter and Saturn as well. But not at Uranus. There the magnetic axis lies 4,800 miles (7,700 kilometers) off center, passing through Uranus about one-third of the way between the planet's center and its surface.[4]

Geophysicists interpret these oddities to mean that the magnetic field of Uranus is generated not at or close to the planet's center but outside of the core.[5] The Earth's magnetic field is thought to come from molten iron and nickel. The magnetic field of Uranus is thought to come from its mantle where water and ammonia may be under sufficient pressure to make them good electrical conductors.

At first scientists thought that the 60-degree tilt of the magnetic field might be just an accident in time. Had *Voyager 2* reached Uranus in the midst of a magnetic field reversal in which the poles switch magnetic polarity, something that happens on Earth about every half-million years?[6]

Voyager 2 used the planet's magnetic field to determine the length of a day on Uranus. As the magnetic field swept over the spacecraft, increasing in intensity whenever a magnetic pole rotated by *Voyager*, scientists could observe that the magnetic field of Uranus spins around once every 17.24 hours. For practical purposes, this cycle is the rotation period of the planet. Uranus has no solid surface and hence no landmarks that repeatedly rotate by to reveal the length of a day.

Spectroscopic measurements of the spin of Uranus from Earth could only approximate the rotational period. To calculate the rotation of Uranus based on cloud motions in the atmosphere was problematical because, as on Earth, wind speed varies with location and time. At present, the fastest winds on Uranus are near the south pole, where the solar heating of the atmosphere is most intense. A year before *Voyager 2*'s encounter, the rotational period of Uranus was variously listed between 10 and 24 hours, with newer estimates suggesting 15 to 17 hours. With its measurement of 17.24 hours, *Voyager 2* refined that figure considerably.

Uranus and Neptune rotate faster than Earth and the other rocky midget planets but not as rapidly as the larger giants, Jupiter and Saturn.

Dayglow

The spacecraft found all sorts of atmospheric glows at Uranus, just as expected based on what the *Voyagers* had detected at Jupiter and Saturn.

Uranus had an aurora, similar to the northern and southern lights on Earth. Subatomic particles from the Sun were diverted by the magnetic field of Uranus toward the planet's magnetic poles, where they plunged into the atmosphere, causing hydrogen molecules, the principal constituent, to glow.

Uranus also exhibited air glow on its daytime face, as ultraviolet energy from the Sun caused some atmospheric atoms and molecules to glow very faintly.

But most interesting was a previously unrecognized atmospheric emission initially given the name *electroglow* and now renamed *dayglow* to emphasize that it happens only when the atmosphere is directly exposed to sunlight. Dayglow had been detected by the *Voyagers* at Jupiter and Saturn but initially misidentified as aurora. *Voyager 2* revealed it unmistakably at Uranus.[7] The exact cause of dayglow is still being debated, but the fluorescence seen comes from hydrogen atoms in the tenuous upper atmosphere only on the sunward side of the planet. The total ultraviolet light released by dayglow from the sunlit atmosphere of Uranus corresponds to a few trillion watts of power. One trillion watts is enough to power 20 million homes at peak demand—all the homes in the New York and Los Angeles metropolitan areas.[8]

The Energy of Uranus

Uranus was expected to be slightly warmer than heating by the distant Sun would allow. Jupiter and Saturn are radiating into space almost twice as much energy as they receive from the Sun.[9] They emit this energy not as visible light but in the form of heat and radio waves. In the case of Jupiter, the source of this radiation is energy released by the continuing decay of radioactive elements within the planet and from the heat as gravity continues to compress its interior. In the case of Saturn, the internal heat is mostly caused by radioactive decay and gravitational compression, but about a third of Saturn's excess radiation comes from the separating mix of hydrogen and helium within the planet. The heavier helium is falling toward the planet's core, creating heat by friction as it rubs against the hydrogen fluid.[10]

Although it is not the size of Jupiter and Saturn, Uranus is a giant planet, so gravitational and radioactive heating could be anticipated. *Voyager 2* did indeed find Uranus slightly warmer than sunlight alone could provide, but not much. Uranus emits only about 15 percent more energy than it receives from the Sun, energy radiated in the infrared and radio wavelengths.

Measurements by *Voyager 2* greatly clarified our perspective on the structure of Uranus. The planet is about 85 percent hydrogen and 12 percent helium by mass—close to the same proportions as the Sun, Jupiter, and Saturn. The bodies of the solar system are truly a family, spawned from the same cloud of gas and dust and differing from one another because of their distances from the Sun.

Hydrogen dominates the atmosphere of Uranus, but the visible "surface" of the planet is a haze layer of acetylene (C_2H_2) and ethane (C_2H_6) formed by sunlight striking methane in the Uranian atmosphere. It is the small amount of methane (2 percent to 3 percent) mixed in with the hydrogen, helium, and other elements and compounds that gives Uranus its blue-green color by absorbing and not reflecting the red portion of

The Structure of Uranus

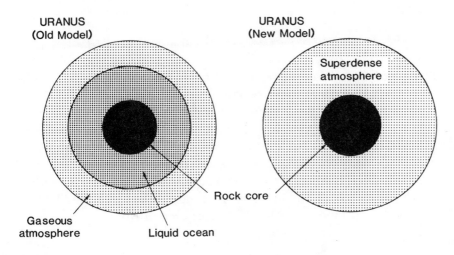

The internal structure of Uranus compared to that of Earth and Jupiter. *Voyager 2* indicated that a two-layer model for the interior of Uranus is correct rather than the earlier three-layer model. (The internal structure of each planet is drawn to scale, but not its size compared to the others. Uranus is about 4 times the diameter of Earth; Jupiter is more than 11.)

the sunlight it receives. The upper atmosphere of Uranus, warmed only feebly by sunlight and the weak internal heat of the planet, is extremely cold—about 350° below zero Fahrenheit (−212° Celsius).

Before *Voyager 2*'s visit to Uranus, the interior of the planet was thought to be at least basically similar to the interiors of Jupiter and Saturn—a hot, rocky core about the size of Earth surrounded by a dense ocean of hydrogen under so much pressure that it behaved like a metal. On top of this dense fluid, where the pressure was less, lay the gaseous atmosphere, mostly hydrogen and helium.

Initial analysis of *Voyager 2* data suggested that this three-layered structure applied to Uranus as well, except that the behavior of the mantle surrounding the core was dominated by liquid water mixed in with the hydrogen and under so much pressure that it was ionized. Because of its electrical charge, this water became a good conductor of electricity. As this giant interior ocean of electrically charged water rotated, said the scientists, Uranus generated its magnetic field.

But late in 1987 that conclusion was dramatically reversed.[11]

The problem is that for a planet that rotates as rapidly as it does, Uranus has relatively little bulge at its equator. Given its speed of rotation, if Uranus had a light atmosphere overlying a dense liquid mantle, the planet should bulge more as it turns. But it doesn't. Therefore, said the new conclusion, Uranus probably does not have a light atmosphere on top of a liquid mantle. Instead the gases of the atmosphere—hydrogen, helium, water, ammonia, and methane—are all mixed together as a superdense atmosphere—a gas, not a liquid—that extends from outside the rocky core all the way to the visible surface of Uranus, where pressure and temperature allow different molecules to condense as clouds. Because Neptune is similar in size and mass, its interior structure is expected to be the same.

The Problem of Tilt

In a solar system where all the planets out to Uranus stand nearly upright on their polar axes as they revolve around the Sun, why does Uranus lie on its side? *Voyager 2* found no evidence to resolve this puzzle.

The still-prevailing view is that Uranus and all the planets were formed from a vast cloud of gas and dust by accretion: They were hit by, and absorbed, many cometlike planetesimals of differing sizes. Some struck near the poles, tending to tilt the planets. In some planets the impacts nearly balanced out, leaving the planets upright as they formed. Others were left with moderate tilts. The succession of collisions left Uranus and Pluto spinning on their sides.

The Moons of Uranus

Before the arrival of *Voyager 2,* Uranus was known to harbor five moons. But Earth-bound telescopes had not been able to resolve the moons' disks, so their diameters could only be approximated. They were substantial in size but far smaller than the four largest satellites of Jupiter, which range from just slightly smaller than our Moon to just slightly larger than the planet Mercury. None was the size of Titan, the largest moon of Saturn, or Triton, the largest moon of Neptune.

Voyager 2 provided the first pictures ever made that showed features on these five previously recognized but little-known moons of Uranus. The spacecraft also discovered ten new satellites of Uranus and two more rings to add to the nine already known.

Uranus is about a thousand times more massive than all its satellites and its ring system put together—very roughly the same ratio as its fellow gas giant planets. But of the four giant planets in our solar system, Uranus is the only one without a giant moon. Even the Moon of Earth, which is 2,160 miles (3,476 kilometers) in diameter and ranks sixth in size among planetary satellites, is more than twice the diameter of the largest Uranian moon. If our Moon were hollow, it would be possible to fit into it all 15 known moons and all the particles in the 11 known rings of Uranus and still have with room left over.

Small they were—but not without many surprises.

The two biggest moons are the two outermost: Oberon and Titania. Almost the same in size, they are otherwise very different. Next, moving inward, are Umbriel and Ariel, almost identical in size and about three-quarters the diameter of Oberon and Titania. But again, size is about all they have in common. The innermost of the major moons is Miranda, smallest of the five—and the weirdest.

The first of the Uranian moons to be discovered had been Oberon and Titania, found on January 11, 1787, by William Herschel, about six years after he had discovered Uranus. This time he was using his 18.8-inch (20-foot focal-length) reflector. Umbriel and Ariel were discovered in 1851 by William Lassell, an English amateur astronomer in the tradition of Herschel.

The names for the moons of Uranus were provided about 1852 by John Herschel, William's son, who borrowed them from English literature rather than Greek and Roman mythology. A German astronomer protested this violation of tradition. The names Oberon and Titania were taken from Shakespeare's *A Midsummer Night's Dream.* Umbriel and Ariel were given names snipped from Alexander Pope's *The Rape of the Lock.* [12] For Miranda, not discovered until 1948 by Gerard P. Kuiper, the source of the name was once again Shakespeare, this time *The Tempest.*

Like most satellites elsewhere in the solar system, the moons of Uranus

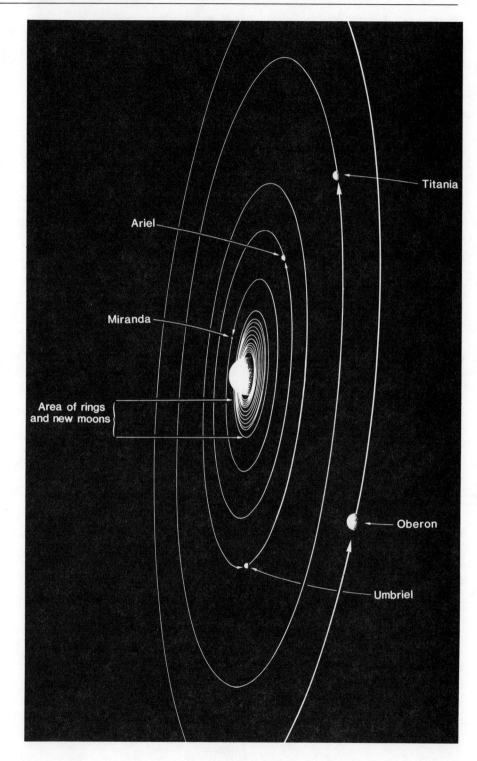

Titania

Ariel

Miranda

Area of rings
and new moons

Oberon

Umbriel

**Uranus, its rings and
moons**

were expected to have nearly circular orbits, to revolve around their planet's equator, and to rotate on their axes in the same amount of time as they revolved so that they always kept the same face toward Uranus (as our Moon always keeps the same face toward Earth). Despite the tilt of Uranus and its retrograde rotation, all 15 of its moons comply with these conventions.[13]

The moons of Uranus were also supposed to be dull. After all, they were small and cold—a good formula for dead worlds. Here were no moons like Saturn's Titan, so large that its gravity could retain an atmosphere. No moons like Jupiter's Io, which was still being pulled periodically like a piece of taffy between Jupiter and the moons Europa and Ganymede so that Io's insides are molten and it belches lava to the surface and into space with a frequency and ferocity unmatched by any other body in the solar system.

Based on all the bodies circling the Sun and especially the other satellites in the solar system, the moons of Uranus were expected to be simple little worlds of rock and ice that had formed along with or soon after Uranus, in time to be pounded by icy and rocky debris left over from the accretion of the planets and the moons. This bombardment should have saturated their surfaces with large and small craters—craters overlapping craters. For moons as small as those of Uranus, it was expected that little had happened since their formation except the impact of an occasional comet onto a surface covered with craters of all sizes.

Larger moons in the solar system were expected to evolve further because of the quantity of radioactive elements they contained. The radioactive decay would have released enormous heat inside the body. As the size of a sphere increases, the surface area and the volume also increase, but the surface area—which sheds heat—increases only by the square of the radius, whereas the volume—which determines how much radioactive material there is—increases by the cube of the radius. Thus, if two objects are formed from the same material, the larger one should have a higher internal temperature because it cannot shed its heat as well. The result is that a planet or large moon might be expected to have melted soon after it formed, with its heavier components sinking toward the core and its lighter materials rising toward the surface. This process is called *differentiation*. External signs of differentiation can often be found in volcanic activity, which has covered part of the surface of the object with relatively smooth material that is obviously younger because it has flooded and erased many of the craters. Differentiation, however, should not have occurred in smaller bodies because the internal heat would not have been great enough.

Radioactive heating steadily subsides over millions of years as the radioactive elements inside a body decay into nonradioactive ones. Unless a moon is of extraordinary size so that its gravity can hold an atmosphere to cause erosion or unless the moon is positioned so that it experiences extensive tidal strain from its planet and fellow moons, the evolution of that satellite is almost at an end. The only changes come from occasional comet impacts[14] and from high-speed particles and ultraviolet energy from the Sun. Impacts create new craters and bury old ones. The solar wind and radiation create chemical changes in some surface materials and generally tend to darken their color.

With modest sizes, between 300 and 1,000 miles (500 to 1,600 kilometers), and in the eternal cold nearly 2 billion miles from the Sun, the moons of Uranus should have been—and were expected to be—cratered heaps that had "died" as soon as they had formed and with only a pocked faceful of scars to show for their passive existence.

But the moons of Uranus forgot to read that script and act accordingly.

Oberon

Oberon, the outermost moon, came close to fitting expectations. Here, as anticipated, were craters of all sizes, some over 60 miles (100 kilometers) in diameter, in suitable proportions to indicate that Oberon had withstood the initial cratering by large and small objects as the solar system formed about 4.6 billion years ago and had endured the continued cratering by smaller objects as the moons completed their formation around the planet.

At the horizon on Oberon was a mountain, probably the central peak of an impact crater perhaps 200 miles (300 kilometers) across, that rose

Oberon, the outermost moon of Uranus, seen in high resolution by Voyager 2.
NASA/Jet Propulsion Laboratory

to an altitude of at least 12 miles (20 kilometers)—a monstrous protrusion more than twice the height of Mount Everest on a world one-eighth the Earth's diameter. The fact that large craters were still visible everywhere on the surface indicated that nothing very much had happened on Oberon for the past 4 billion years.

But Oberon bore a warning that Uranian moons would not conform to expectations. On the floors of a few craters was smooth dark material, indicating that something had welled up from the interior, seeped onto the surface, and solidified. Such a comparatively small moon should not have experienced an interior melt.

Titania

Ostensibly, Titania was the twin of Oberon, almost identical in size, density, color, and reflectivity. Titania was a little closer to Uranus and a tiny bit bigger—1,000 miles (1,610 kilometers) in diameter to Oberon's 960 miles (1,550 kilometers). Neither was half the size of the Earth's Moon. But amid a welter of small craters on Titania were only two or three traces of large craters from the early days of the solar system. And yet Titania must have suffered at least as many large impacts as Oberon. Something had erased those large craters from the face of Titania. How had it happened to Titania but not Oberon?

And that was just the beginning of the contrast. The terrain of Titania was crisscrossed by giant cracks, some 1,000 miles (1,600 kilometers)

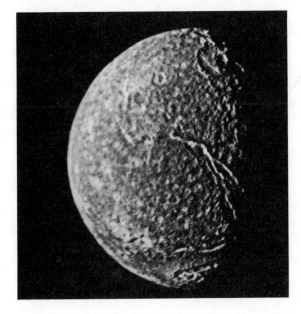

Titania, the largest moon of Uranus, seen in high resolution by *Voyager 2*. The giant cracks, as much as 3 miles deep and 1,000 miles long, expose light-colored material. *NASA/Jet Propulsion Laboratory*

long, 30 miles (50 kilometers) across, and as much as 3 miles (5 kilometers)
deep. (For comparison, the Grand Canyon on Earth is one mile deep.)
These cracks exposed lighter-colored material.

From the way features overlaid features, geologists could piece together
the evolution of Titania. Debris left over as the planets and moons formed
pummeled Oberon and Titania, but Titania was a bleeder. Soft ice oozed
forth, flooding some features. The crust softened and other features
sagged. The heat that caused this partial melting subsided and Titania
froze from the outside in. In great abundance among the chemicals that
rose toward the surface was water. Water is a most peculiar substance:
As it freezes, it expands rather than contracts. The freezing water expanded and stretched the crust until it ruptured in a network of faults,
forming steep scarps and deep grabens. Throughout this period of crustal
fracturing, additional fluids probably poured forth, covering rough terrain and then freezing smooth and hard. But what was the source of the
heat that caused the interior of Titania and perhaps, at least to some
degree, Oberon to melt?

Voyager 2 provided clues by revealing the densities of the moons. Pictures from the space probe, taken at known distances, allowed the dimensions of the major moons to be refined to greater accuracy. Tracking
Voyager 2 by its radio transmissions also allowed celestial dynamicists
to measure how much the spacecraft had been deflected by the gravity
of Oberon and Titania, so that the masses of these two largest moons
could be calculated.

With a knowledge of the mass and volume, scientists could calculate
the satellites' densities—between 1.4 and 1.7 times as great as water. Such
densities are far below those of rocky worlds such as the Earth and Moon.
But they are higher than those of the comparably sized icy moons of
Saturn, so Oberon and Titania must have proportionally more rock in
them. They are perhaps about half rock and half ice. Although the masses
and hence the densities of the other Uranian moons could not be
measured so accurately, it is likely that they have much the same composition. The greater the abundance of rock, the more radioactive
elements would have been incorporated into each moon as it formed,
and thus the greater the likelihood that these moons experienced substantial internal heating due to radioactivity.

The present surface temperatures of the satellites of Uranus are approximately −315°F (80°K). The satellites of Uranus are actually warmer than
the cloud tops of their planet because they have darker surfaces, which
absorb more energy from the Sun. To raise water to its melting point
would require a vast amount of energy. Under ordinary conditions on
Earth, water melts at 32°F (0°C; 273°K)—almost 350°F above the

temperature of the Uranian satellites. Even tidal strain together with radioactive decay cannot account for that much of a temperature difference in such small bodies that rapidly lose so much heat to space. But maybe it was not standard water ice that melted. Perhaps it was methane clathrate—water ice with occasional molecules of methane trapped in the ice crystal lattice. Such a compound melts at a significantly lower temperature, as do other similar compounds such as carbon monoxide clathrate and ammonia hydrate.[15]

Umbriel

Oberon is rather evenly cratered, without much variety to its terrain. Titania has craters but also vast systems of cracks and ice floes—a world of extensive tectonic activity in its early years. One might have expected Umbriel, still closer to Uranus, to continue this progression of increasing geological activity. But the characters of Shakespeare and Pope are capricious, and their satellite namesakes are no different. They defy orderly expectations.

Instead of showing global geologic activity, Umbriel turned out to be almost totally bland. It is the darkest of the major moons, with little variation in its color. It displays no craters with bright rays like those on Oberon and Titania, presumably formed by the relatively recent impact of comets that melted subsurface water ice and splashed the momentarily liquid water across the surface. There still is no generally favored explanation for why Umbriel is so uniformly dark and has so little evidence of tectonic activity while the moons on either side of it exhibit great geologic diversity.

Umbriel, darkest of the Uranian moons, shows craters but little geologic activity— except for two bright features near the top of this high-resolution *Voyager 2* **image. Light-colored material is visible at the bottom of a crater 50 miles in diameter and on the slope of the central peak in a nearby crater.** *NASA/Jet Propulsion Laboratory*

Yet Umbriel is not completely without contrast. There are two bright features visible. One is on the slope of the central peak of a crater. The other is a ring 50 miles (80 kilometers) in diameter that covers the floor of a different crater. From a distance this circular bright spot gives Umbriel the face of an organ grinder's monkey with its little hat on askew. This brighter material must have come from below the surface.

Since little has disturbed the primordial craters of Umbriel, perhaps the dark surface is original as well. With a diameter of only 740 miles (1,190 kilometers), Umbriel is smaller than Oberon and Titania and therefore should not have experienced internal melting and differentiation except under very unusual circumstances. Perhaps, then, the surface we see is the original crust: very dark carbon-rich rock mixed rather evenly with lighter-colored ice.

Alternatively, it may be that the deep gray surface of Umbriel is just a fairly recent coating from an unknown source that blanketed Umbriel— and Umbriel only. Titania and Ariel, the moons on either side of Umbriel, have no such dark cover.

Whether the darkness of Umbriel's surface is primordial or more recent, the bright ring on the crater floor may be evidence that a relatively recent large impact could temporarily melt enough subsurface ice to allow a significant outpouring of lighter-colored materials to the surface.

Ariel

Ariel is Umbriel's twin in size but in no other way. Umbriel is the darkest of the major Uranian moons, reflecting only 19 percent of the light that hits it. Ariel is the lightest of the moons in color, with an albedo of 40 percent. Umbriel retains one of the most heavily cratered—hence oldest—surfaces in the Uranian system. Ariel's surface is one of the least cratered—hence youngest.

So despite its size and position among the satellites of Uranus, Ariel more nearly resembles Titania than Umbriel. Yet the violence done to Ariel's surface is far beyond what Titania experienced.

Virtually all evidence of large craters and much of the evidence for smaller craters has been obliterated on Ariel. Its surface has been remolded more intensively, over a broader area, and through a longer period than Titania's.

Titania shows extensive fault systems. Ariel displays a global network of faults with rift valleys in some places 10 to 20 miles (15 to 30 kilometers) deep. Some areas on Titania have been smoothed by volcanic floes; on Ariel most of the terrain has been resurfaced by a volcanic process. But the "lava" is not molten rock like volcanoes on Earth produce. Instead it is probably a glacierlike mixture of ice and rock only moderately

Ariel has fault valleys up to 20 miles deep that extend most of the way around the moon, as revealed by *Voyager 2*.
NASA/Jet Propulsion Laboratory

warmer than the surface of Ariel. This viscous material probably flowed like a glacier too. In places, it rode up over a crater wall and stopped, forming steep scarps more than half a mile high.

As on Titania, but to a much greater extent, upwelling water (probably in clathrate form) froze and expanded, shattering the crust into systems of spectacular deep, narrow valleys. The landscape of Ariel has the look of devastation.

Where did the heat for this volcanism come from? No one knows for certain. Some of the heat came from the decay of radioactive elements; perhaps part from the gravitational compression of the moon as it formed; maybe some from the impact of debris upon its surface; and some, perhaps most, from tidal strain exerted by its neighboring moon Umbriel if the two were temporarily locked in resonant orbits in the past.

Whatever its cause, the source of this volcanic resurfacing faded away at least 3 billion years ago, leaving the gardening of the terrain to the impact of wayward comets.

Miranda

As surprising as Titania was in contrast to Oberon and as Ariel was in contrast to Umbriel, Miranda was as astonishing a single object as *Voyager* had seen in all its travels. A "brave new world," in the words of Shakespeare's Miranda. Here, helter-skelter, side by side, was almost every kind of exotic terrain in the solar system: sinuous valleys, reminiscent of those on Mars, carved by flowing water; grooves in the landscape like the faults on Jupiter's moon Ganymede; cratered highlands similar to the ancient terrain on Earth's Moon; and much more.

Miranda, innermost of the large moons of Uranus. The bright V-shaped feature (the "chevron") lies close to Miranda's south pole. The south polar regions of Uranus and its satellites were pointed sunward when *Voyager 2* flew past. The chevron lies within one of the three peculiar ovoids that *Voyager 2* discovered on Miranda.

To the left is the ridged and grooved terrain of a much larger ovoid. A third ovoid extends over the horizon to the right.
NASA/Jet Propulsion Laboratory; mosaic by Patricia M. Bridges and Jay L. Inge, U.S. Geological Survey

Voyager 2 flew by Miranda at a distance of 17,500 miles (29,000 kilometers), the closest the spacecraft had been to any of the 51 bodies it had encountered in its eight-and-a-half-year sojourn. Because of this close encounter, the *Voyager 2* mission team could take pictures of Miranda that showed detail down to 2,000 feet (less than one kilometer) across—about the size of a large football stadium. Finer detail could be seen on Miranda than at any of the *Voyagers'* other exploratory sites. And Miranda rewarded the attention amply.

There on Miranda, covering most of the visible surface, was the always-expected mix of large and small craters—indicative of the beating the little moon took after it formed. That much was as it should have been for a small moon. And that was about all there should have been.

But also there, absurdly superimposed on the rolling cratered plains, were three enormous ovoid regions, extending 125 to 200 miles (200 to 300 kilometers) across Miranda—half or more of its diameter. Within these ovoids was light and dark material arranged in ridges, grooves, and scarps, intersecting one another chaotically. There were fewer craters within the ovoids, so the ovoids were apparently a slightly more recent and more localized phenomenon than the earliest cratering. At first glance, two of the ovoids looked like a giant farmer had gone berserk plowing his fields. The third and smallest ovoid, located near the moon's south pole, exhibited a single bright V-shaped feature (dubbed the "chevron"), as if the crazed farmer had laid out an immense boomerang for defense.[16]

Yet the weirdness of Miranda did not end there. The ovoids and the rolling cratered plains were themselves cut by huge systems of fractures that circled the entire moon, creating fault valleys with steep terraced walls. One could stand at the edge of one of these cliffs and gaze down

Miranda is a medley of all the weird terrain in the solar system. Fractures up to 12 miles deep cut through the ovoids and encircle the moon.
NASA/Jet Propulsion Laboratory

Valley walls on Miranda catch the sunlight while night blankets the surrounding area, revealing how high and steep the cliffs are. Miranda is only 300 miles in diameter but has canyons more than 10 times deeper than the Grand Canyon on Earth.
NASA/Jet Propulsion Laboratory

into a canyon 6 to 12 miles (10 to 20 kilometers) deep—roughly ten times the depth of the Grand Canyon on Earth and up to three times the depth of the Mariner Valley chasm on Mars. If an astronaut in the weak gravity of Miranda jumped off a 12-mile-high cliff, he would fall for ten minutes before he hit the valley floor. It would not be a happy landing. At first he would fall slowly, but then gradually he would fall faster and faster until he reached the bottom of the chasm at a speed of 120 miles per hour (200 kilometers per hour).[17]

And just to round out this smorgasbord of a surface, Miranda displayed some evidence of floes from eruptions long ago, although not as extensively as Ariel.

"Isn't it wonderful?" said one scientist admiring Miranda. Said another: "It looks like a satellite designed by a committee."[18]

About all the geologists could agree upon was that Miranda was one of the strangest worlds yet seen. Its face was more what might have been expected from a planet or moon ten times its size. With a diameter of only 300 miles (484 kilometers), Miranda should scarcely have had enough gravity to pull its mass into a spherical shape. Yet Miranda had not been passive after its formation. Here, in the ovoids, the fractures, and the floes, was evidence that it had once had considerable internal heat, enough to let its interior at least partially differentiate.

One explanation for the erratic surface of Miranda was that the satellite was initially formed with a not completely uniform mixture of rock and ice throughout. Then internal heat allowed the start of differentiation. The heavier materials began to sink toward the center and the lighter materials began to float toward the surface, but three to four billion years ago the internal heat was fading and the moon was freezing. The lighter and brighter ice buoyed up to the surface in only a few places to form the ovoids. It was a case of arrested development. Had differentiation continued, the bright ovoid material would have covered the whole moon and smoothed all the terrain.

It is most strange indeed that geologic activity ever began on Miranda or Ariel, considering their small size. Ariel is only one-third the diameter of Earth's Moon, Miranda only one-seventh. They are too small in volume to have had enough radioactive elements to allow for even partial internal melting if their composition resembles the other bodies in the solar system. Yet the evidence of internal heat is undeniable.

Where did it come from? The most likely explanation is that much of the heating was provided by tidal strain induced by Ariel in a resonant orbit with Miranda long ago. If Miranda caught up with and passed Ariel at the same point in its orbit at regular intervals for an extended period of time, the pull on Miranda from Uranus in one direction and from Ariel in the opposite direction would have the effect of flexing the tidal budge of Miranda, creating significant frictional heat inside the body. Tidal heating is the best explanation for the volcanoes on Jupiter's Io, the cracks in the ice of Jupiter's Europa, and the floes that truncated craters on Saturn's Enceladus.

In the present age Miranda, Ariel, and Umbriel are not in tidal resonance, but they may have been at some period in the not-too-distant past. If so, the Miranda-Ariel connection may have given Miranda its haphazard terrain, and the Ariel-Umbriel resonance could have given Ariel its fractured look. Umbriel may in turn have experienced tidal strain imposed by Ariel or perhaps Titania, but Umbriel's greater distance from Uranus may have kept the strain within manageable limits, leaving the satellite with an unstretched face. Thus, despite being the same size, Umbriel and Ariel may have developed differently because they lie at different distances from Uranus.

Ten New Moons

Voyager 2 not only unveiled the five known moons of Uranus; it also discovered ten new ones, tripling the number of documented satellites for Uranus. Yet astronomers had hoped to detect at least 18 new moons.

The reason for such high expectations was the need to explain the nine narrow, sharp-edged rings of Uranus. It was reasonably easy to explain the appearance of Saturn's broad, flat disk of rings. Each particle in the rings is a separate satellite with an orbit all its own. The particles, by the billions, must occasionally collide, thereby altering their orbits. They also knock chips off one another and scatter those fragments onto unique orbits of their own. In this way, a ring of chunks steadily pulverizes itself and widens into a band of debris.

In examining the rings of Saturn over the centuries, astronomers on

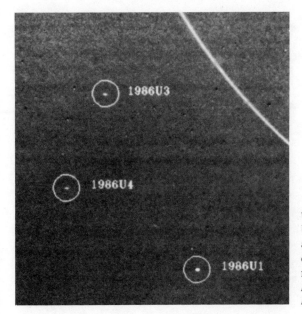

Voyager 2 discovered ten new small moons at Uranus. Three of them are circled here, lying outside the outermost ring of Uranus.
NASA/Jet Propulsion Laboratory

Earth also noticed a series of apparent gaps of a few thousand down to a few hundred miles where there were no ring particles or at least relatively few. But this too was explainable if one relied on the moons of Saturn. Each moon has its orbit. Each ring particle is a tiny moonlet with an orbit too. Imagine a ring particle named Sam with an orbital period of 7.5 hours. Saturn's moon Mimas, in a higher orbit, has a period of 22.5 hours, three times that of Sam. So every time Sam goes one and a half times around Saturn, he catches up with and passes Mimas. Each time he passes Mimas, Sam experiences a gravitational pull outward, away from Saturn. He is pulled into a slightly higher orbit. These tugs always occur at the same two points on opposite sides of Sam's orbit. The effect of these symmetrical tugs by the gravity of Mimas tends to raise Sam's orbit.

Thus Saturn's major inner moons, through their orbital resonance with particles in Saturn's rings, tend to clear out or reduce the number of particles at certain distances in the ring system.

Ring theory was in good shape until the rings of Uranus were detected. Astronomers could understand broad, flat ring systems. They could understand narrow gaps between rings. But here, revealed in the 1977 star occultation by Uranus, were extremely narrow rings with broad gaps. Astronomers tried to explain what they detected by satellite resonance. It didn't work. The moons of Uranus were too small, the gaps were too large, and the rings were too finely "sculpted."

Theoreticians went to work. Peter Goldreich and Scott Tremaine produced an intriguing answer.[19] The particles in each narrow ring were

The complete ring system of Uranus. Nine thin, dark rings had been discovered from Earth. *Voyager 2* found two more.
NASA/Jet Propulsion Laboratory

herded and kept in position by at least one and probably two moons acting as shepherds. Picture Epsilon, the brightest and outermost ring of
Uranus. Left alone, collisions would be constantly slowing some particles
in the rings so that they would fall to lower orbits. Other particles,
however, would be gaining speed by collision and would rise to higher
orbits. Inevitable and continuous collisions among the particles in the
Epsilon Ring or any ring would cause it to spread out—and rather quickly
too.

But now imagine a small moon orbiting Uranus just inside this ring
and a second small moon just outside. The closer an object is to the body
it orbits, the faster it travels. So the inner shepherd would be orbiting
faster than the ring particles. Every time it passes a ring particle, its gravity
gives that particle a little tug—a little extra speed—and that boost causes
the particle to rise to a higher orbit. The inner shepherd uses its gravitational energy to prevent scattered particles from falling inward from the
ring.

The outer shepherd moon, however, is circling more slowly than the
ring particles. Each time a ring particle passes that moon, the moon's
gravity tends to reduce its speed and it begins to fall to a lower orbit.
In this way, particles with excess speed that are rising out of the ring
are slowed and dropped back to the ring once more.

So the outer shepherd shears the outer edge of the ring and the inner
shepherd grooms the inner edge. In this way, a narrow ring can last an
extended period of time.

But the explanation is not yet complete. The conservation of angular
momentum governs both the rings and the shepherd moons. Each time
the inner shepherd adds velocity to a ring particle, the moon loses a
minute amount of energy and falls to a minutely lower orbit. Each time
the outer shepherd retards the velocity of a ring particle, it gains that
same amount of energy and rises to a minutely higher orbit. How then
do the shepherd moons stay in place to continue their ring-preservation
duties? The answer appears to be resonance with the larger, outer moons.

This was the explanation that Goldreich and Tremaine offered for the
thin rings of Uranus. Since the required shepherd moons would be too
small to detect from Earth, it would be up to *Voyager 2* to attempt to find
these moons when it arrived at Uranus in 1986.

But the confirmation of shepherd moons did not wait that long. NASA's
Pioneer 11, the first spacecraft to fly by Saturn, discovered in 1979 that
Saturn had a faint, narrow ring (now known as the F Ring). When *Voyager
1* arrived at Saturn in 1980, it found that the F Ring had a pair of shepherd
moons.

So when *Voyager 2* reached Uranus in 1986, astronomers expected to

Two shepherd moons
(marked), one on each
side of the Uranus'
largest and outermost
(Epsilon) ring, provide
the gravitational effects
that confine the par-
ticles and keep the ring
narrow. Theorists
predicted their ex-
istence; *Voyager 2*
found them for the Ep-
silon Ring but was not
able to see shepherds
for the other Uranian
moons. Perhaps they
are too small.
*NASA/Jet Propulsion
Laboratory*

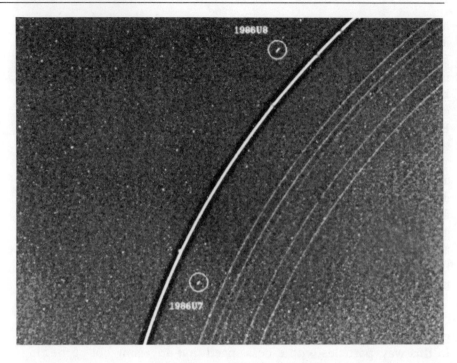

see two shepherd moons for each of the nine known rings of Uranus.

A pair of shepherd moons—about 25 to 30 miles (40 to 50 kilometers) in diameter—was discovered for the Epsilon Ring. Eight other small satellites were discovered, closer to Uranus than the major moons but all beyond the rings. They were not shepherds, and their gravities were too small to significantly affect the rings by resonance.

Where were the expected shepherds? At *Voyager 2*'s closest approach to the rings, its cameras could detect moons larger than about 12 miles (20 kilometers) in diameter, but the shepherds required by the rings of Uranus could be as small as about 10 miles (15 kilometers) in diameter. There may well be small undiscovered objects lurking in orbit around Uranus, especially pairs of shepherd moons dogging each ring, but except for the shepherds of the Epsilon Ring, careful analysis of *Voyager 2*'s full ring-survey images has not revealed them.

So Uranus, with 15 known moons, may yet have twice that number of satellites. But we probably won't know for certain until the successor to *Voyager* reaches that world of many worlds with improved imaging equipment. Unfortunately the United States has no such mission in preparation. There may be no more close-up spacecraft explorations of Uranus or Neptune in our lifetimes.

The first of the ten new moons of Uranus that *Voyager 2* discovered was detected on December 31, 1985, while *Voyager 2* was still three and a half weeks from Uranus. Pending official confirmation, the moon was unpoetically labeled 1985U1. But the mission team dubbed it Puck, raiding Shakespeare's *A Midsummer Night's Dream* once more.

Because of Puck's early detection, its substantial size, and its position closer to Uranus than the five major moons, the picture-taking schedule of *Voyager 2* was modifed to allow for one close-up image of Puck by sacrificing one picture to be taken of Miranda.

The close-up of Puck showed a dark, uneven surface about 105 miles (170 kilometers) across—a little more than one-third the diameter of Miranda. Puck was almost spherical in shape and exhibited some muted large craters. Perhaps the outlines of these comparatively large craters had been eroded over the eons by the impacts of millions of tiny particles whose craters were not visible from a distance of 320,000 miles (515,000 kilometers).

As nearly as *Voyager* could tell, the nine other new moons that it discovered were smaller versions of Puck. They had diameters ranging from about 50 miles (80 kilometers) down to 25 miles (40 kilometers). All lay closer to the planet than the major moons and Puck, and all were very dark in color, with a reflectivity less than the Earth's Moon.

The ten new moons, all much darker than the major moons, are about the same charcoal black color of the rings. The rings and these inner moonlets may therefore have the same composition and the same origin.

Some *Voyager* scientists speculate that the moonlets and ring particles are covered with methane ice whose original light color has changed chemically over the ages through exposure to high-energy protons trapped in the magnetic field of Uranus. This energy breaks down methane into carbon and hydrogen and polymerizes the carbon into long-chain hydrocarbons, black in color, dubbed "star tar" by Carl Sagan, one of the proponents of this theory.

Other *Voyager* scientists explain the dark color of the small satellites and rings as carbon compounds present from the origin of the solar system, rather than recently blackened. It is the same mixture of ice and dark carbonaceous materials that formed Uranus, says planetary scientist Robert Hamilton Brown. He calls this debate between interpretations "tar wars."

Regardless of its origin, the dark color of the moons and rings was one of *Voyager 2*'s most important findings at Uranus. Earlier in 1986, Soviet and European space probes that flew by Halley's Comet discovered that its nucleus was also extremely dark. This blackish hue suggests abundant carbon or carbon compounds, vital for life. Thus, satellites in the outer solar system and their cometary antecedents appear to be emphasizing that our solar system (and others?) formed with the right chemical elements for life to begin wherever conditions would permit.

Busted Moons and Ring Fodder

Eleven dingy rings. There isn't much to them. Prior to the *Voyager 2* flyby, nine rings of Uranus had been known since 1977 when they revealed their existence by taking turns momentarily blocking the light of a star. All were thin in dimensions and material. The Epsilon Ring, the outermost and most substantial of the eleven, varies in width from 14 to 58 miles (22 to 93 kilometers). The other rings have widths of from 0.5 to 7 miles (1 to 12 kilometers).[20] If Uranus were shrunk to the size of a golf ball, the rings would be the width of strands in a spider's web.

The rings of Uranus may be sparse and black as coal, but they are relatively free of dust. In fact, observations by *Voyager* at Uranus showed comparatively few particles smaller than beach balls or chairs. By contrast, Jupiter's ring system is by mass about 50 percent dust particles measuring about one-ten-thousandth of an inch (a few microns) in size—about the dimensions of the tiny solid grains in smoke that make it opaque. Saturn's rings have 10 times less dust than Jupiter's. And the rings of Uranus have about 100 times less dust than those of Saturn.

Voyager 2 could measure the dustiness of the rings as it passed Uranus by looking back so that the sunlight struck one side of the rings while *Voyager* observed from the other. Under this circumstance, good-sized ring chunks (a foot, a yard, a mile in size) are hard to see, but tiny solid flecks of ice the size of dust are conspicuous because they tend to scatter light forward. The effect is like what a moviegoer sees in a darkened theater as the film is projected. Looking down the projector's beam of light toward the screen, one usually sees only reflected brightness from the screen. But from the front or sides of the theater, the light's path from the projector toward the screen is obvious as it illuminates dust in the air.

So the dust in the rings of Uranus—what little there was—showed up when *Voyager 2* put the rings of Uranus between itself and the Sun. This scarcity of dust in the Uranian rings was startling. It indicated that the rings of Uranus must be evolving continuously and rapidly. The particles in any ring system must be colliding, and thereby grinding themselves down. A ring system in equilibrium must contain a sizable amount of fine dust. Jupiter's small dusty ring may be the remnant of collisions and disintegrations that have worn the chunks down to fine powder. Saturn's icy rings contain a balance of large and small fragments. At Uranus the large particles are present, but the small particles are missing. The rings of Uranus are not in collisional equilibrium. The large fragments are colliding and making dust. But something is removing dust from the rings of Uranus almost as fast as it is formed.

Voyager 2 framed the problem. *Voyager 2* found the answer. Its ultraviolet spectrometer showed that the hydrogen atmosphere of Uranus extends in a very tenuous form much farther from the planet than ex-

Past Uranus, *Voyager 2* looked back through the rings toward the Sun. The image revealed dust particles, although far fewer than in the rings of Jupiter and Saturn. Since ring particles continue to form dust by collisions, the dust must be falling into the atmosphere of Uranus. The ring system of Uranus is eroding rapidly.
NASA/Jet Propulsion Laboratory

pected, all the way out through the rings. The cause of this bloated atmosphere was assigned to the phenomenon that creates dayglow. In that process, hydrogen atoms are slowly but steadily escaping from Uranus, and as they do they provide sufficient density to exert a significant drag on the dust particles in the rings. The dust particles are steadily slowed and fall to ever-lower orbits until they disappear from the ring system and vanish into the shroud of gases in the atmosphere of Uranus.

The entire Uranian ring system is rapidly eroding.

Far from Uranus, where Oberon lies, there is little evidence that anything much has happened geologically since the intense meteoroid bombardment of the solar system's early days. Closer to Uranus, Ariel and Miranda are smaller worlds with extended geologic activity written on their faces. Still closer to Uranus are the ten new moons, all tiny by comparison and, to judge by the largest one, all thoroughly battered. Still closer than the moons is the Epsilon Ring, the densest, widest, and brightest of the rings, with two of the newly found ten moons serving as shepherds. And still closer are the remaining ten rings, composed of chunky debris.

But why should the moons of Uranus show evidence of greater, longer, and more disruptive geologic activity the closer to the planet they lie?

The internal heat from the decay of radioactive elements and gravitational compression necessary to melt the interior and remold the surface ought to be greatest in the largest moons. Yet Oberon and Titania are the two outermost and do not show the greatest geologic activity. Instead, the most profound geologic upheaval has occurred on Ariel and Miranda, the two innermost and smallest of the five major moons. Tidal strain induced by Uranus and neighboring moons in resonant orbits may well have been a principal cause. But another factor may have contributed as well.

Miranda and Ariel were battered more severely by impacts than the others, says the hypothesis, for the very reason that they lie closer to Uranus. The debris orbiting the Sun left over from planet accretion was diverted in its course by the enormous mass of Uranus so that it passed closer to the planet, creating a region around Uranus where the density of flying junk was higher and the chances of a moon getting hit were greater. Uranus gravitationally focused a hail of debris on itself and its satellites, especially the innermost ones.

Judging from the ancient face of Oberon and by invoking the concept of gravitational focusing by which Uranus hurled planetesimals upon its huddled satellites, the *Voyager 2* imaging team estimated that, compared to Oberon, Ariel would have received 5 times as many impact craters and Miranda 14 times as many. Uranus was guilty of child abuse.

But how does anyone know about the frequency of cratering events in the Uranian system? The process begins with an estimation of the number of comets passing nearby.

Comets are essentially dirty snowballs, made mostly of water ice with flecks of dust mixed in. The solid nucleus of a typical comet is about 5 to 10 miles (8 to 15 kilometers) in diameter. Based on the orbits of comets observed from Earth, Dutch astronomer Jan H. Oort established in 1950 that all known comets were members of our solar system, held captive by the gravity of the Sun, and not itinerants from outer space just passing through our solar system. Therefore, said Oort, to account for the steady trickle of comets that pass close enough to the Sun for us to see, our planetary system must be surrounded by a sphere of comets, starting beyond Neptune and Pluto and extending halfway to the nearest star—out to a distance of about two light-years.[21] In this realm, called the Oort Cloud, there must be, according to recent estimates, trillions of comets remaining today, even after 4.6 billion years of attrition.

The comets in the Oort Cloud lie at such distances that we cannot detect them from Earth. They travel in such remote orbits that we would never see any of them except that, every once in a very long while, the Sun, dragging its family of planets and satellites along, passes in the vicinity of another star. When that happens, depending on which directions the star and comets are going, the gravity of the passing star accelerates millions of comets and they escape from our solar system forever. But the passing star also decelerates millions of other comets, and they begin a long fall that will carry them over a period of many centuries closer to the Sun on new orbits. Most of those falling millions never get as close to the Sun as is Pluto or Neptune. But the few that do enter the planetary realm of the solar system and penetrate deeply to within Mars' or Jupiter's distance from the Sun show us by their orbits that they are gravitational members of our Sun's family and have come our way from the outer limits of our Sun's gravitational control.

Based on the comets we detect and on statistical probability, for every comet whose orbit starts outbound again at about the distance of Jupiter, there should be twice as many comets that venture no closer to the Sun than Saturn and four times as many that approach no closer than Uranus.

Comets are small in size, so their paths are easily disturbed by the gravity of the giant planets. These perturbations hurl some comets out of the solar system. Other comets will be slowed so that they cannot return to the Oort Cloud. Instead they are trapped, at least temporarily, on elliptical orbits relatively close to the Sun. Before, they had orbital periods of thousands or millions of years. They were long-period comets. Now they are short-period comets, with periods of 200 years or less.

Because the gravity of Uranus usually gets a crack at an inbound long-period comet before Saturn or Jupiter do, many more comets are expected to show orbital evidence of a gravitational encounter with Uranus than with Saturn or Jupiter despite their far greater masses. Some comets have been diverted so that they never venture much farther from the Sun than Jupiter. They are said to be the Jupiter family of comets. So too there are families of comets with aphelia at about the distances of Saturn and Uranus. But because far more comets reach inward only as far as Uranus rather than Saturn or Jupiter and because Uranus gets the first chance to gravitationally disturb all that do, some astronomers estimate that Uranus has a harem of short-term comets 100 times more numerous than Saturn and 600 to 700 times more numerous than Jupiter.

Uranus finds itself constantly in the midst of a snowball fight with iceballs the size of Earth mountains or larger. There are probably a million short-period comets that frequently pass near Uranus.[22] Over time, Uranus and its satellites stand a good chance of getting hit. Uranus faces a larger army of assassins than Jupiter or Saturn, but it has a larger area of space in which to hide and less gravity to draw trouble its way. Jupiter and Saturn may face fewer prowling assassins, but they have smaller orbits along which to scurry to escape a hit and more gravity to focus comet attention toward them. The result is that the number of impacts in the Jovian, Saturnian, and Uranian systems evens out. A square mile on Uranus and its satellites may be expected to be blasted with about the same frequency as a square mile on Jupiter, Saturn, and their satellites.

The frequency of comet cratering can be estimated well enough, comet specialists believe, so that when estimates of comet damage are compared with the observed damage to the moons of the giant planets, conclusions may be drawn. Oberon and Umbriel show too many craters, especially large ones, to have been cratered only by comets. They are survivors of at least most of the earliest formative events at Uranus.

The ten newly found inner satellites of Uranus might well be fragments from moons that shattered about 3 billion years ago. The rings of Uranus are most likely fragments from the ongoing demolition of its satellites. If all the material in the Uranian rings could be scooped up and packed into one large rocky iceball, it would form a body only 18 miles (30 kilometers) in diameter, smaller than any moon yet discovered at Uranus. By comparison, the particles in Saturn's ring system would form a body 180 miles (300 kilometers) in diameter.[23] The rings of Saturn contain a thousand times more mass than the rings of Uranus.

The Price-to-Learning Ratio

Long before *Voyager 2*'s data could be fully analyzed and its discoveries thoroughly appreciated, Uranus was a starlike dot far behind the spacecraft, which was already preparing for its next and final port of call.

From launch through the encounter with Uranus, *Voyager 2* had cost each American $2. It was a remarkable return on an investment.

CHAPTER 10

Appointment with Neptune

"The real heroes are the engineers at JPL who built the wonderful spacecraft that have lasted so long and performed so well."
Theoretician Scott Tremaine
(1988)

"For a spacecraft designed and built back in the days when hand-held calculators were first being marketed, the Voyagers *have been remarkably responsive to the science and engineering demands placed on them."*
Ellis D. Miner, Assistant Project Scientist for *Voyager*
(1986)

Because of its great distance, it has been hard to pry secrets from Neptune. It is about the same size as Uranus but more than half again as far away, so it is about ten times fainter and offers even less of a disk upon which detail might be discerned. One large moon, Triton, was found soon after Neptune was discovered, but a century passed before a second moon, Nereid, was found in 1949.

Neptune moves so slowly in its distant orbit that, since its discovery in 1846, it has not yet had time to complete one revolution around the Sun. That event won't occur until 2011.

For *Voyager 2*, Neptune was a staggering challenge because it stood last in a line of *ifs. If Voyager 2* survived, collected data, and achieved the proper gravitational assist at Jupiter; *if* . . . at Saturn; *if* . . . at Uranus. Each flyby placed its own special demands on the spacecraft's trajectory, and the demands restricted its flight path at the next planet.

If scientific success at Uranus were to match the *Voyagers'* triumphs at Jupiter and Saturn, the researchers needed the spacecraft to pass close to the planet; penetrate deeply into the planet's suspected magnetic field; sail close by the planet's innermost major moon, Miranda; and then swing behind the planet and its rings so that the scientists could use the radio transmission of *Voyager* passing through the planet's ring system and atmosphere to reveal its structure and composition.

Voyager 2's flight by Uranus was also tightly constrained by the spacecraft's need to use the planet for a gravity assist to reach Neptune. But for *Voyager 2* to get just to the vicinity of Neptune was not enough. Researchers wanted a full-fledged scientific investigation, which meant, of course, flying close to the planet, plunging deep into its magnetosphere, and beaming radio signals through its rings (if there were any) and atmosphere. It meant, as well, passing close to Neptune's largest moon, Triton, and flying behind Triton so that *Voyager*'s radio signals could pass through the moon's atmosphere to indicate its structure and composition.

It was hard enough to meet the objectives at Uranus even if one could neglect the gravitational-assist requirements to divert the craft on to Neptune on a precise billion-mile course. To meet all the objectives at both Uranus and Neptune was a lot to ask of one single flight path.

Yet such a flight path was found. It would carry *Voyager 2* only 3,000 miles (4,900 kilometers) above the cloud tops at Neptune's north pole, then behind the planet, and then on past the moon Triton at an altitude of only 25,000 miles (40,000 kilometers).[1] With utmost skill and care, *Voyager 2* could even avoid colliding with the planet, its partial rings, and its moons. It would be the closest planetary flyby in the *Voyager* program. To make it work, *Voyager 2* at Uranus had to hit a point in space at a point in time with phenomenal accuracy. To miss "corridor center" at Uranus by a mile would create an error of 4,000 miles at Neptune. A small miss at Uranus could be corrected later by using the spacecraft's thrusters to adjust speed and direction, but such a maneuver was limited by the fuel remaining.

The accuracy required of the spacecraft navigators at Uranus to place *Voyager 2* on its unique trajectory for Neptune, said Charles Kohlhase, *Voyager* mission planning manager, was a feat comparable to a golfer sinking a thousand-mile putt.

The celestial golfers holed out. When the mission team determined that *Voyager 2* was headed down the corridor only 6 miles (10 kilometers) off center, they canceled the final midcourse correction.

As *Voyager 2* passed 50,700 miles (81,600 kilometers) above the cloud tops of Uranus on January 24, 1986, the gravity of the planet bent the spacecraft's trajectory by 23 degrees and increased its velocity by almost 4,500 miles per hour (2 kilometers per second). *Voyager 2* was on course to Neptune. A billion miles and three and a half years of travel lay ahead.

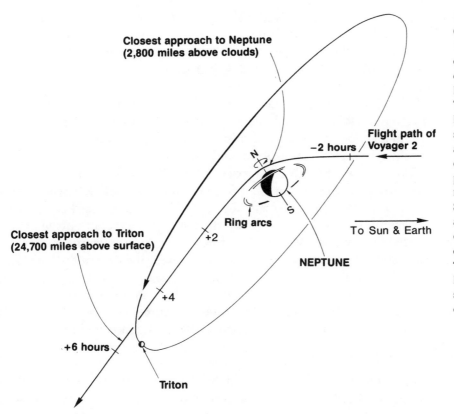

Closest approach to Neptune
(2,800 miles above clouds)

Flight path of Voyager 2

−2 hours

Ring arcs

To Sun & Earth

NEPTUNE

Closest approach to Triton
(24,700 miles above surface)

+2

+4

+6 hours

Triton

Voyager 2 at Neptune. On August 24–25, 1989, *Voyager 2* flew outside the ring arcs, over the north pole of Neptune, then on past Triton. Triton is the only large moon in the solar system to travel around its planet in the direction opposite to its planet's spin and revolution around the Sun. Triton's orbit is also inclined 23 degrees to Neptune's equator. After passing Triton, *Voyager 2* was headed out of the solar system in a southerly direction.

The New Challenge for *Voyager 2*

Hiding near the planetary fringe of our solar system, a billion miles (1.6 billion kilometers) farther out than Uranus, Neptune is about four times too dim ever to be seen with unaided eyes. At a distance from Earth of 2.8 billion miles (4.5 billion kilometers), Neptune presents a disk only 2.3 arc seconds across, so discerning features on the planet is like seeing details on a dime a mile away.

Because it is 30 times more distant from the Sun than is Earth, Neptune receives 900 times less sunlight than our planet and 2.5 times less than Uranus. The Sun in the skies of Earth is a disk measuring about half a degree (30 arc minutes) across. From Neptune the Sun is only one arc minute in diameter—the size of a quarter seen across the length of a football field. Yet the Sun in the sky of Neptune is still about a thousand times brighter than the full Moon in our nighttime sky. Even so, the light levels at Neptune are low—the equivalent of twilight about ten minutes after sundown on a clear day on Earth.[2]

Voyager 2 had three successful planetary encounters behind it, but Neptune posed a new set of obstacles. First, the spacecraft would have to survive the three and a half years of flight between Uranus and Neptune. Second, because of Neptune's greater distance from the Sun, *Voyager 2* would have to take pictures at still-lower light levels. Third, because close approaches to Neptune and Triton were scientifically desirable, the speed of the spacecraft would be greater and the hazard of smeared pictures increased. Finally, the increased distance would make radio communication with the spacecraft even more difficult. At a range of 2.8 billion miles (4.5 billion kilometers), instructions radioed to the spacecraft would take four hours and six minutes to arrive, and the data requested would take another four hours and six minutes to reach the Earth.

The logistics of Earth's first spacecraft to visit Neptune put exceptional pressure on the one remaining crippled onboard radio receiver and on the fault detection and correction systems of the onboard computers. It also put enormous pressure on the team of spacecraft navigators on Earth who, by using *Voyager 2* pictures of the Neptunian moons against their starry backgrounds, would have to determine the craft's exact location, perhaps modify its speed and angle of approach slightly as remaining fuel would permit, and update the craft about the changed target times and angles for the cameras and other instruments.

In the three and a half years between the Uranus and Neptune encounters, improvements to *Voyager 2* and to the communication system on Earth continued. The objective was to get from *Voyager 2* the same quality pictures and the same rate of data transmission from Neptune as had been achieved at Uranus despite the 57 percent greater distance, which more than doubled the problems of transmission and reception. In the perpetual twilight so far from the Sun, *Voyager*'s television cameras would require longer exposures to form pictures. The longest possible time exposure at Uranus without using the tape recorder had been 15 seconds. For Neptune, due to computer reprogramming, the longest exposure time without using the tape recorder could now be several hours.

Voyager 2 was now even steadier as a camera and instrument platform than it had been at Uranus. By firing the thrusters in bursts of only five thousandths of a second to correct its aim, the spacecraft at Uranus was twice as steady as it had been at Saturn. At Neptune, the thrusters would fire in four-millisecond bursts for a further increase in camera-pointing stability of about 20 percent.

Even so, flying close to Triton's expected landscape of features at high speed would lead to blurred pictures, so the *Voyager* scientists and engineers improved target-motion compensation (panning the spacecraft to follow the action) with nodding image motion compensation. Using small thruster bursts, *Voyager* could turn slightly to take a picture, then close its camera shutter and swing back to point its antenna at Earth so that the picture could be transmitted immediately without being stored on the tape recorder. The craft would then nod back to its target to resume picture taking.

But it was not enough just to make improvements to a 12-year-old spacecraft built with early 1970s technology on an extended mission 2 billion miles (3 billion kilometers) and eight years beyond mission requirements. Improvements were made to facilities on Earth as well.

Voyager 2 could not increase its radio-transmitting power, so NASA increased the receiving power on antennae on Earth. At Goldstone, California; Madrid, Spain; and Canberra, Australia, are the tracking stations of NASA's Deep Space Network. When *Voyager 2* flew by Uranus in 1986, each had a steerable radio receiving dish 210 feet (64 meters) in diameter. For the Neptune encounter, NASA enlarged those dishes to 230-foot (70-meter) receivers, increasing reception by about 20 percent. Other modifications to reduce background noise provided the big dishes with a total improvement in receptivity of about 50 percent.

In addition, arrangements were made so that the Goldstone, California, dish would be assisted by the Very Large Array radio-telescope facility in Socorro, New Mexico. The VLA is a system of 27 movable dishes each 82 feet (25 meters) in diameter. The Goldstone and VLA receivers would be linked together to more than double their receiving power to catch the one-tenth of a billionth of a millionth of a watt reaching the array from *Voyager 2* at Neptune. A modern electronic digital watch operates on 20 billion times more power. Help for NASA's Canberra, Australia, dish would come from Australia's 210-foot (64-meter) Parkes Radio Telescope and, when *Voyager 2* passed beyond Neptune and Triton, from the 210-foot (64-meter) dish of Japan's Usuda space-tracking station.

Target Neptune

Uranus and Neptune, said the astronomy textbooks prior to the *Voyager* flyby, are pretty much twins. And so they are in size, in mass, in atmosphere, and in color. It was their similarities that provided a basic set of expectations about what *Voyager 2* would find at Neptune.

Uranus is a little larger in diameter, but Neptune has a slightly greater mass. Both have thick atmospheres composed overwhelmingly of hydrogen and helium flavored with small quantities of other gases, including methane. It is the methane that gives both Uranus and Neptune their blue-green color by absorbing the red wavelengths of sunlight.

But there are also differences—and significant ones.

Uranus and Neptune are similar in size and mass, but because Neptune is smaller in diameter and yet greater in mass, it has a considerably higher density. That density was expected to enhance Neptune's magnetic field and internal heat.

Neptune and Triton (marked by arrow) as seen from Earth with the 120-inch telescope of the Lick Observatory
Lick Observatory photograph

Unlike capsized Uranus, Neptune stands relatively upright as it revolves around the Sun. There is some axial tilt—29 degrees—very similar to the Earth's 23.5 degrees. Unlike Uranus, there is never any sunlight beaming down almost vertically on the Neptunian poles.

When it became possible to sample wavelengths beyond the optical light coming from Neptune, astronomers discovered that the total amount of energy radiating from Neptune was greater than the energy it was receiving from the Sun. The excess energy was in the form of heat and radio waves. Jupiter and Saturn emit about twice as much energy as they receive from the Sun due to heat from their interiors. Uranus emits more energy that it receives, but just barely. At Neptune, at least half of the energy flowing from the planet was from internal heat. It was radiating two to two and a half times more energy than it received. It was not thought that Neptune was particularly warmhearted. It was just that it received so little energy from the Sun that it was easier to detect the planet's own emission. Neptune's internal heat production was thought to be roughly comparable to that of Uranus. The behavior of *Voyager 2* deep in the gravitational and magnetic fields of Neptune would provide new information about the planet's interior structure, which could clarify the source of this internal energy.

And, perhaps because of its greater interior heat, Neptune, unlike Uranus, showed cloud features that were visible from Earth. It was a struggle to see them, but they were there. Jupiter's clouds are exceptionally distinct and colorful. Saturn's clouds are shrouded by haze but still show considerable variation in hues. Ground-based observers occasionally claimed to see features in the atmosphere of Uranus, but they could not be confirmed by most astronomers. When *Voyager 2* arrived at Uranus, its pictures in visible light showed an essentially featureless atmosphere. Only intensive computer enhancement of contrast showed a very modest array of details undiscernible by the unaided eye from the rest of the atmospheric background.

Based on the progression toward weaker atmospheric detail from Jupiter to Saturn to Uranus, one might have expected no cloud details on the colder Neptune. But Neptune didn't care about expectations.

The discovery of cloud details on Neptune was made possible by a new imaging technology called the charge-coupled device (CCD). Soon after its invention in 1969, the CCD began to outperform photographic film, which had been the picture-taking backbone of astronomy for a hundred years. CCDs are small silicon chips divided into many rows and columns. Photons striking each tiny sensitive spot trigger a buildup of electrical charge in proportion to the number of photons received. By measuring the charge at each site, a picture can be constructed. In this way CCDs serve as the heart of supersensitive television cameras. Using CCDs with Earth-based telescopes, astronomers detected on Neptune bright high-altitude clouds that formed and vanished—and provided a means of estimating the rotation of the atmosphere of Neptune at different latitudes.

As on Uranus, the length of a day on Neptune had been hard to measure and was highly uncertain. As a gas giant planet, Neptune was expected to rotate faster than rocky midgets like Earth. As a small gas giant like Uranus, Neptune was expected to rotate slower than the larger gas giants, Jupiter and Saturn. Neptune showed a modest equatorial bulge, which suggested a rotational period as fast as 15 hours.

The extent of the equatorial bulge on Neptune was determined from the planet's occasional occultations of stars. Those same occultations allowed the diameter of Neptune to be measured with respectable accuracy: 30,800 miles (49,600 kilometers).

The determination of Neptune's rotation by spectroscopy and photometry had left considerable uncertainties. Spectroscopy measured how fast Neptune's western limb was rotating toward the Earth and how fast the eastern limb was turning away. Together with the exact diameter of Neptune, these speeds could furnish a reasonable calculation of the rotation of Neptune (or at least its atmosphere).

Photometry measured variations in the light reflected from Neptune so that if it had a long-lived atmospheric feature like Jupiter's Great Red Spot, its appearance and disappearance as the planet turned could reveal

This photograph of Neptune, taken by Heidi B. Hammel with the University of Hawaii's 88-inch telescope on Maura Kea in 1986, was the best ground-based image of Neptune of its time. It showed clouds (bright spots) in Neptune's

southern hemisphere. From these features, Hammel determined the rotation period for Neptune (or at least the atmosphere at that latitude) to be 17 hours.
Courtesy of Heidi B. Hammel, Mauna Kea Observatory

Neptune's rotational period. One photometric measurement suggested that Neptune rotated in 17 hours 43 minutes.[3]

Finally, in 1979, the first cloud features on Neptune were distinguished. Subsequent observations have refined the rotation period of Neptune (or at least its clouds) to about 17 hours.[4]

The Search for Rings at Neptune

With the discovery of the ring systems of Uranus and Jupiter, most astronomers suspected that Neptune would have rings also. Were they so faint, like those of Jupiter, that evidence of their existence would have to await a visit from *Voyager*, or were they substantial enough, like those of Uranus, to be detected from Earth when they occulted a distant star?

Such occultations, however, are much rarer for Neptune than Uranus for two reasons. First, although the two planets are about the same size, Neptune is much farther away from Earth and therefore offers a much smaller apparent disk to eclipse a star. An occultation by Neptune happens only about once a year.

Second, the axial tilt of Uranus helps the chances that its rings will occult a star, while Neptune's tilt does not. Planetary rings lie around their planet's equator. So, in the case of Uranus, for about half of its 84-year orbit, the rings present themselves face on to Earth, increasing the zone in the sky where a stellar occultation can take place. But Neptune stands closer to vertical in its orbit and thus its equatorial rings appear more nearly edge on, reducing the area of the sky they cover and hence the chance they will occult a star.

In 1981, Neptune nearly eclipsed a star, and a team of astronomers was watching intently. The star blinked once as Neptune approached but did not blink again after Neptune glided by. The astronomers announced a probable new moon of Neptune, but they weren't too confident. It wasn't a ring, they reckoned, because a ring would have occulted the star inbound and outbound. Yet for a moon, a very tiny dot, to partially occult a star was exceedingly improbable. Still, there are a lot of stars and such events must happen sometime. And something had indeed happened. But the suspected moon could not be seen directly.[5]

The search for a ring system continued. Neptune occulted a star in 1983 with many astronomers in attendance. No evidence of a ring or third moon was found.

Interested in the problem, an astronomer at the University of Paris, André Brahic, asked for telescope time on July 22, 1984, at the European Southern Observatory on Cerro La Silla, Chile, when Neptune was scheduled to nearly occult another star. His request was denied. But he drew attention to the event and prevailed upon some colleagues who had been assigned to the 40-inch (1-meter) telescope that night to take a break from their research and watch Neptune as it passed the star. There was a flicker before Neptune reached the star—but no flicker as Neptune moved away. The event had lasted about one second. The star's light had been dimmed 35 percent. It was as if there was a ring at Neptune but one that extended only part way around the planet—a partial ring, an arc.

Because of the attention Brahic called to the event, another team of astronomers was also at work that night using the passage of Neptune near the star to search for a ring. This team was only 60 miles (100 kilometers) south of Cerro La Silla, at the Cerro Tololo Inter-American Observatory. Their 36-inch (0.9-meter) telescope carried a sensitive photometer that continuously recorded the light levels on magnetic tape.

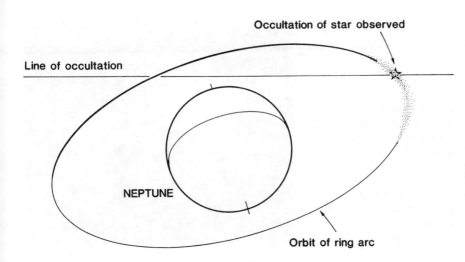

Occultation of star observed

Line of occultation

NEPTUNE

Orbit of ring arc

The "arc ring" system of Neptune was discovered in 1984 when Neptune passed near but not in front of a star. Yet the star was briefly occulted on one side of Neptune but not the other. Astronomers concluded that a thin ring was present but that it extended only part way around Neptune—a ring arc.

For quick reference, it also printed the average light level every 3.4 and 5.0 seconds. The occultation had lasted only about one second. The samples printed by the computer had so nearly averaged out the event that it went undetected.[6] But when the team leader, William B. Hubbard of the University of Arizona, heard about Brahic's positive occultation results at a conference that October, he reexamined the full record of the observation on his magnetic tape, which showed light-level readings every one-hundredth second. The occultation was real and agreed in every detail with the event seen at the European Southern Observatory. And because the same event had been seen by two observing teams at different sites, the occulting object could not be a moon. To partially block the same star simultaneously from slightly different angles would have required no less than two moons positioned for simultaneous grazing occultations with preposterous accuracy. The likelihood of such a coincidence was vanishingly small.

But a partial occultation seen from two sites could be explained by a short narrow stream of debris circling Neptune. Based on the length of the occultation, the ring arc was estimated to be about 15 miles (25 kilometers) across and 100 miles (160 kilometers) long. It was 41,500 miles (67,000 kilometers) from the center of Neptune. At 2.65 Neptune radii from the planet's center, this ring arc was near but beyond the planet's Roche Limit, the distance from a planet within which a large body cannot form due to tidal forces exerted on it by the planet. Because this ring arc lay beyond the Roche Limit for Neptune, the arc was attributed to the breakup of a moon rather than primordial material that could not form into a moon.

Based on the number of searches for a ring that found nothing, Hub-

Artist Paul DiMare pictures a ring system composed of large dark particles and little dust or ice. *Voyager 2* found such a ring system at Uranus. Will the arc rings of Neptune look like this?
© *Paul DiMare*

bard, Brahic, and their collaborators estimated that the ring arc must envelop only about 10 percent of the planet.[7]

The discovery of an arc ring at Neptune provided continued stimulation for occultation observations at every opportunity. Approximately one-quarter of those experiments produced readings that were interpreted as ring fragments, but according to researcher Philip D. Nicholson, only three results were absolutely convincing—and they yielded three separate arc rings at different distances from Neptune. So, as *Voyager 2* approached, there appeared to be at least three arc rings, and perhaps dozens. None of the three best-established arc rings had been seen more than once. The first and outermost to be discovered lay 26,500 miles (42,700 kilometers) above the cloud tops of Neptune. The distances of the inner arcs were highly uncertain.

It was another hard-won victory to wrest information from a tiny blue-green dot almost 3 billion miles (4.8 billion kilometers) away.

But how had partial rings come to be, and how could they persist? The particles closer to Neptune must revolve faster, tending to spread the arc's inner boundary forward along its orbit. The particles farther from Neptune must revolve more slowly, tending to spread the arc's outer boundary backward along the orbit. Jack Lissauer calculated that rotational shearing would spread the particles of the arc into a full ring in less than three years. So what was preventing the arc or arcs from forming a full ring?

Several theoreticians attempted to explain how an arc ring system could last millions of years, perhaps since the formation of the solar system.[8]

Peter Goldreich, Scott Tremaine, and Nicole Borderies offered a mechanism by which one shepherd moon could by resonances stabilize a series of arc rings if the moon's orbit was circular but slightly inclined to the arc ring plane. The mechanism was analogous to the moons Janus and Epimetheus in the Saturn system, which occupy almost precisely the same orbit. As Epimetheus, the smaller of the two, catches up with its companion, it is accelerated by the gravity of Janus and begins to ascend to a slightly higher orbit. As it rises, its orbital velocity declines and it begins to fall behind. In this way Epimetheus never passes and never quite catches up with Janus.

As Epimetheus falls behind, Janus gradually, over a period of years, begins to approach it from behind. The entire process repeats itself, this time with Janus falling behind and Epimetheus gradually catching up. In this way Janus and Epimetheus oscillate closer and farther from one another along the orbit they share.

This same process, said Goldreich, Tremaine, and Borderies, was probably at work in the Neptunian system, except that Epimetheus was replaced by a swarm of particles. Each particle in the arc rings would behave like a tiny moon and exhibit the same kind of oscillation as Epimetheus, catching up with and falling behind its coorbiting moon, which thus acted as shepherd. Astronomers had not yet seen that shepherd moon in the Neptunian system, but perhaps *Voyager 2* would.

Depending on its size, this coorbital shepherd would be able to explain not only a ring arc or arcs at about its own distance from Neptune but also, by resonance, a large number of arc rings at different distances.

According to their calculations, these arc rings would be stable for billions of years, so the partial rings could have been in place since about the time that Neptune formed.

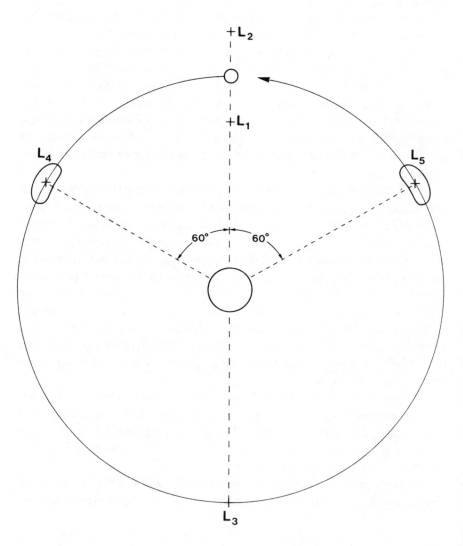

Lagrangian Points. For any two bodies revolving around one another, there are five precise positions where the gravity of the two bodies and centrifugal force will allow small objects to remain. Only the L4 and L5 points are truly stable, however, for small objects disturbed from those points will oscillate near those positions and not fall toward either body.

A different method of sustaining Neptune's peculiar ring arc system was proposed by Jack Lissauer using a fascinating arrangement of shepherd moons. To explain how the arc particles stayed together in a clump along their orbit, Lissauer took his cue from Jupiter. As Jupiter revolves around the Sun, two families of asteroids travel with it in its orbit, one 60 degrees ahead of Jupiter and another 60 degrees behind. These minor planet families of Jupiter are called the Trojan asteroids, and their orbital curiosity was first explained by the Italian-French mathematician Joseph Louis Lagrange in 1772, more than a century before asteroids began to be discovered at the Lagrangian Points.

At these positions the gravity of Jupiter and the gravity of the Sun balance in such a way that particles and moonlets located there remain equidistant from the Sun and Jupiter with stable orbits. Three other gravitationally balanced positions also exist for any body and its orbiting satellite. But of the five, only two provide stable orbits: those that lie along the satellite's orbit and precede and trail it by 60 degrees. The preceding Lagrangian Point is designated L4; the trailer L5.

At Jupiter, the Sun and planet combine to produce gravitationally stable positions for the Trojan asteroids. Lissauer used that scenario for Neptune with the substitution of the ring arc for the Trojan asteroids and

LAGRANGIAN POINTS

In 1772 mathematician Joseph Louis Lagrange discovered a peculiar consequence of the law of gravity when applied to two bodies orbiting one another, such as Jupiter and the Sun. According to his calculations, there would be two positions along the orbit of Jupiter 60 degrees ahead and 60 degrees behind the planet where the gravity of Jupiter and the Sun would cause small objects near those sites to oscillate without falling toward Jupiter or the Sun.

In 1904, 132 years later, asteroids began to be found at those positions, called the Lagrangian Points.

There are a total of five Lagrangian Points for any two bodies revolving around one another. The other three lie along a line connecting the two bodies, as shown in the diagram. These points, however, are not stable for small objects because if the objects are disturbed even slightly from those positions (by the Sun or another planet), they will wander away and not return.

No asteroids have been found at the Lagrangian Points in the Earth-Sun or Earth-Moon systems, but there have been reports of particles detected at the orbital positions 60 degrees ahead (L4) and 60 degrees behind (L5) each of the smaller bodies.

No asteroids have been found at the Lagrangian Points in the Saturn-Sun system either, but the gravities of Saturn and its modest-size moon Tethys work together to hold two moons at Lagrangian Points along Tethys' orbit. Calypso occupies the L4 position and Telesto follows at L5. Both Lagrangian moons are about 15 miles (25 kilometers) in diameter.

Saturn appears to delight in Lagrangian possibilities. The ring-master and its moon Dione combine gravitational forces to hold Helene (about 20 miles in diameter) at Dione's L4 point.

the substitution of Neptune and an undiscovered moon for the Sun and Jupiter. He suggested that the undiscovered moon was 60 degrees behind the arc ring (which would place the arc ring in the L4 position). To accomplish its gravitational duties, this Lagrangian shepherd would have to be about 125 miles (200 kilometers) in diameter—a candidate for *Voyager 2* discovery because it is too small to be seen from Earth.

The Lagrangian shepherd would keep the arc ring particles from spreading out along their orbit around Neptune but would not control the spread of the particles outward and inward into a wide band due to collisions that would accelerate some into higher orbits and decelerate others into lower orbits. Eventually these collisions would propel particles far enough from the stable Lagrangian Points so that the arc rings would be extremely tenuous. So at least one more shepherd moon was necessary to control the radial spread of the arc. Like the shepherds for the full rings at the other gas giants, this shepherd could orbit inside or outside the arc ring. There could be an inner shepherd, an outer shepherd, or both.

Lissauer was forecasting that this shepherd would lie inward of the ring where its greater orbital velocity would cause it periodically to catch up with and pass the arc ring particles and accelerate descending (closer) ones slightly so that they would climb back into the arc ring clump and not decay into Neptune. There was no way to know the size of this shepherd because the required mass would vary according to how far its orbit was from the partial ring. It was probably between 60 and 125 miles (100 and 200 kilometers) in diameter. A shepherd orbiting 600 miles (1,000 kilometers) below the orbit of the arc ring, said Lissauer, would need to be about 75 miles (120 kilometers) in diameter.

Which model, if either, was correct? Lissauer felt that the Goldreich-Tremaine-Borderies hypothesis deserved to be favored because it was more economical in the number of moons it required.[9] Each ring arc in Lissauer's system would be stabilized by two or three shepherd moons, whereas in the Goldreich-Tremaine-Borderies explanation one moon would suffice to stabilize one or many arcs. If *Voyager 2* could photograph the expected shepherd moon or moons of Neptune in or near the arc ring system, it would be possible to settle this question.

Scientists were also anxious to see if *Voyager 2* could photograph the ring arcs themselves. It wouldn't be easy. As measured from their brief occultations of stars, the arcs were certainly very narrow, like the rings of Uranus, and probably very dark as well. With its ability to make closeup pictures and to provide its own radio occultation experiment, it was hoped that *Voyager 2* might reveal the number and structure of Neptune's curious ring fragments and the size and nature of the particles that compose them.

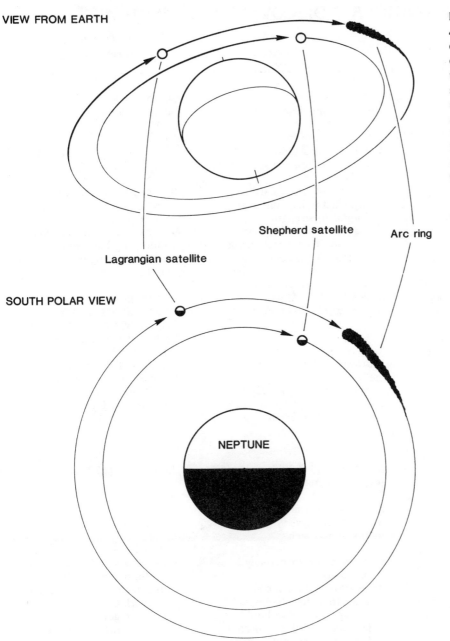

VIEW FROM EARTH

Lagrangian satellite

Shepherd satellite

Arc ring

SOUTH POLAR VIEW

NEPTUNE

In the hypothesis by Jack J. Lissauer, each of Neptune's arc rings could be maintained by the teamwork of two shepherd moons unseen from Earth. The arcs would lie at the leading or trailing Lagrangian Points of one moon that would keep the fragments bunched up along their orbit. A second moon inside or outside the ring-arc orbit would keep the fragments from spreading inward or outward.

Sixteen moons had been confirmed for Jupiter. Seventeen for Saturn. Fifteen for Uranus. But only two moons were known to exist at Neptune.

Triton was discovered by the English brewer and amateur astronomer William Lassell soon after Neptune was found and was named ap-

The Moons of Neptune

SCORECARD FOR *VOYAGER 2* DISCOVERIES AT NEPTUNE

	Best Information before Voyager 2 Encounter	Data from Voyager 2 Encounter
Neptune		
Diameter	30,800 miles (49,600 kilometers)	30,770 miles (49,520 kilometers)
Mass (Earth=1)	17.2	17.15
Density (water=1)	1.76	1.64
Rotation period	17.0 hours (based on clouds); about 18.0 hours suspected for interior	16.11 hours for interior (16.0 to 18.3 hours for clouds)
Magnetic field	not detectable from Earth; suspected to be similar to Uranus' in strength	0.13 gauss average; tilted 47° and offset 55% of distance from center
Rings	3 ring arcs reasonably certain; material fills about 20 percent of orbit; ring particles expected to be black; shepherd moon(s) expected for arcs	4 sparse but complete rings; outer ring has 3 denser segments; ring material dark and dusty
Distance from center of planet	25,000 to 44,000 miles (41,000 to 71,000 kilometers)	39,100; 36,700 to 33,100; 33,100; 30,400 to 24,000(?) miles (62,900; 59,000 to 53,200; 53,200; 49,000 to 38,000(?) kilometers)
Atmospheric composition	hydrogen, helium, methane	hydrogen, helium, methane
Atmospheric features	methane clouds barely discernible away from equator; slight banding expected but not seen from Earth	Great Dark Spot, Little Dark Spot, and smaller white cloud features and dark bands.
Triton		
Diameter	2,200 miles (3,500 kilometers) (highly uncertain)	1,681 miles (2,705 kilometers)
Mass (Earth=1)	0.016	0.0036
Density	2 (highly uncertain)	2.07
Rotation period	5.9 days retrograde	5.9 days retrograde
Atmospheric composition	methane, nitrogen	nitrogen (99.9%), methane (less than 0.1%)
Atmospheric features	pressure and transparency unknown	pressure about 1/60,000 that of Earth; transparent
Surface features	none known; methane and water frost detected; possible nitrogen ice and/or liquid; dark reddish color expected due to methane polymerization	nitrogen ice caps, few craters, network of fractures, active nitrogen geysers, cantaloupe terrain; surface is highly reflective

	Best Information before Voyager 2 Encounter	Data from Voyager 2 Encounter
Nereid		
Diameter	200 miles (300 kilometers) (highly uncertain)	210 miles (340 kilometers)
Mass (Earth=1)	negligible	negligible
Density	2 (highly uncertain)	about 2
Rotation period	unknown	unknown
Atmosphere	none	none
Surface features	none known	none resolvable
Other Satellites		
	perhaps 1	6 (from 260 to 30 miles [420 to 50 kilometers] in diameter)

propriately after the son of Poseidon (Neptune), god of the sea. He and his brothers, the tritons, had the upper bodies of men and the lower bodies of fish—the male version of mermaids.

A second satellite of Neptune was not discovered for more than a century. It was found in 1949 by Gerard P. Kuiper. Thought to be less than 200 miles (about 300 kilometers) in diameter, this small moon was named Nereid after the sea nymphs who served as attendants for Poseidon.

So, prior to *Voyager*'s visit, Neptune was only known to have two moons. *Voyager* was expected to change that. It tripled the number of moons known at Uranus. Neptune's greater distance made the detection of moons smaller than 150 miles (250 kilometers) very difficult from Earth with ground-based telescopes. And it was hard to explain Neptune's arc rings without invoking at least one shepherd moon of respectable size.

There was a feeling that surprises might be in store. What they lacked in number, the moons of Neptune might make up in weirdness.

Triton, the larger and closer of Neptune's two moons, traveled around its planet in a retrograde orbit—circling in the direction opposite to Neptune's orbit around the Sun and rotation on its axis. Triton was the only large satellite in the solar system with this peculiarity.

Nereid was peculiar in its own way. It possessed the most eccentric orbit of any moon in the solar system, passing as close to Neptune as 870,000 miles (1.4 million kilometers), then swinging out to 6.0 million miles (9.7 million kilometers).

Unlike most other satellites, Triton and Nereid did not revolve around their planet's equator but instead occupied substantially inclined orbits.

These anomalies combined to suggest to most planetary astronomers that something catastrophic had happened to the satellite system of Neptune. Perhaps the disruption and damage had been so great that the number of moons waiting to be discovered at Neptune was low—maybe only those required to hold the ring arc system in place.

Triton was big—but exactly how big was uncertain. It was thought to be about 2,200 miles (3,500 kilometers) in diameter. That would have made it considerably larger than Pluto and about the same size as our Moon. Of the satellites in the solar system, Triton was expected to rank between fifth and seventh in size, behind Jupiter's Ganymede, Saturn's Titan, Jupiter's Callisto and Io, and perhaps behind Earth's Moon and Jupiter's Europa. Even if Triton had a larger diameter than our Moon, it probably had less mass because our Moon was denser.

Of all the 54 satellites in the solar system known at that time, only two—Triton and Titan—possessed permanent atmospheres. Infrared studies of Triton by Dale P. Cruikshank and Peter Silvaggio in 1975 identified methane ice on Triton's surface. That led to the realization that Triton must possess an atmosphere. It was not possible to distinguish methane gas from methane ice in the spectrum, yet at the temperature of Triton (estimated at $-360°F$; $55°K$), there had to be enough vaporization of methane ice to provide Triton with at least a very thin atmosphere.

Cruikshank and his colleagues also discovered on Triton the presence of molecular nitrogen (N_2). Much of it also would lie condensed on the surface, but enough would be vaporizing to give Triton a substantial atmosphere, with perhaps one-tenth the surface pressure of the air on Earth.

Thus the atmosphere of Triton was pictured as very similar to what the *Voyagers* found at Titan: a gaseous blanket dominated by nitrogen with a trace of methane.[10] Ultraviolet wavelengths of sunlight and bombardment by charged particles in Neptune's magnetosphere could cause methane in Triton's atmosphere to polymerize into smog, as it had at Titan. But Triton's atmosphere was so much less dense than Titan's that the smog might perhaps have dropped out of the sky, leaving a rich reddish sludge of organic chemicals on the surface on Triton and far less smog in the atmosphere.

The colder temperatures at Triton might indeed produce a bizarre landscape. In identifying methane ice on its surface, Cruikshank and Silvaggio noticed that as Triton rotated in a six-day period, the signal varied so as to indicate that the methane ice did not cover everything. Instead they envisioned the methane ice to be distributed in continent-size patches, between which water ice, rock, soil—and nitrogen—were exposed. The expected temperature range on Triton might allow the nitrogen to be frozen or liquid. Cruikshank suggested that Triton might be dotted with shallow lakes, a few feet deep, of liquid nitrogen. Some astronomers were skeptical because the temperature range for nitrogen as a liquid is very narrow. But what if Triton, son of the sea god Neptune, had such peculiar oceans on its surface?

Would *Voyager 2* glimpse this landscape? Would the atmosphere of Triton be transparent? Over the last few years the light variation from Triton as it rotated had virtually vanished. Scientists worried that as Triton approached its summer season, its atmosphere was becoming hazy. Still, *Voyager*'s spectrometers and the analysis of its radio signals passing through the atmosphere of Triton were expected to provide conclusive information about the gases that blanketed this moon.

If Triton's atmosphere was transparent, *Voyager 2* hoped to see a moon to rival Jupiter's Io, Saturn's Titan, and Uranus' Miranda in spectacle and mystery. Triton must have led a remarkable life. It was the only large moon in the solar system to revolve in a retrograde direction. Triton must have undergone a major gravitational ordeal after it formed. Perhaps *Voyager 2* would see Triton's history written on its surface features.

Late on August 24, 1989, *Voyager 2* passed closer to Neptune than it did to Jupiter, Saturn, Uranus, or any of their moons or rings—only about 3,050 miles (4,900 kilometers) above its cloud tops as it skimmed over Neptune's north pole[11] and headed on for Triton and then the stars. *Voyager 2* had completed its Grand Tour of all four giant planets in our solar system.

11

Voyagers to the Stars

"This is a present from a small distant world . . . We are attempting to survive our time so we may live into yours. We hope someday, having solved the problems we face, to join a community of galactic civilizations. This record represents our hope and our determination, and our good will in a vast and awesome universe."

From President Jimmy Carter's message to extraterrestrial civilizations on the *Voyager* spacecraft record (1977)

Voyager 2's Grand Tour of the outer planets must end with Neptune in 1989. To obtain a gravity assist from Neptune so that *Voyager* could travel on to Pluto would require the spacecraft to fly within 3,100 miles (5,000 kilometers) of the center of Neptune. Since the radius of Neptune is 15,400 miles (24,800 kilometers), this extension of the mission is not practical.

But *Voyager 2*'s mission will not end with the Neptune encounter. Both *Voyager 1* and *Voyager 2* received enough energy from gravity assists at Jupiter to escape from the solar system. Their subsequent planetary encounters have been along trajectories that will permit them to escape the gravitational bonds of the Sun and send them out of our solar system on an endless glide through interstellar space.

The Journey Beyond

But crossing the orbit of Neptune or Pluto does not place the spacecraft beyond the solar system. Beyond the outermost planets lies the Oort Cloud, a reservoir of trillions of comets, extending halfway to the nearest star. Its outer boundary is perhaps 7,000 times the distance of Pluto from

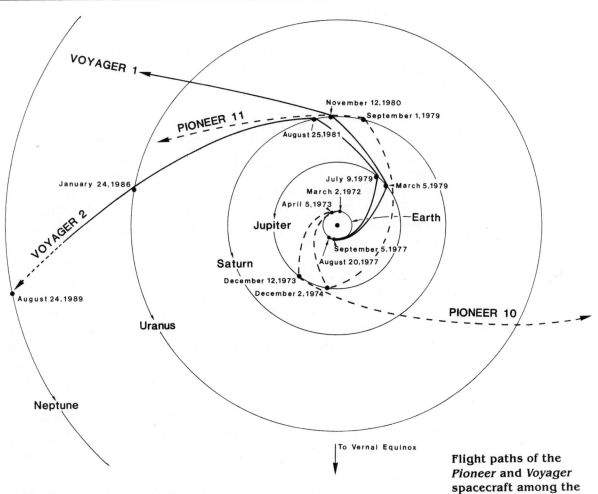

Flight paths of the *Pioneer* and *Voyager* spacecraft among the giant planets

the Sun, yet the comets of the Oort Cloud are held to the solar system by the Sun's gravity. For *Voyager 1* and *Voyager 2*, leaving the solar system is a threshold that lies far in the future.

Yet there is a boundary that both *Voyager* craft may survive to mark. The *Voyagers* are sailing outward with the solar wind at their backs—a breeze of electrons and protons from the Sun racing past them. Near the Earth, the solar wind regularly blows at a million miles per hour (500 kilometers per second). But somewhere, well beyond Neptune, the speed of the solar wind falters as the outbound particles are confined by the pressure of the interstellar gas and magnetic field through which the solar system swims.

This bubble of confinement is the heliopause—effectively the end of the Sun's far outer "atmosphere"—the point where the environment is less that of the Sun than of the combined outpourings of all the other stars in the Milky Way Galaxy. It is an important threshold as the *Voyagers* wend their way toward the stars.[1]

The location of the heliopause—its distance from the Sun—is unknown. No spacecraft escaping from our solar system has yet reached this boundary. Only four spacecraft are outbound with escape velocities. At the beginning of 1988, *Pioneer 10* was about 42 astronomical units from the Sun, *Pioneer 11* was 24, *Voyager 1* was 31, and *Voyager 2* was 24. Thus, both *Voyagers* are already farther from the Sun than *Pioneer 11*, which reached Saturn via gravitational assist from Jupiter by traveling more across the solar system than directly outward. *Voyager 1* will overtake *Pioneer 10* in distance in 1998. *Voyager 2* will overhaul *Pioneer 10* in 2016.[2]

Pioneer 10 is leaving our solar system in a direction nearly opposite to the Sun's motion among the stars. The distance to the heliopause upstream (in the direction the Sun is moving) is expected to be shorter than the distance downstream because the speed of the Sun in the upstream direction causes the pressure of the interstellar medium to be greater, pushing the heliopause inward. Therefore, *Pioneer 10*, headed downstream, may have farther to travel to reach the heliopause than the other craft.

The distance to the heliopause must also be somewhat variable because of the changeable output of the Sun. Faster solar particles push the heliopause outward, while periods of slower-moving particles allow the

The top diagram on the facing page shows the flight paths of the *Voyager* and *Pioneer* spacecraft as they leave the realm of the planets as viewed from north of the solar system. The bottom diagram shows the *Voyager* and *Pioneer* trajectories from the side, 20 degrees above the plane of the solar system, viewed from the vernal equinox. The end of each spacecraft's trajectory marks its position in the year 2000 A.D. Here are the directions (based on the ecliptic) that the spacecraft are headed and their asymptotic speeds.

Spacecraft	Asymptotic Speed (astronomical units per year)	Celestial Latitude	Celestial Longitude
Pioneer 10	2.384	2.909°	83.368°
Pioneer 11	2.214	12.596°	291.268°
Voyager 1	3.501	35.549°	260.778°
Voyager 2	3.386	-47.455°	310.885°

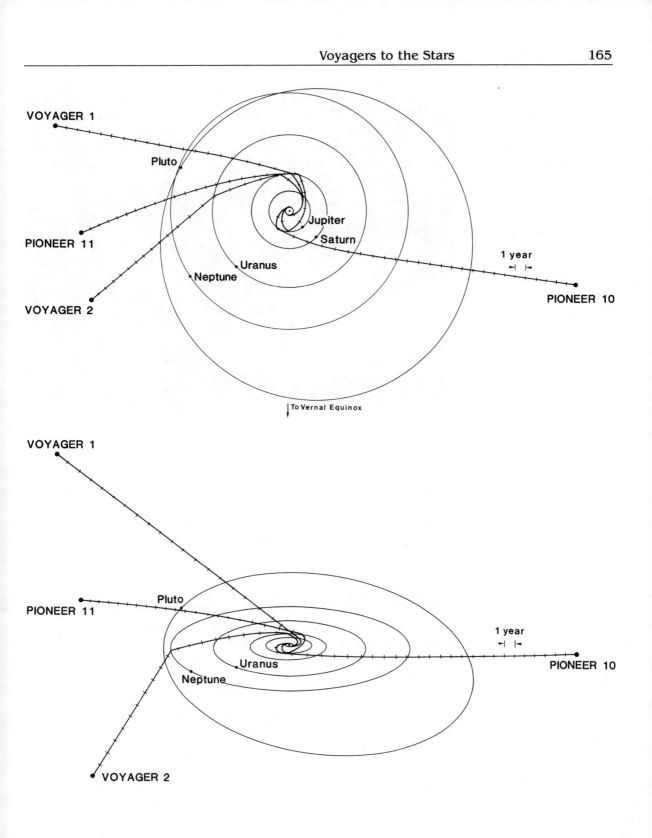

NASA's *Pioneer 10* and *11* and *Voyager 1* and *2* spacecraft are headed out of the solar system. Artist Don Davis portrays *Pioneer 10*, at present the most distant craft, moving outward from the Sun (the brightest star visible) and away from the heart of our Milky Way galaxy.
NASA Ames Research Center

heliopause to contract. Solar scientists think that the heliopause lies at a distance of 100 to 200 astronomical units—100 to 200 times the Earth's distance from the Sun. Neptune orbits at a distance of 30 astronomical units.

Voyager 1 and *Voyager 2*, increasing their distance from the Sun by about 3.5 astronomical units per year, could arrive at the heliopause as early as about 2010. Both craft should continue to have enough electrical power from their nuclear generators for radio transmission and enough fuel for their thrusters to keep their antennae turned toward Earth until about 2010 or 2015. If the heliopause lies at about 100 astronomical units from the Sun, the *Voyagers* may tell us where. Beyond that point, the *Voyagers* will continue outward, but they will be mute and passive.

Yet even at the heliopause, the *Voyagers'* journey of departure from the solar system will scarcely have begun. Beyond them will lie the vast cloud of comets, no less members of the Sun's family than the planets. The Oort Cloud may begin as close to the Sun as 50 astronomical units and extend as far as 135,000, halfway to the nearest star. Even though the *Voyagers* are separating themselves from the Sun at about 10 miles per second (16 kilometers per second), it will be 40,000 years until they are beyond the Oort Cloud and have truly crossed the boundary into interstellar space. Forty thousand years is about the period of time that separates us from Neanderthal Man.

Voyager 2 and the Stars

On its Grand Tour of the giant planets, *Voyager 2* was traveling near the plane of the solar system. But at Neptune, *Voyager 2* passed low over the planet's north pole, and its course was bent southward to encounter Triton. So *Voyager 2* will be headed out of our solar system on a southerly route. It is pointed toward a rather drab region of the sky in the constellation Pavo, the Peacock. To see that part of the heavens, we must be in the southernmost United States or farther south.

Yet, ironically, *Voyager 2*'s first reasonably close stellar encounter will not be with any of the stars in the far southern sky but with a star now located in the northern constellation Andromeda, the Princess. That star, known only by its catalog designation of Ross 248, is a small cool red star with only about one-fifth the mass of our Sun. Find the Great Square of Pegasus and look north one length of the Square—and you will not see Ross 248. With a magnitude of +12.3, it is about 200 times too faint for human eye visibility.

Even though *Voyager 2* will be traveling south and Ross 248 is located in the north, the two are moving toward one another. While *Voyager 2* is consuming 40,000 years in its transit through the Oort Cloud, all the stars in the sky are moving in different directions. The constellations are gradually changing shape beyond recognition. Some of the stars are coming toward us faster than our spacecraft are going to meet them—almost as if they are coming to fetch the *Voyagers*.

Ross 248 is currently 10.3 light-years away, but while *Voyager 2* rushes outward at 33,000 miles per hour (14.8 kilometers per second), Ross 248 is approaching our system at more than five times that speed. No sooner will *Voyager 2* emerge from the Oort Cloud than, 40,176 years from now, it will encounter Ross 248, passing at a distance of 1.7 light-years, closer to *Voyager* than to any subsequent star known. Ross 248 will pass the outskirts of our solar system 3.25 light-years from our Sun, 25 percent closer than our nearest stellar neighbors, the three stars of Alpha Centauri, are to us now. Yet even when Ross 248 reaches that close range, it will be four times too faint for people on Earth to see without a telescope.

Still, its passage may eventually be seen and even felt indirectly as its gravity warps the orbits of millions of comets and redirects some of them inward toward the Sun where they will provide brilliant displays in the skies of Earth and perhaps even impacts on our planet.

Voyager 1 and the Stars

The same kind of stellar encounter awaits *Voyager 1*, even though it is traveling toward a very different part of the sky. It is pointed in the direction of Rasalhague, the brightest star in the constellation Ophiuchus, the Serpent Bearer. But the star headed for a rendezvous with *Voyager 1* is AC+79 3888.[3] This star, with no name other than its catalog listing, is currently to be found in the faint constellation Camelopardalis, the Giraffe. This region of the sky is visible all night long to people living north of the Tropic of Cancer. AC+79 3888 is just a short distance from Polaris, the North Star, and halfway between the bowl of the Big Dipper and the *W* of Cassiopeia. AC+79 3888 is slightly larger and brighter than Ross 248, but it too is a small cool red star with only one-quarter the mass of our Sun. At its present distance of 16.6 light-years, AC+79 3888 is an 11th-magnitude star, nearly a hundred times too faint for the unaided eye to see.

While *Voyager 1* is moving outward at 37,000 miles per hour (16.6 kilometers per second), AC+79 3888 will be traveling toward our solar system at seven times that speed. In 40,272 years, at the same time that *Voyager 2* will be scurrying by Ross 248 more than a quarter of the way around the sky, *Voyager 1* will be only a little more than 1.6 light-years from AC+79 3888, and AC+79 3888 will be just 3 light-years from the Sun.[4] Even so, AC+79 3888 will still be two times too faint for people on Earth to see without a telescope.

A Message from Earth

Quite by accident, both of these first star encounters by the *Voyagers* are with single stars like our Sun—a minority in space, where most stars have one or more gravitationally bound companions. They may well have planetary systems, since we think the process that starts the formation of stars is identical to the process of planet formation.

Yet even with a family of planets, it is very unlikely that Ross 248 and AC+79 3888 provide the right environment for life to exist. Both stars are much smaller than our Sun. They emit so little heat that a planet would have to be at precisely the correct distance with an almost perfectly circular orbit to stay in a habitable zone. Worse still, that planet would be so close to its star that it would be tidally coupled to it, like most moons are to their nearby planets, so that one side of the planet would fry in constant sunlight while the other side would freeze in constant night. Most scientists do not expect life to exist in the solar system of a low-mass red dwarf star.

Even if both these stars illuminate planets populated by intelligent spacefaring beings, it would be extremely unlikely that they would detect a tiny silent spacecraft passing beyond the fringe of their comet clouds.

Voyager 1 and *Voyager 2,* bound out of the solar system, carry sounds and pictures of Earth on a phonograph record to show a civilization that may find the spacecraft what life on our planet is like. Here, a technician is mounting the interstellar message on *Voyager 2.*
NASA

And the stars are so widely separated that there is a vanishingly small chance that either of the *Voyagers* will hit or come very close to a star in the next billion years.

Still, just on the outside chance that some civilization deep in space may retrieve a *Voyager*, each craft is equipped with a special record that gives its finders pictures and sounds from the planet Earth.

The message was designed for NASA by Carl Sagan, Frank Drake, Ann Druyan, Timothy Ferris, Jon Lomberg, and Linda Salzman Sagan. Attached to the side of each *Voyager* is a gold-coated two-sided copper phonograph record, complete with enclosed stylus and cartridge and with instructions etched on its aluminum cover. The record should last a billion years. On it are greetings in 55 different human languages and one whale language; the sounds of Earth—from thunder to frogs to a newborn baby; 90 minutes of music from around the world; and, encoded as vibrations, 118 pictures of our planet and ourselves.[5]

For the beings that find a *Voyager* along its endless journey, the spacecraft will have found a new and eloquent voice—no longer telling its home planet about other worlds but now telling other beings of its origin and the people who sent it outward.

12

The Smallest Planet

"One cannot help but wonder whether this remarkable pair (Neptune and Pluto) holds any further surprises."
Astronomer James G. Williams
(1971)

The Incredible Shrinking Planet

Pluto was hard to find. Of the few who sought to locate a trans-Neptunian planet, most justified their efforts by what seemed to them to be slight but real irregularities in the motion of Uranus even after the perturbations of Neptune were accounted for. Pluto was finally discovered in 1930, culminating a series of searches that began in 1905. But even after its discovery, Pluto, like its mythological namesake, was a shadowy figure, if not downright antisocial. The planet revealed almost nothing to astronomers.

No moon was seen, so it was not possible to calculate Pluto's mass using the law of gravity.[1] Pluto's disk as seen from Earth was too small to measure, so it was not possible to determine the diameter of the planet with any accuracy at all. The planet revealed no surface features. The dimness of the planet and the inability of existing telescopes to see its disk meant that, unless Pluto was absurdly dense, it was too small to be the planet that Lowell and Pickering had predicted. Its mass could not have measurably disturbed the motion of Uranus.

When it was discovered, Pluto was thought to be about the size of Earth. As telescopes grew and techniques improved, the planet stayed elusive, always small enough to avoid precise measurement. It was thought to be three-quarters our size, then half. In 1950, Gerard P. Kuiper tried to

Pluto wanders in front of two galaxies. In the picture on the left (October 28, 1970), Pluto is the starlike object at the top of the galaxy on the right. One day later (picture on right), Pluto has moved to a position where it appears between the two galaxies. James Gunn took the photograph on the left with the 48-inch Schmidt Telescope at the Palomar Observatory. The photo on the right was taken by Karen and Richard Hackney and Alex G. Smith with the 30-inch telescope at the Rosemary Hill Observatory, University of Florida.
(left) Palomar Observatory photograph by James Gunn; (right) Courtesy of Karen Hackney, Richard Hackney, and Alex G. Smith

measure Pluto's disk with the newly operational 200-inch telescope on Palomar Mountain and concluded that Pluto was less than 3,500 miles (5,900 kilometers) in diameter.[2]

In 1955, Merle F. Walker and Robert Hardie at the Lowell Observatory identified fluctuations in the light from Pluto recurring over a period of 6.3867 days. They interpreted this (correctly) as the rotation period of Pluto.[3]

Then, in 1976, astronomers[4] used spectroscopy to identify frozen methane on Pluto's surface, and estimates of the planet's size plunged again. Until that time it had been thought that Pluto was a dark-colored object with low reflectivity like our Moon or Mars or the asteroids. But with methane ice on its surface, Pluto was now thought to be a highly reflective body. If Pluto was reflecting 40 to 50 percent of the light it received yet still was very dim, it had to be even smaller than previously estimated, or more light would have reached the Earth. Pluto was smaller than Mercury. It had fallen to last place in size among the planets in our solar system. Pluto was probably smaller than our Moon.

The existence of methane ice on Pluto led astronomers to the realization that Pluto must have at least some atmosphere. Methane freezes only at extremely low temperatures. At Pluto, where temperatures are 45 to 55° above absolute zero (-379 to $-361°F$; -228 to $-218°C$), methane is frozen but is steadily vaporizing to supply Pluto with an atmosphere. A temperature change of just a few degrees changes the rate of vaporization and the amount of atmosphere greatly. The behavior of methane makes it certain that Pluto has a tenuous atmosphere of methane, but it is very hard spectroscopically to distinguish methane gas from methane ice.

On June 9, 1988, Pluto edged in front of a star, the first confirmed stellar occultation for tiny Pluto since it was discovered. The star's light faded and returned gradually rather than blinking out and then back on suddenly, indicating that Pluto is surrounded by a partially transparent medium—an atmosphere. Methane must be present, but the other and even the principal components of the atmosphere have not yet been determined. Whatever its composition, Pluto's atmosphere can't be extensive. The gravity of Pluto can't hold much.

Still, it is surprising that a planet of such small size—with so little gravity—can retain any atmosphere at all. The atmosphere is certainly not tightly bound to Pluto. The methane gas must be drifting away very gradually as solar energy, weak as it is at Pluto, accelerates some methane molecules to Pluto's escape velocity—a mere 2,700 miles per hour (1.2 kilometers per second). If methane molecules at the top of Pluto's atmosphere are traveling outward and do not collide with other molecules, they are lost. To keep Pluto supplied with its present methane atmosphere since the beginning of the solar system, the planet would have needed a global coating of methane ice at least 2 miles (3 kilometers) thick.[5] As skimpy as Pluto's atmosphere is, astronomers think it is many times thicker now than usual, as Pluto makes its closest approach to the Sun and the warming temperatures vaporize more methane ice. For all but a few years of the planet's 248-year circuit of the Sun, Pluto's atmosphere may lie frozen on the ground.

Measurements following perihelion may indicate whether or not the atmosphere of Pluto is transient. Certainly Pluto's maintenance of an atmosphere is precarious. If it were a little colder, Pluto's atmosphere would freeze to the planet's surface. A little warmer and virtually all of Pluto's wisp of an atmosphere would escape, unless continuously replenished by the evaporation of surface ices.

For nearly half a century after its discovery, Pluto had shrunk from view and defied efforts of familiarity. But gradually, hardworking astronomers (and Pluto's eccentric orbit) coaxed the planet into a more accommodating mood. Suddenly, everything Pluto did seemed almost to beg for attention. Pluto turned out to be something of an exhibitionist.

The Discovery of Pluto's Moon

The crucial breakthrough in Pluto research came on June 22, 1978, when James W. Christy was examining photographs of Pluto he had requested. They had been taken as part of an ongoing effort by the U.S. Naval Observatory to establish a more accurate orbit for the planet.[6] Pluto had been photographed by Anthony V. Hewitt on three different dates using the 61-inch (1.55-meter) Astrometric Reflector at the Naval Observatory's Flagstaff (Arizona) Station. There were two plates for each date and three images of Pluto on each plate. They did not look very promising. The pictures had been marked "poor" because the image of Pluto appeared to be defective. It was elongated. It would be hard to get measurements of Pluto's precise position from a dot that had been elongated asymmetrically as if the image had been smeared when the telescope failed to track it properly as the Earth turned during the 1.5-minute exposure.

But then Christy noticed that the stars around Pluto were not elongated. He looked again at the elongations of the Pluto image. The bulge had changed position. On the April 13 and 20 plates the elongation was to the south. On May 12, the elongation was to the north. Christy toyed with the idea that Pluto had a moon, but he remained skeptical. He discussed his findings with his colleagues, looking for other explanations, but none seemed to fit.

The next day, Christy examined the 50 earlier U.S. Naval Observatory plates of Pluto taken in 1965, 1970, and 1971. Two plates from 1965 showed the bulge. But most interesting were five plates taken during one week in 1970. They showed the elongation progressing clockwise around Pluto in a 6-day period, about the same as Pluto's rotational cycle.[7] Christy sought out his colleague Robert S. Harrington. "Bob," said Christy, "Pluto's got a satellite."[8]

Christy measured the elongation angles carefully so that Harrington could attempt a calculation of the orbit of the satellite. He began with the assumption that the moon's period of revolution was exactly the same

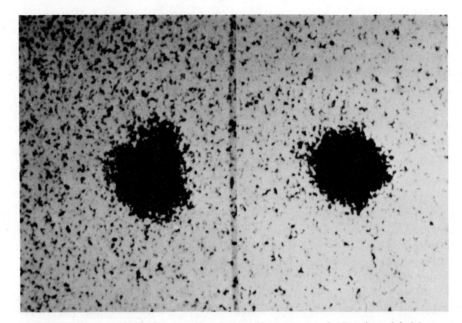

In 1978, James W. Christy noticed that there was a bulge in a highly magnified image of Pluto (left). He noticed that only Pluto, not the background stars (such as one shown to the right), exhibited this distortion. He found elongated images of Pluto on earlier U.S. Naval Observatory photographs. His conclusion: Pluto has a moon. He proposed the name Charon.

Official U.S. Naval Observatory photograph

as Pluto's period of rotation. Using a pocket calculator at home, Harrington computed the satellite's probable orbit and compared it to the elongations that Christy had measured on the photographs. The moon's predicted positions fit the image bulges almost perfectly. "That was great fun," said Harrington.

Pluto had a moon. It proved to be the largest satellite to be discovered since Neptune's moon Triton was found in 1846. No sooner had Harrington computed the moon's orbit than he used its orbit to derive the mass of the Pluto-satellite system. He also noted that Pluto and its moon were gravitationally bound together in a unique way. Moons typically revolve around their planets in the same period of time as they rotate once, so that they always keep the same face pointed at their planet. Unlike any other planet, Pluto also rotates once for every revolution of its moon, so Pluto keeps the same face pointed back at its moon.

A MOMENT OF PERCEPTION
by James W. Christy

From an apparently insignificant detail on a small number of astronomical images came a bonanza of scientific revelations. Pluto, a mystery for 48 years, became a well-understood planetary system within a span of a few days. How did this happen? Why was Charon not seen earlier by the thousands of astronomers who studied Pluto?

The elongation on the images of Pluto that was Charon was minute and hidden from perception by many effects: elongation due to the orbital motion of Pluto during exposure, elongation from imprecise tracking of the telescope during exposure, expansion of the image of Pluto due to poor "seeing" through the atmosphere, distortion of the image from imperfect telescope optics, and distortions from uneven distribution of photographic grains.

The elongation on the images of Pluto was also hidden by the bias in the minds of most astronomers, including myself, that moons did not exist that close to planets and, because many attempts to find a moon of Pluto had failed, that Pluto did not have a moon. Many of us had even been taught that. Thus, even though I had seen several exposures of Pluto with significant elongation, my mind was not yet open to discovery.

From the day that Pluto was discovered in 1930, astronomers had hoped to find a moon of the planet and thus calculate its mass. They made stronger exposures and Pluto's image overwhelmed that of Charon. They made underexposures in which the image of Pluto's companion was undetectable. Also, Pluto was at opposition (closest to Earth) in midwinter through most of the period. During winter, most observatories suffer from poorer "seeing" conditions and optical distortions, both due to thermal gradients in and around the telescopes. Pluto's orbital motion has caused opposition to slowly migrate until, at present, it occurs in the spring.

The discovery exposures of Charon were made in Flagstaff far from opposition in late spring near the end of the observing season for Pluto. Better

James W. Christy, discoverer of Charon, at the U.S. Naval Observatory's Starscan equipment, with which he determined that the bulge in Pluto was a moon.
Courtesy of James W. Christy

seeing conditions occur then in Flagstaff. The exposures were made with a telescope of high optical quality and low thermal coefficient optics. The exposure times just happened to be exactly right for detection of the elongation of the image, which was Charon.

When I first saw these exposures on June 22, 1978, I was looking with the mind and eyes of an astronomer who had examined roughly 50,000 images in recent years. Many of these images had been of double stars exposed in the course of the U.S. Naval Observatory's extensive double-star program. I had seen dual images blended together in all possible circumstances by all combinations of image distortions. My mind was now attuned to two celestial bodies disguised as one. Now I could think: Pluto has a moon.

In our plate collection, I found elongations of Pluto's images on three nights in the spring of 1978, on five nights in one week during 1970, and on two nights in 1965. The 1965 plate envelope had been clearly marked by the observer, "Pluto image elongated." I myself had seen that plate many times, but I had rejected the implication. Each of these nine nights revealed an elongation in a specific direction.

From ten apparently insignificant image distortions and two days of study came a cascade of revelations:

1. In the 1978 exposures, one night showed an elongation to the south; another, about a month later, to the north. Hypothesis: Pluto had a moon orbiting north-south. Strange—almost all other moons in the solar system move in an east-west plane. But no proof of a new moon yet.

2. In the 1970 exposures, five elongations in one week and the elongations progressed completely around Pluto. Conclusion: Pluto has a moon with a probable orbital period of six days.

3. But astronomers had previously determined a light variation of Pluto (presumably its rotation period) of precisely 6.3867 days. Hypothesis: The orbital period of the moon is exactly 6.3867 days.

4. Eureka! The two 1965 elongations, the five 1970 elongations, and the three 1978 elongations are at angles in exact agreement with the 6.3867 day period, according to calculations by Bob Harrington. How can we get so much from such trivial elongations? But the avalanche of conclusions continues.

5. The orbit is north-south with Charon only six Pluto diameters' distance from the planet. Harrington concludes that both bodies are tidally locked. This is also evi-dent from the coincidence of the light curve and the orbital period. Thus, Pluto's pole of rotation is on its side, in the plane of the solar system. More yet.

6. Harrington calculates the mass of Pluto-Charon from the orbital period and the distance. He gets less than one percent of Earth's mass. Therefore, Pluto could not have have caused perturbations in the orbits of Neptune and Uranus.

7. Because a cold planet's density cannot be too low, the small mass leads to a very small diameter for Pluto, approximately 3,000 kilometers, we thought at the time. Charon's brightness is about 20 percent of Pluto's. Conclusion: Charon's diameter is more than a third of Pluto's, making it the largest moon in the solar system relative to its planet and the largest moon discovered since 1846.

8. During the time between the 1965 and 1978 elongations, Pluto's orbital motion around the Sun should change our view of Charon's orbital plane. The 1970 and 1965 elongations were extended farther east-west than those in 1978. The resultant orbital solution by Bob Harrington reveals that Charon's orbit was approximately face on at the time of Pluto's discovery in 1930 and has been closing to the line of sight since then. Conclusion: Eclipsing of Pluto-Charon will commence soon, even though this can occur only once every 124 years!

Thus within a week of Charon's discovery there were roughly a dozen major conclusions made concerning the true nature of Pluto. All of these conclusions have been verified over the last ten years.

What had been a prolonged mystery was quickly and totally unveiled by ten minuscule image distortions. By amazing coincidence, these ten elongations were ideally placed in time for scientific logic to yield correct conclusions.

As the discoverer of Pluto's satellite, it fell to Christy to suggest a name. He wanted to honor his wife Charlene—"Char" to her family. So he proposed the name Charon, the boatman in Greek mythology who ferries the souls of the dead across the River Styx to Pluto's realm in Hades.[9] The name was ideal: Charon as a sentinel for Pluto. It fit well with the lore of Pluto and the tradition of naming planets and moons after Roman and Greek mythological figures.

But the name Charon accidentally led to a problem with pronunciation. Christy had anticipated that Charon would be pronounced like "Char" in Charlene. But the standard Greek and Latin pronunciation of Charon is the same as the name Karen.[10]

Significance of a Moon for Pluto

The discovery that Pluto had a moon was not just fodder for trivia games and an excuse to revise textbooks. The existence of a satellite for Pluto vastly increased what could be known about Pluto from Earth-based observations.

To begin with, a satellite held in orbit by Pluto's gravity meant that scientists for the first time could calculate with some confidence the mass of the Pluto-Charon system.[11] Charon lay at a distance of 12,400 miles (19,980 kilometers) from Pluto and circled with a period of 6.39 days. From these figures, the mass of Pluto could be reasonably estimated. It would take about 450 Plutos to equal the mass of the Earth. Even our Moon is five and a half times more massive than Pluto.

Compared to Pluto, Charon was surprisingly large. Previously, the Earth held the honors for having the largest satellite in proportion to its size. The Moon was more than one-quarter the diameter of Earth and one-eighty-first its mass. No other planet-satellite pair came close to such equality in size. Earthlings talked proudly of their unique twin-planet system—until Charon's discovery. With an estimated diameter of 777 miles (1,250 kilometers) compared to Pluto's 1,457 miles (2,345 kilometers), Charon is more than half the diameter of Pluto and probably has about 15 percent its mass.

Lowell and Pickering had embarked upon their searches for a trans-Neptunian planet because they thought they had detected its perturbations in the motion of Uranus. They had used those irregularities (Pickering used what he thought were Neptune perturbations also) to predict the existence of a ninth planet. Driven by this work, Pluto was found, but its small size worried astronomers that its gravity was too weak to cause detectable perturbations in the motion of Uranus or Neptune. Yet almost no one had anticipated that Pluto had so little mass that the Earth from 3 billion miles (5 billion kilometers) away would exert a greater gravitational force on Neptune than did Pluto, even if Pluto and Neptune could be where their orbits lie closest together. Whether or not the oddities in the motion of Uranus and Neptune were real rather than errors of measurement, it was now absolutely certain that Pluto could not possibly be responsible. Its gravity was far too weak.

But Charon did far more than reveal the mass of Pluto. Before Charon was found, no one knew how Pluto's axis was tipped to its plane of revolution.[12] Did Pluto "stand" nearly vertically on its axis as it revolved around the Sun like seven of the planets, or did it lie on its side like Uranus? Charon, the bulge in the fuzzy image of Pluto, appeared alternately to the north and then to the south. If Charon was orbiting close to the plane of Pluto's equator as almost all moons in the solar system do, that meant that Pluto must have its equator tipped almost north/south as seen from Earth. For Charon to revolve precisely once around Pluto in the same period as Pluto spins once on its axis indicated that Charon must be positioned over Pluto's equator. So Pluto's rotational axis had to lie near the plane of its orbit. Pluto, like Uranus, lies on its side as it orbits the Sun.

The orientation of Charon's orbit also led to a likely explanation of why Pluto was not brightening as fast as expected as it approached perihelion. The closer it is to the Sun, the more light Pluto receives and the larger its angular disk is to reflect sunlight. Pluto should have brightened considerably between 1950 and 1987. It did brighten, but about 32 percent less than expected.

When Charon was discovered, its motion around Pluto showed that Pluto was tipped on its side as it revolved around the Sun. The oblique perspective on Charon's orbit at the time of its discovery in 1978 meant that when the ninth planet was discovered in 1930, Tombaugh must have been viewing the region around Pluto's south pole.[13]

In the late 1980s, with the gradual change of seasons, Pluto's equator is facing the Sun and Earth. The failure of Pluto to brighten as much as expected is thought to be due primarily to this change in perspective. If the poles of Pluto are covered with ice and highly reflective, while the equator is much darker (perhaps in part because it is exposed to almost vertical sunlight as Pluto comes closest to the Sun and has suffered enough vaporization of ices to expose regions of dark surface material), then the shift from viewing a bright polar ice cap to a less reflective equator could explain why Pluto is dimmer than expected.

The orientation of Charon's orbit also alerted astronomers to a rare opportunity that was about to open whereby Pluto and Charon would reveal details on their surfaces. It was a priceless accident of timing. Pluto is so small and distant from Earth that, even when it is closest to the Sun, it is scarcely more than 0.1 arc second across, the size of a baseball seen from 100 miles (160 kilometers) away—too small for its disk to be measured directly from the surface of the Earth through the turbulence of our atmosphere. And Charon is smaller still. How is it possible to chart any detail at all on two worlds when their disks are not discernible?

The opportunity lay in a series of eclipses. When Charon was discovered in 1978, the south pole of Pluto was pointed forward in its direction of travel and a little bit sunward, just enough so that Charon circled Pluto without passing across the surface of Pluto or passing behind Pluto as seen from Earth. But Pluto's poles were pointed toward specific points in the star field. So, as Pluto slowly revolved around the Sun, observers on Earth would look directly first at one pole of Pluto, then its equator, then the other pole, then its equator again—over a period of 248 years. The orientation of Pluto and the orbit of Charon indicated that within a few years Pluto would arrive at a position in its orbit where, as seen from Earth, the orbit of Charon would be nearly edge on to Earth and Charon would be transiting across the face of Pluto and then vanishing behind Pluto in the course of its 6.39-day orbital journey. Those eclipses, watched for by astronomers since 1979, were finally detected in 1985. The results were immediate and dramatic.

Shadow Dance

Eclipse season for Pluto and Charon. As Pluto moves around the Sun, we see Charon's orbit around Pluto from gradually changing angles. Twice in every 248-year revolution of Pluto, the orbit of Charon is edge on to Earth. During this 5-year period, Pluto and Charon take turns eclipsing one another. In the course of each 6.4-day revolution of Charon around Pluto, first Charon passes in front of Pluto, blocking part of it from view, then Charon moves behind Pluto and is occulted. Because of the information about Pluto and Charon that these eclipses provide, it is very fortunate that Charon was discovered in 1978 rather than in 1990.

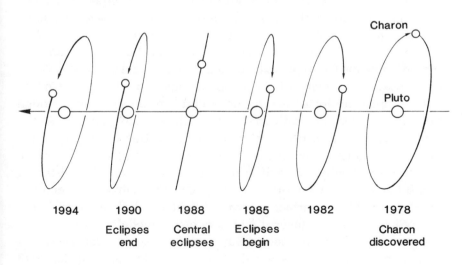

1994	1990	1988	1985	1982	1978
	Eclipses end	Central eclipses	Eclipses begin		Charon discovered

Astronomers carefully measured the amount of light coming from the Pluto-Charon system. The two are brightest when they are side by side to the line of sight—neither blocking the light of nor casting a shadow on the other. When Charon is in transit across the face of Pluto, the combined light of the planet-moon system declines by about 40 percent (about 0.55 magnitude) as Charon blocks part of the reflective surface of Pluto from view. As Charon emerges from transit, the brightness of Pluto-Charon is again at a maximum. Then Charon ducks behind Pluto and the brightness declines again, but only by about 20 percent (about 0.24 magnitude).

The occultation of Charon by Pluto does not subtract from the system as much reflected light as when Charon stands in front of Pluto and blocks a portion from view. Thus Charon must be darker and less reflective than Pluto. Pluto reflects perhaps 46 percent of the light it receives from the Sun; Charon only about 34 percent.

But the gleanings from Pluto-Charon eclipses are far greater than an approximation of comparative reflectivity. Previously, no markings on the surface of Pluto could be resolved by telescope. The only features on Pluto known to exist were the undefined surface oddities that caused Pluto's brightness to vary over its rotation cycle of 6.39 days.

In 1984, Marc W. Buie and Robert Marcialis, working independently, developed computer models of surface features on Pluto that could closely approximate the fluctuations in the planet's 6.39-day light period. Using the discoveries of methane ice on Pluto and the dimming effect as Pluto's equator was oriented more and more toward Earth, both scientists envisioned Pluto with extensive polar caps and a darker equatorial belt. Both also hypothesized that Pluto had two large equatorial spots. Marcialis used two dark spots in his model; Buie used one very large dark spot and a smaller bright spot. Which, if either, was correct?

In the series of eclipses between Charon and Pluto, each transit of Charon across the face of Pluto blocked different terrain from view. When the eclipse season began in 1985, our line of sight caused us to see Charon moving across the north polar region of Pluto. In 1988, midway through the eclipse season, Charon was transiting along Pluto's equator. As the eclipse season ends in 1990, our view will show Charon cutting across Pluto's south polar region. In the course of the eclipse cycle, Charon will have systematically blocked from view the entire Charon-facing hemisphere of Pluto. Gradually emerging as the eclipses proceed is a rough map of Pluto's surface in terms of light and dark features. So far, the gradations in tone favor the Buie two-spot model.

The smaller of the two spots in Buie's model—perhaps 250 miles (400 kilometers) in diameter—is as reflective as the polar caps. The larger of

Pluto is so tiny and distant that telescopes on Earth cannot distinguish its disk; thus no surface features may be discerned on it. But based on light variations as Pluto spins on its axis in 6.4 days and as it revolves around the Sun, Marc W. Buie created a computer model of the surface of Pluto that shows bright polar ice caps, a darker equatorial belt, and two equatorial spots: one bright and the other very large and dark. Here Buie shows the rotation of Pluto bringing the light and dark spots into view. Pluto lies on its side as it revolves around the Sun. Its south pole is to the left. The hemisphere of Pluto with no spots is the one that always faces toward Charon. The present series of eclipses between Pluto and Charon should determine whether Buie's model is correct.
Courtesy of Marc W. Buie, UH/SDSC

Using his computer model of Pluto, Marc W. Buie illustrates the March 19, 1987, transit of Charon across the face of Pluto. Pluto's south pole is to the left. Notice how large Charon is compared to Pluto and that Charon is darker in color. The amount by which the transit of Charon and its shadow reduce the light from Pluto tells astronomers how light or dark the eclipsed surface of Pluto is and allows a rough map to be drawn. The transit event shown here required approximately four hours.
Courtesy of Marc W. Buie, UH/SDSC

the spots is quite dark and has a width of 500 miles (800 kilometers), more than a third the diameter of Pluto. The bright polar caps and equatorial bright spot are interpreted as methane ice. The less reflective equatorial band may be a region partially covered with methane ice, with some exposed dark surface. The large dark equatorial spot might be nearly ice-free terrain where the dark pitted surface of Pluto is most visible.[14]

A Tour of Pluto

If a spacecraft from Earth (call it Orpheus) one day plunges into the realm of Pluto, what will its instruments—or its passengers—see?

Here is some speculation.

We have landed at the equator. The Sun shines brilliantly, far outshining every star in the sky. But at Pluto we notice a difference. Daylight is dim—like the dark overcast of a thunderstorm on Earth. The Sun is so distant that it is no longer a golden orb but now just a dazzlingly bright star in the heavens. For the first time, at the distance of Neptune and Pluto, we can see the Sun for what it is—a star.[15] We are so far away that the Sun is scarcely more than a point of light. Yet the other stars are still so distant that the Sun outshines the brightest of them by a factor of 10 million. After all, if we were on our way from the Sun to the nearest star, reaching Pluto would be like a runner completing the first 15 feet (4.7 meters) of a marathon. The comparison between the Sun and stars can be made directly because the stars can be seen in the sky at the same time as the Sun. Pluto's atmosphere is so thin that there is almost no scattered light to obscure the stars.

Here, with Pluto as close to the Sun as it can get, the Sun is about 900 times fainter than it appears on Earth. Still, the Sun shines 400 times more brightly on Pluto than the full Moon shines on Earth.[16] We can read a book in the sunlight on Pluto. But we must be careful not to cast a shadow on the page. The atmosphere on Pluto is so minimal that there are too few gas molecules and too little dust to scatter the sunlight and keep shadows from being absolutely black. What the sunlight falls on, we can see. What is in shadow disappears, unless Charon is visible and in a full enough phase to provide shadow-illuminating light. Contrasts on Pluto are very stark, like the Apollo astronauts found on the Moon. A rule for visitors to Pluto: Don't step into shadows. It would be easy to fall into a crater we could not see.

On our approach for landing on Pluto, we saw both of the polar ice caps, extending well toward the equator. Infrared measurements from Earth indicated that Pluto was partially covered by frozen methane, and much of that methane ice now lies at the poles, where the sunlight is now falling most obliquely and warming the highly volatile methane least well. It was not possible to tell during our approach whether the frozen methane was a deep ice field or a thin coating of methane frost.

With Pluto near perihelion, temperatures on the planet are near a maximum where the Sun is highest in the sky, which just happens to be at the equator. The temperatures are not exactly balmy—about 370° below zero Fahrenheit (−223° Celsius).

We have chosen to land at the equator because there is less frozen methane here, so that the surface of Pluto lies exposed. It is a sharp contrast to the bright white polar caps. The equatorial region is, on the whole, two to three times less reflective, with tones varying over large and small areas. Our overall impression of color is neutral medium gray, much lighter than the charcoal gray soil on Earth's Moon, but far off white. As we look harder, some, maybe much, of Pluto's gray surface seems to be just a tinge reddish brown, suggesting that the soil contains significant quantities of carbon and carbon compounds.

Pluto is certainly a battered world. Craters and debris are everywhere. Mapping from orbit should tell us whether the planet is saturated with craters and has changed little over the 4.6 billion years since the solar system began or whether it has erased some or many of its scars by surface upheavals due to internal processes rather than passively enduring a steady pounding from passing comets. If Pluto is little changed since the formation of the solar system, it could tell us much about the cloud of gas and dust from which the Sun and planets formed.

Craters of all sizes dominate the landscape. The rubble littering the barren ground everywhere is debris from eons of impacts. The horizon is hilly and uneven, with a suggestion of a couple of small flat-topped mountains projecting over the horizon—probably the rims of large craters. It may be that our landing site is within an ancient large crater—it is hard to tell. How well named Pluto is. The desolate frozen landscape, the dim and eerie light—it is not hard to imagine that the god Pluto lives here.

As we begin to walk about, we feel very light on our feet, and with each step we take, we bounce high above the ground. We have seen videotapes of the Apollo astronauts bounding across the Moon in one-sixth Earth gravity. Pluto's surface gravity is even weaker: less than one-third of our Moon's and only 5 percent what we experience on Earth. Here on Pluto, a 160-pound (73-kilogram) man weighs 8 pounds (3.6 kilograms). On Earth, from a standing start, we could jump about a foot (0.3 meter) into the air. With a flexible lightweight spacesuit on Pluto, we could jump about 20 times as high. Garage jumping could become a popular sport.

We will have to be careful not to venture too far from our lander without a homing device. Distance is hard to judge on a world where there are no familiar objects like houses to give a sense of scale and no haze to make the horizon look distant. Besides, on a small world like Pluto, the horizon not only looks sharp and nearby, it is truly very close. If we wander just 2.5 miles (4 kilometers) from our spacecraft, an astronaut standing on the ground there would lose sight of us below the horizon.[17]

One of our crucial experiments here will be to drill a hole in Pluto and pull out a core sample to see what lies below the surface. The abundance of water elsewhere in the outer solar system, including Charon, and the modest density of Pluto point to water being a major component of the planet, although its presence on Pluto has not yet been confirmed because the spectrum of methane overwhelms the spectral bands of water. Does frozen water lie trapped below the surface? Perhaps much of the terrain upon which we are standing is water ice mixed with flecks of carbon and other compounds, which gives it a darker cast.

Over there—and, yes, elsewhere, now that we look closely—are white frosty patches. We bounce over for a closer look. (It's hard to stop bouncing.) It is a thin layer of methane frost in beautiful large crystals. The sublimation of methane from ice to gas provides Pluto with a very tenuous atmosphere. Some of the methane vaporizing here will drift toward the poles and freeze on the ground there until the changing seasons bring summer to the north pole in 2051. But by then, Pluto will be much farther from the Sun and less methane will sublimate. Pluto's poles stay covered with methane ice throughout the planet's 248-year period of revolution.

On our descent for landing, flying along Pluto's equator, we saw (in our continuing speculation) a large white feature, perhaps 250 miles (400 kilometers) across. It looked like a refugee from the polar ice caps. Yet we knew to watch for it. It was predicted by Buie's two-spot model of Pluto, based on light variations as the planet rotates. The roughly circular shape of this intensely white spot suggests an impact feature. Has it filled with ice welling up from below, like that bright crater on Uranus' Umbriel? Is it a young feature that has not yet had time to darken from exposure to sunlight and fast-traveling subatomic particles from the Sun and stars? Why it should be so different from the surrounding terrain is not obvious.

We hope to explore that equatorial bright spot later, but we have deliberately landed near an even larger feature and are making our way there now. On light/dark maps of Pluto it appeared as an extremely dark spot perhaps 500 miles (800 kilometers) across—more than a third the diameter of Pluto.

Computer models of Pluto's surface used circular spots for convenience to approximate the sizes and positions of features that could provide the planet with the light variations it shows. Does an actual feature exist where the model shows a huge dark circular spot? A giant impact basin has this shape. Imagine it, stretched out before us: an enormous crater, its walls and floors pocked by other craters. We are surrounded by desolation. This crater is so immense that it quickly stretches out of sight beyond the horizon in front of us and to our sides. It must be primarily this dark feature that created the light variations from Pluto that first allowed the length of its day to be measured at 6.4 Earth days. But if this basin was formed by impact, how could Pluto have survived the shock? At the very least, the impact would have caused such upheavals within Pluto that the scar would have been erased.

Whatever surface features may correspond to the small bright spot and large dark spot in Buie's model, they are located on the side of Pluto always facing away from Charon. We return to the side of Pluto where Charon can always and only be seen—a hemisphere with only slight contrasts.

Moonlight

We look up at Charon in the sky, 20 times closer to Pluto than our Moon is to Earth. It is an impressive sight. Charon may rank twelfth in size among moons in the solar system, but it is so close to Pluto—only 11,650 miles (18,800 kilometers) above Pluto's equator—that it appears larger than any other moon appears from the surface of its planet. Charon covers almost 4 degrees in Pluto's sky—eight times as wide as our Moon appears from Earth. On our planet, you can hold a pea out at arm's length and completely eclipse our Moon. On Pluto, to block Charon from view, you would need a billiard ball.

It was no surprise that Charon rotates in the same period of time as it revolves so that it always presents the same hemisphere to Pluto. All the inner satellites and all the major satellites in the solar system have synchronous rotation and revolution because they are tidally coupled to their planets. A planet's gravity creates a slight tidal bulge in its moons and pulls on that bulge so that the moons cannot turn it away from the planet. One side of the satellite always faces the planet and the other side always faces away while the planet rotates rapidly, so that the moon rises and sets for all parts of the planet.

But Pluto furnished a surprise. Pluto and Charon are so close to twins in size and so close together that Charon's gravity induces a bulge in Pluto. The bulge is great enough that Pluto is tidally coupled to Charon just as Charon is tidally coupled to Pluto. Thus, Pluto always shows the same face to Charon just as Charon always shows the same face to Pluto. It is the only example of mutual tidal coupling in the solar system.[18] The result is that for an astronaut standing on Pluto, Charon is either always visible or never visible. If it is visible from that location, Charon never rises or sets and always stands at the same place above the horizon. If

NO TIDAL COUPLING (Not to scale)

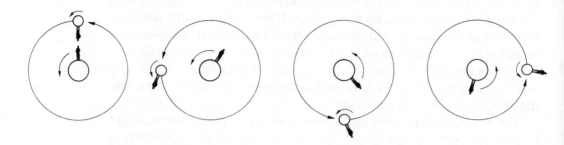

SATELLITE TIDALLY COUPLED: EARTH/MOON SYSTEM
(Moon shows only one side to Earth)

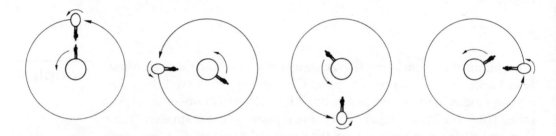

PLANET AND SATELLITE BOTH TIDALLY COUPLED: PLUTO/CHARON SYSTEM
(Both bodies show only one side to each other)

Planet-moon systems
with and without tidal
coupling

Charon is not visible from the astronaut's landing site, it will never rise,
and the astronaut will have to make a pilgrimage to the proper side of
Pluto to enjoy moonlight.

We have deliberately landed on the hemisphere of Pluto where Charon
is always seen. Charon far outshines all other bodies in the sky except
the Sun. And it is close enough to show surface features even without

a telescope. The shadows we see on Charon reveal an uneven, cratered landscape. Like Pluto, Charon is light gray, although somewhat darker and more even in color than Pluto, as was known from measurements made from Earth using the Pluto-Charon eclipses. The very slightly reddish brown hue of Pluto is missing from Charon—or at least from Charon's Pluto-facing side, that is the only side we get to see from the surface of Pluto. Missing too from Charon is the methane frost which partially covers Pluto. With Charon's smaller mass and therefore weaker gravity, whatever methane ice there was at the surface has evaporated.[19] Perhaps this in part explains why Charon is less reflective. The escaping methane has exposed frozen water to view.

On Earth, we are used to the rising and setting of the Sun, Moon, and stars as our planet turns. On Pluto, the Sun rises and sets, if somewhat slowly, but Charon stays fixed in the sky.[20] It never rises or sets, thanks to tidal coupling. As Charon revolves once around Pluto in 6.4 days, Pluto spins once around on its axis in that same period of time. The result is that Charon hangs almost stationary in the sky while the Sun and stars glide slowly past in the background. Because Charon is so large in the sky, stars are frequently blocked from view. These stellar occultations are the only eclipses visible during the 120-year gap between seasons of solar and lunar eclipses.

From the vantage point of Earth, Pluto and Charon pass in front of and behind one another very rarely. The Earth experiences solar and lunar eclipses at least four times and sometimes as many as seven times a year. Because of Pluto's axial tilt and Charon's position over Pluto's equator, the pair go for almost 120 years without their shadows ever falling upon one another. Then, in a period roughly six years long, Charon's orbit is nearly edge on to Earth and every 6.39-day orbit Charon makes carries it across the face of Pluto and then around behind Pluto. The result is an eclipse frenzy. Serendipitously, that eclipse season began in 1985, soon after Charon was discovered and while Pluto and Charon were near perihelion (hence easiest to study). The eclipse season will continue into October 1990. After 1990 there will be no more occultations or transits of the pair until about 2109, and then Pluto will be its farthest from the Sun and its least accommodating for study from Earth.

For an astronaut on Pluto in 1988, at the peak of the present eclipse season, a solar eclipse is a stirring sight. The Sun is by far the brightest object in the sky, but in apparent size, it seems to be no more than a starlike dot. The rotation of Pluto carries this dazzling point of light closer and closer to the huge disk of Charon until it disappears—dimming out at Charon's limb in a little less than 30 seconds.[21] With the Sun passing behind the widest part of Charon's disk, the total phase of this solar eclipse would last 1 hour 37 minutes. (The total phase of solar eclipses on Earth last a maximum of 7 minutes.)

During an eclipse of the Sun on Pluto, Charon would look like a giant dark hole in the sky, marked only by the absence of stars. It would be dark but not black because it would be illuminated by reflected light from Pluto. The corona—the outer atmosphere of the Sun, which makes solar eclipses seen from Earth so beautiful—would be visible only just after the Sun vanished and just before it reappeared. At mid-eclipse, the disk of Charon covers the entire orbit of the Earth. The corona is far too faint at that distance from the Sun to peer around the edges of Charon.

The Origin of Pluto

How could this strange double-planet system have developed? The rest of the planets in our solar system lie in a plane that is so wide and yet so flat that if it were shrunk to a size you could hold in your hand, the solar system out through Neptune would be about the size and thickness of a *Time* magazine. But Pluto violates that analogy.

Of all the planets, the inclination (17.2 degrees) and the eccentricity (0.25) of Pluto's orbit is the greatest. Its orbit is so elliptical that Pluto sails out to a distance of 49.3 astronomical units—almost 4.6 billion miles (7.4 billion kilometers) from the Sun. Since its last aphelion in 1866, the year after the conclusion of the Civil War, the elliptical orbit of Pluto has been carrying it ever closer to the Sun. On January 21, 1979, Pluto passed inside the orbit of Neptune—the only planet that crosses the orbit of another. Pluto will spend 20 years closer to the Sun than Neptune and will not resume its usual distinction as the outermost planet until May 14, 1999. When *Voyager 2* reaches Neptune on August 24, 1989,[22] it will literally be visiting the farthermost planet from the Sun.

The modest size of Pluto that was emerging after its discovery and its excursion within the orbit of Neptune suggested to some astronomers that Pluto's ancestry could be traced back to Neptune.

In 1934, Issei Yamamoto of Japan proposed in a lecture that Pluto was an escaped moon of Neptune. Yamamoto suggested that a star passed close to Neptune, causing Neptune to fall to an orbit closer to the Sun. The encounter also forced Triton into a retrograde orbit and cast Pluto out onto a planetary orbit centered on Neptune's original distance from the Sun (in agreement with Bode's Law for an eighth planet).[23]

In 1936, Raymond A. Lyttleton of England attempted to explain Pluto's curious orbit by suggesting that Pluto had originally been a moon of Neptune but that a near collision between Triton and Pluto had gravitationally accelerated Pluto out of the Neptunian system and had radically altered the course of Triton so that it now moved around Neptune in the opposite direction—the largest satellite with retrograde motion and the only satellite with that orbital anomaly that lies close to a planet.

In 1956, Gerard P. Kuiper agreed that Pluto had come from the Neptunian system, escaping as the planets completed their formation. But Kuiper saw no need for a near collision with Triton to eject Pluto. Instead he thought that Pluto had abandoned Neptune when the Sun began to shine. The Sun's radiation and particles had, he said, swept away the light gases at Neptune, reducing the planet's mass by a factor of 40. Neptune then had too little mass to retain Pluto by gravity.[24]

Many astronomers, however, were uncomfortable with the idea that Pluto had come from the Neptune system. They pointed out that when Pluto crosses the path of Neptune, it is always 8.9 astronomical units north of Neptune's orbit on its way inbound to perihelion and 6.1 astronomical units north of Neptune's orbit outbound. At its closest, Pluto is about as close to Neptune's orbit as the Earth is to Jupiter when they are on opposite sides of the Sun. The orbits of Neptune and Pluto never intersect like a road at a railway crossing. Instead the passage is more like a bridge high above the railroad track. When it moved temporarily inside the orbit of Neptune in 1979, Pluto passed far above the path of Neptune, and Neptune was nowhere near that point in its orbit.

If Pluto crosses above Neptune's orbit at a minimum distance of 6.1 astronomical units, it would seem that every once in a long while Pluto and Neptune must come as close to one another as 6.1 astronomical units. But according to careful mathematical analysis and computer simulation, Pluto and Neptune can never get closer to one another than 16.7 astronomical units—almost the distance from the Earth to Uranus.[25]

Picture Pluto's orbit as a moderately elongated ellipse made of stiff wire. Normally, a planet revolves around its orbit like a bead strung on the wire while the entire orbit—the stiff wire—very slowly rotates (precesses) like a very fat hour hand on a clock.

The reason that Neptune and Pluto never come close together is that the size of the gravitational forces that Neptune, Uranus, Saturn, and Jupiter exert on Pluto and the timing of those forces do not allow Pluto's orbit to precess but only to oscillate within a very narrow range. This confinement appears to be permanent, so Pluto's and Neptune's orbits can never and have never come close to actually intersecting so that a collision or close encounter would be possible. Further, the rhythmic gravitational effects of the outer planets slightly adjust the size and shape of Pluto's orbit, and thus its period of revolution, so that Neptune is never nearby when Pluto crosses over Neptune's orbit.

Curiously, Neptune and Pluto are closest to one another when Pluto is near aphelion—about as far beyond the orbit of Neptune as it can get.

Pluto can actually come closer to Uranus (10.6 astronomical units) than it can to Neptune.

Recently, astronomers have used supercomputers to calculate the paths of Pluto and Neptune hundreds of millions of years backward into the past and forward into the future, trying to take into account the gravitational perturbations they caused in each other's orbit and the perturbations that the other giant planets caused in theirs. These studies have found no incident where Neptune or Pluto were precariously close to one another.[26]

The discovery of Charon greatly changed the perspective on Pluto's origins, just as it changed many perceptions of Pluto. First, the motion of Charon showed that Pluto was even smaller than previously imagined. There was no way that Pluto, as a moon of Neptune, could have reversed Triton's orbital direction. With such a low mass, if Pluto, as a moon of Neptune, had ever received an acceleration from a close encounter with

IS PLUTO A PLANET?

As information about Pluto has increased, the size attributed to Pluto has decreased. It is certainly the smallest planet, far smaller than Mercury. It is considerably smaller in size and mass than our Moon. At the same time, Pluto has shrunk in the estimation of some astronomers to the point that they are calling for the expulsion of Pluto from the ranks of planethood and its demotion to the category of asteroid.

How does Pluto fit in with the minor planets? Lousy. First of all, it's too large. It is more than twice the diameter of the largest asteroid, Ceres. Even Charon, Pluto's moon, is larger than Ceres. In fact, Pluto has about three times more mass than all the asteroids in the solar system put together.

Second, Pluto is in the wrong place to be an asteroid. The vast majority of minor planets orbit the Sun between Mars and Jupiter. The only known minor planet beyond Jupiter that doesn't return to this asteroid belt for part of its orbit is Chiron, whose circuit carries it from just inside the orbit of Saturn to just inside the orbit of Uranus. It never gets within a billion miles (1.6 billion kilometers) of Pluto. Chiron's mean distance from the Sun (13.7 astronomical units) places it closer to the asteroid belt than to Pluto.

If a second asteroid belt is discovered beyond Neptune and if Pluto is fairly typical of the size and composition of those minor planets, then it might make sense to recategorize Pluto as an outer asteroid. But Clyde Tombaugh and, 40 years later, Charles Kowal diligently searched the heavens for Pluto-sized objects beyond Neptune. They found none, and it is most likely that objects even close to that size do not exist or at least are very rare.

Pluto is different from the known asteroids in other ways as well. Its much greater mass allows it to retain a moon and a tenuous atmosphere.

Pluto just doesn't qualify as an asteroid. We learn little or nothing about the structure of the solar system by approaching Pluto as a minor planet.

How then does Pluto fare as a comet? Better, but still poor. Pluto's distance from the Sun places it not too far inward from the possible inner edge of the Oort Cloud of comets. Pluto's composition and the ellipticity and inclination of its orbit are somewhat cometlike. But again, Pluto is far too large. The nucleus of a typical comet is perhaps 5 to 10 miles its master, Pluto would have been ejected from the solar system, not just the Neptunian family.

Since gravitational interaction within the Neptune system between Triton and Pluto would not have been powerful enough to have caused the peculiar orbits of Neptune's satellites, Robert S. Harrington and Thomas C. Van Flandern in 1979 proposed a different source of energy. They suggested that Triton, Pluto, and Charon were indeed once moons of Neptune but that their orbits had been disrupted by an outside intruder—an undiscovered tenth planet with two to five times the mass of Earth. Pluto and Charon were ejected from the Neptune system close enough together to be gravitationally bound.

But most astronomers now believe that Pluto and Triton are planetesimals left over from the beginning of our solar system. Other planetesimals that reached their size merged together to form still-larger bodies such as Uranus and Neptune. Pluto (with its satellite Charon) was

---

(8 to 15 kilometers) across. Pluto is about 1,457 miles (2,345 kilometers) in diameter.

Pluto is also somewhat too dense. Comets are dirty snowballs with a density close to that of water. Pluto's density is twice as great, indicating that it is about 70 percent rock and 30 percent ice. Its density is similar to Triton's and Neptune's and intermediate between those of comets and asteroids.

Pluto—as well as Uranus, Neptune, and their icy satellites—probably originated from the accretion of comets, just as Earth and the other rocky midget planets near the Sun probably formed from rocky planetesimals of which the asteroid belt is the least altered remnant. But no one considers the Earth an asteroid even though its progenitors were asteroid-like. So, likewise, it would be unhelpful to classify Pluto as a comet.

There is simply nothing to be gained by excluding Pluto from planethood. There is no asteroid belt known beyond Neptune for which Pluto can serve as a charter member. Even if Pluto is an overgrown comet, it is far too large to be representative of that species. Therefore, to designate Pluto as an asteroid or comet is to make it an orphan—too different from its brethren for useful comparison. To desig-

nate Pluto an asteroid or a comet is to ensure that it will virtually drop from treatment in classrooms and schoolbooks, and a new generation of children will grow up thinking of Pluto as a "mistake," if they have any awareness of Pluto at all.

And then think how easy it will be to convince any Congress that NASA deserves funds to send a spacecraft to an extremely distant asteroid.

No. Pluto is a planet—by orbit and by size. It is best understood—and taught in astronomy courses—as a probable example of a large outer solar system planetesimal, the kind of object formed from cometlike bodies in the outer planetary realm at the beginning of our solar system. Most of these planetesimals merged with others to mold the comet conglomerates we now call Uranus, Neptune, and their moons.

But there may be a pair of planetesimals that did not coalesce further. Pluto and Charon have potential value to science not as representatives of a class of asteroids or comets but as large, nearly pristine planetesimals—the objects from which gas giant planets and their moons are made.

locked by the gravity of the outer planets in a resonant orbit that protected it from collision with and accretion into a larger planet. William B. McKinnon has suggested that Triton survived until planet formation was nearly complete but then passed close by Neptune, was slowed by the gas and dust remaining around the planet, and was captured by Neptune's powerful gravitational field into a retrograde orbit.

Such a capture would have caused intense heating inside Triton, melting the interior and allowing the newly acquired satellite to differentiate. If so, the surface of Triton should still attest to its stressful early life. Pictures and measurements from *Voyager 2* at Triton may indicate whether it was indeed captured by Neptune.[27]

Although Pluto never experienced the stresses imposed on Triton by Neptune, its interior too has probably undergone major changes since accretion. The presence of low-density methane ice everywhere on the surface of Pluto and yet the substantial density of the planet, about twice that of water, suggests to McKinnon and Steve Mueller that Pluto's interior must have melted and separated into layers.

Pluto's density indicates that it is composed of much more rock than

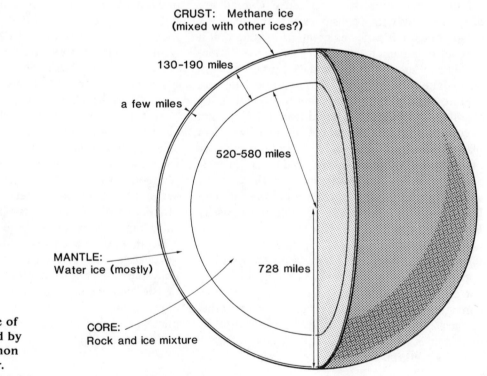

CRUST: Methane ice
(mixed with other ices?)

130–190 miles

a few miles

520–580 miles

728 miles

MANTLE:
Water ice (mostly)

CORE:
Rock and ice mixture

Internal structure of Pluto as proposed by William B. McKinnon and Steve Mueller.

ice. The quantity of rock is great enough so that the decay of radioactive elements soon after the planet formed must have caused Pluto's interior to differentiate, with the denser rocky materials sinking toward the center and the lighter ices floating toward the surface. With methane ice concentrated toward the surface, slow vaporization could have kept Pluto supplied with a thin methane atmosphere since the solar system began.[28]

McKinnon and Mueller also suggest that Charon was once part of Pluto. A large planetesimal wandering through the outer solar system smashed into the original, larger Pluto. But the orbital velocities of objects so far from the Sun are not so great that the collision would have scattered the debris widely. Instead, the fragments of the original Pluto, continuing to orbit together, could have reaccreted but into two smaller bodies orbiting one another—Pluto and Charon.

As perhaps the only remaining large planetesimals left in the outer solar system, Triton and Pluto-Charon could be closely related. Since Pluto will soon be gliding farther from the Sun again and since no spacecraft to visit it has yet been planned, it may be that Triton is our best clue to the nature of Pluto, unless Triton's capture by Neptune has changed it too greatly to provide useful comparisons.

A Mission to Pluto?

On September 12, 1989, Pluto will celebrate perihelion, its closest approach to the Sun, when it reaches a distance of 2.75 billion miles (4.4 billion kilometers). Astronomers—professional and amateur—will join the celebration because Pluto at perihelion is seven times brighter than at aphelion. When it is farthest from the Sun, Pluto sinks to magnitude 15.9 and a 22-inch (56-centimeter) telescope is about the minimum size required to study the distant planet. At perihelion Pluto is expected to reach a maximum magnitude of 13.6, so an 8-inch (20-centimeter) telescope should just be able to discern it.[29]

During 1999, Pluto will return to its role as the outermost planet, gradually sliding back into the darkness of distance that helped to hide it from discovery and then from understanding for so many years. The next decade or two offers a rare window of opportunity to study what for 228 out of its 248-year orbit is the most remote planet in our solar system.

Will there be a space probe to visit Pluto and Charon in the near future? NASA has no plans, but the Soviet, European, Japanese, and Chinese space programs are expanding. Now is the time for a mission to Pluto, while the planet is still about as close to the Sun as it ever gets. Send a spacecraft to Pluto soon and save 1 billion miles (1.6 billion kilometers) over the average distance from the Earth to Pluto. That's a savings of greater than the distance between the Earth and Saturn.

A direct flight from the Earth to Pluto using a least-energy orbit would take 40 years. But by using Jupiter for a gravity assist, the time for the journey would be cut to 10 to 15 years, and far less energy would be required. The next launch window for a Jupiter-assist flight to Pluto is in the late 1980s—but no spacecraft has been built. The next opportunity will come in 12 years when Jupiter completes another revolution of the Sun and begins to overtake Pluto once more. Perhaps there will be an orbiter and lander mission on its way to the outermost planet and its outsized moon in the year 2001.

CHAPTER 13

Is There a Tenth Planet?

*"The finding of Pluto was an important discovery, but
what you did not find out there is even more important."*
Astronomer Gerard P. Kuiper to Clyde Tombaugh
(1950)

As soon as Tombaugh had discovered Pluto and reconfirmed it with new photographs, he resumed his systematic photographic survey in Cancer and Leo where he had left off. This self-assigned use of time was probably a good release of nervous energy because almost four weeks would pass between the moment he delightedly called across the hall to Lampland and the actual announcement of a ninth planet. However, said Tombaugh, "I suspended blinking, thinking the search was over—so I thought. I was getting tired of the tedious blinking anyway."[1]

After ten weeks of excitement, the pressure for information from other observatories and from journalists had subsided. One day in late May 1930, Vesto Slipher went to Tombaugh and made a request: "I would like you to resume searching. There might be more planets out there like Pluto. Start where you left off in February." Tombaugh was pleased: "The staff now had complete confidence in my work. I had examined two million stars. To cover the wider area, I had at least twenty million stars to go." That number proved to be an underestimate.

He steadily expanded his search north and south of the ecliptic to take in all the sky visible from Flagstaff. He kept a special eye out for the several planets that William H. Pickering had predicted. "As I was to learn over the next thirteen years in the resumed search," wrote Tombaugh, "not one of his other planets existed."

Tombaugh worked on resolutely: "After the experience with greed involved in the Pluto discovery, I could see that even in astronomy, it was a dog-eat-dog situation. After all the sacrifices made by the Lowell family and the staff, I was determined that if there were more planets to be found, they would be found at the Lowell Observatory."

By April of 1938, Tombaugh had photographed with the 13-inch telescope and examined with the blink microscope 35 million stars. By July of 1943 he had photographed the entire sky visible from Flagstaff, from Canopus to Polaris. But his tolerance for blinking was steadily dropping. Once he could maintain concentration for five to six hours per day. A few years after the discovery of Pluto, he had to cut back to three to four hours. Now he could endure only two hours a day. "I was burning out," he said.

In July 1943, in the midst of World War II, Clyde Tombaugh, now 37 years old, was drafted to teach navigation for the Navy in Flagstaff. With that event, said Tombaugh, "my planet searching ended forever."

His final tally of individual stars photographed and blinked numbered 45 million—90 million paired images. He had spent 7,000 hours at the blink microscope, the equivalent of doing nothing else for an eight-hour working day for three and a half years.

In his 14 years at the blink comparator, Tombaugh had found:

1 new globular star cluster
5 new open star clusters
1 new supercluster of 1,800 galaxies
several new small clusters of galaxies
1 new comet
about 775 new asteroids
and
1 new planet

Because of his careful and dogged years of search, Tombaugh was confident that no planet brighter than magnitude 16.5 existed within his field of coverage. Only a planet in an almost polar orbit and situated near the south pole (not visible from Flagstaff) could have escaped his detection. A planet the size of Jupiter would have been detected at 470 astronomical units (12 times Pluto's distance from the Sun). He could have picked up a Neptune-size planet at 7 times the distance of Neptune. He could have seen a planet the size of Pluto at 1.5 times Pluto's average distance from the Sun. "Other planets like Pluto do not appear to exist out to a distance of 60 astronomical units," Tombaugh concluded,

Beyond 60 astronomical units, said Tombaugh, more Pluto-like planets could exist, but their perturbations, like Pluto's, would be immeasurable. The only means to find them would be by a comprehensive observational search of lengthy, tedious, and costly proportions.

But if Pluto wasn't massive enough to have caused the irregularities in the motion of Uranus and (according to William H. Pickering) the motion of Neptune as well, what *was* causing those discrepancies? Had Planet X been missed?

As it gradually became apparent that Pluto was too small to be the culprit, predictions for the existence of a tenth planet began to appear fairly steadily, most based on new analyses of the orbital discrepancies.[2]

Some of the scientists who think there is evidence that points toward a trans-Plutonian planet and who have been most active recently in pursuit of Planet 10 are Thomas C. Van Flandern and Robert S. Harrington, Daniel P. Whitmire and John J. Matese, John D. Anderson, and Conley Powell. Each came to the conclusion that a tenth planet exists by a different route, but the planet each envisioned had much in common with the others.

The Quest Goes On

Piecing Scattered Clues Together

His work at the Almanac Office of the U.S. Naval Observatory kept Tom Van Flandern close to peculiarities in planetary orbits. The outer planets were uncooperative. The calculated orbits for Neptune would fit its observed position and provide useful predictions for a few years, but by the end of ten years, the predicted positions were considerably in error. A calculated orbit for Uranus would fit for one whole revolution of the planet but, maddeningly, would not fit the previous or a subsequent revolution. The orbits of some short-period comets also, he felt, showed the effects of perturbations that could not be explained by the gravity of known planets or by the jet effect of ice on rotating comets vaporizing so that it slightly alters the comets' orbits. Van Flandern became convinced about 1976 that the discrepancies in the motion of Uranus and Neptune were real and not just errors of measurement.

He then called the anomalies in the motions of Uranus, Neptune, and the comets to the attention of his Naval Observatory colleague Robert S. Harrington and suggested the idea of a tenth planet. Harrington was skeptical at first, but the discovery of a moon for Pluto showed that the mass of Pluto was far too small to disturb Uranus, Neptune, or distant comets.

Van Flandern and Harrington began their collaboration with a study of the peculiarities in the Neptune system. The newly calculated mass of Pluto had demolished Lyttleton's already seriously undermined idea that Pluto was once a satellite of Neptune along with Triton and that a gravitational encounter between Triton and Pluto had reversed the orbital motion of Triton and hurled Pluto out into its own orbit around the Sun. Pluto didn't have the mass to turn Triton around.

Could the gravitational energy to force Triton into retrograde revolu-

Thomas C. Van Flandern
Courtesy of Thomas C. Van Flandern

Robert S. Harrington
Official U.S. Naval Observatory photograph

tion have come from an outside source—the same source that they felt was disturbing the outer planets? Could that intruder have been a planet?

They made computer simulations of planets of different sizes intruding into the Neptunian system at different distances, speeds, and angles. From their computations emerged a nominee—a planet with two to five times the mass of Earth in a highly inclined and elliptical orbit 50 to 100 astronomical units from the Sun with an orbital period of about 800 years.[3] In one brief visit long ago, the intruder had reversed the motion of Triton, warped the orbit of Nereid, and cast the moon Pluto out of the Neptune family onto a planetary orbit of its own. Charon, they suspected, was either an additional satellite of Neptune expelled along with Pluto so that they captured one another; or, alternatively, the intensity of the intruding planet's tidal strain had caused Pluto to break in two, with Charon as the smaller fragment. For Van Flandern there was a third alternative: Charon might be a former satellite of the intruder planet that was transferred to Pluto's control as Pluto and the intruder sped away after the encounter.

With their inclined, eccentric path, Harrington and Van Flandern felt, Pluto and Charon hinted at their past by returning four times a millennium to a position near the scene of the crime—the place from which they were kidnapped and abandoned, the place of their birth.

The ideas of Van Flandern and Harrington then began to diverge. Van Flandern continued to think that the marauding planet had formed beyond Neptune at the beginning of the solar system. Harrington thought that Planet 10 had formed between the orbits of Uranus and Neptune.

As to commencing a search for Planet 10, Van Flandern felt it was too early. More data was needed, such as an improved determination of the mass of Neptune, which *Voyager 2* should furnish. Also needed was much more mathematical analysis to demonstrate that a tenth planet had to exist and where it could be found.

Harrington preferred to approach the problem of locating the suspected planet by brute force—supplying a computer with thousands of orbits to crunch in order to find those orbits that might be possible. He began searching for Planet 10 in October 1979, using the Naval Observatory's 15-inch (38-centimeter) astrograph (a wide-field photographic survey telescope) in Washington, D.C. In 1980, he continued, using the 24-inch (61-centimeter) Curtis Schmidt Telescope at the Cerro Tololo Inter-American Observatory in Chile. Additional searches were mounted in 1981 and 1984 with the 15-inch telescope in Washington, D.C., and then in 1986 and 1987 with the 8-inch (20-centimeter) double astrograph of the U.S. Naval Observatory's Black Birch site in New Zealand. He examined all the plates on a blink comparator and has, in his words, "nothing to show for my efforts."[4]

He and Van Flandern still agree that Planet 10 should be a frozen methane, ammonia, and water world somewhat like Uranus and Neptune but of lower mass—perhaps two to five times the mass of Earth. To remain so far unseen, Planet 10 must be nearing aphelion on its highly elliptical orbit, so that it is near minimum brightness. Still, for an icy body its size, this tenth planet should be about magnitude 13, some six times brighter than Pluto when it was found. Van Flandern suggests that a trans-Plutonian planet could be dark in color, reflecting light so poorly that it would be no brighter than 16th or 17th magnitude—fainter than Pluto at its discovery.

Harrington is not driven on in his quest by utter confidence in the irregularities in the motions of the outer planets. He thinks they are real but admits they are slight. Imagine, he says, observing from Washington, D.C., and identifying a drunk coming out of a Baltimore bar by his stagger. That's the size of the alleged perturbations in the motions of Uranus and Neptune. It may be, he feels, that these discrepancies are errors in converting older observations to a common reference frame. But he is encouraged to keep hunting by the computer simulation he and Van Flandern performed, that found that a single planet of modest mass passing only once through the Neptune system could account for the present motions of Triton, Nereid, and Pluto.

And if he finds Planet 10, what will he name it? "Humphrey," he says. The name was inspired by "Humphrey the Camel," a somewhat off-color song from the 1960s. But Humphrey isn't exactly a traditional Roman or Greek name. "Well," he says, "I considered Zorba." When searching for a tenth planet, Harrington feels, commitment is necessary, but it doesn't pay to take yourself too seriously.[5]

The Killer Planet

In 1985 two more researchers postulated a tenth planet, but they approached the issue from a different direction. Daniel P. Whitmire and John J. Matese, at the University of Southwestern Louisiana, had been active in the controversy about the cause of mass extinctions on Earth, such as the one about 65 million years ago that wiped out the dinosaurs.

In 1980, Luis W. Alvarez, Walter Alvarez, Frank Asaro, and Helen V. Michel had proposed that the impact of an object from space had thrown so much dust into the atmosphere that the Sun was blocked from view. It was black as night for months. In the dark and cold, plants died. Animals that depended on the plants died. Animals that depended on other animals died. More than half the species of plants and animals on Earth perished at that time. The Alvarezes, Asaro, and Michel felt that the assassin was an asteroid perhaps 6 miles (10 kilometers) in diameter.[6]

But the extinction that claimed the dinosaurs and so much of life 65

**John J. Matese (left)
and Daniel P. Whitmire**
*Courtesy of Daniel P.
Whitmire and John J.
Matese*

million years ago was only one of many mass extinctions that the Earth
has experienced in the last 250 million years. In 1984, David M. Raup
and J. John Sepkoski, Jr., presented evidence that large-scale oblitera-
tions of life on our planet have occurred approximately every 28 million
years.[7]

Two different teams of researchers immediately recognized that asteroid
collisions with Earth are too infrequent to cause mass extinctions every
28 million years and that there was no mechanism to get asteroids to
hit the Earth with regularity. But comets could, if something was disturbing them. They proposed that the periodic mass extinctions were triggered by an unseen star within our solar system, bound to our Sun by
gravity, just as the planets are. After all, a majority of the stars in the
universe are binary or multiple star systems.

One team of researchers was Marc Davis, Piet Hut, and Richard A.
Muller; the other team was Daniel P. Whitmire and Albert A. Jackson
IV. Their proposals were independent, simultaneous, and very similar.
The Sun's companion had to be a star of low mass and hence low
brightness to remain unidentified when it was by far the closest star to
the Sun. This star had an elliptical orbit that carried it in as close as 0.5
light-year (about 30,000 astronomical units) to the Sun and then out to
a distance of 2.4 light-years (more than halfway to the nearest star) in
a period of 28 million years.

In the course of its travels, this star would at perihelion career through
the densest portion of the Oort Cloud of comets, accelerating millions
of them out of the solar system but decelerating millions of others, forcing them to fall in closer to the Sun so that some hit the Earth with momen-
tous consequences for the evolution of life. Davis, Hut, and Muller dubbed

this small but lethal hypothetical star Nemesis, "after the Greek goddess who relentlessly persecutes the excessively rich, proud, and powerful. We worry," they added, "that if the companion is not found, this paper will be our nemesis."[8]

There is, however, no consensus among paleontologists and geologists about the causes of mass extinctions and whether mass extinctions and cratering episodes occur at regular intervals. The controversy continues at a lively pace into the present.

Were mass extinctions caused by comet showers triggered by a companion star for our Sun? One of the early attacks on this hypothesis came from analyses of the stability of a companion star on such an elliptical orbit that carried it more than half the distance to the nearest star. It was doubtful that it could survive in such an orbit from the beginning of the solar system because the Sun's gravity at that distance is very weak. Stars and clouds of interstellar gas and dust passing near the solar system would have disrupted the regularity of the twin star's period and, rather quickly, would have torn it away from the Sun.

In proposing a "death star" hypothesis, Whitmire had already recognized the problem of a companion star's orbital stability. He and John J. Matese sought an alternative: What if the culprit were a planet instead? Instead of Sun 2 scattering comets with a plunge from the fringes into the densest regions of the Oort Cloud, this Planet 10 would disrupt comet orbits by scratching the innermost portion of the Oort Cloud from inside, in particular a disk of comets thought to lie in the plane of the solar system with orbits not far beyond Neptune and Pluto.

Yet Pluto takes only 248 years to orbit the Sun. How could a planet not too far beyond Pluto take 28 million years to complete a circuit? According to the law of gravity, it couldn't. Even a planet several times the distance of Pluto cannot revolve around the Sun that slowly. But the entire orbit of a planet will revolve due to the gravity of neighboring planets, and this precession can proceed very slowly.

Visualize Planet X on an elliptical orbit perpendicular to the plane of the solar system. If the plane of the solar system is a table top, then the orbit of Planet X is standing on its head. We see the table top at eye level edge on and the orbit of Planet X face on. In that headstand position, Planet X does not disturb any disk of ancient comets that lie in the plane of the solar system not far beyond Neptune and Pluto. But eventually it will disturb the comets in the disk because the gravity of the outer planets causes the entire orbit of Planet X to precess. The tilt of the orbit will stay inclined to the plane of the solar system by, say, 90 degrees, but the orbit will gradually pivot around like a very fat hour hand on a clock. It will pivot through the plane of the table and down, then back up through the plane of the table and back to its initial headstand position. In a multiple-exposure photograph, the ellipses of Planet X's orbit would form a rosette.

In the course of that precession, the outer portion of the orbit (the end of the fat hour hand) would slide through the comet disk only at the nine and three o'clock positions, sending swarms of comets in all directions only during those two relatively brief periods when the planet's aphelion is in or near the plane of the comet disk. If the orbit of Planet X completes one precession cycle in 56 million years, it will cause two periods of comet showers for the inner solar system—one every 28 million years.

But what would be the size of the orbit of a planet with an orbital precession of 56 million years? To their surprise, say Whitmire and Matese, the average distance of this planet from the Sun turned out to be only about 80 astronomical units (about twice the distance of Pluto). Its 700-year orbit would be substantially inclined (perhaps 45 degrees) and elliptical (slightly more than Pluto's). It would range far enough to chop through the comet disk when precession placed it in the proper position, but it was also close enough to the Sun to be detectable. The orbit of this Planet X would be stable.

It was at this point, say Matese and Whitmire, they noticed that their hypothetical planet was practically identical to the one proposed by Harrington and Van Flandern to explain a completely different set of problems. Harrington and Van Flandern's tenth planet was intended to solve

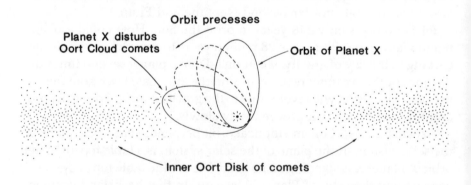

According to Daniel P. Whitmire and John J. Matese, Planet X has an elliptical orbit which is highly inclined to the plane of the solar system. The precession of that orbit causes it to pass through the disk of the inner Oort Cloud of comets, disturbing their orbits and causing comet showers for the inner solar system. Comet impacts on Earth from these showers, they believe, are responsible for periodic mass extinctions of life on our planet.

the irregularities in the positions of Uranus and Neptune, the strange orbits of Neptune's satellites, and the peculiar orbit of Pluto. Whitmire and Matese felt they had found a tenth planet in their data. Harrington and Van Flandern felt they had found a tenth planet in their very different data. Yet the two planets were essentially the same. Matese and Whitmire found in this convergence a great boost to their confidence.

They agree with Harrington and Van Flandern that there is a trans-Plutonian planet of substantial size to be found. No object in the solar system has caused more trouble. Imagine a Most Wanted poster for this fugitive planet.

WANTED on cosmic charges:

- Disturbing the motion of Uranus and Neptune.
- Smuggling short-period comets (like Halley's) into the inner solar system.
- Suspected of trespassing at Neptune, driving Triton and Nereid berserk, and kidnapping Pluto.
- Repeated assaults on Earth with deadly comets, causing periodic mass extinctions of life.

DESCRIPTION of fugitive: One to five Earth masses; eccentric, with odd inclination; likes to leave subtle clues to tantalize astronomers; lives in trans-Plutonia, constantly on move, no known address, might repeat movements every 700 years; knows how to hide.
NOTE: Substantial reward for information leading to his arrest.

Finding one planet, in the opinion of Whitmire and Matese, could solve many crimes.[9]

An analysis by Eugene M. Shoemaker and Ruth F. Wolfe, however, argues that even with a mass of five Earths, Planet X could not cause comet showers, a possible cause of mass extinctions on Earth. Pointing to other studies, they concluded that the purported inconsistencies in the motions of Uranus and Neptune do not indicate a tenth planet, that a planet of equal or greater mass than Earth would be so bright that it could hardly have escaped previous discovery, and that a planet larger than Earth would be unlikely to have formed beyond Pluto.[10] Matese and Whitmire counter that their own analyses show that a Planet X with five Earth masses could cause comet showers, that a planet with low reflectivity or one located deep in the southern sky could have escaped detection, and that the study that indicated an Earth-size planet could not form beyond Pluto also cannot account for the existence of Uranus and Neptune.

Watching for a Spacecraft to Quiver

John Anderson
Courtesy of John Anderson

In 1987 a new proponent of a tenth planet emerged on the scene. John Anderson at the Jet Propulsion Laboratory was working with NASA's *Pioneer 10* and *11* spacecraft, which had preceded the *Voyagers. Pioneer 10* flew by Jupiter. *Pioneer 11* flew by Jupiter and converted its close passage into a gravity assist to Saturn. Both craft are now headed out of the solar system in nearly opposite directions, and *Pioneer 10* is already beyond the orbits of the planets.

Anderson tracked the departing probes by their radio signals for five years to see if either was deflected from its course by gravity waves moving across the cosmos or by the gravity of a trans-Plutonian planet. Neither craft exhibited any sign of unusual perturbation.

Anderson therefore concluded that a tenth planet most likely does exist! A positive conclusion from what seemed like negative evidence.

Two years earlier, the interpretation of this data by Anderson and E. Myles Standish, Jr., had been negative: "A three-year analysis of radio tracking data from the Pioneer 10 spacecraft . . . fails to reveal the presence of Planet X."[11]

But now Anderson felt that the slight unpredictabilities in the motion of the outer planets that U.S. Naval Observatory astronomers had called attention to could best be explained by the existence of a tenth planet. Therefore, the lack of perturbations in the spacecraft provided information about the unseen planet's path.

The Jet Propulsion Laboratory had calculated highly accurate orbits for Uranus and Neptune by including only observations from 1910 to the present and by excluding earlier observations. Anderson had confidence in almost all the observational data—new and old. He therefore concluded that an unseen outer planet had been disturbing Uranus and Neptune before and during the nineteenth century but that the planet was now too far away for its gravitational effects to be noticeable on the planets or even on the two tiny and distant *Pioneer* craft.

Thus Planet 10, he surmised, must have a highly elliptical orbit that carries it far enough away to be undetectable now but periodically brings it close enough to leave its disturbing signature on the paths of the outer planets. He put the orbital period at 700 to 1,000 years. The suspect planet also had to have a highly inclined orbit so as to have produced no detectable deflection of either of the *Pioneers*. Finally, to create the planet perturbations reported in the Naval Observatory data, he concluded that the planet must have a mass of about five Earths. This Planet X is now far away, nearing aphelion, where its gravitational effects are unnoticeable. Its perturbations on the outer planets won't be detected again until about the year 2600.

For the time being, this distant planet, if it exists, has left us few, if any, clues as to where in the sky to search for it. Anderson hopes that, as the two *Voyager* craft sail out beyond the planets, they may help to pin down the location of Planet X.

The most recent of the proposals for a tenth planet is also the most traditional in methodology. Conley Powell is an aerospace engineer for Teledyne-Brown Engineering in Huntsville, Alabama, who specializes in astrodynamics. He calculates orbits. So slight discrepancies in the motions of the outer planets that U.S. Naval Observatory astronomers could not explain as observational errors were fascinating to him. He discarded the Neptune residuals from consideration even though Harrington and Van Flandern thought them significant because he felt that, with less than one full revolution completed since it was discovered, Neptune's precise orbit was still too uncertain. The orbit of Uranus, however, was much better known, and he began an analysis of the discrepancies between the predicted and actual positions of Uranus in the tradition of Adams, Le Verrier, and Lowell, with the hope that the position of a tenth planet could be determined mathematically.

As the Jet Propulsion Laboratory mathematicians had shown, the observations of Uranus after 1910 provide much more orbital accuracy than early ones. Powell therefore assigned less weight to early visual and even early photographic observations and more weight to twentieth-century Uranus position records, based on probable errors in the data as computed according to statistical theory. It was not, he felt, a question of the disturbing planet getting farther away during the past 80 years. The data improvement about 1910 was too sudden to be attributed to the growing distance of a tenth planet. It was due instead, he thought, to new techniques used to pinpoint planet positions.

Powell's calculations showed Planet X with 2.9 Earth masses at a distance from the Sun of 60.8 astronomical units, giving a period of revolution of 494 years.[12] He was intrigued that this number was approximately twice the period of Pluto and three times the period of Neptune—suggesting that the planet he thought he saw in the data had an orbit stabilized by mutual gravitational resonance with its nearest neighbors despite their vast separation.

His calculations for a tenth planet also provided an orbit inclined by only 8.3 degrees (less than Pluto's) and only slightly eccentric (but not firm enough to warrant a number). The orbital resonance of Planet 10 and the unspectacular nature of its derived orbit gave him confidence that this unseen planet was real.

This solution to his calculations called for the trans-Plutonian planet

Reanalyzing the Motion of Uranus

Conley Powell
Courtesy of Conley Powell

to be in Gemini, ironically the same part of the sky where Uranus and Pluto were found. It would be brighter than Pluto when it was discovered.

At the request of Conley Powell, the Lowell Observatory agreed to search for the hypothesized planet near the spot that Powell's calculations indicated on the survey photographs made by Clyde Tombaugh. Had Tombaugh missed the tenth planet? Beginning in August 1987, under the supervision of Edward Bowell, Norman Thomas used a blink comparator to search approximately 1,000 square degrees of sky. Nothing was found.

Undaunted, Powell reexamined his data. He was dissatisfied with his inability to derive more than a vague value for the eccentricity of the orbit of his suspected tenth planet. So he let his computer "have its head" in a sequence of approximations that produced a still better fit of the residuals. What emerged was a significantly different prediction.

Planet 10 was now smaller, closer, and brighter. His new solution predicted a planet with 87 percent the mass of Earth. With a mean distance of 39.8 astronomical units, a period of 251 years, and an eccentricity of 0.26, Powell's planet would follow almost exactly the path of Pluto. Like Pluto, it would even spend part of its circuit inside the orbit of Neptune. Powell is fascinated by the similarities between his new prediction and the final predictions for a ninth planet by Lowell and Pickering.

This tenth planet, Powell calculates, should be located at present in the eastern part of the constellation Leo, the Lion, with a comparatively bright magnitude of 12.2. "It's hard to see how Tombaugh could have missed it," says Powell. Although the unseen planet would have been well toward aphelion during Tombaugh's search, it would have been close to the ecliptic and brighter than magnitude 13. Says Powell, "Either Tombaugh was mistaken in thinking that he could not have missed a planet brighter than 16th magnitude or my calculations are mistaken."

Powell thinks that a search for the planet predicted by his revised computation is premature. He first wants to refine his calculations using new data he has just received from Bob Harrington—the post-1910 residuals of Uranus calculated by the Jet Propulsion Laboratory for navigational use in the *Voyager 2* encounter with Uranus.

If his planet is found, he would like to name it Persephone. But if his calculations lead to no planet discovery, would that suggest that the Uranus residuals are erroneous? No, says Powell, it is hard to believe that these discrepancies are not significant. More likely, he feels, his gravitational model of the outer solar system is wrong, perhaps because there is an eleventh planet out there whose gravitational effects are confusing matters.

There is yet another serious scientific search in progress for a trans-Plutonian planet, but it is being conducted without the belief or theoretical calculations that such a planet really exists. This investigation is being carried out by Thomas J. Chester and Michael Melnyk of the Jet Propulsion Laboratory. It is perhaps the least orthodox of all.

On January 25, 1983, NASA launched the Infrared Astronomical Satellite (IRAS), a joint endeavor by the United States, the Netherlands, and Great Britain. Scientists realized that this 22-inch (57-centimeter) telescope with infrared sensors would have a reasonable chance of detecting a tenth planet if it exists. A distant planet would receive and reflect very little sunlight and therefore be hard to find with optical telescopes and photography. But the meager energy it absorbed from the Sun and converted to heat could make this planet stand out clearly in infrared wavelengths. Many research projects were conducted on IRAS before it ran out of liquid helium to cool its special infrared detectors in November 1983, as expected.[13] Regardless of whether they were examining galaxies, nebulae, or stars, many of the astronomers checked the IRAS data for a possible tenth planet. As Chester explained, "Everyone wanted to be rich and famous."

It wasn't easy. IRAS recorded some 600,000 objects. Finding a tenth planet among them is like finding a poppy seed in a bin of sesame seeds. Almost. There were some sensible ways to improve the odds. As they proceeded with their principal investigations, astronomers kept their eyes open for objects in the expected low-temperature range. They looked for objects that moved. No tenth planet was found.

Looking for Heat

Thomas J. Chester and Michael Melnyk (right)
Gaylin Laughlin

Plate 16. Saturn and its exquisite ring system as seen by *Voyager 2.* The two bluish dots below Saturn are its moons Rhea and Dione.
NASA/Jet Propulsion Laboratory

Plate 17. Even more detail in the ring system of Saturn is visible in this *Voyager 2* view after closest encounter. Saturn can never be seen from this angle on Earth.
NASA/Jet Propulsion Laboratory

Plate 18. The *Voyager* spacecraft revealed that Saturn's ring system is composed of thousands of rings, as this false color picture clearly shows.
NASA/Jet Propulsion Laboratory

Plate 19. The richly banded world of Jupiter, as seen by *Voyager 1.* The Great Red Spot, a giant storm more than twice the size of Earth, and many lesser storms (white and reddish spots) are clearly visible. Also visible are three moons of Jupiter: reddish Io is near the right edge of Jupiter; Europa is the whitish dot near the right edge of the picture; and Callisto is a tiny dot below Jupiter and to the left.
NASA/Jet Propulsion Laboratory

Plates 20 and 21. Io, Jupiter's innermost large moon, as photographed by *Voyager 1.* Active volcanoes on Io, such as the one seen on the horizon (Plate 21), hurl gas and debris more than 100 miles (160 kilometers) above the moon's sulfur-covered surface. Said one scientist: "I've seen better-looking pizzas."
NASA/Jet Propulsion Laboratory

Plates 22 and 23. Europa, just a little smaller than Earth's Moon, looks like a fractured billiard ball in these *Voyager* pictures. Beneath the icy surface may lie liquid water. The fractures in Europa's crust are probably caused by the tidal strain created by Jupiter, Io, and Ganymede.
NASA/Jet Propulsion Laboratory

Plates 24 and 25. Ganymede, Jupiter's largest satellite and the largest moon in the solar system. The ridges and grooves seen by the *Voyagers* indicate a world where chunks of crust moved about and collided with one another.
NASA/Jet Propulsion Laboratory